Introduction to Mass Communication

Introduction to Mass Communication

Media Literacy and Culture

Stanley J. Baran
San Jose State University

Mayfield Publishing Company
Mountain View, California
London • Toronto

For Kimb Massey,
in and out of the classroom,
the finest teacher I've ever known.

Copyright © 1999 by Mayfield Publishing Company

Library of Congress Cataloging-in-Publication Data

Baran, Stanley J.
     Introduction to mass communication : media literacy and culture /
Stanley Baran.
          p. cm.
     Includes bibliographical references and index.
     ISBN 1-55934-960-3 (alk. paper)
     1. Mass media.   2. Mass media and culture.   3. Media literacy.
     I. Title
P90.B284   1998   98-34578
     302.23—dc21   CIP

Manufactured in the United States of America
10   9   8   7   6   5   4   3   2   1

Mayfield Publishing Company
1280 Villa Street
Mountain View, California 94041

Sponsoring editor, Holly J. Allen; *production editor,* Carla White Kirschenbaum; *developmental editors,* Kathleen Engelberg and Elisa Adams; *manuscript editor,* Kay Mikel; *text designer,* Ellen Pettengell; *design manager,* Jeanne M. Schreiber; *art editor,* Robin Mouat; *photo researcher,* Brian Pecko; *illustrators,* John Nelson, John and Judy Waller, Victory Productions, and Lineworks, Inc.; *manufacturing manager,* Randy Hurst. The text was set in 10/13 New Aster by GTS Graphics, Inc. and printed on 50# Chromatone LG by Banta Book Group, Menasha.

Brief Contents

Contents

part 2   Media, Media Industries, and Media Audiences   61

part 4   Mass Mediated Culture in the Information Age   313

Preface

The media literacy movement is receiving a great deal of attention today. A special Winter 1998 issue of the *Journal of Communication* was devoted to media literacy, and several new books on the topic have appeared. Media literacy is emphasized now in primary and secondary education, with 38 states mandating coverage in school curricula. But as someone who has taught Introduction to Mass Communication or Introduction to Mass Media at the college level every year since 1973, I can say with authority that media literacy has been a part of university media education for more than two decades. The course has long been designed to fulfill the following goals:

- to increase students' knowledge and understanding of the mass communication process and the mass media industries;
- to increase students' awareness of how they interact with those industries and with media content to create meaning;
- and to help students become more skilled and knowledgeable consumers of media content.

These are all aspects of media literacy as it is now understood. This text makes explicit what has been implicit for so long: that media literacy skills can and should be taught directly and that, as we enter the twenty-first century, media literacy is an essential survival skill for everyone in our society.

Perspective

This focus on media literacy grows naturally out of a *cultural perspective* on mass communication. This text takes the position that media, audiences, and culture develop and evolve in concert. The current prevailing notion in the discipline of mass communication is that, while not all individuals are directly affected by every media message they encounter, the media nonetheless do have important cultural effects. Today, the media are accepted as powerful forces in the process through which we come to know ourselves and one another. They function both as a forum where issues are debated and as the storytellers that carry our beliefs across time and space. Through these roles, the media are central to the creation and maintenance of both our dominant culture and our various bounded cultures.

This cultural orientation toward mass communication and the media places much responsibility on media consumers. In the past, people were considered either as victims of media influence or as impervious to it. The cultural orientation asserts that audience members are as much a part of the mass communication process as are the media technologies and industries. As important agents in the creation and maintenance of their own culture, audience members have an obligation not only to participate in the process of mass communication but also to participate actively, appropriately, and effectively. In other words, they must bring media literacy— the ability to effectively and efficiently comprehend and use mass media— to the mass communication process.

Features

The pedagogical features of this book are designed to support and improve media literacy skills. Every chapter (with the exception of Chapters 1 and 2) concludes with a special section devoted to the development of a specific media literacy skill selected for its relevance to the subject of the chapter. For example, Chapter 4, Newspapers, offers guidelines for interpreting the relative placement of newspaper stories. Chapter 8, Television, discusses how to identify staged news events on television. Other media literacy topics include recognizing product placements in movies, listening critically to radio "shock jocks," evaluating news based on anonymous sources, and using e-mail effectively.

Several kinds of boxes are used in the book to support media literacy as well as to highlight topics of special interest. One series of boxes, entitled "Using Media to Make a Difference," focuses on how media industry practitioners and audience members have employed the mass communication process to advance important social, political, and cultural causes. For example, Chapter 6, Film, highlights the African American films and film industry that grew up in response to the D. W. Griffith film *The Birth of a Nation*. Chapter 10, Advertising, showcases the advertising campaign that saved the Grand Canyon from being turned into a vast lake in the 1960s. Other examples described in these boxes include the creation of *Sesame Street*, the founding of Mothers Against Drunk Driving, the effect of Oprah Winfrey's televised book club on book sales, and the Blue Ribbon Campaign for Online Freedom of Speech, Press, and Association. In all of these boxes, we see how thoughtful professionals and active consumers have used the media to work for social change.

A second series of boxes, entitled "Cultural Forum," highlights important media-related cultural issues that are currently debated in the mass media. A "Cultural Forum" box in Chapter 1, for example, looks at the globalization of ownership of the U.S. mass media. Other "Cultural Forum" boxes explore such topics as the cultural implications of the rerelease of the *Star Wars* trilogy in 1997, the debate over warning labels on rock music, and the increasing commercialization of the Internet.

A third series of boxes, "Media Echoes," is designed to show that similar issues, controversies, and debates surface again and again in the history of the mass media. The trial of John Peter Zenger in 1735, for example, is echoed in the trial of Larry Flynt in 1988, with issues of libel, truth-telling, and freedom of speech at stake in both cases. The 1920s public relations campaign to encourage women to smoke is echoed by the recent Joe Camel advertising campaign to enlist teenage smokers, and again, similar issues are raised.

Learning Aids

Several types of learning aids are included in the book to support student learning and to enhance media literacy skills.

- Lists of relevant World Wide Web sites at the end of every chapter enable students to locate additional resources and encourage students to practice using the Internet.

- Photo essays raise provocative questions for students to consider.

- Important Resources, an annotated listing of books and articles for further reading, provides additional information for students.

- Chapter Reviews allow students to make sure they have focused on each chapter's most important material.

- Questions for Review further highlight important content and provide a review of key points.

- Questions for Critical Thinking and Discussion encourage students to investigate their own cultural assumptions and media use and to engage one another in debate on critical issues.

- Key terms are printed in bold type in the text, defined where they appear, and included in an extensive glossary at the end of the book.

- The Codes of Ethics of several of the major media industry self-regulatory bodies are included in an appendix at the end of the book.

- An exhaustive list of references is also provided at the end of the book.

Organization

Introduction to Mass Communication: Media Literacy and Culture is divided into four parts. Part One, Laying the Groundwork, as its name implies, provides the foundation for the study of mass communication. Chapter 1, Mass Communication, Culture, and Mass Media, defines important concepts and establishes the basic premises of the cultural perspective on mass communication with its focus on media literacy. Chapter 2, Media Literacy and Culture, provides an overview of the development of mass communication and the media and elaborates on the meaning and implications of media literacy.

Part Two, Media, Media Industries, and Media Audiences, includes chapters on the individual mass media technologies and the industries that have grown up around them—books (Chapter 3), newspapers (Chapter 4), magazines (Chapter 5), film (Chapter 6), radio and sound recording (Chapter 7), and television (Chapter 8). All of these chapters open with a short history of the medium and continue with discussions of the medium and its audiences, the scope and nature of the medium, and current trends in the industry and technology. Each chapter concludes with a section on developing a media literacy skill specifically related to that medium. Throughout each chapter there is a focus not just on the industry and technology but also on cultural issues and the interaction of culture, medium, and audience. For example, in Chapter 4, the issue of "redlining" in the newspaper industry is raised. Newspapers today must attract readers who are demographically appealing to advertisers. But what does this "industrial reality" mean to readers who do not fit that mold? What happens when newspapers abandon their traditional role as the voice of the community? Can our democracy function if segments of its citizenry are excluded from political and cultural discourse? These and numerous other questions arise when audience, culture, and medium are considered together.

Part Three, Supporting Industries, carries this same approach into two related areas—public relations (Chapter 9) and advertising (Chapter 10). As in the medium-specific chapters, each of these chapters begins with a brief history, continues with a discussion of audience, the scope of the industry, and current trends, and concludes with guidelines on developing relevant media literacy skills.

Part Four, Mass Mediated Culture in the Information Age, tackles several important areas. Chapter 11, Theories of Mass Communication, provides a short history of mass communication theory and compares and evaluates the field's major theories. Chapter 12, Mass Communication Research and Effects, explains the different forms of mass communication research and explores the ongoing debate over media effects. The chapter considers such topics as media and violence, media and gender and racial/ethnic stereotyping, and media and the electoral process.

Chapter 13, Media Freedom, Regulation, and Ethics, provides a detailed discussion of the First Amendment, focusing on refinements in interpretation and application made over the years in response to changes in technology and culture. The chapter analyzes such topics and issues as privacy, the use of cameras in the courtroom, and changing definitions of indecency. The chapter concludes with an extended discussion of media ethics and professionalism.

Chapter 14, The Internet, looks at the new online computer technologies and how they are reshaping the traditional mass communication process. Included are discussions of such current topics as cyberaddiction, online advertising and selling, controlling Internet expression, and copyright problems.

Chapter 15, The Changing Global Village, examines several issues we are currently facing as a result of advances in technology. Branching off from the opposing perspectives of Marshall McLuhan and cybermaven William Gibson, the chapter looks at how technology operates as a double-edged sword. Issues of personal identity, privacy, and democracy are considered, as are the growing technology and information gaps among different groups of people in the culture. The chapter also looks at media systems in other parts of the world and concludes with a discussion of local cultural integrity versus cultural imperialism.

Supplements

A full array of supplemental material for students and instructors accompanies this text.

- An *Instructor's Resource Guide* provides teaching aids for each chapter, including learning objectives, key terms and concepts, lecture ideas, video suggestions, and a guide to using the Media Literacy Worksheets. Also included in the guide are more than 70 transparency masters and a test bank of more than 1000 test items.

- A computerized test bank offers the test items in either Macintosh or Windows formats. Questions can be edited and new questions can be added.

- A World Wide Web site (www.mayfieldpub.com/baran) includes PowerPoint® slides, electronic transparencies, a syllabus builder for the instructor, an online study guide and hot links to media resources for the student, and more.

- An instructor's CD-ROM (compatible with both Macintosh and IBM computers) offers electronic versions of the *Instructor's Resource Guide*, PowerPoint® slides, electronic transparencies, and study questions for students.

- Media Literacy Worksheets provide practical activities to help students develop their media literacy skills, and a Media Consumption Journal. The worksheets can be shrink-wrapped with the text at no cost to the student.

- *The Mayfield Quick Guide to the Internet for Communication Students*, by John Courtright and Elizabeth Perse, offers instruction and tips on using the Internet, with a focus on addresses and sites of interest to communication students. The guide can be shrink-wrapped with the text at no cost to the student.

- A companion reader, *Readings in Mass Communication*, by Kimberly Massey, offers 46 thought-provoking articles that support the main themes in this book. The reader can be shrink-wrapped with the text at a discounted price to the student.

- Videos are available to qualified adopters.

Acknowledgments

Any project of this magnitude requires the assistance of many people. The early drafts of the text were written in England, while I was teaching in my university's Semester Abroad program, and in Germany, where I was in residence as a Senior Fulbright Fellow at the Institut für Journalismus und Kommunikation at the Hochschule für Musik und Theater in Hannover. In England, my colleague Dennis Jaehne, from San Jose State's Communication Studies department, provided thoughtful counsel on culture and communication. The program's local administrator in Bath, Dawn Stollar, and her husband, Derek, the program's history lecturer, set me on the trail of a number of sources important to the early chapters. In Germany, Institut Director Klaus Schönbach and professor Sylvia Knobloch provided ready ears for—and not infrequent improvement of—my ideas.

Naturally, I depended greatly on library resources. The staffs at the University of Bath and at San Jose State University were unwaveringly professional and helpful.

Reviewers, too, are an indispensable part of the creation of a good textbook. Although I didn't know them by name, I found myself in long distance, anonymous debate with several superb thinkers, especially about some of the text's most important concepts. Their collective keen eye and questioning attitude sharpened each chapter to the benefit of both writer and reader. (Any errors or misstatements that remain in the book are of course my sole responsibility.) Now that I know who they are, I would like to thank the reviewers by name: David Allen, Illinois State University; Sandra Braman, University of Alabama; Tom Grimes, Kansas State University; Kirk Hallahan, Colorado State University; Katharine Heintz-Knowles, University of Washington; Paul Husselbee, Ohio University; Seong Lee, Appalachian State University; Rebecca Ann Lind, University of Illinois at Chicago; Maclyn McClary, Humboldt State University; Guy Meiss, Central Michigan University; Debra Merskin, University of Oregon; Scott R. Olsen, Central Connecticut State University; Ted Pease, Utah State University; Linda Perry, *Florida Today* newspaper; Elizabeth Perse, University of Delaware; Tina Pieraccini, State University of New York-College at Oswego; Michael Porter, University of Missouri; Peter Pringle, University of Tennessee at Chattanooga; Neal Robison, Washington State University; Linda Steiner, Rutgers University; and Don Tomlinson, Texas A & M University.

I've written text and trade books for a number of different publishers, and each experience, while different, has been rewarding. The professionals at Mayfield, while the technical equals of the best I have known over 25 years of writing, surpass all others in their unfailing good humor, kindness, and individual charm. My editor, Holly Allen, waited for me to *want* to write this book. If I had known how skilled a colleague and delightful a friend she would be, I would have been ready years sooner. Mayfield's developmental editors also contributed to the book. Kate

Engelberg brought an enviable intellectual and stylistic sharpness to my work, Elisa Adams gave new meaning to "attention to detail" and "precision," and Susan Shook did an admirable job bringing together the supplements package. My production editor, Carla White Kirschenbaum, was always ready to help me and prod me when necessary. My copy editor, Kay Mikel, further refined the text. Credit for the imaginative visual look of this book goes to three talented people, photo researcher Brian Pecko, art director Jeanne Schreiber, and art editor Robin Mouat. Their graphic ideas helped make my writing easier to understand.

My most important colleague through all this, however, has been my wife, San Jose State University radio-TV professor Kimb Massey. She is a master of the cyberworld and a superb teacher. The former skill improved the text's content, the latter its tone and approach. These are only two of the reasons I've dedicated this book to her. The others are our marriage, which has made me a better person, and the gift of our daughter, Simmony, whose simple existence requires that I consider and reconsider what kind of world we will leave for her. I've written this text in the hope that it helps make the future for her and her friends better than it might otherwise have been.

part 1

Laying the Groundwork

Mass Communication, Culture, and Mass Media

The clock radio jars you awake. It's vintage REM, the last few bars of "It's the End of the World As We Know It." The laughing deejay shouts at you that it's 7:41 and you'd better get going. But before you do, he adds, listen to a few words from your friends at Fry's Electronics, home of fast, friendly, courteous service—"We will beat any competitive price!"

In the living room, you find your roommate has left the television on. You stop for a moment and listen: the Supreme Court has refused to hear an affirmative action appeal, your U.S. representative is under investigation for sexual harassment, and you deserve a break today at McDonald's. As you head toward the bathroom, your bare feet slip on some magazines littering the floor—*Wired, Rolling Stone, Newsweek*. You need to talk to your roommate about picking up!

After showering, you quickly pull on your Levi's, lace up your L.A. Gear cross-trainers, and throw on a B.U.M. Equipment pullover. No time for breakfast; you grab a Nature Valley granola bar and the newspaper and head for the bus stop. As the bus rolls up, you can't help but notice the giant ad on its side: *Die Hard IX—Kill Before You're Killed*. Rejecting that as a movie choice for the weekend, you sit down next to a teenager listening to music on his headphones and playing a video game. You bury yourself in the paper, scanning the lead stories and the local news and then checking out *Doonesbury* and *Dilbert*.

Hopping off the bus at the campus stop, you run into Chris from your computer lab. You walk to class together, talking about last night's *X-Files*.

It's not yet 9:00, and already you're awash in media messages.

In this chapter we define communication, interpersonal communication, mass communication, media, and culture and explore the relationships among them and how they define us and our world. We investigate how communication works, how it changes when technology is introduced into the process, and how differing views of communication and mass communication can lead to different interpretations of their power. We also discuss the opportunities mass communication and culture offer us and the responsibilities that come with those opportunities. Always crucial, these issues are of particular importance now, when we find ourselves in a period of remarkable development in new communication technologies.

Finally, we discuss the changing nature of contemporary mass communication and its implications for both communication industries and media consumers.

What Is Mass Communication?

"Does a fish know it's wet?" influential cultural and media critic Marshall McLuhan would often ask. The answer, he would say, is "No." The fish's existence is so dominated by water that only when water is absent is the fish aware of its condition (and then it's too late).

So it is with people and mass media. The media so fully saturate our everyday lives that we are often unconscious of their presence, not to mention their influence. Media inform us, entertain us, delight us, annoy us. They move our emotions, challenge our intellects, insult our intelligence. Media often reduce us to mere commodities for sale to the highest bidder. Media help define us; they shape our realities.

A fundamental theme of this book is that media do none of this alone. They do it *with* us as well as *to* us through mass communication, and they do it as a central—many critics and scholars say *the* central—cultural force in our society.

COMMUNICATION DEFINED

In its simplest form, **communication** is the transmission of a message from a source to a receiver. For more than 50 years now, this view of communication has been identified with the writing of political scientist Harold Lasswell (1948). He said that a convenient way to describe communication is to answer these questions:

- *Who?*
- Says *what?*
- In *which* channel?
- To *whom?*
- With *what effect?*

Expressed in terms of the basic elements of the communication process, communication occurs when:

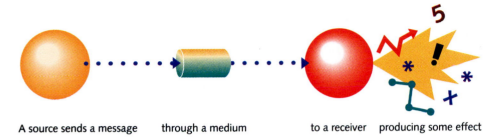

A source sends a message   through a medium   to a receiver   producing some effect

Straightforward enough, but what if the source is a professor who insists on speaking in a technical language far beyond the receiving students' level of skill? Obviously, communication does not occur. Unlike mere message-sending, communication requires the response of others. Therefore, there must be a *sharing* (or correspondence) of meaning for communication to take place.

A second problem with this simple model is that it suggests that the receiver passively accepts the source's message. However, if our imaginary students don't comprehend the professor's words, they respond with "Huh?" or look confused or yawn. This response, or **feedback,** is also a message. The receivers (the students) now become a source, sending their own message to the source (the offending professor) who is now a receiver. Hence, communication is a *reciprocal* and *ongoing process* with all involved parties more or less engaged in creating shared meaning. Communication, then, is better defined as *the process of creating shared meaning.*

Communication researcher Wilbur Schramm, using ideas originally developed by psychologist Charles E. Osgood, developed a graphic way to represent the reciprocal nature of communication (Figure 1–1). This depiction of **interpersonal communication**—communication between two or a few people—shows that there is no clearly identifiable source or receiver. Rather, because communication is an ongoing and reciprocal process, all the participants, or "interpreters," are working to create meaning by *encoding*

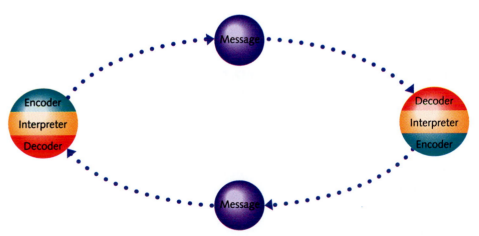

Figure 1–1 Osgood and Schramm's Model of Communication. *Source:* McQuail & Windhal, 1986, p. 14.

and *decoding* messages. A message is first **encoded,** that is, transformed into an understandable sign and symbol system. Speaking is encoding, as are writing, printing, and filming a television program. Once received, the message is **decoded;** that is, the signs and symbols are interpreted. Decoding occurs through listening, reading, or watching that television show.

The Osgood-Schramm model demonstrates the ongoing and reciprocal nature of the communication process. There is, therefore, no source, no receiver, and no feedback. This is because as communication is happening, both interpreters are simultaneously source and receiver. There is no feedback because all messages are presumed to be in reciprocation of other messages. Even when your friend starts a conversation with you, for example, it can be argued that it was your look of interest and willingness that communicated to her that she should speak. In this example, it is improper to label either you or your friend as the source—Who really initiated this chat?—and, therefore, it is impossible to identify who is providing feedback to whom.

Not every model can show all aspects of a process as complex as communication. Missing from this representation is **noise**—anything that interferes with successful communication. Noise is more than screeching or loud music when you're trying to read. Biases that lead to incorrect decoding, for example, are noise, as is newsprint that bleeds through from page 1 to page 2.

Encoded messages are carried by a **medium,** that is, the means of sending information. Sound waves are the medium that carries our voice to friends across the table; the telephone is the medium that carries our voice to friends across town. When the medium is a technology that carries messages to a large number of people—as newspapers carry the printed word and radio conveys the sound of music and news—we call it a **mass medium** (the plural of medium is **media**). The mass media we use regularly include radio, television, books, magazines, newspapers, movies, sound recordings, and computer networks. Each medium is the basis of a giant industry, but other related and supporting industries also serve them and us—advertising and public relations, for example. In our culture we use the words *media* and *mass media* interchangeably to refer to the communication industries themselves. We say, "The media entertain" or "The mass media are too conservative (or too liberal)."

MASS COMMUNICATION DEFINED

We speak, too, of mass communication. **Mass communication** is the process of creating shared meaning between the mass media and their audiences. Schramm recast his and Osgood's general model of communication to help us visualize the particular aspects of the mass communication process (Figure 1–2). This model and the original Osgood and Schramm scheme have much in common—interpreters, encoding, decoding, and messages—but it is their differences that are most significant for our understanding of how mass communication differs from other forms

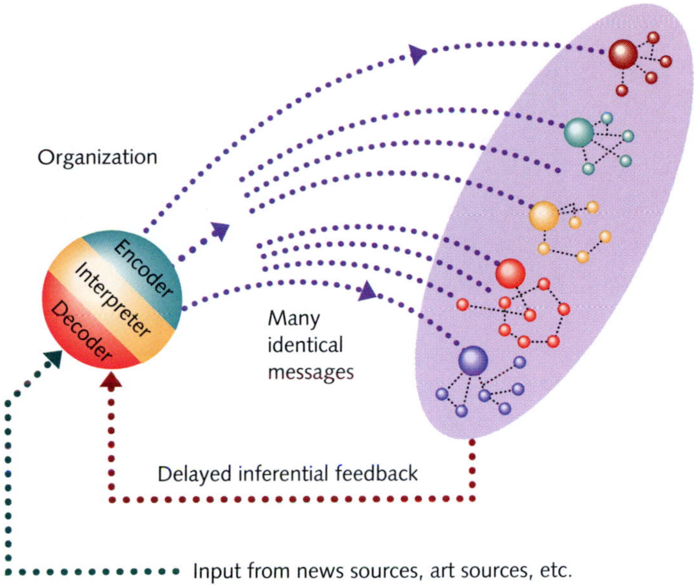

Figure 1–2 Schramm's Model of Mass Communication. *Source:* McQuail & Windhal, 1986, p. 31.

Organization

Encoder
Interpreter
Decoder

Many identical messages

Delayed inferential feedback

Input from news sources, art sources, etc.

The mass audience

Many receivers, each decoding, interpreting, encoding

Each connected with a group in which the message is reinterpreted and often acted upon

of communication. For example, where the original model has "message," the mass communication model offers "many identical messages." Additionally, the mass communication model specifies "feedback," whereas the interpersonal communication model does not. When two or a few people communicate face-to-face, the participants can immediately and clearly recognize the feedback residing in the reciprocal messages (our boring professor can see and hear the students' disenchantment as they listen to the lecture). Things aren't nearly as simple in mass communication.

In Schramm's mass communication model, feedback is represented by a line labeled delayed **inferential feedback.** This feedback is indirect rather than direct. Television executives, for example, must wait a day, at the very minimum, and sometimes a week or a month, to discover the ratings for new programs. Even then, the ratings only measure how many sets are tuned in, not whether people liked or disliked the programs. As a result, these executives can only infer what they must do to improve programming; hence the term "inferential feedback." Mass communicators are also subject to additional feedback, usually in the form of criticism in other media, such as a television critic writing a column in a newspaper.

The differences between the individual elements of interpersonal and mass communication change the very nature of the communication process. How those alterations influence the message itself and how the likelihood of successfully sharing meaning varies are shown in Figure 1–3. For example, the immediacy and directness of feedback in interpersonal communication free communicators to gamble, to experiment with different approaches. Their knowledge of one another allows them to tailor their messages as narrowly as they wish. As a result, interpersonal communication is often personally relevant and possibly even adventurous and challenging. In contrast, the distance between participants in the mass communication process, imposed by the technology, creates a sort of

	Interpersonal Communication You invite a friend to lunch.		Mass Communication Aaron Spelling produces *Melrose Place.*	
	Nature	**Consequences**	**Nature**	**Consequences**
Message	Highly flexible and alterable	You can change it in midstream. If feedback is negative, you can offer an alternative. Is feedback still negative? Take a whole new approach.	Identical, mechanically produced, simultaneously sent Inflexible, unalterable The completed *Melrose Place* episode that is aired.	Once in the can, *Melrose Place* cannot be changed. If a plot line or other communicative device isn't working with the audience, nothing can be done.
Interpreter A	One person—in this case, you	You know your mind. You can encode your own message to suit yourself, your values, your likes and dislikes.	A large, heirarchically structured organization—in this case, Aaron Spelling Productions.	Who really is Interpreter A? Aaron Spelling? The writers? The director? The actors? The network and its standards and practices people? The sponsors? All must agree, leaving little room for individual vision or experimentation.
Interpreter B	One or a few people, usually in direct contact with you and, to a greater or lesser degree, known to you—in this case, Chris	You can tailor your message specifically to Interpreter B. You can make relatively accurate judgments about B because of information present in the setting. Chris is a vegetarian; you don't suggest a steak house.	A large, heterogeneous audience known to Interpreter A only in the most rudimentary way, little more than basic demographics—in this case, several million *Melrose Place* viewers	Communication cannot be tailored to the wants, needs, and tastes of all audience members or even those of all members of some subgroup. Some more or less generally acceptable standard is set.
Feedback	Immediate and direct yes or no response	You know how successful your message is immediately. You can adjust your communication on the spot to maximize its effectiveness.	Delayed and inferential Even overnight ratings too late for this episode of *Melrose Place* Moreover, ratings limited to telling the number of sets tuned in	Even if the feedback is useful, it is too late to be of value for this episode. In addition, it doesn't suggest how to improve the communication effort.
Result	Flexible, personally relevant, possibly adventurous, challenging, or experimental		Constrained by virtually every aspect of the communication situation A level of communication most likely to meet the greatest number of viewers' needs A belief that experimentation is dangerous A belief that to challenge the audience is to risk failure	

Figure 1–3 Elements of Interpersonal Communication and Mass Communication Compared.

"communication conservatism." Feedback comes too late to allow for corrections or alterations in communication that fails. The sheer number of people in many mass communication audiences makes personalization and specificity difficult. As a result, mass communication tends to be more constrained, less free. This does not mean, however, that it is less potent than interpersonal communication in shaping our understanding of ourselves and our world.

Media theorist James W. Carey recognized this and offered a **cultural definition of communication** that has had a profound impact on the way communication scientists and others have viewed the relationship between communication and culture. Carey wrote, *"Communication is a symbolic process whereby reality is produced, maintained, repaired and transformed"* (Carey, 1975, p. 10).

Carey's definition asserts that communication and reality are linked. Communication is a process embedded in our everyday lives that informs the way we perceive, understand, and construct our view of reality and the world. Communication is the foundation of our culture.

What Is Culture?

Culture is the learned behavior of members of a given social group. Many writers and thinkers have offered interesting expansions of this definition. Here are four examples, the first three from anthropologists, the last from a performing arts critic. These definitions highlight not only what culture *is* but also what culture *does*:

> Culture is the learned, socially acquired traditions and lifestyles of the members of a society, including their patterned, repetitive ways of thinking, feeling and acting. (M. Harris, 1983, p. 5)

> Culture lends significance to human experience by selecting from and organizing it. It refers broadly to the forms through which people make sense of their lives, rather than more narrowly to the opera or art of museums. (R. Rosaldo, 1989, p. 26)

> Culture is the medium evolved by humans to survive. Nothing is free from cultural influences. It is the keystone in civilization's arch and is the medium through which all of life's events must flow. We are culture. (E. T. Hall, 1976, p. 14)

> Culture is an historically transmitted pattern of meanings embodied in symbolic forms by means of which [people] communicate, perpetuate, and develop their knowledge about and attitudes toward life. (C. Geertz cited in Taylor, 1991, p. 91).

CULTURE AS SOCIALLY CONSTRUCTED SHARED MEANING

Virtually all definitions of culture recognize that culture is *learned*. Recall the opening vignette. Even if this scenario doesn't exactly match your early mornings, you probably recognize its elements. Moreover, all of us are familiar with most, if not every, cultural reference in it. *The X-Files, Rolling Stone*, McDonald's, L.A. Gear, *Dilbert*, REM—all are points of reference, things that have some meaning for all of us. How did this come to be?

Creation and maintenance of a more or less common culture occurs through communication, including mass communication. When we talk to our friends; when a parent raises a child; when religious leaders instruct their followers; when teachers teach; when grandparents pass on recipes; when politicians campaign; when media professionals produce content that we read, listen to, and watch, meaning is being shared and culture is being constructed and maintained.

FUNCTIONS AND EFFECTS OF CULTURE

Culture serves a purpose. It helps us categorize and classify our experiences; it helps define us, our world, and our place in it. In doing so culture can have a number of sometimes conflicting effects.

Limiting and Liberating Effects of Culture   A culture's learned traditions and values can be seen as patterned, repetitive ways of thinking, feeling, and acting. Culture limits our options and provides useful guidelines for behavior. For example, when conversing, you don't consciously consider, "Now, how far away should I stand? Am I too close?" You just stand where you stand. After a hearty meal with a friend's family, you don't engage in mental self-debate, "Should I burp? Yes! No! Arghhhh. . . ." Culture provides information that helps us make meaningful distinctions about right and wrong, appropriate and inappropriate, good and bad, attractive and unattractive, and so on. How does it do this?

Obviously, through communication. Through a lifetime of communication we have learned just what our culture expects of us. The two examples given here are positive results of culture's limiting effects. But culture's limiting effects can be negative, such as when we are unwilling or unable to move past patterned, repetitive ways of thinking, feeling, and acting, or when we entrust our "learning" to teachers whose interests are selfish, narrow, or otherwise not consistent with our own.

U.S. culture, for example, values thinness in women. How many women endure weeks of unhealthy diets and succumb to potentially dangerous surgical procedures in search of a body that for most is physically unattainable? How many men (and other women) never get to know, like, or even love those women who cannot meet our culture's standards of thinness and beauty?

Now consider how this situation may have come about. Our mothers did not bounce us on their knees when we were babies, telling us that thin

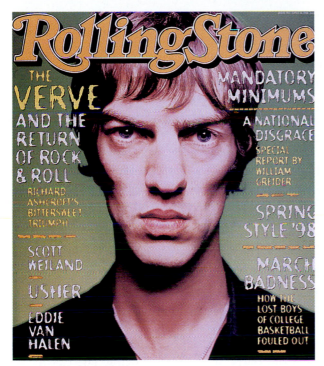

These images have meaning for all of us, meaning that is socially constructed through communication in our culture. How many can you recognize? What specific meaning or meanings does each have for you? How did you develop each meaning? How closely do you think your meanings match those of your friends? Of your parents? What value is there—if any—in having shared meaning for these things in our everyday lives?

DILBERT © United Feature Syndicate, Inc.

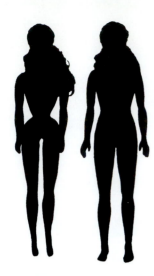

The Barbie doll (*left*) represents an unattainable ideal for American girls. In 1991, a rival, the Happy to Be Me doll (*right*), appeared on the scene. Happy's creator wanted to present a more realistic image to young, impressionable minds. Do you think the American public was ready for Happy?

was good and fat was bad. Think back, though, to the stories you were told and the television shows and movies on which you grew up. The heroines (or, more often, the beautiful love interests of the heroes) were invariably tall and thin. The bad guys were usually mean and fat. From Disney's depictions of Snow White, Cinderella, Beauty, Tinker Bell, and Pocahontas to the impossible dimensions of Barbie, the message is embedded in the conscious (and unconscious) mind of every girl and boy. Thin is in! In a recent reversal—either because it tired of the controversy or because it finally understood its possibly negative contribution to young girls' self-concept—Mattel, Barbie's manufacturer, announced in 1997 that it would henceforth give the doll more realistic body proportions.

This message—thin is in—and millions of others come to us primarily through the media, and although the people who produce these media images are not necessarily selfish or mean, their motives are undeniably financial. Their contribution to our culture's repetitive ways of thinking, feeling, and acting is most certainly not primary among their concerns when preparing their communication.

Culture need not only limit. That media representations of female beauty often meet with debate and disagreement points up the fact that culture can be liberating as well. This is so because cultural values can be contested.

Especially in a pluralistic, democratic society such as ours, the **dominant culture**—the one that seems to hold sway with the majority of people—is often openly challenged. People do meet, find attractive, like, and even love people who don't fit the standard image of beauty. Additionally, the media sometimes present images that suggest different ideals of beauty and success. Actress Janeane Garofalo; comedienne and talk show host Rosie O'Donnell; Christine Lahti, who plays Dr. Kate Austin on television's *Chicago Hope;* talk show host and influential broadcasting executive Oprah Winfrey; and singer-actress Bette Midler all represent alternatives to our culture's idealized standards of beauty, and all have undeniable appeal (and power) on the big and small screens. Liberation from the limitations imposed by culture resides in our ability and willingness to learn and use *new* patterned, repetitive ways of thinking, feeling, and acting; to challenge existing patterns; and to create our own.

Defining, Differentiating, Dividing, and Uniting Effects of Culture

Have you ever made the mistake of calling a dolphin, porpoise, or even a whale a fish? Maybe you've heard others do it. This error occurs because when we think of fish we think, "lives in the water" and "swims." Fish are defined by their "aquatic culture." Because water-residing, swimming dolphins and porpoises share that culture, we sometimes forget that they are mammals, not fish.

We, too, are defined by our culture. We are citizens of the United States; we are Americans. If we travel to other countries, we will hear ourselves labeled "American," and this label will conjure up stereotypes and expectations in the minds of those who use and hear it. The stereotype,

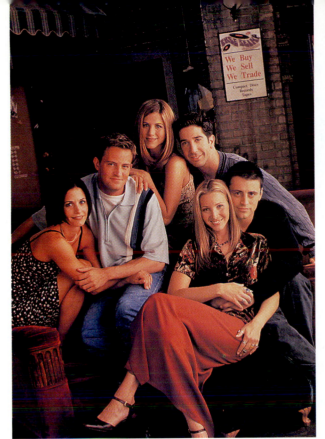

Friends, Sabrina the Teenage Witch, and *Silk Stalkings*—These three television programs are aimed at different audiences, yet in each the characters share certain traits that mark them as attractive. Must people in real life look like these performers to be considered attractive? Successful? Good? The nine people shown are all slender, tall, and young. Yes, they're just make-believe television characters, but the producers of the shows on which they appear chose these people—as opposed to others—for a reason. What do you think it was? How well do you measure up to the cultural standard of beauty and attractiveness represented here? Do you ever wish that you could be just a bit more like these people? Why or why not?

Rosie O'Donnell, Oprah Winfrey, and *Chicago Hope*'s Christine Lahti are prominent women whose presentation in the media suggests different cultural ideals of beauty and success. Each represents an alternative to our culture's idealized standards of beauty. How attractive do you find each woman to be? What is it about each that appeals to you?

whatever it may be, will probably fit us only incompletely, or perhaps hardly at all—perhaps we are dolphins in a sea full of fish. Nevertheless, being American defines us in innumerable important ways, both to others (more obviously) and to ourselves (less obviously).

Within this large, national culture, however, there are many smaller, **bounded cultures.** For example, we speak comfortably of Italian neighborhoods, fraternity row, the South, and the suburbs. Because of our cultural understanding of these categories, each expression communicates something about our expectations of these places. We think we can predict with a good deal of certainty the types of restaurants and shops we will find in the Italian neighborhood, even the kind of music we will hear escaping from open windows. We can predict the kinds of clothes and cars we will see on fraternity row, the likely behavior of shop clerks in the South, and the political orientation of the suburb's residents. Moreover, the people within these cultures usually identify themselves as members of those bounded cultures. An individual may say, for example, "I am Italian American" or "I'm from the South." These smaller cultures unite groups of people and allow them to see themselves as different from other groups around them. Thus, culture also serves to differentiate us from others.

In the United States, we generally consider this a good thing. We pride ourselves on our pluralism and our diversity and on the richness of the cultural heritages represented within our borders. We enjoy moving from one bounded culture to another or from a bounded culture to the dominant national culture and back again.

Problems arise, however, when differentiation leads to division. Just as culture is constructed and maintained through communication, it is also communication (or miscommunication) that turns differentiation into

division. We all know how communication can hurt, how words can convey lack of respect. Los Angeles police detective Mark Fuhrman's now notorious testimony in the O. J. Simpson murder trial in 1996 is, sadly, a perfect example. Citing evidence of Fuhrman's habitual use of derogatory labels for African Americans, Simpson's lawyers effectively argued that a culture (the L.A. police department) that fostered a man like Fuhrman and allowed him to exist without censure could not possibly have been fair in its investigation of Simpson. The jury agreed; the nation was divided—along racial lines.

Yet, U.S. citizens of all colors, ethnicities, genders and gender preferences, nationalities, places of birth, economic strata, and intelligences often get along; in fact, we *can* communicate, *can* prosper, *can* respect one another's differences. Culture can divide us, but culture also unites us. Our culture represents our collective experience. We converse easily with strangers because we share the same culture. We speak the same language, automatically understand how far apart to stand, appropriately use titles or first or last names, know how much to say, and know how much to leave unsaid. Through communication with people in our culture, we internalize cultural norms and values—those things that bind our many diverse bounded cultures into a functioning, cohesive society.

Defining Culture   From this discussion of culture comes the definition of culture on which the remainder of this book is based:

> Culture is the world made meaningful; it is socially constructed and
> maintained through communication. It limits as well as liberates us; it

differentiates as well as unites us. It defines our realities and thereby shapes the ways we think, feel, and act.

Mass Communication and Culture

Culture defines our realities, but who contributes to the construction and maintenance of culture? Because culture is constructed and maintained through communication, it is in communication that cultural power resides. And because mass media are such a significant part of the modern world, more and more attention is being paid to the interaction between mass communication and culture.

EXAMINING MASS COMMUNICATION AND CULTURE

Since the introduction of the first mass circulation newspapers in the 1830s, media theorists and social critics have argued about the importance and power of the media industries and mass communication. In their most general form, these debates have been shaped by three closely related dichotomies.

Micro- versus Macro-Level Effects People are concerned about the effects of media. Does television cause violence? Do beer ads cause increased alcohol consumption? Does pornography cause rape? The difficulty here is with the word "cause." Although there is much scientific evidence that media cause many behaviors, there is also much evidence that they do not.

As long as we debate the effects of media only on individuals, we remain blind to media's greatest influences (both positive and negative) on the way we live. For example, during the 1995 television season, in which tough dramatic action programs such as *Law & Order* and *Walker, Texas Ranger* were attracting large audiences, the media violence issue heated up with Attorney General Janet Reno's public attack on "irresponsible broadcasters." The lineups of the major television networks featured a number of new drama programs. Television people called them "gritty," "hard-hitting," and "realistic." Others saw them as too sexy, too violent, too exploitative. Dick Wolf, executive producer of the popular but controversial television hit *Law & Order*, found his show at the middle of the storm. In an interview with cable channel A&E's *Investigative Reports*, Wolf argued: "I grew up on Tom and Jerry, and I haven't climbed into a tower and pulled a gun on people."

Who can argue with this? For most people media have relatively few *direct* effects at the personal or **micro level.** But we live in a culture in which people *have* shot people or are willing to use violence to settle disputes, at least in part because of the cultural messages embedded in our media fare. The hidden, but much more important, impact of media operates at the cultural or **macro level.** Violence on television contributes to

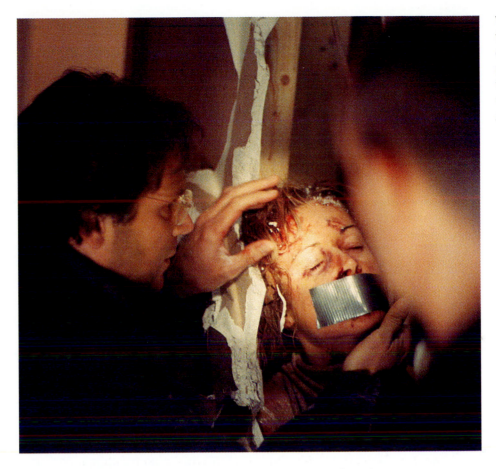

What are the effects of televised violence? The debate swirls as different people mean different things by "effects." This violent scene is from *Millenium*.

the cultural climate in which real-world violence becomes more acceptable. Sure, perhaps none of us have shot people from atop a tower. But do you have bars on the windows of your home? Are there parts of town where you would rather not walk alone? Do you vote for the "tough on crime" candidate over the "education" candidate?

The micro-level view is that televised violence has little impact because most people are not directly affected. The macro-level view is that televised violence has a great impact because it influences the cultural climate.

Administrative versus Critical Research **Administrative research** asks questions about the immediate, observable influence of mass communication. Does a commercial campaign sell more cereal? Does an expanded Living section increase newspaper circulation? Did *Beavis and Butt-Head* inspire a little boy to burn down his house and kill his baby sister? For decades the only proofs of media effects that science (and therefore the media industries, regulators, and audiences) would accept were those with direct, observable, immediate impacts. Nearly 60 years ago, however, Paul Lazarsfeld, the "Father of Social Science Research" and possibly the most important mass communication researcher of all time, warned of the danger of this narrow view. He believed that **critical research**—asking larger questions about what kind of nation we are building, what kind of people

CALVIN AND HOBBES • Bill Watterson

we are becoming—would serve our culture better. Writing long before the influence of television and information access through the World Wide Web, he stated:

> Today we live in an environment where skyscrapers shoot up and elevateds (commuter trains) disappear overnight; where news comes like shock every few hours; where continually new news programs keep us from ever finding out details of previous news; and where nature is something we drive past in our cars, perceiving a few quickly changing flashes which turn the majesty of a mountain range into the impression of a motion picture. Might it not be that we do not build up experiences the way it was possible decades ago. . . ? (1941, p. 12)

Administrative research concerns itself with direct causes and effects; critical research looks at larger, possibly more significant cultural questions. As Figure 1–4 shows, cartoon character Calvin understands the distinction well.

Transmissional versus Ritual Perspective Last is the debate that led Professor Carey to articulate his cultural definition of communication. The **transmissional perspective** sees media as senders of information for the purpose of control; that is, media either have effects on our behavior or they don't. The **ritual perspective,** Carey wrote, views media not as a means of transmitting "messages in space" but as central to "the maintenance of society in time." Mass communication is "not the act of imparting information but the representation of shared beliefs" (1975, p. 6). In other words, the ritual perspective is necessary to understand the *cultural* importance of mass communication.

Consider an ad for Budweiser beer. What message is being transmitted? Buy Bud, of course. So people either do or don't buy Bud. The message either controls or does not control people's beer-buying behavior. That is the transmissional perspective. But what is happening culturally in that ad? What reality about alcohol and socializing is shared? Can young people really have fun in social settings without alcohol? What constitutes a good-looking man or woman? What does success look like in the United States? The ritual perspective illuminates these messages—the culturally important content of the ad.

The transmissional message in this beer ad is obvious—buy Budweiser. The ritual message is another thing altogether. What is it?

MASS COMMUNICATION OPPORTUNITIES AND RESPONSIBILITIES

Because culture can limit and divide or liberate and unite, it offers us infinite opportunities to use communication for good—if we choose to do so. Carey wrote,

> Because we have looked at each new advance in communication technology as opportunities for politics and economics, we have devoted them, almost exclusively, to government and trade. We have rarely seen them as opportunities to expand [our] powers to learn and exchange ideas and experience. (1975, pp. 20–21)

Who are "we" in this quote? *We* are everyone involved in creating and maintaining the culture that defines us. *We* are the people involved in mass media industries and the people who comprise their audiences. Together we allow mass communication not only to occur but to contribute to the creation and maintenance of culture.

Everyone involved has an obligation to participate responsibly. For people working in the media industries, this means professionally and ethically creating and transmitting content. For audience members, it means behaving as critical and thoughtful consumers of that content. Two ways to understand our opportunities and our responsibilities in the mass communication process are to view the mass media as our cultural storytellers and to conceptualize mass communication as a forum.

Mass Media As Cultural Storytellers A culture's values and beliefs reside in the stories it tells. Who are the good guys? Who are the bad guys? How many of your childhood heroines were chubby? How many good guys

Figure 1–5 Storytellers play an important role in helping us define ourselves.

BALLARD STREET **Jerry Van Amerongen**

There we are, huddled around the tribal campfire, telling and retelling the stories of our people.

dressed in black? How many heroines lived happily ever after without marrying Prince Charming? Probably not very many. Our stories help define our realities, shaping the ways we think, feel, and act. Storytellers have a remarkable opportunity to shape culture (Figure 1–5). They also have a responsibility to do so in as professional and ethical a way as possible.

At the same time, you, the audience for these stories, also have opportunities and responsibilities. You use these stories not only to be entertained but to learn about the world around you, to understand the values, the way things work, and how the pieces fit together. You have a responsibility to question the tellers and their stories, to interpret the stories in ways consistent with larger or more important cultural values and truths, to be thoughtful, to reflect on the stories' meanings and what they say about you and your culture. To do less is to miss an opportunity to construct your own meaning and, thereby, culture.

For many years, for example, the makers of Fritos corn chips advertised their product using very brief stories (commercials) that had as the lead character an animated Mexican outlaw, the Frito Bandito. To many he was only a cartoon character, an imaginary spokesperson for an insignificant snack food. What was there to think about, to reflect on? To many others who share our culture, however, the Frito Bandito was the televised personification of the worst stereotype of people of Mexican descent—small, dark, violent, and sneaky. Only when people began to question and reject the manufacturer's 30- and 60-second stories of a corn chip crazed outlaw did the Frito Bandito disappear.

Mass Communication As Cultural Forum   Imagine a giant courtroom where we discuss and debate our culture—what it is, and what we want it to be. What do we think about welfare? single motherhood? labor unions? nursing homes? What is the meaning of "successful," "good," "loyal," "moral," "honest," "beautiful," "patriotic"? We have cultural definitions or understandings of all these things and more. Where do they come from? How do they develop, take shape, and mature?

Mass communication has become a primary forum for the debate about our culture. Logically, then, the most powerful voices in the forum have the most power to shape our definitions and understandings. Where should that power reside—with the media industries or with their audiences? If you answer "media industries," you must demand that members of these industries act professionally and ethically. If you answer "audiences," you must insist that individual audience members have an obligation to be thoughtful and critical of the media messages they consume. The forum is only as good, fair, and honest as those who participate in it.

Scope and Nature of Mass Media

No matter how we choose to view the process of mass communication, it is impossible to deny that an enormous portion of our lives is spent in interaction with mass media. On a typical Sunday night, 37 million people in the United States will tune in a prime time television show. Television sets are in 98% of all our homes, VCRs in over 80%. The television set is on for more than 7½ hours a day in a typical U.S. household. Two thirds of all U.S. adults will read a newspaper each day; two thirds will listen to the radio for some part of every day. A movie like *Titanic* can earn $920 million in 10 weeks in ticket sales alone. The Web site for the film *Independence Day* received 2.5 million "hits" a day when the movie was in the theaters. The average person spends 3,344 hours a year—57% of his or her waking hours—consuming mass media content (Figure 1–6).

Despite the pervasiveness of mass media in our lives, many of us are dissatisfied with or critical of the media industries' performance and much of the content provided. A 1995 survey conducted by the Times-Mirror Center for the People and the Press concluded that "two out of three members of the public had nothing good to say about the media."

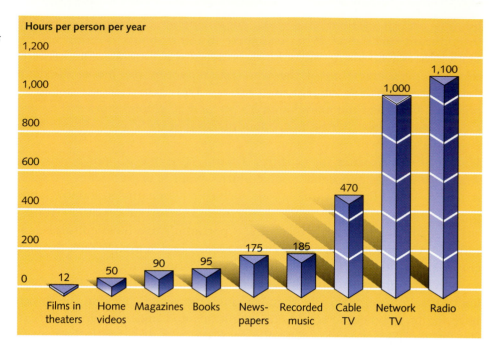

Figure 1–6 United States Media Consumption. *Source: Census Bureau Statistical Abstract of the U.S. and RADAR.*

Hours per person per year

Films in theaters: 12
Home videos: 50
Magazines: 90
Books: 95
Newspapers: 175
Recorded music: 185
Cable TV: 470
Network TV: 1,000
Radio: 1,100

Our ambivalence—we criticize, yet we consume—comes in part from our uncertainties about the relationships among the elements of mass communication. What is the role of technology? What is the role of money? And what is *our* role in the mass communication process?

THE ROLE OF TECHNOLOGY

To some thinkers, it is machines and their development that drive historical, economic, and cultural change. This idea is referred to as **technological determinism.** Certainly there can be no doubt that movable type contributed to the Protestant Reformation and the decline of the Catholic Church's power in Europe or that television changed the way members of American families interact. Those who believe in technological determinism would argue that these changes in the cultural landscape were the inevitable result of new technology.

But others see technology as more neutral and claim that the way people *use* technology is what gives it significance. This perspective accepts technology as one of many factors that shape historical, economic, and cultural change; technology's influence is ultimately determined by how much power it is given by the people and cultures that use it.

This disagreement about the power of technology is at the heart of the controversy surrounding the new communication technologies. Are we more or less powerless in the wake of advances like the Internet, the World Wide Web, and instant global audio and visual communication? If we are at the mercy of technology, the culture that surrounds us will not be of our making, and the best we can hope to do is make our way reasonably well in a world outside our own control. But if these technologies are indeed neutral and their power resides in *how* we choose to use them, we can utilize them responsibly and thoughtfully to construct and maintain whatever kind of culture we want.

Technology does have an impact on communication. At the very least it changes the basic elements of communication (see Figure 1–3). What technology does not do is relieve us of our obligation to use mass communication responsibly and wisely.

THE ROLE OF MONEY

Money, too, alters communication. It shifts the balance of power; it tends to make audiences products rather than consumers.

The first newspapers were financially supported by their readers; the money they paid for the paper covered its production and distribution. But in the 1830s a new form of newspaper financing emerged. Publishers began selling their papers for a penny—much less than it cost to produce and distribute them. Because so many more papers were sold at this bargain price, publishers could "sell" advertising space based on their readership. What they were actually selling to advertisers wasn't space on the page—it was readers. How much they could charge advertisers was directly related to how much product (how many readers) they could produce for them.

This new type of publication changed the nature of mass communication. The goal of the process was no longer for audience and media to create meaning together. Rather, it was to sell those readers to a third participant—advertisers.

Some observers think this was a devastatingly bad development, not only in the history of mass communication but in the history of democracy. It robbed people of their voice, or at least made the voices of the advertisers more powerful. Others think it was a huge advance for both mass communication and democracy because it vastly expanded the media, broadening and deepening communication. Models showing these two different ways of viewing mass communication are presented in the box "Audience As Consumer or Audience As Product." Which model makes the most sense to you? Which do you think is the most accurate?

The goals of media professionals will be questioned repeatedly throughout this book. For now, keep in mind that ours is a capitalist economic system and that media industries are businesses. Movie producers must sell tickets, book publishers must sell books, and even public broadcasting has bills to pay.

This does not mean, however, that the media are or must be slaves to profit. Our task is to understand the constraints placed on these industries

Audience As Consumer or Audience As Product?

People base their judgments of media performance and content on the way they see themselves fitting into the economics of the media industry. Businesses operate to serve their consumers and make a profit. The consumer comes first, then, but who *is* the consumer in our mass media system? This is a much debated issue among media practitioners and media critics. Consider the following models.

	Producer	Product	Consumer
Basic U.S. Business Model	A manufacturer. . .	produces a product. . .	for consumers who choose to buy or not. The manufacturer must satisfy the consumer. Power resides here.
Basic U.S. Business Model for Cereal: Rice Krispies As Product, Public As Consumer	Kellogg's. . .	produces Rice Krispies. . .	for us, the consumers. If we buy Rice Krispies, Kellogg's makes a profit. Kellogg's must satisfy us. Power resides here.
Basic U.S. Business Model for Television (A): Audience As Product, Advertisers As Consumer	NBC. . .	produces audiences (using its programming). . .	for advertisers. If they buy NBC's audiences, NBC makes a profit. NBC must satisfy its consumers, the advertisers. Power resides here.
Basic U.S. Business Model for Television (B): Programming As Product, Audience as Consumer	NBC. . .	produces (or distributes) programming. . .	for us, the audience. If we watch NBC's shows, NBC makes a profit. NBC must satisfy us. Power resides here.

The first three models assume that the consumer *buys* the product; that is, the consumer is the one with the money and therefore the one who must be satisfied. The last model makes a different assumption. It sees the audience, even though it does not buy anything, as sufficiently important to NBC's profit-making ability to force NBC to consider its interests above others' (even those of advertisers). Which model do you think best represents the economics of U.S. mass media?

by their economics and then demand that, within those limits, they perform ethically and responsibly. We can do this only by being thoughtful, critical consumers of the media.

Current Trends in Mass Communication

Today, technology and money continue to alter the mass communication process. There is a growing concentration of ownership, rapid globalization, increased audience fragmentation, and a steady erosion of traditional distinctions among media. We will return to these themes in later chapters, but here we will discuss them in terms of their impact on the mass communication process.

CONCENTRATION OF OWNERSHIP

Ownership of media companies is increasingly concentrated in fewer and fewer hands. Through mergers, acquisitions, buyouts, and hostile takeovers, a very small number of large conglomerates is coming to own more and more of the world's media outlets. For example, in 1996 Westinghouse bought CBS for $5.4 billion, creating a broadcasting giant owning 15 television and 39 radio stations capable of reaching over one third of all the homes in the United States.

In that same year Disney bought Capital Cities/ABC, and Time Warner bought Turner Broadcasting. The Time Warner/Turner merger brought together under one corporate parent TBS Superstation; TNT Cable Network; the Cartoon Network; New Line Cinema; Castle Rock Entertainment; Savoy Pictures; BHC Stations; Hanna-Barbera Cartoons; CNN; Headline News; CNN International; Turner Classic Movies; the Airport Channel; Warner Brothers' movie studios, television, animation, and home video companies; the record labels Warner, Elektra, WEA International, and Atlantic; the magazines *Time, People, Life, Sports Illustrated,* and *Fortune;* Time Life Books and video; HBO; HBO Video; HBO Independent Productions; the Pathfinder Web site; Time Warner Cable, the country's second largest cable company; and pieces of 3DO, Atari, and the Sega Channel. Other examples abound.

The potential impact of this **oligopoly**—a concentration of media industries into an ever smaller number of companies—on the mass communication process is enormous. What becomes of shared meaning when the people running communication companies are more committed to the financial demands of their corporate offices than they are to their audiences, who are supposedly their partners in the communication process? What becomes of the process itself when the media companies grow more removed from those with whom they communicate? And what becomes of the culture that is dependent on that process when concentration has limited the diversity of perspective and information?

Influential media critic Ben Bagdikian argues that media conglomeration severely disrupts the mass communication process, limiting the voice of the people and placing enormous power in the hands of the giant media monopolies. He wrote,

> When he first opened the Soviet Union's media to dissenting ideas in the mid-1980s, Mikhail Gorbachev could not have predicted the ultimate impact. To the surprise of the world, and of Gorbachev himself, his policy of *glasnost* helped dissolve one of the most powerful empires in modern

times. The explosive change was triggered by millions of people hearing alternative ideas, among them ideas that resonated powerfully with their private feelings. . . . With the country suddenly flooded with free criticism and new public ideas, millions of formerly passive Soviet citizens saw their private desires legitimated by reflection in the mass media. . . . But, ironically, in much of the developed democratic world, the commercial media have taken on characteristics of the old Soviet media. Left to their own devices, a small number of the most powerful firms have taken control of most of their countries' printed and broadcast news and entertainment. They have their own style of control, not by official edict or state terror, but by uniform economic and political goals. They have their own way of narrowing political and cultural diversity, not by promulgating official dogma, but by quietly emphasizing ideas and information congenial to their profits and political preferences. Although they are not their countries' official political authorities, they have a disproportionate private influence over the political authorities and over public policy. (1992, pp. 239–240)

GLOBALIZATION

Closely related to the concentration of media ownership is globalization. It is primarily large, multinational conglomerates that are doing the lion's share of media acquisitions. The potential impact of globalization on the mass communication process speaks to the issue of diversity of expression. Will distant, anonymous, foreign corporations, each with vast holdings in a variety of nonmedia businesses, use their power to shape news and entertainment content to suit their own ends? Opinion is divided. Some observers feel that this concern is misplaced—the pursuit of profit will force these corporations to respect the values and customs of the nations and cultures where they operate. Some observers have a less optimistic view. They point to the 1998 controversy surrounding the publication of *East and West* as a prime example of the dangers of media globalization.

The book's author, Chris Patten, was Britain's last governor to Hong Kong before that colony was returned to Chinese control in 1997. Patten was given a fat advance from publisher HarperCollins, a subsidiary of multinational media conglomerate News Corporation (see the box on "The Globalization of Ownership of U.S. Mass Media"), to write a book detailing his years of service. HarperCollins's analysis of early chapters of the manuscript was glowing, with its top editors calling the book a "sure best seller." But then the publisher abruptly and mysteriously dumped the project, calling it boring, below standard, and unlikely to sell.

Patten sued, and subsequent press reports, citing internal News Corporation memos, illuminated the root of the problem. Once News Corporation executives, including Chairman Rupert Murdoch, saw the text of *East and West*, they thought it too critical of the Chinese government. Patten faulted Beijing for what he saw as its lack of commitment to democracy. This was troublesome for News Corporation because it had significant business dealings with those same leaders and had ambitions of even more. In fact, as News Corporation critics were delighted to point out, the company had a history of attempting to placate the Chinese government, already having pulled BBC World Television from its Asian television service because that respected news source had aired a speech critical of China's human rights record.

Although Patten immediately found another publisher for *East and West* (Macmillan), newspapers and broadcast outlets around the world gave the story full play. The affair, however, was ignored by News Corporation's many media outlets.

The U.S. media holdings of four multinational corporations are shown in the box "The Globalization of Ownership of U.S. Mass Media." Of which of these were you aware?

AUDIENCE FRAGMENTATION

The nature of the other partner in the mass communication process is changing too. The audience is becoming more fragmented, its segments more narrowly defined. It is becoming less of a mass audience.

Before the advent of television, radio and magazines were national media. Big national radio networks brought news and entertainment to the entire country. Magazines like *Life, Look,* and the *Saturday Evening Post* once offered limited text and many pictures to a national audience. But television could do these things better. It was radio with pictures; it was magazines with motion. To survive, radio and magazines were forced to find new functions. No longer able to compete on a mass scale, these media targeted smaller audiences that were alike in some important characteristic, and therefore more attractive to specific advertisers. So now we have magazines like *Ski* and *Internet World,* and radio station formats such as Country, Urban, and Lithuanian. This phenomenon is known as **narrowcasting, niche marketing,** or **targeting.**

Technology has wrought the same effect on television. Before the advent of cable television, people could choose from among the three commercial broadcast networks—ABC, CBS, NBC—one noncommercial public broadcasting station, and, in larger markets, maybe an independent station or two. Now, with cable, satellite, and VCRs, people have literally thousands of viewing options. The television audience has been fragmented. To attract advertisers, each channel now must find a more specific group of people to make up its viewership. Nickelodeon targets kids, for example; Nick at Night appeals to baby boomers; Fox Television aims at young urban viewers; and Bravo seeks upper-income older people.

If the nature of the media's audience is changing, then the mass communication process must also change. The audience in mass communication is typically a large, varied group about which the media industries know only the most superficial information. What will happen as smaller, more specific audiences become better known to their partners in the

The Globalization of Ownership of U.S. Mass Media

Several international conglomerates have significant holdings in U.S. media companies whose names are quite familiar. Here are the holdings of just four.

BERTELSMANN (GERMANY)

Books	Magazines	Recordings	Multimedia
Bantam	*McCall's*	RCA Records	America Online
Doubleday	*YM*	BMG Music	Rocket Science
Dell	*Family Circle*	BMG Catalogue	BMG Interactive
Random House	*Fitness*	Arista	
Knopf	*Parents*	Killer Tracks	
Crown			
Ballantine			
Times Books			
Fodor's			
The Modern Library			
Times Business			
Princeton Review			
Everyman's Library			
Pantheon			
Villard			
Schocken			
Vintage			
Harmony Books			
Clarkson N. Potter			
Del Rey			
Fawcett			
Bell Tower			

NEWS CORPORATION (AUSTRALIA)

Magazines	Multimedia	Newspapers
Triangle Publications	Delphi	*Boston Herald*
TV Guide	MCI Online	*New York Post*

Books	Video/Film	Recordings
HarperCollins	20th Century Fox	20th Century Fox Records
Basic Books	Fox (Network) Television	
Regan Books	Fox Video	
Westview Press	Fox Cable Network	
	f/x Cable Network	
	22 television stations:	
	KBRC, Birmingham, AL	
	KTTV, Los Angeles, CA	
	KDVR, Denver, CO	
	KFTC, Fort Collins, CO	
	WFLD, Chicago, IL	
	WFXT, Boston, MA	
	WNYW, New York, NY	
	WGHP, High Point, NC	
	WTXF, Philadelphia, PA	
	WHBQ, Memphis, TN	
	KRIV, Houston, TX	
	KSTU, Salt Lake City, UT	

SEAGRAM (CANADA)

Books	Video/Film	Recordings
Putnam	MCA	MCA Records
Berkley Group	Universal	Geffen
	Cinema International	Uni Distribution
	United International	PolyGram
	MCA TV	Decca
	USA Cable Network	Kapp
		Jersey
		GRP
		Rising Tide
		Interscope
		A&M
		Deutsche Grammophon
		Island
		Mercury
		Motown

Multimedia

Universal Interactive

Interplay

SONY (JAPAN)

Video/Film	Recordings	Multimedia
Columbia Pictures	CBS Records	Sony
Sony Pictures Classics	Columbia Records	
TriStar Pictures	Sony	
Columbia TriStar Television	Relativity	
Columbia TriStar Home Video	Chaos	
Loews Theaters	Epic	
	TriStar Music	
	WTG	

What implications do you see for the trend represented by these holdings?

Sources: Various, including *Village Voice,* 16 January 1996; *Broadcasting & Cable Yearbook,* 1997; and online.

process of making meaning? What will happen to the national culture that binds us as we become increasingly fragmented into demographically targeted **taste publics**—groups of people bound by little more than an interest in a given form of media content?

EROSION OF DISTINCTIONS AMONG MEDIA

David Bowie first released his 1996 single "Telling Lies" online, rather than on disc. HBO produces first-run films for its own cable television channel, immediately releasing them on tape for VCR rental. Both former *New Republic* editor Michael Kinsley and former Republican presidential hopeful Pete DuPont publish political magazines exclusively on the Web. Stephen King and his publisher, Viking Press, published the horrormeister's 1993 story *Umney's Last Case* exclusively on the Internet. The *Mighty Morphin Power Rangers* is as much a 30-minute television commercial for licensed merchandise, like toys and clothes, as it is a Saturday morning cartoon.

You can read the *New York Times* or *Time* magazine and hundreds of other newspapers and magazines on your computer screen. Manufacturers now produce WebTV, allowing families to curl up in front of the big screen for online entertainment and information. Cable television delivers high-fidelity digitized music by DMX. *500 Nations* was a television film designed to promote a CD-ROM-based educational package about Native Americans. Where people once had to buy game cartridges for Sega and other video games, now these games can be played interactively on cable television. The Mighty Ducks is an NHL hockey team, a TV cartoon show, and a series of Hollywood movies. Teens and young adults enthusiastically read 'zines, hybrids of newspapers and magazines.

The traditional lines between media are disappearing. Conglomeration is one reason. If one company owns newspapers, an online service, television stations, book publishers, a magazine or two, and a film company, it has a strong incentive to get the greatest use from its content, whether news, education, or entertainment, by using as many channels of delivery as possible. The industry calls it **synergy,** and it is the driving force behind several recent mergers and acquisitions in the media and telecommunications industries. In 1997, for example, computer software titan Microsoft paid $1 billion for a 6% interest in cable television operation US West. Microsoft's goal in this and other similar purchases (it already owned part of cable giant Comsat Corporation and, at the time, was negotiating for a one-third stake in TCI Cable) is to make cable and the Internet indistinguishable.

Another reason for the merging of media is audience fragmentation. A mass communicator who finds it difficult to reach the whole audience can reach its component parts through various media. A third reason is the audience itself. We are becoming increasingly comfortable receiving information and entertainment from a variety of sources. Will this expansion and blurring of traditional media channels confuse audience members, further tilting the balance of power in the mass communication process toward the media industries? Or will it give audiences more power—power to choose, power to reject, and power to combine information and entertainment in individual ways?

Concentration of ownership, globalization of media, audience fragmentation, and the erosion of traditional distinctions among the media are forcing all parties in the mass communication process to think critically about their positions in it. Those in the media industries face the issue of professional ethics, discussed in Chapter 13. Audience members confront the issue of media literacy, a topic at the core of Chapter 2.

Chapter Review

Communication is the process of creating shared meaning. All communication is composed of the same elements, but technology changes the nature of those elements. Communication between a mass medium and its audience is mass communication, a primary contributor to the construction and maintenance of culture. James Carey's articulation of the "cultural definition" of communication enriched our understanding of how mass communication functions in our lives.

As the learned behavior of a given social group, culture is the world made meaningful. It resides all around us; it is socially constructed and is maintained through communication. Culture limits as well as liberates us; it differentiates as well as unites us. It defines our realities and shapes the ways we think, feel, and act.

Although culture and communication are interrelated, the influence of mass communication has long been in dispute. Still debated are micro- versus macro-level effects, administrative versus critical research, and the transmissional versus the ritual perspective.

Because we construct and maintain our culture largely through mass communication, mass communication offers us remarkable opportunities, but with them come important responsibilities. As our culture's dominant storytellers or as the forum where we debate cultural meanings, media industries have an obligation to operate professionally and ethically. Audience members, likewise, have the responsibility to consume media messages critically and thoughtfully.

The proponents of technological determinism argue that technology is the predominant agent of social and cultural change. Opponents of this view believe that technology is only one part of the mix and that how people use technology is the crucial factor in determining its power. The new communication technologies, which promise to reshape our understanding of mass communication, are controversial for that very reason.

Money, too, shapes the mass communication process. Questions arise about the nature of the partnership between media professionals and their audiences when audiences are seen as products to be sold to a third party (advertisers) rather than as equal members in the process. Ultimately, however, ours is a capitalist economic system, and the media, as profit-making entities, must operate within its limits and constraints. Our task is to understand this and demand that, within these limits, media operate ethically and responsibly. This is especially crucial today as technological and economic factors—concentration of ownership, globalization of media, audience fragmentation, and erosion of traditional distinctions among media—promise to further alter the nature of mass communication.

Questions for Review

1. What is culture? How does culture define people?
2. What is communication? What is mass communication?
3. What are encoding and decoding? How do they differ when technology enters the communication process?
4. What does it mean to say that communication is a reciprocal process?
5. What is James Carey's cultural definition of communication? How does it differ from other definitions of that process?
6. What three dichotomies define the debate surrounding media effects?
7. What do we mean by mass media as cultural storyteller?
8. What do we mean by mass communication as cultural forum?
9. How did the advent of penny newspapers in 1830 change the nature of the mass communication process?
10. What is concentration of ownership? media globalization? audience fragmentation?

Questions for Critical Thinking and Discussion

1. Do you feel inhibited by your bounded culture? by the dominant culture? How so?
2. Think about your reaction to the O. J. Simpson verdicts. Can you separate your feelings from your racial or ethnic identity? Why or why not? Have you ever discussed your views on these controversial decisions with a person from a different racial or ethnic group? Describe that experience. Do you see our culture as unified or divided?
3. Who were your childhood heroes and heroines? Why did you choose them? What cultural lessons did you learn from them?
4. Critique the definition of culture given in this chapter. What would you personally add? subtract?
5. What are the qualities of a thoughtful and reflective media consumer? Do you have these characteristics? Why or why not?

Important Resources

Alexander, J. C., & Seidman, S. (1990). *Culture and society: Contemporary debates.* **New York: Cambridge University Press.** A collection of 31 essays drawn from other sources. Various perspectives, such as Marxism, postmodernism, and structuralism, are employed in examining culture's influence on how people and groups organize their daily lives.

Carey, J. W. (1989). *Communication as culture: Essays on media and society.* **Boston, MA: Unwin Hyman.** A collection of essays and lectures from the "founder" of the cultural approach to media studies in the United States. Taken together, they present a strong basis for approaching mass communication and technology from the cultural or ritual perspective.

Gerbner, G., Mowlana, H., & Nordenstreng, K. (Eds.). (1993). *The global media debate.* **Norwood, NJ: Ablex.** An edited volume containing several essays of various levels of sophistication. Issues range from the cultural impact of increased globalization on native cultures to the technological advances driving the trend.

Real, M. R. (1996). *Exploring media culture: A guide.* **Thousand Oaks, CA: Sage.** Examines the interaction between popular culture and the mass media. Investigates the cultural role of media and content, such as Hollywood movies, the Internet, and MTV, as a means of helping the public become more skilled "readers" of the media.

Culture and the Media Web Sites

Read more about Ben Bagdikian's *Media Monopoly:*

http://www.socialchange.net.au.tcc/books_and_Articles/Articles/3928.htm

Cultural reaction to Barbie can be found in several Web sites. Two interesting places to start are:

The Barbie List

http://www.silverlink.net/~crash/barbies/136-160.html

The Barbie Closet

http://www.spesh.com/barbie/barburl.htm

Media Literacy and Culture

Baby-sitting your 3-year-old niece was *not* how you wanted to spend your Saturday night. But family is family, so here you are, watching television with a little kid.

"What do you want to watch?" you ask.

"MTV!" she cheers.

"No. You're too young."

"*X-Files*!"

"No. It's too scary for little kids like you."

"Mommy lets me watch."

"Are you telling me the truth?"

"No. How 'bout HBO?"

"Compromise. How about Disney?"

"What means *compromise*?"

"It means we'll watch Disney." You punch up the Disney Channel with the remote and settle in to watch what looks like an adolescent action show. Three preteen sleuths are in a low-speed car chase, pursuing a bad guy of some sort.

When the chase takes them into a car wash, your niece asks, "Why are they dreaming?"

"What?!"

"Why are those people dreaming?"

"They're not dreaming."

"Then why is the picture going all woosie-like?"

"That's not woosie-like. That's the brushes in the car wash going over the windshield. The camera is showing us what they're seeing. It's called POV, point of view. It's when the camera shows what the characters are seeing."

"I know that! But why are they dreaming? When the picture goes all woosie-like, it means that the people are dreaming!"

"Says who?"

"Says everyone. And when the music gets louder, that means the show's gonna be over. And when the man talks real loud, that means it's a commercial. And when stars and moons come out of the kitty's head, that means it hurts."

"Can we just be quiet for a little bit?"

"And when there's blood, it's really catsup. And when the. . . ."

"If I let you watch MTV, will you quiet down?"

"Cool. Deal."

"Are you really only 3?"

"And a half."

In this chapter we investigate how we can improve our media literacy skills. Before we can do this, however, we must understand why literacy, in and of itself, is important. Throughout history, literacy has meant power. When communication was primarily oral, the leaders were most often the best storytellers. The printing press ushered in the beginnings of mass communication, and in this primarily print-based environment, power and influence migrated to those who could read.

As literacy spread through various cultures, power began to fragment. The world became increasingly democratic. In today's modern, mass mediated cultures, literacy is still important, but there are now two forms of literacy—literacy as traditionally understood (the ability to read) and media literacy.

Let's begin by looking at the development of writing and the formation of **literate culture.** An expanding literate population encouraged technological innovation; the printing press transformed the world. Other communication technology advances have also had a significant impact; however, these technologies cannot be separated from how people have used them. Technology can be used in ways beneficial and otherwise. The skilled, beneficial use of media technologies is the goal of media literacy.

A Cultural History of Mass Communication

Our quick trip through the history of mass communication begins at the beginning, in cultures whose only form of communication was oral.

ORAL CULTURE

Oral or **preliterate cultures** are those without a written language. Virtually all communication must be face-to-face, and this fact helps to define the culture, its structure, and its operation. Whether they existed thousands of years ago before writing was developed or still function today (for example, among certain Eskimo peoples and African tribes where **griots,** or "talking chiefs," provide oral histories of their people going back hundreds of years), oral cultures are remarkably alike. They share these characteristics:

The meaning in language is specific and local. As a result, communities are closely knit, and their members are highly dependent on each other for all aspects of life.

Knowledge must be passed on orally. People must be *shown* and *told* how to do something. Therefore, skilled hunters, farmers, midwives, and the like hold a special status; they are the living embodiments of culture.

Memory is crucial. As repositories of cultural customs and traditions, elders are revered; they are responsible for passing knowledge on to the next generation.

Myth and history are intertwined. Storytellers are highly valued; they are the meaning makers, and, like the elders, they pass on what is important to the culture.

What does the resulting culture look like? People know each other intimately and rely on one another for survival. Roles are clearly defined. Stories teach important cultural lessons and preserve important cultural traditions and values. Control over communication is rarely necessary, but when it is, it is easily achieved through social sanctions.

THE INVENTION OF WRITING

Writing, the first communication technology, complicates this simple picture. More than 5,000 years ago, alphabets were developed independently in several places around the world. **Ideogrammatic** (picture-based) **alphabets** appeared in Egypt (as hieroglyphics), Sumeria (as cuneiform), and urban China.

Ideogrammatic alphabets require a huge number of symbols to convey even the simplest idea. Their complexity meant that only a very select few, an intellectual elite, could read or write. For writing to truly serve effective and efficient communication, one last advance was required.

The Sumerians were international traders, maintaining trade routes throughout known Europe, Africa, and Asia. The farther the Sumerian people traveled, the less they could rely on face-to-face communication and the greater their need for a more precise writing form. Sumerian cuneiform slowly expanded, allowing symbols to represent sounds rather than objects and ideas. Appearing around 1800 B.C., these were the first elements of a **syllable alphabet**—an alphabet employing sequences of vowels and consonants, that is, words.

The syllable alphabet as we know it today slowly developed, aided greatly by ancient Semitic cultures, and eventually flowered in Greece around 800 B.C. Like the Sumerians long before them, the Greeks perfected

This Sumerian cuneiform dates from 700 years before the birth of Christ.

their easy alphabet of necessity. Having little in the way of natural resources, the Greek city-states depended and thrived on bustling trade routes all around the Aegean and Mediterranean Seas. For orders to be placed, deals arranged, manifests compiled, and records kept, writing that was easy to learn, use, and understand was necessary.

A medium was necessary to carry this new form of communication. The Sumerians had used clay tablets, but the Egyptians, Greeks, and Romans eventually employed **papyrus,** rolls of sliced strips of reed pressed together. Around 100 B.C. the Romans began using **parchment,** a writing material made from prepared animal skins, and by A.D. 100 the Chinese had developed a paper made from rags. This technology made its way to Europe through various trade routes some 600 years later.

LITERATE CULTURE

With the coming of **literacy**—the ability to effectively and efficiently comprehend and use written symbols—the social and cultural rules and structures of preliterate times began to change. People could accumulate a permanent body of knowledge and transmit that knowledge from one generation to another. Among the changes that writing brought were these:

Meaning and language became more uniform. The words "a bolt of cloth" had to mean the same to a reader in Mesopotamia as they did to one in Sicily. Over time, communities became less closely knit and their members less dependent on one another. The definition of "community" expanded to include people outside the local area.

This Egyptian funeral papyrus depicts the weighing of a heart when a person dies.

Communication could occur over long distances and long periods of time. With knowledge being transmitted in writing, power shifted from those who could show others their special talents to those who could write and read about them.

The culture's memory, history, and myth could be recorded on paper. With written histories, elders and storytellers began to lose their status, and new elites developed. Homer (some historians believe he was actually several scribes), for example, compiled in written form several generations of oral stories and histories that we know as the *Iliad* and the *Odyssey*.

What did the resulting culture look like? It was no longer local. Its members could survive not only by hunting or farming together but by commercial, political, or military expansion. Empires replaced communities. There was more compartmentalization of people based on what they did to earn a living—bakers baked, herders herded, merchants sold goods. Yet, at the same time, role and status were less permanently fixed. Slaves who learned to read to serve their masters took on new duties for those masters and rose in status.

Power and influence now resided not in the strongest hunter, wisest elder, or most engaging storyteller but in those who could read and write; that is, power and influence now rested with those who were literate. They could best engage in widespread official communication, and they wrote the histories and passed on cultural values and lessons. With this change from preliterate to literate culture, the first stirrings of a new political philosophy were born. Reading and writing encouraged more open and robust debate, political exchange, and criticism of the powerful; in other words, it fostered democracy.

It's important to remember that in the newly literate cultures, communication was still quite limited. An orator could address at most a few hundred people at a time. Writers could reach only those literate few who held their handwritten scrolls or letters. The printing press would change this, making it possible to duplicate communication, thereby expanding our ability to communicate with one another.

THE GUTENBERG REVOLUTION

It is impossible to overstate the importance of Johannes Gutenberg's development of movable metal type. Historian S. H. Steinberg wrote in *Five Hundred Years of Printing*:

> Neither political, constitutional, ecclesiastical, and economic, nor sociological, philosophical, and literary movements can be fully understood without taking into account the influence the printing press has exerted upon them. (1959, p. 11)

This page from a Gutenberg Bible shows the exquisite care the printer used in creating his works. The artwork in the margins is hand-painted, but the text is mechanically printed.

Marshall McLuhan expressed his admiration for Gutenberg's innovation by calling his 1962 book *The Gutenberg Galaxy*. In it he argued that the advent of print is the key to our modern consciousness. Why was Gutenberg's invention so important? Simply because it allowed *mass* communication.

The Printing Press Printing and the printing press existed long before Gutenberg perfected his process in or around 1446. The Chinese were using wooden block presses as early as A.D. 600 and by A.D. 1000 had movable clay type. A simple movable metal type was even in use in Korea in the 13th century. Gutenberg's printing press was a significant leap forward, however, for two important reasons.

Gutenberg was a goldsmith and a metallurgist. He hit upon the idea of using metal type crafted from lead molds in place of type made from wood or clay. This was an important advance. Not only was metal type durable enough to print page after page but letters could be arranged and rearranged to make any message possible. And Gutenberg was able to produce virtually identical copies.

In addition, Gutenberg's advance over Korean metal mold printing was one of scope and intention. The Korean press was used to produce attractive artwork. Gutenberg saw his invention as a way to produce books—many books—for profit. He was, however, a poor businessman. He stressed quality over quantity, in part because of his reverence for the book he was printing, the Bible. He used the highest quality paper and ink and turned out far fewer volumes than he otherwise could have.

Other printers, however, quickly saw the true economic potential of Gutenberg's invention. The first Gutenberg Bible appeared in 1456. By the end of that century, 44 years later, printing operations existed in 12 European countries, and the continent was flooded with 20 million volumes of some 35,000 different titles.

The Impact of Print   Although Gutenberg developed his printing press with a limited use in mind, printing Bibles, the cultural effects of mass printing have been profound.

Handwritten or hand copied materials were expensive to produce, and the cost of an education, in time and money, had made reading an expensive luxury. However, with the spread of printing, written communication was available to a much larger portion of the population, and the need for literacy among the lower and middle classes grew. The ability to read became less of a luxury and more of a necessity; eventually literacy spread, as did education. Soldiers at the front needed to be able to read the emperor's orders. Butchers needed to understand the king's shopping list. So the demand for literacy expanded, and more (and more types of) people learned to read.

Tradespeople, soldiers, clergy, bakers, and musicians all now had business at the printer's shop. They talked. They learned of things, both in conversation and by reading printed material. As more people learned to read, new ideas germinated and spread, and cross-pollination of ideas occurred.

More material from various sources was published, and people were freer to read what they wanted when they wanted. Dominant authorities—

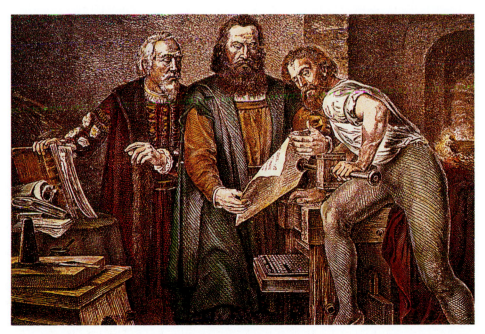

Johannes Gutenberg takes the first proof from his printing press.

the Crown and the Church—were now less able to control communication and, therefore, the culture. New ideas about the world appeared; new understandings of the existing world flourished.

In addition, duplication permitted standardization and preservation. Myth and superstition began to make way for standard, verifiable bodies of knowledge. History, economics, physics, and chemistry all became part of the culture's intellectual life. Literate cultures were now on the road to modernization.

Printed materials were the first mass-produced product, speeding the development and entrenchment of capitalism. We live today in a world built on these changes. Use of the printing press helped fuel the establishment and growth of a large middle class. No longer were societies composed of rulers and subjects; printing sped the rise of democracy. No longer were power and wealth functions of birth. Power and wealth could now be created by the industrious. No longer was political discourse limited to accepting the dictates of Crown and Church. Printing had given ordinary people a powerful voice.

THE INDUSTRIAL REVOLUTION

By the mid-18th century, the printing press had become one of the engines driving the Industrial Revolution. Print was responsible for building and disseminating bodies of knowledge, leading to scientific and technological developments and the refinement of new machines. In addition, industrialization reduced the time necessary to complete work, and this created something heretofore unknown to most working people—leisure time.

Industrialization had another effect as well. As workers left their sunrise-to-sunset jobs in agriculture, the crafts, and trades to work in the newly industrialized factories, not only did they have more leisure time but they had more money to spend on their leisure. Farmers, fishermen, and tile makers had to put their profits back into their jobs. But factory workers took their money home, some of which was spendable. Combine leisure time and expendable cash with the spread of literacy and the result is a large and growing audience for printed *information* and *entertainment*. By the late 19th century, a mass audience and the means to reach it existed.

"Modern" Communication Technologies

Every major advance in mass communication technology has affected the cultures that used it, just as the printing press changed Western Europe. Today, many experts argue that television and computers are equal in influence to Gutenberg's marvel. Whether you agree or not, there is no doubt that the introduction of mass market newspapers and magazines, motion pictures, radio, television, and computers has created a world markedly different from that which existed before their arrival. All media will be examined in detail in upcoming chapters, but here are some thumbnail sketches of the cultural impact of these new modes of communication.

NEWSPAPERS, MAGAZINES, MOTION PICTURES, AND RADIO

The printing press made newspapers and magazines possible, but it was technological and social changes brought about by industrialization that gave us *mass market* newspapers and magazines. As these media were beginning to flourish in the late 19th and early 20th centuries, motion pictures and radio were also developing. Taken together, these communication technologies spoke to and for the growing lower- and middle-class populations of the United States. This was a time of remarkable transformation.

The westward migration that had begun in the 1840s was in full force, and immigrants from Asia and Europe were pouring into the United States in search of jobs and opportunity. Former slaves and their children began moving north to the great industrial cities in the late 1860s, looking for freedom and dignity as well as work. Industry was producing consumer products, like electric lights and telephones, that once were only dreams. Organized labor was agitating for a greater say in workers' lives. Government was struggling to deal with duties and responsibilities unimagined 20 years earlier.

Into the middle of this volatile brew came the new mass market media. Foreign-speaking immigrants and unschooled laborers could be informed and entertained by movies or radio; minimal reading skill was required.

Mass circulation newspapers brought everyday people into the cultural dialogue, as depicted in this 1873 painting by Edgar Degas, *The Interior of the Cotton Market in New Orleans.*

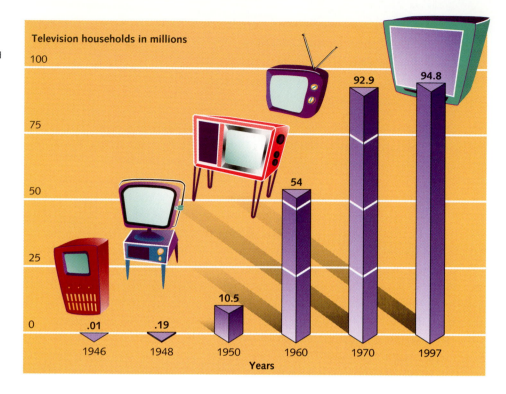

Figure 2–1 Growth of Television in the United States. *Source:* Census data and *Broadcasting & Cable Yearbook;* various years.

Television households in millions

Years

Mass market newspapers and magazines were simple to read and full of pictures and cartoons, accessible even to newly literate immigrants and un-educated former slaves. Movies were silent, requiring no reading ability at all, and radios in the 1920s were inexpensive to own and demanded nothing more of listeners than the ability to hear. For the first time in history, an entire population was able to participate in cultural communication.

Mass market newspapers and magazines, motion pictures, and radio helped unify a rapidly expanding, pluralistic, multi-ethnic country; created and nourished the U.S. middle class; and established, supported, and solidified the roots of the U.S. consumer economy.

TELEVISION

Television was no less influential. Its diffusion throughout U.S. homes was phenomenal. Figure 2–1 shows this remarkable rate of growth.

Television was virtually nonexistent in 1945 at the end of World War II, with only 10,000 sets in people's homes, and those exclusively in major urban areas. A short 14 years later, 54 million households had televisions. The country that welcomed television was as much in a state of transformation as the one that had already greeted mass market newspapers, magazines, movies, and radio.

World War II further removed the United States from its primarily rural, small-town identity. It was fast becoming a global industrial giant. More people now worked shorter weeks (40 hours) and had increased leisure time—and money to spend. The manufacturing capabilities refined

Television may not have "caused" the Civil Rights movement, but Dr. Martin Luther King's adroit use of the medium's ability to brings scenes like this into people's homes surely aided the cause.

for the war effort were retooled for the manufacture of consumer products—cars, golf clubs, sportswear—that took advantage of this free time and money. Because people needed to know about these new products in order to buy them, advertising expanded.

Minorities who had fought for freedom in Europe and Asia demanded it at home. Some women who had entered the workforce while the men were at war remained on the job, but many others returned to their homes in the 1950s. However, by the 1960s and 1970s women were questioning their domestic role. This, as well as economic necessity, contributed to the re-entry of women into the workforce in even greater numbers. The trend toward both Mom and Dad working outside the home was set. People left their small towns to move nearer the factories, and traditional communities began to dissolve. Historically important anchors like school and church lost their hold over children, and thanks to the postwar baby boom, there were teenagers aplenty when television became a mass medium.

Television became a true mass medium in 1960, reaching into 90% of all U.S. homes. At that time the United States was characterized by social and racial unrest. The youth revolution of "sex, drugs, and rock 'n roll" took hold in that decade, as did economic growth accompanied by rampant commercialism and consumerism. There were dramatic rises in violence of all kinds, especially teen violence and juvenile delinquency. Television was smack in the middle of this social and cultural sea change.

Did the new medium *cause* this transformation? No, television did not cause these profound alterations in our culture. To make that argument is to take the transmissional view. But if we apply Carey's ritual perspective (see Chapter 1) to an example from that era, the success of the Civil Rights movement, it is easy to understand the cultural importance of mass communication in our lives.

It is impossible to imagine the Civil Rights movement succeeding without the ugly televised pictures of Southern cops and their dogs descending on Dr. Martin Luther King Jr. and his peaceful marchers. The ability of television to convey "representations of shared belief" was central to Dr. King's strategy. He believed that Americans were basically good and fair and that they shared a fundamental belief in freedom and equality. Dr. King's plan worked; people of conscience were shocked at scenes of non-resisting marchers being bludgeoned. After seeing televised news reports from Selma, Alabama, President John F. Kennedy is reported to have turned to his brother, Attorney General Robert Kennedy, and said, "We must now act. The American people will not stand for this." He then dedicated the power of his office to the movement.

COMPUTER NETWORKS

The United States of the late 1990s, much like the country that greeted television, is a nation in transition. It has "won" the Cold War, but its citizens aren't coming home to a changed culture as they did in 1945; they never left. Yet the rules have changed anyway. The United States does not stand supreme as it did after World War II. Rather, it is one player in the global economy, struggling to assert dominance. In this cause the nature of work has changed. The service industries—retailing, telecommunications, social services—now provide more jobs than does manufacturing.

In the midst of this change are the new computer technologies. The information society, the electronic superhighway, the information infrastructure, and virtual reality were unimagined 20 years ago. Individuals can communicate electronically in an instant with one person or 10 million people. People search for and retrieve information from the world's most sophisticated libraries, newspapers, and databases without ever leaving

We have yet to realize the full impact of the new computer technologies. For example, many of us are familiar with virtual reality, pictured here, as an amusing diversion. But scientists foresee far more significant uses for this digital wonder.

The Dangers of Papyrus

New communication technologies invariably are met with concern. Today's debate surrounds the impact of the Internet and the World Wide Web. On April Fools' Day 1997, the *ABC Evening News* offered this report:

> WORLD NEWS NOW (THEN) Egypt's emerging papyrus technology continues to alarm parents and law enforcement. A new bill introduced today would let the government regulate material found on papyrus. Legislators said paperspace, as it is known to so-called writers, is becoming a haven for monotheists, con artists, and worse, hoping to prey on the young and the gullible. A little bit later in the broadcast we will have some tips on how to shield your children from offensive and dangerous material found on the papyrus.

Clearly, this is a humorous take on the current debate over the Internet in our cultural forum. What is your own opinion?

their homes. Many workers telecommute, rarely visiting the office. More and more, homes are *becoming* people's offices. We are an **information society**—a society wherein the creation and exchange of information is the dominant social and economic activity.

We can't be certain yet how this information society will evolve, but many issues are already being debated, as you will see in Chapters 13, 14, and 15. For example, what becomes of those who cannot afford to be linked, wired, and online? Will computer technologies divide the nation into information haves and have-nots? What new communities will develop? Who owns information? What skills will be needed to succeed professionally and personally? To what extent should government be involved in creating and maintaining computer networks? Should there be official policing of content?

These are questions about the use and control of a new medium. Throughout history, whenever new communication technologies have been introduced, societies have inevitably confronted similar questions (see the box "The Dangers of Papyrus"). The concern, obviously, is with how best to use the strengths of the emerging medium and how to minimize its disruptive potential. This is just one element, albeit an important one, of media literacy.

Media Literacy

Television influences our culture in innumerable ways. One of its effects, according to many people, is that it has encouraged violence in our society. For example, according to a *New York Times* survey from 1996, U.S. television viewers overwhelmingly (more than 80%) say there is too much violence on television. Yet almost without exception, the local television news program that has the largest proportion of violence in its nightly newscast is the ratings leader. "If it bleeds, it leads" has become the motto for much of local television news. It leads because people watch.

So, although many of us are quick to condemn improper media performance or to identify and lament its harmful effects, we rarely question our own role in the mass communication process. We overlook it because we participate in mass communication naturally, almost without conscious effort. We possess high-level interpretive and comprehension skills that make even the most sophisticated television show, movie, or magazine story understandable and enjoyable. We are able, through a lifetime of interaction with this medium, to *read media texts*. Recall the opening vignette. That 3-year-old was already exhibiting a fairly high level of skill at reading television texts. Maybe her skills aren't as sophisticated as yours—she did not know POV, for example—but in her short life she has already become a fairly skilled viewer.

Media literacy is a skill we take for granted, but like all skills, it can be improved. And if we consider how important the mass media are in creating and maintaining the culture that helps define us and our lives, it is a skill that *must* be improved.

ELEMENTS OF MEDIA LITERACY

Earlier we defined literacy as the ability to effectively and efficiently comprehend and use written symbols. With the development of nonprint-based media, however, that definition must be expanded to include the ability to effectively and efficiently comprehend and utilize *any form of communication*. When speaking specifically of participation in mass communication, this ability is called **media literacy.**

Media literacy can mean somewhat different things to different observers, as shown in the box "Defining Media Literacy." What each of its definitions has in common, however, is the idea that media consumers must develop the "ability" or "facility" to better interpret media content. So, for our purposes, media literacy is the ability to effectively and efficiently comprehend and utilize mass media content.

Media scholar Art Silverblatt (1995) identified five fundamental elements of media literacy. To these we will add two more. Media literacy includes these characteristics:

Defining Media Literacy

Media literacy takes on slightly different meanings depending on the orientation of the person or organization doing the defining. Here are four useful definitions currently in play in the cultural forum. How would you assess the worth of each? Identify the one most useful for you and defend your choice.

From the *National Telemedia Council* (1992, p. 12), a professional association designed to promote media literacy:

The ability to choose, to understand—within the context of content, form/style, impact, industry and production—to question, to evaluate, to create and/or produce and to respond thoughtfully to the media we consume.

From the *Aspen Institute's National Leadership Conference on Media Literacy* (1992, p. 1), a foundation dedicated to improving the social and cultural life of U.S. citizens:

The ability of a citizen to access, analyze, and produce information for specific outcomes.

From the *Cultural Environment Movement* ("The People's Charter," 1996, p. 1), a public interest group devoted to increasing literacy as a way to combat corporate takeover of media:

The right to acquire information and skills necessary to participate fully in public deliberation and communication. This requires facility in reading, writing, and storytelling; critical media awareness; computer literacy, and education about the role of communication in society.

From the *National Communication Association* (1996, p. 2), a professional scholarly organization composed largely of university academics:

Being a critical and reflective consumer of communication requires an understanding of how words, images, graphics, and sounds work together in ways that are both subtle and profound. Mass media such as radio, television, and film and electronic media such as the telephone, the Internet, and computer conferencing influence the way meanings are created and shared in contemporary society. So great is this impact that in choosing how to send a message and evaluate its effect, communicators need to be aware of the distinctive characteristics of each medium.

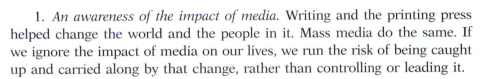

1. *An awareness of the impact of media.* Writing and the printing press helped change the world and the people in it. Mass media do the same. If we ignore the impact of media on our lives, we run the risk of being caught up and carried along by that change, rather than controlling or leading it.

2. *An understanding of the process of mass communication.* If we know the components of the mass communication process and how they relate to one another, we can form expectations of how they can serve us. What are the rights, duties, and obligations of the media industries? of the audience? How do different media limit or enhance messages? Which forms of feedback are most effective, and why?

3. *Strategies for analyzing and discussing media messages.* To consume media messages thoughtfully, we need a foundation on which to base thought and reflection. If *we* make meaning, we must possess the tools with which to make it (for example, understanding the intent and impact of film and video conventions like camera angles and lighting, or the

Media Literacy As the Struggle for Power

Some approaches to media literacy are avowedly political; that is, they see media literacy in terms of the struggle between disadvantaged audiences and powerful media industries. The Cultural Environment Movement, a coalition of 150 independent organizations with supporters in 64 countries, and Paper Tiger Television, a group that uses public access television to boost media literacy, are two examples. Here are their approaches to media literacy. Are these the rantings of paranoid, anti-media zealots, or do these approaches have merit?

The Cultural Environment Movement ("The People's Charter," 1996, p. 4) issued its *Viewers' Declaration of Independence* at its Founding Convention. Here are excerpts:

Viewers' Declaration of Independence

This declaration originated at the Founding Convention of the Cultural Environment Movement (CEM) in St. Louis, Missouri, U.S.A., on March 17, 1996. It was revised following suggestions by a committee elected at the convention.

> We hold these truths to be self-evident:
>
> That all persons are endowed with the right to live in a cultural environment that is respectful of their humanity and supportive of their potential.
>
> That all children are endowed with the right to grow up in a cultural environment that fosters responsibility, trust, and community rather than force, fear, and violence.
>
> That when the cultural environment becomes destructive of these ends, it is necessary to alter it.

Such is the necessity that confronts us. Let the world hear the reasons that compel us to assert our rights and to take an active role in the shaping of our common cultural environment.

1. Humans live and learn by stories. Today they are no longer hand-crafted, home-made, community-inspired. They are no longer told by families, schools, or churches but are the products of a complex mass-production and marketing process. Scottish patriot Andrew Fletcher once said, "If one were permitted to make all the ballads, one need not care who should make the laws of a nation." Today most of our "ballads"—the myths and stories of our culture—are made by a small group of global conglomerates that have something to sell.

2. This radical transformation of our cultural environment has changed the roles we grow into, the way we employ creative talent, the way we raise our children, and the way we manage our affairs. Communication channels proliferate but technologies converge and media merge. Consolidation of ownership denies entry to newcomers, drives independents out of the mainstream, and reduces diversity of content. Media blend into a seamless homogenized cultural environment that constrains life's choices as much as the degradation of the physical environment limits life's chances.

3. This change did not come about spontaneously or after thoughtful deliberation. It was imposed on an uninformed public and is enshrined in legislation rushed through Congress without any opportunity for public scrutiny or debate about its consequences and world-wide fallout. The airways, a global commons, have been given away to media empires.

strategy behind the placement of photos on a newspaper page). Otherwise meaning is made for us; the interpretation of media content will then rest with its creator, not with us.

4. *An understanding of media content as a text that provides insight into our culture and our lives.* How do we know a culture and its people, attitudes, values, concerns, and myths? We know them through communication. For modern cultures like ours, media messages increasingly dominate that communication, shaping our understanding of and insight into our culture. Some groups feel so strongly about the power of the media to shape culture that they have attempted to take back some of that

4. In exchange for that give-away, we are told, we get "free" entertainment and news, but in truth, we pay dearly, both as consumers and as citizens. The price of soap we buy includes a surcharge for the commercials that bring us the "soap opera." We pay when we wash, not when we watch. And we pay even if we do not watch or do not like the way of life promoted. This is taxation without representation. Furthermore, the advertising expenditures that buy our media are a tax-deductible business expense. Money diverted from the public treasury pays for an invisible, unelected, unaccountable, private Ministry of Culture making decisions that shape public policy behind closed doors.

5. The human consequences are also far-reaching. They include cults of media violence that desensitize, terrorize, brutalize and paralyze: the promotion of unhealthy practices that pollute, drug, hurt, poison, and kill thousands every day: portrayals that dehumanize, stereotype, marginalize and stigmatize women, racial and ethnic groups, gays and lesbians, aging or disabled or physically or mentally ill persons, and others outside the cultural mainstream.

6. These distortions of the democratic process divert attention from the basic needs, problems and aspirations of people. They conceal the drift toward ecological suicide; the silent crumbling of our vital infrastructure; the cruel neglect of children, poor people, and other vulnerable populations; the invasions of privacy at home and in the workplace; the growing inequalities of wealth and opportunity; the profits made from throwing millions of people on the scrapheap of the unemployed; the commercialization of the classroom; and the downgrading of education and the arts.

7. Global marketing formulas, imposed on media workers and foisted on the children of the world, colonize, monopolize and homogenize cultures everywhere. Technocratic fantasies mask social realities that further widen the gaps between the information rich and the information poor.

8. Repeated protests and petitions have been ignored or dismissed as attempts at "censorship" by the media magnates who alone have the power to suppress and to censor. No constitutional protection or legislative prospect will help us to loosen the noose of market censorship or to counter the repressive direction the "culture wars" are taking us. We need a liberating alternative.

We, therefore, declare our independence from a system that has drifted out of democratic reach. Our CEM offers the liberating alternative: an independent citizen voice in cultural policymaking, working for the creation of a free, fair, diverse, and responsible cultural environment for us and our children.

Paper Tiger Television was founded in 1981, and at that time issued its *Manifesto*, which reads in part:

> The power of mass culture rests on the trust of the public. This legitimacy is a paper tiger. Investigation into the corporate structures of the media and critical analysis of their content is one way to demystify the information industry. Developing a critical consciousness about the communications industry is a necessary first step toward democratic control of information resources. (online: *http://www.papertiger.org*)

power themselves. See the box "Media Literacy As the Struggle for Power" for more information about two such groups.

5. *The ability to enjoy, understand, and appreciate media content.* Media literacy doesn't mean living the life of a grump, liking nothing in the media, or always being suspicious of harmful effects and cultural degradation. We take high school and college classes to enhance our understanding and appreciation of novels; we can do the same for media texts.

Learning to enjoy, understand, and appreciate media content includes the ability to use **multiple points of access**—to approach media content from a variety of directions and derive from it many levels of meaning. Thus, we control meaning making for our own enjoyment or appreciation. For example, we can enjoy the *Star Wars* trilogy as an exciting space adventure, pitting the rebels against the Empire. But we can also understand these films as superb examples of sophisticated, high-budget Hollywood filmmaking. Or we can access them at the point of their cultural meaning. What, for example, does a character like Han Solo say about our reverence for independence and daring?

In fact, television programs like *The Larry Sanders Show, Spin City, The X-Files,* and *Star Trek: The Next Generation, Voyager,* and *Deep Space Nine* are specifically constructed to take advantage of the media literacy skills of sophisticated viewers while providing entertaining fare for less skilled consumers. The same is true for films like *Fargo* and *Pulp Fiction,* magazines like *Mondo 2000,* and the best of jazz, rap, and rock. *Larry Sanders* and *Spin City* are produced as television comedies, designed to make people laugh. But they are also intentionally produced in a manner that provides more sophisticated, media literate viewers with opportunities to make more personally interesting or relevant meaning. Anyone can laugh while watching these programs, but some people can investigate hypocrisy in show business and the meaning of friendship *(Larry Sanders),* or they can examine what goes on inside politics and the ability of an openly gay person to perform professionally in the workplace *(Spin City).*

6. *An understanding of the ethical and moral obligations of media practitioners.* To make informed judgments about the performance of the media, we also must be aware of the competing pressures on practitioners as they do their jobs. We must understand the media's official and unofficial rules of operation. In other words, we must know, respectively, their legal and ethical obligations. Return, for a moment, to the question of televised violence. It is legal for a station to air graphic violence. But is it ethical? If it is unethical, what power, if any, do we have to demand its removal from our screens? Dilemmas such as this are discussed at length in Chapter 13.

7. *Development of appropriate and effective production skills.* Traditional literacy assumes that people who can read can also write. Media literacy also makes this assumption. Our definition of literacy (of either type) calls not only for effective and efficient comprehension of content but for its effective and efficient *use.* Therefore, media literate individuals should develop production skills that allow them to create useful media messages. If you have ever tried to make a narrative home video—one that tells a story—you know that producing content is much more difficult than consuming it. Even producing a taped answering machine message that isn't embarrassing is a daunting task for many people.

This element of media literacy may seem relatively unimportant at first glance. After all, if you choose a career in media production, you'll get training in school and on the job. If you choose another calling, you may never be in the position of having to produce content. But most professions

The Larry Sanders Show is a television program about a television program in which actors such as Rosanne play themselves to Garry Shandling's Larry Sanders. When the fictional show airs during the real television program, it is shot on videotape. When the action is behind the scenes, it is shot on film. Why do you think the producers go to this trouble? And what's going on in *Pulp Fiction?* Time shifts, scenes presented nonchronologically, and absurd plot twists, all are used intentionally to meet the demands of more sophisticated moviegoers while still providing great entertainment for the larger audience. Both are fine examples of content designed expressly to be read from different points of access.

Newspapers, magazines, and television news shows intentionally used this dramatic picture of a dead U.S. Marine being dragged through a Somalian street to generate an emotional response among viewers. But even though the image said very little about U.S. military involvement in that war-torn land, its publication and airing led to a change in U.S. foreign policy in Somalia. Why?

now employ some form of media, either to disseminate information, for use in training, to enhance presentations, or to keep in contact with clients and customers. The Internet and the World Wide Web (Chapter 14) in particular require effective production skills of their users—at home, school, and work—because online receivers can and do easily become online creators.

MEDIA LITERACY SKILLS

Consuming media content is simple. Push a button and you have television pictures or music on a radio. Come up with enough cash and you can see a movie or buy a magazine. Media literate consumption, however, requires a number of specific skills:

1. *The ability and willingness to make an effort to understand content, to pay attention, and to filter out noise.* As we saw in Chapter 1, anything that interferes with successful communication is called noise, and much of the noise in the mass communication process results from our own consumption behavior. When we watch television, often we are also doing other things, such as eating, reading, or chatting on the phone. We drive while we listen to the radio. Obviously, the quality of our meaning making is related to the effort we give it.

2. *An understanding of and respect for the power of media messages.* The mass media have been around for more than a century and a half. Just about everybody can enjoy them. Their content is either free or relatively inexpensive. Much of the content is banal and a bit silly, so it is easy to dismiss media content as beneath serious consideration or too simple to have any influence.

We also disregard media's power through the **third person effect**—the common attitude that others are influenced by media messages but we are not. That is, we are media literate enough to understand the influence of mass communication on the attitudes, behaviors, and values of others but not self-aware or honest enough to see it in our own lives.

3. *The ability to distinguish emotional from reasoned reactions when responding to content and to act accordingly.* Media content is often designed to touch us at the emotional level. We enjoy losing ourselves in a good song or in a well-crafted movie or television show; this is among our great pleasures. But because we react emotionally to these messages doesn't mean they don't have serious meanings and implications for our lives.

We can use our feelings as a point of departure for meaning making. We can ask, "Why does this content make me feel this way?" For example, Secretary of State Madeleine Albright often talks of the **CNN effect**—the ability of television pictures to move people so powerfully that important military and political decisions are driven by those pictures rather than by well-reasoned policy considerations. Television pictures are intentionally shot and broadcast for their emotional impact. Reacting emotionally is appropriate and proper. But then what? What do these pictures tell us about the larger issue at hand?

4. *Development of heightened expectations of media content.* We all use media to tune out, waste a little time, and provide background noise. When we decide to watch television, we are more likely to turn on the set and flip channels until we find something passable than we are to read the listings to find a specific program to view. When we're at the video store, we often settle for anything because "It's just a rental." When we expect little from the content before us, we tend to give meaning making little effort and attention.

5. *A knowledge of genre conventions and the ability to recognize when they are being mixed.* The term **genre** refers to the categories of expression within the different media, such as "the evening news," "documentary," "horror movie," or "entertainment magazine." Each genre is characterized by certain distinctive, standardized style elements—the **conventions** of that genre. The conventions of the evening news, for example, include a short, upbeat introductory theme and one or two good-looking people sitting at a space-age desk. When we hear and see these style elements, we expect the evening news. We can tell a documentary film from an entertainment movie by its more serious tone and the number of "talking heads." We know by their appearance—the use of color and the amount of text on the cover— which magazines offer serious reading and which provide entertainment.

Knowledge of these conventions is important because they cue or direct our meaning making. For example, we know to accept the details in a documentary film about the sinking of the *Titanic* as more credible than those found in a Hollywood movie about that disaster.

This skill is also important for a second reason. Sometimes, in an effort to maximize audiences (and therefore profits) or for creative reasons, media content makers mix genre conventions. Are Oliver Stone's *Nixon* and *JFK* fact or fiction? Is Geraldo Rivera a journalist, a talk show host, or a showman? Is *G.I. Joe* a kid's cartoon or a 30-minute commercial? *Hard Copy* and *Inside Edition* look increasingly like *Dateline NBC* and the *CBS Evening News*. Reading media texts becomes more difficult as formats are co-opted.

6. *The ability to think critically about media messages, no matter how credible their sources.* It is crucial that media be credible because, in a democracy where the people govern, the media are central to the governing process. This is why the news media are sometimes referred to as the fourth branch of government, complementing the executive, judicial, and legislative branches. This does not mean, however, that we should believe everything they report. But it is often difficult to arrive at the proper balance between wanting to believe and accepting what we see and hear unquestioningly, especially when frequently we are willing to suspend disbelief and are encouraged by the media themselves to see their content as real and credible.

The sets of each of these newscasts share certain characteristics. Yet we know them to be very different types of programs with quite different definitions of what constitutes news. Why do you think the producers of *Hard Copy* employ the conventions of more traditional news programs such as *ABC News Overnight?*

Consider the *New York Times* motto, "All the News That's Fit to Print," and the title "Eyewitness News." If it's all there, it must all be real, and who is more credible than an eyewitness? But if we examine these media, we would learn that the *Times* in actuality prints all the news that fits (in its pages) and that the news is, at best, a very selective eyewitness.

7. *A knowledge of the internal language of various media and the ability to understand its effects, no matter how complex.* Just as each media genre has its own distinctive style and conventions, each medium also has its own specific internal language. This language is expressed in **production values**—the choice of lighting, editing, special effects, music, cam-

era angle, location on the page, and size and placement of headline. To be able to read a media text, you must understand its language. We learn the grammar of this language automatically from childhood; for example, "the picture going all woosie-like" from the opening vignette.

Let's consider two versions of the same movie scene. In the first, a man is driving a car. Cut to a woman lying tied up on a railroad track. What is the relationship between the man and woman? Where is he going? With no more information than these two shots, you know automatically that he cares for her and is on his way to save her. Now, here's the second version. The man is driving the car. Fade to black. Fade back up to the woman on the tracks. Now what is the relationship between the man and the woman? Where is he going? It's less clear that these two people even have anything to do with each other. We construct completely different meanings from exactly the same two pictures because the punctuation (the quick cut/fade) differs.

Media texts tend to be more complicated than these two scenes. The better we can handle their grammar, the more we can understand and appreciate texts. The more we understand texts, the more we can be equal partners with media professionals in meaning making.

THE MEDIA LITERATE PERSON

Developing solid media literacy skills should lead to several important outcomes. Silverblatt (1995) provides a scheme for the kinds of critical awareness we should develop. The media literate person:

- Is well informed about media coverage issues.
- Is aware of his or her daily contact with the media and their influence on lifestyles, attitudes, and values.
- Effectively interprets media messages to derive insight into their meaning.
- Develops a sensitivity to media content trends as a means of learning about his or her culture.
- Remains abreast of ownership, financial, and regulatory issues impacting the media industries.
- Considers the role of the media in his or her individual decision making.

Beyond this critical awareness, media literate people *discuss media* with the people around them; *make informed, critical choices* from among many media options; and, where necessary and appropriate, *engage in social action,* such as writing letters, canceling subscriptions, and registering official complaints with appropriate self- and outside regulatory agencies. A model of media literacy combining all these elements and skills is shown in Figure 2–2.

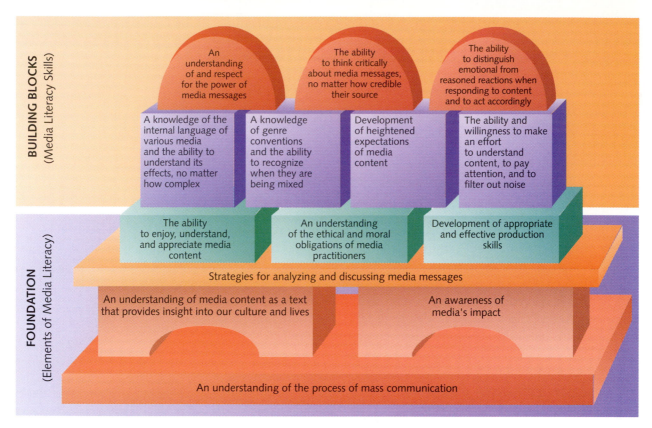

BUILDING BLOCKS (Media Literacy Skills)

An understanding of and respect for the power of media messages

The ability to think critically about media messages, no matter how credible their source

The ability to distinguish emotional from reasoned reactions when responding to content and to act accordingly

A knowledge of the internal language of various media and the ability to understand its effects, no matter how complex

A knowledge of genre conventions and the ability to recognize when they are being mixed

Development of heightened expectations of media content

The ability and willingness to make an effort to understand content, to pay attention, and to filter out noise

The ability to enjoy, understand, and appreciate media content

An understanding of the ethical and moral obligations of media practitioners

Development of appropriate and effective production skills

Strategies for analyzing and discussing media messages

FOUNDATION (Elements of Media Literacy)

An understanding of media content as a text that provides insight into our culture and lives

An awareness of media's impact

An understanding of the process of mass communication

Figure 2–2 A Model of Media Literacy. This model graphically represents some of the themes investigated in this chapter. The entire media literacy enterprise has at its base *an understanding of the process of mass communication.* Upon this rests its second most fundamental set of elements, *an understanding of media content as a text that provides insight into our culture and lives,* and *an awareness of media's impact.* Once media message consumers acquire these three elements, the remainder should logically follow. Individuals may alter the relative position of the remaining foundational elements and building blocks to suit their personally determined consumption strategies.

Chapter Review

In oral or preliterate cultures language was local and specific; knowledge, history, and myth were transmitted orally; memory was crucial; and elders and storytellers, as repositories of cultural values and beliefs, occupied positions of elevated status.

Writing changed the way cultures are organized and the way they function. Meaning and language became more uniform. When knowledge, history, and myth were transmitted in writing, the literate became the new elite. With writing also came the beginnings of democracy.

Gutenberg's invention of the printing press around 1446 gave writing new power. The ability to read became a necessity for people at all levels of society; literacy and education spread. The newly literate began to interact, both as people and in their ideas. As more material was published, people had more variety of thought presented to them, and they were freer to read what they wanted when they wanted.

The Industrial Revolution spread the power of print, but it also helped create a middle class with discretionary income to spend on information and entertainment. By the end of the 19th century a mass audience and the means to reach it existed.

The communication technologies that followed the printing press—newspapers, magazines, motion pictures, radio, television, and computer networks—had their own impacts. Mass market newspapers, magazines, motion pictures, and radio helped to geographically and culturally unify the rapidly expanding, pluralistic, multiethnic United States; aided in the creation and nourishment of its middle class; and helped establish, support, and solidify the roots of our consumer economy.

Television was central to the transformation of the United States into a true consumer economy after World War II. But the influence and power of all the mass media, as well as the new computer communication technologies, raise questions about their use and control. People who are more media literate can better answer these questions for themselves and their culture.

Media literacy is composed of an awareness of the impact of the media on individuals and society; an understanding of the process of mass communication; strategies for analyzing and discussing media messages; an awareness of media content as a "text" that provides insight into contemporary culture; cultivation of enhanced enjoyment, understanding, and appreciation of media content; development of an understanding of the ethical and moral obligations of media practitioners; and development of appropriate and effective production skills.

Media literacy requires mastery of several skills: the ability and willingness to make an effort to understand content, to pay attention, and to filter out noise; an understanding of and respect for the power of media messages; the ability to distinguish emotional from reasoned reactions when responding to content and to act accordingly; development of heightened expectations of media content; a knowledge of genre conventions and the ability to recognize when conventions are being mixed; the ability to think critically about media messages, no matter how credible their source; and a knowledge of the internal language of various media and the ability to understand its effects, no matter how complex.

The outcomes of the development of media literacy are an increase in critical awareness, more and improved discussion about media, better choices from among media's content, and social action.

Questions for Review

1. Characterize the communication and organizational styles of preliterate cultures. Where does power reside in these cultures?
2. What social, cultural, and economic factors boosted the development and spread of writing?
3. How did literacy change communication and the organization of preliterate cultures? Characterize the newly literate cultures.
4. How did the printing press make possible mass communication?
5. What was the impact of printing on the culture of Western Europe?
6. What was the role of the Industrial Revolution in furthering literacy? the development of the middle class? democracy?
7. What is media literacy? What are its components?
8. What is meant by multiple points of access? What does it have to do with media literacy?
9. What are some specific media literacy skills?
10. What is the difference between genres and production conventions? What do these have to do with media literacy?

Questions for Critical Thinking and Discussion

1. Consider the changes brought about by the shift from oral to literate cultures. How similar or different do you think the changes will be as we move to a more fully computer literate culture?
2. What is technology's double edge? Can you see it in the media that you use today?
3. How media literate do you think you are? What about those around you—your parents,

for example, or your best friend? What are your weaknesses as a media literate person?

4. Can you take a piece of media content from your own experience and explain how you approach it from multiple points of access?

5. How do you choose which television programs you watch? How thoughtful are your choices? How do you choose videos? movies? How thoughtful are you in these circumstances?

Important Resources

Davis, R. E. (1976). *Response to innovation: A study of popular argument about new mass media.* **New York: Arno Press.** A fascinating examination of popular press reaction to the introduction of movies, talkies, radio, and television. Thousands of quotes are used to demonstrate that concern greeting these technologies varied very little.

Eisenstein, E. L. (1979). *The printing press as an agent of change: Communications and cultural transformations in early-modern Europe.* **Cambridge: Cambridge University Press.** The classic work on the impact of printing. Even though it is serious scholarship, it is a readable look at and analysis of Gutenberg's technology and its cultural impact.

Innis, H. A. (1972). *Empire and communications.* **Toronto: University of Toronto Press.** A classic work examining how the spread of communication facilitated the spread of political and military influence. It is serious scholarship, but well written and accessible to college level readers.

Harpley, A. (1990). *Bright ideas; media education.* **Jefferson City, MO: Scholastic Books.** Media literacy is making its way into primary and secondary schools. This is one example of how teaching media literacy is being integrated into school curricula.

Potter, W. J. (1998). *Media literacy.* **Thousand Oaks, CA: Sage.** A detailed and thorough discussion of media literacy—what it is, how to develop it, and how to teach it.

Silverblatt, A. (1995). *Media literacy.* **Westport, CN: Praeger.** Portions of Chapter 2 in this book depend heavily on the ideas expressed clearly and intelligently by Silverblatt in this excellent primer. Together with the Potter book mentioned here, these are two of the best sources on media literacy available anywhere.

Silverblatt, A., & Enright Eliceiri, E. M. (1997). *Dictionary of media literacy.* **Westport, CT: Greenwood Press.** A reference book containing concepts, terms, organizations, and issues important to media literacy.

Media Literacy Web Sites

Center for Media Education	*http://www.cme.org/cme*
CineMedia	*http://www.gu.edu.au/gwis/cinemedia/CineMedia.home.html*
Cultural Environment Movement	*http://www.cemnet.org*
Media Alliance	*http://www.media-alliance.org*
Media Awareness Network	*http://www.schoolnet.ca/medianet*
Media Education Foundation	*http://www.igc.org/mef*
Media Foundation	*http://www.adbusters.org*
Media Literacy On-line Project	*http://interact.uoregon.edu/MediaLit/HomePage*
National Communication Association	*http://natcom.org*
Paper Tiger Television	*http://www.papertiger.org*
Strategies for Media Literacy Web Page	*http://kqed.org/fromKQED/Cell/ml/home.html*

part 2

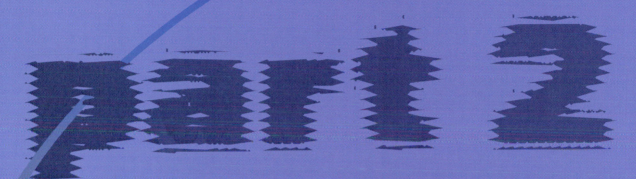

Media, Media Industries, and Media Audiences

Books

The video began when you hit the play button on the remote control. But the folks who rented the movie before you failed to rewind. So there you were, watching an arresting scene from François Truffaut's 1967 adaptation of Ray Bradbury's (1953/1981) science fiction classic *Fahrenheit 451*.

At first you couldn't make out what was happening. A group of people were wandering about, and each person was talking to him- or herself. You recognized actress Julie Christie, but the other performers and what they were saying were completely unfamiliar. You stayed with the scene. The trees were bare. Snow was falling, covering everything. Puffs of steam floated from people's mouths as they spoke, seemingly to no one. As you watched a bit more, you began to recognize some familiar phrases. These people were reciting passages from famous books! Before you could figure out why they were doing this, the film ended.

So you rewound and watched the entire video, discovering that these people *were* the books they had memorized. In this near future society, all books had been banned by the authorities, forcing these people—book lovers all—into hiding. They hold the books in their heads because to physically hold them is a crime. If discovered with books, people are jailed and the books are set afire—Fahrenheit 451 is the temperature at which book paper burns.

Moved by the film, you go to the library the next day and check out the book itself. Bradbury's main character, Guy Montag, a fireman who until this moment had been an official book burner himself speaks a line that stays with you, even today. After he watches an old woman burn to death with her forbidden volumes, he implores his ice cold, drugged, and television-deadened wife to understand what he is only then realizing. He

In the now not so distant future of *Fahrenheit 451*, people must memorize the content of books because to own a book is illegal.

pleads with her to see: "There must be something in books, things we can't imagine, to make a woman stay in a burning house; there must be something there" (1981, pp. 49–50).

In this chapter we examine the history of books, especially in terms of their role in the development of the United States. We discuss the importance that has traditionally been ascribed to books, as well as the scope and nature of the book industry. We address the various factors that shape the contemporary economics and structures of the book industry. Finally, we discuss a media literacy issue specific to the book—aliteracy.

A Short History of Books

As we saw in the last chapter, use of Gutenberg's printing press spread rapidly throughout Europe in the last half of the 15th century. But the technological advances and the social, cultural, and economic conditions necessary for books to become a major mass medium were three centuries away. As a result, it was a printing press and a world of books not unlike that in Gutenberg's time that first came to the New World in the 17th century.

BOOKS IN COLONIAL NORTH AMERICA

The earliest colonists came to America primarily for two reasons—to escape religious persecution and to find economic opportunities unavailable to them in Europe. Most of the books they carried with them to the New World were religiously oriented. Moreover, they brought very few books at all. Better educated, wealthier Europeans were secure at home. Those willing to make the dangerous journey tended to be poor, uneducated, and largely illiterate.

There were other reasons early settlers did not find books central to their lives. One was the simple fight for survival. In the brutal and hostile land to which they had come, leisure for reading books was a luxury for which they had little time. People worked from sunrise to sunset just to live. If there was to be reading, it would have to be at night, and it was folly to waste precious candles on something as unnecessary to survival as reading. In addition, books and reading were regarded as symbols of wealth and status and therefore not priorities for people who considered themselves to be pioneers, servants of the Lord, or anti-English colonists. The final reason the earliest settlers were not active readers was the lack of portability of books. Books were heavy, and few were carried across the ocean. Those volumes that did make it to America were extremely expensive and not available to most people.

The first printing press arrived on North American shores in 1638, only 18 years after the Plymouth Rock landing. It was operated by a company called Cambridge Press. Printing was limited to religious and government documents. The first book printed in the Colonies appeared in 1644—*The Whole Booke of Psalms*, sometimes referred to as the *Bay Psalms Book*. Among the very few secular titles were those printed by Benjamin Franklin 90 years later. *Poor Richard's Almanack*, which first appeared in 1732, sold 10,000 copies annually. The *Almanack* contained short stories, poetry, weather predictions, and other facts and figures useful to a population more in command of its environment than those first settlers. As the Colonies grew in wealth and sophistication, leisure time increased, as did affluence and education. Franklin also published the first true novel printed in North America, *Pamela*, written by English author Samuel Richardson. Still, by and large books were religiously oriented or pertained to official government activities such as tax rolls and the pronouncements of various commissions.

The primary reason for the lack of variety was the requirement that all printing be done with the permission of the colonial governors. Because these men were invariably loyal to King George II, secular printing and criticism of the British Crown or even of local authorities was never authorized, and publication of such writing meant jail. Many printers were

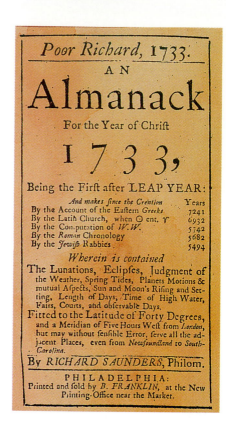

First published in 1732, Benjamin Franklin's *Poor Richard's Almanack* offered readers a wealth of information for the upcoming year.

imprisoned—including Franklin's brother James—for publishing what they believed to be the truth.

The printers went into open revolt against official control in March 1765 after passage of the Stamp Act. Designed by England to recoup money it spent waging the French and Indian War, the Stamp Act mandated that all printing—legal documents, books, magazines, and newspapers—be done on paper stamped with the government's seal. Its additional purpose was to control and limit expression in the increasingly restless Colonies. This affront to their freedom, along with the steep cost of the tax—sometimes doubling the cost of a publication—was simply too much for the colonists. The printers used their presses to run accounts of antitax protests, demonstrations, riots, sermons, boycotts, and other antiauthority activities, further fueling revolutionary and secessionist sympathies. In November 1765—when the tax was to take effect—the authorities were so cowed by the reaction of the colonists that they were unwilling to enforce it.

Anti-British sentiment reached its climax in the mid-1770s, and books were at its core. Short books, or pamphlets, motivated and coalesced political dissent. In 1774 England's right to govern the Colonies was openly challenged by James Wilson's *Considerations on the Nature and Extent of the Legislative Authority of the British Parliament*, John Adams's *Novanglus Papers*, and Thomas Jefferson's *A Summary View of the Rights of British America*. Most famous of all was Thomas Paine's 47-page *Common Sense*. It sold 120,000 copies in the first three months after its release to a total population of 400,000 adults. Between 1776 and 1783 Paine also wrote a series of pamphlets called *The American Crisis*. *Common Sense* and *The American Crisis* made Paine the most widely read colonial author during the American Revolution.

The Early Book Industry After the War of Independence, printing became even more central to political, intellectual, and cultural life in major cities like Boston, New York, and Philadelphia. To survive financially, printers also operated as booksellers, book publishers, and sometimes as postmasters who sold stationery and even groceries. A coffee house or tavern often was attached to the print shop. The era was alive with political change, and printer/bookshops became clearinghouses for the collection, exchange, and dissemination of information.

The U.S. newspaper industry grew rapidly from this mix, as we'll see in Chapter 4. The book industry, however, was slower to develop. Books were still expensive, often costing the equivalent of a working person's weekly pay, and literacy remained a luxury. However, due in large measure to a movement begun before the Civil War, compulsory education had come to most states by 1900. This swelled the number of readers, which

British-born writer, patriot, and revolutionary leader Thomas Paine wrote *Common Sense* and *The American Crisis* to rally his colonial compatriots in their struggle against the British.

increased demand for books. This increased demand, coupled with a number of important technological advances, brought the price of books within reach of most people. In 1861 the United States had the highest literacy rate of any country in the world (58%), and 40 years later at the start of the 20th century, 9 out of every 10 U.S. citizens could read.

Improving Printing   The 1800s saw a series of important refinements to the process of printing. Continuous roll paper, which permitted rapid printing of large numbers of identical, standardized pages, was invented in France at the very beginning of the century. Soon after, in 1811, German inventor Friedrich Koenig converted the printing press from muscle to steam power, speeding production of printed material and reducing its cost. In 1830 Americans Thomas Gilpin and James Ames perfected a wood grinding machine that produced enough pulp to make 24 miles of paper daily, further lowering the cost of printing. The final pieces of this era's rapid production–cost reduction puzzle were fit in the later part of the century. German immigrant Ottmar Mergenthaler introduced his **linotype** machine in the United States in 1884. Employing a typewriter-like keyboard, the linotype allowed printers to set type mechanically rather than manually. Near the same time, **offset lithography** was developed. This advance made possible printing from photographic plates rather than from heavy and relatively fragile metal casts.

The Flowering of the Novel The combination of technically improved, lower cost printing (and therefore lower cost publications) and widespread literacy produced the flowering of the novel in the 1800s. Major U.S. book publishers Harper Brothers and John Wiley & Sons—both in business today—were established in New York in 1817 and 1807, respectively. And books such as Nathaniel Hawthorne's *The Scarlet Letter* (1850), Herman Melville's *Moby Dick* (1851), and Mark Twain's *Huckleberry Finn* (1884) were considered by their readers to be equal to or better than the works of famous European authors such as Jane Austen, the Brontës and Charles Dickens.

The growing popularity of books was noticed by brothers Irwin and Erastus Beadle. In 1860 they began publishing novels that sold for 10 cents. These **dime novels** were inexpensive, and because they concentrated on frontier and adventure stories they attracted growing numbers of readers. Within 5 years of their start, Beadle & Company had produced over 4 million volumes of what were also sometimes called **pulp novels** (Tebbel, 1987). Advertising titles like *Malaeska: Indian Wife of the White Hunter* with the slogan "Dollar Books for a Dime!" the Beadles democratized books and turned them into a mass medium.

The Coming of Paperback Books Dime novels were "paperback books" because they were produced with paper covers. But publisher Allen Lane invented what we now recognize as the paperback in the midst of the Great Depression in London when he founded Penguin Books in 1935. Four years later, publisher Robert de Graff introduced the idea to the United States. His Pocket Books were small, inexpensive (25 cents) reissues of books that had already become successful as hardcovers. They were sold just about everywhere—newsstands, bookstores, train stations, shipping terminals, and drug and department stores. Within weeks of their introduction, de Graff was fielding orders of up to 15,000 copies a day (Tebbel, 1987). Soon, new and existing publishers joined the paperback boom. Traditionalists had some concern about the "cheapening of the book," but that was more than offset by the huge popularity of paperbacks and the willingness of publishers to take chances. For example, in the 1950s and '60s, African American writers such as Richard Wright and Ralph Ellison were published along with controversial works like *Catcher in the Rye*. Eventually, paperback books became the norm, surpassing hardcover book sales for the first time in 1960. According to *Publishers Weekly*, 60% of all books bought in 1997 were paperbacks.

Paperbacks today are no longer limited to reprints of successful hardbacks. Many books begin life as paperbacks. The John Jakes books *The Americans* and *The Titans,* for example, were issued initially as paperbacks and later reissued in hardcover. Paperback sales today top 1 million volumes a day, and bookstores generate half their revenue from these sales.

Books and Their Audiences

The book is the least "mass" of our mass media in audience reach and in the magnitude of the industry itself, and this fact shapes the nature of the relationship between medium and audience. Publishing houses, both large and small, produce narrowly or broadly aimed titles for readers, who buy and carry away individual units. This more direct relationship between publishers and readers renders books fundamentally different from other mass media. For example, because books are less dependent than other mass media on attracting the largest possible audience, books are more able and more likely to incubate new, challenging, or unpopular ideas. As the medium least dependent on advertiser support, books can be aimed at extremely small groups of readers, challenging them and their imaginations in ways that many sponsors would find unacceptable in advertising-based mass media. Because books are produced and sold as individual units—as opposed to a single television program simultaneously distributed to millions of viewers or a single edition of a mass circulation newspaper—more "voices" can enter and survive in the industry. This medium can sustain more voices in the cultural forum than can other mass media.

THE CULTURAL VALUE OF THE BOOK

The book industry is bound by many of the same financial and industrial pressures that constrain other media, but books, more than the others, are in a position to transcend those constraints. In *Fahrenheit 451* Montag's boss, Captain Beatty, explains why all books must be burned. "Once," he tells his troubled subordinate, "books appealed to a few people, here, there, everywhere. They could afford to be different. The world was roomy. But then the world got full of eyes and elbows and mouths" (Bradbury, 1981, p. 53). Bradbury's firemen of the future destroy books precisely because they *are* different. It is their difference from other mass media that makes books unique in our culture. Although all media serve the following cultural functions to some degree (for example, people use self-help videos for personal development and popular music is sometimes an agent of social change), books traditionally have been seen as a powerful cultural force for these reasons:

- *Books are agents of social and cultural change.* Free of the need to generate mass circulation for advertisers, offbeat, controversial, even revolutionary ideas can reach the public. For example, Andrew Macdonald's *Turner Diaries* is the ideological and how-to bible of the antigovernment militia movement in the United States. Nonetheless, this radical, revolutionary book is openly published, purchased, and discussed. For a look at the role of other books in social movements, see the box "The Role of Books in Social Movements."

- *Books are an important cultural repository.* Want to definitively win an argument? Look it up. We turn to books for certainty and truth about the world in which we live and the ones about which we want to know. Which countries border Chile? Find the atlas. Stevie Nicks' band before Fleetwood Mac? Look in *The Rolling Stone Illustrated History of Rock and Roll.*

- *Books are our windows on the past.* What was the United States like in the 19th century? Read Alexis de Tocqueville's *Democracy in America.* England in the early 1800s? Read Jane Austen's *Pride and Prejudice.* Written in the times they reflect, these books are more accurate representations than are available in the modern electronic media.

- *Books are important sources of personal development.* The obvious forms are self-help and personal improvement volumes. But books also speak to us more individually than advertiser-supported media because of their small, focused target markets. *Our Bodies,*

Media Echoes

The Role of Books in Social Movements

In the 15th and 16th centuries, reformers used one book—the Bible—to create one of history's most important revolutions, the Protestant Reformation. Of course, the reformers did not write this book, but their insistence that it be available to people was a direct challenge to the ruling powers of the time. Englishman John Wycliffe was persecuted and burned at the stake in the mid-1300s for translating the Bible into English. Two hundred years later, another Englishman, William Tyndale, so angered Church leaders with his insistence on printing and distributing English-language Bibles that the Church had his dead body exhumed, strangled, burned at the stake, and thrown in a river.

Before printed Bibles became generally available in the 16th and 17th centuries, Bibles and other religious tracts were typically chained to some unmoveable piece of the church. Church leaders said this was done because people desperate for the Word of God would steal them, denying others access. If this was true, why were Wycliffe and Tyndale persecuted for trying to *expand* access? Historians, both secular and religious, now believe that the reason **chained Bibles** existed was to ensure that reading and interpreting their contents could be supervised and controlled. The established elites feared the power of the printed word.

This was also the case during the American Revolution, as we've seen in this chapter, as well as when the country rejected a 200-year evil, slavery. Harriet Beecher Stowe published the realistically painful story of slavery in America in 1852. Her *Uncle Tom's Cabin* had first appeared in two parts in an antislavery magazine, but its greatest impact was as a book hungrily read by a startled

Chained Bibles and other handprinted books in England's Hereford Chapel.

Ourselves, introduced by the Boston Women's Health Book Collective in the very earliest days of the modern feminist movement, is still published today. *Dr. Spock's Baby and Child Care* has sold more than 30 million copies. J. D. Salinger's *Catcher in the Rye* was the literary anthem for the baby boomers in their teen years, as is William Gibson's *Neuromancer* for many of today's cyber youth. It is unlikely that any of these voices would have found their initial articulation in commercially sponsored media.

- *Books are wonderful sources of entertainment and escape.* Arthur C. Clarke, John Grisham, Judith Krantz, J. R. R. Tolkien, and Stephen King all specialize in writing highly entertaining and imaginative novels. The enjoyment found in the works of writers Joyce Carol Oates *(On Boxing, We Were the Mulvaneys),* John Irving *(The World According to Garp, Hotel New Hampshire, A Prayer for Owen Meany),*

public. *Uncle Tom's Cabin* sold 20,000 copies in its first 3 weeks on the market, and 300,000 copies in its first year, eventually reaching sales of 7 million.

It was the tale of a kind, literate slave, Uncle Tom. Tom's reward for his intelligence and his goodness was death at the hands of evil slave owner Simon Legree. A fine work of literature, *Uncle Tom's Cabin* galvanized public feelings against slavery. Abolitionist sentiment was no longer the domain of the intellectual, social, and religious elite. Everyday people were repulsed by the horrors of slavery. One of Stowe's most ardent readers was Abraham Lincoln, who, as president, abolished slavery.

Books have traditionally been at the center of social change in the United States. Horatio Alger's rags-to-riches stories excited westward migration in the 1800s. Upton Sinclair's *The Jungle* and other muckraking books brought about significant health and labor legislation in the early 1900s. John Steinbeck's *The Grapes of Wrath* took up the cause of migrant farmers in the post-Depression 1930s. Alex Haley's *The Autobiography of Malcolm X* and Ralph Ellison's *Invisible Man* were literary mainstays of the 1960s Civil Rights era, as was Betty Friedan's *Feminine Mystique* for the women's movement. In the 1970s, the paperback publication of *The Pentagon Papers* hastened the end of the Vietnam War.

The role of books in important social movements is echoed in Chapter 5 in the discussion of magazine muckrakers.

This promotional flier calls *Uncle Tom's Cabin* "the greatest book of the age," a fair assessment, given its impact on the times and U.S. history.

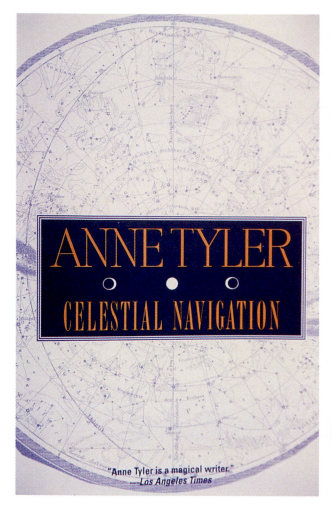

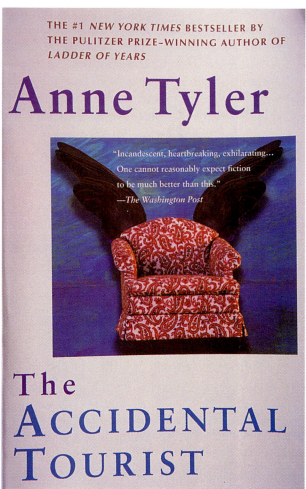

Anne Tyler's books are not only serious literature but are entertaining reading as well. *The Accidental Tourist* was popular not only as a book but also as a feature film.

Pat Conroy *(The Prince of Tides, Beach Music),* and Anne Tyler *(Celestial Navigation, The Accidental Tourist)* is undeniable.

- *Books are mirrors of culture.* Books, along with other mass media, reflect the culture that produces and consumes them.

CENSORSHIP

Because of their influence as cultural repositories and agents of social change, books have often been targeted for censorship. A book is censored when someone in authority limits publication of or access to it. Censorship can and does occur in many situations and in all media (more on this in Chapter 13). But because of the respect our culture traditionally holds for books, book banning takes on a particularly poisonous connotation in the United States.

Reacting to censorship presents a dilemma for book publishers. Publishers have an obligation to their owners and stockholders to make a profit. Yet, if responsible people in positions of authority deem a certain book unsuitable for readers, shouldn't publishers do the right thing for the larger society and comply with demands to cease its publication? This was the argument presented by morals crusader Anthony Comstock in 1873 when he established the New York Society for the Suppression of Vice. It was the argument made in 1953 when U.S. Senator Joseph McCarthy demanded the removal of more than 100 books from U.S. diplomatic libraries because of their "procommunist" slant. (Among them was Thomas Paine's *Common Sense*.) It is the argument offered today for the death sentence pronounced by Iran's late Ayatollah Khomeini on Salman Rushdie for his 1989 *Satanic Verses*.

According to the American Library Association Office of Intellectual Freedom and the American Civil Liberties Union, among the library and school books most frequently targeted by modern censors are *The Diary of Anne Frank*, Mark Twain's *The Adventures of Huckleberry Finn*, George Orwell's *1984*, John Steinbeck's *Of Mice and Men*, Kurt Vonnegut's *Slaughterhouse Five*, Harper Lee's *To Kill a Mockingbird*, Shakespeare's *Macbeth*, and children's favorite *In the Night Kitchen* by Maurice Sendak. The 50 most frequently banned books in the United States between 1990 and 1992 are shown in Figure 3–1. With how many are you familiar? Which ones have you read? What is it about each of these books that might have brought it to the censors' attention?

Book publishers can confront censorship by recognizing that their obligations to their industry and to themselves demand that they resist censorship. The book publishing industry and the publisher's role in it is fundamental to the operation and maintenance of our democratic society. Rather than accepting the censor's argument that certain voices require silencing for the good of the culture, publishers in a democracy have an obligation to make the stronger argument that free speech be protected and encouraged. The short list of frequently censored titles in the previous paragraph should immediately make it evident why the power of ideas is worth fighting for.

Scope and Structure of the Book Industry

Over 50,000 new and reprinted book titles are issued in the United States each year.

CATEGORIES OF BOOKS

The Association of American Publishers divides these books into several sales categories:

- *Book club editions* are books sold and distributed (sometimes even published) by book clubs. There are currently more than 300 book clubs in the United States. These organizations offer trade, professional, and more specialized titles, for example, books for aviation

BANNED BOOKS

1. *Impressions,* edited by Jack Booth et al.
2. *Of Mice and Men,* by John Steinbeck
3. *The Catcher in the Rye,* by J. D. Salinger
4. *The Adventures of Huckleberry Finn,* by Mark Twain
5. *The Chocolate War,* by Robert Cormier
6. *Bridge to Terabithia,* by Katherine Paterson
7. *Scary Stories in the Dark,* by Alvin Schwartz
8. *More Scary Stories in the Dark,* by Alvin Schwartz
9. *The Witches,* by Roald Dahl
10. *Daddy's Roommate,* by Michael Willhoite
11. *Curses, Hexes, and Spells,* by Daniel Cohen
12. *A Wrinkle in Time,* by Madeleine L'Engle
13. *How to Eat Fried Worms,* by Thomas Rockwell
14. *Blubber,* by Judy Blume
15. *Revolting Rhymes,* by Roald Dahl
16. *Halloween ABC,* by Eve Merriam
17. *A Day No Pigs Would Die,* by Robert Peck
18. *Heather Has Two Mommies,* by Leslea Newman
19. *Christine,* by Stephen King
20. *I Know Why the Caged Bird Sings,* by Maya Angelou
21. *Fallen Angels,* by Walter Myers
22. *The New Teenage Body Book,* by Kathy McCoy and Charles Wibbelsman
23. *Little Red Riding Hood,* by Jacob Grimm and Wilhelm Grimm
24. *The Headless Cupid,* by Zilpha Snyder
25. *Night Chills,* by Dean Koontz
26. *Lord of the Flies,* by William Golding
27. *A Separate Peace,* by John Knowles
28. *Slaughterhouse-Five,* by Kurt Vonnegut
29. *The Color Purple,* by Alice Walker
30. *James and the Giant Peach,* by Roald Dahl
31. *The Learning Tree,* by Gordon Parks
32. *The Witches of Worm,* by Zilpha Snyder
33. *My Brother Sam Is Dead,* by James Lincoln Collier and Christopher Collier
34. *The Grapes of Wrath,* by John Steinbeck
35. *Cujo,* by Stephen King
36. *The Great Gilly Hopkins,* by Katherine Paterson
37. *The Figure in the Shadows,* by John Bellairs
38. *On My Honor,* by Marion Dane Bauer
39. *In the Night Kitchen,* by Maurice Sendak
40. *Grendel,* by John Gardner
41. *I Have to Go,* by Robert Munsch
42. *Annie on My Mind,* by Nancy Garden
43. *The Adventures of Tom Sawyer,* by Mark Twain
44. *The Pigman,* by Paul Zindel
45. *My House,* by Paul Zindel
46. *Then Again, Maybe I Won't,* by Judy Blume
47. *The Handmaid's Tale,* by Margaret Atwood
48. *Witches, Pumpkins, and Grinning Ghosts: The Story of the Halloween Symbols,* by Edna Barth
49. *One Hundred Years of Solitude,* by Gabriel García Márquez
50. *Scary Stories 3: More Tales to Chill Your Bones,* by Alvin Schwartz

Figure 3–1 Most Banned Books in the 1990s. Shown here are the 50 books most frequently challenged in U.S. schools and public libraries between 1990 and 1992. *Source:* Foerstel, H. N. (1994). *Banned in the U. S. A.: A Reference Guide to Book Censorship in Schools and Public Libraries.* Westport, CT: Greenwood Press.

aficionados and expensive republications of classic works. The Book of the Month Club, started in 1926, is the best known; the Literary Guild and the Reader's Digest Book Club are also popular.

- *El-hi* are textbooks produced for elementary and high schools.
- *Higher education* are textbooks produced for colleges and universities.
- *Mail order books,* like those advertised on television by Time-Life Books, are delivered by mail and usually are specialized series (*The War Ships*) or elaborately bound special editions of classic novels.

- *Mass market paperbacks* are typically published only as paperbacks and are designed to appeal to a broad readership; many romance novels, diet books, and self-help books are in this category.

- *Professional books* are reference and educational volumes designed specifically for professionals such as doctors, engineers, lawyers, scientists, and managers.

- *Religious books* are volumes such as Bibles, catechisms, and hymnals.

- *Standardized tests* are guide and practice books designed to prepare readers for various examinations such as the SAT or the Bar exam.

- *Subscription reference books* are publications such as the *Encyclopedia Britannica*, atlases, and dictionaries bought directly from the publisher rather than purchased in a retail setting.

- **Trade books** can be hard- or softcover and include not only fiction and most nonfiction, but cookbooks, biographies, art books, coffee-table books and how-to books.

- *University press* books come from publishing houses associated with and often underwritten by universities. They typically publish serious nonfiction and scholarly books. The University of Chicago Press and the University of California Press are two of the better known university presses, and the Oxford University Press is the oldest publisher in the world.

In 1996 total U.S. book sales reached $20.75 billion, a 4% increase over the year before (Figure 3–2). Only one category, adult hardcover, failed to grow in sales.

FROM IDEA TO PUBLICATION

The ideas that ultimately become the books that fit these different categories reach publishers in a number of ways. Sometimes they reach an **acquisitions editor** (the person charged with determining which books a publisher will publish) unsolicited. This means that ideas are mailed or phoned directly to the acquisitions editor by the author. Many of the larger and better publishers will not accept unsolicited ideas from aspiring writers unless they first secure the services of an agent, an intermediary between publisher and writer. Increasingly, acquisitions editors are determining what books *they* think will do well and seeking out writers who can meet their needs.

At some publishing houses, acquisitions editors have the power to say "yes" or "no" based on their own judgment of the value and profitability of an idea. At many others, these editors must prepare a case for the projects they want to take on and have them reviewed and approved by a review or proposal committee. These committees typically include not only "book people" but marketing, financial, production, and administrative professionals who judge the merit of the idea from their own perspectives. Once

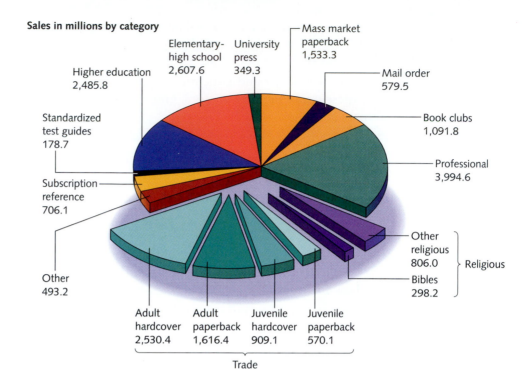

Figure 3–2 Book Sales in the United States, 1996. *Source:* Association of American Publishers News, Feb. 24, 1997.

Sales in millions by category

Elementary-high school 2,607.6

University press 349.3

Mass market paperback 1,533.3

Mail order 579.5

Book clubs 1,091.8

Professional 3,994.6

Higher education 2,485.8

Standardized test guides 178.7

Subscription reference 706.1

Other 493.2

Other religious 806.0

Bibles 298.2

Religious

Adult hardcover 2,530.4

Adult paperback 1,616.4

Juvenile hardcover 909.1

Juvenile paperback 570.1

Trade

the acquisitions editor says "yes," or is given permission by the committee to do so, the author and the publisher sign a contract.

Now the book must be written (if it is not already completed). An editor (sometimes the acquiring editor, sometimes not) is assigned to assist the author in producing a quality manuscript. Some combination of the publisher's marketing, promotions, and publicity departments plan the advertising campaign for the book. When available, review copies are sent to appropriate reviewers in other media. Book tours and signings are planned and scheduled. Copy for sales catalogues is written to aid salespeople in their attempts to place the book in bookstores.

All this effort is usually aimed at the first few months of a book's release. The publisher will determine in this time if the book will succeed or fail with readers. If the book appears to be a success, additional printings will be ordered. If the book has generated little interest from buyers, no additional copies are printed. Bookstores will eventually return unsold copies to the publisher to be sold at great discount as **remainders.**

Current Trends in Book Publishing

The contemporary book industry is characterized by several important economic and structural factors. Among the most important are conglomeration, increasing commercialization and demand for profits, the growth of small presses, restructuring of retailing, and changes in readership.

CONGLOMERATION

More than any other medium, the book industry was dominated by relatively small operations. Publishing houses were traditionally staffed by fewer than 20 people, the large majority by fewer than 10. Today, however, although more than 20,000 businesses call themselves book publishers, only 2,000 produce four or more titles a year. The industry is dominated now by a few giants: Hearst Books, the Penguin Group, Bantam Doubleday Dell, Time Warner Publishing, Farrar, Straus & Giroux, Harcourt General, HarperCollins, and Simon & Schuster. Each of these giants was once, sometimes with another name, an independent book publisher. All are now part of large national or international corporate conglomerates (Figure 3–3).

Opinion is divided on the benefit of corporate ownership. The positive view is that the rich parent company can infuse the publishing house with necessary capital, allowing it to attract better authors or to take gambles on new writers that would, in the past, have been impossible. Another plus is that the corporate parent's other media holdings can be used to promote and repackage the books for greater profitability.

The negative view is that as publishing houses become just one in the parent company's long list of enterprises, product quality suffers as important editing and production steps are eliminated to maximize profits. Before conglomeration, publishing was often described as a **cottage industry;** that is, publishing houses were small operations, closely identified with their personnel—both their own small staffs and their authors. The cottage imagery, however, extends beyond smallness of size. There was a quaintness and charm associated with publishing houses—their attention to detail, their devotion to tradition, the care they gave to their façades (their reputations). The world of corporate conglomerates has little room for such niceties, as profit dominates all other considerations.

Random House, once an independent book publisher, is now owned by the German conglomerate Bertelsmann, owner of about 40 other media outlets such as RCA Records and *McCall's* magazine. A former editor, Andre Schiffrin (1996), wrote of the change from independent to subsidiary, "The drive for profit fits like an iron mask on our cultural output" (p. 29).

COMMERCIALIZATION AND DEMAND FOR PROFITS

The threat from conglomeration is seen in the parent company's overemphasis on the bottom line—that is, profitability at all costs. Unlike in the days when G. P. Putnam's sons and the Schuster family actually ran the houses that carried their names, critics fear that now little pride is taken

Privately held; George Hearst, Jr., chairman

HEARST

HEARST BOOKS
1995 combined revenues: $160 million (est.)

AVON BOOKS
WILLIAM MORROW & CO.
Hearst Books
Hearst Books International
Hearst Marine Books
Quill Trade

■ ■ ■

Newspapers
Albany (NY) *Times Union, Beaumont* (TX) *Enterprise, Edwardsville* (IL) *Intelligencer, Houston Chronicle, Huron* (MI) *Daily Tribune, Laredo* (TX) *Morning Times, Midland* (MI) *Daily News, Midland* (TX) *Reporter-Telegram, Plainview* (TX) *Daily Herald, San Antonio Express-News, San Francisco Examiner, Seattle Post-Intelligencer;* 7 weeklies

■

Magazines
Esquire, Good Housekeeping, Colonial Homes, Cosmopolitan, Country Living, Country Living Gardener, ESPN, House Beautiful, Marie Claire (with Marie Claire Album), Motor Boating & Sailing, Popular Mechanics, Redbook, SmartMoney (with Dow Jones), Sports Afield, Town & Country, Victoria, and Harper's Bazaar. Also, 9 magazines in the U.K. and 81 international editions

■

Cable
Part owner of Lifetime (50% with Disney); A&E and History Channel (37.5% with Disney and NBC); ESPN; ESPN2; and ESPNEWS (20% with Disney); one foreign channel (partially owned)

■

Stations
7 TV stations; 6 radio stations

■

TV Production
24-hour news channel in New England; entertainment programming (*Flash Gordon*)

■

Multimedia
Kidsoft (kid's software, 29.4%; Netscape (1.5%); Books That Work (how-to software, 17.5%) I/Pro (Internet provider; minority interest)

■

Comics
King Features Syndicate (*Blondie, Beetle Bailey*) and others

■

Other
Timber, ranching, and real estate in California

1995 revenues:
$2.3 billion

Figure 3–3 The Media Nation: Publishing. *Source: The Nation,* March 17, 1997.

C.E.O. Rupert Murdoch controls about 30% of stock

NEWS CORPORATION

HARPERCOLLINS
1995 revenues: $550 million (est.)

HARPERCOLLINS
Harper Reference
Harper Perennial
Harper Business
Basic Books
Harper Prism
Regan Books
Harper San Francisco
Westview Press

Newspapers
New York Post; The (London) *Times, The Sun,* and others, together accounting for 30% of newspaper sales in the U.K.; more than 200 wholly and partially owned papers in Australia and New Zealand; papers in Fiji and Papua New Guinea (partially owned); inserts for 622 U.S. papers

Magazines
Pacific Islands Monthly, Premiere (50%), *TV Guide, The Weekly Standard;* 40% of 18 weekly and monthly magazines in Australia, New Zealand, and Europe

Television
Fox Network; Twentieth Century Fox Television (*The X-Files; Chicago Hope*)

Cable & Satellite Television
In the U.S.: fXM:Movies from Fox; in partnership

1995 revenues:
$9 billion

NEWS CORPORATION

with TCI-owned Liberty Media (50%) for: Fox Sports Net, Fox Sports International and fX; Fox Kids Worldwide (50%), Fox News Channel; in partnership with MCI (50%) to develop ASkyB, satellite TV in the U.S.; STAR TV, satellite TV that reaches all of Japan, China, India, Southeast Asia and into Africa; BSkyB (40%), satellite TV in the U.K., which holds 49% interest (with Kirch Gruppe) in Germany's DF1; developing JSkyB in Japan (50% with Softbank); FOXTEL (50%) cable operator and two sports networks (50%) in Australia; Canal FOX, cable TV in Latin America

Television Stations
22, including 1 in each of the top 4 markets (N.Y., L.A., Chicago, Phila.)

Motion Pictures
Twentieth Century Fox, Fox 2000, Fox Searchlight Pictures, Fox Family Films, Fox Studios Australia

Multimedia
CD publishing; about 20 Web sites (including iGuide)

Other
Sheep farming; paper production (46.2% of Australia's only newsprint plant); an Australian airline (50%)

PEARSON PLC

THE PENGUIN GROUP
Combined 1995 revenues: $617 million (est.)

VIKING PENGUIN	**PUTNAM BERKELEY**
Studio	G. P. Putnam's Sons
DUTTON/SIGNET/	Grosset/Putnam
PLUME	Boulevard
Dutton	Price Stern Sloan
Donald I. Fine	Jeremy P. Tarcher
Signet	Berkley Books
Onyx	Jove
Topaz	Ace
Plume	Perigee
Meridian	HP Books
Mentor	**RIVERHEAD BOOKS**

Newspapers
The Financial Times; newspapers and magazines in Spain and France; financial newspaper in South Africa

Magazines
The Economist (50%)

Television Production
Thames Television (*The Bill*); Grundy Worldwide (*Neighbors*); Financial Times Television (all in U.K.); ACI in L.A.; BSkyB (4%); Hong Kong's TVB (10%); U.K.'s Channel 5 (24% with others)

Satellite Television
BBC Prime; BBC World (6% with BBC)

Motion Pictures
Phoenix Pictures (20%)

Multimedia
Mindscape

Financial
Lazard Frères & Co. (9% profit interest); Lazard Brothers (in U. K.) 50%

Theme Parks/Amusements
Port Aventura theme park in Spain (40%); Madame Tussaud's wax museum, the London Planetarium, Rock Circus, Alton Towers, Warwick Castle, Chessington World of Adventures (all in U.K.); Madame Tussaud's Scenerama (in Amsterdam); Madame Tussaud's 42nd St. (coming to N.Y.C.)

1995 (est.) revenues:
$2.8 billion

VIACOM

SIMON & SCHUSTER

1995 revenues $832.7 million (est.)

SIMON & SCHUSTER	POCKET BOOKS
Lisa Drew Books	Star Trek
Scribner	Minstrel Books
Touchstone	Archway
Fireside	Folger Shakespeare
Aguilar	Library
Libros en Español	Washington
THE FREE PRESS	Square Press
Lexington Books	MTV Books
Martin Kessler Books	Pocket Star Books

Also, largest educational publisher in U.S. (1995 sales over $1 billion)

■ ■ ■

Motion Pictures: Paramount Pictures

■

Movie Theaters

Famous Players in Canada; UCI (50% with MCA) and Films Paramount in Europe; Cinamerica (50% with Time Warner) in western U.S.

■

Cable

MTV; M2: Music Television; VH1; Nickelodeon; Nick at Nite's TV Land; Showtime; FLIX; Sci-Fi Channel (50% with Seagrams); Comedy Central (50% with Time Warner); The Movie Channel; Sundance Channel (45% with PolyGram & Robert Redford); USA Network (50% with Seagrams); Paramount Channel (in U.K. with BSkyB)

■

Television

UPN Network (50% with Chris Craft) includes 152 affiliates, reaching 92% of U.S. TV homes; Spelling Entertainment (*Melrose Place, Beverly Hills, 90210*), 75%; Paramount Television syndication (*Cheers, I Love Lucy*) and production (*Frasier, Entertainment Tonight*)

■

TV Stations: 11

■

Radio Stations: 10

■

Home Video

Blockbuster stores; Paramount Home Video

■

Other Entertainment

Theme parks (Kings Dominion, Kings Island, Great America, Carowinds, Canada's Wonderland)

1995 revenues:
$11.3 billion

BERTELSMANN AG

BANTAM DOUBLEDAY DELL

1995 revenues: $670 million (est.)

BANTAM BOOKS	DELL
DOUBLEDAY	Delacorte Press
Anchor Books	The Dial Press
Currency Books	Delta
Nan A. Talese Books	Island Books
Image Books	Laurel
	BROADWAY BOOKS

RANDOM HOUSE

1995 revenues: $1.26 billion (est.)

RANDOM HOUSE	ALFRED A. KNOPF
The Modern Library	Everyman's Library
Times Books	Pantheon
Times Business	Villard
Princeton Review	Schocken
CROWN	Vintage
Crown Trade Paperbacks	FODOR'S
Harmony Books	BALLANTINE
Clarkson N. Potter	Del Rey
Bell Tower	Fawcett

One of Germany's largest trade publishers. Also, 2.5 million book club members worldwide in the Literary Guild and other book clubs in the U.S., most of Western Europe, Canada, Australia, New Zealand and, beginning 1996, in China (70% with state-run company)

Magazines

Family Circle, McCall's, Parents, Child, Fitness, American Homestyle and Garden, Ser Padres Network, YM; 34 magazines in Germany, including Stern and Der Spiegel (part owner); magazines in France, Spain, England, Italy, and Poland. About 40 professional magazines

Newspapers

Six dailies in Germany; part ownership of papers in Hungary and Slovakia

Television

CLT-UFA (50%); largest European broadcaster, with television and radio stations and television programming branches

Music

Arista, RCA, others (14% of music sold worldwide); music publishing

Multimedia

Includes partnership with America Online in Europe; publishes reference CDs

Other

Printing; CDs for data storage

1995 revenues:
$19.26 billion

Ted Turner holds 10% of stock, TCI chairman John Malone and Seagrams each control 9%, and L.A. investment firm The Capital Group has 7.5%

TIME WARNER

TIME WARNER PUBLISHING
1995 revenues: $325 million (est.)

WARNER BOOKS
Warner Treasurers
Warner Vision
Aspect

LITTLE, BROWN
Bullfinch
Back Bay

MAIL-ORDER BOOKS

Time-Life Books
Oxmoor House

Book-of-the-Month Club
Sunset Books

Motion Pictures
Warner Bros. (75%), Castle Rock Entertainment, New Line Cinema, library of MGM, RKO, and pre-1950 Warner Bros. films

Cable & Satellite TV
CNN, Headline News, CNNfn, CNN Airport Network, CNN Interactive, CNN/SI, CNN Newsource, TBS Superstation, Cinemax, Comedy Central (50%), Court TV (33.3%), Sega Channel (33%), Turner Classic Movies, TNT, Cartoon Network, HBO (75%); Primestar (31% with others) satellite TV in U.S.

Cable Franchises
12.1 million subscribers *(about 20% of U.S. TV homes)*

TV Programming
Warner Bros. television (*Friends* and *ER*); WB Television Network with (Chicago) Tribune Broadcasting (84% of U.S. TV homes); Warner Bros. Television Animation (75%), Telepictures Production, Hanna-Barbera Cartoons (*The Flintstones, The Jetsons*), World Championship Wrestling, Turner Original Productions, Turner Sports, Turner Learning (noncommercial daily newscasts for schools)

Music
Atlantic, Elektra, Warner labels (22% of U.S. music sales)

Radio: CNNRadio

Magazines
Asiaweek, Baby Talk, Coastal Living, Cooking Light, Dancyu, DC Comics, Entertainment Weekly, Fortune, Health, Hippocrates, In Style, Life, Money, Parenting, People, People en Español, President, Progressive Farmer, Southern Living, Southern Accents, Sports Illustrated, Sports Illustrated for Kids, Sunset, This Old House, Time, Time for Kids, Weight Watchers, Who

Theme Parks: Six Flags (49%)

Sports: Atlanta Braves, Atlanta Hawks, Goodwill Games

Other
Home video and satellite, CD-ROM production, some retail stores

1995 revenues:
$8.1 billion

Privately held by Dieter von Holtzbrinck, president

HOLTZBRINCK

FARRAR, STRAUS & GIROUX
Hill & Wang
Noonday Press
North Point Press

ST. MARTIN'S PRESS
Robert Wyatt Books
Thomas Dunne Books

HENRY HOLT & CO.
Metropolitan Books

1995 combined revenues:
$267 million (est.)

Major trade publisher in Germany and the U.K.

Newspapers
Dailies and weeklies in Germany, including *Die Zeit* and *Tagesspiegel*

Magazines
Scientific American

Multimedia
Part owner of N.Y. firm Voyager

Television
Part owner of #2-rated channel in Germany

1995 (est.) revenues:
$2 billion

EDUCATIONAL PUBLISHERS

(Firms that no longer concentrate on trade publishing)

HARCOURT GENERAL
Publishes some trade books under both Harcourt Brace and the Harvest imprint. Publishes extensively in education (8.6% of U.S. market in 1995) and professional areas

McGRAW-HILL
Publishes some trade, and extensively in education (11% of U.S. market in 1995) and professional areas

---

in the content of books and that risk-taking (tackling controversial issues, experimenting with new styles, finding and nurturing unknown authors) is becoming rarer and rarer.

Chairperson of the Writing Seminars at Johns Hopkins University, Mark Miller (1997), wrote, "This is the all important difference between then and now: As book lovers and businessmen, [publishers] did the high-yield trash so as to subsidize the books they loved (although those books might also sell). No longer meant to help some finer things grow, the crap today is not a means but (as it were) the end" (p. 14). To Miller and other critics of conglomeration, the industry seems overwhelmed by a blockbuster mentality—lust for the biggest selling authors and titles possible, sometimes with little consideration for literary merit. Judith Krantz, for example, received a $3.2 million advance for *Princess Daisy*; Mary Higgins Clark, $35 million from Simon & Schuster for six books; Colin Powell, $6.5 million from Random House for his autobiography; Tom Clancy, $2.5 million for *Without Remorse*; Stephen King, $10 million *each* for his next four titles; Ronald Reagan, $8 million for his memoirs; O. J. Simpson's ex-girlfriend Paula Barbieri, $3 million from Little, Brown for her musings. "Where the [small] houses prized the subtle labor of their editors, the giants want their staff not poring over prose but signing big names over lunch" (Miller, 1997, p. 13). As the resources and energies of publishing houses are committed to a small number of superstar writers and blockbuster books, smaller, more interesting, possibly more serious or important books do not get published. If these books cannot get published, they will not be written. We will be denied their ideas in the cultural forum.

Publishers attempt to offset these large investments through the sale of **subsidiary rights;** that is, the sale of the book, its contents, and even its characters to filmmakers, paperback publishers, book clubs, foreign publishers, and product producers like T-shirt, poster, coffee cup, and greeting card manufacturers. The industry itself estimates that many publishers would go out of business if it were not for the sale of these rights. Writers like Michael Crichton *(Jurassic Park)*, John Grisham *(The Client)*, and Gay Talese *(Thy Neighbor's Wife)* can command as much as $2.5 million for the film rights to their books. Although this is good for the profitability of the publishers and the superstar authors, critics fear that those books with the greatest subsidiary sales value will receive the most publisher attention. The story of a book published as much for its subsidiary rights potential as for its value as a blockbuster is told in the box "The Making of a Blockbuster: *Scarlett.*"

As greater and greater sums are tied up in blockbusters, and as subsidiary rights therefore grow in importance, the marketing, promotion, and public relations surrounding a book become crucial. This leads to the additional fear that only the most promotable books will be published— the stores are flooded with O. J. Simpson books, celebrity picture books, unauthorized biographies of celebrities, and tell-all autobiographies from the children of famous people.

The Making of a Blockbuster: *Scarlett*

In search of that next blockbuster, publishers are increasingly initiating projects, a reversal of the more traditional and common sequence in which authors or their agents bring books to them. The most famous (and financially richest) example is that of *Scarlett*.

In 1991 Warner Books wanted to capitalize on the continuing popularity of the 1936 book *Gone with the Wind* by Margaret Mitchell, as well as on the 1939 movie of the same name starring Vivien Leigh and Clark Gable. Warner knew the book had sold more than 28 million copies since publication, making it one of the best-selling books of all time, and that it was still selling 40,000 hardcover and 250,000 paperback volumes a year. The movie, a film classic, was a nationwide video rental mainstay. To the publisher, this was a property worth exploiting—a blockbuster lurked somewhere in the astounding popularity of this story.

First, the potential new book needed an author. Several were considered. Alexandra Ripley, author of three successful romantic novels set in the historic South, was the choice, chosen largely for her success with female readers of romance books. She was given a $4.9 million advance, somewhat more than the $500 Mitchell had received nearly 60 years before.

Then the book needed a title. Focus groups composed primarily of female romance novel readers and women who did not typically read such books were asked to choose between different options.

Then a promotion and publicity plan was drawn up. Warner anticipated unfriendly reviews. After all, the project had already encountered quite a bit of criticism as a cheap commercial trick and a rip-off of a "real" book. To ensure that there was no negative criticism to blunt the book's early success, the publisher refused to provide the customary advance copies to media, critics, or bookstore buyers. Signs in bookstores telling people to reserve their copy and an excerpt published in *Life* magazine were all the public saw of the book until September 25, 1991, the date of its release.

Once in bookstores, *Scarlett: The Sequel to Margaret Mitchell's Gone with the Wind,* sold more copies more quickly than any book in history—1.2 million copies in 6 weeks. By Christmas sales had topped 2 million.

And the payoff for the project the book initiated? At least $5 million on the hardcover and an equal amount on the paperback, booming sales on author Ripley's other novels (also published by Warner), and millions more from the made-for-TV movie produced by Warner Brothers Films.

For months *Scarlett* was in the cultural forum. Much of the discussion was critical of Warner Books, in particular, and the meaning of this project for the world of books in general. Did you read *Scarlett?* If so, what did you think of it? What do you think of projects such as this? Do you accept the argument that as long as people are reading *something* there is a chance they will read other things? Are vehicles like *Scarlett* a practical means of building the reading habit, or are they what media critic and New York University professor Todd Gitlin (1997) calls "dumb-down" books?

The importance of promotion and publicity has led to an increase in the release of **instant books.** What better way to unleash millions of dollars of free publicity for a book than to base it on an event currently on the front page and the television screen? Publishers see these opportunities and then initiate the projects. Several instant books were on the shelves within days of the O. J. Simpson verdict and the death of Princess Diana. Kerry Strug had *Landing on My Feet: A Diary of Dreams* in stores within weeks of her 1996 Atlanta Olympics performance. The Persian Gulf War spawned several instant books. Airman Scott O'Grady's crash and rescue in Bosnia produced the instant book *Basher Five-Two: The True Story of F-16 Fighter Pilot Captain Scott O'Grady.* News events including the Jonestown massacre, the assassination of John Lennon, and Oliver North's testimony on the Iran-Contra affair have also spawned instant books. Lost in the flood of instant books, easily promotable authors and titles, and

Joanne Whalley Kilmer and Timothy Dalton dance in television's *Scarlett* while Clark Gable and Vivien Leigh do the same in the original movie *Gone with the Wind.*

Soon after her dramatic performance in the 1996 Atlanta Olympics, gymnast Kerry Strug went from Olympic athlete to hard-back book author with the publication of *Landing on My Feet: A Diary of Dreams.*

Typical of thousands of small publishing houses, Ten Speed Press offers an array of interesting, odd, or otherwise "small" books that larger publishers may ignore.

FRONTLIST

VODOU
Visions and Voices of Haiti

by Phyllis Galembo;
introduction by Gèrdes Fleurant

Priestesses, zombies, snakes, and swamps. Voodoo, or *vodou*, the dazzlingly symbolic spiritual tradition of many Afro-Caribbean peoples, has 10 x 10 inches,
February

LONG SLIM SLIMY ONES, SHORT FAT JUICY ONES
The Complete Guide to Worms in Your Garden

by Loren Nancarrow and Janet Hogan Taylor

We would like to introduce the modest hero of the new organic gardening revolution: the worm. After spilling the secrets of natural pest control in DEAD SNAILS **March**

THE GARDENCYCLE: 1999

by Seeds of Change

A marvelous keepsake that marries practicality and beauty, THE GARDENCYCLE daily diary is nothing less than the consummate guide and companion to a gardener's year, with space for recording personal garden information, handy 144 pages, full color,

blockbusters, critics argue, are books of merit, books of substance, and books that make a difference.

GROWTH OF SMALL PRESSES

The overcommercialization of the book industry is mitigated somewhat by the rise in the number of smaller publishing houses. Although these smaller operations are large in number, they account for a very small proportion of books sold (remember the 18,000 houses that annually imprint fewer than four titles). They cannot compete in the blockbuster world. By definition *alternative*, they specialize in specific areas such as the environment, feminism, gay issues, and how-to. They can also publish writing otherwise uninteresting to bigger houses, such as poetry and literary commentary. Relying on specialization and narrowly targeted marketing, books like Ralph Nader and Clarence Ditlow's *The Lemon Book*, published by Moyer Bell, and Claudette McShane's *Warning! Dating May Be Hazardous to Your Health*, published by Mother Courage Press, not only can earn healthy sales but also can make a difference in their readers' lives.

RESTRUCTURING OF BOOK RETAILING

There are approximately 20,000 bookstores in the United States, but the number is dwindling as small independent operations find it increasingly difficult to compete with chains like Bookstop, Barnes & Noble, Borders, Books-A-Million, and Crown. Nearly one-half of U.S. bookselling is accounted for by Barnes & Noble and Borders alone (Institute for Alternative Journalism, 1996, p. 4), and over half is accounted for by chain stores (Figure 3–4). These larger operations are typically located in malls

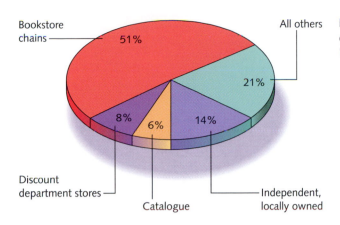

Bookstore chains — 51%

All others — 21%

Figure 3–4 Where We Buy Our Books. *Source: Publishers Weekly,* May 12, 1997, p. 13.

Discount department stores — 8%

Catalogue — 6%

Independent, locally owned — 14%

Many major chain bookstores now emulate the comfort and charm of an independent store. Barnes & Noble's bookstores offer customers a clean, well-lighted place to peruse their products and sip a latté.

that have heavy pedestrian traffic. Their size allows them to purchase inventory cheaply and then offer discounts to shoppers. Because their location attracts shoppers, they can also profitably stock nonbook merchandise such as audio- and videotapes, CDs, computer games, calendars, magazines, and greeting cards for the drop-in trade. But high volume, high traffic operations tend to deal in high volume books. To book traditionalists, this only encourages the industry's blockbuster mentality. When the largest bookstores in the country order only the biggest sellers, the small books get lost. When floor space is given over to Garfield coffee mugs and Sharon Stone calendars, there is even less room for small but potentially interesting books.

Although the independent bookstore share of total U.S. retail sales fell from 32.5% in 1991 to 14% in 1997, many continue to prosper. Using their size and independence to their advantage, they counter the chains with

Figure 3–5 Innovations originally instituted by independent booksellers have redefined "the bookstore." Reprinted with permission of King Features Syndicate.

expert, personalized service provided by a reading-loving staff, coffee and snack bars, cushioned chairs and sofas for slow browsing, and intimate readings by favorite authors (Figure 3–5). In fact, so successful have these devices been that the big stores now are copying them. Still, the big operations cannot or will not emulate some strategies. Specialization is one. Religious, feminist, and animal-lover bookstores exist. The in-store book club for children or poetry fans, for example, is another small-store strategy.

Another alternative to the big mall chain store is buying books online. Amazon *(http://www.amazon.com)* of Seattle is the best known of the new online book sales services. Thorough, fast (it guarantees 2-day delivery), and well stocked (it lists 2.5 million titles and its motto is "Every Book Under the Sun"), Amazon boasts low overhead and that means better prices for readers. In addition, its Web site offers book buyers large amounts of potentially valuable information. Once online, customers can identify the books that interest them, read synopses, check reviews from multiple sources, and read comments not only from other readers but sometimes from the authors and publishers as well. Of course, they can also order books. Some other popular online bookstores can be found at *http://powells.com* and *http://www.books.com.*

Although big bookselling chains have their critics, they also have their defenders. At least the big titles, CDs, and cheap prices get people into bookstores, the argument goes. Once folks begin reading, even if it is trashy stuff, they might move on to better material. People who never buy books will never read books. (For a look at another force in the book industry, see the box "The Oprah Effect.")

CHANGES IN BOOK READERSHIP

This defense of the commercialization of books and bookselling—whatever it takes, get people buying books—has some merit, because even though the United States has the highest level of literacy in the world, very few

The best-known and most successful of the online booksellers, Amazon.com offers potential buyers a wealth of information and services.

of us read books, and even fewer read books regularly. This is a media literacy issue.

DEVELOPING MEDIA LITERACY SKILLS
Combating Aliteracy

Nearly 300 million hardcover books are bought annually in the United States. Overall book sales continue to increase, reaching over $20 billion in 1997. The typical U.S. reader reads books for 110 hours a year and spends more than $100 on those volumes. These numbers might suggest that the book as a medium is in good shape. But this is not necessarily the case.

The rise in sales is due in large part to the flood of how-to, self-help, and cookbooks. Three hundred million books is about one book per person, and this includes "required reading" such as text, professional, and reference books—categories that, when combined, dwarf other types of books. One hundred ten hours a year is just 18.5 minutes a day. One hundred dollars a year is less than two dollars a week. The Gallup company reports that of all the English-speaking peoples in the world, U.S. citizens read the fewest books. Fewer than one person in five in the United States aged 18 years and older is currently reading a book. Half of all U.S. adults manage only one book a year, and only one in five of these reads books regularly.

Very few people in the United States are illiterate, that is, unable to read. But half the population will not read a book this year. The media literacy issue most specific to books, then, is not so much illiteracy as **aliteracy,** possessing the ability to read but being unwilling to do so. This is culturally problematic for two reasons. First, given the role books have played for centuries as a major force in the social, political, and intellectual development of the cultures that have used them, can any culture afford to ignore books? Totalitarian governments ban and burn books because they are repositories of ideas, ideas that can be read and considered with limited outside influence or official supervision. What kind of culture develops when, by their own refusal to read books, people figuratively save the dictators the trouble of striking the match?

Some communication theorists argue that this is a needless fear. Their position is that newer media have simply taken on many of the cultural and social change duties that were once the sole province of books. Television, film, and computer networks keep people connected to and active

Using Media to Make a Difference

The Oprah Effect

We've seen that books have been used to make a difference—political, social, and cultural—at several points throughout this chapter. But this is a story of how a giant in one medium is using her clout to make a difference in another.

As do all talk show hosts, Oprah Winfrey frequently devotes episodes of her highly rated daytime television program to authors of nonfiction books. However, on one occasion in 1993, Winfrey aired a show featuring fiction writers, and fewer viewers than usual tuned in for *"Authors I'd Like to Have Dinner With."*

In 1996 the program's format was revamped, allowing voracious reader Winfrey a "floating" segment in which she could pursue a topic for as little or as long as she and her audience were interested. Winfrey decided this would be a good opportunity to try novel-

ists again. "'I started thinking about it again one morning in the shower,'" the host of the *Oprah Winfrey Show* said. "'It would be great if we could do this book club and do what I've always wanted to do: sit down with authors I really love'" (Kinsella, 1997, p. 276).

The initial entry on "Oprah's Book Club" was a first novel, *The Deep End of the Ocean,* by Jacquelyn Mitchard. This was soon followed by Toni Morrison's *Song of Solomon,* Jane Hamilton's *The Book of Ruth,* and Wally Lamb's *She's Come Undone.* To everyone's surprise, few of her estimated 14 million daily viewers abandoned the show, *and* sales of the featured books skyrocketed. Winfrey took this as a sign that she had taken on a "new mission." She told *Publishers Weekly,*

I feel strongly that, no matter who you are, reading opens doors and provides, in your own personal sanctuary, an opportunity to explore and feel things, the way other forms of media cannot. I want books to become part of my audience's lifestyle, for reading to become a natural phenomenon with them, so that it is no big deal. (Kinsella, 1997, p. 277)

Ever mindful of television's visual demands, the Book Club is presented in part at a dinner that takes on the style of the book. Winfrey and the author talk, and

in their cultures. But, counter book traditionalists, these other media, because of their heavy reliance on advertising support, will enter only the narrowest of opinions into the cultural forum. As Beatty expounded on the death of the book in *Fahrenheit 451*, "[b]ut the public, knowing what it wanted, spinning happily, let the comic book survive. And the three-dimensional sex magazine, of course. There you have it, Montag. It didn't come from the Government down. There was no dictum, no declaration, no censorship, to start with, no!" (Bradbury, 1981, p. 56).

Chapter Review

The colonists, due to widespread illiteracy, high cost, and official control, were not a book-oriented population. The American Revolution changed that and ushered in the beginnings of the book industry. The combination of technical advances such as roll paper, the steam printing press, linotype, offset lithography, and increased literacy after the Civil War produced the flowering of the novel in the 1800s, firmly establishing the relationship between readers and medium.

Books are divided into several categories (trade, professional, el-hi, higher ed, standardized

then both engage in a discussion with *Oprah Winfrey Show* audience members. The author also appears on Oprah On-line to further discuss the book with Oprah viewers. So successful as television is the Book Club that cable channel Lifetime began airing specially edited one-hour versions of the dinners.

Have Winfrey and the Book Club made a difference? A buyer for Chicago-based chain Barbara's Bookstores said, "She really does seem to be bringing in new people, and they're people who specifically said they wouldn't otherwise have bought a book at all" (Kinsella, 1997, p. 276). Barnes & Noble's director of merchandise said that "a good percentage of shoppers coming in for Book Club titles are new readers. Seventy-five percent of the people who buy the Book Club title are buying something else, too," he reported. "They shop, they browse, they engage in conversation with our booksellers, and then they come back" (p. 276).

So influential has Oprah's Book Club become that Winfrey finally gave in to publishing industry requests that she let publishers know well in advance which books she will feature to allow printing of sufficient copies. The industry has even given their television-boosted sales a name—*The Oprah Effect*.

Oprah's Book Club

tests, religious, book club, mail order, subscription reference, mass market paperbacks, and university press). Although more than 20,000 companies call themselves book publishers, only 2,000 produce four or more titles a year. The scope and structure of the contemporary book industry is characterized by conglomeration, increasing commercialization and demand for profits, the growth of small presses, the restructuring of book retailing, and changes in the nation's book reading habits. Our unwillingness to read books is a major media literacy issue.

Questions for Review

1. What were the major developments in the modernization of the printing press?
2. Why were the early colonists not a book reading population?
3. What was the Stamp Act? Why did colonial printers object to it?
4. What factors allowed the flowering of the American novel as well as the expansion of the book industry in the 1800s?
5. Who developed the paperback in England? in the United States?
6. Name six reasons books are an important cultural resource.
7. What are the major categories of books?
8. What is the impact of conglomeration on the book industry?
9. What are the products of increasing commercialization and demands for profit in the book industry?
10. What is meant by aliteracy?

Questions For Critical Thinking and Discussion

1. Do you envision books ever again having the power to move the nation as they did in Revolutionary or antislavery times? Why, or why not?
2. How familiar are you with the early great American writers such as Hawthorne, Cooper, and Thoreau? What have you learned from these writers?
3. Are you proud of your book reading habits? Why, or why not?
4. Where do you stand in the debate on the over-commercialization of the book? To what lengths should publishers and booksellers go to get people to read?
5. Under what circumstances is censorship permissible? Whom do you trust to make the right decision about what you should and should not read? If you were a librarian, under what circumstances would you "pull" a book?

Important Resources

Publishers Weekly. The "bible" of the book publishing and selling industries. It typically contains a wealth of facts and figures, much inside industry information, and numerous readable feature articles.

Scribner, C. (1990). *In the company of writers: A life in publishing.* **New York: Scribners.** A readable autobiographical account of the publishing industry. It is particularly interesting as it covers publishing's transformation from cottage industry to corporate control.

Tebbel, J. (1972, 1975, 1978, 1981). *A history of book publishing in the United States,* **4 vols. New York: Bowker.** Everything you ever wanted to know about the book industry and readership in four excellently researched and documented volumes.

The writers market, **Cincinnati, OH: F & W Publishing.** Indispensable for would-be writers and successful authors alike. Contains the names and addresses of all the nation's leading publishers and offers valuable how-to and insider essays on making a career as an author.

Book Information Web Sites

Association of American Publishers	*http://www.publishers.org/*
Publishers Weekly	*http://www.bowker.com/catalogue/home/entries/mag_42_1.html*
Book Industry Study Group	*http://www.bookwire.com/bisg/research-resources/statistical.html*
Internet Book Information Center	*http://sunsite.unc.edu/ibc/IBC-homepage.html*
Bookwire	*http://www.bookwire.com/news.articles$pub3*
Banned Books Online	*http://www.cs.cmu.edu/People/spok/banned-books.html*
Freedom to Read	*http://www.lib.udel.edu/ud/freedom/freedom.html*

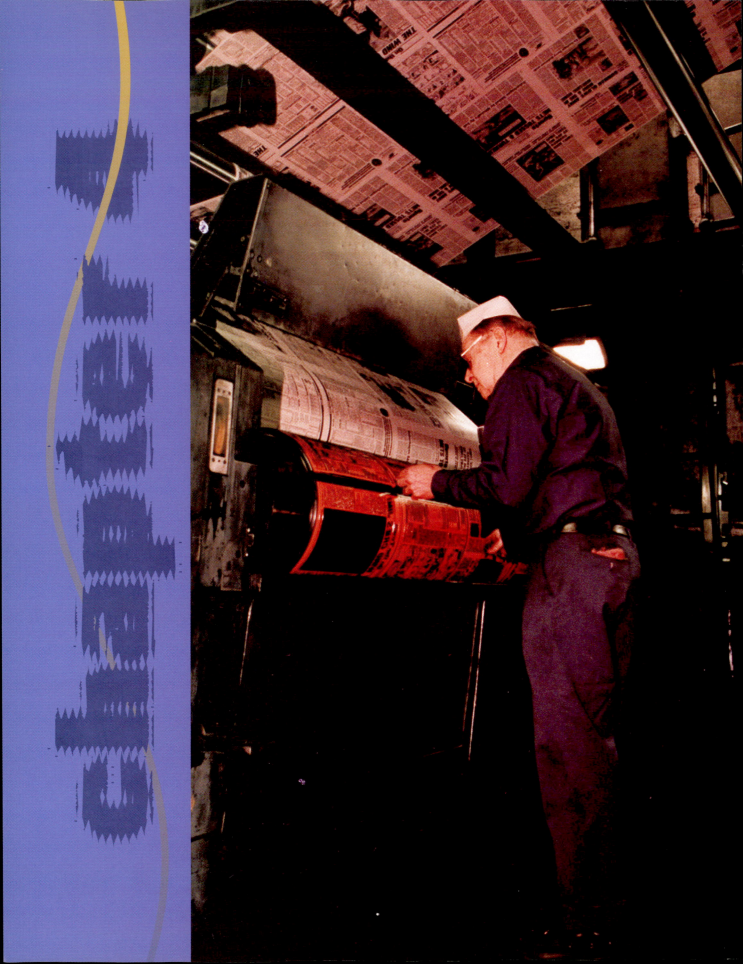

Newspapers

New at the newspaper, you really want to make your mark. You go to your boss, the city editor, in hopes of enlisting his support for your plan. He is enthusiastic, and together you pitch your idea to the executive editor. The three of you sit at a work table in her cluttered office. She asks the city editor to explain the proposal, but he defers to you. The pressure weighs on your lungs, but there's an excitement in your heart that reminds you of why you wanted to be a journalist in the first place. You begin.

"We're always being criticized for doing too much soft news, not enough depth and detail."

She nods.

"We're accused of covering political campaigns like horse races. Who's in front, who's running well— that sort of thing."

She nods again.

"People claim we in the media, especially newspapers, don't listen to them enough."

More nods.

"Circulation figures have been flat for some time." This was a risk— the boss could take it as a criticism of her work—but being a journalist is about putting yourself on the line. You wait for, and receive, a begrudging nod. So you continue, "We need to give people a reason to read us."

"Good setup," says the executive editor. "Now get to the point."

"I'm proposing an exercise in civic journalism, using the paper as a proactive force in the community."

"OK. Shoot."

"We have a big gubernatorial election coming up, right? So let's poll a thousand registered voters and ask what issues they most care about. Then we take the top three or four issues and create a series of questions we can ask the candidates in interviews. Then we write stories based on their responses to the very issues the people want to know about." After a pause that strikes you as a bit too long, you begin to weaken. "OK, maybe it needs some work. It was just an idea. Maybe if we can . . ."

"Stop," she interrupts, "I think it's an excellent idea. You can serve as a researcher for the team that manages the project. We'll call it 'Your Voice, Your Vote' and run the stories on the front page for a month before the election. Good work!"

For weeks you're the paper's hotshot young go-getter. Although you didn't get to write them, the reports on crime, drugs, education, and taxes are sharply crafted and well received. The readers like what you're doing; so do the politicians, who seem relieved to be spared a "personalities" campaign. Circulation, both newsstand and subscription, climbs a bit; ad revenues rise even more.

Then journalists from around the country offer their opinions. The paper has abdicated its professional responsibility by allowing a poll to dictate coverage. It's pandering to readers by allowing them to dictate newsworthiness. You've undermined candidates' personal political judgment. You've ignored issues that are equally or more important. What about race, for example? Your newspaper is accused of limiting public debate, engaging in self-serving pseudojournalism for the purpose of boosting revenues, and attempting to control the public agenda.

It may or may not be true, but your star seems to be shining a bit less brightly now. And all you wanted was to do good newspaper work.

In this chapter we examine the relationship between the newspaper and its readers. We start with a look at the medium's roots, beginning with the first papers, following them from Europe to colonial America, where many of the traditions of today's free press were set. We study the cultural changes that led to creation of the penny press and to competition between these mass circulation dailies that gave us "yellow journalism."

We then review the modern newspaper in terms of its size and scope. We discuss different types of newspapers and the importance of newspapers as an advertising medium. The wire and feature services, important providers of newspaper content, are also highlighted.

We then detail how the relationship between medium and audience is shifting as a result of the loss of competition within the industry, attempts at civic journalism, the positive and negative impacts of technology, the prospects for online newspapers, and changes in the nature of newspaper readership. Finally, we test our media literacy skill through a discussion of how to read the newspaper, for example, interpreting the relative positioning of stories.

A Short History of Newspapers

The opening vignette makes an important point about contemporary newspapers—they are working hard to secure new identities for themselves in an increasingly crowded media environment. As a medium and as an industry, newspapers are poised at the edge of a significant change in their role and operation. The changing relationship between newspapers and readers is part of this upheaval. Newspapers have faced similar challenges more than once in the past and have survived.

THE EARLIEST NEWSPAPERS

In Caesar's time Rome had a newspaper. The **Acta Diurna** (actions of the day), written on a tablet, was posted on a wall after each meeting of the Senate. Its circulation was one, and there is no reliable measure of its total readership. However, it does show that people have always wanted to know what was happening and that others have helped them do so.

The newspapers we recognize today have their roots in 17th-century Europe. **Corantos,** one-page news sheets about specific events, were printed in English in Holland in 1620 and imported to England by British booksellers who were eager to satisfy public demand for information about Continental happenings that eventually led to what we now call the Thirty Years' War.

Englishmen Nathaniel Butter, Thomas Archer, and Nicholas Bourne eventually began printing their own occasional news sheets, using the same title for consecutive editions. They stopped publishing in 1641, the same year that regular, daily accounts of local news started appearing in other news sheets. These true forerunners of our daily newspaper were called **diurnals.**

Political power struggles in England at this time boosted the fledgling medium, as partisans on the side of the monarchy and those on the side of Parliament published diurnals to bolster their positions. When the monarchy prevailed, it granted monopoly publication rights to the *Oxford Gazette,* the official voice of the Crown. Founded in 1665 and later renamed the *London Gazette,* this journal used a formula of foreign news, official information, royal proclamations, and local news that became the model for the first colonial newspapers.

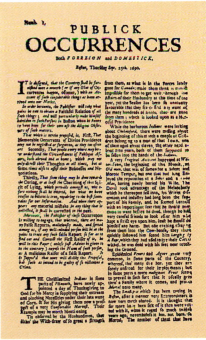

The first daily newspaper to appear in the 13 colonies, *Publick Occurrences Both Foreign and Domestick,* lasted all of one edition.

Colonial Newspapers In Chapter 3 we saw how bookseller/print shops became the focal point for the exchange of news and information and how this led to the beginning of the colonial newspaper. It was at these establishments that **broadsides** (sometimes referred to as **broadsheets**), single-sheet announcements or accounts of events imported from England, would be posted. In 1690 Boston bookseller/printer (and coffee house owner) Benjamin Harris printed his own broadside, *Publick Occurrences Both Foreign and Domestick.* Intended for continuous publication, the country's first daily lasted only one day. Harris had been critical of local and European dignitaries, and he had also failed to obtain a license.

Benjamin Franklin published America's first political cartoon—"Join, or Die," a rallying call for the Colonies—in his *Pennsylvania Gazette* in 1754.

JOIN, or DIE.

More successful was Boston Postmaster John Campbell, whose 1704 *Boston News-Letter* survived until the Revolution. The paper featured foreign news, reprints of articles from England, government announcements, and shipping news. It was dull, and it was also expensive. Nonetheless, it established the newspaper in the Colonies.

The *Boston News-Letter* was able to survive in part because of government subsidies. With government support came government control, but the buildup to the Revolution helped establish the medium's independence. In 1721 Boston had three papers. James Franklin's *New-England Courant* was the only one publishing without authority. The *Courant* was popular and controversial, but when it criticized the Massachusetts governor, Franklin was jailed for printing "scandalous libels." When released, he returned to his old ways, earning himself and the *Courant* a publishing ban, which he circumvented by installing his younger brother Benjamin as nominal publisher. Ben Franklin soon moved to Philadelphia, and without his leadership the *Courant* was out of business in three years. Its lasting legacy, however, was in proving that a newspaper with popular support could indeed challenge authority.

In Philadelphia Benjamin Franklin established a print shop and later, in 1729, took over a failing newspaper, which he revived and renamed the *Pennsylvania Gazette*. By combining the income from his book shop and printing businesses with that from his popular daily, Franklin could run the *Gazette* with significant independence. Even though he held the contract for Philadelphia's official printing, he was unafraid to criticize those in authority. In addition, he began to develop advertising support, which also helped shield his newspaper from government control by decreasing its dependence on official printing contracts for survival. Ben Franklin demonstrated that financial independence could lead to editorial independence. It was not, however, a guarantee.

In 1734 *New York Weekly Journal* publisher John Peter Zenger was jailed for criticizing that Colony's royal governor. The charge was seditious libel, and the verdict was based not on the truth or falsehood of the printed words but on whether they had been printed. The criticisms had been published, so Zenger was clearly guilty. But his attorney, Andrew Hamilton, argued to the jury, "For the words themselves must be libelous, that is, false, scandalous and seditious, or else we are not guilty." Zenger's peers agreed, and he was freed. The case of Peter Zenger became a symbol of colonial newspaper independence from the Crown, and its power was evident in the refusal by publishers to accept the Stamp Act in 1765 (see Chapter 3). For more on this colonial newspaperman, see the box "Truth As a Defense Against Libel: The Zenger Trial."

Newspapers After Independence After the Revolution, the new government of the United States had to determine for itself just how free a press it was willing to tolerate. When the first Congress convened under the new Constitution in 1790, the nation's founders debated, drafted, and adopted the first 10 amendments to the Constitution, called the **Bill of Rights.** The **First Amendment** reads:

> Congress shall make no law respecting an establishment of religion, or prohibiting the free exercise thereof; or abridging the freedom of speech, or of the press; or the right of the people peacefully to assemble, and to petition the Government for a redress of grievances.

But a mere eight years later, fearful of the subversive activities of foreigners sympathetic to France, Congress passed a group of four laws known collectively as the **Alien and Sedition Acts.** The Sedition Act made illegal writing, publishing, or printing "any false scandalous and malicious writing" about the president, Congress, or the federal government. So unpopular were these laws to a people who had just waged a war of independence against similar limits on their freedom of expression that they were not renewed when Congress reconsidered them two years later in 1800. We will examine in detail the ongoing commitment to the First Amendment, freedom of the press, and open expression in the United States in Chapter 13.

THE MODERN NEWSPAPER EMERGES

At the turn of the 19th century, urbanization, growing industries, movement of workers to the cities, and increasing literacy combined to create an audience for a new kind of paper. Known as the **penny press,** these one-cent newspapers were for everyone. Benjamin Day's September 3, 1833, issue of the *New York Sun* was the first of the penny papers. Day's

Media Echoes

Truth as a Defense Against Libel: The Zenger Trial

Young German immigrant John Peter Zenger started publishing New York's second paper, the *Weekly Journal*, in 1733 with encouragement from several anti-Crown merchants and business people who wanted a voice to counter William Bradford's Crown-supported *Gazette*. Zenger had been an apprentice under Bradford, whose official title was "King's Printer to the Province of New York."

Zenger did his new job well. He was constantly and openly critical of New York's British-born governor, William Cosby. Soon he was arrested and jailed for seditious libel. For the nine months he was imprisoned, he continued to edit his paper, run on the outside by his wife.

This trial began on August 4, 1735, and at first it did not go well for Zenger. His two original lawyers were disbarred because they argued that the judge, appointed by Cosby, should step down. Zenger's supporters then hired 80-year-old Philadelphia attorney Andrew Hamilton. Hamilton was not only a brilliant lawyer and orator but an astute reader of contemporary political sentiment. He built his defense of the accused printer on growing colonial anger toward Britain. Actually he had little choice. As the law stood, Zenger *was* guilty. British law said that printed words could be libelous, even if true, if they were inflammatory or negative. Truth, Hamilton argued, is a defense against libel. Otherwise how could anything other than favorable material about government ever be published? Moreover, he added, why should the colonists be bound by a British law they had not themselves approved?

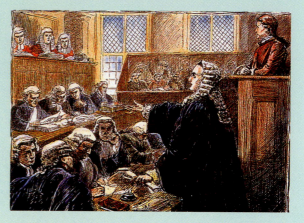

John Peter Zenger, sitting in the dock, is defended by Andrew Hamilton.

To make his point Hamilton said, "Power may justly be compared to a great river, while kept within its due bounds, is both beautiful and useful. But when it overflows its banks, it is then too impetuous to be stemmed, it bears down all before it, and brings destruction and desolation wherever it comes."

The jury ruled Zenger not guilty, making it clear to the British and their colonial supporters that the colonists would no longer accept their control of the press.

Two hundred and fifty years later, different people are still fighting for press freedom. The Zenger trial is echoed in Chapter 13 in the travails of Larry Flynt and in Chapter 15 in the account of murdered journalists in Argentina.

innovation was to sell his paper so inexpensively that it would attract a large readership, which could then be "sold" to advertisers. Day succeeded because he anticipated a new kind of reader. He filled the *Sun's* pages with police and court reports, crime stories, entertainment news, and human interest stories. Because the paper lived up to its motto, "The Sun shines for all," there was little of the political and business information that had characterized earlier papers.

Soon there were penny papers in all the major cities. Among the most important was James Gordon Bennett's *New York Morning Herald.* Although more sensationalistic than the *Sun,* the *Herald* pioneered the correspondent system, placing reporters in Washington, D.C., and other major U.S. cities as well as abroad. Correspondents filed their stories by means of the telegraph, invented in 1844.

Horace Greeley's *New York Tribune* was an important penny paper as well. Its nonsensationalistic, issues-oriented and humanitarian reporting established the mass newspaper as a powerful medium of social action.

The People's Medium People typically excluded from the social, cultural, and political mainstream quickly saw the value of the mass newspaper. The first African American newspaper was *Freedom's Journal,* published initially in 1827 by John B. Russwurum and the Reverend Samuel Cornish. Forty others soon followed, but it was Frederick Douglass who made best use of the new mass circulation style in his newspaper, *The Ram's Horn,* founded expressly to challenge the editorial policies of Benjamin Day's *Sun.* Although this particular effort failed, Douglass had established himself and the minority press as a viable voice for those otherwise silenced. Douglass's *North Star,* founded in 1847 with the masthead slogan "Right is of no Sex—Truth is of no Color—God is the Father of us all, and we are all Brethren," was the most influential African American newspaper before the Civil War.

Native Americans found early voice in papers such as the *Cherokee Phoenix,* founded in 1828 in Georgia, and the *Cherokee Rose Bud,* which began operation 20 years later in Oklahoma.

Volume 1, Number 1 of Benjamin Day's *New York Sun,* the first of the penny papers.

Throughout this period of the popularization of the newspaper, numerous foreign language dailies also began operation, primarily in major cities where immigrants tended to settle. Sloan, Stovall, and Startt (1993) report that in 1880 there were more than 800 foreign language newspapers publishing in German, Polish, Italian, Spanish, and various Scandinavian languages.

The First Wire Services   In 1849 six large New York papers, including the *Sun*, the *Herald*, and the *Tribune*, decided to pool efforts and share expenses collecting news from foreign ships docking at the city's harbor. After determining rules of membership and other organizational issues, in 1856 the papers established the first news gathering (and distribution) organization, the New York Associated Press. Other domestic **wire services** followed—the Associated Press in 1900, the United Press International in 1907, and the International News Service in 1909.

This innovation, with its assignment of correspondents to both foreign and domestic bureaus, had a number of important implications. First, it greatly expanded the breadth and scope of coverage a newspaper could offer its readers. This was a boon to dailies wanting to attract as many readers as possible. Greater coverage of distant domestic news helped unite an expanding country while encouraging even more expansion. The United States was a nation of immigrants, and news from people's homelands drew more readers. Second, the nature of reporting began to change. Reporters could now produce stories by rewriting—sometimes a little, sometimes a lot—the actual on-the-spot coverage of others. Finally, newspapers were able to reduce expenses (and increase profits) because they no longer needed to have their own reporters in all locations.

Yellow Journalism   In 1883 Hungarian immigrant Joseph Pulitzer bought the troubled *New York World*. Adopting a populist approach to the news, he brought a crusading, activist style of coverage to numerous turn-of-the-century social problems—growing slums, labor tensions, and failing farms, to name a few. The audience for his "new journalism" was the "common man," and he succeeded in reaching readers with light, sensationalistic news coverage, extensive use of illustrations, and circulation building stunts and promotions (for example, an around-the-world balloon flight). Ad revenues and circulation figures exploded.

Soon there were other new journalists. William Randolph Hearst applied Pulitzer's successful formula to his *San Francisco Examiner*, and then in 1895 he took on Pulitzer himself in New York. The competition between Hearst's *Morning Journal* and Pulitzer's *World* was so intense that it debased newspapers and journalism as a whole, which is somewhat ironic in that Pulitzer later founded the prize for excellence in journalism that still bears his name.

Drawing its name from the Yellow Kid, a popular cartoon character of the time, **yellow journalism** was a study in excess—sensational sex, crime, and disaster news, giant headlines, heavy use of (often fabricated)

MAINE EXPLOSION CAUSED BY BOMB OR TORPEDO?

Capt. Sigsbee and Consul-General Lee Are in Doubt---The World Has Sent a
Special Tug, With Submarine Divers, to Havana to Find Out---Lee Asks for
an Immediate Court of Inquiry---Capt. Sigsbee's Suspicions.

CAPT. SIGSBEE, IN A SUPPRESSED DESPATCH TO THE STATE DEPARTMENT, SAYS THE ACCIDENT WAS MADE POSSIBLE BY AN ENEMY.

Dr. E. C. Pendleton, Just Arrived from Havana, Says He Overheard Talk There of a Plot to Blow Up the Ship---Capt.
Zalinski, the Dynamite Expert, and Other Experts Report to The World that the Wreck Was Not
Accidental---Washington Officials Ready for Vigorous Action if Spanish Responsibility
Can Be Shown---Divers to Be Sent Down to Make Careful Examinations.

Several of yellow journalism's excesses—dramatic graphics, bold headlines, the reporting of rumor—are evident in this front page from Joseph Pulitzer's *New York World.* Many historians believe that the sinking of the Maine was engineered by yellow journalist William Randolph Hearst, publisher of the *New York Morning Journal,* in order to create a war that his papers could cover as a way to build circulation.

photos and illustrations, and reliance on cartoons and color. It was successful at first, and other papers around the country adopted all or part of its style. Although public reaction to the excesses of yellow journalism soon led to its decline, traces of its popular features remain. Large headlines, big front page pictures, extensive use of photos and illustrations, and cartoons are characteristic even of today's best newspapers.

The years between the era of yellow journalism and the coming of television were a time of remarkable growth in the development of newspapers. From 1910 to the beginning of World War II, daily newspaper subscriptions doubled, and ad revenues tripled. In 1924, the American Society of Newspaper Editors issued the "Canons of Journalism and Statement of Principles" in an effort to restore order and respectability after the yellow era. The opening sentence of the Canons was, "The right of a newspaper to attract and hold readers is restricted by nothing but considerations of public welfare." The wire services internationalized. United Press International started gathering news from Japan in 1909 and was covering South America and Europe by 1921. In response to the challenge of radio and magazines for advertising dollars, newspapers began consolidating into **newspaper chains**—papers in different cities across the country owned by a single company. Hearst and Scripps were among the most powerful chains in the 1920s. But the next major shift in newspapers as a medium was brought about by television.

Newspapers and Their Audiences

Sixty million newspapers are sold daily in the United States, and 6 of 10 people report reading a paper every day. The industry that produces those newspapers looks quite different from the one that operated before television became a dominant medium. There are now fewer papers. There are now different types of papers. More newspapers are part of large chains. What has not changed is why people read the newspaper. Researcher Bernard Berelson's classic 1949 study of what missing the paper means speaks for today's newspaper readers as well. Readers use the newspaper:

- To get information about and interpretation of public affairs
- As tools for daily living (for example, advertising, radio and movie listings, and announcements of births, deaths, and weddings)
- For relaxation and escape
- For prestige (newspaper content is raw material for conversation)
- For social contact (from human interest stories and advice columns)

As we saw in Chapter 2, the advent of television coincided with several important social and cultural changes. Shorter work hours, more leisure, more expendable cash, movement to the suburbs, and women joining the workforce in greater numbers all served to alter the newspaper–reader relationship. Overall, circulation rose from 48 to 62 million between 1945 and 1970 (and has remained steady since), but the amount of time people spent reading their papers decreased. People were reading only 20% of the stories, spending less than 30 minutes a day with the paper, and only 15 minutes was focused primarily on the paper itself. Circulation for big city papers dropped, and many closed shop. As newspapers struggled to redefine themselves in the expanding television era, the number of chains grew from 60, controlling 42% of the daily circulation, to 157, controlling 60% of the daily circulation (*Editor & Publisher International Yearbook*, various years; *Statistical Abstracts of the United States*, various years).

Scope and Structure of the Newspaper Industry

Today there are 12,246 newspapers operating in the United States. Of these, 1,710 (14%) are dailies, 9,011 (74%) are weeklies, and 705 (12%) are semiweekly. The dailies have a combined circulation of 60.7 million, the weeklies 54.6 million. The average weekly has a circulation of just over 7,000. **Pass-along readership**—readers who did not originally purchase the paper—brings 132 million people a day in touch with a daily and 200 million a week in touch with a weekly. However, overall circulation has remained the same despite a growing population. In 1990 there were only 0.7 newspaper subscriptions per U.S. household compared to 1.12 in 1960 (*Editor & Publisher International Yearbook*, 1995). To maintain their success and to ensure their future, newspapers have had to diversify.

TYPES OF NEWSPAPERS

We've cited statistics about dailies and weeklies, but these categories actually include many different types of papers. Let's take a closer look at some of these types of papers.

USA Today offers brief reports for people on the go. Despite its great commercial success, its critics refer to it as McPaper.

National Daily Newspapers We typically think of the newspaper as a local medium, our town's paper. But three national daily newspapers enjoy large circulations and significant social and political impact. The oldest and most respected is the *Wall Street Journal*, founded in 1889 by Charles Dow and Edward Jones. Today, as then, its focus is on the world of business, although its definition of business is broad. With a circulation of 1.8 million, the *Journal* is the biggest daily in the United States, and an average household income of its readers of $146,300 makes it a favorite for upscale advertisers.

The *Christian Science Monitor*, begun in 1908, continues to hold to its founding principle as a paper of serious journalism. Begun as a high-minded alternative to Boston's yellow papers by Mary Baker Eddy, founder of the Christian Science religion, it was international in coverage and national in distribution from the start. Today, with its dwindling number of subscribers now totaling 150,000, it grows smaller.

The newest and most controversial national daily is *USA Today*. It calls itself "The Nation's Newspaper," but its critics derisively call it "McPaper" because of what they see as its lack of depth, apparent dependence on style over substance, and reliance on stories of no more than a dozen sentences. The paper's daily circulation of 1.4 million suggests that, critics aside, readers welcome its mix of short, lively, upbeat stories; full color graphics; state-by-state news and sports briefs; and liberal use of easy-to-read illustrated graphs and tables. Begun in 1982 to appeal to business travelers and others on the run, *USA Today* depends primarily on single-issue rather than subscriber sales, with airport news racks a primary sales point.

Large Metropolitan Dailies To be a daily, a paper must be published at least five times a week. As we can see in Figure 4–1, the big city dailies as a whole are losing circulation, with the heavy losses of the evening papers offsetting increases for the morning papers. Many old, established papers, including the *Cleveland Press*, the *Philadelphia Bulletin*, and the *Washington Star*, have stilled their presses in recent years. When the *Chicago Daily News* closed its doors, it had the sixth highest circulation in the country.

Figure 4–1 also shows how both number of and circulation of dailies have changed in the last two and a half decades. As big cities cease to be industrial centers, homes, jobs, and interests have turned away from downtown. Those large metropolitan dailies that are succeeding have used a number of strategies to cut costs and to attract and keep more suburban-oriented readers. (For a look at a questionable cost-cutting measure, see the box "Shunning Low-Income Readers: Smart Business or Self-Defeating Strategy?") Several papers, like the *Boston Globe*, produce an "all-day newspaper," with multiple editions throughout the day, accommodating everyone's work, commute, or home schedule.

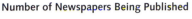

Number of Newspapers Being Published

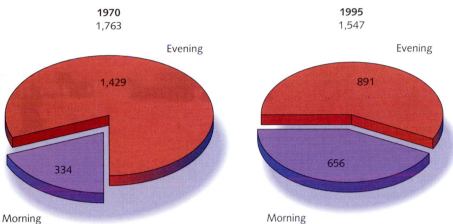

Figure 4–1 Daily Newspapers, Number and Circulation, 1970–1995. *Source:* Adapted from *Editor & Publisher International Yearbook*, 1995.

Number of Newspaper Readers (in millions)

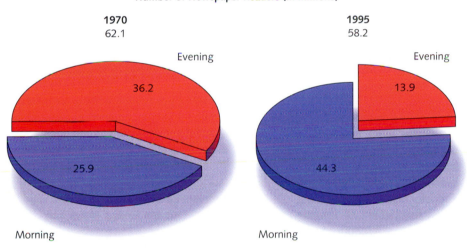

Almost all papers publish **zoned editions**—suburban or regional versions of the paper—to attract readers and to combat competition for advertising dollars from the suburban papers. Many big city dailies have gone as far as to drop the city of their publication from their name. Where is *The Tribune* published? Oakland, California, and Scranton, Pennsylvania, and Warren, Ohio, and Wisconsin Rapids, Wisconsin, each produces a paper called *The Tribune,* but these papers have dropped the city name from their mastheads.

The *New York Times* is a special large metropolitan daily. It is a paper local to New York, but the high quality of its reporting and commentary, the reach and depth of both its national and international news, and the solid reputations of its features (such as the weekly *Times Magazine* and the *Book Review*) make it the nation's newspaper of record.

Shunning Low-Income Readers: Smart Business or Self-Defeating Strategy?

Newspapers attempt to attract readers with a variety of tactics. Changing their look, producing more lifestyle features, and writing shorter, snappier stories are a few examples. They also use sales and marketing techniques—for example, discounts, direct mail advertising, and telephone solicitation. But as newspapers compete for revenues in a media-saturated world, many papers are faced with a difficult choice—one that is quietly discussed inside the industry but that deserves an airing in the larger cultural forum as well.

Two truths of newspaper economics are now in conflict. Newspapers have historically built their circulations on lower income readers. They have recently been increasingly attentive to the demographic demands of advertisers. The result is that many papers are reducing the number of copies they produce to eliminate "fringe circulation." One way they accomplish the less-is-more strategy is by refusing home delivery and refusing to market their papers to some low-income neighborhoods, denying low-income people discounts available to others, forcing these people to pay in advance for subscriptions, and neglecting to produce for these less desirable areas the kinds of zoned editions that are common for more upscale ones. Production and delivery expenses then go down without damaging ad revenues.

Asked if neglected inner city readers weren't being disadvantaged, Newspaper Association of America (NAA) chief economist Miles Groves responded sadly, "Isn't that the American way, for the poor to pay more?" (Cranberg, 1997, p. 52). *Washington Post* ombudsman Geneva Overholsers accused papers that use these strategies of "adopting redlining: they simply cease to serve areas of little interest to advertisers" (p. 54). Former editor of the *Orlando Sentinel* and the *Chicago Tribune*, James Squires, calls this redlining "the dirty little secret of newspapering" (p. 54). *Austin-American Statesman* editor Richard Oppel decried this abandonment of "the middle-class and lower-middle-class readers who have been the traditional core of newspaper readership. Newspapers should be at the center of common experience and a common narrative in our communities" (p. 54).

Newspaper vending boxes such as these are increasingly rare in many poorer urban areas as some papers intentionally limit their circulation to neighborhoods that are more demographically attractive to advertisers.

Some observers believe that the problem will solve itself economically. As the United States becomes increasingly ethnically diverse, newspapers will be foolish to ignore any group of readers. The NAA recently published an economic analysis entitled "Diversity, A Business Imperative" in which it argued, "By the year 2010, nearly one out of every two children under 5 years of age will belong to an ethnic minority group. These young people are the ones the newspaper industry must learn to attract as readers and as employees" (Cranberg, 1997, p. 53).

Enter your voice in the forum. Are you content to let economics solve this problem, or do you see these practices as a violation of public trust by a medium that has long claimed a special role in democracy? If you were a newspaper editor, how far would you go to put service over profit?

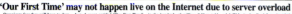

Most major dailies challenge suburban newspapers with targeted regional editions of their own. Here the *San Jose Mercury News* takes on the *Palo Alto Daily News* with its southbay edition, carrying stories on an East Palo Alto fire and Stanford athletics.

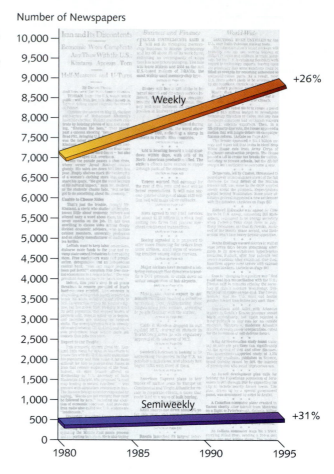

Figure 4–2 Growth of Weeklies and Semiweeklies, 1980–1995. *Source:* Adapted from Gale Research, Inc. *1995 Gale Directory of Publications and Broadcast Media.*

Suburban and Small Town Dailies As the United States has become a nation of transient suburb dwellers, so too has the newspaper been suburbanized. Since 1985 the number of suburban dailies has increased by 50%, and one, Long Island's *Newsday,* is the seventh largest paper in the country with a circulation of nearly 800,000.

Small town dailies operate much like their suburban cousins if there is a nearby large metropolitan paper; for example, the *Lawrence Eagle-Tribune* publishes in the shadow of Boston's two big dailies. Its focus is the Merrimack River Valley in Massachusetts, 25 miles northwest of Boston. If the small town paper has no big city competition, it can serve as the heart of its community.

Weeklies and Semiweeklies Many weeklies and semiweeklies have prospered because advertisers have followed them to the suburbs (Figure 4–2). Community reporting makes them valuable to those people who identify more with their immediate environment than they do with the neighboring big city. Suburban advertisers like the narrowly focused readership and more manageable advertising rates.

Many weeklies and semiweeklies, although not suburban, prosper through this same combination of meeting the needs of both readers and advertisers. Certainly there are daily ethnic newspapers, but ethnic newspapers typically tend to be weeklies. Especially in urban areas where the big dailies are scurrying to attract and hold the suburban readers, Spanish language and African American weeklies are operating profitably. There are approximately 160 Spanish language and 170 African American newspapers publishing today (*Editor & Publisher International Yearbook*, 1997).

Another common type of weekly operates as the alternative press. The offspring of the underground press of the 1960s antiwar, antiracism, pro-drug culture, the alternative press is redefining itself. The most successful among them—*The Village Voice*, the *L.A. Weekly*, the *Boston Phoenix*, and the *Seattle Weekly*—succeed by attracting upwardly mobile young people and young professionals, not the disaffected counterculture readers who were their original audiences. The Association of Alternative Weeklies (AAW) now represents 104 established alternative papers with a circulation of over 5.5 million. Questioning its own alternative label, AAW director Kate Hawthorne told *Columbia Journalism Review*, "We've become our parents" (Gremillion, 1995, p. 34). Now challenging the "old guard" alternatives are the Generation X weeklies, including Seattle's *The Stranger* and Dallas's *The Met*.

THE NEWSPAPER AS AN ADVERTISING MEDIUM

The reason we have the number and variety of newspapers we do is that readers want them. When newspapers prosper financially, the reason is that advertisers see their value. Figure 4–3 shows that more advertising dollars find their way to newspapers than to any other medium. There are two reasons for this beyond high circulation numbers.

First, newspapers are local in nature. Supermarkets, local car dealers, department stores, movie theaters, and other local merchants who want to offer a coupon turn automatically to the paper. Approximately 65% of daily newspaper space is advertising. Of that space, 60% is for local retail advertising, and another 25% is classified, which is overwhelmingly local. The second reason many advertisers favor newspapers is that their own industry research has identified the newspaper as the medium most often used by consumers when making a specific purchasing decision.

THE WIRE AND FEATURE SERVICES

Much of the 35% of the newspaper that is not advertising space is filled with content provided by outside sources, specifically the wire and feature services. Wire services, as we've already seen, collect news and distribute it to their members. (They draw their name from the way they originally distributed material—by telephone wire. Today material is more likely to

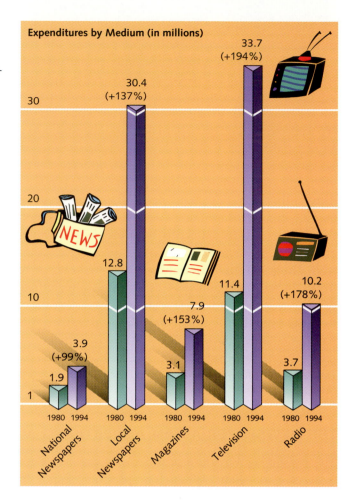

Figure 4–3 Advertising Expenditures by Medium, 1980–1994. *Source:* Adapted from McCann-Erickson, Inc., for *Advertising Age,* Crain Communications, Inc.

Expenditures by Medium (in millions)

	National Newspapers	Local Newspapers	Magazines	Television	Radio
1980	1.9	12.8	3.1	11.4	3.7
1994	3.9 (+99%)	30.4 (+137%)	7.9 (+153%)	33.7 (+194%)	10.2 (+178%)

come by computer network or satellite.) Unlike the early days of the wire services, today's member is three times more likely to be a broadcast outlet than a newspaper. These radio and television stations receive voice and video as well as written copy. In all cases, members receive a choice of material, most commonly national and international news, state and regional news, sports, business news, farm and weather reports, and human interest and consumer material.

The feature services, called **feature syndicates,** do not gather and distribute news. Instead, they operate as clearinghouses for the work of columnists, essayists, cartoonists, and other creative individuals. Among the material provided (by wire, by computer, or physically in packages) are opinion pieces such as Ellen Goodman or Molly Ivins commentaries; horoscope, chess, and bridge columns; editorial cartoons such as the work of Scott Willis and Ben Sergeant; and comics, the most common and popular form of syndicated material. Among the major syndicates, the best known are The *New York Times* News Service, King Features, Newspaper Enterprise Association (NEA), and the *Washington Post* News Service.

Current Trends in Newspaper Publishing

Loss of competition within the industry, civic journalism, technology, and the evolution of newspaper readership are altering not only the nature of the medium but also its relationship with its audiences.

LOSS OF COMPETITION

The newspaper industry has seen a dramatic decline in competition. This has taken two forms: loss of competing papers and concentration of ownership. In 1923 more than 60% of the cities that had newspapers had two or more competing (having different ownership) dailies. Now only 2% have competing papers. With circulation and advertising revenues leveling out for urban dailies, very few cities can support more than one paper. Congress attempted to reverse this trend with the 1970 Newspaper Preservation Act, which allowed **joint operating agreements (JOAs).** A JOA permits a failing paper to merge most aspects of its business with a successful local competitor as long as their editorial and reporting operations remain separate. The philosophy is that it is better to have two more or less independent papers in one city than to allow one to close. Eighteen of the 40 cities that now have competing dailies have JOAs, including San Francisco, Pittsburgh, El Paso, and Cincinnati.

The concern, naturally, is about editorial diversity. Cities with only one newspaper have only one newspaper editorial voice. This runs counter to two long-held American beliefs about the relationship between a free press and its readers:

- Truth flows from a multitude of tongues.
- The people are best served by a number of antagonistic voices.

What becomes of political, cultural, and social debate when there are neither multiple nor antagonistic (or at least different) voices? Media critic Robert McChesney (1997) offered this answer: "As ownership concentrated nationally in the form of chains, journalism came to reflect the partisan interests of owners and advertisers, rather than the diverse interests of any given community" (p. 13).

The trend toward newspaper concentration is troubling to many observers. The nation's 160 newspaper chains control 80% of daily newspaper circulation, own the 9 biggest circulation papers in the country, and own over 1,200 of the nation's 1,547 dailies.

Chains are not new. Hearst owned several big city papers in the 1880s, but at that time most cities enjoyed significant competition between papers. Now that most communities have only one paper, nonlocal chain or conglomerate control of that voice is more problematic. Among the larger chains are Gannett (82 dailies), Knight-Ridder (31), Newhouse (26), Times Mirror (22), New York Times (26), Scripps Howard (21), and Thomson Newspapers (18). Additional concern is raised about chain ownership when the chain is also a media conglomerate, owning several different types of media outlets as well as other nonmedia companies. Will the different media holdings speak with one corporate voice? Will they speak objectively, and will they cover at all the doings of their nonmedia corporations?

Chains do have their supporters. Although some critics see big companies as more committed to profit and shareholder dividends, others see chains such as Knight-Ridder, winner of numerous Pulitzer Prizes and other awards, as turning expanded economic and journalistic resources toward better service and journalism. Some critics see outside ownership as uncommitted to local communities and issues, but others see balance and objectivity (especially important in one-paper towns). Ultimately, we must recognize that not all chains operate alike. Some operate their holdings as little more than profit centers; others see profit residing in exemplary service. Some groups require that all its papers toe the corporate line; others grant local autonomy. Gannett, for example, openly boasts of its dedication to local management control.

CIVIC JOURNALISM

The opening vignette was based on an actual example of **civic journalism**—a newspaper actively engaging the community in reporting important civic issues—which was attempted in 1994 by a group of newspapers in North Carolina (Effron, 1997). These efforts at "interactive journalism" are motivated in part by a drive to strengthen the identity of the paper as an indispensable local medium, thereby attracting readers and boosting revenues. This activism further differentiates newspapers from other media (especially from online information delivery services, which are essentially passive) in the chase of advertising dollars. But papers are also trying civic journalism specifically to do good for the communities of which they themselves are members.

Civic journalism happens in a number of ways. Some newspapers devote significant resources to in-depth and long-running coverage of crucial community issues, interviewing citizens as subjects of the stories and inviting comment and debate through various "Hotline" or "Open Forum" sections of their papers. Other newspapers establish citizen councils to advise them on missed opportunities for coverage. Others assemble citizen panels that meet at regular intervals throughout a political campaign or other ongoing story. Citizen reaction to developments in those events is reported as news. Still others establish citizen roundtables to provide insight on crucial issues, for example, race and education. In these discussions people from different constituencies in the community—often holding quite conflicting perceptions of the problem—come together to talk out their differences. This interaction is reported as news, and the papers' editorial writers offer commentary and suggestions for solution.

As we also saw in the vignette, civic journalism is not universally embraced by the newspaper community. Critics contend that too much professional journalistic judgment is given away to people whose interests and concerns are too personal and too narrow. Others claim that the heavy focus on a particular issue in civic journalism distorts the public agenda (see the box "Covering the Issue of Race"). Still, the civic journalism "experiment" continues.

IMPACT OF TECHNOLOGY

Technology has been both ally and enemy to newspapers. Television forced newspapers to change the way they did business and served their readers. Now, online computer networks pose the greatest challenge to this medium. Online job hunting and auto sales services are already cutting into classified advertising profits of newspapers. The Internet and the World Wide Web provide readers with more information and more depth, and with greater speed, than the traditional newspaper.

As a result, the traditional newspaper is reinventing itself using these very same technologies. In the mid-1980s several big publishers experimented with **videotext** and **teletext services.** These are paperless newspapers, or news on demand, delivered by computer video screen. Unfortunately, they were not very successful. Knight-Ridder lost 5 years and $50 million on its Viewtron experiment. Time, Inc., and the Times Mirror Company had similar failures. Videotext was simply too expensive, too hard to use, and ultimately unnecessary: The newspaper was still there, you could read it on the bus, and you could cut out recipes and cartoons.

But the widespread diffusion of small, portable inexpensive computers, coupled with the expanded use of the Internet and World Wide Web (see Chapter 14) has rekindled interest in new forms of newspaper delivery. Knight-Ridder is back in the online information service business, as are the Dow Jones Company, the Associated Press, and Gannett. Many major newspapers now offer online versions of their publications. As of November 1997, *Editor & Publisher Directory of Online Newspapers* listed and provided Internet links to 2,560 online newspapers around the world, including online papers in every state *(http://www.mediainfo.com/ephome/npaper/nphtm/online.htm).*

The *San Jose Mercury News* Newshound and the *Fort Worth Star-Telegram* Startext, for example, permit readers to access actual stories from a given edition, search for related reports from past editions, call up additional data on stories, and read alternative points of view. Online papers can be interactive, customized, and available on demand. They can combine text, pictures, moving images, and sound. They offer unlimited space, freeing reports to be as long and as detailed as reporters and readers want. They can serve multiple communities, either geographic ones or those built around specific interests.

John V. Pavlik (1997), executive director of the Center for New Media at Columbia University, sees online newspapers traveling through three stages of life. Stage 1 consisted of publications simply reproducing their paper editions online. Stage 2 consisted of repackaging and possibly broadening what was available in the printed version. Stage 3, now just under way, has newspapers developing "original news content designed specifically for the Web as a new medium of communication" (p. 36).

Many industry observers see this last phase as essential in attracting young people—a group that does not typically have the newspaper habit, as we'll soon see—to newspapers. The expansion of online newspaper service is being slowed by money. No newspaper in the United States is currently turning a profit with its online service.

Technology serves both these new services and traditional newspapers in numerous ways. Computers and satellites greatly aid collection and distribution of news. News copy and other content, complete with appropriate layout, is now sent from editor to printing plants (and to online data

Using Media to Make a Difference

Covering the Issue of Race

Wichita Falls, Texas, has a population of about 100,000, 81% of whom are White and 11% of whom are African American. However, Carroll Wilson, editor of the daily 38,000 circulation *Times Record News,* was dismayed that the races seemed separate, distrustful of one another, and, in the case of the African Americans, embittered. His solution was to use his paper to not only "dig beneath the deceptively calm state of race relations" in the community but also to "provide context for a conversation about race" (Dalton, 1997, p. 54).

Here are a few of the problems his community faced:

- The town was still battling to meet the demands of a 1970 federal court-ordered school desegregation plan.

- African American unemployment was 14.3%, compared to 5.4% for nonminorities.

- Only 3 of the town's 178 police officers were Black.

- The large majority of African Americans left town soon after high school graduation.

Wilson chose Leah Quin, a 25-year-old reporter three years out of college, to head a project the paper called "About Face: Wichita Falls in Black & White." The result was a series of 17 stories that ran on 9 con-

secutive days in March 1997. The opening headline set the tone for what was to come: Silent Divide: Thirty Years After Integration, Blacks and Whites in Wichita Falls Still Are Leading Separate Lives, Divided Not by Laws But by Mutual Misunderstanding.

The paper did not spare itself scrutiny. One part of the series examined the contribution of the *Times Record News* to the chasm—all 12 reporters were White—and Wilson promised to correct the imbalance. As late as 1968 the paper refused to publish photographs of Blacks. Dr. Martin Luther King Jr.'s photo wasn't shown, even after his assassination; White losers to Black boxers Sugar Ray Robinson and Joe Louis were pictured, not their Black victors. Among its other stories were reports on interracial relationships in business and religion, school imbalance, Black distrust of the local criminal justice system, and racism at nearby Sheppard Air Force Base.

Did the paper make a difference? African American Brenda Jarrett, executive director of a community youth center, felt it did: "We pulled our heads out of the sand and I think that's wonderful. The first step to recovery is admitting, and yes, racism is a disease" (p. 55). Claude Foster, president of the local NAACP, agreed, praising the paper for "regenerating the discussion" on community race relations (p. 55). Mayor Kay Yeager, however, felt differently, complaining that the stories were written from "a pretty one-sided point of view" and that they exaggerated racial difficulties in Wichita Falls (p. 55).

Editor Wilson's own evaluation was mixed: "Nothing's happened, nothing's changed and yes, I'm disappointed. I'm proud of us, we did what a good newspaper should have done—raise hell and do the traditional things that many of us have lost sight of" (p. 55).

services), both locally and over distances, with the stroke of a computer key. Computers have made layout and printing faster and more accurate, helping to control newspaper production costs.

To the chagrin of the established papers, readily available, easy to use, and inexpensive computer hardware and software can now be combined to do **desktop publishing,** small-scale print design, layout, and production. The medium is decentralized and more varied, giving readers more and better choices of news sources and coverage. Either because of or in spite of these technological developments, traditionalists believe that there will always be paper newspapers. They cite the portability of newspapers, their ability to provide a large amount of different kinds of clearly categorized content in one place, and their relative permanence (you can start a story, put it down, read it later, then reread it after that) as major reasons newspapers will continue to find an audience.

CHANGES IN NEWSPAPER READERSHIP

A more pessimistic view of the future of newspapers is that as newspapers have reinvented themselves and become more user-friendly, more casual, more lifestyle-oriented, and more in touch with youth they have become inessential and unimportant, just another commodity in an

Is this the future of the newspaper? The *San Jose Mercury News* offers its online version, *Mercury Center,* to a worldwide readership, providing detailed coverage of stories that also appear in its traditional paper newspaper.

overcrowded marketplace of popular, personality-centered media. The shift in tone of the modern newspaper is a direct result of another force that is altering the medium–audience relationship—changes in the nature of newspaper readership.

Publishers know well that newspaper readership in the United States is least prevalent among younger people. Fewer than 30% of 18- to 29-year-olds read a daily paper. Fewer than 50% of 30- to 44-years-olds do so (in 1972 the proportion was 75%). The problem facing newspapers, then, is how to lure young people (readers of the future) to their pages. Online papers might be one solution, but the fundamental question remains: Should newspapers give these readers what they *should* want or what they *do* want?

Some newspapers confront this problem directly. They add inserts or sections directed toward, and sometimes written by, teens and young people. This is good business. But traditionalists disagree with another youth-targeted strategy—altering other, more serious (presumably more important) parts of the paper to cater to the infrequent and nonnewspaper reader. As more newspaper professionals adopt a market-centered approach—using readership studies, focus groups, and other tests of customer satisfaction to design their papers—they increasingly find themselves criticized for "cheapening" both the newspaper as a medium and journalism as an institution.

What happens to journalistic integrity, critics ask, to community service, to the traditional role of newspapers in our democracy, when front pages are given over to reports of starlets' affairs, sports heroes' retirements, and full-color photos of plane wrecks because this is what younger readers want? As topics of interest to the 18- to 35-year-old reluctant reader and nonreader are emphasized, what is ignored? What happens to depth, detail, and precision as stories get shorter and snappier? What kind of culture develops on a diet of **soft news** (characterized by opinion, background, and "color") rather than **hard news** (characterized by factual accounting, data, and information)?

The "softening" of newspapers raises a potential media literacy issue. The media literate person has an obligation to be aware of the impact newspapers have on individuals and society and to understand how the text of newspapers offers insight into contemporary culture. We might ask ourselves: Are we getting what we asked for? What do we as a people and as individuals want from our newspaper? Do we understand the role newspapers play in our democratic process? Are we fully aware of how newspapers help shape our understanding of ourselves and our world?

In a 1787 letter, Thomas Jefferson wrote to a colleague, "Were it left to me to decide whether we should have a government without newspapers or newspapers without government, I should not hesitate to prefer the latter." Would he write that about today's newspaper, a newspaper increasingly designed to meet the wants, needs, and interests of younger, occasional newspaper readers or those who do not read at all?

There is the alternative view, however—that there is no problem here at all. Ever since the days of the penny press, newspapers have been dom-

Does this front page represent soft news run amok or an effort to give readers what they want? Two days after 86 people were killed at the Branch Davidian compound in Waco, Texas, in the midst of a statewide primary election, and with an array of world news available, the top story in this San Francisco newspaper—front page, above the fold, *and* above the banner— is the trade of a star football player.

inated by soft news. All we are seeing today is an extension of what has always been. Moreover, nonreaders are simply going elsewhere for the hard news and information that were once the sole province of newspapers. They're going online, to television, and to specifically targeted sources, including magazines and newsletters.

DEVELOPING MEDIA LITERACY SKILLS
Interpreting Relative Placement of Stories

Newspapers tell readers what is significant and meaningful through their placement of stories in and on their pages. Within a paper's sections (for example, front, leisure, sports, and careers), readers almost invariably read pages in order (that is, page 1, then page 2, and so on). Recognizing this, papers place the stories they think are most important on the earliest pages. Newspaper jargon for this phenomenon has even entered our everyday language. "Front page news" means the same thing in the pressroom as in the living room.

San Francisco Examiner

NEA rejects merger with AFT

Would have created largest teachers union

By Robert Greene
ASSOCIATED PRESS

NEW ORLEANS — The National Education Association soundly rejected a merger that would have created the nation's largest single teachers' union and a powerful force within organized labor.

Well over half the delegates to the NEA's representative assembly voted against the merger with the American Federation of Teachers. Sunday's vote was 5,624 against and 4,091 for, or 58 percent to 42 percent. Approving the merger would have required a two-thirds majority because the 141-year-old organization's constitution would have had to be changed.

The outcome was a blow to NEA president Robert F. Chase, who had put the weight of the union leadership behind the merger. Opponents feared the merger would have cost the organization its unique identity and institutions while taking a leap into the unknown.

Chase urged delegates to lay aside their differences and move on with their business.

"The decision was made on an issue. It was not based on personalities," he said. "When decisions are

GONE FISHIN', NO MATTER WHAT

Don Turner, who came to Florida from Columbus, Ohio, for a car race that was postponed by the wildfires, fishes at Ormond Beach in smoke-filled air Sunday.
AP/DAVID J. PHILLIP

The fire-weary turn to God

Evacuated Florida residents seek solace in state's

valuable stuff. But that all can be replaced. That doesn't bother me. I keep smiling."

State officials estimate that nearly 2,000 fires have damaged or destroyed 213 homes and busi-

Gov. Lawton Chiles said Sunday on CNN. "We were afraid yesterday morning that we literally could lose the whole county."

Fourth of July weekend travel was disrupted throughout the

uation. We are asking for one more day," said Craig Fugate, chief of preparedness and response for division of emergency management.

Haralampus wouldn't have a home to go back to even if he could

Officials seeking videos of fair shooting

Suspect in custody; victims recovering in area hospitals

FROM EXAMINER STAFF AND WIRE REPORTS

PLEASANTON — Authorities are asking fairgoers who were in the carnival area of Saturday night's Alameda County Fair to share any videotapes they may have shot when a gunman opened fire, wounding eight people.

Alameda County Sheriff's Department Lt. Dave Hoig said even videos that appear to show nothing may be helpful.

He identified the suspect being held in the shooting as Jamal Desmond Johnson, 23, of Richmond. A former police officer who now works for the carnival followed the gunman after witnessing the shooting, officials said. A sergeant arrived on the scene and Johnson was taken into custody.

Hoig said that Johnson had a record of drug arrests in Contra Costa County.

The shooting forced cancellation of scheduled fireworks Saturday and turned the festive fair atmosphere into frantic and fearful chaos.

The fracas apparently began after the shooter had an argument

---

San Francisco Chronicle
NATION

SCOTT OSTLER

Hey, It's Good To Be Back Home Again

I just flew back from vacation and boy, is my Visa card tired.

Oh God, he's going to bore us with stories about his vacation.

No, the slides speak for themselves. And frankly, my personal life is none of your business. The ancient treasure I recovered will be tied up in courts for years, the circus people I rescued swore me to secrecy, and the blimpjacking wasn't all my fault. So what's there to say?

I'm semi-rested and faintly tanned, my batteries are recharged, maybe overcharged, leaking acid and throwing off sparks.

A guy shouldn't have to go from vacation to reality instantly. Everyone should get a transition week.

Coming off vacation, you are vaguely annoyed and disappointed that your place of work has hummed along just fine without you. Some people — co-workers, your boss, a spouse — were not even aware you were away.

BY ROBIN WEINER/FOR THE CHRONICLE

Big Teacher Unions Still Unjoined

NEA delegates reject merger with the AFT

By Steven Greenhouse
New York Times

New Orleans

Delegates at the National Education Association's convention voted overwhelmingly yesterday against merging with the American Federation of Teachers, frustrating plans to create a stronger organization to fight what union leaders see as an unprecedented assault against public education.

The vote, which would have created the largest union in American history with 3.3 million members, is a serious blow to the leadership's designs of creating a unified voice to combat a wave of critics, most notably supporters of vouchers, a growing movement to allow use of taxpayer money to help pay for students to attend private schools

"The vast majority of delegates . . . want to see

Two papers in the same city on the same day give different treatment to wire stories about the same event—the merger of a teacher's union. What can you discern from the placement each paper gave to its report of this event?

The placement of stories on a page is also important. English readers read from top to bottom and from left to right. Stories that the newspaper staff deem important tend to be placed "above the fold" and toward the left of the page. This is an important aspect of the power of newspapers to influence public opinion and of media literacy. As you'll see in Chapter 11, relative story placement is a factor in **agenda setting**—the way newspapers and other media influence not only what we think but what we think about.

Two pages from different newspapers published on the same day in the same city are shown on page 118. Both chose to report a wire service story on the failed merger of two giant teacher's unions, but notice the different treatments given this story in these two newspapers. What judgments can you make about the importance each daily placed on this story? How might *Chronicle* readers have interpreted this event differently from readers of the rival *Examiner*?

A media literate newspaper reader should be able to make similar judgments about other layout decisions. The use of photos suggests the importance the editors assign to a story, as do the size and wording of headlines, the employment of jumps (continuations to other pages), and placement of a story in a given section. A report of a person's death on the front page, as opposed to the international section or in the obituaries, carries a different meaning, as does an analysis of an issue placed on the front page as opposed to the editorial page.

Chapter Review

In this chapter we examined how European Corantos and diurnals led to the creation of what we now know as the newspaper. In the Colonies, broadsides posted at print shops developed into the first American newspaper, *Publick Occurrences*, in 1690.

Pre-Revolution America saw the development of many contemporary press traditions—criticism of public officials, advertising as a financial base, and independence from government control. The commitment to newspaper freedom was codified in the United States in the First Amendment and tested in the Alien and Sedition Acts of 1798.

The modern newspaper emerged in 1833 when Benjamin Day published the *New York Sun* and sold copies for one cent. His penny press took advantage of important cultural and social change in the United States and ushered in the era of mass circulation newspapers. However, competition for that circulation led to much journalistic abuse in the form of yellow journalism. Still, the newspaper had become established as a medium for all the people, a fact capitalized on by Native

American and foreign language publishers and African American publishers such as Frederick Douglass.

Between the era of yellow journalism and World War II, newspaper chains developed, the ASNE wrote its Canons, and the wire services internationalized. But it was war-wrought social and cultural change, coupled with the advent of television, that provided the next big shift in the newspaper–reader relationship. Although overall newspaper circulation now holds steady, the number of urban daily papers is falling as is their circulation. Their loss is a gain for suburban and small town dailies and weeklies, reflecting changes in our lifestyle and work habits. National daily newspapers also drain readers and advertising revenue from big city dailies. Nevertheless, newspapers still attract the greatest amount of ad revenue of all the media and are the medium of choice for many advertisers. Up to 65% of newspaper space may be given over to advertising,

(continued)

with the remainder filled out with content often provided by wire services and feature syndicates.

The newspaper–reader relationship is again on the brink of a major change. Competition is declining in the industry because few cities have competing papers. Where competing papers do exist, they sometimes operate under joint operating agreements. Chains now dominate the medium, controlling fully 80% of all circulation. Many papers are experimenting with civic journalism to reinforce their commitment to their local communities.

Technology in the form of television was no friend to newspapers, but now computers, satellite, and online information services not only help reduce cost and inefficiency in newspaper production and distribution but promise to reshape the information collection and distribution functions of newspapers.

Finally, declining readership among younger people poses an important dilemma for professionals who produce the newspaper. Should they give readers (and nonreaders) what they want or what they should want? A related literacy issue arises as media literate readers are obligated to make themselves aware of the impact newspapers have on individuals and society and to understand how the newspaper text offers insight into contemporary culture.

Questions for Review

1. What are Acta Diurna, Corantos, diurnals, and broadsheets?
2. What is the significance of *Publick Occurrences Both Foreign and Domestick,* the *Boston News-Letter,* the *New-England Courant,* the *Pennsylvania Gazette,* and the *New York Weekly Journal*?
3. What factors led to development of the penny press? to yellow journalism?
4. What are the similarities and differences between wire services and feature syndicates?
5. When did newspaper chains begin? Can you characterize them as they exist today?
6. What are the different types of newspapers?
7. Why is the newspaper an attractive medium for advertisers?
8. What is a JOA?
9. What are videotext and teletext? desktop publishing?
10. What is hard and soft news?

Questions for Critical Thinking and Discussion

1. Compare why you use the newspaper to Berelson's list. Do his reasons people use the paper reflect your own use?
2. What are your favorite syndicated features? Why?
3. Does your town have competing dailies? If yes, how does that competition manifest itself? If not, what do you think you're missing? Does your town have a JOA situation? If yes, can you describe its operation?
4. Where do you stand on the debate over chains? Are they good or bad for the medium?
5. Have you ever used a newspaper's online information service? How would you describe your experience?

Important Resources

Bogart, L. (1991). ***Preserving the press: How daily newspapers mobilized to keep their readers.*** **New York: Columbia University Press.** An interesting book by a respected media historian that examines how newspapers have dealt with various challenges to their ability to hold their readers.

Columbia Journalism Review. A quarterly magazine of reporting and commentary on issues in journalism. Covering all media, not only newspapers, it is lively and provocative.

Editor & Publisher. This weekly magazine bills itself as the bible of "the Fourth Estate" and "the only independent weekly journal of newspapering." It typically offers interesting stories about the business side of newspapering, valuable statistics, and commentary on contemporary issues.

Harris, M., & O'Malley, T. (1997). *Studies in newspaper and periodical history.* Westport, CT: Greenwood Press. A collection of essays and research reports that examine newspaper history from 1770 to 1970. Chapters deal with international as well as U.S. publications.

Journalism History. A scholarly but readable quarterly focusing primarily on U.S. journalism history. It has fine review sections on books and media about the subject.

Quill. Published by the Society of Professional Journalists, *Quill* calls itself "a magazine that surveys and interprets today's journalism while stimulating its readers to collective and individual action for the good of our profession." As such, in addition to timely reporting and commentary, it offers several excellent professionally-oriented features such as regular columns on freedom of information, technology, and improving writing.

Squires, J. D. (1993). *Read all about it! The corporate takeover of America's newspapers.* New York: Times Books. A novel-like account of changes in the operation of newspapers and how they serve their readers, by the former editor of the *Orlando Sentinel* and the *Chicago Tribune*.

Tebbel, J. (1969). *The compact history of the American newspaper.* New York: Hawthorn. Now a bit dated, but an invaluable guide to early newspaper history.

Washington Journalism Review. A quarterly review of journalism in the United States, this magazine pays particular attention to issues of news coverage of national events.

Newspaper Information Web Sites

American Society of Newspaper Editors	*http://www.asne.org/*
National Newspaper Association	*http://www.oweb.com/nna/*
Newspaper Association of America	*http://www.naa.org/*
Links to National Newspapers	*http://www.uwsp.edu/stuorg/pointer/STUFF/NEWSLINKS.HTM*

Magazines

You've been out of school a few years, and you are doing OK. You're paying your bills, and your job, while not particularly exhilarating, satisfies you. Then you meet some people who ask you to help them with their magazine.

They have put out a few issues of what they'd hoped would be a new kind of magazine, and they need more brain power. "We were really angry and frustrated at the cynicism and dumbing down of the media. We thought there's got to be an alternative, something real," said one of your new partners (Leland, 1995, p. 71). Their plan is to make their bimonthly an outlet for serious but engaging writing and, by constantly redefining the magazine, a satire of the contemporary U.S. magazine scene.

Your first issue as a member of the team is the "Sell Out" issue. There is a liquor ad on the cover and a commercial sponsor for every page (Virgin Records welcomes you to page 12), even every staffer (Lisa Salmon, copy editor, appears courtesy of Tanqueray). There are stories on the presidential election, race, Michael Moore, investment banking, the digital revolution, television news, the culture of camp—serious stuff.

Good stuff too. The *Chicago Tribune,* the *Washington Post, USA Today, Harper's Magazine,* and *Newsweek* all do stories on the little magazine that could. You are riding high. You've proven to yourself and to the world that you can put out a good magazine. Now it is time to see if you can produce a financially successful one. You need money to expand circulation, but you don't have enough circulation to raise ad rates. You approach potential investors and national publishers, but they are wary. They praise your talent and your brains, but your magazine, they say, is "not advertiser friendly." They doubt that even with more circulation you can attract more advertising than you already have.

After 16 issues your magazine ceases publication.

This vignette is based on the true story of a group of young people—

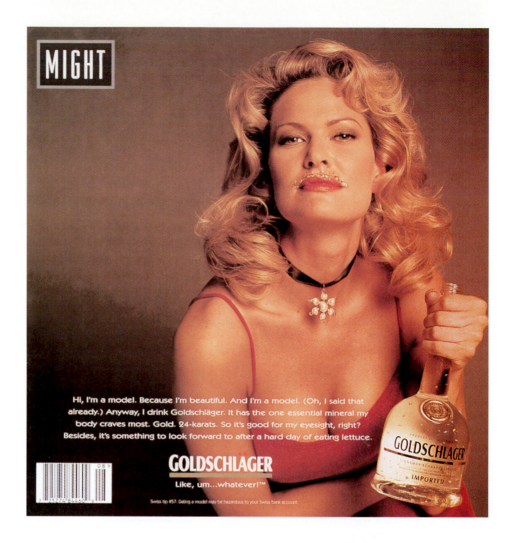

Marny Requa, David Eggars, David Moody, and Paul Tullis—who founded
Might in 1993, a hip, wry, San Francisco-based magazine. According to
senior editor Tullis, "Might was a call to the publishing industry to see if
a magazine with no celebrity profiles, fashion spreads, or product reviews
could get the money it needed to reach the audience it had found. The
answer was a resounding, unqualified NO" (CJR Grapevine, 1997, p. 23).

In the contemporary world of consumer magazines, being good isn't
enough. To succeed, a publication must both be good *and* appeal to a specialized readership with relatively narrow interests. These homogeneous
audiences are particularly attractive to advertisers. In this chapter we
examine the dynamics of the contemporary magazine industry and its
audiences. We study the medium's beginnings in the Colonies, its pre-Civil
War expansion, and its explosive growth between the Civil War and World
War I. This was the era of great mass circulation magazines, but it was
also the era of powerful writers known as muckrakers.

Influenced by television and by the social and cultural changes that
followed World War II, the magazine took on a new, more narrowly

focused nature, which provided the industry with a growing readership and increased profits. We detail the various categories of magazines, discuss circulation research, look at the ways the industry protects itself from competition from other media, and how advertisers influence editorial decisions. Finally, we investigate some of the editorial decisions that should be of particular interest to media literate magazine consumers.

A Short History of Magazines

Magazines were a favorite medium of the British elite by the mid-1700s, and two prominent colonial printers hoped to duplicate that success in the New World. In 1741 in Philadelphia, Andrew Bradford published *American Magazine, or a Monthly View of the Political State of the British Colonies*, followed by Benjamin Franklin's *General Magazine, and Historical Chronicle, for All the British Plantations in America*. Composed largely of reprinted British material, these publications were expensive and aimed at the small number of literate colonists. Lacking an organized postal system, distribution was difficult, and neither magazine was successful. *American Magazine* produced three issues, *General Magazine,* six. Yet between 1741 and 1794, 45 new magazines appeared, although no more than 3 were published in the same time period. Entrepreneurial printers hoped to attract educated, cultured, moneyed gentlemen by copying the successful London magazines. Even after the Revolutionary War, U.S. magazines remained clones of their British forerunners.

THE EARLY MAGAZINE INDUSTRY

In 1821 the *Saturday Evening Post* appeared; it was to continue for the next 148 years. Among other successful early magazines were *Harper's* (1850) and *Atlantic Monthly* (1857). Cheaper printing and growing literacy fueled expansion of the magazine as they had the book (see Chapter 3). But an additional factor in the success of the early magazines was the spread of social movements such as abolitionism and labor reform. These issues provided compelling content, and a boom in magazine publishing began. In 1825 there were 100 magazines in operation; by 1850 there were 600. Because magazine articles were increasingly focused on matters of importance to U.S. readers, magazines like the *United States Literary Gazette* and *American Boy* began to look less like London publications and more like a new and unique product. Journalism historians John Tebbel and Mary Ellen Zuckerman (1991) called this "the time of significant beginnings" (p. 13); it was here that the magazine developed many of the characteristics we associate with it even today. Magazines and the people who staffed them began to clearly differentiate themselves from other publishing endeavors (such as books and newspapers). The concept of specialist writers took hold, and their numbers rose. In addition, numerous and detailed illustrations began to fill the pages of magazines.

Still, these early magazines were aimed at a literate elite interested in short stories, poetry, social commentary, and essays. The magazine did not become a true national mass medium until after the Civil War.

THE MASS CIRCULATION ERA

The modern era of magazines can be divided into two parts, each characterized by a different relationship between the medium and the audience.

Mass circulation popular magazines began to prosper in the post-Civil War years. In 1865 there were 700 magazines publishing; by 1870 there were 1,200; by 1885 there were 3,300. Crucial to this expansion was the women's magazine. Suffrage—the right to vote for women—was the social movement that occupied its pages, but a good deal of content could also be described as how-to for homemakers. Advertisers, too, were anxious to appear in the new women's magazines, hawking their brand name products. First appearing at this time are several magazines still familiar today, including *Ladies' Home Journal, Good Housekeeping*, and *McCall's*.

There were several reasons for this phenomenal growth. As with books, widespread literacy was one reason. But the Postal Act of 1879, which permitted mailing magazines at cheap second-class postage rates, and the spread of the railroad, which carried people and publications westward from the east coast, were two others. A fourth was the reduction in cost. As long as magazines sold for 35 cents—a lot of money for the time—they were read largely by the upper class. However, a circulation war erupted between giants *McClure's, Munsey's Magazine*, and *The Saturday Evening Post*. Soon they, as well as *Ladies' Home Journal, McCall's, Woman's Home Companion, Collier's*, and *Cosmopolitan*, were selling for as little as 10 and 15 cents, which brought them within reach of many working people. On October 2, 1893, *Munsey's* ran a newspaper ad in the *New York Sun* announcing: "*Munsey's Magazine* at ten cents a copy and one dollar a year inaugurates a new era in magazine publishing. . . . It has found the substratum—the solid rock foundation. No first rate magazine can ever go lower."

This 1870s price war was made possible by the newfound ability of magazines to attract growing amounts of advertising. As we'll see in Chapter 10, social and demographic changes in the post-Civil War era—urbanization, industrialization, the spread of roads and railroads, and development of consumer brands and brand names—produced an explosion in the number of advertising agencies. These agencies needed to place their messages somewhere. Magazines were the perfect outlet because they were read by a large, national audience. As a result, circulation—rather than reputation, as had been the case

This *McClure's* cover captures the spirit of the Roaring Twenties as well as the excitement of the burgeoning magazine industry.

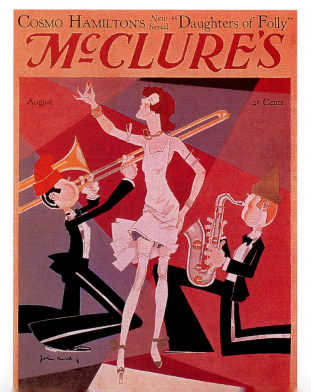

COSMO HAMILTON'S *New Serial* "Daughters of Folly"

McCLURE'S

August · 25 Cents

before—became the most important factor in setting advertising rates. Magazines kept cover prices low to ensure the large readerships coveted by advertisers. The fifth reason for the enormous growth in the number of magazines was industrialization, which provided people with leisure and more personal income.

Magazines were truly America's first *national* mass medium, and like books they served as an important force in social change, especially in the **muckraking** era of the first decades of the 20th century (see the box "Taking on the Giants: Muckraking in the Magazines"). Theodore Roosevelt coined this label as an insult, but the muckrakers wore it proudly, using the pages of *The Nation, Harper's Weekly, The Arena*, and even mass circulation publications like *McClure's* and *Collier's* to agitate for change. Their targets were the powerful. Their beneficiaries were the poor.

The mass circulation magazine grew with the nation. From the start there were general interest magazines such as *The Saturday Evening Post*, women's magazines such as *Good Housekeeping*, pictorial magazines such as *Life* and *Look*, and digests such as *Reader's Digest*, which was first published in 1922 and offered condensed and tightly edited articles for people on the go in the Roaring Twenties. What these magazines all had in common was the size and breadth of readership. They were mass market, mass circulation publications, both national and affordable. As such, magazines helped unify the nation. They were the television of their time—the dominant advertising medium, the primary source for nationally distributed news, and the preeminent provider of visual, or photo, journalism.

Between 1900 and 1945, the number of families who subscribed to one or more magazines grew from 200,000 to more than 32 million. New and important magazines continued to appear throughout these decades. For example, African American intellectual W. E. B. DuBois founded and edited *The Crisis* in 1910 as the voice of the National Association for the Advancement of Colored People (the NAACP). *Time* was first published in 1923. Its brief review of the week's news was immediately popular (it was originally only 28 pages long). It made a profit within a year.

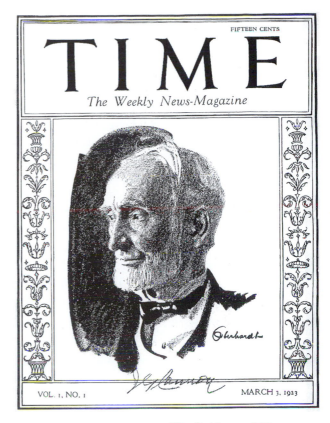

The first issue of *Time*.

THE ERA OF SPECIALIZATION

In 1956 *Collier's* declared bankruptcy and became the first mass circulation magazine to cease publication. But its fate, as well as that of other mass circulation magazines, had actually been sealed in the late 1940s and 1950s following the end of World War II. Profound alterations in the nation's culture—and, in particular, the advent of television—changed the relationship between magazines and their audience. No matter how large their circulation, magazines could not match the reach of television. Magazines did not have moving pictures or visual and oral storytelling. Nor could magazines match television's timeliness. Magazines were weekly, whereas television was continuous. Nor could they match television's novelty. In the beginning *everything* on television was of interest to viewers. As a result, magazines began to lose advertisers to television.

The audience changed as well. As we've seen, World War II changed the nature of American life. The new, mobile, product-consuming public was less interested in the traditional Norman Rockwell world of *The Saturday Evening Post* (closed in 1969) and more in tune with the slick, hip world of narrower interest publications such as *GQ* and *Self,* which spoke to them in and about their new and exciting lives. And because World War II had further urbanized and industrialized America, people—including millions of women who had entered the workforce—had more leisure and more money to spend. They could spend both on a wider array of personal

Media Echoes

Taking on the Giants: Muckraking in the Magazines

At the start of the 20th century, corruption and greed in business and politics were creating some of the worst abuses this country had ever seen—unsafe food, inhumane child labor practices, unregulated drug manufacture and sale, exploitation of workers, a lack of safety standards in the workplace, blatant discrimination against African Americans, and a disregard for human and civil rights. Industrial giants, the so-called Robber Barons, amassed fortunes through mammoth monopolies controlling mining, manufacturing, banking, railroads, food packing, and insurance.

Why didn't the government step in and stop these abuses? Local politicians and police were in the pay of the industries. The federal government was also hamstrung. At the time, U.S. Senators were selected by the legislatures of the individual states. For the right price, an industry could make sure that people favorable to its interests were selected by those legislatures to serve in the Senate. The buying and selling of seats ensured that the Senate would block any attempts to pass legislation designed to break up monopolies or remedy social ills.

Echoing the role of books in social change, magazines, particularly popular mass market magazines, took

leadership in challenging these powerful interests and advocating reform. Reaching a nationwide audience, *McClure's, American Magazine,* and *Collier's* shocked and outraged the public with their exposés. Historian Louis Filler (1968) called the crusading magazine articles of writers such as Ida Tarbell, Upton Sinclair, Lincoln Steffens, Jack London, and others "literary rather than yellow"(p. 31). That is, rather than adopting the overexcited, excessive tone of the yellow journalism of the day, these were well written, well researched, and well argued. Articles and series such as Steffens's "The Shame of the Cities," Tarbell's "The History of the Standard Oil Company," Sinclair's novel *The Jungle* (on unclean food and abuse of workers), and Edwin Markham's "The Hoe-Man in the Making" (on unsafe and inhumane child labor practices) galvanized the nation.

One of the greatest successes of magazine journalism was spurred by what we would now consider an unlikely source. However, it produced an amendment to the U.S. Constitution.

A series of articles begun in *Cosmopolitan* in March 1906 changed the way U.S. senators were elected, ensuring passage of reform legislation. "The Treason of the Senate" accused U.S. senators of treason for giving

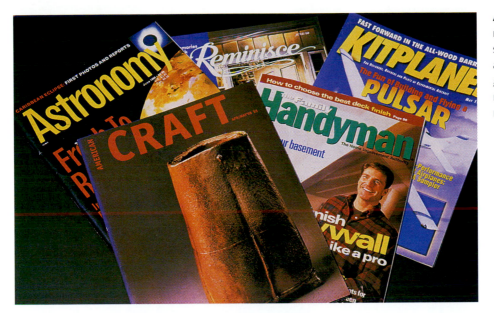

A wide array of specialized magazines exists for all lifestyles and interests. Here are only five of the 12,000 general interest consumer magazines available to U.S. readers.

aid and comfort to "the enemies of the nation." Within days of hitting the newsstands, every issue of *Cosmopolitan* had been sold, and President Teddy Roosevelt was compelled to respond to the charges. In a speech delivered on March 17, Roosevelt condemned "the man with the muckrake [who in] magazines makes slanderous and mendacious attack upon men in public life and upon men engaged in public work" (Filler, 1968, p. 252). Thus did the crusading writers and journalists come to be known as "muckrakers." Roosevelt's anguish was no match for the public's anger. In 1913 the 17th Amendment, mandating popular election of senators, was ratified.

The efforts of the muckrakers and the magazines that spread their writing produced legislation and policies that have helped define the world as we know it. They were influential in passage of the Pure Food and Drug Act and the Hepburn Railroad Bill in 1906, the Federal Reserve Bill in 1913, the Clayton Anti-Trust Act in 1914, and numerous child labor laws.

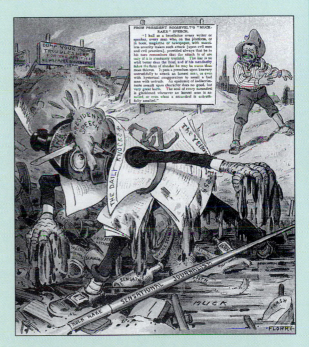

Though President Roosevelt meant the epithet as an insult, the Muckrakers wore the title with pride.

129

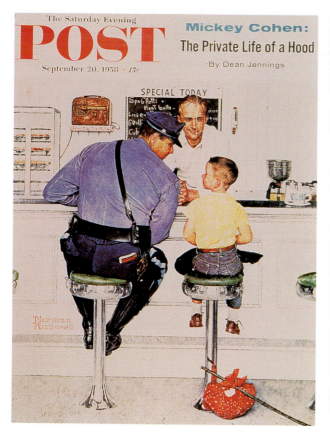

The Saturday Evening
POST
September 20, 1958 · 75¢

Mickey Cohen:
The Private Life of a Hood
·By Dean Jennings·

SPECIAL TODAY

Norman Rockwell

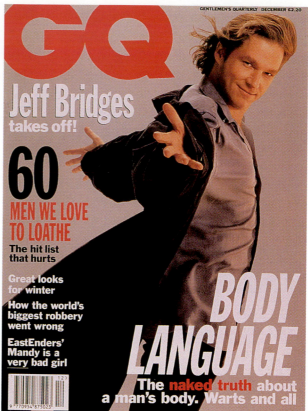

GENTLEMEN'S QUARTERLY   DECEMBER £2.20

GQ

Jeff Bridges takes off!

60

MEN WE LOVE TO LOATHE
The hit list that hurts

Great looks for winter

How the world's biggest robbery went wrong

EastEnders' Mandy is a very bad girl

BODY LANGUAGE
The **naked truth** about a man's body. Warts and all

A change in people's tastes in magazines reflects some of the ways the world changed after World War II. Norman Rockwell's America was replaced by *GQ*'s and Michael Jackson's.

Who Loved Ya, Baby? Telly Savalas, 1922-1994

FEBRUARY 7, 1994 $2.39

People weekly

MICHAEL'S DANGEROUS DEAL
Hounded by charges of child abuse, the King of Pop makes a bargain that could cost him his credibility—and his future

Michael Jackson and his teenage accuser (right) attended an awards show in 1993

interests *and* on magazines that catered to those interests. Where there was once *Look* (closed in 1971) and *Life* (closed in 1972 but resurrected as a monthly pictorial magazine in 1978), there was now *Flyfishing, Surfing, Ski,* and *Easyrider.* The industry had hit on the secret of success: specialization and a lifestyle orientation.

Magazines and Their Audiences

Exactly who are the audiences for magazines? Magazine industry research indicates that among people with at least some college, 94% read at least one magazine and average more than 11 different issues a month. Nearly the same figures apply for households with annual incomes of over $40,000 and for people in professional and managerial careers, regardless of educational attainment. The typical magazine reader is at least a high school graduate, is married, owns his or her own house, is employed full time, and has an annual household income of just under $40,000. Advertisers find magazine readers an attractive, upscale audience for their pitches.

How people use magazines also makes them an attractive advertising medium. People report:

- Reading magazines as much for the ads as for the editorial content, keeping them available for up to four months
- Passing them along to an average of four similar adults
- Being very loyal, which translates into increased esteem for those advertisers in the pages of their favorite publications

Scope and Structure of the Magazine Industry

In 1950 there were 6,950 magazines in operation. The number now exceeds 22,000, some 12,000 of which are general interest consumer magazines. Of these, 800 produce three fourths of the industry's gross revenues. Contemporary magazines are typically divided into three broad types:

- *Trade, professional, and business magazines* carry stories, features, and ads aimed at people in specific professions and are either distributed by the professional organizations themselves *(American Medical News)* or by media companies such as Whittle Communications and Time Warner *(Progressive Farmer).* The number of publications in this category is larger than that of any other.
- *Industrial, company, and sponsored magazines* are produced by companies specifically for their own employees, customers, and stockholders, or by clubs and associations specifically for their members.

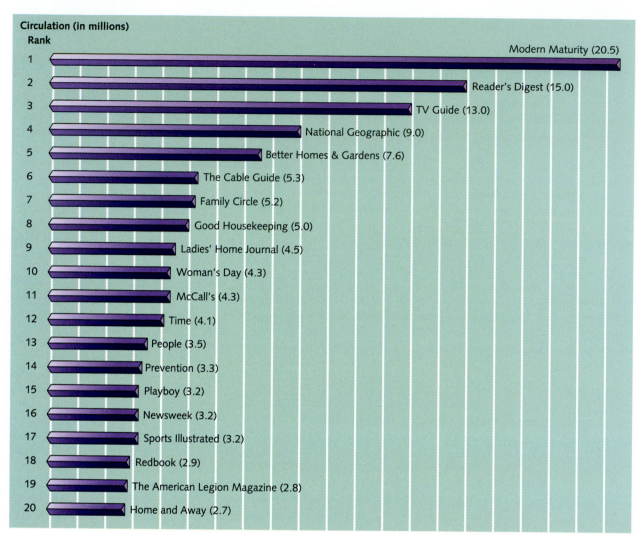

Circulation (in millions)

Rank	Magazine
1	Modern Maturity (20.5)
2	Reader's Digest (15.0)
3	TV Guide (13.0)
4	National Geographic (9.0)
5	Better Homes & Gardens (7.6)
6	The Cable Guide (5.3)
7	Family Circle (5.2)
8	Good Housekeeping (5.0)
9	Ladies' Home Journal (4.5)
10	Woman's Day (4.3)
11	McCall's (4.3)
12	Time (4.1)
13	People (3.5)
14	Prevention (3.3)
15	Playboy (3.2)
16	Newsweek (3.2)
17	Sports Illustrated (3.2)
18	Redbook (2.9)
19	The American Legion Magazine (2.8)
20	Home and Away (2.7)

Figure 5–1 The 20 Magazines with the Highest Paid Circulation (1996). *Source: Advertising Age online statistics, January 1998.*

The Leader, for example, is the magazine of the Fireman's Fund insurance company. *Modern Maturity* is the magazine for members of the American Association of Retired People (AARP).

- *Consumer magazines* are sold by subscription and at newsstands, bookstores, and other retail outlets including supermarkets, garden shops, and computer stores. *Sunset Magazine* and *Wired* fit here, as do *Road & Track, US, TV Guide,* and *The New Yorker* (Figure 5–1).

CATEGORIES OF CONSUMER MAGAZINES

The industry typically categorizes consumer magazines in terms of their targeted audiences. Of course, the wants, needs, interests, and wishes of those readers determine the content of each publication. Although these categories are neither exclusive (where do *Chicago Business* and *Sports*

Illustrated for Women fit?) nor exhaustive (what do we do with *Hot Rod* and *National Geographic*?), they are at least indicative of the cascade of options. Here is a short list of common consumer magazine categories along with examples of each type.

Alternative magazines: *Mother Jones, The Utne Reader*

Celebrity and entertainment magazines: *People, Entertainment Weekly*

Children's magazines: *Highlights, Ranger Rick*

Computer magazines: *Internet, PC World*

Business/money magazines: *Money, Black Enterprise*

Ethnic magazines: *Hispanic, Ebony*

Family magazines: *Fatherhood, Parenting*

Fashion magazines: *Bazaar, Elle*

General interest magazines: *Reader's Digest, Life*

Geographic magazines: *Texas Monthly, Bay Area Living*

Gray magazines: *Modern Maturity*

Literary magazines: *Atlantic, Harper's*

Men's magazines: *GQ, Field & Stream, Playboy*

News magazines: *Time, U.S. News & World Report, Newsweek*

Political opinion magazines: *The Nation, National Review*

Sports magazines: *Sport, Sports Illustrated*

Sunday newspaper magazines: *Parade, USA Weekend*

Women's magazines: *Working Woman, Good Housekeeping, Ms.*

Youth magazines: *Seventeen, Tiger Beat*

ONLINE MAGAZINES

Another category, **Webzines,** or online magazines, has recently emerged, made possible by the Internet. Many magazines, among them *Time* and *Mother Jones,* now produce online editions offering special interactive features not available to their hard copy readers. In addition, several strictly online magazines have been attempted. For example, former *New Republic* editor Michael Kinsley moved from Washington (D.C.) to Washington (state) to publish an exclusively online magazine called *Slate* for Microsoft *(http://www.slate.com).* Several journalists from the *San Francisco Examiner* joined with Silicon Valley entrepreneurs to begin *Salon Magazine (http://www.salonmagazine.com),* aimed at affluent, hip, Internet-savvy readers and specializing in books, travel, politics, and sex. *Salon* has published articles by famous authors such as Amy Tan *(Joy Luck Club)* and John LeCarré *(Smiley's People, The Spy Who Came in From the Cold).*

Webzines have yet to succeed financially. Those produced by existing paper magazine publishers serve primarily as an additional outlet for

Salon is a typical example of the online-only magazines trying to make it in an increasingly crowded media environment.

existing material, a way to extend the reach of the parent publication. Exclusively online magazines have yet to produce a profit, and many industry analysts think it will be a long time before they do. David Coursey, publisher of *Coursey.com*, an electronic newsletter about Silicon Valley, said of online magazines, "Think of it as a steeplechase on a dark, moonlit night. You face the same hurdle every other kind of publication faces. But what readers want is different, your relationship with advertisers is different, and you're dealing with an immature market" (Herhold, 1997, p. 1E).

There are several hurdles specific to purely online magazines. Because Internet and World Wide Web users have become accustomed to free access to sites, Webzines have yet to find a successful means of charging for subscriptions. *Slate* dropped its plan to do so when faced with a 1997 reader revolt. Second, as opposed to Webzines produced by paper magazines, purely online magazines must generate original content, an expensive undertaking, yet they compete online for readers and advertisers as equals with Webzines subsidized by paper magazines. In addition, purely online magazines must also compete with all other Web sites on the Internet. They are but one of an infinite number of choices for potential readers. And finally, of the total annual U.S. expenditure on advertising (approximately $160 billion), only $500 million is spent on the Web in its entirety. There may simply be too little commercial support to sustain this new form of magazine.

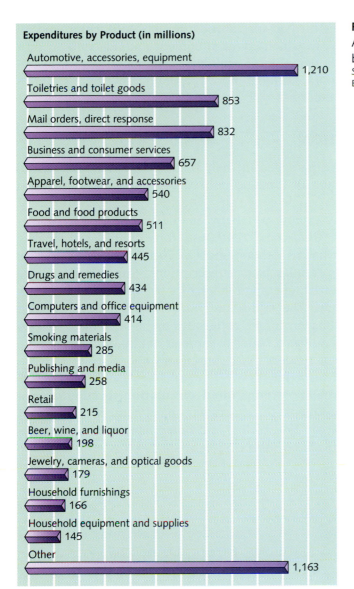

Expenditures by Product (in millions)

Automotive, accessories, equipment — 1,210
Toiletries and toilet goods — 853
Mail orders, direct response — 832
Business and consumer services — 657
Apparel, footwear, and accessories — 540
Food and food products — 511
Travel, hotels, and resorts — 445
Drugs and remedies — 434
Computers and office equipment — 414
Smoking materials — 285
Publishing and media — 258
Retail — 215
Beer, wine, and liquor — 198
Jewelry, cameras, and optical goods — 179
Household furnishings — 166
Household equipment and supplies — 145
Other — 1,163

Figure 5–2 Magazine Advertising Expenditures by Product (1994). *Source:* Publishers Information Bureau, Inc., New York, NY.

Magazine Advertising

Magazine specialization exists and succeeds because the demographically similar readership of these publications is attractive to advertisers who wish to target ads for their products and services to those most likely to respond to them. This is a lucrative situation for the magazine industry. In 1993 magazines sold more than $7.6 billion in advertising space, up from $2.8 billion in 1980. (But for the story of a magazine with no advertising, see the box "Suzuki Samurai versus *Consumer Reports.*") Five and a half percent of all advertising expenditures in U.S. media is placed with magazines. How those billions of dollars are spread among different types of products is shown in Figure 5–2.

Magazines are often further specialized through **split runs,** special versions of a given issue in which editorial content and ads vary according to some specific demographic or regional grouping. *Time*, for example, has at least 8 regional editions, more than 50 state editions, and 8 professionally oriented editions.

TYPES OF CIRCULATION

Magazines price advertising space in their pages based on **circulation,** the total number of issues of a magazine that are sold. These sales can be either subscription or single-copy sales. On the whole, the number of magazines sold is fairly evenly split between the two, but some magazines, *Woman's Day, TV Guide,* and *Penthouse,* for example, rely heavily on single-copy sales, whereas others, such as *Reader's Digest,* earn as much as 60% of their revenues from subscriptions. Subscriptions have the advantage of an assured, ongoing readership, but they are sold below the cover price and have the additional burden of postage included in their cost to the publisher. Single-copy sales are less reliable, but to advertisers they are sometimes a better barometer of a publication's value to its readers. Single-copy readers must consciously choose to pick up an issue, and they pay full price for it.

A third form of circulation, **controlled circulation,** occurs when a magazine is provided at no cost to readers who meet some specific set of advertiser-attractive criteria. Free airline and hotel magazines fit this category. Although they provide no subscription or single-sales revenue, these

Using Media to Make a Difference

Suzuki Samurai versus *Consumer Reports*

Very few magazines survive today without accepting advertising. Those that are ad-free insist that freedom from commercial support allows them to make a greater difference in the lives of their readers. *Ms.*, for example, cannot advocate development of strong, individual females if its pages carry ads that suggest beauty is crucial for women's success. But it is *Consumer Reports* that makes this case most strongly—it must be absolutely free of outside influence if its articles about consumer products are to maintain their well-earned reputation for fairness and objectivity. This reputation was put to the test when automobile manufacturer Suzuki went to war with the magazine and its publisher, Consumer Union.

In 1988 *Consumer Reports* tested a number of sports utility vehicles for safety. Several passed the magazine's difficult evaluation, but the Suzuki Samurai did not. The Samurai tipped up severely and repeatedly in a series of avoidance-maneuver tests. *Consumer Reports* rated the Samurai "not acceptable" in its July 1988 issue. Later that same year, the National Highway Transportation and Safety Administration (NHTSA) accepted Consumer Union's petition that it develop minimum stability standards to prevent rollover in all vehicles. Six years later, in 1994, the NHTSA abandoned its plans to develop such a standard, citing the high

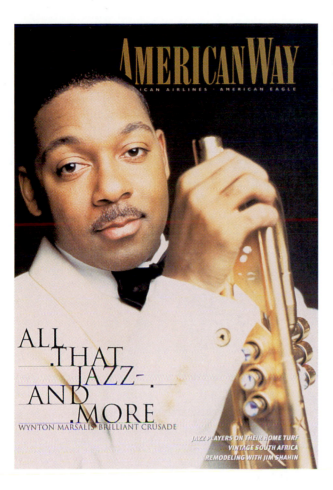

ALL
THAT
JAZZ—
AND
MORE

WYNTON MARSALIS' BRILLIANT CRUSADE

JAZZ PLAYERS ON THEIR HOME TURF
VINTAGE SOUTH AFRICA
REMODELING WITH JIM SHAHIN

Controlled circulation magazines, like American Airlines' in-flight publication *American Way*, take advantage of readers' captivity.

cost to manufacturers in meeting proposed rules. Instead, argued the NHTSA, an "informed public" would, through its purchases of certain vehicles rather than others, produce the necessary change.

Grudgingly accepting the NHTSA market-based solution, *Consumer Reports* continued its testing as a way to inform the public, despite lawsuits and attacks from Suzuki. Those attacks, and *Consumer Reports'* reputation, were challenged in a 1997 lawsuit.

A 31-year-old Samurai passenger, Katie Rodriguez, was paralyzed from the neck down in a rollover accident on a Missouri highway. She sued Suzuki. Despite testimony from its own expert witnesses that there had been 147 deaths and 7,000 injuries resulting from Samurai rollover accidents, the manufacturer made the "unscientific and rigged" *Consumer Reports* research the center of its defense. In its closing arguments, Suzuki lawyers claimed that Rodriguez's suit and other

suits against the company (more than 175 to that date) had been the direct result of the magazine's unfair rating in 1988.

But when the jury began its deliberations, one of the first exhibits it asked for was that same 1988 *Consumer Reports* article. When they returned their verdict, jurors awarded Ms. Rodriguez $25 million in compensatory damages and another $11.9 million in punitive damages.

Did the magazine make a difference? Although the NTHSA has yet to develop mandatory antirollover safety standards, *Consumer Reports* believes that the unanimous jury verdict against the Suzuki Samurai shows that it did.

Source: This box was developed from material available on *Consumer Reports'* Web site *http://www.consumer.org*.

magazines are an attractive, relatively low-cost advertising vehicle for companies seeking narrowly defined, captive audiences.

MEASURING CIRCULATION

Regardless of how circulation occurs, it is monitored through research. The Audit Bureau of Circulation (ABC) was established in 1914 to provide reliability to a booming magazine industry playing loose with self-announced circulation figures. The ABC provides reliable circulation figures as well as important population and demographic information. Other research companies, including Simmons Market Research Bureau and Standard Rate and Data Service, also generate valuable data for advertisers and magazines. Circulation data are often augmented by measures of **pass-along readership,** which refers to readers who neither subscribe nor buy single copies but who borrow a magazine or read one in a doctor's office or library.

Current Trends in Magazine Publishing

The forces that are reshaping all the mass media have had an impact on magazines as well. In the magazine industry, alterations in how it does business are primarily designed to help magazines compete with television in the race for advertising dollars.

MEETING COMPETITION FROM TELEVISION

As we've seen, the move toward specialization in magazines was forced by the emergence of television as a mass audience, national advertising medium. Ironically, it is television that once again threatens the preeminence of magazines as a specialized advertising medium. Specifically, the challenge comes from cable television. Advertiser-supported cable channels survive using precisely the same strategy as magazines—they deliver to advertisers a relatively large number of consumers who have some important demographic trait in common. Similar competition, although still insignificant, is also coming from specialized online content providers such as ESPNET SportsZone and The Discovery Channel Online. Magazines are well positioned to fend off these challenges for several reasons.

First is internationalization, which expands a magazine's reach, making it possible for magazines to attract additional ad revenues for content that, essentially, has already been produced. Internationalization can happen in one of several ways. Some magazines, *Time,* for example, produce one or more foreign editions in English. Others enter cooperative agreements with overseas companies to produce native-language versions of essentially U.S. magazines. For example, Time Warner and the French company Hachette cooperate to publish a French-language *Fortune.* Often U.S. magazines prepare special content for foreign language editions.

The look alone of this magazine's cover makes it clear that it is the German version of what we know in the U.S. as *Psychology Today.*

Reader's Digest, for example, has 25 different editorial staffs who produce 48 worldwide editions in 19 languages. The internationalization of magazines will no doubt increase as conglomeration and globalization continue to have an impact on the magazine industry as they have on other media businesses.

Second is technology. Computers and satellites now allow instant distribution of copy from the editor's desk to printing plants around the world. The result—almost immediate delivery to subscribers and sales outlets—makes production and distribution of even more narrowly targeted split runs more cost effective. This is an efficiency that cable television and online information services have yet to match.

Third is the sale of subscriber lists and a magazine's own direct marketing of products. Advertisers buy space in specialized magazines to reach a specific type of reader. Most magazines are more than happy to sell those readers' names and addresses to those same advertisers as well as to others who want to contact readers with direct mail pitches. Many magazines use their own subscriber lists for the same purpose, marketing products of interest to their particular readership. Cable television, even the most specialized channels, cannot easily identify individual audience members; therefore, they cannot sell their names.

Advertorials Aimed at Young Girls

The issue of development of healthy self-esteem and body image for young girls is frequently debated in the cultural forum. We saw in Chapter 1, for example, that Mattel, manufacturer of the popular Barbie, has changed the doll's physique in response to complaints that it fosters unrealistic standards and expectations in children. Consider your attitudes on this debate as you evaluate the following situation.

Chicago-based 'Teen magazine's 1993 media kit makes the case for the use of advertorials. Read their presentation, aimed at prospective advertisers, and think about how comfortable you are with the practice.

> 'TEEN's advertorial services are top-notch! Last year we produced 150 advertorial pages . . . that's more advertorial pages than any other national magazine. 'TEEN has its own advertorial staff: three editors whose only responsibility is the creation and production of advertorial pages. We work with both client and agency from preliminary layouts through the day of the shoot to the final selection of film, copy and color corrections.

Why Advertorials Will Work For You

- 'TEEN advertorials are designed to look like our editorial pages. Our editors know the looks our readers like and the advertorial pages are presented in this style.

- The advertorials can take your campaign one step further by providing additional information that is not provided in your advertisement. Additionally, they dramatically increase the frequency of your advertising message. (as cited in Silverblatt, 1995, p. 138)

Are you at all troubled that this potentially misleading content appears in a magazine aimed at young, relatively unsophisticated media consumers? Why, or why not?

Do you think the first explanation of why advertorials work—advertorials are designed to look like editorial pages—implies an overt effort to deceive readers?

Examine the advertorial's construction. What physical attributes characterize the models? How quickly did you find the "advertisement" disclaimer?

Imagine yourself as a 12-year-old. Do you think you could tell the difference between this advertisement and other editorial content in the magazine? Do you think you would have associated the Sears logo on the second page with the pictures and text on the first? Do you think this is an important issue? Why, or why not?

An article or an ad? Can you tell? Could a twelve-year-old reader make the distinction?

Cultural Forum

ADVERTORIALS

Publishers and advertisers sometimes use advertorials as a means of boosting the value of a magazine as an advertising medium. **Advertorials** are ads that appear in magazines that take on the appearance of genuine editorial content. Sometimes they are a page or less, sometimes inserts composed of several pages. They frequently carry the disclaimer "Advertisement," but it is usually in small print. Sometimes the disclaimer is no more than the advertiser's logo in a page corner. The goal is to put commercial content before readers, cloaked in the respectability of editorial content. The question for readers is clear: Is an item journalism or is it advertising?

Critics of advertorials argue that this blurring of the distinction between editorial and commercial matter is a breach of faith with readers (see the box "Advertorials Aimed at Young Girls"). Moreover, if the intent is not deception, why is the disclaimer typically small; why use the editorial content format at all? Defenders contend that advertorials are a well-entrenched aspect of contemporary magazines. The industry considers them not only financially necessary in an increasingly competitive media market but proper as well. No one is hurt by advertorials. In fact, they often deliver useful information. Advertisers are free in America to use whatever legal and truthful means available to sell their products. Magazines always label the paid material as such. And readers aren't idiots, defenders claim, they know an ad when they see one.

ADVERTISER INFLUENCE OVER MAGAZINE CONTENT

Controversial, too, is the influence that some advertisers attempt to exert over content. This influence is always there, at least implicitly. A magazine editor must satisfy advertisers as well as readers. One common way advertisers' interests shape content is in the placement of ads. Airline ads are moved away from stories about plane crashes. Cigarette ads rarely appear near articles on lung cancer. In fact, it is an accepted industry practice for a magazine to provide advertisers with a "heads up," alerting them that soon-to-be-published content may prove uncomfortable for their businesses. Advertisers can then request a move of their ad, or pull it and wait to run it in the next issue.

Complementary copy—content that reinforces the advertiser's message, or at least does not negate it—is problematic when creating such copy becomes a major influence in a publication's editorial decision making. This happens in a number of ways. Editors sometimes engage in self-censorship, making decisions about how stories are written and which stories appear based on the fear that specific advertisers will be offended. Some magazines, *Architectural Digest,* for example, identify companies by name in their picture caption copy only if they are advertisers. But many critics inside and outside the industry see increased crumbling of the wall between advertising demands and editorial judgment.

They point to the growing practice of advertisers demanding (and magazines granting) the right to prescreen content. Colgate-Palmolive, for example, refuses to place ads in a "media context" containing "offensive" sexual content or other material it feels is "antisocial or in bad taste." It requires its advertising agencies to prescreen content for these taboos, but those agencies need not define them for the magazines (Baker, 1997, p. 31). In February 1997 Chrysler's advertising agency, PentaCom, mailed a letter to all the magazines in which it places ads, stating, "In an effort to avoid potential conflicts, it is required that Chrysler Corporation be alerted in advance of any and all editorial content that encompasses sexual, political, social issues or any editorial that might be construed as provocative or offensive. Each and every issue that carries Chrysler advertising requires a written summary outlining major theme/articles appearing in upcoming issues" (p. 30). PentaCom, which annually places more than $270 million of Chrysler advertising in 100 magazines, demanded that executives of those publications sign and return its letter as acknowledgment of their acceptance of this requirement. Chrysler's head of consumer media relations said that every publication that received the letter agreed to its terms (p. 30).

The question raised by critics is, "How can a magazine function, offering depth, variety, and detail, when Colgate-Palmolive and Chrysler are joined by dozens of other advertisers, each demanding to preview content, not for its direct comment on matters of importance to their businesses, but for controversy and potential offensiveness?" (p. 30). Milton Glaser, cofounder of *New York* magazine, offered one answer, "It will have a devastating effect on the idea of a free press and of free inquiry" (p. 30).

DEVELOPING MEDIA LITERACY SKILLS
Recognizing the Power of Graphics

Detecting the use of and determining the informational value of advertorials is only one reason media literacy is important when reading magazines. Another necessary media literacy skill is the ability to understand how graphics and other artwork provide the background for interpreting stories. The notorious June 27, 1994, *Time* O. J. Simpson cover—where artists altered Simpson's facial tones on an L.A. police department mug shot—is one controversial example of how graphics are used to create meaning. The magazine said it wanted to show the "real" O. J., free of the glamour and hype that usually surround him. Critics claimed that darkening Simpson's face was designed to play to the ugly stereotype of African Americans as criminals. Media literate readers might also ask, "How does changing what was a 'real' photograph make the subject seem more real?"

The December 1, 1997, cover of *Newsweek* offered a less well-known but equally compelling example of graphics sleight-of-hand. That issue featured Bobbi McCaughey, mother of the Iowa septuplets born November 19, 1997. Artists at that magazine "repaired" McCaughey's teeth. Their intent was to present the new mother in the best possible light. There was no inflammatory issue of racial stereotyping in this instance, but the Iowa woman's multiple birth was not without controversy. Although much of the media treated her as a hero and the babies' births as a wonderful event, many observers took a different view. Doctors had advised McCaughey against the dangerous and premature births. The event was not a miracle of nature—as much of the media had packaged it—but the result of taking fertility drugs. Questions were raised about the ability of a working-class family to support such a large number of children. Media critics complained that the alteration in McCaughey's appearance helped shape people's interpretation of the event and mask a number of other important issues.

New York Times columnist Frank Rich (1997) labeled the alteration "e.c.," or emotional correctness.

> Since it's e.c. that Iowans be portrayed as the epitome of neighborly American generosity—with their governor, Terry Branstad, leading the gift giving to the McCaughey family—few dare note the estimated 9,000-plus homeless Iowan children who are being stripped of aid rather than showered with it even as donations roll in for the magnificent seven. It's also e.c. to applaud those selfless American corporations that are giving the McCaugheys a "fully loaded" Chevrolet van, Pampers, Gerber baby food and all the rest. So what if corporate America until last week ignored a mother who gave birth to sextuplets in Washington, D.C., back in May? When a black urban mother has more babies than she can afford, she's not an automatically e.c. magazine cover subject; she's more likely to be branded as a welfare queen. (p. A25)

The *Newsweek* cover from December 1, 1997. The publication's graphic improvement of Bobbi McCaughey's teeth proved more controversial than the magazine's editors had expected.

Do you agree? Did you see this particular *Newsweek* cover? If so, what was your reading of it? Do you accept the magazine's rationale for altering the photo? Do you believe that the magazine, at the least, had an obligation to inform its readers of its editorial decision to restructure reality?

Chapter Review

The colonial magazine was not particularly successful, and those that did exist were copies of popular British magazines. But in the years after the Revolutionary War, the magazine as we know it today had its start. After the Civil War, a great explosion in popular magazines occurred. The Postal Act of 1879, widespread literacy, a price war among the leading magazines, industrialization, and urbanization combined to fuel growth in this industry.

As the first national mass medium in the United States, magazines were an important force in the social change of the progressive era of the first decades of the 20th century, due to the writings and successes of the muckrakers. The giant mass circulation magazines of the time were the dominant advertising medium, the primary outlet for nationally distributed news, and the sole national provider of photojournalism.

After the coming of television, magazines changed. Despite the death of once powerful publications like *Collier's* and *The Saturday Evening Post*, the industry prospered. The keys to its success were specialization and development of a lifestyle orientation.

The 22,000 magazines in operation today include trade, professional, and business magazines; industrial, company, and sponsored magazines; and consumer magazines. The top 800 consumer magazines account for three quarters of the industry's revenues and exist in a variety of categories, from alternative to youth magazines. Webzines, or online magazines, are now appearing as well.

Magazines flourish because advertisers value their homogeneous audiences. Magazines further narrow their readership through split runs, special versions of the same issue targeted toward specific geographic areas or professions.

Space is sold in magazines on the basis of circulation. Magazines circulate through subscriptions, single-copy sales, and controlled circulation. Whatever the means of distribution, research groups such as the Audit Bureau of Circulation and Simmons determine and verify the true circulation numbers, taking care to include pass-along readership.

Other media, particularly cable television and certain online content providers, currently challenge the preeminence of magazines as a specialized advertising medium. But the industry meets this competition through internationalization of its publications, improved production and distribution technologies, use of their own computer networks, and by selling their lists of subscribers. But the greatest strength against their competitors is the nature of the magazine audience. Advertisers value magazine readers because they are educated, have high incomes, read magazines *for* the ads, keep magazines available for months, pass them along to similar people, and tend to be loyal to their magazines and to those who advertise in them.

Many magazines attract additional advertising by offering advertorials, ads that appear to be editorial content. This practice is of importance to the literate media consumer. Advertorials, as well as a variety of other editorial decisions, shape the meaning of all content. The use of artwork and graphics is intended to convey specific impressions. The 1997 *Newsweek* cover of Iowa septuplet mother Bobbi McCaughey is an excellent but controversial example of this technique.

Questions for Review

1. How would you characterize the content of the first U.S. magazines?

2. Who were Ida Tarbell, Upton Sinclair, Lincoln Steffens, and Jack London? What movement

did they represent, and what were some of its accomplishments?

3. What factors fueled expansion of the magazine industry at the beginning of the 20th century?

4. What factors led to the demise of the mass circulation era and the development of the era of specialization?

5. What are the three broad types of magazines?

6. Why do advertisers favor specialization in magazines?

7. In what different ways do magazines internationalize their publications?

8. What attributes make the contemporary magazine reader attractive to advertisers?

9. Which two media currently challenge the preeminence of magazines as a specialized advertising medium? Why?

10. What is an advertorial? What is its function?

Questions for Critical Thinking and Discussion

1. Can you think of any contemporary crusading magazine or muckraking writers? Compared to those of the progressive era, they are certainly less visible. Why is this the case?

2. How well do you fit the profile of the average magazine reader?

3. Which magazines do you read? Draw a demographic profile of yourself based only on the magazines you regularly read.

4. Which side do you take in the advertorial debate? Why?

5. Are you troubled by the practice of altering photographs? Can you think of times when it might be more appropriate than others?

Important Resources

Janello, A., & Jones, B. (1991). *The American magazine.* **New York: Harry N. Abrams.** A thorough examination of the operation of the magazine industry and an interesting study of how magazines develop their particular look and style.

Nourie, A., & Nourie, B. (Eds.). (1990). *American mass market magazines.* **Westport, CT: Greenwood Press.** A collection of essays and reports covering many important issues in contemporary magazines, including minority magazines and internationalization.

Tebbel, J. (1969). *The American magazine: A compact history.* **New York: Hawthorn Books.** Written by an eminent print historian, this book is considered by many to be the definitive popular discussion of the development of magazines in the United States.

Winship, J. (1987). *Inside women's magazines.* **London: Pandora Press.** The style and content of women's magazines is examined from a critical perspective in this readable, picture-filled book.

Magazine Information Web Sites

The Utne Reader	*http://www.utne.com*
Audit Bureau of Circulation	*http://www.accessabc.com*
Editor & Publisher	*http://www.mediainfo.com*
Magazine CyberCenter (online magazine newsstand)	*http://www.magamall.com/*
Life **Magazine Home Page**	*http://pathfinder.com/Life/lifehome.html*
Link to the Top 100 Computer Magazines	*http://www.internetvalley.com/top100mag.html*
Wired Magazine Homepage	*http://www.wired.com*

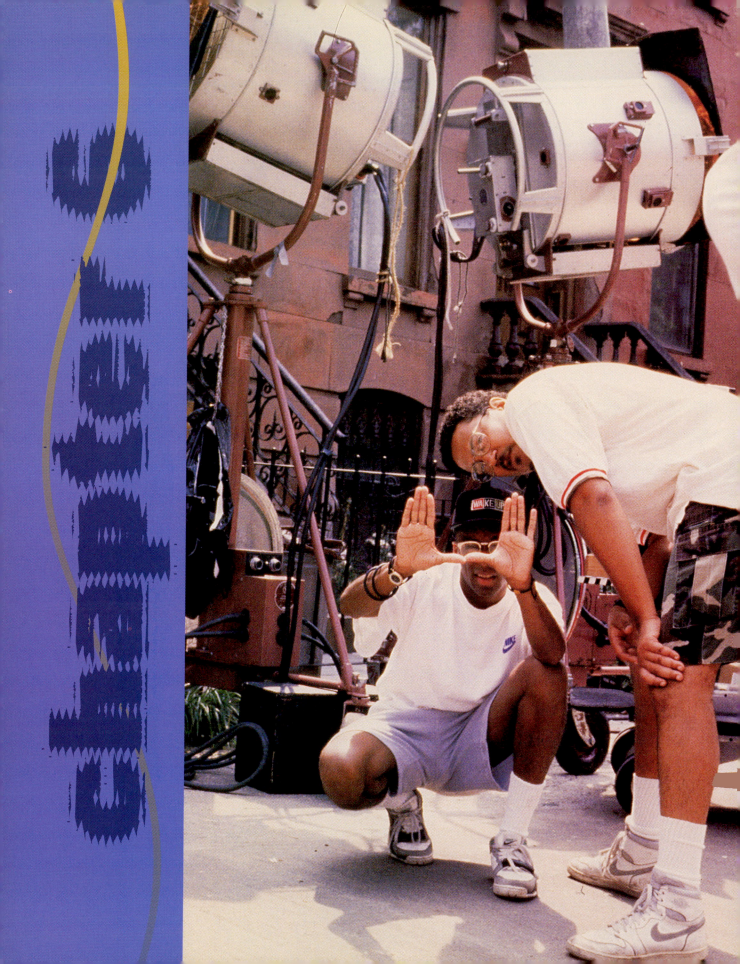

Film

Paris is cold and damp on this December night, three days after Christmas in 1895. But you bundle up and make your way to the Grand Café in the heart of the city. You've read in the morning paper that brothers Auguste and Louis Lumière will be displaying their new invention that somehow makes pictures move. Your curiosity is piqued.

Tables and chairs are set up in the basement room of the café, and a white bedsheet is draped above its stage. The Lumières appear to polite applause. They announce the program: *La Sortie des usines Lumière, (Quitting Time at the Factory); Le Repas de bébé,* featuring a Lumière child eating; *L'Arroseur arrosé,* about a practical joking boy and his victim, the gardener; and finally *L'Arrivée d'un train en gare,* the arrival of a train at a station.

The lights go out. Somewhere behind you, someone starts the machine. There is some brief flickering on the suspended sheet and then . . . you are completely awestruck. There before you—bigger than life-size—photographs are really moving. You see places you know to be miles away. You spy on the secret world of a prankster boy, remembering your own childhood. But the last film is the most impressive. As the giant locomotive rushes toward the audience, you and most of the others are convinced you are about to be crushed. There is panic. People are ducking under their chairs, screaming. Death is imminent!

The first paying audience in the history of motion pictures has just had a lesson in movie watching.

The Lumière brothers were excellent mechanics, and their father owned a factory that made photographic plates. Their first films were little more than what we would now consider black and white home movies. As you can tell from their titles, they were simple stories. There was no editing; the camera was simply turned on, then turned off. There were no fades, wipes, or flashbacks. No computer graphics, no dialogue, and no music. And yet much of the audience was terrified by the oncoming cinematic locomotive. They were illiterate in the language of film.

We begin our study of the movies with the history of film, from its entrepreneurial beginnings, through introduction of its narrative and visual language, to its establishment as a large, studio-run industry. We detail Hollywood's relationship with its early audiences and changes in the structure and content of films resulting from the introduction of television. We then look at contemporary movie production, distribution, and exhibition systems, the influence of the major studios, and the economic pressures on them in an increasingly multimedia environment. We examine the special place movies hold in our culture and how ever-younger audiences and the films that target them may affect our culture. Recognizing the use of product placement in movies is the basis for improving our media literacy skill.

A Short History of the Movies

We are no longer illiterate in the grammar of film, nor are movies as simple as the early Lumière offerings. Consider the sophistication necessary for filmmakers to produce a computer-generated movie such as *Toy Story* and the skill required for audiences to read *Pulp Fiction*'s shifts in time, unconventional camera angles, and other twists and turns. How we arrived at this contemporary medium–audience relationship is a wonderful story.

Early newspapers were developed by businesspeople and patriots for a small, politically involved elite that could read, but the early movie industry was built largely by entrepreneurs who wanted to make money entertaining everyone. Unlike television, whose birth and growth were predetermined and guided by the already well-established radio industry (see Chapter 8), there were no precedents, no rules, and no expectations for movies.

Return to the opening vignette. The audience for the first Lumière movies did not "speak film." Think of it as being stranded in a foreign

The Lumière's *L'Arrivee d'un train en gare*. As simple as early films were, their viewers did not have sufficient film literacy to properly interpret, understand, and enjoy them. This scene supposedly sent people screaming and hiding to avoid being crushed by the oncoming train.

country with no knowledge of the language and cultural conventions. You would have to make your way, with each new experience helping you better understand the next. First you'd learn some simple words and basic customs. Eventually, you'd be able to better understand the language and people. In other words, you'd become increasingly literate in that culture. Beginning with that Paris premiere, people had to become film literate. They had to develop an understanding of cinematic alterations in time and space. They had to learn how images and sound combined to create meaning. But unlike visiting in another culture, there was no existing cinematic culture. Movie creators and their audiences had to grow up together.

THE EARLY ENTREPRENEURS

In 1873 former California Governor Leland Stanford needed help winning a bet he had made with a friend. Convinced that a horse in full gallop had all four feet off the ground, he had to prove it. He turned to well-known photographer Eadweard Muybridge, who worked on the problem for four years before finding a solution. In 1877 Muybridge arranged a series of still cameras along a stretch of race track. As the horse sprinted by, each camera took its picture. The resulting photographs won Stanford his bet, but more important, they sparked an idea in their photographer. Muybridge was intrigued by the appearance of motion created when photos are viewed sequentially. He began taking pictures of numerous kinds of human and animal action. To display his work, Muybridge invented the **zoopraxiscope,** a machine for projecting slides onto a distant surface.

Muybridge's horse pictures. When these plates were placed sequentially and rotated, they produced the appearance of motion.

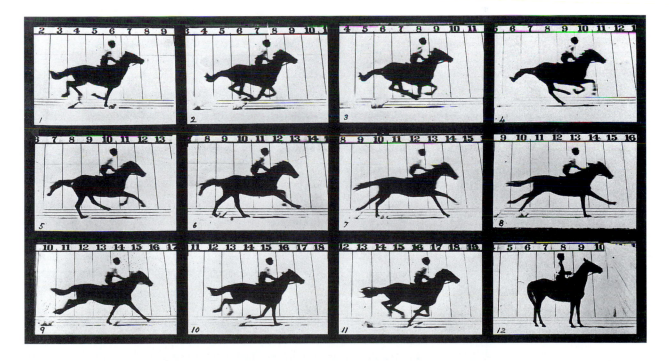

When people watched the rapidly projected, sequential slides, they saw the pictures as if they were in motion. This perception is the result of a physiological phenomenon known as **persistence of vision,** in which the images our eyes gather are retained in the brain for about ¼ of a second. Therefore, if photographic frames are moved at 24 frames a second, people perceive them as actually in motion. This phenomenon had been identified and studied in the early 1800s by several European thinkers and scientists, including Peter Mark Roget, author of the *Thesaurus* that still bears his name. But it was Muybridge who made the first important application of that fact.

Muybridge eventually met the prolific inventor Thomas Edison in 1888. Edison quickly saw the scientific and economic potential of the zoopraxiscope and set his top scientist, William Dickson, to the task of developing a better projector. But Dickson correctly saw the problem as one of developing a better system of *filming*. He understood that shooting numerous still photos, then putting them in sequential order, then redrawing the images they held onto slides was inherently limiting. Dickson combined Hannibal Goodwin's newly invented celluloid roll film with George Eastman's easy-to-use Kodak camera into a motion picture camera that took 40 photographs a second. He used his **kinetograph** to film all types of theatrical performances, some by unknowns and others by famous entertainers such as Annie Oakley and Buffalo Bill Cody. Of course, none of this would have been possible if it were not for photography itself.

The Development of Photography   The process of photography was first developed by French inventor Joseph Nicéphore Niépce around 1816. Although there had been much experimentation in the realm of image making at the time, Niépce was the first person to make practical use of a camera and film. He photographed natural objects and produced color prints. Unfortunately, his images would last only a short time.

Niépce's success, however, attracted the attention of countryman Louis Daguerre, who joined with him to perfect the process. Niépce died before the 1839 introduction of the **daguerreotype,** a process of recording images on polished metal plates, usually copper, covered with a thin layer of silver iodide emulsion. When light reflected from an object passed through a lens and struck the emulsion, the emulsion would etch the image on the plate. The plate was then washed with a cleaning solvent, leaving a positive or replica image.

In the same year as Daguerre's first public display of the daguerreotype, British inventor William Henry Fox Talbot introduced a paper film process. This process was actually more important to the development of photography than the metal film system, but the daguerreotype received widespread attention and acclaim and made the public enthusiastic about photography.

The **calotype** (Talbot's system) used translucent paper, what we now call the negative, from which several prints could be made. In addition, his film was much more sensitive than Daguerre's metal plate, allowing

Typical of daguerreotypes, this plate captures a portrait. The method's long exposure time made all but the most stationary subjects impossible to photograph.

for exposure times of only a few seconds as opposed to the daguerreotype's 30 minutes. Until calotype, virtually all daguerreotype images were still lifes and portraits, a necessity with long exposure times.

The final steps in the development of the photographic process necessary for true motion pictures were taken, as we've just seen, by Goodwin in 1887 and Eastman in 1889 and were adapted to motion pictures by Edison scientist Dickson.

Thomas Edison Edison built the first motion picture studio near his laboratory in New Jersey. He called it Black Maria, the common name at that time for a police paddy wagon. It had an open roof and revolved to follow the sun so the performers being filmed would always be illuminated.

The completed films were not projected. Instead, they were run through a **kinetoscope,** a sort of peep show device. Often they were accompanied by music provided by another Edison invention, the phonograph. Patented in 1891 and commercially available three years later, the kinetoscope quickly became a popular feature in penny arcades, vaudeville halls, and big city Kinetoscope Parlors. This marked the beginning of commercial motion picture exhibition.

The Lumière Brothers The Lumière brothers made the next advance. Their initial screenings demonstrated that people would sit in a darkened room to watch motion pictures projected on a screen. The brothers from Lyon envisioned great wealth in their ability to increase the number of

Scene from *A Trip to the Moon*. Narrative came to the movies through the inventive imagination of Georges Méliès.

people who could simultaneously watch a movie. In 1895 they patented their **cinematographe,** a device that both photographed and projected action. Within weeks of their Christmastime showing, long lines of enthusiastic moviegoers were waiting for their makeshift theater to open. Edison recognized the advantage of the cinematographe over his kinetoscope, so he acquired the patent for an advanced projector developed by U.S. inventor Thomas Armat. On April 23, 1896, the Edison Vitascope premiered in New York City, and the American movie business was born.

THE COMING OF NARRATIVE

The Edison and Lumière movies were typically only a few minutes long and showed little more than filmed reproductions of reality—celebrities, weight lifters, jugglers, and babies eating. They were shot in fixed frame (the camera did not move), and there was no editing. For the earliest audiences, this was enough. But soon the novelty wore thin. People wanted more for their money. French film maker Georges Méliès began making narrative motion pictures, that is, movies that told a story. At the end of the 1890s he was shooting and exhibiting one-scene, one-shot movies, but soon he began making stories based on sequential shots in different places. He simply took one shot, stopped the camera, moved it, took another shot, and so on. Méliès is often called the "first artist of the cinema" because he brought narrative to the medium in the form of imaginative tales such as *A Trip to the Moon* (1902).

Scene from *The Great Train Robbery.* Porter's masterpiece introduced audiences to editing, intercutting of scenes, moving cameras . . . and the western.

Méliès had been a magician and caricaturist before he became a filmmaker, and his inventive movies showed his dramatic flair. They were extravagant stage plays where people disappeared and reappeared and other wonders occurred. *A Trip to the Moon* came to America in 1903, and U.S. moviemakers were quick not only to borrow the idea of using film to tell stories but to improve on it.

Edwin S. Porter, an Edison Company cameraman, saw that film could be an even better storyteller with more artistic use of camera placement and editing. His 12-minute *The Great Train Robbery* (1903) was the first movie to use editing, intercutting of scenes, and a mobile camera to tell a relatively sophisticated tale. It was also the first western. This new narrative form using **montage**—tying together two separate but related shots in such a way that they took on a new, unified meaning—was an instant hit with audiences. Almost immediately hundreds of **nickelodeons,** some having as many as 100 seats, were opened in converted stores, banks, and halls across the United States. The price of admission was one nickel, hence the name. By 1905 cities like New York were opening a new nickelodeon every day. From 1907 to 1908, the first year in which there were more narrative than documentary films, the number of nickelodeons in the United States increased tenfold. With so many exhibition halls in so many towns serving such an extremely enthusiastic public, many movies were needed. Literally hundreds and hundreds of new **factory studios,** or production companies, were started.

Because so many movies needed to be made and rushed to the nickelodeons, people working in the industry had to learn and perform virtually all aspects of production. There was precious little time for, or

The Ku Klux Klan was the collective hero in D.W. Griffith's *The Birth of a Nation.* This cinematic masterpiece and ground-breaking film employed production techniques never before used; however, its racist theme mars its legacy.

profitability in, the kind of specialization that marks contemporary film-making. Writer, actor, cameraman D. W. Griffith perfected his craft in this environment. He was quickly recognized as a brilliant director. He introduced innovations such as scheduled rehearsals before final shooting and production based on close adherence to a shooting script. He lavished attention on otherwise ignored aspects of a film's look—costume and lighting—and used close-ups and other dramatic camera angles to transmit emotion.

All his skill came together in 1915 with the release of *The Birth of a Nation.* Where Porter had used montage to tell a story, Griffith used it to create passion, move emotions, and heighten suspense. The most influential silent film ever made, this 3-hour epic was 6 weeks in rehearsal and 9 weeks in shooting, cost $125,000 to produce (making it the most expensive movie made to date), was distributed to theaters complete with orchestral music score, had a cast of thousands of humans and animals, and had an admission price well above the usual 5 cents—$3. It was the most popular and profitable movie made until unseated in 1939 by *Gone with the Wind.* Along with other Griffith masterpieces, *Intolerance* (1916) and *Broken Blossoms* (1919), *The Birth of a Nation* set new standards for the American film. They took movies out of the nickelodeons and made them big business. At the same time, however, *The Birth of a Nation* represented the basest aspects of U.S. culture because it included an ugly, racist portrayal of African Americans and a sympathetic treatment of the Ku Klux Klan. The film inspired protests in front of theaters across the country and criticism in some newspapers and magazines, and African Americans fought back with their own films (see the box "African American Response to D. W. Griffith: The Lincoln and Micheaux Film Companies"). Nevertheless, *The Birth of a Nation* found acceptance by the vast majority of people.

THE BIG STUDIOS

In 1908 Thomas Edison, foreseeing the huge amounts of money that could be made from movies, founded the Motion Picture Patents Company (MPPC), often called simply the Trust. This group of 10 companies under Edison's control, holding the patents to virtually all existing filmmaking and exhibition equipment, ran the production and distribution of film in the United States with an iron fist. Anyone who wanted to make or exhibit a movie needed Trust permission, which typically was not forthcoming. In addition, the MPPC had rules about the look of the movies it would permit: they must be one reel, approximately 12 minutes long, and must adopt a "stage perspective"; that is, the actors must fill the frame as if they were in a stage play.

Many independent film companies sprang up in defiance of the Trust, including Griffith's in 1913. To avoid MPPC scrutiny and reprisal, these companies moved to California. This westward migration had other benefits. Better weather meant longer shooting seasons. Free of MPPC standards, people like Griffith who wanted to explore the potential of film in longer than 12-minute bits and with imaginative use of the camera were free to do so. In 1917 the MPPC was declared an illegal monopoly and died. It was already dead, in fact, because the independent movies were simply bigger and better. In addition, because the Trust would not allow identification of its on-screen performers, the competing independent actors and actresses had become popular, recognizable stars that audiences wanted to see. At the time of the demise of the Trust, Mary Pickford and Charlie Chaplin were each making more than $1 million a year. The star system was entrenched, as were the now powerful production companies, and the studio system was born.

The studios controlled the movie industry from California. Thomas H. Ince (maker of the William S. Hart westerns), Griffith, and comedy genius Mack Sennett formed the Triangle Company. Adolph Zukor's Famous Players in Famous Plays—formed when Zukor was denied MPPC permission to distribute one of his films—joined with several other independents and a distribution company to become Paramount. Other independents joined to create the Fox Film Company (soon called 20th Century Fox) and Universal. Although films were still silent, by the mid-1920s there were more than 20,000 movie theaters in the United States, and more than 350,000 people were making their living in film production. More than 1,240,000 feet of film was shot each year in Hollywood, and annual domestic U.S. box office receipts exceeded $750 million.

The industry prospered not just because of its artistry, drive, and innovation but because it used these to meet the needs of a growing audience. At the beginning of the 20th century, generous immigration rules, combined with political and social unrest abroad, encouraged a flood of European immigrants who congregated in U.S. cities where the jobs were and where people like themselves who spoke their language lived. American farmers, largely illiterate, also swarmed to the cities as years of drought and farm failure left them without home or hope. Jobs in the big mills and factories, although unpleasant, were plentiful. These new city dwellers had money and the need for leisure activities. Movies were a nickel, required no ability to read or to understand English, and offered glamorous stars and wonderful stories from faraway places.

Foreign political unrest proved to be a boon to the infant U.S. movie business in another way as well. In 1914 and 1915, when the California studios were remaking the industry in their own grand image, war raged in Europe. European moviemaking, most significantly the influential French, German, and Russian cinema, came to a halt. European demand for movies, however, did not. American movies, produced in huge numbers for the hungry home audience, were ideal for overseas distribution. Because so few in the domestic audience could read English, few printed titles were used in the then-silent movies. Therefore, little had to be changed to satisfy foreign moviegoers. Film was indeed a universal language, but more important, the American film industry had firmly established itself as the world leader, literally within 20 years of the Lumière brothers' first screening.

Using Media to Make a Difference

African American Response to D. W. Griffith: The Lincoln and Micheaux Film Companies

The African American community did not sit passively in the wake of D. W. Griffith's 1915 cinematic but hateful wonder, *The Birth of a Nation*. The NAACP fought the film in court and on the picket line, largely unsuccessfully. But other African Americans decided to use film to combat *Birth*. The first was Emmett J. Scott, a quiet, scholarly man. He sought money from the country's black middle class to produce a short film showing the achievements of African Americans. His intention was to attach his film, *Lincoln's Dream*, as a prologue to screenings of the Griffith film. Together with screenwriter Elaine Sterne, Scott eventually expanded the project into a feature length movie. He approached Universal Studios with his film but was rejected.

With independent backing from both Black and White investors, the film was released in 1918. Produced by an inexperienced cast and crew working on a production beset by bad weather and technical difficulties, the retitled *The Birth of a Race* filled 12 reels of film and ran more than 3 hours. Its publicity hailed it as "The Greatest and Most Daring of Photoplays . . . The Story of Sin . . . A Master Picture Conceived in the Spirit of Truth and Dedicated to All the Races of the World" (Bogle, 1989, p. 103). It was an artistic and commercial failure. Scott, however, had inspired others.

Even before *The Birth of a Race* was completed, the Lincoln Motion Picture Company was incorporated, in Nebraska in 1916 and in California in 1917, by brothers Noble P. and George Johnson. Their tack differed from Scott's. They understood that their Black films would never be allowed on "White" screens, so they produced movies designed to tell Black-oriented stories to Black audiences. They might not be able to convince White America of Griffith's error, but they could reassure African Americans that their views could find expression. Lincoln's first movie was *The Realization of a Negro's Ambition*, and it told the story of Black American achievements. The Johnson brothers turned U.S. racism to their advantage. Legal segregation in the

CHANGE COMES TO HOLLYWOOD

As was the case with newspapers and magazines, the advent of television significantly altered the movie–audience relationship. But the nature of that relationship had been shaped and reshaped in the three decades between the coming of sound and the coming of television.

The Talkies   The first sound film was one of three films produced by Warner Brothers. It may have been *Don Juan* (1926), starring John Barrymore, distributed with synchronized music and sound effects. Or perhaps Warner's more famous *The Jazz Singer* (1927), starring Al Jolson, which had several sound and speaking scenes (354 words in all) but was largely silent. Or it may have been the 1928 all-sound *Lights of New York*. Historians disagree because they cannot decide what constitutes a sound film.

There is no confusion, however, about the impact of sound on the movies and their audiences. First, sound made possible new genres—musicals, for example. Second, as actors and actresses now had to really act, performance aesthetics improved. Third, sound made film production

south and de facto segregation in the north had led to an explosion of Black theaters. These movie houses needed content. Lincoln helped provide it by producing 10 three-reelers between 1916 and 1920.

Two more notable film companies began operation, hoping to challenge Griffith's portrayals at least in Black theaters. Oscar Micheaux founded the Micheaux Film and Book Company in 1918 in Chicago and soon produced *The Homesteader*, an eight-reel film based on the autobiographical novel he'd written three years earlier. It was the story of a successful Black homestead rancher in South Dakota. But Micheaux was not content to boost Black self-esteem. He was determined to make "racial photoplays depicting racial life" (as cited in Sampson, 1977, p. 42). In 1920 he released *Within Our Gates*, a drama about the southern lynching of a Black man. Censored and denied a screening in dozens of cities both north and south, Micheaux was undeterred. In 1921 he released the eight-reeler *The Gunsaulus Mystery*, based on a well-known murder case in which a Black man was convicted.

These early film pioneers used their medium to make a difference. They challenged the interpretation of history being circulated by the most popular movie in the world, they provided encouragement and entertainment to the African American community, and they began the long tradition of Black filmmaking in the United States.

A scene from *The Realization of a Negro's Ambition.*

a much more complicated and expensive proposition. As a result, many smaller filmmakers closed shop, solidifying the hold of the big studios over the industry. In 1933, 60% of all U.S. films came from Hollywood's eight largest studios. By 1940, they were producing 76% of all U.S. movies and collecting 86% of the total box office. As for the audience, in 1926, the year of *Don Juan's* release, 50 million people went to the movies each week. In 1929, at the height of the Great Depression, the number had risen to 80 million. By 1930, when sound was firmly entrenched, the number of weekly moviegoers had risen to 90 million (Mast & Kawin, 1996).

Scandal The popularity of talkies, and of movies in general, inevitably raised questions about their impact on the culture. In 1896, well before sound, *The Kiss* had generated a great moral outcry. Its stars, John C. Rice and May Irwin, were also the leads in a popular Broadway play, *The Widow Jones,* which closed with a climactic kiss. The Edison Company asked Rice and Irwin to recreate the kiss for the big screen. Newspapers and politicians were bombarded with complaints from the offended. Kissing in the theater was one thing; in movies it was quite another! The then-newborn industry responded to this and other calls for censorship with various forms of self-regulation and internal codes. But in the early 1920s more Hollywood scandals forced a more direct response.

In 1920 "America's Sweetheart" Mary Pickford obtained a questionable Nevada divorce from her husband and immediately married the movies' other darling, Douglas Fairbanks, himself newly divorced. In 1920 and

Al Jolson, in black face, starred in the 1927 *The Jazz Singer,* one of three claimants to the title of first sound movie.

1921 comedian Fatty Arbuckle was involved in police problems on two coasts. The first was apparently hushed up after a $100,000 gift was made to a Massachusetts district attorney, but the second involved a murder at a San Francisco hotel party thrown by the actor. Although he was acquitted in his third trial (the first two ended in hung juries), the stain on Arbuckle and the industry remained. Then, in 1922, actor Wallace Reid and director William Desmond Taylor both died in what the newspapers referred to as "a mysterious fashion" in which drugs and sex were thought to have played a part. The cry for government intervention was raised. State legislatures introduced more than 100 separate pieces of legislation to censor or otherwise control movies and their content.

Hollywood responded in 1922 by creating the Motion Picture Producers and Distributors of America (MPPDA) and appointing Will H. Hays—chairman of the Republican party, a Presbyterian church elder, and a former postmaster general—president. The Hays Office, as it became known, undertook a vast effort to improve the image of the movies. Stressing the importance of movies to national life and as an educational medium, Hays promised better movies and founded a committee on public relations that included many civic and religious leaders. Eventually, in 1934, the Motion Picture Production Code (MPPC) was released. The MPPC forbade the use of profanity, limited bedroom scenes to married couples, required that skimpy outfits be replaced by more complete costumes, delineated the length of screen kisses, ruled out scenes that ridiculed public officials or religious leaders, and outlawed a series of words from "God" to "nuts," all enforced by a $25,000 fine (see the box "Self-Censorship in Hollywood: The Movie Ratings").

New Genres, New Problems By 1932 weekly movie attendance had dropped to 60 million. The Depression was having its effect. Yet the industry was able to weather the crisis for two reasons. The first was its creativity. New genres held people's interest. The feature documentaries such as *The Plow that Broke the Plains* (1936) spoke to audience needs to understand a world in seeming disorder. Musicals such as *42nd Street* (1933) and screwball comedies such as *Bringing Up Baby* (1938) provided easy escapism. Gangster movies such as *Little Caesar* (1930) reflected the grimy reality of Depression city streets and daily newspaper headlines. Horror films such as *Frankenstein* (1931) articulated audience feelings of alienation and powerlessness in a seemingly uncontrollable time. Socially conscious comedies such as *Mr. Deeds Goes to Town* (1936) reminded moviegoers that good could still prevail, and the **double feature** with a **B-movie**—typically a less expensive movie—was a welcome relief to penny-pinching working people.

The movie business also survived the Depression because of its size and power, both residing in a system of operation called **vertical integration.** Using this system, studios produced their own films, distributed them through their own outlets, and exhibited them in their own theaters. In effect, the big studios controlled a movie from shooting to screening, guaranteeing distribution and an audience regardless of quality.

When the 1930s ended, weekly attendance was again over 80 million, and Hollywood was churning out 500 pictures a year. Moviegoing had become a central family and community activity for most people. Yet the end of that decade also brought bad news. In 1938 the Justice Department challenged vertical integration, suing the big five studios—Warner Brothers, MGM, Paramount, RKO, and 20th Century Fox—for restraint of trade; that is, they accused the studios of illegal monopolistic practices. The case would take 10 years to decide, but the movie industry, basking in the middle of its Golden Age, was under attack. Its fate was sealed in 1939 when the Radio Corporation of America (RCA) made the first public broadcast of television from atop the Empire State Building. The impact of these two events was profound, and the medium would have to develop a new relationship with its audience to survive.

Hollywood Goes to War   During World War II Hollywood was a model citizen. Director Frank Capra (*Mr. Smith Goes to Washington,* 1939) joined the Army to make the immortal and influential *Why We Fight* series of propaganda movies. Countless numbers of before and behind the camera talent joined the war effort, in and out of uniform. War bonds were sold in

Media Echoes

Self-Censorship in Hollywood: The Movie Ratings

In 1952 in *Burstyn v. Wilson* the Supreme Court declared that film is "a significant medium for the communication of ideas" designed to "entertain as well as to inform." Movies were finally granted First Amendment protection (undoing the 1915 Supreme Court judgment in *Mutual Film Corp. v. Ohio Industrial Commission,* which had ruled that movies were merely novelty and entertainment, unworthy of protection as expression). The significance of the ruling was that government at all levels was prohibited from denying filmmakers their right of free expression.

The Supreme Court decision did not affect the industry's own censorship, however. In 1953 director Otto Preminger and United Artists decided to challenge that self-imposed denial of freedom. Preminger and his studio sought the MPPC certificate of approval for *The Moon Is Blue,* a saucy sex comedy starring William Holden and David Niven. Adapted from a popular Broadway play, it was the tale of a woman who flaunted her virginity, and its humor resided in its double entendre and innuendo. Because the film contained words like "virgin" and "mistress," the MPPC denied Preminger and United Artists, forbidding them to release the movie. They released it anyway. Audiences were not overly fond of *The Moon Is Blue,* but the MPPC had not halted its distribution or exhibition, nor did it punish the filmmakers in any effective manner.

In 1955 Preminger and United Artists again battled the MPPC, this time over *The Man with the Golden Arm,* a stark and powerful film starring Frank Sinatra as a drug addict and Eleanor Parker as his crippled wife. The MPPC denied the movie permission to be released because of its portrayal of unsavory morals. Director and studio again defied the industry censors, putting the film in theaters. It was a smash hit, both critically and at the box office. The MPPC was proven powerless, its control of movie content broken for good.

During this time, Hollywood was challenging television with the production of message movies about controversial social problems including racism, juvenile delinquency, and alcohol abuse. But despite *Burstyn v. Wilson,* the industry still feared government intrusion.

theater lobbies. At the unnecessary request of the Office of War Information Bureau of Motion Picture Affairs, feature films and even cartoons stressed the greatness of the United States and its industrial might; demonized the Japanese, Germans, and Italians; encouraged and entertained the troops; and inspired the home front workers to greater levels of productivity. In 1946, one year after the end of World War II, more than 90 million people a week were filling the theaters and fattening Hollywood bank accounts.

The boom quickly turned bust as television, the Paramount case, and the "red scare" delivered three successive blows to the industry.

Television When World War II began, the government took control of all patents for the newly developing technology of television as well as of the materials necessary for its production. The diffusion of the medium to the public was therefore halted, but its technological improvement was not. In addition, the radio networks and advertising agencies, recognizing that the war would end some day and that the future was in television, were preparing for that day. When the war did end, the movie industry found itself competing not with a fledgling medium but with a technologically

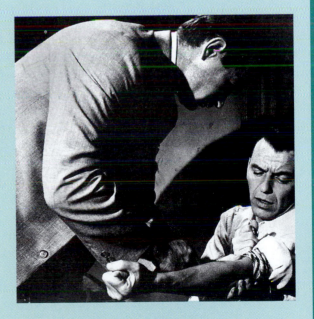

Frank Sinatra shoots heroin into his arm in the 1955 *The Man with the Golden Arm.*

Its solution was to develop a different kind of self-regulation, and in 1966 the Motion Picture Association of America's (MPAA) rating system was born.

No longer were moviemakers told what they could and could not do. Instead, audiences were being alerted to what filmmakers were doing. The idea was to give filmmakers as much artistic freedom as they wanted, but to provide moviegoers with some indication of the nature of a film's content. The rating system, which has seen some alteration since its introduction, is familiar today to everyone who goes to a movie or rents a video:

G	general audiences
PG	parental guidance; for mature audiences
PG–13	parental guidance advised for children under 13 years old
R	restricted; no one under 17 years old admitted unless accompanied by an adult
NC–17	no children under 17; replaces the old X rating

Development of an informational rating system by the film industry is echoed in Chapter 14 in the account of the Internet rating system for computer users.

and economically sophisticated one. As we saw in Chapter 1, the number of homes with television sets grew from 10,000 in 1946 to more than 10 million in 1950 and 54 million in 1960. Meanwhile, by 1955 movie attendance was down to 46 million people a week, fully 25% below even the worst attendance figures for the Depression years.

The Paramount Decision   In 1948, a full 10 years after the case had begun, the Supreme Court issued its Paramount Decision, effectively destroying the studios' hold over moviemaking. Vertical integration was ruled illegal, as was **block booking,** the practice of requiring exhibitors to rent groups of movies, often inferior, to secure a better one. The studios were forced to sell off their exhibition businesses (the theaters). Before the Paramount Decision, the five major studios owned 75% of the first-run movie houses in the United States; after it, they owned none. Not only did they no longer have guaranteed exhibition, but other filmmakers now had access to the theaters, producing even greater competition for the dwindling number of movie patrons.

Red Scare   The U.S. response to its postwar position as world leader was fear. So concerned were some members of Congress that communism would steal the people's rights that Congress decided to steal them first. The Hollywood chapter of the virulent anticommunism movement we now call McCarthyism (after the Republican senator from Wisconsin, Joseph McCarthy, its most rabid and public champion) was led by the House Un-American Activities Committee (HUAC) and its chair, J. Parnell Thomas (later imprisoned for padding his congressional payroll). First convened in 1947, HUAC had as its goal to rid Hollywood of communist influence. The fear was that communist, socialist, and "leftist" propaganda was being inserted secretly in entertainment films by "reds," "fellow travelers," and "pinkos." Many of the industry's best and brightest talents were called to testify before the committee and were asked, "Are you now or have you ever been a member of the Communist Party?" Those who came to be known as the Hollywood 10, including writers Ring Lardner Jr. and Dalton Trumbo and director Edward Dmytryk, refused to answer the question, accusing the committee, by its mere existence, of being in violation of the Bill of Rights. All were jailed. Rather than defend its First Amendment rights, the film industry abandoned those who were even mildly critical of the "red scare," jettisoning much of its best talent at a time when it could least afford to do so. In the fight against television, movies became increasingly tame for fear of being too controversial.

The industry was hurt not only by its cowardice but also by its short-sightedness. Hungry for content, the television industry asked Hollywood to sell it old features for broadcast. The studios responded by imposing on themselves the rule that no films could be sold to television and no working film star could appear on "the box." When it could have helped to shape early television viewer tastes and expectations of the new medium, Hollywood was absent. It lifted its ban in 1958.

Fighting Back The industry worked mightily to recapture audiences from television using both technical and content innovations. Some of these innovations remain today and serve the medium and its audiences well. These include more attention to special effects, greater dependence on and improvements in color, and CinemaScope (projecting on a large screen two and one half times wider than it is tall). Among the forgettable technological innovations were 3-D and smellovision (wafting odors throughout the theater).

Innovation in content included spectaculars with which the small screen could not compete. *The Ten Commandments* (1956), *Ben Hur* (1959), *El Cid* (1960), and *Spartacus* (1960) filled the screen with many thousands of extras and lavish settings. Now that television was catering to the mass audience, movies were free to present challenging fare for more sophisticated audiences. The "message movie" charted social trends, especially alienation of youth (*Blackboard Jungle*, 1955; *Rebel Without a Cause*, 1955) and prejudice (*12 Angry Men*, 1957; *Imitation of Life*, 1959; *To Kill a Mockingbird*, 1962). Changing values toward sex were examined (*Midnight Cowboy*, 1969; *Bob and Carol and Ted and Alice*, 1969), as was the new youth culture rejection of middle-class values (*The Graduate*, 1967; *Goodbye Columbus*, 1969) and its revulsion/attraction to violence (*Bonnie and Clyde*, 1967). The movies as an industry had changed, but as a medium of social commentary and cultural impact, they may have grown up.

Movies and Their Audiences

We talk of Hollywood as the "dream factory," the makers of "movie magic." We want our lives and loves to be "just like in the movies." The movies are "larger than life," movie stars are much more glamorous than

Warren Beatty eats some lead in the climax of the 1967 hit movie *Bonnie and Clyde.*

television stars. The movies, in other words, hold a very special place in our culture. Movies, like books, are a culturally special medium, an important medium. In this sense the movie–audience relationship has more in common with that of books than with that of television. Just as people buy books, they buy movie tickets. Because the audience is in fact the true consumer, power rests with it in film more than it does in television.

For better or worse, today's movie audience is increasingly a young one. The typical moviegoer in the United States is a teenager or young adult. These teens and 20-somethings, while comprising less than 20% of the total population, represent more than 30% of the tickets bought. It's no surprise, then, that new screens sprout at malls, where teens and even younger people can be dropped off for a day of safe entertainment. Many movies are aimed at kids—*The Santa Clause, Home Alone, Who Framed Roger Rabbit?, Space Jam;* all the *Rambos, Batmans,* and *Supermans;* anything with Jim Carrey; all the movies based on television shows or comic books. Until the 1998 blockbuster *Titanic,* the biggest money making movies of all time—*E.T. The Extra-Terrestrial* (1982), the *Star Wars* films, the various *Indiana Jones* movies, *Ghostbusters, Jurassic Park,* and *Independence Day*—were all fantastic adventure films that appeal to younger people. The question asked by serious observers of the relationship between film and culture is whether the medium is increasingly dominated by the wants, tastes, and needs of what amounts to an audience of children. What becomes of film as an important medium, one with something to say, one that challenges people?

Industry defenders point to Steven Spielberg, a man with several of the 10 biggest box office hits in history to his credit. He is also the source of *The Color Purple* (1985), *Schindler's List* (1993), and *Saving Private Ryan* (1998). His blockbuster successes earn him the clout in Hollywood to make these important movies. Industry defenders additionally argue that the income generated by youth-oriented box office hits is available for financing and distributing small, important movies such as *Eve's Bayou* (1997), *In the Company of Men* (1997), and *The Ice Storm* (1997).

Here are film critic Jonathan Romney's (1997) comments in *The Guardian.*

> Hollywood in 1996 was truly represented by lumbering leviathans such as *Independence Day, Mission: Impossible,* and *Twister*—not movies so much as attrition campaigns pursued with relentless F/X power, and without a single enduring idea to distinguish them. . . . Look at the reality: While those three films topped US/Canada box office for 1996 (*Independence Day* chalking a cool $306 million), *The English Patient* grossed a mere $24 million, putting it in the mid-70s on the chart, while *Secrets and Lies* ($5 million) is around the 150 mark, three places above a delicacy called *Bordello of Blood.*
>
> So don't expect Hollywood to change its ways just yet. . . . In the boardroom, business goes on as usual. In 1997, that business involves sequels to *Jurassic Park, Alien, Home Alone,* and *Speed,* plus remakes of *Zorro, Godzilla, The Absent Minded Professor,* and one of the 1960s most conspicuous flops, *Dr. Doolittle.* There are two volcano epics imminent: one, *Dante's*

Peak, is a re-fry of the *Twister* formula, with ash and digital lava replacing flying cows. (p. 2)

Romney is obviously critical of contemporary Hollywood. A thoughtful reader, however, can see that he places blame on the audience as well. We return to some of the issues he raises in later sections of this chapter.

Scope and Nature of the Film Industry

Hollywood's record year of 1946 saw the sale of more than 4 billion tickets. Today, about 1 billion people will see a movie in a U.S. theater. Domestic box office in 1997 was $6.42 billion, a 13% increase over 1996. Twelve movies in 1996, including *The First Wives Club*, *The Birdcage*, *The Nutty Professor*, *Independence Day*, and *Twister*, exceeded $100 million at the box office (Romney, 1997).

THREE COMPONENT SYSTEMS

The movie business today enjoys significant financial health for two reasons. The first is improvements in its three component systems—production, distribution, and exhibition. The second, discussed in the next section, is that the movie industry has learned to live with television.

Production   Production is the making of movies. More than 500 feature length films are produced in the United States each year, a large increase over the early 1980s, when, for example, in 1985 288 features were produced. As we'll see later in this chapter, significant revenues from home video are one reason for the increase, as is growing conglomerate ownership that demands more product for more markets.

Technology, too, has affected production. Most Hollywood films are shot on videotape. In most cases this taping is done in conjunction with shooting the movie on film and is used as a form of immediate feedback for directors and cinematographers.

Another influence of technology can be seen in films such as *Twister* (1996), *Independence Day* (1996), *Lost World* (1997), and *Spawn* (1997). Digital filmmaking has made grand special effects not only possible but expected. Stunning special effects, of which *Titanic* (1997) is a fine example, can make a good movie an excellent one. The downside of computer-generated special effects is that they can greatly increase production costs. *Spawn*, for example, cost more than $40 million to make; *Titanic*, more than $200 million. In fact, the Motion Picture Association of America calculates that the cost of making a Hollywood feature film rose 148% between the years 1987 and 1997. Many film critics blame this increase for rises in ticket prices and a diminishing willingness to take creative chances in a big budget film.

Critics assailed *Titanic* for its weak story line and two-dimensional characters—the real stars of the highest grossing movie of all time were the special effects.

Distribution   Distribution was once as simple as making prints of films and sending them to theaters. Now it means supplying these movies to television networks, cable and satellite networks, and makers of videocassettes and videodiscs. The sheer scope of the distribution business ensures that large companies (most typically the big studios themselves) will dominate. In addition to making copies and guaranteeing their delivery, distributors now finance production and take responsibility for advertising and promotion and for setting and adjusting release dates. The advertising and promotion budget for a Hollywood feature usually equals 50% of the production costs. Spending $30 million to tout a Hollywood movie, for example, is not uncommon, and the investment is seen as worthwhile. *Mission: Impossible* returned $450 million in box office receipts in its first year of release, *Twister* $500 million, and *Independence Day*, $800 million.

Exhibition   There are currently about 22,800 movie screens in the United States. About 80% of theaters have two or more screens and average 340 seats in front of each. In the wake of the Reagan administration policy to deregulate the business, which undid the Paramount Decision in the 1980s, one half are now owned by a studio, a trend that is continuing. For example, in September of 1997 Sony, which already owned once-independent Lowes, Star Theaters, and Magic Johnson Theaters, merged with former independent giant Cineplex Odeon to form Lowes Cineplex Entertainment, the world's largest movie theater company. Screens not owned by a studio are typically part of large theater chains, for example, Syufy. Together, the seven largest chains, including studio-owned chains, control more than 80% of U.S. ticket sales.

It is no surprise to any moviegoer that exhibitors make much of their money on concession sales of items that typically have an 80% profit margin. This is why matinees and budget nights are attractive promotions for theaters. A low-priced ticket pays dividends in overpriced popcorn and Goobers.

THE STUDIOS

Studios are at the heart of the movie business and increasingly are regaining control of the three component systems of the industry. There are major, minimajor, and independent studios. The majors, who finance their films primarily through the profits of their own business, include Warner Brothers, Columbia, Paramount, 20th Century Fox, Universal, MGM/UA, and Disney. The minimajors include Polygram, TriStar, Cannon, Lorimar,

Spike Lee, here on the set of the 1989 *Do the Right Thing*, has repeatedly demonstrated that independent films can investigate important themes and take creative risks while at the same time entertaining audiences and earning solid revenues.

and Touchstone. These companies combine their own money with outside financing to make movies. Together the majors and minimajors account for 80% to 90% of annual U.S. movie revenue. Although the majors each produce 15 to 20 films of their own every year, one half to two thirds of the movies on U.S. theater screens come from the independents. The majors, however, finance much of the independent film companies' production and control distribution of their films, not only to domestic and foreign theaters but to television and home video as well.

Although independents provide the majority of our movies, they produce only about 10% of the box office revenue. Independent studios find the money to make their movies from outside sources. If they are successful, like Spike Lee (*Malcolm X*, 1992; *Jungle Fever*, 1991; *Crooklyn*, 1994) or Quentin Tarantino (*Pulp Fiction*, 1994; *Jackie Brown*, 1997), for example, much of that funding can come from the major studios. More often funding is obtained from a distribution company, bank, or other outside sources. Lee himself raised the entire $175,000 needed for the production of *She's Gotta Have It* (1986), a movie that eventually made $8 million at the box office. The story of how Robert Townsend financed *Hollywood Shuffle* (1987) with his savings account and credit cards is now Hollywood legend.

Independent films tend to have smaller budgets. Often this leads to much more imaginative filmmaking and more risk taking than the big studios are willing to do. The 1969 independent film *Easy Rider*, which cost $370,000 to produce and made over $50 million in theater rentals, began the modern independent film boom. *Pulp Fiction* cost $8 million to make and earned $210 million in box office receipts. Four of the five nominations for Best Picture Oscars in 1997 were independents: *The English Patient, Fargo, Shine*, and *Secrets and Lies*. Describing independent films, *Entertainment Weekly* Hollywood reporter Lisa Schwarzbaum (1997) said,

> At its simplest, an independent film can be defined as one made outside the Hollywood system. On the one hand this means there's no Paramount or Warner Bros. safety net to catch a falling director. On the other, it ensures that no pinhead business-school grad can reduce a director to nervous tics with notes about "third act problems." Independent films are not only independent of big publicity departments to help sell the wares, but they're also free from the kind of audience testing, second-guessing, and endemic messing around that so regularly make big-budget movies so safely *boring*. (pp. 8–9)

Current Trends in Moviemaking

Reporter Schwarzbaum's affection for independent films is shared by many contemporary film critics who see several trends—especially increased conglomeration and the influence of television—reshaping the film industry in ways not to their liking. Other critics, however, point to record box office figures as a sign of the economic and artistic health of this industry.

CONGLOMERATION AND THE BLOCKBUSTER MENTALITY

Each of the majors is a part of a large conglomerate. Paramount is owned by Viacom, 20th Century Fox is part of the Rupert Murdoch collection of companies, Warner Brothers is part of the huge Time Warner/Turner merger discussed in Chapter 1, and Disney is now part of the giant conglomerate formed in the 1996 Disney/Capital Cities/ABC union. Much of this conglomeration takes the form of international ownership. Japanese company Matsushita owns Universal Pictures and its parent company MCA Entertainment. MGM/UA is owned by an Italian company, Columbia by Japanese Sony, and Fox by Murdoch's Australian company. According to many critics, this combination of conglomeration and foreign ownership forces the industry into a **blockbuster mentality**—filmmaking characterized by reduced risk taking and more formulaic movies. Business concerns are said to dominate artistic considerations as accountants and financiers make more and more of the decisions once made by creative people. The common outcomes of this blockbuster mentality are several.

Concept Movies The marketing and publicity departments of big companies love **concept films**—movies that can be described in one line. *Twister* is about a giant, rogue tornado. *The Lost World* is about giant, rogue dinosaurs. *Space Jam* (1996) is Michael Jordan and Warner Brothers cartoons.

Independent films dominated the 1997 Academy Awards, with *Fargo* taking the Oscar for Best Actress and Best Original Screenplay.

International ownership and international distribution contribute to this phenomenon. High concept films that depend little on characterization, plot development, and dialogue are easier to sell to foreign exhibitors than are more sophisticated films. *Twister* and *Jurassic Park* play well everywhere. Big name stars also have international appeal. That's why they can command huge salaries. The importance of foreign distribution cannot be overstated. Only 2 in 10 U.S. features make a profit on U.S. box office. Much of their eventual profit comes from overseas sales. Kevin Costner's *Waterworld* (1995), for example, pulled in only $88 million domestically but made another $175 million overseas. Sharon Stone's *Sliver* (1993) grossed $36 million at home but $78 million abroad. Sylvester Stallone's *Daylight* (1996) cost $80 million to make and returned only $33 million domestically. Yet international rentals brought in $111 million. More than 32% of the income from the exhibition of U.S. movies comes from abroad.

Audience Research Before a movie is made, its concept, plot, and characters are subjected to market testing. Often multiple endings are produced and tested with sample audiences by companies such as National Research Group and Marketcast. New scenes of Michael Keaton's *Beetlejuice* (1988) were shot and the story line was altered in response to research on teen audiences. The question raised by film purists is what has become of the filmmaker's genius? What separates these market-tested films from any other commodity?

Sequels and Remakes Nothing succeeds like success. How many *Mighty Ducks* have there been? *Sister Acts? Die Hards? Lethal Weapons? Aliens? Beverly Hills Cops?* Jerry Lewis's 1963 *The Nutty Professor* was reborn as Eddie Murphy's 1996 *The Nutty Professor.* Disney remade its own *101 Dalmatians. Sleepless in Seattle* (1993) is a remake of *An Affair to Remember* (1957), a movie it uses as part of its own plot. The 1997 rerelease of the 20-year-old *Star Wars* trilogy is a sequel of a series of sequels and is seen by some critics as representing the ultimate failure of contemporary Hollywood, a view that is challenged by other observers (see the box "The Rerelease of *Star Wars:* Sign of Success or Symptom of Failure?").

Television and Comic Book Remakes Nothing succeeds like success. That, and the fact that teens and preteens make up the largest proportion of the movie audience, is why so many movies are adaptations of television shows and comic books. In the last few years *The Beverly Hillbillies, The Munsters, The Flintstones, The Shadow, The Fugitive, The Saint, Mission: Impossible, George of the Jungle, Leave It to Beaver, Lost in Space* (and its sequel), *Sgt. Bilko, Beavis and Butt-head, McHale's Navy, Mr. Magoo, The Brady Bunch, Dragnet,* and *Wayne's World* have moved from small to big screen. *The Addams Family, Dennis the Menace, Richie Rich, Batman,* and *Superman* have traveled from the comics, through television, to the silver screen. *Tank Girl, Barb Wire, Spawn, X Men, Men in Black, Kull the Conqueror, Steel,* and *The Crow* have moved directly from comics to movies. Movies from comics are especially attractive to studios because of their built-in merchandise tie-in appeal.

Merchandise Tie-Ins   Films are sometimes produced as much for their ability to generate interest for nonfilm products as for their intrinsic value as movies. *Star Wars* remained a merchandising gold mine even before its 1997 rerelease. *Jurassic Park* (1993) and its sequel *The Lost World* generated millions of dollars in sales of plastic dinosaurs and other items. Studios often believe that it is riskier to make a $7 million film with no merchandising potential than a $100 million movie with greater merchandising appeal.

Product Placement   Many movies are serving double duty as commercials. We'll discuss this phenomenon in detail later in the chapter as a media literacy issue.

LIVING WITH TELEVISION

So intertwined are today's movie and television industries that it is often meaningless to discuss them separately. As much as 70% of the production done by the studios is for television, Paramount's various *Star Trek* series and Fox's entire television network being two prime examples. But the growing relationship between **theatrical films**—those produced originally for theater exhibition—and television is the result of technological changes in the latter. Satellite, cable, pay-per-view, videodisc, digital videodisc (DVD), and videocassette have provided immense distribution and exhibition opportunities for the movies. Nineteen percent of studio revenues come from domestic VCR, cable, and satellite rentals alone. Today's distributors make only one third of their income from rentals to movie houses. Home video accounts for 43%, various television outlets another 23%. Video sales (to individuals and tape rental stores) are a lucrative business as well. While still earning box office income in theaters, *Independence Day* was being offered for sale on tape for $22.98. The studios maximize their tape profits with trailers for their other video and in-theater films and with commercials. Box office failures can turn loss to profit with good video sales. *Striptease* (1996), *Showgirls* (1995), *Cotton Club* (1984), and *Dune* (1984) all became profitable in this fashion.

DEVELOPING MEDIA LITERACY SKILLS
Recognizing Product Placements

The Nokia personal communicator is one of the stars of the 1997 *The Saint*. The BMW Z3 is featured in *GoldenEye* (1996). Etch-a-Sketch boosted annual sales from 2.5 million units in 1994 to 3.5 million units

The Rerelease of *Star Wars:* Sign of Success or Symptom of Failure?

In the mid-1970s, Universal and United Artists both rejected George Lucas's script for *Star Wars* as "uncommercial." Before the 1997 rerelease of the 20-year-old blockbuster and its two sequels, *The Empire Strikes Back* (1980) and *Return of the Jedi* (1983), these films were already among the top 10 box office hits of all time. How successful were they?

- George Lucas is the second most profitable moviemaker in history based on the initial release of these three movies alone.

- *Star Wars* alone originally grossed $323 million worldwide, the trilogy $1.3 billion.

- In 1996, the year before the rerelease of the trilogy, *Star Wars* action figures were the second biggest selling toy in the world after Barbie. Licensing rights to *Star Wars* have brought in more than $4 billion.

- The average American has seen the original *Star Wars* seven times.

- *The Return of the Jedi,* which cost $32.5 million to make in 1983, earned $45,311,004 in its first week of release, representing a $13 million profit in seven days. The movie also set a single day record of $8,440,105 on its opening Sunday.

How successful were the rereleased movies?

- The rereleased *Star Wars* took in $37.3 million in its first weekend.

- Within one week of *Empire's* rerelease, it and *Star Wars* were atop the box office chart, the first time in history that a movie and its sequel were numbers 1 and 2.

- The original and rereleased movies have grossed $11.5 billion worldwide.

With its huge success, *Star Wars* became the focus of debate in the cultural forum. Observers critical of the rerelease saw a Hollywood so devoid of anything to say that it was now in the business of repackaging and remarketing what it was saying 20 years before. Additional criticism came not from the fact of the rerelease per se but of *Star Wars* itself. *Star Wars* may not have been the best movie ever made, but it may have been the most important movie ever made because of how its success changed Hollywood. Many critics saw the release of the original, in the words of writer David Gritten, as "the day the rot set in." According to this view, *Star Wars:*

- Started the industry trend of domination by big action, special effects, summer mega-hit releases

- Turned the youth audience into Hollywood's prime market

- Established the blockbuster as the true measure of a studio's success; "small" movies were no longer made by the studios

- Set first-week grosses as the measure for success; a slow first week means fewer additional screens; movies no longer have time to develop a following; therefore, complex, interesting films don't get made

- Made movies with strong product tie-in potential the industry's Holy Grail

- Turned film from a medium of expression into an event

Film critic Quentin Curtis (1997) summed up the complaints in his review of the rereleased *Star Wars* for the *Daily Telegraph:*

in 1995 through its placement in *Toy Story.* James Bond in *Tomorrow Never Dies* (1997) uses an Ericson mobile phone, checks the time on a Seamaster Omega watch, wears a Brioni tuxedo, drives a BMW 750iL sedan and a BMW motorcycle, flies American Airlines, drinks Smirnoff vodka, rents a car from Avis with his Visa credit card, and watches a Heineken beer truck explode—all for a fee.

The practice of placing brand name products in movies is not new; Katharine Hepburn throws Gordon's gin into the river in the 1951 *The*

Star Wars

Like many of the most evil influences, George Lucas' *Star Wars* isn't of itself wholly bad. Released now in a "special edition" 20 years after it first came out, the movie has virtues that shine as brilliantly as its reworked special effects—its darting neon lasers and light-sabers—as well as its vices as black as Darth Vader's cape. You only have to remember the context of *Star Wars*'s release—a Hollywood capable of producing such serious fare as *Chinatown* (1974) and *Taxi Driver* (1976)—to measure the damage. With its thin characters, thick coating of special effects and vast marketing operation, *Star Wars* paved the way for today's wall-to-wall blockbusters. (p. 26)

The alternate view is that *Star Wars*, its sequels, and the rerelease proved to Hollywood that it was able to meet audience wants and needs while still producing a profit. Maybe the critics want movies to be something different from those preferred by the vast number of moviegoers. Enter your voice in the forum. How would you answer critics like Curtis on the value of *Star Wars*?

African Queen, and Spencer Tracy is splashed with Coca-Cola in the 1950 *Father of the Bride.* But in today's movie industry product placement has expanded into a business in its own right. In 1997 there were 92 product placement agencies operating in Hollywood, and even an industry association, the Entertainment Resources and Marketing Association (ERMA). The attraction of product placements for sponsors is obvious. For one flat fee paid up front, a product that appears in a movie is in actuality a commercial that lives forever—first on the big screen, then on television and

Product placement carries over from the big screen to other media. JVC's DMV1 video camera played a prominent role in the movie *The Lost World,* enabling the company to use that movie publicity as the basis for its advertising in print.

cable, and then on purchased and rented videotapes and discs. The commercial is also likely to have worldwide distribution.

Many people in and outside the movie industry see product placement as inherently deceptive. "Why not identify the ads for what they are?" they ask. From a media literacy standpoint, the issue is the degree to which artistic decisions are being placed second to obligations to sponsors. Film critic Glenn Lovell (1997) wrote, "Scripts are being doctored and camera angles changed to accommodate manufacturers paying for props or promotional campaigns. It's a classic case of the tail wagging the dog" (p. 7G). David Peoples, the screenwriter for *Blade Runner,* a cinematic testimonial to product placement, calls the practice a "racket . . . a horrifying compromise" (p. 7G). A "hot" Hollywood director who asked critic Lovell not to use his name said, "I've worked with producers who would sell their soul to get a major placement. I say, 'Forget it.' If movie stars want to do commercials, they should do them, and get paid" (p. 7G). One famous example of a sponsor dictating content is Reebok's lawsuit against Sony's TriStar Pictures. The shoe maker was angry that a mock ad for its product did not appear in the 1996 hit *Jerry Maguire,* as originally called for in the script. The producers said that the film-ending spot did not test well with audiences and was cut for "creative reasons." But rather than fight the suit, TriStar settled out of court, agreeing that all subsequent television and video versions of the movie would carry the excised footage.

Knowing how media content is funded and how that financial support shapes content is an important aspect of understanding the mass communication process. Therefore, an awareness of the efforts of the movie industry to maximize income from their films is central to good film literacy.

Consider, for example, the following product placements. If you saw these movies, did you recognize the placements?

Apple PowerBooks in *Mission: Impossible*

Kawasaki Motorcycles in *Spawn*

Marlboros in *My Best Friend's Wedding*

Ray Bans in *Men in Black*

UPS in *A Time to Kill*

Taco Bell in *Batman & Robin*

Dunkin' Donuts in *Good Will Hunting*

Nissan, Sony, Casio PhoneMate, Fisher-Price, and Ford in *Home Alone 3*

Dr. Pepper in *Forrest Gump*

Does it trouble you that content is altered, even if sometimes only minimally, to allow for these brand identifications? To what extent would script alterations have to occur to accommodate paid-for messages before you find them intrusive? Do you think it is fair or honest for a moviemaker who promises you film content in exchange for your money to turn you into what amounts to a television viewer by advertising sponsors' products? At least in television, by law, all commercial messages must be identified as such, and the sponsors of those messages must be identified. Do you think such a rule ought to apply to movies?

Literate film consumers may answer these questions differently, especially as individuals hold film in varying degrees of esteem—but they should answer them.

Chapter Review

The movies were developed by entrepreneurs, people seeking to earn profits by entertaining audiences. Among the first to make a movie was Eadweard Muybridge, whose sequential action photographs inspired Edison laboratory scientist William Dickson to develop a better filming system, the kinetograph. The next advance came from the Lumière brothers, whose cinematographe allowed projection of movies. Another Frenchman, Georges Méliès, brought narrative to movies, and the medium's storytelling abilities were heightened by Americans Edwin S. Porter and D. W. Griffith.

Film soon became a large, studio controlled business on the west coast, where it had moved to take advantage of good weather and to escape the control of the Motion Picture Patents Company. The industry's growth was a product of changes in the U.S. population, political turmoil overseas, the introduction of sound, and the development of new, audience pleasing genres.

After World War II the industry underwent major changes due to the loss of audience to television, the red scare, and the Paramount Decision. The industry was forced to remake itself. At first Hollywood resisted television, but soon studios learned that television could be a profitable partner. Today, the major studios are responsible for much of the film industry's production and distribution. They are also involved in exhibition.

The modern film industry is experiencing the same trend toward conglomeration and internationalization as are other media, and content is influenced by that fact. A blockbuster mentality leads to reliance on concept films, audience research, sequels and remakes, movies based on comic books and television shows, merchandise tie-ins, and product placements. Profits are additionally boosted by overseas distribution and sales to other media such as videocassettes, videodiscs, DVD, satellite, pay-per-view, and television.

The audience for the movies is increasingly a young one, and movie content reflects this reality. Many observers fear that the traditional, elevated role movies have played in our culture is in danger as a result. The same pressures for profit that raise this fear also lead to the potentially misleading practice of product placement and, therefore, to the increased importance of media literacy.

Questions for Review

1. What is the significance of these people to film history? Leland Stanford, Eadweard Muybridge, William Dickson, the Lumière brothers, Louis Daguerre, Joseph Niépce, William Henry Fox Talbot, Hannibal Goodwin, George Eastman.
2. What are the kinetograph, kinetoscope, cinematographe, daguerreotype, calotype, and nickelodeon?
3. What were Méliès's, Porter's, and Griffith's contributions to film as a narrative medium?
4. What was the Motion Picture Patents Company, and how did it influence the content and development of the movie industry?
5. What societal, technical, and artistic factors shaped the development of movies before World War II?
6. How did Hollywood scandals and the red scare shape the medium's content?
7. What is vertical integration? How was it ended and reinstated?
8. What are the three component systems of the movie industry?
9. What are major and minimajor studios? What is an independent?
10. What are concept films? product tie-ins? product placement?

Questions for Critical Thinking and Discussion

1. How do you think the entrepreneurial motivation of the early movie pioneers shaped the relationship of the medium with its audience?
2. Hollywood was an open propaganda agent for the military during World War II. Do you think a mass medium should serve a government in this way? Why, or why not?
3. Hollywood suffered under strict content control and now has shed those restrictions. What restrictions do you think are reasonable for the movies? Why?
4. What do you think of the impact of the blockbuster mentality on movies? Should profit always be the determining factor in producing movie content? Why, or why not?
5. Do you agree with critics like Romney that Hollywood movies are getting less interesting? Do you agree with his argument that Hollywood is simply going where the money is; that is, that the audience plays a role in the quality of that performance?

Important Resources

Balio, T. (1979). *The American film industry.* Madison, WI: University of Wisconsin Press. The classic history of the film industry through World War II and the coming of television.

Ceplair, L., & Englund, S. (1980). *The inquisition in Hollywood: Politics in the film community.* New York: Doubleday. A look at the red scare's corrosive influence on Hollywood, on both the personal and the professional levels.

Cineaste. A quarterly calling itself "America's magazine for the art and aesthetics of the cinema," its pages focus on film criticism and theory. It offers reviews, interviews, and essays on contemporary issues of film narrative and look.

Film Comment. Published by the Film Society of Lincoln Center, this bimonthly features essays, reviews, and commentary on contemporary movies as well as essays on film theory and criticism. It also covers many of the world's important film festivals.

Film Culture. Calling itself "America's independent motion picture magazine," this magazine is published "irregularly." When it does come out, it frequently devotes all or a large part of an issue to articles and essays on one topic, following them with an in-print debate by appropriate filmmakers and critics.

Film Quarterly. For readers serious about film, this magazine specializes in interviews, history, and aesthetic theory. It also presents well-informed reviews of books about film.

Gomery, D. (1986). *The Hollywood studio system.* **New York: St. Martin's Press.** An analysis of the workings and power of the studio system, written for a general readership; entertaining as well as instructive.

Sklar, R. (1994). *Movie-made America: A cultural history of American movies.* **New York: Vintage Books.** Considered the authoritative history of the social and cultural impact of movies since its first edition in 1974, this book is readable but intellectually challenging. It has long earned rave reviews from popular as well as scholarly critics.

Film Information Web Sites

The Cult Film Site	*http://sepnet.com/rcramer/index.htm*
Cyberflicks	*http://www.cyberflicks.com/links.htm*
Entertainment Network News at the Movies	*http://www.enn2.com/movies.htm*
HollywoodNet	*http://hollywoodshopping.com/*
Hollywood Online	*http://www.hollywood.com/*
Hollywood Reporter	*http://www.hollywoodreporter.com*
Internet Movie Database	*http://www.imdb.com*
Motion Picture Association of America Home Page	*http://www.mpaa.org/mpaa.html*
MovieWeb	*http://movieweb.com*

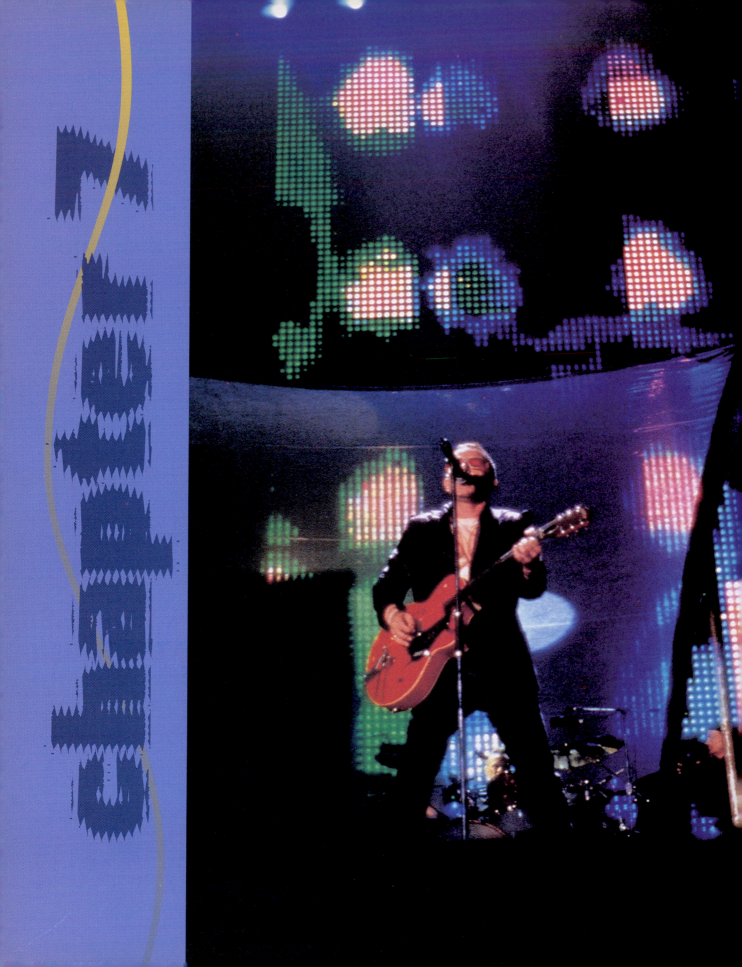

Radio and Sound Recording

"Can we listen to the radio?"

"We are listening to the radio."

"I mean something other than this."

"You want music?"

"Yes, please, anything but public radio. Too much talk."

"OK. Here."

"What! That's the classical music station!"

"What's wrong with that?"

"Nothing . . . much."

"What's that supposed to mean, 'Nothing . . . much?'"

"Nothing . . . much. Let me choose."

"OK. You find a station."

"Fine. Here."

"What's that?!"

"It's the New Hot One. KISS 100. All the hits all the time."

"That's not music."

"You sound like my parents."

"I don't mean the stuff they play isn't music, I mean the deejay is yammering away."

"Hang on. A song is coming up. Anyway, this is funny stuff."

"I don't find jokes about minority wheelchair races funny."

"It's all in fun."

"Fun for whom?"

"What's *your* problem today?"

"Nothing, I just don't find that kind of stuff funny. Here, I'll find something."

"What's that?"

"The jazz station."

"Give me a break. How about sports talk?"

"Nah. How about all news?"

"No way. How about the all talk station?"

"Why, you need another fix of insulting chatter?"

"How about silence?"

"Yeah, how about it?"

In this chapter we study the technical and social beginnings of both radio and sound recording. We revisit the coming of broadcasting and see how the growth of regulatory, economic, and organizational structures led to the medium's golden age.

The heart of the chapter covers how television changed radio and produced the medium with which we are now familiar. We review the scope and nature of contemporary radio, especially its rebirth as a local, fragmented, specialized, personal, and mobile medium. We examine how these characteristics serve advertisers and listeners. The chapter then explores the relationship between radio and the modern recording industry and the way new technologies serve and challenge both media. The popularity of shock jocks inspires our discussion of media literacy.

A Short History of Radio and Sound Recording

The particular stations you disagree about may be different, but almost all of us have been through a conversation like the one in the opening vignette. Radio, the seemingly ubiquitous medium, matters to us. Because we often listen to it alone, it is personal. Radio is also mobile. It travels with us in the car, and we take it along in our Walkman. Radio is specific as well. Stations aim their content at very narrowly defined audiences. But these are characteristics of contemporary radio. Radio once occupied a very different place in our culture. Let's see how it all began.

PREHISTORY OF RADIO

The roots of radio can be found in science and technology. Radio pioneers were more interested in the physics of sound and electrical waves than in mass communication. Toward the end of the 1800s, innovators throughout the world were experimenting with the possibility of a **wireless telegraph** and **wireless telephony.** In 1844 the American inventor Samuel Morse had introduced the telegraph, which made long-distance communication a reality. Telegraph messages were composed of electrical impulses—dots and dashes—and were carried on wires strung from poles. The challenge was then to produce long-distance communication *without* wires, and to do it with voices instead of impulses. Alexander Graham Bell exhibited his new invention, the telephone, at the Philadelphia Centennial Exhibition in 1876. Bell, a teacher of the deaf whose original goal had been to develop an effective hearing aid, demonstrated that voices could be transmitted. Now the race was on for wireless long-distance communication.

Many different wireless systems were tried. Mahlon Loomis received the first U.S. patent for the wireless in 1872. He sent signals through water and ground. This **conduction system** was ultimately too limiting and, like Nathan Stubblefield and other early technicians and tinkerers who saw conduction as the secret to wireless, Loomis has become a historical footnote. What was needed was a system that would allow signals to be reliably sent and received through the air, a **radiation system.**

Scottish physicist and mathematician James Clerk Maxwell predicted that radio waves existed, demonstrating with published equations in 1864 that a radiation system was possible using electromagnetically sent signals. In 1887 German physicist Heinrich Hertz demonstrated that Maxwell's equations were correct. He sent and received wireless signals over short distances in his laboratory. In the early 1890s, French physicist Édouard Branly developed a much improved receiver, and before the decade ended, English physicist Sir Oliver Lodge perfected the principle of tuning, allowing the transmitter and the receiver to operate on the same wavelength.

The "Father of Radio," Guglielmo Marconi, son of a wealthy Italian diplomat and his Irish wife, read the scientific reports associated with these developments. Unlike earlier pioneers, however, Marconi was interested not in the theory of sending signals through the air but in actually doing it. His improvements over earlier experimental designs allowed him to send and receive telegraph code over distances as great as 2 miles by 1896. His native Italy was not interested in his invention, so he used his mother's contacts in Great Britain to find support and financing there. England, with a global empire and the world's largest navy and merchant fleets, was naturally interested in long-distance wireless communication. With the financial and technical help of the British, Marconi successfully transmitted across the English Channel in 1899 and across the Atlantic in 1901. Wireless was now a reality. Marconi was satisfied with his advance, but other scientists saw the transmission of *voices* by wireless as the next hurdle, a challenge that was soon surmounted.

In 1903 Reginald Fessenden, a Canadian, invented the **liquid barretter,** the first audio device permitting reception of wireless voices. His 1906 Christmas Eve broadcast from Brant Rock, a small New England coastal village, was the first public broadcast of voices and music. His listeners were ships at sea and a few newspaper offices equipped to receive the transmission.

Later that same year American Lee DeForest invented the **audion tube,** a vacuum tube that improved and amplified wireless signals. Now the reliable transmission of clear voices and music was a reality. But

Guglielmo Marconi

DeForest's second important contribution was that he saw radio as a means of *broadcasting*. The early pioneers, Marconi included, had viewed radio as a device for point-to-point communication, for example, from ship to ship or ship to shore. But in the 1907 prospectus for his radio company DeForest wrote, "It will soon be possible to distribute grand opera music from transmitters placed on the stage of the Metropolitan Opera House by a Radio Telephone station on the roof to almost any dwelling in Greater New York and vicinity. . . . The same applies to large cities. Church music, lectures, etc., can be spread abroad by the Radio Telephone" (Adams, 1996, pp. 104–106). Soon, countless "broadcasters" went on the air. Some broadcasters were giant corporations, looking to dominate the medium for profit; some were hobbyists and hams, playing with the medium for the sheer joy of it. There were so many "stations" that havoc reigned. Yet the promise of radio was such that the medium continued to mature until World War I, when the government ordered "the immediate closing of all stations for radio communications, both transmitting and receiving."

EARLY SOUND RECORDING

The 1870s also saw the beginning of sound recording. In 1877 prolific inventor Thomas Edison patented his "talking machine," a device for duplicating sound that used a hand-cranked grooved cylinder and a needle. The mechanical movement caused by the needle passing along

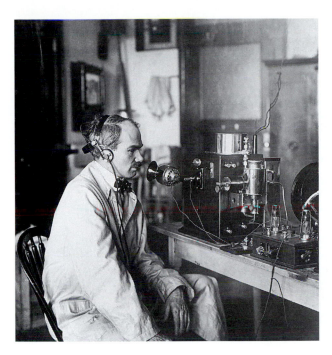

Lee DeForest

the groove of the rotating cylinder and hitting bumps was converted into electrical energy that activated a diaphragm in a loudspeaker and produced sound. The drawback was that only one "recording" could be made of any given sound; the cylinder could not be duplicated. In 1887 that problem was solved by German immigrant Emile Berliner, whose gramophone used a flat, rotating, wax-coated disc that could easily be copied or pressed from a metal master. Two equally important contributions to recording made by Berliner were development of a sophisticated microphone and (through his company, RCA Victor Records) the import from Europe of recordings by famous opera stars. Now people had not only a reasonably priced record player but records to play on it. The next advance was introduction of the two-sided disc by the Columbia Phonograph Company in 1905. Soon there were hundreds of phonograph or gramophone companies, and the device, by either name, was a standard feature in U.S. homes by 1920. More than 2 million machines and 107 million recordings were sold in 1919 alone. Public acceptance of the new medium was enhanced even more by development of electromagnetic recording in 1924 by Joseph P. Maxwell at Bell Laboratory.

The parallel development and diffusion of radio and sound recording is significant. For the first time in history radio allowed people to hear the words and music of others who were not in their presence. On recordings they could hear words and music that may have been created days, months, or even years before.

In 1887 Emile Berliner developed the flat disc gramophone and a sophisticated microphone, both important to the widespread public acceptance of sound recordings for the home. Nipper, the trademark for his company, RCA Victor, is on the scene even today.

THE COMING OF BROADCASTING

The idea of broadcasting—that is, transmitting voices and music at great distances to a large number of people—predated the development of radio. Alexander Graham Bell's telephone company had a subscription music service in major cities in the late 1800s, delivering music to homes and businesses by telephone wires. A front-page story in an 1877 edition of the *New York Daily Graphic* suggested the possibilities of broadcasting to its readers. The public anticipated and, after DeForest's much publicized successes, was eager for music and voices at home. Russian immigrant David Sarnoff, then an employee of American Marconi, recognized this desire and in 1916 sent his superiors what has become famous as the "Radio Music Box Memo." In this memo Sarnoff wrote of

> a plan of development which would make radio a "household utility" in the same sense as the piano or phonograph. The idea is to bring music into the house by wireless. . . . The receiver can be designed in the form of a simple "Radio Music Box" and arranged for several different wavelengths, which should be changeable with the throwing of a single switch or pressing of a single button. (Sterling & Kitross, 1990, p. 43)

The introduction of broadcasting to a mass audience was delayed in the first two decades of the 20th century by patent fights and lawsuits. DeForest and Fessenden were both destroyed financially by the conflict. Yet when World War I ended, an enthusiastic audience awaited what had become a much improved medium. In a series of developments that would be duplicated for television at the time of World War II, radio was trans-

This cover of an 1877 newspaper proved prophetic in its image of speakers' ability to "broadcast" their words.

formed from an exciting technological idea into an entertainment and commercial giant. To aid the war effort, the government took over the patents relating to radio and continued to improve radio for military use. Thus, refinement and development of the technical aspects of radio continued throughout the war. Then, when the war ended in 1919, the patents were returned to their owners—the bickering was renewed.

Concerned that the medium would be wasted and fearful that a foreign company (British Marconi) would control this vital resource, the government forced the combatants to merge. American Marconi, General Electric, American Telephone & Telegraph, and Westinghouse (in 1921)—each in control of a vital piece of technology—joined to create the Radio Corporation of America (RCA). RCA was a government-sanctioned monopoly, but its creation avoided direct government control of the new medium. Twenty-eight-year-old David Sarnoff, author of the Radio Music Box Memo, was made RCA's commercial manager. The way for the medium's popular growth was paved; its success was guaranteed by a public that, because of the phonograph, was already attuned to music in the home and, thanks to the just concluded war, was awakening to the need for instant, wide-ranging news and information.

On September 30, 1920, a Westinghouse executive, impressed with press accounts of the number of listeners who were picking up broadcasts

The wireless-telegraphy room of the *Titanic*. Despite the heroic efforts of wireless operator Jack Philips, scores of people died needlessly in the sinking of that great ocean liner because the ships in its vicinity did not man their receivers.

from the garage radio station of their engineer Frank Conrad, asked him to move his operation to the Westinghouse factory and expand its power. Conrad did so, and on October 27, 1920, experimental station 8XK in Pittsburgh, Pennsylvania, received the first commercial radio license to broadcast. On November 2 this station, KDKA, made the first commercial radio broadcast, announcing the results of the presidential election that sent Warren G. Harding to the White House.

REGULATION

As the RCA agreements demonstrated, the government had a keen interest in the development, operation, and diffusion of radio. At first government interest focused on point-to-point communication. In 1909 almost all the passengers on the wireless-equipped *Republic* were saved as the ship sank off the east coast of the United States. The vessel had used its radio to call for help from nearby ships. Soon after, Congress passed the Wireless Ship Act of 1910, requiring that all ships using U.S. ports and carrying more than 50 passengers have a working wireless and operator. Of course, the wireless industry did not object, as the legislation boosted sales. After the *Titanic* struck an iceberg in the North Atlantic in 1912 and it was learned that hundreds of lives were lost needlessly because many ships in the area had left their radios unattended, Congress passed the Radio Act of 1912, which not only strengthened the rules regarding shipboard wireless but also required that wireless operators be licensed by the Secretary of Commerce and Labor.

The Radio Act of 1912 established spheres of authority for federal and state governments, provided for allocating and revoking licenses and fining violators, assigned frequencies for operation, and set the hours during which a station was authorized to broadcast. The government was in the business of regulating what was to become broadcasting.

The 1910 Act had boosted sales. But the 1912 Act imposed control, and many broadcasters objected. Two legal challenges to government regulatory authority eventually followed, *Hoover v. Intercity Radio Co., Inc.* in 1923 and *U.S. v. Zenith Radio Corp. et al.* in 1926. The broadcasters won both, effectively negating the federal government's power to license. President Calvin Coolidge ordered the cessation of government regulation of radio despite his belief that chaos would descend on the medium.

Coolidge proved prophetic. The industry's years of flouting the 1912 Act had led it to the brink of disaster. Radio sales and profits dropped dramatically. Listeners were tired of the chaos. Stations arbitrarily changed frequencies, power, and hours of operation, and there was constant interference between stations, which was often intentional. Radio industry leaders petitioned Commerce Commissioner Herbert Hoover and, according to historian Erik Barnouw (1966)—who titled his book on radio's early days *A Tower of Babel*—"encouraged firmness" in government efforts to regulate and control the competitors. The government's response was a series of four National Radio Conferences involving industry experts, public officials, and government regulators. These conferences produced the Radio Act of 1927. Order was restored, and the industry prospered. But the broadcasters had made an important concession to secure this saving intervention. The 1927 Act authorized them to *use* the channels, which belonged to the public, but not to *own* them. Broadcasters were thus simply the caretakers of the airwaves, a national resource.

The Act further stated that when a license was awarded the standard of evaluation would be the *public interest, convenience, or necessity*. The Federal Radio Commission (FRC) was established to administer the provisions of the Act. This **trustee model** of regulation is based on two premises (Bittner, 1994). The first is the philosophy of **spectrum scarcity.** Because broadcast spectrum space is limited and not everyone who wants to broadcast can, those who are granted licenses to serve a local area must accept regulation. The second reason for regulation revolves around the issue of influence. Broadcasting reaches virtually everyone in society. By definition, this ensures its power.

The Federal Communications Act of 1934 replaced the 1927 legislation, substituting the Federal Communications Commission (FCC) for the FRC and cementing its regulatory authority, which continues today.

ADVERTISING AND THE NETWORKS

While the regulatory structure of the medium was evolving, so were its financial bases. The formation of RCA had ensured that radio would be a commercial, profit-based system. The industry supported itself through the sale of receivers; that is, it operated radio stations in order to sell radios. The problem was that once everybody had a radio, people would stop buying them. The solution was advertising. On August 22, 1922, New York station WEAF accepted the first radio commercial, a 10-minute spot for Long Island brownstone apartments. The cost was $50.

The sale of advertising led to establishment of the national radio networks. Groups of stations, or **affiliates,** could deliver larger audiences, realizing greater advertising revenues, which would allow them to hire bigger stars and produce better programming, which would attract larger audiences, which could be sold for even greater fees to advertisers. RCA set up a 24-station network, the National Broadcasting Company (NBC), in 1926. A year later it bought AT&T's stations and launched a second network, NBC Blue (the original NBC was renamed NBC Red). The Columbia Broadcasting System (CBS) was also founded in 1927, but it struggled until 26-year-old millionaire cigar maker William S. Paley bought it in 1928, making it a worthy competitor to NBC. The fourth network, Mutual, was established in 1934 largely on the strength of its hit western, *The Lone Ranger.* Four midwestern and eastern stations came together to sell advertising on it and other shows; soon Mutual had 60 affiliates. Mutual differed from the other major national networks in that it did not own and operate its own flagship stations (called **O&O**s, for owned and operated). By 1938 the four national networks had affiliated virtually all the large U.S. stations and the majority of smaller operations as well. These corporations grew so powerful that in 1943 the government forced NBC to divest itself of one of its networks. It sold NBC Blue to Life Saver candy maker Edward Noble, who renamed it the American Broadcasting Company (ABC).

The fundamental basis of broadcasting in the United States was set:

- Radio broadcasters were private, commercially owned enterprises, rather than government operations.
- Governmental regulation was based on the public interest.
- Stations were licensed locally but programmed by national networks.
- Entertainment and information were the basic broadcast content.
- Advertising formed the basis of financial support for broadcasting.

THE GOLDEN AGE

The networks ushered in radio's golden age. Although the 1929–1939 Great Depression damaged the phonograph industry, with sales dipping to as few as 6 million records in 1932, it helped boost radio. Phonographs and records cost money, but once a family bought a radio, a whole world of entertainment and information was at their disposal, free of charge. The number of homes with radios grew from 12 million in 1930 to 30 million in 1940, and half of them had not one but two receivers. Ad revenues rose from $40 million to $155 million over the same period. Between them, the four national networks broadcast 156 hours of network-originated programming a week. New genres became fixtures during this period: comedy *(The Jack Benny Show, Fibber McGee and Molly),* audience participation *(Professor Quiz, Truth or Consequences, Kay Kyser's Kollege of Musical*

Knowledge), children's shows *(Little Orphan Annie, The Lone Ranger)*, soap operas *(Oxydol's Ma Perkins, The Guiding Light)*, and drama (Orson Welles's *Mercury Theater of the Air*). News, too, became a radio staple. Prior to the 1933 **Biltmore agreement,** newspapers, fearing competition from the powerful new medium, refused to make their stories available to radio stations, and many would not carry radio schedules. The Biltmore agreement settled the war, limiting radio to brief news reports at specific, limited times of the day, ensuring the dominance of newspapers as a journalistic medium. Still, news had come to the airwaves.

Radio and Sound Recording in World War II   The golden age of radio shone even more brightly after Pearl Harbor was bombed by the Japanese in 1941, propelling the United States into World War II. Radio was used to sell war bonds, and much content was aimed at boosting the nation's morale (see the box "Radio Goes to War"). The war increased the desire for news, especially from abroad. At the same time the war caused a paper shortage, reducing advertising space in newspapers. No new stations were licensed during the war years, and the 950 existing broadcasters reaped all the broadcast advertising revenues as well as additional ad revenues that otherwise would have gone to newspapers. Ad revenues were up to $310 million by the end of World War II in 1945.

Sound recording benefited during the war as well. Prior to World War II, recording in the United States was done either directly to master metal disc or on wire recorders, literally magnetic recording on metal wire. But GIs brought a new technology back from occupied Germany, a

Indicative of radio's golden age is Harold Huber, here in 1947 portraying Agatha Christie's master detective, Hercule Poirot, in CBS' *Mystery of the Week.*

tape recorder that used an easily handled plastic tape on a reel. In 1947, Columbia Records introduced a new 33⅓ rpm (rotations-per-minute) long-playing plastic record perfected by Peter Goldmark. A big advance over the previous standard of 78 rpm, it was more durable than the older shellac discs and played for 23 rather than 3½ minutes. Columbia offered the technology free to all other record companies. RCA refused the offer, introducing its own 45 rpm disc in 1948. It played for only 3⅓ minutes and had a huge center hole requiring a special adapter. Still, RCA persisted in its marketing, causing a speed war that was settled in 1950 when the two

Using Media to Make a *Difference

Radio Goes to War

Radio in the 1940s was what television is today—the nation's primary in-home medium of entertainment and information. It was only natural, then, that when the United States went to war so too did radio, in both its entertainment and news functions.

Within months after war was declared, the Office of War Information (OWI) was established by President Franklin Delano Roosevelt. Among its divisions was the Radio Bureau. The bureau's task was to "steer" radio with "suggestions." As a result, voluntarism characterized radio's war effort.

In entertainment programming radio served in three ways. First, numerous special appeal programs were broadcast. Major film and radio stars would perform in appeals for the sale of war bonds, enlistment, and resource conservation. Best known is the 57 appearances in one day by movie and radio personality Kate Smith, a telethon event in which she sold more than $112 million in bonds. Second, war-related material was regularly inserted in existing comedy, variety, and dramatic programming. It was a rare family in a soap opera, comedy, or dramatic series that did not have a son or daughter in uniform, or that did not have to contend with the travails of war rationing. Variety shows featured war-related songs such as "He Wears a Pair of Silver Wings," used service people in

their routines, or were broadcast from military bases. Radio's third form of entertainment service was new, war-oriented stories such as *This Is War!*, a "13-week series of hour-long programs aired on 700 stations . . . on all four networks" (Sterling & Kitross, 1990, p. 213). Twenty million listeners a week tuned in to these stories and dramatizations.

News and information, however, were the arenas where the reach and immediacy of radio best served the nation at war. The four national networks—NBC Red and Blue, CBS, and Mutual—increased the total number of news and information hours they broadcast annually from 2,396 in 1940 (before the war) to 5,522 in 1944 (the last full year of hostilities). The number of regularly scheduled newscasts rose from 70 15-minute reports a week to 145 (Sterling & Kitross, 1990, p. 215). Many stations, and the CBS network, reduced the number of commercial minutes they sold on news broadcasts, considering songs, jingles, and other "undue gaiety" out of place amidst serious news of death and fighting. Special OWI-sponsored documentaries were produced. For example, *This Is Our Enemy* and *You Can't Do Business with Hitler* were made available for free to hundreds of stations.

The most lasting legacy of radio in those dramatic years was its on-the-spot coverage. Edward R. Murrow's live broadcasts from European capitals were already well known before the United States officially entered the fight, and with some restrictions on what he could report, they continued throughout the early years of U.S. involvement. The CBS correspondent's live coverage of the Battle of Britain—reported as bombs fell around him—not only informed home listeners but inspired them to support an ally toward whom they had originally felt only limited concern.

giants compromised on 33⅓ as the standard for classical music and 45 as the standard for pop.

Television Arrives   When the war ended and radio licenses were granted again, the number of stations grew rapidly to 2,000. Annual ad revenues reached $454 million in 1950. Then came television. Network affiliation dropped from 97% in 1945 to 50% by the mid-1950s, as stations "went local" in the face of television's national dominance. National radio advertising income dipped to $35 million in 1960, the year that television found

Edward R. Murrow

Kate Smith

Radio broadcast the Allied invasion of North Africa in November 1942 and the Battle of the Bulge in 1944. Radio followed the D-Day invasion troops through Europe and the victorious Allied armies and navies as they moved across the Pacific toward Japan.

It was Murrow again, though, who provided the most moving commentary of the war's end. He broadcast the liberation of the Nazi death camps. These are a few words from his report on April 15, 1945:

If you are at lunch, or if you have no appetite to hear what the Germans have done, now is a good time to switch off the radio, for I propose to tell you of Buchenwald. . . . I was told that this building once stabled 80 horses. There were 1,200 men in it, five to a bunk. The stink was beyond all description. . . . In another part of the camp they showed me the children, hundreds of

them. Some were only six. One rolled up his sleeve, showed me his number. It was tattooed on his arm. B-6030, it was. . . . Murder had been done at Buchenwald. God alone knows how many men and boys have died there during the last 12 years. Thursday I was told there were more than 20,000 in the camp. There had been as many as 60,000. Where are they now? . . . I pray you believe what I have said about Buchenwald. I have reported what I saw and heard, but only part of it. For most of it I have no words. (as cited in Sterling & Kitross, 1990, pp. 218–219)

Radio made a difference. It helped maintain morale in the early years of the war when enemy successes outnumbered those of the Allies. It kept the public informed, supported the troops with money, recruits, and material, and brought home the horror of war.

191

its way into 90% of U.S. homes. If radio were to survive, it would have to find new functions.

Radio and Its Audiences

Radio has more than survived; it has prospered by changing the nature of its relationship with its audiences. The easiest way to understand this is to see pre-television radio as television is today—nationally oriented, broadcasting an array of recognizable entertainment program formats, populated by well-known stars and personalities, and consumed primarily in the home, typically with people sitting around the set. Post-television radio is local, fragmented, specialized, personal, and mobile. Where pre-television radio was characterized by the big national networks, today's radio is dominated by formats, a particular sound characteristic of a local station.

Who is radio's audience? Today, 95% of all U.S. citizens 12 years old and over listen to the radio for an average of 3 hours a day. Teens 17 and younger average 2 hours 19 minutes a day; men 18 and over, 3 hours 29 minutes; and women 18 and over, 3 hours 17 minutes. Teenagers and adults listen an average of 22 hours a week. The majority of us, more than 60%, get our first news of the day from radio. Most listening is done away from home.

Scope and Nature of the Radio Industry

There are 12,276 radio stations operating in the U.S. today: 4,724 commercial AM stations; 5,591 commercial FM stations; and 1,961 noncommercial FM stations.

There are two radios for every person in the United States. The industry as a whole sells more than $11 billion a year of ad time *(Broadcasting & Cable Yearbook 1997)*.

FM, AM, AND NONCOMMERCIAL RADIO

Although there are only about 18% more commercial FM stations than commercial AM stations, the FMs attract about twice as many listeners. This has to do with the technology behind each. The FM (frequency modulation) signal is wider, allowing the broadcast not only of stereo but also of better fidelity to the original sound than the narrower AM (amplitude modulation) signal. As a result, people attracted to music, a radio staple, gravitate toward FM. People favoring news, sports, and information tend to find themselves listening to the AM dial. AM signals travel farther than

FM signals, making them perfect for rural parts of the country. But rural areas tend to be less heavily populated, and most AM stations serve fewer listeners. The FCC approved stereo AM in 1985, but relatively few people have AM stereo receivers. There seems to be little demand for news, sports, and information in stereo.

FM came about as a result of the work begun in 1923 by inventor-innovator Edwin Armstrong. By 1935 Armstrong was demonstrating his technology, as well as stereo radio, to his financial benefactor, RCA's David Sarnoff. But RCA rejected this potential competitor to its AM domain to focus on television instead. So Armstrong turned to GE, and together they put the first FM station, W2XMN, on the air in 1939. The war interrupted diffusion of FM, however, and at the end of the war, the FCC rededicated the part of the broadcast spectrum that had been used for FM to the hot new medium—television. This effectively rendered the half million existing FM radios useless. FM was slow to recover.

In 1961 in an attempt to help FM compete more strongly with AM, the FCC approved FM stereo broadcasts. In 1962 it imposed a partial freeze on the allocation of new AM licenses, making the freeze permanent in 1968. And from 1963 to 1967 the FCC put its **nonduplication rule** into action. Until that time, most FMs were part of **AM/FM combos,** wherein two stations simultaneously broadcast identical content. The AM licensees were content just to keep the FM stations out of the hands of potential competitors. Under the nonduplication rules, holders of an AM and an FM license in the same market were forced to broadcast different content at least 50% of the time. The AMs were already successful, so the content was changed on the FMs, typically to rock and roll, which attracted a growing audience of portable transistor radio listeners. In 1945 there were 50 FM stations on the air; in 1960 there were 785; in 1965 there were 1,300. By the mid-1970s FM had 70% of the audience and 70% of radio ad revenues. Today more than 75% of the total radio audience listens to FM radio.

Many of the stations audiences tune in to are noncommercial—that is, they accept no advertising. When the national frequency allocation plan was established during the deliberations leading to the 1934 Communications Act, commercial radio broadcasters persuaded Congress that they alone could be trusted to develop this valuable medium. They promised to make time available for religious, children's, and other educational programming. No frequencies were set aside for noncommercial radio to fulfill these functions. At the insistence of critics who contended that the commercial broadcasters were not fulfilling their promise, in 1945 the FCC set aside all FM frequencies between 88.1 and 91.9 megahertz (the left-hand portion of the dial) for noncommercial radio. Today these 1,961 noncommercial stations not only provide local service but many offer national network quality programming through affiliation with National Public Radio (NPR), Public Radio International (PRI), or through a number of smaller national networks, for example, Pacifica Radio.

RADIO IS LOCAL

No longer able to compete with television for the national audience in the 1950s, radio began to attract a local audience. Because it costs much more to run a local television station than a local radio station, advertising rates on radio tend to be much lower than on television. Local advertisers can afford radio more easily than they can television, which increases the local flavor of radio.

RADIO IS FRAGMENTED

Radio stations are widely distributed throughout the United States. Virtually every town—even those with only a few hundred residents—has at least one station. The number of stations licensed in an area is a function of both population and proximity to other towns. Tiny Long Beach, Mississippi, has one FM station. White Bluff, Texas, has one AM station. Chicago has 19 AMs and 30 FMs, and New York City has 17 AM and 28 FM stations. This fragmentation—many stations serving many areas—makes possible contemporary radio's most important characteristic, its ability to specialize.

RADIO IS SPECIALIZED

When radio became a local medium, it could no longer program the expensive, star-filled genres of its golden age. The problem now was how to program a station with interesting content and do so economically. A disc jockey playing records was the best solution. But stations soon learned that a highly specialized, specific audience of particular interest to certain advertisers could be attracted with specific types of music. **Format** radio was born. Of course, choosing a specific format means accepting that many potential listeners will not tune in. But in format radio the size of the audience is secondary to its composition.

Broadcasting & Cable Yearbook 1997 recognizes 91 different formats, from the most common, which include country & western (C&W), top 40, album-oriented rock, and all talk, to the somewhat uncommon, for example, Ukrainian and bluegrass. Many stations, especially those in rural areas, offer **secondary services** (formats). For example, a C&W station may broadcast a religious format for 10 hours on Saturday and Sunday.

Format radio offers stations many advantages beyond low-cost operations and specialized audiences that appeal to advertisers. Faced with falling listenership or declining advertising revenues, a station can simply change deejays and discs. Neither television nor the print media have this content flexibility. When confronted with competition from a station with a similar format, a station can further narrow its audience by specializing its formula even more. Many mid-size and large markets have album-oriented rock (AOR), hard rock, alternative rock, classic rock, heavy metal, and soft rock stations. There are country, contemporary country, outlaw country, album country, Spanish country, and young country (YC) stations.

Music format radio requires a disc jockey. Someone has to spin the discs and provide the talk. In a sense, deejays were there from the very start. Early experimenters such as DeForest often played records such as *The Star Spangled Banner* and *Yankee Doodle* when testing the reach of their transmitters. From 1912 to 1917 in San Jose, California, Charles Herrold experimented with radio and ran a wireless school. His students broadcast regularly scheduled shows whose content was published in the newspaper. The "World's First Disc Jockey," Herrold's assistant Ray Newby, would ad lib, spin records, and read newspaper headlines. When listeners called in to report that they were receiving the signal, he would play their requests. In an even more striking forerunner of what was to come, Herrold's wife Sybil ("First Woman to Broadcast") would borrow requested records from a local record store at no cost in exchange for promoting them to the listeners of the weekly *Little Hams Program*. In the 1930s personalities like Martin Block in New York and Al Jarvis in Los Angeles were airing "ballrooms of the imagination," spinning popular dance discs.

But the modern deejay is the invention of Todd Storz, who bought KOHW in Omaha, Nebraska, in 1949. He turned the radio personality/music formula on its head. Before Storz, radio announcers would talk most of the time and occasionally play music to rest their voices. Storz wanted more music, less talk. He thought radio should sound like a jukebox—the same few songs people wanted to hear played over and over again. His top 40 format, which demanded strict adherence to a **playlist** (a predetermined sequence of selected records) of popular music for young people, up-tempo pacing, and catchy production gimmicks, became the standard for the post-television popular music station. Some people credit Gordon McLendon of KLIF in Dallas with perfecting top 40 as well as inventing format radio.

RADIO IS PERSONAL

With the advent of television the relationship of radio and its audience changed. Whereas families had gathered around the radio set to listen together, we now listen to the radio alone. We select personally pleasing formats, and we listen as an adjunct to other personally important activities. Radio personalities talk to us personally as well. They play our requests, wish us happy birthday, and play contests with us.

RADIO IS MOBILE

The mobility of radio accounts in large part for its personal nature. We can listen anywhere, at any time. We listen at work, while exercising, while sitting in the sun. By 1947 the combined sale of car and alarm clock radios exceeded that of traditional living room receivers, and in 1951 the annual production of car radios exceeded that of home receivers for the first time. It has continued to do so every year since.

 The Business of Radio

The distinctive characteristics of radio serve its listeners, but they also make radio a thriving business.

RADIO AS AN ADVERTISING MEDIUM

Advertisers enjoy the specialization of radio because it gives them access to homogeneous groups of listeners to whom products can be pitched. Since the entrenchment of specialized formats, there has not been a year in which annual **billings**—dollars earned from the sale of airtime—have declined. In 1996 total radio billings were $11.4 billion. Advertisers bought

Media Echoes

Problems with Radio Ratings

Once radio became an advertising-based medium, some way was needed to count listeners so advertising rates could be set. The first rating system, the Crossleys, was begun in 1930 at the behest of the Association of National Advertisers, a group suspicious of broadcasters' own self-serving, exaggerated reports of audience size. Within 10 years, Hooper and Pulse were also offering radio ratings. All used random telephone calls, a method that ignored certain segments of the population (the rich and the poor, for example) and that could not accurately tap mobile use of the medium (such as listening in the car). In 1949 these companies and their methods were replaced by the American Research Bureau, later renamed Arbitron.

Arbitron mails diaries to willing listeners in every local market in the country and asks them to note what they listen to every 15 minutes for a period of one week. Arbitron reports:

- **Average quarter-hour:** the number of people listening to a station in each 15-minute segment

- **Cume:** the cumulative audience or number of people listening to a station for at least 5 minutes in any one day

- **Rating:** the percentage of the total population of a market reached

- **Share:** the percentage of people listening to radio who are tuned in to a particular station

These measures are sophisticated, but the use of diaries incurs some problems. Lying is one; forgetting is another. Uneven diary return rates among different types of audiences is a third. Yet advertisers and radio stations need some standard measure of listenership to set rates. Therefore, the ratings—flaws and all—are accepted as the final word, and both ratings services and broadcasters profit from their use.

As soon as a medium encounters a dip in audience numbers, however, the ratings come under scrutiny and are blamed for the problem. This was the case for radio, and it is the case for television, as you'll see echoed in Chapter 8.

When it first began losing audience to television, radio tried to ignore the problem. The cover from the

local time worth $9.1 billion (80% of all billings), national spots worth $1.9 billion (for example, Prestone Antifreeze buys time on several thousand stations in winter areas), and network time worth $426 million. The cost of time is based on the ratings, an often controversial reality in radio (see the box "Problems with Radio Ratings").

Radio is an attractive advertising medium for reasons other than its delivery of a homogeneous audience. Radio ads are inexpensive to produce and therefore can be changed, updated, and specialized to meet specific audience demands. Ads can also be specialized to different times of the day. For example, a hamburger restaurant may have one version of its commercial for the morning audience, in which its breakfast menu is touted, and a different version for the evening audience driving home, dreading the thought of cooking dinner. Radio time is inexpensive to buy, especially when compared to television. An audience loyal to a specific format station is presumably loyal to those who advertise on it. Radio is the listeners' friend; it travels with them and talks to them personally.

August 12, 1953, issue of *Broadcasting/Telecasting* vividly demonstrates this technique—the medium is said to be as strong as ever, as central to people's lives as always. But there was no ignoring the continuing and growing loss of listeners. At the September 17 meeting of the NBC Radio Affiliates in Chicago, and after 15 years of using the ratings to make huge profits, new NBC President David Sarnoff (1953) offered this analysis of the dramatic drop in radio listenership:

> Our industry from the outset has been plagued by rating systems which do not say what they mean and do not mean what they say. They develop figures which give an appearance of precision, even unto decimal points, until you read the fine print.
>
> Unhappily these figures are seized upon by the advertising community as a substitute for analysis and judgment. They are used as the main standard for advertising values in broadcasting, and millions of dollars are spent or withheld each year on the basis of a drop or rise of a few ratings points! . . . Ratings, today, simply do not reflect the *real* audience. (p. 108)

The problem, in other words, was not the television-fueled exodus of millions of listeners—it was the ratings!

The Iowa radio station that bought space on the cover of the industry's "bible," *Broadcasting/Telecasting*, wanted readers to believe all was well in radioland in 1953.

Fans debate whether Todd Storz or Gordon McClendon first invented the DJ. But there is no dispute that Alan Freed, first in Philadelphia and then in New York, established the DJ as a star. Freed, here in a 1958 photo, is credited with introducing America's White teenagers to rhythm 'n blues artists like Chuck Berry and Little Richard, and ushering in the age of rock 'n roll.

DEREGULATION AND OWNERSHIP

The business of radio is being altered by deregulation and changes in ownership rules. To ensure that there were many different perspectives in the cultural forum, the FCC had long limited the number of radio stations one person or company could own to one AM and one FM locally and seven AMs and seven FMs nationally. These numbers were revised upward in the late 1980s, and controls were almost totally eliminated by the Telecommunications Act of 1996. Now, thanks to this **deregulation** there are no national ownership limits, and one person or company can own as many as eight stations in one market, depending on the size of the market. This situation has allowed **duopoly**—one person or company owning and managing multiple radio stations in a single market—to explode. It has also permitted the rapid growth of group owners, such as Capcities/ABC (21 stations), CBS (19), Group W (18), and Infinity (17).

Scope and Nature of the Recording Industry

When the deejays and top 40 formats saved radio in the 1950s, they also changed for all time popular music and, by extension, the recording industry. Disc jockeys were color-deaf in their selection of records. They introduced record buyers to rhythm 'n blues in the music of African American

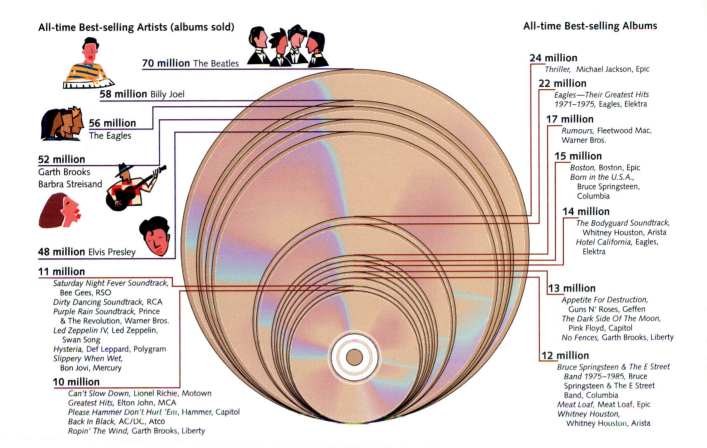

All-time Best-selling Artists (albums sold)

70 million The Beatles

58 million Billy Joel

56 million The Eagles

52 million Garth Brooks Barbra Streisand

48 million Elvis Presley

11 million
Saturday Night Fever Soundtrack, Bee Gees, RSO
Dirty Dancing Soundtrack, RCA
Purple Rain Soundtrack, Prince & The Revolution, Warner Bros.
Led Zeppelin IV, Led Zeppelin, Swan Song
Hysteria, Def Leppard, Polygram
Slippery When Wet, Bon Jovi, Mercury

10 million
Can't Slow Down, Lionel Richie, Motown
Greatest Hits, Elton John, MCA
Please Hammer Don't Hurt 'Em, Hammer, Capitol
Back In Black, AC/DC, Atco
Ropin' The Wind, Garth Brooks, Liberty

All-time Best-selling Albums

24 million
Thriller, Michael Jackson, Epic

22 million
Eagles—Their Greatest Hits 1971–1975, Eagles, Elektra

17 million
Rumours, Fleetwood Mac, Warner Bros.

15 million
Boston, Boston, Epic
Born in the U.S.A., Bruce Springsteen, Columbia

14 million
The Bodyguard Soundtrack, Whitney Houston, Arista
Hotel California, Eagles, Elektra

13 million
Appetite For Destruction, Guns N' Roses, Geffen
The Dark Side Of The Moon, Pink Floyd, Capitol
No Fences, Garth Brooks, Liberty

12 million
Bruce Springsteen & The E Street Band 1975–1985, Bruce Springsteen & The E Street Band, Columbia
Meat Loaf, Meat Loaf, Epic
Whitney Houston, Whitney Houston, Arista

Figure 7–1 All-Time Best Selling Albums and Artists.
Source: Recording Industry Association of America, January 10, 1998.

artists like Chuck Berry and Little Richard. Until the mid-1950s the work of these performers had to be **covered**—rerecorded by White artists such as Perry Como—before it was aired. Teens loved the new sound, however, and it became the foundation of their own subculture as well as the basis for the explosion in recorded music (Figure 7–1).

Today more than 5,000 U.S. companies are producing and releasing 900 million tapes and discs of recorded music on more than 2,600 labels. More than 60,000 stores sell recorded music, and U.S. customers annually buy 36% of the world's recorded music. Thirty-three percent of the recorded music that is bought is rock, 17% African American-oriented urban contemporary, and 16% country.

THE MAJOR RECORDING COMPANIES

Six major recording companies control 90% of the recorded music market in the United States. Each is part of a larger conglomeration of media and other businesses, and all but one are foreign owned:

- **CBS** is owned by Japanese company Sony and produces discs under the labels Columbia, Epic, and WTG.

- **Capitol,** owned by EMI (England) and Paramount, produces discs under its own label as well as Chrysalis.

- **MCA,** owned by Seagram (Canada), has labels MCA, Decca, Kapp, Jersey, Geffen, UNI, GRP, Rising Tide, and Interscope.
- **PolyGram** is also owned by Seagram and has A&M, Deutsche Grammophon, Island, Mercury, and Motown among its labels.
- **RCA Records** and its label Arista are owned by Bertelsmann (Germany).
- **Warner Music,** with its labels Atco, Atlantic, East West, Elektra, Giant, Nonesuch, Reprise, and Sire, is owned by American company Time Warner.

Critics voice concern over conglomeration and internationalization in the music business, which centers on the traditional cultural value of music, especially for young people. Multibillion dollar conglomerates typically are not rebellious in their cultural tastes nor are they usually willing to take risks on new ideas. These duties have fallen primarily to the independent labels, companies such as Windham Hill, Real World Records, and IRS. Still, problems with the music industry–audience relationship remain.

Cultural homogenization is the worrisome outcome of virtually all the world's influential recording being controlled by a few profit-oriented giants. If bands or artists cannot immediately deliver the goods, they aren't signed. So derivative artists and manufactured groups dominate, for example, Paula Abdul, Boyzone, and N Sync.

The *dominance of profit over artistry* worries many music fans. When a major label must spend millions to sign a bankable group such as the Rolling Stones ($28 million), Michael Jackson ($65 million), or Aerosmith ($50 million), it typically pares lesser known, potentially more innovative artists from its roster. This can lead to *infringement of artistic freedom.* When established artists cause controversy, for example, Ice-T with "Cop Killer," the majors simply dump them, as did Time Warner. The message is get in line and stay in line (see the box "Album Warning Labels: Child Protection or Censorship?").

Promotion overshadows the music, say the critics. If groups or artists don't come across well on MTV or otherwise are a challenge to promote (for example, they do not fit an easily recognizable niche), they aren't signed. The solution is to create marketable artists from scratch, such as En Vogue and the Spice Girls. Promoting tours is also an issue. If bands or artists do not have corporate sponsorship for their tours, there is no tour. If musicians do not tour, they cannot create an enthusiastic fan base. But if they do not have an enthusiastic fan base, they cannot attract the corporate sponsorship necessary to mount a tour. This makes radio even more important for the introduction of new artists and forms of music, but radio, too, is increasingly driven by profit-maximizing format narrowing and therefore dependent on the major labels' definition of playable artists. This situation led radio critic Brad Kava (1996, p. 22) to call today's deejays and program directors "little more than trained monkeys working for the record compa-

Huge record company payments to proven acts like the Rolling Stones may be taking resources away from newer, less well-known musicians.

nies" because of their penchant for playing only those artists behind whom the big companies have put their full promotional weight.

REVENGE OF THE BUYERS

In December 1995 the double CD *The Beatles Anthology I* sold 855,797 copies and had $22 million in sales in its first seven days of release. Volume II sold another 442,000 units in March of the following year, refueling interest in Volume I. Together, the two sets sold 16 million copies in six months. But that was the recording industry's last big hurrah; 1996 proved to be the year of the buyers' revenge. From 1986 until 1996, annual sales had grown from $4 billion to $12 billion, fed largely by older buyers restocking their collections with CD reissues of their favorite vinyl records. Then sales went flat. Five of the six major labels began laying off staff. The younger music buying audience wanted the next new sound, and the big record companies were unable to find it. This had happened before, in 1979, when the disco craze fizzled, leaving popular music without a center. Rock was saved then by the antiestablishment punk and new wave movements out of England (a country, incidentally, that did not have format-dominated radio). This new music, commercialized by the Talking Heads, Elvis Costello, the Police, and others, plus the introduction of MTV, gave the record industry a saving push. Both rock in the '60s and punk in

Album Warning Labels: Child Protection or Censorship?

The Parents' Music Resource Center (PMRC) was founded in 1985 by the wives of several prominent Washington politicians. Most visible were Tipper Gore, wife of then Senator Al Gore, and Susan Baker, wife of Ronald Reagan's Secretary of State, James Baker. The PMRC's particular concern was the danger posed to young people by heavy metal and rap music. In newspaper essays, television and radio talk shows, and Congressional testimony, it argued that youth were being negatively affected by popular music lyrics centering on eroticism, homosexuality, sadism, sex, violence, and suicide. Teens, and even younger children, were particularly susceptible to these influences because of how they listened—repetitively and through headphones. Together, the PMRC claimed, this created "a direct, unfettered freeway straight to the mind" (Walser, 1993, p. 141).

Despite their calls for "cleaning up" rock and rap lyrics, PMRC leaders Gore and Baker remained committed to freedom of expression. "We are strong advocates of [the First Amendment and] its protection of free speech and free expression," they wrote. "We do not and have not advocated or supported restrictions on those rights. We have never proposed government action" ("Rock Out Censorship," 1998).

The record industry's response to the PMRC, coming in 1990, mirrored that of the movie industry. It chose self-regulation and placed warning labels on the front of albums and CDs to alert buyers and listeners to the presence of potentially offensive lyrics. The labels immediately became known as "Tipper-stickers."

Although endorsed by the music industry's umbrella organization (the Record Industry Association) and the PMRC, and sufficient to forestall even the most unob-trusive federal legislation, the labels remain controversial, more so than the self-rating systems of the movie business and those that would come later to television. One reason resides in rap and rock's particular role in the culture. An editorial in *Rolling Stone* argued:

> Viewed in the context of the past 30 years, these activities can be seen as just another attempt to muzzle rock 'n roll by people who neither like the music nor understand it. As a vital and often raw form of expression, rock tends to dance on the outer edge of what society finds acceptable. It always has. We must make sure that it always does. ("Rock Out Censorship," 1988)

A second reason for the controversy surrounding the stickers is the suspicion that labeling will lead to other, more restrictive control. The Web pages of Rock Out Censorship (ROC) (http://www.charink.com/roc) offer the warning of rocker John "Cougar" Mellencamp: "They've started with the pretense that it's sex and violence they're after. But in the long run they're going to start censoring anything political." And the funkadelic rhythm 'n blues singer George Clinton adds: "Think! It ain't illegal yet!"

A third reason is the simple rejection of censorship. *Chicago Tribune* columnist Clarence Page writes on the ROC Web site, "I think the republic will survive *Me So Horney*. Whether it will survive efforts by overzealous lawmakers to 'protect' us is less certain." On the same Web site, *New York Times* writer Tom Wicker comments, "States moving toward record labeling laws may protest that they are not trying to restrict artists or expression. But freedom of expression is surely diminished if the freedom to listen is limited."

the '80s emerged from the cultural "shadows." There is now concern that a new form of music is unlikely to emerge from the contemporary recording industry due to its heavy corporate base.

Current Trends and New Technologies in Radio and Sound Recording

Emerging and changing technologies have affected the production and distribution aspects of both radio and sound recording.

Critics of the stickers have had their worst fears confirmed. Soon after labeling began, the state of Washington passed a restrictive Erotic Music Bill (which was immediately declared unconstitutional). The Pennsylvania House of Representatives debated a bill that would have outlawed the sale of stickered albums. Other states have taken up similar legislation. None has yet been successful, but in November 1997, the U.S. Senate opened hearings on popular music lyrics, taking testimony from a father who linked his son's suicide to the music of the controversial band Marilyn Manson.

Enter your voice in the cultural forum. Is there anything wrong with warning labels on albums such as Marilyn Manson's *Anti-Christ Superstar* and the al-legedly racist, misogynistic works of many "gangsta rappers"? Shouldn't people be alerted to the presence of potentially troublesome material? *Anti-Christ Super-star* sold 1 million copies in its first year of release, and Marilyn Manson was *Rolling Stone*'s New Artist of the Year in 1996. Stickers haven't hurt this "death rock" band. But do labels encourage a form of self-censor-ship? Will artists intentionally limit what they write and sing to avoid a sticker that might hurt sales? Marilyn Manson has had concerts canceled in more than a dozen states by public officials concerned about their music and reputation. Have stickers identified it as a problem band? Finally, how important is popular music as a cultural force? Does music deserve the same pro-tections as other forms of media content?

Marilyn Manson at Giants Stadium in June 1997.

THE IMPACT OF TELEVISION

We have seen how television fundamentally altered radio's structure and rela-tionship with its audiences. Television, specifically cable channel MTV, changed the recording industry too. MTV's introduction in 1981 helped pull the industry out of its disastrous 1979 slump. However, it altered the radio–record company relationship, and many hits are now introduced on MTV rather than on radio. In addition, the look of concerts has changed. No longer is it sufficient to pack an artist or group into a hall or stadium with a few thousand screaming fans. Now a concert must be an extravagant

What's most important in this 1997 U2 concert in Sarajevo? the music? the video? the staging? the experience itself?

multimedia event approximating the sophistication of an MTV video. This means that fewer acts take to the road, changing the relationship between musicians and fans.

SATELLITE AND CABLE

The distribution of radio content by satellite has aided the rebirth of the radio networks. Music and other forms of radio content can be distributed quite inexpensively to thousands of stations. As a result, one "network" can provide very different services to its very different affiliates. ABC, for example, maintains five full-service networks: American Contemporary Radio Network, American FM Radio Network, American Entertainment Radio Network, ESPN Radio Network, and American Information Radio Network. Together the five networks reach 140 million listeners a week on 2,900 different stations in 90 countries. Westwood One, which bought the NBC Radio Network in 1987 and added it to its already large and varied networking and program syndication operations, counts among its affiliates 60% of the stations in the United States. The low cost of radio production and satellite distribution, however, makes establishment of other, even more specialized networks possible.

Satellite has another application as well. Many listeners now receive "radio" through their cable televisions in the form of **DMX (Digital Music Express),** and the technology already exists for direct home and even automobile delivery of audio by **digital audio radio service (DARS).** The FCC has already allocated spectrum space for the service, but its diffusion is slowed by uncertainty over listener demand.

DIGITAL TECHNOLOGY

In 1978 the basis of both industries changed from analog to **digital recording.** That is, sound went from being preserved as waves, whether

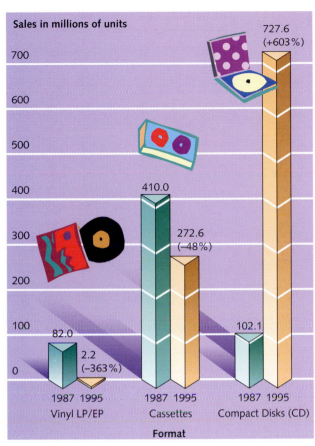

Sales in millions of units

700

600

500

400

300

200

100

0

727.6
(+603%)

410.0

272.6
(−48%)

82.0

2.2
(−363%)

102.1

| 1987 | 1995 | 1987 | 1995 | 1987 | 1995 |

Vinyl LP/EP   Cassettes   Compact Disks (CD)

Format

Figure 7–2 Sales of Recorded Music by Units, 1987–1995.

Source: Recording Industry Association of America, New York *(Statistical Abstracts of the U.S. 1997).*

physically on a disc or tape or through the air, to conversion into 1s and 0s logged in millisecond intervals in a computerized translation process. When replayed at the proper speed, the resulting sound was not only continuous but pristine—no hum, no hiss. The CD, or compact disc, was introduced in 1983 using digital coding on a 4.7 inch disc read by a laser beam. In 1986 *Brothers in Arms* by Dire Straits became the first million selling CD. In 1988 the sale of CDs surpassed that of vinyl discs for the first time, and today CDs account for more than 56% of all music sales (Figure 7–2).

Digital audio tape (DAT), introduced in the early 1970s, offers digital quality sound purity on minicassettes, not only to buyers of manufactured tapes but to home tapers as well. Although DAT tapes must be played on DAT recorders that cost about $1,000, the price of those machines is coming down. DAT makes high fidelity taping of complete digitally recorded albums on digitally broadcast radio stations and taping of borrowed CDs a threat to the recording industry's profits. At the insistence of the recording industry, the federal government therefore kept DAT out of the United States for years after its development. In 1992 Congress passed a "taping tax" of 1% on all sales of blank tapes, DAT and otherwise, that would be paid to music rights holders to compensate for revenues lost to home taping.

Online shoppers can visit *www.cdnow.com* to explore, research, and purchase music.

Digital technology, in the form of computers, offers other challenges to the recording industry. One is the production of recorded music by individuals using everyday home computers and digital equipment. For example, in England in January 1997, Jyoti Mishra (aka White Town) mailed copies of his home-produced *Your Woman* to radio stations. Four weeks later it was Number 1 on the United Kingdom's Top 10 after being picked up by the BBC and played in heavy rotation. Mishra was quickly signed by EMI, but his success demonstrated that digital technology is allowing artists to be less dependent on record industry support to get their music before the public than they once were.

A second digitally based challenge to the record industry status quo comes from the use of the Internet and the Web for music promotion and distribution. N2K Entertainment, for example, maintains a number of online music sites, among them Music Boulevard *(http://www.musicboulevard.com)*, Rocktropolis *(http://www1.rocktropolis.com)*, and Jazz Central Station *(http://www.jazzcentralstation.com)*. With the appropriate software, listeners can sample, download, and tape music from these and similar sites. As improvements in online transmission of high quality audio are made, these sites may eventually be used for the direct online digital release of music—music recorded directly onto CD or DAT, bypassing the record company altogether.

DEVELOPING MEDIA LITERACY SKILLS
Listening to Shock Jocks

The proliferation of shock jocks—outrageous, rude, crude radio personalities—offers an example of the importance of media literacy that may not be immediately apparent. Yet it involves four different elements of media literacy: development of an awareness of media's impact, cultivation of an understanding of media content as a text that provides insight into our culture and our lives, awareness of the process of mass communication, and an understanding of the ethical demands under which media professionals operate (Chapter 2). Different media literate radio listeners judge the shock jocks differently, but they all take time to examine their work and their role in the culture.

The literate listener asks this question of shock jocks and the stations that air them: "At what cost to the culture as a whole, and to individuals living in it, should a radio station program an offensive, vulgar personality to attract listeners and, therefore, profit?" Ours is a free society, and freedom of expression is one of our dearest rights. Citing their First Amendment rights as well as strong listener interest, radio stations have made Howard Stern and other shock jocks like him the fashion of the day. Stern, for example, took poorly rated WXRX in New York to Number 1, and, as Infinity Broadcasting's top attraction, he is syndicated throughout the country. He is free to pray for cancer to kill public officials he does not like; to joke constantly about sexual and other body functions; to make sexist, homophobic, and misogynistic comments; and to insult guests and callers. The FCC has fined stations that carry his show more than $1 million, a move called harassment and censorship by his supporters, but one that boosts Stern's public profile and profits.

Media literate listeners must ask themselves if Stern's "Guess the Jew" contest is just a joke. They must ask themselves if his public prayer for the spread of FCC Commissioner Alfred Sike's prostate cancer is just hyperbole. When he teases female guests about the size and shape of their body parts, is this just an example of his provocative interviewing style? When he speaks dismissively about Hispanics and African Americans, is this just a device to tease listeners?

If you're Jewish, if one of your parents has cancer, if you're a member of a minority group targeted by Stern, the answer to these questions may not make a difference. But you have a choice, say Stern and other shock jock defenders: You can switch the station or turn off the radio. This poses a problem for the media literate listener. Literacy demands an understanding of the importance of freedom not only to the operation of our media system but also to the functioning of our democracy. Yet literacy also means that you cannot discount the impact of the shock jocks. Nor can you assume that their expression does not represent a distasteful side of our culture and ourselves.

Literate media consumers also know that Howard Stern and the other shock jocks exist because people listen to them. They are popular for a reason. Are programs such as Stern's merely a place where the culture is contested (Chapter 1)? Are they a safe place for the discussion of the forbidden, for testing cultural limits? In fact, a literate listener can make the argument that Stern and others like him play an important cultural role.

Do you listen to shock jocks? If you do, how do you justify that listenership? Media literate radio listeners ask and answer these questions.

Chapter Review

The roots of radio lie in science and technology. The search for wireless telephony and wireless telegraph led to advances by James Maxwell, Heinrich Hertz, Édouard Branly, and Oliver Lodge, culminating in Guglielmo Marconi's success around 1896. Marconi's wireless was in turn improved by Reginald Fessenden and Lee DeForest. At about the same time, sound recording was also being perfected. Thomas Edison patented a cylinder sound recorder in 1877, and Emile Berliner introduced the gramophone 10 years later. Both technologies soon found their way into U.S. homes, with broadcasting becoming firmly established at the end of World War I.

Advertising had become the economic base of radio by the 1920s. Regulation of the airwaves came in the form of the Radio Acts of 1910, 1912, and 1927. The Communications Act of 1934 formalized the core concepts of the spectrum as a national resource and radio as a public service medium. The organizational structure of the new industry also was formed early, as national networks CBS, NBC Red and Blue, and Mutual soon provided the content for most U.S. stations. These came together in the 1930s to create the golden age of radio, a period of influence and prosperity that lasted until the end of World War II. But the social changes that followed the war as well as the introduction of television changed almost every aspect of radio.

The 12,276 radio stations operating in the United States today are either commercial FM, commercial AM, or noncommercial FM stations. FM was virtually eliminated when television was introduced, but government rules plus the new youth music of the 1960s turned FM into the most listened to radio form. Whatever its form, radio survives today because it is local, fragmented, specialized (dominated by formats), personal, and mobile. These characteristics make it an attractive medium for advertisers, and recent deregulatory moves have made radio even more successful commercially.

The same youth culture that helped radio succeed in the postwar era also fueled the growth and success of the recording industry. Today there are 5,000 recording companies in the United States, but 90% of the market for recorded music is controlled by six major companies, five of which have international ownership. This concentration has raised concern over cultural homogenization, the dominance of profit over artistry, and an emphasis on promotion rather than the music itself.

Both radio and the recording industry have prospered due to technological advances. Television gave radio its new personality and, through MTV, reinvigorated the music business. Satellite delivery of music directly to radio stations, homes, and cars has made possible the proliferation of radio networks. Advances in digital recording make for better fidelity but also open up the threat of piracy and home recording, both challenges facing the recording industry. The large audience for shock jocks poses a dilemma for media literate listeners who must remain aware of the impact of the media and what the content of shock jock shows says about us as a culture and as individuals.

Questions for Review

1. Who were James Clerk Maxwell, Heinrich Hertz, Édouard Branly, Sir Oliver Lodge, Guglielmo Marconi, Reginald Fessenden, and Lee DeForest?
2. How were the sound recording developments of Thomas Edison and Emile Berliner similar? How were they different?
3. What is the significance of KDKA and WEAF?
4. How do the Radio Acts of 1910, 1912, and 1927 relate to the Communications Act of 1934?
5. What were the five defining characteristics of the American broadcasting system as it entered the golden age of radio?
6. How did World War II and the introduction of television change radio and recorded music?
7. What are the nonduplication rule and duopoly?
8. What does it mean to say that radio is local, fragmented, specialized, personal, and mobile?

9. What are the six major recording companies in the United States?

10. How have cable and satellite affected the radio and recording industries? computers and digitalization?

Questions for Critical Thinking and Discussion

1. Would you have favored a noncommercial basis for our broadcasting system? Why? If you are familiar with the noncommercial system of another country, how would you describe its content?

2. Are you primarily a commercial AM, commercial FM, or noncommercial FM listener? Which are your favorite formats? Why?

3. What do you think of the argument that control of the recording industry by a few multinational conglomerates inevitably leads to cultural homogenization and the ascendance of profit over music?

4. Have you ever been part of a radio ratings exercise? If yes, how honest were you? how thorough? how precise?

5. How much regulation do you believe is necessary in U.S. broadcasting? If the airwaves belong to the people, how can we best ensure that license holders perform their public service functions?

Important Resources

Barnouw, E. (1968). *The golden web: A history of broadcasting in the United States, 1933–1953.* **New York: Oxford University Press.** The second volume of what stands as the definitive study of broadcast history in the United States, this book reads like a novel and is valuable to fans as well as scholars.

Billboard. The weekly business guide of the record industry, it is typically full of short, interesting stories and great statistics.

Broadcasting and Cable Magazine. This weekly magazine for radio, television, and cable offers insightful articles on regulation, economics, programming, technology—virtually every aspect of contemporary broadcasting. Its "Where Things Stand" feature is a handy reference on evolving issues.

Downbeat. Written for the listener rather than for industry professionals, this weekly covers the recording and music scenes with flair and depth. Particularly strong in its jazz coverage.

Godfrey, D. G., & Leigh, F. A. (1998). *Historical dictionary of American radio.* **Westport, CT: Greenwood Press.** Dozens of leading scholars of mass communication have contributed to this comprehensive resource on U.S. radio history. Entries are cross-referenced and indexed. Pertinent Internet sites are also listed.

Szatmary, D. P. (1991). *Rockin' in time: A social history of rock and roll.* **Englewood Cliffs, NJ: Prentice Hall.** A social and cultural history of rock, it is detailed, well researched, and provides a good foundation for placing various artists in the "big picture" of popular music of the last 40 years.

Radio and Recording Information Web Sites

CD Now	*http://www.cdnow.txt*
Underground Music Archive	*http://www.iuma.com/*
100 Years of Radio History	*http://web.lconn.com/rtb/history.htm*
Gigaplex (album and artist statistics)	*http://www.gigaplex.com/10top/10album.htm*
Rock Out Censorship/Record Labeling	*http://www.xnet.com/~paigeone/noevil/labeling.html*
Billboard Magazine	*http://www.billboard.com/*
National Association of Broadcasters	*http://www.nab.org*

Television

You and about 100 million other people watched a special one-hour edition of ABC's *Ellen* on April 30, 1997. After months of teasing both on the show and in the press, Ellen, played by comedienne Ellen DeGeneres, came out of the closet. She revealed that she was gay, the first lead character of a network television show to do so. Battle lines had been drawn. Among those supporting Ms. DeGeneres was President Bill Clinton. Just four days before, at the annual White House correspondents' dinner, the president publicly embraced DeGeneres and her partner, actress Anne Heche, in a powerfully symbolic photo opportunity. Oprah Winfrey, k d lang, and Demi Moore took walk-on roles on the TV episode to show solidarity. *Los Angeles Times* television critic Howard Rosenberg wrote that Ms. DeGeneres "has an opportunity to diminish prejudice on a level not previously seen in TV" (as cited in de Vries, 1997, p. 22). Among those opposed to Ms. DeGeneres were television evangelist Jerry Falwell, who called the actress "Ellen Degenerate." A few advertisers, notably Chrysler and JC Penney, refused to run commercials on the episode, and some ABC affiliates refused to air it.

Regardless of people's feelings about homosexuality, almost everyone had an opinion about Ellen—the show, the character, and the actress. Was this a brave act? Was this a cynical ploy to grab audience for a show that was slipping in the ratings? Why on television? Why in prime time? What does this mean to the gay community? What was the president doing in the middle of this anyway? Why was Ms. DeGeneres front page news in most major papers, the lead story on the three network news shows, and on the cover of magazines from *TV Guide* to *Time?*

What's the fuss? It's just a TV show; it's only television. Who cares? The answer is simple: everybody. There's no such thing as "just a TV show."

"It's only television" has no meaning. The Nixon-Kennedy debates, the explosion of the shuttle Challenger, *Friends*, the Vietnam War, President Nixon's resignation, *Bonanza*, the Gulf War, election results, the Super Bowl, "who shot JR?", Kirk Cameron, the O. J. trial, "don't have a cow," the FBI raid on Waco, Oklahoma City, *The X-Files, Mystery Science Theater 3000,* the Reverend Martin Luther King, Jr., Adolph Hitler, Bozo the Clown—all these things are part of our culture, part of our consciousness, part of our personal and social history. And we know them all from television. It isn't real until it's on the screen.

This chapter traces the development of television, from early experiments with mechanical scanning to the electronic marvel that sits in virtually all our homes. We trace the rapid transformation of television into a mature medium after, and because of, World War II, as well as several events early in its existence that changed and cemented its character—the quiz show scandals, *I Love Lucy,* McCarthyism, and reliance on the Nielsen ratings.

The remarkable reach of television accounts for its attractiveness as an advertising medium. We discuss this reach, and we explore the network–affiliate relationship, program producers, how a show gets on the air, and the syndication business. We encounter new television technologies and their promise to change the interaction between medium and audience. Because they were a catalyst for passage of the 1996 Telecommunications Act, we also examine the television-related provisions of that act. Finally, we discuss television literacy in terms of the practice of staging the news.

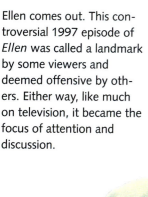

Ellen comes out. This controversial 1997 episode of *Ellen* was called a landmark by some viewers and deemed offensive by others. Either way, like much on television, it became the focus of attention and discussion.

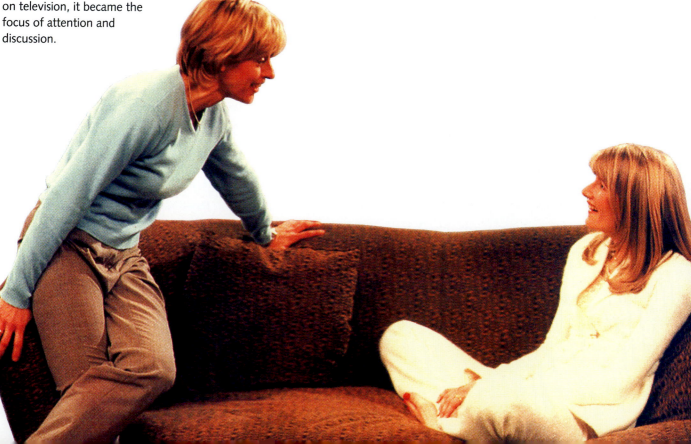

A Nipkow disc.

A Short History of Television

After the printing press, the most important invention in communication technology to date has been television. Television has changed the way teachers teach, governments govern, religious leaders preach, and the way we organize the furniture in our homes. Television has changed the nature, operation, and relationship to their audiences of books, magazines, movies, and radio. The computer, with its networking abilities, may overtake television as a medium of mass communication, but television defines even its future. Will the promise of the Web be drowned in a sea of commercials? Can online information services deliver faster and better information than television? Even the computer screens we use look like television screens, and we await better quick-time videos, WEB-TV, online video conferencing, and the new and improved video computer game. Before we delve deeper into the nature of this powerful medium and its relationship with its audience, let's examine how television developed as it did.

MECHANICAL AND ELECTRONIC SCANNING

In 1884 Paul Nipkow, a Russian scientist living in Berlin, developed the first workable device for generating electrical signals suitable for the transmission of a scene that people could see. His **Nipkow disc** consisted of a rotating scanning disc spinning in front of a photoelectric cell. It produced 4,000 picture dots **(pixels)** per second, producing a picture composed of 18 parallel lines. Although his mechanical system proved too limiting, Nipkow demonstrated the possibility of using a scanning system to divide a scene into an orderly pattern of transmittable picture

Philo Farnsworth and Vladimir Zworykin, pioneers in the development of television.

elements that could be recomposed as a visual image. (This is still the operational basis for modern television.) British inventor John Logie Baird was able to transmit moving images using a mechanical disc as early as 1925, and in 1928 he successfully sent a television picture from London to Hartsdale, NY.

Electronic scanning came either from another Russian or from a U.S. farm boy; historians disagree. Vladimir Zworykin, an immigrant living near Pittsburgh and working for Westinghouse, demonstrated his **iconoscope tube,** the first practical television camera tube, in 1923. In 1929 David Sarnoff lured him to RCA to head the electronics research lab, and it was there that Zworykin developed the **kinescope,** an improved picture tube. At the same time, young Philo Farnsworth had moved from Idaho to San Francisco to perfect an electronic television system, the design for which he had shown his high school science teacher when he was 15 years old. In 1927, at the age of 20, he made his first public demonstration—film clips of a prize fight, scenes from a Mary Pickford movie, and other graphic images. The "Boy Wonder" and Zworykin's RCA spent the next decade fighting fierce patent battles in court. In 1939 RCA capitulated, agreeing to pay Farnsworth royalties for the use of his patents.

In April of that year, at the World's Fair in New York, RCA made the first public demonstration of television in the form of regularly scheduled two-hour NBC broadcasts. These black and white broadcasts consisted of cooking demonstrations, singers, jugglers, comedians, puppets—just about anything that could fit in a hot, brightly lit studio and demonstrate motion. People could buy television sets at the RCA Pavilion at prices ranging from $200 for the 5-inch screen to $600 for the deluxe 12-inch screen model. The FCC granted construction permits to the first two commercial stations in 1941, but World War II intervened. As we saw in Chapter 2, however, technical development and improvement of the new medium continued.

THE FREEZE OF 1948 TO 1952

When World War II ended in 1945 there were nine commercial stations authorized by the FCC, six of which were on the air. Then came the deluge. The FCC was flooded with hundreds of applications for television licenses at the same time it realized the inability of its prewar technical and regulatory standards to meet that demand. In 1948 the FCC declared a **television freeze,** a six-month period in which it would authorize no new stations while it solved four pressing problems: developing an industry standard for color, reducing interference between stations in nearby cities operating on the same channel, finding spectrum space for additional channels and assigning those channels, and reserving channels for educational television. The freeze lasted four years, ending in 1952 with the publication of the **Sixth Report and Order,** the fundamental blueprint for the technical operation of television.

Developing Color   CBS and RCA had been competing since the earliest days to be first to produce a practical system of color television. At the time of the freeze, the already available CBS system was mechanical—it employed rotating colored discs that separated colors and sent them to a single tube. The still developing RCA system was electronic—it used electronic filters to divide a scene into colors and send them to three tubes, one red, one green, and one blue. In 1947 the FCC chose the RCA system as the nation's standard because its more sophisticated engineering promised greater improvement in the future. RCA continued to produce black and white sets but promised to have color available very soon. The FCC eventually tired of waiting for the promised RCA system and ruled that the CBS color television should be the new standard. There was no demand for the new color sets, however. Manufacturers would not make them because they were small and clumsy, those that were produced were too expensive, and there were very few programs broadcast in color. In 1953, after the freeze, the FCC rescinded its decision and made the RCA system the standard, allowing color television to develop rapidly.

Dealing with Interference   The FCC imposed limits on how close to one another two television stations operating on the same channel could be (170, 190, or 220 miles, depending on the part of the country). No stations were put off the air, but several had to change channels.

Allocating Spectrum Space and Assigning Channels   The fact that stations operating on the same channel now had to have so much distance between them meant that more channels would have to be made available. (The atmosphere above the earth is divided into the **broadcast spectrum**— layers of frequencies for radio, and channels for television—to which the FCC grants permission to transmit.) An increased number of channels was made available by authorizing use of the 70 UHF channels. The FCC refused, however, to move *all* television to UHF, although many people advocated doing so. This had the effect of institutionalizing the power of the national television networks from the medium's earliest days as they had already secured affiliate relationships with virtually all the existing VHF stations. The networks ignored the new UHF stations, and as a result, so did the viewers.

The FCC then created an assignment table, allocating channels throughout the United States on a city-by-city basis. All parts of the country would have television service from at least two sources. Cities of reasonable size would have at least one but preferably two channels. UHF and VHF frequencies would be intermixed.

Providing for Educational Television   Recalling the failure of the 1934 Communications Act to provide educational radio with usable AM frequencies, the FCC reserved channels for educational television at a rate of one educational license for every four commercial assignments.

THE 1950s

In 1952 108 stations were broadcasting to 17 million television homes. By the end of the decade, there were 559 stations, and nearly 90% of U.S. households had televisions. In the 1950s more television sets were sold in the United States (70 million) than there were children born (40.5 million) (Kuralt, 1977). The technical standards were fixed, stations proliferated and flourished, the public tuned in, and advertisers were enthusiastic. The content and character of the medium were set in this decade as well:

- Carried over from the radio networks, television genres included variety shows, situation comedies, dramas (including westerns and cop shows), soap operas, and quiz shows.

- Two new formats appeared: feature films and talk shows. Talk shows were instrumental in introducing radio personalities to the television audience, which could see its favorites for the first time.

- Television news and documentary remade broadcast journalism as a powerful force in its own right, led by CBS's Edward R. Murrow

(*See It Now*, 1951) and NBC's David Brinkley and Chet Huntley. Huntley and Brinkley's 1956 coverage of the major political conventions gave audiences an early glimpse of the power of television to cover news and history in the making.

Four other events from the 1950s would permanently shape how television operated: the quiz show scandals, the appearance of *I Love Lucy*, McCarthyism, and establishment of the ratings system.

The Quiz Show Scandal and Changes in Sponsorship   Throughout the 1950s the networks served primarily as time brokers, offering airtime and distribution (their affiliates) and accepting payment for access to both. Except for their own news and sports coverage, the networks relied on outside agencies to provide programs. An advertising agency, for example, would hire a production company to produce a program for its client. That client would then be the show's sponsor—*The Kraft Television Theatre* and *Westinghouse Studio One* are two examples. The agency would then pay a network to air the program over its national collection of stations. This system had enriched the networks during the heyday of radio, and they saw no reason to change.

But in 1959 the quiz show scandal, enveloping independently produced, single advertiser-sponsored programs, changed the way the networks did business. Popular shows like *The $64,000 Question* and *Twenty One* had been rigged by advertisers and producers to ensure that favored contestants would defeat unpopular ones and to artificially build tension where a mismatch was anticipated. Audiences were shocked to learn that winners had been provided with the quiz questions and answers before the broadcasts. Congress held hearings. The reputation of the new medium was being tarnished. The networks used this "embarrassment" as their excuse to eliminate the advertisers and ad agencies from the production and distribution processes. Because audiences held the networks responsible for what appeared under their names, the networks argued that they were obligated to control their schedules. The networks themselves began commissioning or buying the entertainment fare that filled their schedules. This has been the case ever since, but some historians claim that the networks realized quite early the wealth that could be made from **spot commercial sales** (selling individual 60-second spots on a given program to a wide variety of advertisers) and were simply looking for an excuse to remove the advertisers from content decision making.

In either case, the content of television was altered. Some critics argue that this change to spot sales put an end to the "golden age of television." When sponsors agreed to attach their names to programs, *Alcoa Presents* or the *Texaco Star Theater*, for example, they had an incentive to demand high-quality programming. Spot sales, with network salespeople offering small bits of time to a number of different sponsors, reduced the demand for quality. Because individual sponsors were not identified with a given show, they had no stake in how well it was made—only in how many viewers it attracted. Spot sales also reduced the willingness of the networks to try innovative or different types of content. Familiarity and predictability attracted more viewers and, therefore, more advertisers.

There is a counterargument, however. It goes like this. Once the financial well-being of the networks became dependent on the programming they aired, the networks themselves became more concerned with program quality, lifting television from its dull infancy (remembered now as the "golden age" only by those small, early audiences committed to serious character-driven televised drama). Different historians and critics offer arguments for both views.

I Love Lucy *and More Changes*   In 1951 CBS asked Lucille Ball to move her hit radio program, *My Favorite Husband*, to television. Lucy was willing but wanted her real-life husband, Desi Arnaz, to play the part of her

Running from 1947 until 1958, NBC's *Kraft Television Theatre* was among the golden age's most respected live anthology dramas. *Top left*, Richard Kiley and Everett Sloane; *lower left*, Ossie Davis; *lower right*, Walter Matthau and Nancy Walker.

video spouse. The network refused (some historians say the network objected to the prime time presentation of an "interracial" marriage—Desi Arnaz was Cuban—but CBS denies this). But Lucy made additional demands. Television at the time was live—images were typically captured by three large television cameras, with a director in a booth choosing between the three available images. Lucy wanted her program produced in the same manner—in front of a live audience with three simultaneously running cameras—but these cameras would be *film* cameras. Editors could then review the three sets of film and edit them together to give the best combination of action and reaction shots. Lucy also wanted the production to take place in Hollywood, the nation's film capital, instead of New York, the television center at the time. CBS was uncertain about this departure from how television was typically produced and refused these requests as well.

I Love Lucy was significant for far more than its comedy. Thanks to Lucille Ball's shrewd business sense, it became the foundation for the huge syndicated television industry.

Lucy and Desi borrowed the necessary money and produced *I Love Lucy* on their own, selling the broadcast rights to CBS. In doing so the woman now best remembered as "that zany redhead" transformed the business and look of television:

- Filmed reruns were now possible, something that had been impossible with live television, and this, in turn, created the syndication industry.

- The television industry moved from New York, with its stage drama orientation, to Hollywood, with its entertainment film mindset. More action, more flash came to the screen.

- Weekly series could now be produced relatively quickly and inexpensively. A 39-week series could be completed in 20 or 24 weeks, saving money on actors, crew, equipment, and facilities. In addition the same stock shots—for example, certain exterior views—could be used in different episodes.

McCarthyism: The Growing Power of Television The red scare that cowed the movie business also touched television, aided by the publication in 1950 of *Red Channels: The Report of Communist Influence in Radio and Television*, the work of three former FBI agents operating a company called American Business Consultants. Its 200 pages detailed the procommunist sympathies of 151 broadcast personalities, including Orson Welles and newsman Howard K. Smith. Advertisers were encouraged to avoid buying time from broadcasters who employed these "red sympathizers." Like the movie studios, the television industry caved in. The networks employed security checkers to look into people's backgrounds, refused to hire "suspect" talent, and demanded loyalty oaths from performers. In its infancy television had taken the safe path. Many gifted artists were denied not only a paycheck but also the opportunity to shape the medium's content.

Ironically, it was this same red scare that allowed television to demonstrate its enormous power as a vehicle of democracy and freedom. Joseph McCarthy, the Republican junior senator from Wisconsin whose tactics gave this era its name, was seen by millions of viewers as his investigation of "Reds" in the U.S. Army was broadcast by all the networks for 36 days in 1954. Daytime ratings increased 50% (Sterling & Kittross, 1990). At the same time, Edward R. Murrow used his *See It Now* to expose the senator's lies and hypocrisy. As a consequence of the two broadcasts, McCarthy was ruined; he was censured by his Senate colleagues and later died the lonely death of an alcoholic. Television had given the people eyes and ears—and power—where before they had had little. The Army–McCarthy Hearings and Murrow's challenge to McCarthyism are still regarded as two of television's finest moments.

The Nielsen Ratings The concept of computing ratings was carried over from radio (see Chapter 7) to television, but the ratings as we know them today are far more sophisticated. The A.C. Nielsen Company began in 1923

as a product testing company, which soon branched into market research. In 1936 Nielsen started reporting radio ratings and was doing the same for television by 1950.

Nielsen offers a variety of services. The best known are the **ratings.** It reports three types of ratings. **Overnights** are instant ratings gathered from homes in several major urban centers. **Pocketpieces** are ratings based on a national sample that are computed and reported every two weeks. **MNA reports** (multinetwork area reports) are computations based on the 70 largest markets (Walker & Ferguson, 1998). To produce the ratings, Nielsen selects 5,000 households thought to be representative of the entire U.S. viewing audience. From its days as a radio ratings company, Nielsen used a measuring device called the **audimeter,** which recorded when the television set was turned on, the channel to which it was tuned, and the time of day. As discussed in the box "The Problems with the Nielsen Ratings," this was a most elementary counting—it said little about who was watching. In September 1987 Nielsen introduced the **peoplemeter,** a device requiring each member of a television home to press buttons to record his or her individual viewing. (Parents or guardians are responsible for recording children's choices.) The information recorded is sent to Nielsen by telephone lines, and the company can then determine the program watched, who was watching it, and the amount of time each viewer spent with it.

To draw a more complete picture of the viewing situation and to measure local television viewing, Nielsen conducts diary surveys of viewing patterns four times a year. These **sweeps periods** are in February, May, July, and November. During sweeps, diaries are distributed to thousands of sample households in selected markets. Viewers are asked to write down what they're watching and who is watching it. The diary data are then combined with the peoplemeter data to help stations set their advertising rates for the next three months.

Some people complain that a sample of 5,000 households is simply too small to reflect the viewing patterns of millions of Americans. In truth, the sample is large enough, and is selected carefully enough, to ensure *statistical* accuracy within a few percentage points. For 50 years this had been good enough to warrant acceptance by the television industry. However, the entire conduct and value of the ratings has recently come under serious challenge from those same broadcasters.

A second, more important measure of television's audience is its **share,** which is a direct reflection of a particular show's competitive performance. Share doesn't measure viewers as a percentage of *all* television households (as do the ratings). Instead, the share measures a program audience as a percentage of the *television sets in use* at the time it airs. It tells us what proportion of the *actual* audience a program attracts, indicating how well a particular program is doing on its given night, in its time slot, against

Media Echoes

The Problems with the Nielsen Ratings

From the very beginning television ratings have been criticized for factors other than the small number of homes used in their computation. More important questions have to do with what ratings are measuring in the first place, and how the results are used. Audimeter ratings did not measure whether anyone was actually *watching* at a given time. Its replacement technology, the peoplemeter, also has limitations. Punch-in protocols for nonfamily members are sufficiently complex that many users simply fail to acknowledge the presence of additional viewers, or they substitute a family member's code for the guest code. The diary is flawed as well; its value is dependent on the active involvement of viewers. Lack of interest, forgetfulness, and lying can and do occur. Equally important, diaries offer viewers no opportunity to comment on likes and dislikes.

All three systems have an additional problem. Participation in the ratings distorts how and what people watch. Knowing that your viewing choices are being scrutinized, or in the case of the diary writing down bits of information before and after you watch, naturally changes the viewing situation. Moreover, 50% of those who are asked to participate refuse to do so. This raises the question of the representativeness of the sample, that is, how well it matches the entire viewing population (an issue discussed further in Chapter 12).

The *use* of the ratings is also controversial. They are a device for setting advertising rates, not measures of program popularity or worth. The ratings say nothing about what a show means to its viewers. Yet industry and viewers alike often confuse these interpretations.

Still, the television industry was satisfied with the ratings until the introduction of cable and VCR divided the audience to such an extent that the ratings were in danger of becoming meaningless. The Nielsen Company had used a standard sample of 1,200 homes for 35 years. But as the audience became more and more fragmented, it increased the number of metered homes to 4,000. The increase in sample size and the use of the peoplemeter combined to produce more accurate figures, and in 1990 great declines in the number of viewers for ABC, CBS, and NBC were demonstrated.

its competition (Figure 8–1). For example, *The Tonight Show with Jay Leno* normally gets a rating of around 9—terrible by prime time standards—but because it's on when fewer homes are tuned in, its share of 40 (40% of the homes with sets in use) is very high.

Television and Its Audiences

The 1960s saw some refinement in the technical structure of television, which influenced its organization and audience. In 1962 Congress passed **all-channel legislation,** which required that all sets imported into or manufactured in the United States be equipped with both VHF and UHF receivers. This had little immediate impact; U.S. viewers were now hooked on the three national networks and their VHF affiliates (DuMont closed shop in 1955). Still, UHF independents and educational stations were able to at least attract some semblance of an audience. The UHF independents would have to wait for the coming of cable to give them clout. Now that the educational stations were attracting more viewers, they began to look

Now the big networks, long enriched by the ratings, saw them as flawed. They should be "open to interpretation," they said. The sample is "too small," they complained. In early 1996 Nielsen increased the number of metered homes to 5,000. The networks then protested that the new ratings overrepresented the young and technically savvy because the peoplemeter was more complex than either the audimeter or diary and young people were more skilled at using it. This criticism may have been true, but these young people were in fact the very viewers who were abandoning the networks for cable, VCR, and satellite.

Just as the radio networks questioned the rating system they had long embraced when television began to erode their audience (Chapter 7), the television networks are doing the same as they now lose audience to other media. NBC and Fox have threatened Nielsen with lawsuits over their falling numbers, and in December 1996 ABC, CBS, NBC, and Fox ran this full-page ad in the media industry's most important publications.

The network's loss of confidence in Nielsen coincided with their loss of viewers.

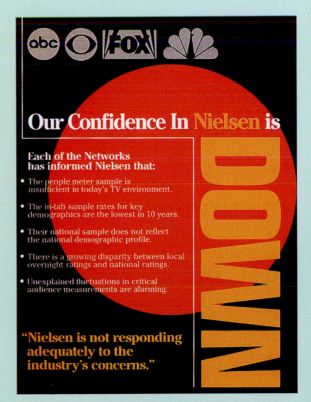

Our Confidence In Nielsen is DOWN

Each of the Networks has informed Nielsen that:

- The people meter sample is insufficient in today's TV environment.
- The in-tab sample rates for key demographics are the lowest in 10 years.
- Their national sample does not reflect the national demographic profile.
- There is a growing disparity between local overnight ratings and national ratings.
- Unexplained fluctuations in critical audience measurements are alarming.

"Nielsen is not responding adequately to the industry's concerns."

Figure 8–1 Computing Ratings and Shares.

Ratings and shares can be computed using these formulas:

$$\text{Rating} = \frac{\text{Households tuned in to a given program}}{\text{All households with television}}$$

$$\text{Share} = \frac{\text{Households tuned in to a given program}}{\text{All households tuned in to television at that time}}$$

Here's an example. Your talk show is aired in a market that has 1 million television households; 400,000 are tuned in to you. Therefore,

$$\frac{400,000}{1,000,000} = .40, \text{ or a rating of 40.}$$

At the time your show airs, however, there are only 800,000 households using television. Therefore, your share of the available audience is

$$\text{Share} = \frac{400,000}{800,000} = .50, \text{ or a rating of 50.}$$

If you can explain why a specific program's share is always higher than its rating, then you understand the difference between the two.

less educational in the strictest sense of the word and began programming more entertaining cultural fare (see the box "The Creation of *Sesame Street*"). The Public Broadcasting Act of 1967 united the educational stations into an important network, the Public Broadcasting Service (PBS), which today has over 300 affiliates.

The 1960s also witnessed the immense social and political power of the new medium to force profound alterations in the country's consciousness and behavior. Particularly influential were the Nixon–Kennedy campaign debates of 1960, broadcasts of the aftermath of the Kennedy assassination and his funeral in 1963, the 1969 transmission of Neil Armstrong's walk on the moon, and the use of television at the end of the decade by civil rights and anti-Vietnam War leaders.

The 1960s also gave rise to a descriptive expression often used today when television is discussed. Speaking to the 1961 convention of the National Association of Broadcasters, John F. Kennedy's new FCC Chair, Newton Minow, invited broadcasters to

> sit down in front of your television set when your station goes on the air and stay there without a book, magazine, newspaper, profit and loss sheet, or ratings book to distract you, and keep your eyes glued to that set until the station signs off. I can assure you that you will observe a **vast wasteland.**

Whether one agrees or not with Mr. Minow's assessment of television, then or now, there is no doubt that audiences continue to watch:

- There are 98 million television households in the United States; 99% have color, nearly 75% have more than one set.
- A television is on for an average of 7.5 hours a day in each U.S. household.
- A top-rated program, *ER*, for example, will typically draw more than 30 million viewers per episode.
- A family of three or more people typically watches television 60 hours a week.

There can be no doubt, either, that television is successful as an advertising medium:

- Total 1996 billings were $27.9 billion: $14.7 billion in national network sales, $6.6 billion in national non-network sales, $6.6 billion in local sales, and $1.9 billion in national syndication sales.
- The average 30-second prime time network television spot costs $100,000 (spots on a top-rated series cost $325,000; low-rated spots average about $50,000).
- Ad time on the 1998 Super Bowl Broncos–Packers broadcast cost $1.3 million for 30 seconds.
- Thirty-second spots on the May 1998 final episode of *Seinfeld* sold for $1.5 million.
- A 30-second local spot can fetch up to $20,000 on a top-rated special in a major market.

The great success of television as an advertising medium has as much to do with its scope and nature as it does with its public appeal.

Scope and Nature of the Television Industry

Today, as it has been from the beginning, the business of television is dominated by a few centralized production, distribution, and decision-making organizations. These **networks** link affiliates for the purpose of delivering and selling viewers to advertisers. The large majority of the 1,189 commercial stations in the United States is affiliated with a national broadcasting network: ABC has 229 affiliates, NBC 211, CBS over 200, and Fox has 144. Scores more are affiliated with UPN (Universal-Paramount) and Warner, start-up networks not yet programming full schedules of content. Although cable has introduced us to dozens of new "cable networks"—ESPN, MTV, Comedy Central, and A&E, to name a few—most programs that come to mind when we think of television were either conceived, approved, funded, produced, or distributed by the broadcast networks.

Using Media to Make a Difference

The Creation of Sesame Street

In 1968 a public affairs program producer for Channel 13 in New York City identified a number of related problems that she believed could be addressed by a well-conceived, well-produced television show.

Joan Ganz Cooney saw that 80% of 3- and 4-year-olds, and 25% of 5-year-olds, in the United States did not attend any form of preschool. Children from financially disadvantaged homes were far less likely to attend preschool at these ages than their more well-off peers. Children in these age groups who did go to preschool received little academic instruction; preschool was the equivalent of organized recess. Large numbers of U.S. children, then, entered first grade with no formal schooling, even though education experts had long argued that these were crucial years in their intellectual and academic development. In addition, the disparity in academic preparedness between poor and other children was a national disgrace.

What did these children do instead of going to preschool? Ms. Cooney knew that they watched television. But she also knew that "existing shows for 3- through 5-year-old children . . . did not have education as a primary goal" (Ball & Bogatz, 1970, p. 2). Her idea was to use an interesting, exciting, visually and aurally stimulating television show as an explicitly educational tool "to promote the intellectual and cultural growth of preschoolers, particularly disadvantaged preschoolers" and to "teach children how to think as well as what to think" (Cook et al., 1975, p. 7).

Ms. Cooney established a nonprofit organization, the Children's Television Workshop (CTW), and sought funding for her program. Several federal agencies, primarily the Office of Education, a number of private foundations including Carnegie and Ford, and public broadcasting contributed $13.7 million for CTW's first four years.

After much research into producing a quality children's television show and studying the best instructional methods for teaching preschool audiences, CTW unveiled *Sesame Street* during the 1969 television season. It was an instant hit with children and parents. The *New Republic* said, "Judged by the standards of most other programs for preschoolers, it is imaginative, tasteful, and witty" (cited in Ball & Bogatz, 1970, p.3). *Reader's Digest* said, "The zooming popularity of

Local affiliates carry network programs (they are said to **clear time**) for a number of reasons.

1. Networks make direct payments to affiliates for airing their programs. For example, NBC pays **compensation** to its affiliates for airing *Frasier*. (Compensation has diminished dramatically in recent years as the networks have been losing audience to cable and other alternatives; many affiliates now receive no compensation.)

2. Networks allow affiliates to insert locally sold commercials in a certain number of specified spots in their programs. The affiliates are allowed to keep all the money they make from these local spots.

3. Financial risk resides with the network, not with the affiliate.

4. Affiliates enjoy the prestige of their networks and use this to their financial advantage. Not only do affiliates charge higher advertising rates for local programming that borders a network offering (for example,

Sesame Street has created a sensation in U.S. television" (p. 3). *Saturday Review* gave its "Television Award" to *Sesame Street* "for the successful illustration of the principle that a major allocation of financial resources, educational research and creative talent can produce a widely viewed and popular series of regular programs for preschool children with an immediate payoff in cognitive learning" (p. 4). Originally scheduled for one hour a day during the school week, within months of its debut *Sesame Street* was being programmed twice a day on many public television stations, and many ran the entire week's schedule on Saturdays and Sundays.

Did Ms. Cooney and her show make a difference? Several national studies demonstrated that academic performance in early grades was directly and strongly correlated with regular viewing of *Sesame Street*. The commercial networks began to introduce educational fare into their Saturday morning schedules. ABC's *Grammar Rock*, *America Rock* (on U.S. history), and *Multiplication Rock* were critical and educational successes at the time, and a traditional children's favorite, CBS's *Captain Kangaroo*, started airing short films influenced by *Sesame Street* on a wide variety of social and personal skills. *Sesame Street* went international and appears even today in almost every developed nation in the world.

Even *Sesame Street's* primary failure was a product of its success. Research indicated that *all* children benefited socially and academically from regular viewing.

The *Sesame Street* gang.

But middle- and upper-class children benefited more than did the disadvantaged children who were a specific target for the show. *Sesame Street* was accused of widening the gap between these children, rather than improving the academic performance of those most in need.

Eyewitness News at 6 that immediately follows *CBS Evening News with Dan Rather*), but they typically charge more for local spots at other times of the day than can independent stations in the same market.

5. Affiliates get network quality programming. Few local stations can match the promotional efforts of the networks; few locally produced programs can equal the budget, the glamour, and the audience appeal of network programming.

THE NETWORKS AND PROGRAM CONTENT

Networks control what appears on the vast majority of local television stations, but they also control what appears on non-network television, that is, when affiliates program their own content. In addition, they influence what appears on independent stations and on cable channels. This non-network material not only tends to be network-*type* programming but most often is programming that originally aired on the networks themselves (called **off-network** programs).

Why do network and network-type content dominate television? *Availability* is one factor. There is 45 years' worth of already successful network content available for airing on local stations. A second factor is that the *production and distribution* mechanisms that have long served the broadcast networks are well established and serve the newer outlets just as well as they did NBC, CBS and ABC. The final reason is us, the audience. The formats we are most comfortable with—our television tastes and expectations—have been and continue to be developed on the networks.

HOW A PROGRAM GETS ON THE AIR

The four national networks receive about 4,000 proposals a year for new television series. Of these, fewer than 100 will be filmed as pilots, or trial programs. Perhaps 20 will make it onto the air. Only half of these will last 13 weeks, a typical season run. In a particularly good year, at most 3 or 4 will succeed well enough to be called hits.

The way a program typically makes it onto the air has changed little since the networks took control of programming after the quiz show scandal. First, an independent producer has an *idea*. That idea is then *shopped* to one of the four big commercial networks. If the network is persuaded, it *buys the option* and asks for a written *outline* in which the original idea is refined. If still interested, the network will order a full *script*. If it approves that script, it will order the production of a *pilot,* and then subject that one episode to rigorous testing by its own and independent audience research organizations. Based on this research, networks will often demand changes, for example, writing out characters who tested poorly or beefing up story lines that the test audiences particularly liked.

If the network is still interested—that is, if it believes the show will be a hit—it orders a set number of episodes and *schedules* the show. In the early days of television, an order might be for 26 or 39 episodes. But

Star Trek's Deep Space Nine, Voyager, Next Generation, and the original series. Among the most successful syndicated programs in history, the technical look and feel of the three latter Star Treks is equal to that of traditional network drama.

as production costs climbed, 13 episodes became the norm, although untested program ideas or producers who are not fully established might get orders for only 2 or 3 episodes. This is called **short ordering.**

At any point in this process, the network can decline interest. Moreover, the network invests very little of its own money during the developmental stages of a program. Even when a network orders a package of episodes, including those for an established hit that has been on for years, it typically pays producers only half of the show's entire production costs. In other words, producers engage in deficit financing—they *lose* money throughout the development process and continue to lose even more the longer their show stays on the network schedule.

The reason television program producers participate in this expensive enterprise is that they can make vast amounts of money in **syndication,** the sale of their programs to stations on a market-by-market basis. Even though the networks control the process from idea to scheduling and decide how long a show stays in their lineups, producers continue to own the rights to their programs. Once enough episodes are made (generally about 50, which is the product of four years on a network), producers can sell the syndicated package to the highest bidder in each of the 210 U.S. television markets, keeping all the revenues for themselves. This is the legacy of Lucille Ball's business genius.

The price of a syndicated program depends on the market size, the level of competition between the stations in the market, and the age and popularity of the program itself. The station buys the right to a specified number of plays, or airings. After that, the rights return to the producer to be sold again and again.

A program that has survived at least four years on one of the networks has proven its popularity, has attracted a following, and has accumulated enough individual episodes so that local stations can offer weeks of daily scheduling without too many reruns. The program is a moneymaker. *The Bill Cosby Show,* for example, will ultimately make a half billion dollars in syndication. *Seinfeld* will generate over one billion dollars.

Many critics of television argue that it is this deficit financing system that keeps the quality of content lower than it might otherwise be. A producer must attract the interest of a network with an idea that is salable on the network's schedule today, while incurring years of financial loss in hopes of having content that will be of interest to syndication viewers 4, 5, or even 10 years in the future. There is little incentive to gamble with characters or story lines; there is little profit in pushing the aesthetic boundaries of the medium.

NEW TELEVISION TECHNOLOGIES

The process by which programs come to our screens is changing, because the central position of networks in that process has been altered. In 1978 ABC, CBS, and NBC drew 92% of all prime time viewers. In 1988, they collected 70%. Today, their share is 57% of the audience. New television technologies—cable, VCR, DVD, satellite, and even the remote control—have upset the long-standing relationship between medium and audience.

Cable Cable television has reshaped the face of modern television. In 1948 television salesman John Walson began Panther Mountain Cable to bring signals from Philadelphia to his town of Mahanoy City, Pennsylvania. He could not sell sets if people could not find channels. Within two years there were 14 such cable companies in the United States, all designed to improve reception through the **distant importation of signals** (delivering stations from distant locales). Today 74% of all U.S. homes—76 million cable households or 240 million viewers in 34,000 communities—are wired for cable reception. The **pass-by rate,** the percentage of homes that have access to one of the country's 11,800 cable systems that choose to take it, is 77%. The cable industry took in $4.5 billion in gross revenue in 1996 (*Broadcasting & Cable Yearbook 1997*). The precable television audience had very few choices—three commercial networks, public television, and an independent station or two sitting way out on the end of the UHF dial—but today's cable audience has 100 or more channel options. These new outlets provide channels for innovative, first-run series such as HBO's *Arli$$* and *Oz* and Showtime's *Fast Track* and *The Hunger.*

In addition, with the increased diffusion of **fiber optic** cable, which uses signals carried by light beams over glass fibers, 500-channel cable systems are becoming technologically feasible. By its mere existence, cable offers alternatives that were not available on broadcast networks.

Eric Roberts and B.D. Wong in HBO's *Oz.* The cable channels produce their own first run series, often more sophisticated than the shows that appear on network television.

Gillian Anderson and David Duchovny in *The X-Files.* A hit on Fox, the program established the fourth network as a leader among young, urban viewers.

EMPOWERING THE INDEPENDENTS   Cable has had another, more subtle but every bit as powerful impact on the networks. Cable has helped equalize the size of the audience for independent and affiliated stations. NBC affiliate Channel 4 might appear as cable channel 11 and sit next to independent Channel 44 (cable channel 12). This erases the long-standing audience bias for the VHF channels. The fact that the network affiliate is now only one of many options further diminishes the distinction between it and its independent neighbors. Seventy-three independent stations were on the air in 1972. Today there are more than 400. These newly powerful independents have helped create a viable fourth television network, Fox, and have nurtured development of the first-run syndication business.

FOX   In the early days of television there were other commercial networks (DuMont and Mutual), but only ABC, CBS, and NBC survived the 1950s. Ever since, speculators and dreamers have planned a "fourth network," but its development was hampered by the lack of available VHF channels. As cable eradicated the distinction between VHF and UHF, media magnate Rupert Murdoch was quick to move, uniting his own chain of stations with powerful independents in important markets. The new Fox Television Network won viewers away from its competitors with innovative and popular programming such as *The Simpsons, In Living Color, Melrose Place,* and *The X-Files.* The existence of Fox led to a change in the rules of program ownership; it therefore promises to dramatically alter the process of how shows make it to the air.

In 1970, concerned that ABC, CBS, and NBC held a virtual monopoly over the production and distribution of television content, the FCC limited their ownership of the entertainment shows they aired, hoping that many independent producers bringing shows to the Big Three would result in a more diverse array of programming. Fox, however, was not bound by these limits when it began operation in 1985 because the FCC wanted to give the new network every chance to survive. Because the traditional networks were losing audiences to cable and other alternatives, the Big Three lobbied the Commission for change, pointing to Fox's success. Finally, in 1993, the FCC passed the **Financial Interest and Syndication Rules** or **Fin-Syn.** Now the networks may produce and own the syndication rights to up to 50% of their prime time entertainment fare. ABC, for example, owns all or part of *Ellen, Home Improvement,* and *The Wonderful World of Disney.* NBC owns all or part of *Working* and *Homicide: Life on the Street,* CBS has interests in *Dr. Quinn, Medicine Woman, Touched by an Angel,* and *Walker, Texas Ranger,* Fox owns *The X-Files, The Simpsons,* and *Millennium.*

The impact of this change for what appears on television screens is unclear. The networks claim that content will get better. When it is their production money and potential syndication profits at risk, networks say they will be more likely to stay with a high quality or innovative show until it finds an audience. Producers argue the opposite—that quality will suffer for two reasons. First, because independent producers will have less of a stake in future syndication money, they will not take innovative chances today. Second, because the networks will want to guarantee their own future syndication income, they will keep the shows they own on the air longer with minimal concern for quality.

FIRST-RUN SYNDICATION   Syndicated programming is coming into viewers' homes in several new and important ways. In the era of network domination, **first-run syndication** was rarely attempted, except for game and talk shows. There was no need; a reservoir of already proven off-network fare was there for the choosing. But the increase in the number of independent stations hungry for quality fare, combined with their new financial clout, has made first–run syndication common. Paramount's *Star Trek: The Next Generation* would often beat network programming in the ratings, and its sequels, *Star Trek: Deep Space Nine* and *Star Trek: Voyager,* air on about 200 stations each. *Baywatch, Babylon 5,* and *The Journeys of Hercules* habitually rank in the top 10 most watched syndicated programs, right next to *Seinfeld* and *Wheel of Fortune.* First-run syndication is attractive because producers do not have to run the gauntlet of the network programming process, and they keep 100% of the income.

Satellites have also boosted the number and variety of programs in first-run syndication. Game and talk shows, standard first-run fare in the past, have proliferated and been joined by programs such as *Hard Copy* and *Inside Edition,* reality (or tabloid) shows distributed daily by satellite to hundreds of stations. These shows are inexpensive to make, inexpensive to distribute, and easily **stripped** (broadcast at the same time five nights a week). They allow an inexhaustible number of episodes with no repeats and are easy to promote ("Secret photos of Michael Jackson's new baby. Tune in at 7:30").

VCR   Introduced commercially in 1976, videocassette recorders (VCRs) now sit in more than 82% of U.S. homes. In some places, Flagstaff, Arizona,

Xena: The Warrior Princess has been extremely successful in first-run syndication.

for example, they are in more than 97% of homes. There are approximately 30,000 video rental stores in the United States, and annual revenues for videocassette sales and rentals exceed $12 billion (Figure 8–2). Naturally, viewing rented and purchased videos further erodes the audience for traditional over-the-air television. The good news for the television industry, however, is that VCRs allow **time-shifting,** or taping a show for later viewing. Sixty-five percent of taping from television is from network affiliated stations *(Broadcasting & Cable Yearbook 1997).* Therefore, content (and commercials) that might otherwise have been missed can still be viewed. However, VCRs also permit **zipping**—that is, fast-forwarding through taped commercials.

DVD   In March 1996 DVD went on sale in U.S. stores. DVD might stand for digital video disc, digital versatile disc, or (according to its developers) it might stand for nothing at all, being merely a series of letters that sounds "high tech" (Apar, 1997). The 5-inch DVD discs look exactly like audio CDs and deliver high quality digital images and sound. Discs can be rented or purchased. Using a DVD player that looks much like a VCR machine, viewers can stop images with no loss of fidelity; can subtitle a movie in a number of languages; can search for specific scenes from an on-screen picture menu; and can access information tracks that give background on the movie, its production, and its personnel. In addition, scenes and music that may not have been used in the theatrical release of a movie are often included on the disc, as are alternative endings.

The diffusion of DVD is slowed by a number of factors. Cost is one. Most people already have VCR machines and tapes, and many do not consider the technical strengths and improved sound of DVD sufficient to warrant an expensive changeover. The lack of content is another. Even though Fox is the only major studio refusing to make its films available on DVD, there were only 1,500 titles available at the end of 1998. Until more titles

Figure 8–2 All-Time Most Popular Movie Videos through 1996.

Source: Alexander & Associates/Video Flash, New York, N.Y. *(Statistical Abstracts of the U.S. 1997).*

Top 10 Rentals

1. *Top Gun*
2. *Pretty Woman*
3. *True Lies*
4. *Ghost*
5. *The Little Mermaid*
6. *Terminator II: Judgment Day*
7. *Cinderella*
8. *Beauty and the Beast*
9. *Dances With Wolves*
10. *Batman*

Top 10 Purchased

1. *The Lion King*
2. *Snow White and the Seven Dwarfs*
3. *Aladdin*
4. *Independence Day*
5. *Jurassic Park*
6. *Toy Story*
7. *Beauty and the Beast*
8. *Men in Black*
9. *Pocahontas*
10. *Star Wars Trilogy*

are available to consumers, they will be slow in buying players. Until there are more players, studios will be slow in making their titles available. Still, viewers bought 200,000 DVD players in 1997, and video industry analysts predict that by 2001 DVD players will be in 12 million U.S. homes (Lieberfarb, 1997).

Remote Control Another in-home technology whose impact is being felt by the television industry is the remote control, currently in more than 90% of American homes. Viewers increasingly **zap** commercials, jumping to another channel with a mere flick of a finger. Two thirds of all viewers

DIRECTV® CHANNEL LINE UP
(keep this close by!)

Ch. 100-199	DIRECT TICKET Pay Per View		Ch. 221	Turner Classic Movies		Ch. 237	WAM! – encore7
Ch. 202	CNN		Ch. 222	Romance Classics*		Ch. 238	BRAVO
Ch. 203	COURT TV		Ch. 225	STARZ! East		Ch. 239	Independent Film Channel
Ch. 204	Headline NEWS		Ch. 226	STARZ! West		Ch. 240	Arts & Entertainment
Ch. 206	ESPN		Ch. 227	STARZ! 2 East*		Ch. 241	The History Channel
Ch. 208	ESPN 2		Ch. 228	STARZ! 2 West*		Ch. 242	The Disney Channel East
Ch. 211	DIRECTV Sports Channel		Ch. 230	HIT MOVIES – encore1		Ch. 243	The Disney Channel West
Ch. 212	TNT		Ch. 231	HIT MOVIES – encore1 WEST*		Ch. 245	Discovery Channel
Ch. 213	Home Shopping Network		Ch. 232	LOVE STORIES – encore2		Ch. 246	The Learning Channel
Ch. 214	Home & Garden Television		Ch. 233	WESTERNS – encore3		Ch. 247	Cartoon Network
Ch. 215	TV Food Network*		Ch. 234	MYSTERY – encore4		Ch. 248	Animal Planet*
Ch. 217	E! Entertainment Television		Ch. 235	ACTION – encore5		Ch. 253	USA Network
Ch. 220	American Movie Classics		Ch. 236	TRUE STORIES & DRAMA—encore6		Ch. 254	Sci-Fi Channel

Figure 8–3 DBS Offerings. DirecTV offers subscribers scores of video and audio channels on eight tiers or levels. © DirecTV. Current as of April 10, 1997.

zap commercials. The remote control also facilitates **grazing** (watching several programs simultaneously) and **channel surfing** or **cruising** (traveling through the channels focusing neither on specific programs nor on the commercials they house). The advertising industry estimates that at least half the audience misses television commercials because of these maneuvers.

Direct Broadcast Satellite (DBS) The technology for the direct delivery of television signals from satellites to homes has long existed. However, its diffusion has been hampered by the easy availability of cable, the cost and size of receiving dishes, and the inability to deliver local stations by satellite. With development of a small, affordable receiving dish, DirecTV began DBS service in 1994, offering 150 channels. It was soon joined by USSB, PrimeStar, AlphaStar and EchoStar. Rupert Murdoch's American Sky Broadcasting (ASkyB) began using digital compression of its signals in 1996 to make room for local stations in its menu of channels, overcoming that particular deficiency. The offerings of one DBS outlet, DirecTV, are shown in Figure 8–3.

TELECOMMUNICATIONS ACT OF 1996

The appearance of these broadcast alternatives was an important factor in moving Congress to overwhelming passage of sweeping legislation designed to overhaul the 1934 Communications Act. Among the most important television provisions of the Telecommunications Act of 1996 were decisions on the use of the broadcast spectrum, deregulation of cable television, and children's programming rules.

The Broadcast Spectrum   The airwaves belong to the people. Therefore, when broadcasters wanted additional spectrum space to transmit high definition digital television **(HDTV),** many in Congress felt they should pay for the privilege. HDTV promised more than better pictures at home. The digital compression of signals would allow broadcasters to transmit six or seven channels of programming in the band where they now transmit one. The power and profit potentials were enormous. Proponents of the sale predicted that $70 billion could be collected by auctioning the necessary frequencies, and the money could be put toward reducing the federal deficit, funding new children's and educational television program services, and wiring every school in the country to the Internet. The broadcasters, however, argued that the cost of buying the frequencies would have been an unfair burden in their competition with computer network companies, who also wanted to enter the HDTV business with online delivery to personal computers and **WEB-TV,** high definition television sets connected to the Internet that serve as "family-sized" monitors.

Declaring its intent to revisit the sale issue later, Congress gave the spectrum space to the broadcasters free in what Senator Bob Dole called "a multibillion dollar giveaway" and the "worst form of corporate welfare." Conservative columnist William Safire called the gift a "ripoff . . . on a scale vaster than dreamed of by yesteryear's robber barons" (Hickey, 1996, p. 40).

Later, in the summer of 1997, several broadcasters, including ABC, announced that they would give up their HDTV plans and use the additional spectrum space to offer a number of pay services, for example, channels that deliver stock quotes. Angry Washington politicians called hearings on the "double cross," and the industry reaffirmed its promise to use the spectrum space for HDTV.

Cable Deregulation   The Telecommunications Act of 1996 immediately deregulated systems with fewer than 50,000 subscribers, and the remainder of the nation's systems were free of rate rules by March of 1996. Less to the cable industry's liking, however, was provision in the act allowing telephone companies to compete with cable companies for the delivery of television programming.

Children's Television   The act also dealt with the difficult issue of children's television. Responding to public pressure (the *New York Times* reported at the time that 80% of the population thought there was too much sex and violence on television), Congress required the industry to develop its own rating system for television shows and to equip all new television sets with technology (known as the **V-chip**) that would allow parents to program out those categories of content they did not want their children to see. The debate surrounding the V-chip and the rating system on which its operation is based are discussed in the box "The V-Chip and the Content Rating Wars."

The V-Chip and the Content Rating Wars

The Telecommunications Act of 1996 mandated installation of an electronic content screening device in new television sets. The result was the so-called V-chip, which in itself is not controversial. What has sparked intense debate in the cultural forum is the content rating scheme that activates the filter.

It was important to government regulators and the television industry that the television rating system be industry generated. Broadcasters have First Amendment rights that the government respects and the industry wishes to protect. "I feel very strongly that the government should not be involved in this," President Clinton commented (Fleming, 1996, p. 6). So major broadcasting, cablecasting, and production professionals established a TV ratings implementation group to devise a labeling scheme. They put Jack Valenti—head of the Motion Picture Association of America and author of the MPAA movie code—in charge. The implementation group met for a year with television effects researchers, parent groups, and child advocates.

These interested parties unanimously wanted the rating scheme to be content-based. That is, they wanted the labels to inform parents about what was actually in the shows. A national study by the National Parent Teacher Association found that 80% of surveyed parents wanted content-based ratings, as did a poll conducted by the Roper Center for Public Opinion Research (Kunkel, 1997).

When the industry group presented its ratings scheme in December 1996, it was age-based rather than content-based. A content-based code would have been descriptive, labeling programs for their degree and type of violence, sex, adult language, and nudity. The age-based code, however, presented only the program producer's overall judgment about the suitability of a show for a specific age group. That's when the controversy started. Mr. Valenti told the public, "I can tell you right now, we're not going to use any other television rating system except the one we're going to announce" (Fleming, 1996, p. 6).

Why would the television industry be opposed to providing as much information to parents as possible to help them make wise decisions about their children's viewing? The industry offered two explanations. The first was its desire to keep the rating scheme as simple as possible, and age provided recognizable, easily understood categories. The second was the sheer volume

DEVELOPING MEDIA LITERACY SKILLS
Recognizing Staged News

Broadcasting & Cable Yearbook 1997 reports that 70% of the American public "turns to TV as the source of most of its news. . . 54% rank it as the most believable news source" (p. xxi). Television news can be immediate and dramatic, especially when events being covered lend themselves to visual images. But what if they don't? News may be journalism, but television news is also a television *show,* and as such it must attract viewers. Television news people have an obligation to truthfully and accurately inform the public, but they also have an obligation to attract a large number of people so their station or network is profitable.

Even the best television journalists cannot inform a public that does not tune in, and the public tunes in to see pictures. Television professionals, driven to get pictures, often walk the fine ethical line of **news staging;** that is, recreating some event that is believed to or could have happened. Sometimes news staging takes simple forms; for example, a reporter may narrate an account of an event he or she did not witness while video of that event is played. The intended impression is that the reporter is on the

of content that had to be rated—all programming other than news and sports.

Critics rejected these arguments. The video game industry labels material by content, as does the Internet (Chapter 14). Are parents of kids who watch television somehow less capable than those whose children play video games or surf the Net? Volume of content should not be a problem, they added, because all content has to be rated anyway. If a producer previews his or her show to give it an age-based label, the same amount of time can be used to give it a content-based code.

Advocates of content-based codes point to profits as the primary reason why the industry favored its age-based scheme:

> By clouding the reasons why a program is rated in a certain way, as well as by providing only the vaguest information about what types of violence or sex are shown, the controversies surrounding actual program ratings can be minimized. Imagine the economic implications for broadcasters if people who didn't want their children to see violence on TV actually had an effective way of blocking all violent programs. Ratings would go down and advertising dollars would decline. That's an unacceptable outcome for the broadcasters. So the strategy is to deliver a rating system, but to limit it to categories so imprecise that they never really reduce viewership of a program. (Kunkel, 1997, p. B5)

Some broadcasters, however, did listen to the public. In October 1997 most of the nation's largest broadcast and cable networks voluntarily introduced content-based codes as an addition to the age-based labels. On these channels, when the code appears on the upper left corner of the screen for 15 seconds at the beginning of a program, it is accompanied by the letters FV (fantasy violence), S (sexual situations), L (coarse language), V (violence), or D (suggestive dialogue).

Enter your voice in the forum. Do you think the V-chip is necessary? Is it an infringement of broadcasters' free expression rights? Do you think an age- or content-based code is better? Why shouldn't broadcasters, engaged in a legal business, do whatever they can to protect profits? If you were a program producer, would you use content-based labels? If so, how would you justify that use to your company's stockholders?

scene. What harm is there in this? It's common practice on virtually all U.S. television news shows. But how much of a leap is it from that to ABC's 1994 broadcast of reporter Cokie Roberts, wrapped tightly in winter clothes, seemingly reporting from Capitol Hill on a blustery January night when she was in fact standing in a nearby Washington studio, her "presence" at the scene staged by computer digital technology?

The broadcasters' defense is, "This is not staging in the sense that the *event* was staged. What does it matter if the reporter was not actually on the spot? What was reported actually did happen." Some media literate viewers may accept this argument, but another form of news staging exists that is potentially more troublesome—re-creation. In 1992 the producers of *Dateline NBC* re-created the explosion of a GMC truck, justifying the move with the argument that similar explosions "had happened" (Chapter 13). In the mid-1990s a Denver news show ran footage of a pit bull fight it had arranged and defended its action on the ground that these things "do happen." *ABC Evening News* simulated surveillance camera recordings of U.S. diplomat Felix Bloch handing over a briefcase to a shady character on the street to accompany a 1989 report on Bloch's arrest on espionage charges. The simulation was accurate down to the detail of a

ABC's Peter Jennings does a "stand up" report on events that he may or may not have seen take place in the scene behind him. Most broadcasters have no trouble with this form of news staging. Media literate viewers, however, must determine for themselves how comfortable they are with this and other more "creative" forms of turning real world events into video images.

surveillance camera's dark, grainy look and the time code numbers racing in the corner of the picture. This staging was justified with the claim that it "could have happened."

Where do media professionals draw the line? What happens to the public's trust in its favorite news source as the distinctions between fact and fiction, reality and illusion, and reporting and re-creating disappear? Does labeling staged events as "re-creations" or "simulations" solve the problem?

If you see a televised news story labeled as re-creation or simulation, what leads you to trust the re-creator's or simulator's version? Media literate people develop strategies to analyze content, deciding where *they* draw the line and rejecting staged news that crosses it. The news producer must balance service to the public against ratings and profit, but viewers must balance their desire for interesting, stimulating visuals against confidence that the news is reported rather than manufactured.

Why did ABC feel compelled not only to have Ms. Roberts appear to report from in front of the Capitol Building but also to have it seem, by her dress, that she was quite cold? Did the network think viewers would not have accepted a report on the issues from Ms. Roberts seated in a studio? There are two possible explanations for staging such as this. One is the need to meet television audience demands for visuals. The second explanation is the assumption, widely held by television professionals, that people are incapable of reading, accepting, interpreting, and understanding important issues unless they are presented in a manner that meets viewers' expectations of the news. If this is accurate, media literate viewers must reconsider their expectations of the medium. If this assumption about viewers is incorrect, media literate people must make that clear to those who produce the news, either by choosing news programs that avoid staging or by protesting to those that do.

Chapter Review

Mechanical methods of television transmission were developed as early as 1884 by Paul Nipkow, but it was the electronic scanning developed by Zworykin and Farnsworth that moved the medium into its modern age. World War II delayed the diffusion of television but hastened its technical development. At the end of the war, a mature medium, complete with network structure, formats, stars, and economic base, was in place. So explosive was the growth of television that in 1948 the FCC froze new station permits to allow time to develop a plan for the orderly and efficient growth of this new technology. In this period a standard for color television was adopted, interference problems were solved, new spectrum space was opened, and channels were set aside for noncommercial broadcasting. By 1960, 559 stations were being watched by 90% of all homes in the United States.

During this time, the quiz show scandal, Lucille Ball's production innovations, McCarthyism, and the onset of the ratings served to define the new medium's character.

The business of television is still dominated by the networks, although their power is in decline. New television technologies promise the greatest changes, not only in the business of television but in the relationship between medium and audience. Cable has eroded the network audience share by providing numerous alternatives for viewers, empowering the independents, allowing for creation of a powerful fourth network, and

giving life to the first-run syndication business. VCR and DVD have further eroded the audience of the networks and allow viewers to time-shift and zip. The remote control permits zapping, grazing, and channel surfing. And direct broadcast satellite, hampered at first by the success of cable and the size and cost of receiving dishes, is now a young but well-entrenched technology.

These new technologies served as a catalyst for the passage of the 1996 Telecommunications Act, which gave additional spectrum space to broadcasters for the development of HDTV, deregulated cable, and required a rating system for television programs and the manufacture of television sets with content-blocking capabilities (the V-chip).

News staging raises several issues for media literate viewers. Staging can be seemingly harmless, such as reporters narrating accounts of events they were not at to give the appearance that they are on the scene. But literate television viewers must make their own judgments about more questionable practices such as re-creations and simulations.

Questions for Review

1. What is the importance of each of the following to the history of television: Paul Nipkow, John Logie Baird, Vladimir Zworykin, Philo Farnsworth, and Newton Minow?
2. Why did the FCC call the 1948 television freeze? What issues did it hope to resolve?
3. What was the impact on television of the quiz show scandal, *I Love Lucy*, McCarthyism, and the Nielsen ratings?
4. How are the ratings taken? What are some complaints about the ratings system?
5. What is the nature of the network–affiliate relationship? What does each provide for the other?
6. How does a program typically make it to the air? How does syndication figure in this process?
7. How have cable, VCR, DVD, remote control, and DBS affected the networks?
8. What are some of the changes in television wrought by cable?
9. What is first-run syndication?
10. What are some of the television-related provisions of the 1996 Telecommunications Act?

Questions for Critical Thinking and Discussion

1. How different do you think today's television might be had the FCC moved all television channels to the UHF spectrum during the freeze? Would this necessarily be a good thing?
2. Do you agree with Newton Minow's assessment of television? If so, what can be done to improve the medium's performance?
3. As an independent producer, what kind of program would you develop for the networks? How immune do you think you could be from the pressures that exist in this process?
4. How should Congress distribute spectrum space, through sale or through free distribution? What difference does this make to viewers?

5. Is news staging ever permissible? If not, why not? If yes, under what conditions? Have you ever recognized a report as staged when it was not so identified? Describe what you saw.

Important Resources

Broadcasting & Cable Magazine. This weekly magazine for radio, television, and cable offers insightful articles on regulation, economics, programming, and technology—virtually every aspect of contemporary broadcasting. Its "Where Things Stand" feature is a handy reference on evolving issues.

Barnouw, E. (1970). ***The image empire: A history of broadcasting in the United States, from 1953.*** **New York: Oxford University Press.** This third volume of the definitive study of broadcast history in the United States focuses on the beginning of television; it reads like a novel and is valuable to fans as well as scholars.

Barnouw, E. (1990). ***Tube of plenty: The evolution of American television.*** **New York: Oxford University Press.** This popular and readable book is Barnouw's effort to condense those parts of his landmark trilogy that deal with television into one volume. Barnouw also used this book to update the reader on what had happened in television between the publication of the trilogy and 1990.

Davis, D. (1993). ***The five myths of television power: Or why the medium is not the message.*** **New York: Simon & Schuster.** Written for general readers with some understanding of the workings of television, this book offers challenges to a number of assumptions that the industry and many viewers take for granted. Does television give people what they want? Do the ratings reflect a program's popularity? Do commercials work?

MacDonald, J. F. (1993). ***One nation under television: The rise and decline of network TV.*** **Chicago, IL: Nelson-Hall.** An entertaining examination of what the author calls "the most important social and cultural force in the United States during the last four decades." It is a history of television that centers on the networks. Particularly interesting is its insider look at how programming decisions were made during different stages of the medium's and the country's life.

Newcomb, H. (1994). ***Television: The critical view.*** **New York: Oxford University Press.** A collection of critical essays on most aspects of television's operation and programming, this book is meant for television-sophisticated readers. It has been through many editions, a testimony to its popularity and the timeliness of its contents.

Reel, A. F. (1979). ***The networks: How they stole the show.*** **New York: Charles Scribner's.** An excellent, readable, and opinionated study of how the networks took over television at a time when the medium was young. Special interest is given to the regulatory decisions that shaped television's early character. Don't let the date dissuade you.

Television Information Web Sites

100 Years of Television History	*http://web.lconn.com/rtb/tv.htm*
Radio Television News Directors Association	*http://www.rtnda.org/rtnda/ethics.html*
The TV Internet Resource Guide	*http://www.tvnet.com/ITVG/itvg.html*
A. C. Nielsen Company	*http://www.nielsenmedia.com*
International Radio & Television Society	*http://www.irts.org*
Children's Television Workshop	*http://www.ctw.org*
ABC	*http://www.abc.com*
NBC	*http://www.nbc.com*
CBS	*http://www.cbs.com*
Fox	*http://www.fox.com/white.html*

part 3

Supporting Industries

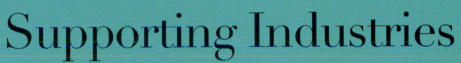

Public Relations

You've seen a lot of war movies and television documentaries about World War II and Vietnam. There are occasional news clips from countries torn by ethnic or civil strife. These images are all so far away, either in time or place. But this is different. This is your own country preparing for war—war, with all its overtones of bravery, heroism, and patriotism. But also war with its other reality—bombs, death, and suffering. There's no military draft, so you don't have to fight. But you're a good citizen. You care about your country, and you're working to come to some conclusion on the wisdom of U.S. military intervention in this battle between two distant countries in the volatile Middle East.

You've read that the public is evenly split on the question of going to war with Iraq to reclaim Kuwait. President Bush has sanctions in place against Iraq for its August 1990 invasion of the tiny oil-rich country. They seem to have little effect. Some experts say give sanctions more time. Others argue for war.

Then you see news reports that cement your opinion. On CNN, the evening network news broadcasts, the front page of most U.S. newspapers, and in all the news magazines is the image and testimony of teenager Nayirah al-Sabah. The petite Kuwaiti girl is testifying before the U.S. House of Representatives Human Rights Caucus, telling of Iraqi atrocities at the hospital where she worked in Kuwait City. The occupying army regularly tortured young people with electricity, she sobs. Her most chilling revelation is of infanticide. Iraqi troops, she says, had invaded her hospital and dumped newborn babies out of their cribs and incubators, leaving them to die painful deaths on the hospital floor.

Within days her story is repeated hundreds of times by those who want stronger action against Iraq and its despotic leader, Saddam Hussein.

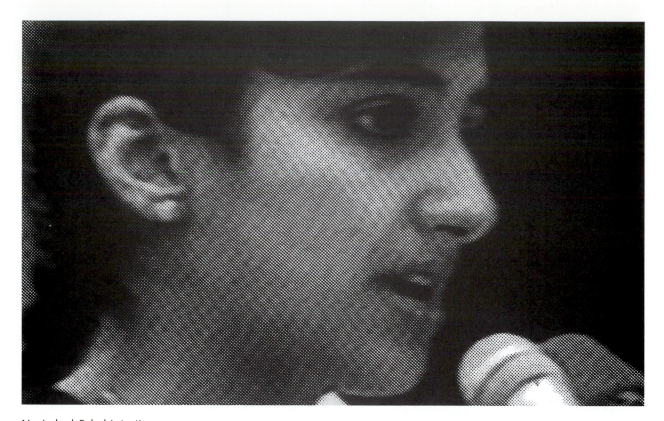

Nayirah al-Sabah's testimony helped fuel passions for the war against Iraq. It was later discovered that she was less than truthful. When asked about her appearance before Congress, her father, the Kuwaiti Ambassador to the United States and Canada, defended his daughter, "If I wanted to lie, or if we wanted to lie, if we wanted to exaggerate, I wouldn't use my daughter to do so. I could easily buy other people to do it."

Public opinion, matching your own feelings, begins to shift toward the military action the United States would soon take.

In this chapter we investigate the public relations industry and its relationship with mass media and their audiences. We first define public relations. Then we study its history and development as the profession matured from its beginnings in hucksterism to a full-fledged, communication-based industry. We see how the needs and interests of the profession's various publics became part of the public relations process. We also define exactly who those publics are. The scope and nature of the industry is detailed. Types of public relations activities and the organization of a typical public relations operation are described. Trends such as globalization and specialization are studied, as is the impact of new communication technologies on the industry. Finally, we discuss trust in public relations. In our media literacy skill we study video news releases—what they are, and how to identify them.

Defining Public Relations

Nayirah al-Sabah's Congressional testimony is one of the most successful yet controversial efforts of public relations. At the conclusion of the Gulf War, several facts surrounding the young woman and her testimony came to light, not the least of which was that the baby killing never happened.

No doubt the invaders had killed and tortured thousands of people, but al-Sabah had never witnessed the massacre of newborns she so emotionally described. A postwar investigation determined that the incident most likely had never happened. Other facts fueled the controversy. Al-Sabah was not necessarily the traumatized waif she appeared to be when speaking to Congress and the public. She was in fact the daughter of Kuwait's ambassador to the United States and Canada, whose government-in-exile desperately wanted U.S. military help. The teenager had been coached for her testimony by a public relations company hired by the Kuwaitis to move U.S. public opinion. In fact, the public relations company Hill and Knowlton had brought al-Sabah to the attention of a member of the House of Representatives, who then convened the hearings. In addition, Hill and Knowlton alerted the media to her explosive testimony, ensuring live coverage from CNN as well as a tidal wave of other print and broadcast reports.

Questions were also raised about the PR firm's client in this case, Citizens for a Free Kuwait. Critics contended that the public relations giant itself had manufactured the group as a more respectable front for its actual client, a group of wealthy Kuwaitis who had fled their homeland when the invasion began.

Hill and Knowlton succeeded in serving its client. Public opinion was molded and moved in the desired direction. But had the company been honest and fair with the public? Did the ends it desired justify the means it employed? In collecting its $11.9 million fee from this client, had Hill and Knowlton given the industry another black eye?

One of the ironies of public relations, both as an activity and as an industry, is that it has such terrible public relations. We dismiss information as "just PR." Public relations professionals are frequently equated with snake oil salespeople, hucksters, and other willful deceivers. They are referred to both inside and outside the media industries as **flacks.** Yet virtually every organization and institution—big and small, public and private, for profit and volunteer—uses public relations as a regular part of its operation. Many have their own public relations departments. The term "public relations" carries such a negative connotation that most independent companies and company departments now go by the name "public affairs," "corporate affairs," or "public communications."

The problem rests, in part, on confusion over what public relations actually is. There is no universally accepted definition of public relations because it can be and is many things—publicity, research, public affairs, media relations, promotion, merchandising, and more. Much of the contact media consumers have with public relations occurs when the industry defends people and companies who have somehow run afoul of the public. England's Prince Charles hired a public relations firm in 1996 to boost the image of his unpopular mistress Camilla Parker-Bowles, Exxon used a vast PR army to minimize its responsibility for the environmentally disastrous 1989 oil spill from its tanker *Exxon Valdez* disaster, and politicians and partisan groups habitually use public relations to shape the news.

Odwalla's prompt, honest public relations campaign to communicate with its public may have saved additional lives. It did save the 16-year-old company and the jobs of its employees.

Yet when seven people died from cyanide poisoning after taking tainted Tylenol capsules in 1982, a skilled and honest public relations campaign by Johnson & Johnson (makers of Tylenol) and its public relations firm, Burson-Marsteller, saved the brand and restored trust in the product. In late 1996, when Odwalla fresh apple juice was linked to the death of a young child, that company's instant, direct, and honest campaign to identify and eliminate the source of the contamination and rebuild public confidence saved the company and thousands of jobs. The public relations campaign by Mothers Against Drunk Driving (MADD) led directly to passage of tougher standards in virtually every state to remove drunk drivers from the road and to provide stiffer sentences for those convicted of driving under the influence. Dramatic reductions in the number of alcohol-related traffic accidents resulted from this effort (see the box "The MADD Campaign").

The industry itself recognizes the confusion surrounding what public relations actually is. Various public relations professional organizations have made efforts over the years to develop a succinct yet thorough definition of this industry. In one such effort, that of the Foundation for Public Relations Research and Education, 65 public relations professionals sifted through 472 different definitions (Harlow, 1976). The definition that we will use, however, is that offered by public relations educator S. Watson Dunn (1986). This definition includes two elements that individually appear in almost all other definitions, *communication* and *management:*

> Public relations is a management function that uses two-way communication to mesh the needs and interests of an institution or person with the needs and interests of the various publics with which that institution or person must communicate. (p. 5)

A Short History of Public Relations

The history of this complex field can be divided into four stages: early public relations, the propaganda-publicity stage, early two-way communication, and advanced two-way communication (Dunn, 1986). These four stages have combined to shape the character of this industry.

EARLY PUBLIC RELATIONS

Archaeologists in Iraq have uncovered a tablet dating from 1800 B.C. that today we would call a public information bulletin. It provided farmers with information on sowing, irrigating, and harvesting their crops. Julius Caesar fed the people of the Roman Empire constant reports of his achievements to maintain morale and to solidify his reputation and position of power. Genghis Khan would send "advance men" to tell stories of his might, hoping to frighten his enemies into surrendering.

Public relations campaigns abounded in colonial America and helped to create the Colonies. Merchants, farmers, and others who saw their own advantage in a growing colonial population used overstatement, half-truths, and lies to entice settlers to the New World. *A Brief and True Report of the New Found Land of Virginia,* by John White, was published in 1588 to lure European settlers. The Boston Tea Party was a well-planned media event organized to attract public attention for a vital cause. Today we'd call it a **pseudo-event,** an event staged specifically to attract public attention. Benjamin Franklin organized a sophisticated campaign to thwart the

The December 16, 1773, Boston Tea Party was one of the first successful pseudo-events in the new land. Had cameras been around at the time, it would also have been a fine photo op.

Stamp Act, the Crown's attempt to limit colonial press freedom (Chapter 3), using his publications and the oratory skills of criers. *The Federalist Papers* of John Jay, James Madison, and Alexander Hamilton were originally a series of 85 letters published between 1787 and 1789, which were designed to sway public opinion in the newly independent United States toward support and passage of the new Constitution, an early effort at issue management. George Washington employed the public relations

Using Media to Make a Difference

The MADD Campaign

After Candy Lightner's child was killed in a drunk driving accident in 1980, she sought out others like herself, mothers who had lost children to the volatile mix of cars and alcohol. What she hoped they could do was provide each other with emotional support and campaign to ensure that other parents would never know their grief. Thus, Mothers Against Drunk Driving (MADD) was born.

There are now more than 400 chapters of MADD in the United States and a number of foreign groups as well. Individuals and businesses contribute over $40 million a year to MADD's efforts, which include a variety of educational, public relations, and victims' assistance programs. MADD's primary public information

campaign, Project Red Ribbon, which runs during the Thanksgiving to Christmas to New Year's holiday season, annually distributes more than 30 million red ribbons. People tie them to the rear view mirrors, door handles, and radio antennae of their cars. This reminder encourages people not to drive if under the influence of drugs or alcohol, to call a cab if necessary, or even to take away a friend's car keys if he or she is drunk. The ribbon also serves as a sign of solidarity against the terrors of drunk driving. MADD has enlisted in Project Red Ribbon such major corporations as Welch's, 7-Eleven Stores, and the national trucking company Consolidated Freightways Motorfreight.

Among MADD's publics are teenagers. With its parallel organization, Students Against Drunk Driving (SADD), MADD targets this high-risk group through various educational campaigns and in the media aimed at teen audiences. The organization also conducts public information campaigns aimed at adult drivers and repeat drunk drivers, often in conjunction with state and other authorities. It also assists legislators in their efforts to pass drunk driving legislation. Finally, two more of MADD's publics are public servants such as police and

skills of Mason Weems in 1800 to burnish his reputation in a glowing and often fictitious biography of the Father of Our Country. (Among Weems's inventions was the cherry tree / "I cannot tell a lie" myth.) In all these examples, people or organizations were using communication to inform, to build an image, and to influence public opinion.

THE PROPAGANDA-PUBLICITY STAGE

Mass circulation newspapers and the first successful consumer magazines appeared in the 1830s, expanding the ability of people and organizations to communicate with the public. In 1833, for example, Andrew Jackson hired former newspaperman Amos Kendall as his publicist and the country's first presidential press secretary in an effort to combat the aristocrats who saw Jackson as too common to be president.

Abolitionists sought an end to slavery. Industrialists needed to attract workers, entice customers, and enthuse investors. P. T. Barnum, convinced that "a sucker is born every minute," worked to lure them into his shows. All used the newspaper and the magazine to serve their causes.

paramedics, who must deal with the effects of drunk driving, and the families and friends who have lost loved ones in alcohol- or drug-related driving accidents.

Has MADD made a difference? Since 1988, numerous prime time television programs have featured episodes about the dangers of drunk driving. MADD's professional staff has served as script advisor to these programs. MADD was instrumental in passage of the federal Drunk Driving Prevention Act of 1988, offering states financial incentives to set up programs that would reduce alcohol- and drug-related automobile fatalities. This legislation also made 21 the national minimum legal drinking age. MADD successfully campaigned for the Victim's Crime Act of 1984, making compensation from drunk drivers to victims and their families federal law.

There are two even more dramatic examples of how successful Lightner's group has been. There have been significant reductions in the number of alcohol- and drug-related auto fatalities in every year since MADD was founded—a nearly 8% drop from 1982 to 1990, for example. But MADD's cultural impact shows most strongly in the way people treat drunk drivers. It is no

MADD reaches its various publics in a variety of ways.

longer "cool" to talk about how smashed we got at the party, or how we can't believe we made it home. Almost every evening out with a group of friends includes a designated driver. Drunk drivers are considered nearly as despicable as child molesters. Many in public relations, traffic safety, and law enforcement credit MADD's public relations efforts with this change.

251

Politicians recognized that the expanding press meant that a new way of campaigning was necessary. In 1896 presidential contenders William Jennings Bryan and William McKinley both established campaign headquarters in Chicago from which they issued news releases, position papers, and pamphlets. The modern national political campaign was born.

It was during this era that public relations began to acquire its deceitful, huckster image. A disregard for the public and the willingness of public relations experts to serve the powerful fueled this view, but public relations began to establish itself as a profession during this time. The burgeoning press was its outlet, but westward expansion and rapid urbanization and industrialization in the United States were its driving forces. As the railroad expanded to unite the new nation, cities exploded with new people and new life. Markets, once small and local, became large and national.

As the political and financial stakes grew, business and government became increasingly corrupt and selfish—"The public be damned" was William Vanderbilt's public comment when asked in 1882 about the effects of changing the schedule of his New York Central Railroad. The muckrakers' revelations badly tarnished the images of industry and politics. Massive and lengthy coal strikes led to violence and more antibusiness feeling. In the heyday of the journalistic exposé and the progressive movement (Chapter 5), government and business both required some good public relations.

In 1889 Westinghouse Electric established the first corporate public relations department, hiring a former newspaper writer to engage the press and ensure that company positions were always clear and in the public eye. Advertising agencies, including N. W. Ayer & Sons and Lord and Thomas, began to offer public relations services to their clients. The first publicity company, The Publicity Bureau, was opened in Boston in 1906 and later expanded to New York, Chicago, Washington, St. Louis, and Topeka to help the railroad industry challenge federal regulations that it opposed.

The railroads had still other problems, and they turned to *New York World* reporter Ivy Lee for help. Beset by accidents and strikes, the Pennsylvania Railroad usually responded by suppressing information. Lee recognized, however, that this was dangerous and counterproductive in a time when the public was already suspicious of big business, including the railroads. Lee escorted reporters to the scene of trouble, established press centers, distributed press releases, and assisted reporters in obtaining additional information and photographs.

When a Colorado coal mine strike erupted in violence in 1913, the press attacked the mine's principal stockholder, New York's John D. Rockefeller, blaming him for the shooting deaths of several miners and their wives and children. Lee handled press relations and convinced Rockefeller to visit the scene to talk (and be photographed) with the strikers. The strike ended, and Rockefeller soon was being praised for his sensitive intervention. Eventually Lee issued his *Declaration of Principles*, arguing

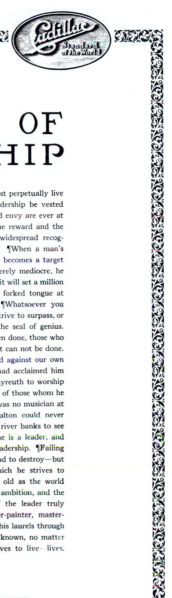

1915 Penalty of Leadership Cadillac image ad. This campaign was an early but quite successful example of image advertising—using paid ads to build goodwill for a product.

that public relations practitioners should be providers of information, not purveyors of publicity.

Not all public relations at this time was damage control. Henry Ford began using staged events like auto races to build interest in his cars, started *Ford Times* (an in-house employee publication), and made heavy use of image advertising.

Public relations in this stage was typically one-way, from organization to public. Still, by the outbreak of World War I, most of the elements of today's large-scale, multifunction public relations agency were in place.

World War I brought government into large scale public relations. Even today, the CPI's posters—like this one encouraging citizens to support the war effort through war bonds—are recognized.

AND THEY THOUGHT WE COULDN'T *FIGHT*

VICTORY LIBERTY LOAN

EARLY TWO-WAY COMMUNICATION

Although the U.S. public largely supported the nation's position in World War I, President Woodrow Wilson recognized the need for public relations in support of the war effort. In 1917 he placed former newspaperman George Creel at the head of the newly formed Committee on Public Information (CPI). Creel assembled opinion leaders from around the country to advise the government on its public relations efforts and to help shape public opinion. The committee sold Liberty Bonds and helped increase membership in the Red Cross. It engaged in public relations on a scale never before seen, using movies, public speakers, articles in newspapers and magazines, and posters.

About this time public relations pioneer Edward Bernays began emphasizing the value of assessing the public's feelings toward an organization. He would then use this knowledge as the basis for the development of the public relations effort. Together with Creel's committee, Bernays's work was the beginning of two-way communication in public relations—that is, public relations talking to people and, in return, listening to them when they talked back. Public relations professionals began representing their various publics to their clients, just as they represented their clients to those publics.

There were other advances in public relations during this stage. During the 1930s, President Franklin D. Roosevelt, guided by advisor Louis McHenry Howe, embarked on a sophisticated public relations campaign to win support for his then-radical New Deal policies. Central to Roosevelt's effort was the new medium of radio. The Great Depression that plagued the country throughout this decade once again turned public opinion against business and industry. To counter people's distrust, many more corporations established in-house public relations departments; General Motors opened its PR operation in 1931. Public relations professionals turned increasingly to the newly emerging polling industry founded by George Gallup and Elmo Roper to better gauge public opinion as they constructed public relations campaigns and to gather feedback on the effectiveness of those campaigns. Gallup and Roper successfully applied newly refined social science research methods—advances in sampling, questionnaire design, and interviewing (Chapter 12)—to meet the business needs of clients and their publics.

The growth of the industry was great enough and its reputation sufficiently fragile that the National Association of Accredited Publicity Directors was founded in 1936. The American Council on Public Relations was established three years later. They merged in 1947, creating the Public Relations Society of America (PRSA), the principal professional group for today's public relations professionals.

World War II saw the government undertake another massive campaign to bolster support for the war effort, this time through the Office of War Information (OWI). Employing techniques that had proven successful during World War I, the OWI had the additional advantage of public opinion polling, fully established and powerful radio networks and their stars, and a Hollywood eager to help. Singer Kate Smith's war bond radio telethon (Chapter 7) raised millions, and director Frank Capra produced the *Why We Fight* film series for the OWI (Chapter 6).

During this era both public relations and Ivy Lee suffered a serious blow to their reputations. Lee was the American public relations spokesman for Germany and its leader, Adolf Hitler. In 1934 Lee was required to testify before Congress to defend himself against the charge

Better known for hits such as *Mr. Smith Goes to Washington* and *It's a Wonderful Life*, director Frank Capra brought his moviemaking talents to the government's efforts to explain U.S. involvement in World War II and to overcome U.S. isolationism. His *Why We Fight* documentary series still stands as a classic of the form.

that he was a Nazi sympathizer. He was successful, but the damage had been done. As a result of Lee's ties with Germany, Congress passed the Foreign Agents Registration Act in 1938, requiring anyone who engages in political activities in the United States on behalf of a foreign power to register as an agent of that power with the Justice Department.

ADVANCED TWO-WAY COMMUNICATION

Post-World War II U.S. society was confronted by profound social change and expansion of the consumer culture. It became increasingly important for organizations to know what their clients were thinking, what they liked and disliked, and what concerned and satisfied them. As a result, public relations turned even more decidedly toward integrated two-way communication, employing research, advertising, and promotion.

As the public relations industry became more visible, it opened itself to closer scrutiny. Best-selling novels like *The Hucksters* and *The Man in the Gray Flannel Suit* (and the hit movies made from them) painted a disturbingly negative picture of the industry and those who worked in it. Vance Packard's best-selling book *The Hidden Persuaders*, dealing with both public relations and advertising, further eroded PR esteem. As a result of public distrust of the profession, Congress passed the Federal Regulation of Lobbying Act in 1946, requiring, among other things, that those who deal with federal employees on behalf of private clients disclose those relationships. And as the industry's conduct and ethics came under increasing attack, the PRSA responded with a code of ethics in 1954 and an accreditation program in 1962. Both, with modification and improvement, stand today.

The modern era of public relations is characterized by other events as well. More people buying more products meant that greater numbers of

Criticism of public relations found its way into popular culture through a number of popular films and books. This scene is from the movie *The Hucksters*.

people were coming into contact with a growing number of businesses. As consumer markets grew in size, the basis for competition changed. Texaco, for example, used advertising to sell its gasoline. But because its products were not all that different from those of other oil companies, it also sold its gasoline using its good name and reputation. Increasingly, then, advertising agencies began to add public relations divisions. This change served to blur the distinction between advertising and PR.

Women, who had proved their capabilities in all professional settings during World War II, became prominent in the industry. Anne Williams Wheaton was associate press secretary to President Eisenhower; Leone Baxter was president of the powerful public relations firm Whitaker and Baxter. Companies and their executives and politicians increasingly turned to television to burnish their images and shape public opinion. Nonprofit, charitable, and social activist groups also mastered the art of public relations. The latter used public relations especially effectively to challenge the PR power of targeted businesses. Environmentalist, civil rights, and women's rights groups and safety and consumer advocate organizations were successful in moving the public toward their positions and, in many cases, toward action.

SHAPING THE CHARACTER OF PUBLIC RELATIONS

Throughout these four stages in the development of public relations, several factors combined to shape the identity of public relations, influence the way the industry does its job, and clarify the necessity for PR in the business and political world. These factors include:

Advances in Technology. Advances in industrial technology made possible mass production, distribution, and marketing of goods.

Advances in communication technology (and their proliferation) made it possible to communicate more efficiently and effectively with ever larger and more specific audiences.

Growth of the middle class. A growing middle class, better educated and more aware of the world around it, required information about people and organizations.

Growth of organizations. As business, organized labor, and government grew bigger after World War II, the public saw them as more powerful and more remote. As a result, people were naturally curious and suspicious about these forces that seemed to be influencing all aspects of their lives.

Better research tools. The development of sophisticated research methodologies and statistical techniques allowed the industry to know its audiences better and to better judge the effectiveness of public relations campaigns.

Professionalization. Numerous national and international public relations organizations helped professionalize the industry and clean up its reputation.

Public Relations and Its Audiences

Virtually all of us consume public relations messages on a daily basis. Increasingly, the video clips we see on the local evening news are provided by a public relations firm or the PR department of some company or organization. The content of many of the stories we read in our daily newspaper or hear on local radio news comes directly from PR-provided press releases. The charity food drive we support, the poster encouraging us toward safe sex, and the corporation-sponsored art exhibit we attend are all someone's public relations effort. Public relations professionals interact with seven categories of publics (Dilenschneider & Forrestal, 1987):

Employees. An organization's employees are its life blood, its family. Good public relations begins at home with company newsletters, social events, and internal and external recognition of superior performance.

Stockholders. Stockholders own the organization (if it is a public corporation). They are "family" as well, and their goodwill is necessary for the business to operate. Annual reports and stockholder meetings provide a sense of belonging as well as information.

Communities. An organization has neighbors where it operates. Courtesy, as well as good business sense, requires that an organization's neighbors be treated with friendship and support. Information meetings, company-sponsored safety and food drives, and open houses strengthen ties between organizations and their neighbors.

Media. Very little communication with an organization's various publics can occur without the trust and goodwill of professionals in the mass media. Press packets, briefings, and facilitating access to organization newsmakers build that trust and goodwill.

Government. Government is "the voice of the people" and, as such, deserves the attention of any organization that deals with the public. From a practical perspective, governments have the power to tax, regulate, and zone. Organizations must earn and maintain the goodwill and trust of the government. Providing information and access through reports, position papers, and meetings with personnel keep government informed and build its trust in an organization. The government is also the target of many PR efforts, as organizations and their lobbyists seek favorable legislation and other action (see the box "Public Relations and Gun Control").

Investment community. Corporations are under the constant scrutiny of those who invest their own money, invest the money of others, or make recommendations on investment. The value of a business and its ability to grow are functions of the investment community's respect for and trust in it. As a result, all PR efforts that build an organization's good image speak to that community.

Customers. Consumers pay the bills for companies through their purchase of products or services. Their goodwill is invaluable. That makes good PR, in all its forms, invaluable.

Scope and Structure of the Public Relations Industry

Today some 170,000 people identify themselves as working in public relations, and more than 80% of major U.S. companies have public relations departments, some housing as many as 400 employees (Figure 9–1). There are over 4,000 public relations firms in the United States, the largest employing as many as 1,000 people. Most, however, have fewer, some as few as four employees.

There are full service public relations firms and those that provide only special services. Media specialists for company CEOs, newspaper clipping services, and makers of video news releases are special service providers. Public relations firms bill for their services in a number of ways. They may charge an hourly rate for services rendered, or they may be on call, charging clients a monthly fee to act as their public relations counsel. Hill and Knowlton, for example, has a minimum $5,000 a month charge. Third are **fixed-fee arrangements,** wherein the firm performs a specific set of services for a client for a specific and prearranged fee. Finally, many firms bill for **collateral materials,** adding a surcharge as high as 17.65% for handling printing, research, and photographs. For example, if it costs

Public Relations and Gun Control

Few issues are as hotly debated in the cultural forum as individual gun ownership, and few voices in the debate are as powerful as that of the National Rifle Association. A public interest group over 100 years old, the National Rifle Association sponsors shooting clubs, marksmanship programs, and gun safety classes. It is recognized by the U.S. Olympic Committee as the national governing body for competitive shooting in the United States. It has authored a code of ethics for hunters and serves as a primary certifying body for hunting and target shooting instructors, referees, and counselors. Among its high visibility members are former presidents Ronald Reagan and George Bush and Hollywood legend Charlton Heston.

For the last several decades, however, the NRA has been best known for its fierce and effective lobbying efforts dedicated to limiting restrictions on firearms. "Guns don't kill people; people kill people" has been its theme. Working to protect what it sees as people's right to carry guns, the NRA bases its position on the Second Amendment to the U.S. Constitution, which says that "a well-regulated militia, being necessary to the security of a free State, the right of the people to keep and bear arms shall not be infringed." Although there is controversy as to the intent of this amendment, the NRA has found a good deal of support—2.8 million members, an $87 million annual budget, three magazines with annual ad revenues of $7 million, and an expensive office building in Washington, DC.

Challenging the NRA on the national level is Handgun Control Inc. (HCI), also based in Washington. Best known for its successful support of the 1993 Handgun Violence Prevention Act, HCI lobbies Congress in opposition to the NRA, identifies and supports political candidates who support tighter gun control, publishes periodic reports indicating which legislators have taken NRA money and how much, and distributes a quarterly newsletter, *Washington Report,* and other gun safety and gun control material.

HCI's victory over the NRA in the passage of the 1993 legislation known as the Brady Bill marked a turning point in the gun control debate. The Brady Bill was passed despite a filibuster by NRA-backed congresspeople; politicians no longer fear the group as they once did. Membership has flattened or is in decline, as are revenues. Has the NRA met its match in the HCI, or has it, with its zealous, unbending opposition to all gun control efforts, been its own worst PR?

A majority of U.S. citizens, regardless of age, gender, or location, favor federal gun control; there are more guns in the United States than there are people. The United States is the only developed nation in the world that does not license, register, or otherwise regulate gun ownership. Nearly 65% of all murders involve a gun, and almost all U.S. police and other law enforcement agencies favor strict control of guns. The NRA has fought several controversial battles in the face of these realities.

The NRA opposed the Brady Bill's 5-day waiting period and personal background check for a gun purchase. It fought a ban on plastic handguns that could be used to evade metal detectors in airports and other public places (the legislation was called the Terrorist Firearms Prevention Act). It opposed restrictions on teflon-coated "cop killer" bullets that can pierce bulletproof vests. It challenged a ban on the manufacture and sale of snub-nosed and inexpensive handguns, known as Saturday Night Specials. It fought restrictions on automatic and assault weapons.

Especially in light of growing public sentiment in favor of stricter control of guns, these inflexible positions may be hurting the effectiveness of the NRA. Its position has long been that any infringement of Second Amendment rights will only open the door to even more control. But an increasing number of politicians and members of the public are asking, "What do cop killer bullets and plastic handguns have to do with the Second Amendment?"

If you were to advise the NRA on its public relations, would you advocate that it moderate its stance on those issues that seem to turn off the public? If you were to advise HCI, what strategy would you recommend to exacerbate the NRA's difficulties in these areas? For each client, how would you go about getting useful feedback from the public on this emotionally charged issue?

Best-known for its effective lobbying, the NRA also conducts a full array of public relations activities.

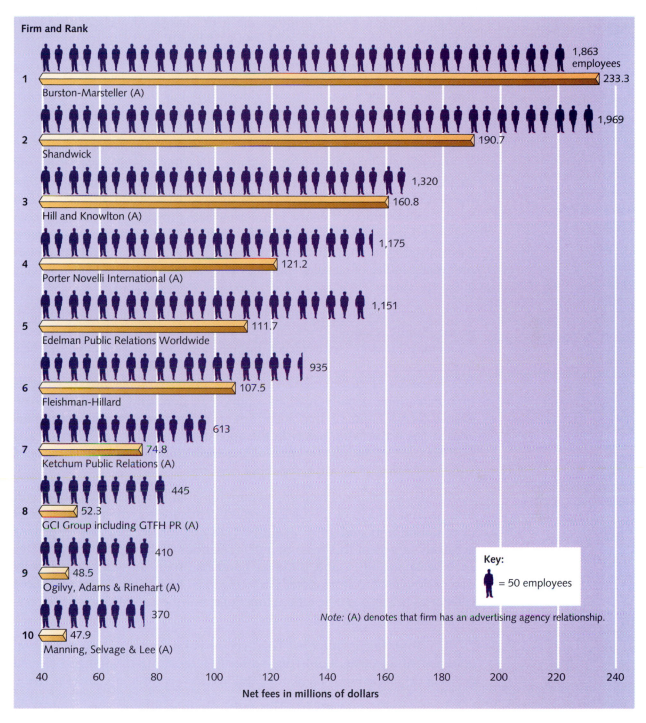

Firm and Rank

1 Burston-Marsteller (A) — 1,863 employees — 233.3

2 Shandwick — 1,969 — 190.7

3 Hill and Knowlton (A) — 1,320 — 160.8

4 Porter Novelli International (A) — 1,175 — 121.2

5 Edelman Public Relations Worldwide — 1,151 — 111.7

6 Fleishman-Hillard — 935 — 107.5

7 Ketchum Public Relations (A) — 613 — 74.8

8 GCI Group including GTFH PR (A) — 445 — 52.3

9 Ogilvy, Adams & Rinehart (A) — 410 — 48.5

10 Manning, Selvage & Lee (A) — 370 — 47.9

Key:
= 50 employees

Note: (A) denotes that firm has an advertising agency relationship.

40   60   80   100   120   140   160   180   200   220   240

Net fees in millions of dollars

Figure 9–1 Ten Largest PR Firms in the United States, 1996. Source: *O'Dwyer's Directory of Public Relations Firms, 1996.*

$3,000 to have a poster printed, the firm charges the client $3,529.50 ($3,000 + [$3,000 × .1765] = $3,000 + $529.50).

PUBLIC RELATIONS ACTIVITIES

Regardless of the way public relations firms bill their clients, they earn their fees by offering all or some of these 14 interrelated services identified by the PRSA.

1. *Publicity.* Publicity is the practice of getting media coverage for the client. Often it is a quest for good publicity, having the client throw out the first ball at a baseball game, for example. Just as often, however, it can be the more difficult task of countering bad publicity by getting media coverage for the client's point of view in front of the public. When Pepsi was rocked by a product tampering hoax in 1993, adroit publicity about the impossibility of needles making their way into cans of Pepsi quickly killed the furor.

2. *Communication.* Central to two-way public relations is communication. Public relations firms or departments have as a fundamental activity communicating with target publics and advising clients in their interaction with them. In the 1970s, for example, Mobil Oil public affairs vice president Herb Schmertz started the practice of placing *advertorials* in publications usually read by opinion leaders and the public alike. (Recall from Chapter 5 that advertorials are opinion pieces in space purchased like advertising but with the appearance of editorial content.) His goal was to communicate—free of the media filter—Mobil's views on a variety of subjects to various publics

3. *Public affairs.* The public affairs function includes interacting with officials and leaders of the various power centers with whom a client must deal. Community and government officials and leaders of pressure groups are likely targets of this form of public relations. Public affairs emphasizes social responsibility and building goodwill, such as when a company donates money for a computer lab to the local high school. The next three categories are also public affairs functions, but they are defined by the target publics they influence.

4. *Government relations.* This type of public affairs work focuses on government agencies. **Lobbying**—directly interacting to influence elected officials or government regulators and agents—is often a central activity.

5. *Community relations.* This type of public affairs work focuses on the communities in which the organization exists. If a city wants to build a new airport, for example, those whose land will be taken or devalued must be satisfied. If they are not, widespread community opposition to the project may develop.

6. *Minority relations.* Public affairs activities are directed toward specific racial minorities in this type of work. When Denny's restaurant chain

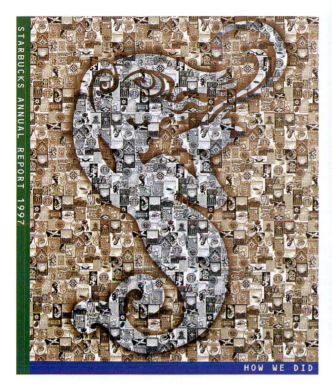

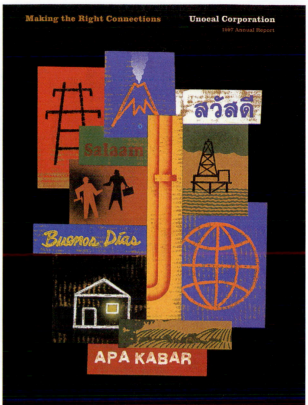

Annual reports from Starbucks and Unocal. Corporate annual reports are one product of financial public relations.

was beset by numerous complaints of racial discrimination during the 1990s, it undertook an aggressive campaign to speak to those who felt disenfranchised by the events. A secondary goal of its efforts, which were aimed largely at the African American community, was to send a message to its own employees and the larger public that this was the company line, that discrimination was wrong, that everybody was welcome in Denny's.

7. *Financial public relations.* Practiced primarily by corporate organizations, financial PR is the enhancement of communication between investor-owned companies and their shareholders, the financial community (for example, banks, annuity groups, and investment firms), and the public. Much corporate strategy, such as expansion into new markets and acquisition of other companies, is dependent upon good financial public relations.

8. *Industry relations.* Companies must interact not only with their own customers and stockholders but also with other companies in their line of business, both competitors and suppliers. In addition, they must also stand as a single voice in dealing with various state and federal regulators. For example, groups as disparate as the Texas Restaurant Association, the American Petroleum Institute, and the National Association of Manufacturers all require public relations in dealing with their various publics. The goal is the maintenance and prosperity of the industry as a whole (Figure 9–2).

Figure 9–2 The fictitious Acme Fishhook Research Council in this Robotman cartoon is a good example of an organization that engages in industry relations public relations activities. Robotman reprinted by permission of Newspaper Enterprise Association, Inc.

9. *Press agency.* Being a press agent means attracting attention to the client, usually through planning or staging some activity. The 10K Fun Run sponsored by the local newspaper is the product of press agency, as is the politician cutting the ribbon at a new bridge.

10. *Promotion.* Similar in some ways to press agency, promotion differs in that its goal is to create support or goodwill for the client as opposed to merely garnering attention. Ronald McDonald Houses, where families of hospitalized children can stay free of cost, are a promotional tool of McDonald's Restaurants. They earn the hamburger chain attention, but at the same time, they earn it much goodwill.

11. *Media relations.* As the number of media outlets grows and as advances in technology increase the complexity of dealing with them, public relations clients require help in understanding the various media, in preparing and organizing materials for them, and in placing those materials. In addition, media relations requires that the public relations professional maintain good relationships with professionals in the media, understand their deadlines and other restraints, and earn their trust.

12. *Issues management.* Often an organization is as interested in influencing public opinion about some larger issue that will eventually influence its operation as it is in the improvement of its own image. Issues management typically uses a large-scale public relations campaign designed to move or shape opinion on a specific issue. Usually the issue is an important one that generates deep feelings. Death penalty advocates (both pro and con) employ a full range of communication techniques to sway people to their side. Mobil's advertorials sometimes address environmentalism and public transportation—important issues in and of themselves, but also important to the future of a leading manufacturer of gasoline.

13. *Propaganda.* This word has primarily negative connotations, but **propaganda**—the generation of more or less automatic responses to given symbols—is used by the good guys as well as the bad. For example, their soldiers are cowards who hurt the innocent; ours are freedom fighters

Our Children's Stories

Tanya liked to play outside at the House while she recovered from a bone marrow transplant.

Tanya is a bright and joyful seven year old from Sonora, but already in second remission with rhabdomyosarcoma. She was referred to Lucile Salter Packard Children's Hospital at Stanford when a bone marrow transplant was considered.

The transplant was done in early October and Tanya was released from the Hospital a few days before Halloween. At the Ronald McDonald House Tanya pirouetted around in her ballerina costume, climbed the big oak in the courtyard and enjoyed the warmth and support of the House, while recovering from her bone marrow transplant operation.

birth defect, with an artery connected to the wrong chamber of his heart. His breathing difficulties were due to his heart using only two chambers instead of the necessary four. He was brought to the Lucile Salter Packard Children's Hospital for corrective surgery.

The surgery to repair the artery was not complicated, but when it was time to remove Alex from the heart-lung

Alex, who owes his life to an emergency heart transplant, returns to the Hospital, and security of the Ronald McDonald house, several times a year to be evaluated. He is a vibrant, active six year old who enjoys being read to by his mom…truly a miracle of medicine.

Four-month old Alex was having difficulty breathing. He was tentatively diagnosed with asthma and underwent a chest x-ray and sonogram to evaluate his situation. He was found to have a

bypass machine, his repaired heart would not beat, and Alex had to be put on full life support. His parents were notified of his dire situation. The only hope was a heart transplant with a

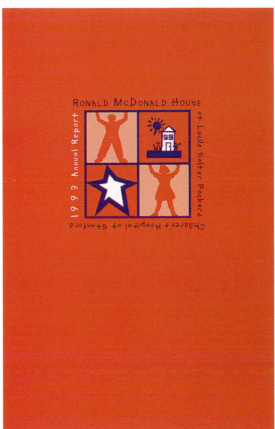

RONALD McDONALD HOUSE
1993 Annual Report
at Lucile Salter Packard
Children's Hospital at Stanford

The best public relations can serve both client and the public, as demonstrated by this Ronald McDonald House promotional material.

doing God's work. Because propagandists want an automatic reaction free of reflection, ethical public relations professionals today avoid the practice as essentially manipulative and unfair.

14. *Advertising.* Public relations professionals often use advertising, but advertising and PR are not the same. The major difference is one of control. Advertising is controlled communication; advertisers pay for ads to appear in specific media exactly as they want. Public relations tends to be less controlled. The PR firm cannot control how or where its press release is used by the local paper. It could not control how the media would react to Pepsi's claims of innocence in the product tampering hoax of 1993. Advertising becomes a public relations function when its goal is to build an image or to motivate action, as opposed to its usual function of selling products. The Smokey the Bear forest fire prevention campaign is a well-known successful public relations advertising campaign.

Advertising and public relations obviously overlap even for manufacturers of consumer products. Chevrolet must sell cars, but it must communicate with its various publics as well. Exxon sells gasoline. But in the wake of the *Valdez* disaster, it needed serious public relations help. One result of the overlap of advertising and public relations is that advertising agencies increasingly own their own public relations departments or firms

This is a very successful, long running advertising campaign. It is also a very successful, long running public relations campaign.

Only you can prevent forest fires.

SMOKEY

U.S. Department of Agriculture – Forest Service and Your State Forester 72-CFFP-16

or associate closely with a PR company. Seven of the top 10 highest earning public relations firms are subsidiaries of advertising agencies (see Figure 9–1). For example, Burson-Marsteller is owned by Young & Rubicam.

Another way that advertising and public relations differ is that advertising people typically do not set policy for an organization. Advertising people *implement* policy after organization leaders set it. In contrast, public relations professionals usually are part of the policy decision process because they are the liaison between the organization and its publics. Effective organizations have come to understand that even in routine decisions the impact on public opinion and subsequent consequences can be of tremendous importance. As a result, public relations has become a management function, and a public relations professional typically sits as a member of a company's highest level of management.

ORGANIZATION OF A PUBLIC RELATIONS OPERATION

Public relations operations come in all sizes. Regardless of size, however, the typical PR firm or department will have these types of positions (but not necessarily these titles):

Executive. This is the chief executive officer who, sometimes with a staff, sometimes alone, sets policy and serves as the spokesperson for the operation.

Account executives. Each account has its own executive who provides advice to the client, defines problems and situations, assesses the needs and demands of the client's publics, recommends a communication plan or campaign, and gathers the PR firm's resources in support of the client.

Creative specialists. These are the writers, graphic designers, artists, video and audio producers, and photographers—anybody necessary to meet the communication needs of the client.

Media specialists. Media specialists are aware of the requirements, preferences, limitations, and strengths of the various media used to serve the client. They find the right media for clients' messages.

Larger public relations operations may also have these positions as need demands:

Research. The key to two-way public relations communication rests in research—assessing the needs of a client's various publics and the effectiveness of the efforts aimed at them. Polling, one-on-one interviews, and **focus groups** where small groups of a targeted public are interviewed provide the PR operation and its client with feedback.

Government relations. Depending on the client's needs, lobbying or other direct communication with government officials may be necessary.

Financial services. Very specific and sophisticated knowledge of economics, finance, and business or corporate law is required to provide clients with dependable financial public relations.

Current Trends in Public Relations

GLOBALIZATION, SPECIALIZATION, AND NEW TECHNOLOGIES

As it has in the media industries themselves, globalization has come to public relations, both in the form of foreign ownership and in the reach of PR firms' operations into foreign countries. Hill and Knowlton (owned by British company WPP Group) and the U.S. firm Burston-Marsteller both maintain major operations around the world. Burston-Marsteller, for example, operates 63 offices in 32 countries. Rowland Company Worldwide is owned by English advertising agency Saatchi & Saatchi. Shandwick, the second highest earning PR firm in the United States, is based in London.

A second trend in public relations is specialization. As we've seen, the PRSA identifies 14 activities of public relations professionals, but it also acknowledges that specialization could expand that list. This specialization takes two forms. The first is defined by issue. For example, environmental public relations is attracting ever larger numbers of people, both to the side of environmentalists and to the side of industry. Ketchum Public Relations attracts corporate clients in part because of its reputation as a firm with superior **greenwashing** skills. That is, Ketchum is particularly adept at countering the public relations efforts aimed at its clients by environmentalists.

The second impetus driving specialization has to do with the increasing number of media outlets used in public relations campaigns that rely on new and emerging technologies. Online information and advertising are a growing part of the total public relations media mix, as are **video news releases** and videoconferencing. Television, in the form of the **satellite-delivered media tour,** where spokespeople can be simultaneously interviewed by a worldwide audience connected to the on-screen interviewee via telephone, has further extended the reach of public relations. In addition, desktop publishing has greatly expanded the number and type of available print outlets. All require professionals with quite specific skills.

Media Echoes

Boosting Smoking among Women

Into the early 1900s, smoking was seen as an unsavory habit, permissible for men, never for women. But with the turn of the century, women too wanted to light up. Advertising campaigns first began targeting female smokers in 1919. The American Tobacco Company slogan "Reach for a Lucky instead of a sweet" along with ads designed to help women understand that they could use cigarettes to keep their figures were targeted at this new market. The rush to smoke was also fueled by the fight for suffrage; women wanted equality. The right to vote was an important goal, but if men could smoke without a fight, why couldn't women?

As more women began to smoke, antismoking crusades attempted to deter them. The protection of women's morality, not their health, inspired the crusaders. Many cities forbade the use of tobacco by women in public places. Yet the number of women who started smoking continued to grow. George

Washington Hill, head of American Tobacco, wanted this lucrative market to continue to expand, and he wanted to own as large a part of it as possible. He turned to public relations and Edward Bernays.

A nephew of Sigmund Freud, Bernays was employed to conduct psychological research aimed at understanding the relationship between women and cigarettes. He learned that women saw cigarettes as symbols of freedom, as the representation of their unfair treatment in a man's world, and as a sign of their determination to be accepted as equal.

Bernays had several objectives: (1) to let the public know that it was quite all right for women to smoke; (2) to undercut the bans on public smoking by women that existed in many places; and (3) to position Lucky Strikes cigarettes as a progressive brand.

In meeting these goals, Bernays perpetrated a publicity stunt that is still heralded as a triumphant coup among public relations practitioners. New York City

TRUST IN PUBLIC RELATIONS

We began our discussion of public relations with the admission that the profession bears a negative reputation (see the box "Boosting Smoking among Women"). Edward Bernays's call for greater sensitivity to the wants and needs of the various publics and Ivy Lee's insistence that public relations be open and honest were the industry's first steps away from its huckster roots. The post–World War II code of ethics (Appendix A) and accreditation programs were a second and more important step. Yet Bernays himself was dissatisfied with the profession's progress. The "Father of Public Relations" died in 1995 at the age of 103. He spent the greater part of his last years demanding that the industry, especially the PRSA, police itself. In 1986 Bernays wrote,

> Under present conditions, an unethical person can sign the code of the PRSA, become a member, practice unethically—untouched by any legal sanctions. In law and medicine, such an individual is subject to disbarment from the profession. . . . There are no standards. . . . This sad situation makes it possible for anyone, regardless of education or ethics, to use the term "public relations" to describe his or her function. (p. 11)

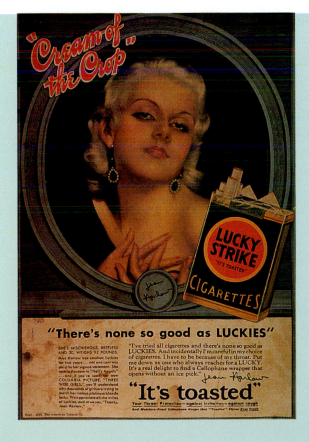

"There's none so good as LUCKIES"

SHE'S MISCHIEVOUS, RESTLESS AND 20, WEIGHS 112 POUNDS. Miss Harlow has smoked Luckies for two years . . . not one cent was paid for her signed statement. She rose to stardom in "Hell's Angels" . . . and, if you see her new COLUMBIA PICTURE, "THREE WISE GIRLS," you'll understand why thousands of girls are trying to match her riotous platinum blonde locks. We appreciate all she writes of Luckies, and so we say, "Thanks, Jean Harlow."

"I've tried all cigarettes and there's none so good as LUCKIES. And incidentally I'm careful in my choice of cigarettes. I have to be because of my throat. Put me down as one who always reaches for a LUCKY. It's a real delight to find a Cellophane wrapper that opens without an ice pick."

Jean Harlow

"It's toasted"

Your Throat Protection — against irritation — against cough
And Moisture-Proof Cellophane Keeps that "Toasted" Flavor Ever Fresh

Copr., 1931, The American Tobacco Co.

had a ban on public smoking by females. Because of, rather than despite, this, Bernays arranged for 10 socially prominent young women to enter the 1929 annual Easter Parade down Fifth Avenue as the "Torches of Liberty Contingent." As they marched, the debutantes lit their Lucky "torches of freedom" and smilingly proceeded to puff and walk. For reporters on the scene, this made for much better news and photos than the usual little kids in their spring finery. The blow for female emancipation was front page news, not only in New York, but nationally. The taboo was dead.

Later in his life, Bernays would argue that had he known of the link between cigarette smoking and cancer and other diseases, he would never have taken on American Tobacco as a client. We will see in Chapter 10 whether his strategy—and his later misgivings—are echoed in contemporary efforts to expand the market for cigarettes.

Lucky Strike used advertising and an effective public relations campaign to break the taboo on women smokers.

The Father of Public Relations, Edward Bernays, used the last years of his long career and life to campaign for improved industry ethics.

Many people share Bernays's concern. In the United States the number of public relations people exceeds the number of journalists (170,000 to 130,000). Estimates from both inside and outside the industry claim that from 50% to 90% of the stories we read in the paper or see on television originate entirely or in part from a public relations operation in the form of either a printed or a video news release. Critics further contend that 40% of what we read and see appears virtually unedited, leading PR professionals to boast that "the best PR is invisible" and "the best PR ends up looking like news" (Stauber & Rampton, 1995, p. 2).

This state of affairs led journalist and former *Mother Jones* editor Mark Dowie to write in his introduction to John Stauber and Sheldon Rampton's *Toxic Sludge Is Good For You: Lies, Damn Lies and the Public Relations Industry,*

> PR has become a communications medium in its own right, an industry designed to alter perception, reshape reality, and manufacture consent. It is run by a fraternity carefully organized so that only insiders can observe their peers at work. . . . It is critical that consumers of media in democratic societies understand the origin of information and the process by which it is mediated, particularly when they are being deceived. (1995, pp. 2–4)

If it is true that the public is being systematically deceived by public relations, the cultural implications could not be more profound. What becomes of the negotiation function of culture, wherein people debate and discuss their values and interests in the cultural forum, if public relations gives some voices advantages not available to others? Dowie suggests the remedy for this potential problem: Consumers must make themselves aware of "the origin of information and the process by which it is mediated" (p. 4). As we've seen throughout this book, we would expect nothing less of a media literate person.

 DEVELOPING MEDIA LITERACY SKILLS

Recognizing Video News Releases

Recognizing and correctly interpreting **video news releases** is another way to build media literacy. Video news releases are preproduced reports about a client or its product that are distributed free of charge to television stations on videocassette. Typically they:

- Look exactly like genuine news reports, employing the visual and aural conventions viewers typically associate with television news.

- Are narrated by a speaker whose voice, intonation, and delivery match those of bona fide television news reporters.

- Carry the voice-over on a separate audio channel so the station can delete the original narration and have its own anchor or reporter narrate to give the appearance that the report originated locally.

- Are accompanied by a script in the event the local station wants its own reporter or anchor to do the narration but needs help in writing it.

- Come free of titles or other graphics because local stations have their own logos and video character type faces.

Video news releases can be used in their entirety or in part, and most providers consider even a 5-second excerpt (a long time in television news) to be a success.

Defenders argue that as television news operations scale back their staffs because of the demands for greater profit brought about by conglomeration and other market forces, these reports are one of the few ways local news can acquire visuals and details about subjects of interest to the public. Critics, however, point to the deception inherent in the production of a piece designed expressly to look like something it isn't—original broadcast journalism.

At the very least the news department that uses such a report must identify its source and determine whether the presentation is objective enough to classify as news. The problem for the viewer is twofold. First,

Figure 9–3 This Tom Tomorrow comic satirizes one of the most controversial tools used by public relations firms—the self-promoting video news release. Legal, and sometimes providing useful information, these video clips test the viewer's media literacy skills.

when outside material is broadcast, it is common for the news show to include the name of its provider at the end of the program. "Film and video provided by" is familiar to anyone who watches television news. But the long list of names that follows makes matching the source and the content difficult.

The second problem for the viewer is that stations often find themselves under great internal pressure to classify a report as objective. Many large market and even some medium and small market stations broadcast three half-hour news shows an evening; typically at 5:30, 6:30, and 10 or 11 P.M. A growing number of stations now air a 60-minute news show at 10 or 11 P.M. Filling all that time with interesting and different visuals is a daunting task. There is great incentive for station executives, therefore, to find objectivity where little may exist (Figure 9–3).

In the end literate media consumers must depend on the ethics of the station that uses news releases and their own skill at reading them. In those instances where a reporter or an anchor acknowledges the outside source of a report while it airs, viewers must determine what level of trust they want to give the report. Not all video news releases are false or misleading. If we accept that they are created to further particular individual or organization interests, they can provide useful information. In those cases where the outside source is not identified or is identified apart from the report, literate viewers should question not only the report but the value of a news operation that has such limited regard for journalistic convention and so little respect for viewers.

The question that remains, however, is how to identify a video news release when the station does not do so. This is actually a relatively easy skill to acquire. You are watching a video news release when:

- A report is accompanied by visuals that are not from the station's area.

- No local station personnel appear in the report.

- There is no verbal or visual attribution (for example, "These scenes are from our sister station in Muncie" or the CNN logo in the corner of the screen).

- The report appears in the part of the newscast typically reserved for soft or feature stories.

Chapter Review

Because public relations is and does many different things, there is no universally accepted definition of this industry. In this chapter we define public relations as a management function that uses two-way communication to mesh the needs and interests of an institution or person with the needs and interests of the various publics with which that institution or person must communicate.

Public relations has matured from a huckster's activity into an industry attempting to develop and maintain professionalism among its practitioners. It has passed through four stages in this process: early public relations, the propaganda-publicity stage, early two-way communication, and advanced two-way communication.

Some 170,000 people work in contemporary public relations in the United States. There are over 4,000 public relations firms, and most major companies have in-house PR operations. The 14 activities typically carried out by PR operations are publicity, communication, public affairs, government relations, community relations, minority relations, financial public relations, industry rela-

tions, press agency, promotion, media relations, issues management, propaganda, and advertising. One way public relations differs from advertising is that public relations typically has a policy-making or management function in an organization, which advertising lacks.

The publics addressed by public relations include employees of the organization, its stockholders, the communities in which it operates, the media it depends on, the government, the investment community, and its customers.

Public relations operations typically employ an executive, account executives, creative specialists, and media specialists. Some larger operations will also have people in research, government relations, and financial services.

Globalization, specialization, and new communication technologies are altering the nature of the industry, but one thing that has not changed since its early days is the question of trust. The proliferation of video news releases is only one ethical question facing the profession. Their existence poses a challenge to the literate media consumer.

Questions for Review

1. Good definitions of public relations should contain what two elements?
2. What are the four stages in the development of the public relations industry?
3. Who are Ivy Lee, George Creel, and Edward Bernays?
4. What are the CPI and OWI? What is their importance to the development of public relations?
5. Who are George Gallup and Elmo Roper?
6. What is the difference between public relations and advertising? between press agency and promotion?
7. What are some specific divisions of public relations' public affairs activities?
8. Who are public relations' publics? What are their characteristics?
9. What positions typically exist in a public relations operation?
10. How have new communication technologies influenced the public relations industry?

Questions for Critical Thinking and Discussion

1. Did you see or read any of Nayirah al-Sabah's testimony? Did you believe her? Were your opinions about war with Iraq influenced by her stories? What is your reaction now that it has been revealed that her testimony may not have been completely true?
2. Propaganda is avoided by ethical PR people because it depends on an automatic, nonreflective reaction to a message or symbol. Can you think of industry, government, or interest group propaganda efforts that do exist? What symbols or messages typically generate these automatic responses?
3. If a video news release is fair, objective, and informative, does that justify the implicit deception in its use as a news report? Explain your view.
4. Reread the Dowie quote from page 270. Do you agree with his assessment of the profession? What is your feeling about public relations? When do you think it is useful for the culture? When do you think it is harmful?
5. Would you consider a career in public relations? If not, why not? If yes, what attracts you to this profession? Is there a specific aspect of its operation that interests you more than others? Why?

Important Resources

Center, A. H., & Jackson, P. (1995). *Public relations practices: Managerial case studies and problems.* **Englewood Cliffs, NJ: Prentice Hall.** A college-level textbook that uses some of the most famous PR efforts—for example, those involving the *Exxon Valdez* oil spill and Union Carbide's disastrous industrial accident at Bhopal, India—and many less well known but effective campaigns to lay out the basics of the industry. The ethics and responsibility sections are thoughtfully written.

Culbertson, H. M., Jeffers, D. W., Stone, D. B., & Terrell, M. (1993). *Social, political, and economic contexts in public relations: Theories and cases.* **Hillsdale, NJ: Lawrence Erlbaum.** A detailed examination of public relations as it operates in the culture. Much attention is given to the business of PR, but much is also directed at its roles and functions in various aspects of the modern business and social environment.

International Public Relations Review. Calling itself the "international journal of corporate and public affairs," this quarterly presents articles on both public relations within specific countries and public relations in countries other than one's own.

Public Relations Quarterly. A half-scholarly, half-trade journal that specializes in applied research and serious commentary on the profession from within and without.

Public Relations Review. A journal of research and commentary, published five times a year, that presents applied industry research and critical comment from academics.

pr reporter. This weekly typically takes on a specific public relations problem—for example, a hoax aimed at Girl Scout Cookies or public dissatisfaction with colleges and universities—for each of its issues and details either how one campaign addressed it or offers several opinions on how the problem might be handled. It bills itself as a "cutting edge newsletter of public relations, public affairs, and communication strategies."

Public Relations Information Web Sites

Public Relations Agencies and Resources on the WWW *http://www.webcom/impulse/prlist.html*

Canadian Public Relations Society *http://www.cprs.ca/conx.htm*

Public Relations Society of America *http://www.seflin.org/prsa/prsa.1.html*

Public Relations Students Society of America *http://www.prssa.org/prssacod.htm*

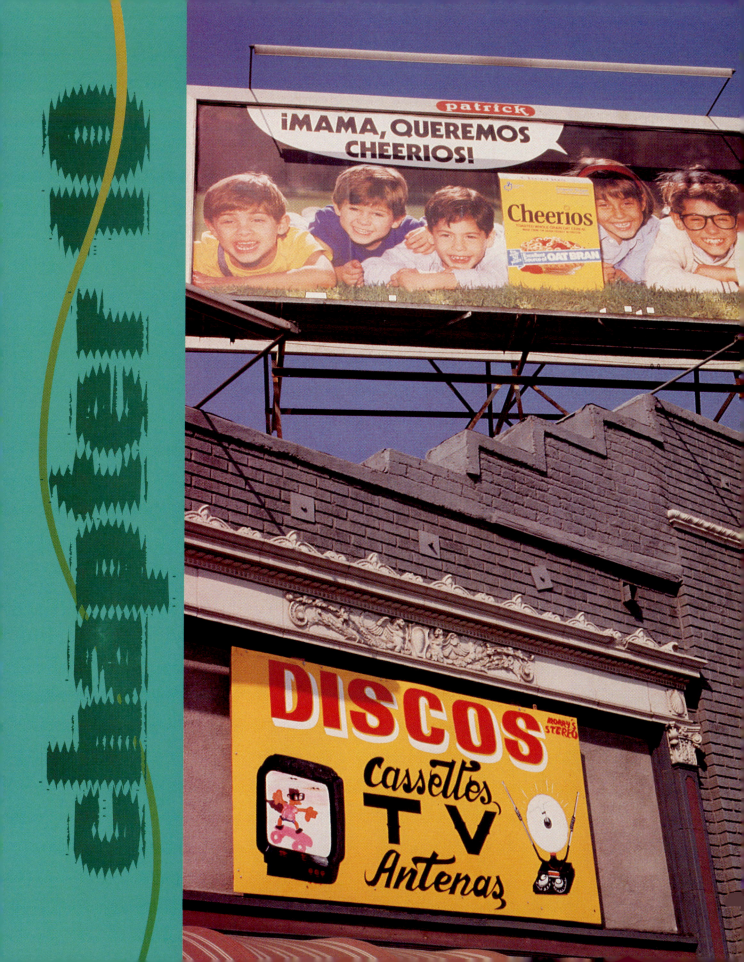

Advertising

Your roommates, both advertising majors, challenge you. "We bet you $10 that you can't go all of tomorrow without seeing an ad."

You think, "I'll just stay away from radio and television—no problem, considering I have a cassette player in my car and tons of homework to do." That leaves newspapers and magazines, but you can avoid their ads simply by not reading either for 24 hours. Online ads? You'll simply stay unlinked. "What about billboards?" you counter.

"We won't count them," your roomies graciously concede, "but everything else is in."

You shake hands and go to bed planning your strategy. This means no cereal in the morning—the Cheerios box has a McDonald's ad on it. There'll be no bus to school. Not only are the insides packed with ads, but a lot of buses are now covered in vinyl wrap ads that let riders see out the windows but turn buses into gigantic rolling commercials. Can't walk either. There are at least two ad kiosks on the way. It'll cost you more than $10 to take a cab, but this is about winning the bet, not about money. Cab it will be! You sleep well, confident victory is yours.

The next evening, over pizza, you hand over your $10.

"What was it?" gloats one of your companions. "Sneak a peek at TV?"

"No," you say, and then you begin the list: The cab had an ad for a radio station on its trunk and a three-sided sign on its roof touting the pizza joint you're sitting in, a chiropractor, and American Airlines. Inside, it had an electronic digital display hanging from the ceiling, pushing the lottery. The sidewalk near campus had the message "From here it looks like you could use some new underwear—Bamboo Lingerie" stenciled on it in water-soluble iridescent red paint. The restrooms on campus have Volkswagen ads pasted on their walls. Your ATM receipt carried an ad for a brokerage firm. You encountered a Domino's Pizza ad on the back of the cash register receipt you got at the store; the kiwi you bought there had a sticker on it reminding you to buy Snapple. The shopping basket had a realtor's pitch pasted to the side; even the little rubber bar you used to separate your kiwi and mineral water from the groceries of the shopper in front of you had an ad on each of its four sides.

"Easiest $10 we ever made," smile your roommates.

In this chapter we examine the history of advertising, focusing on its maturation with the coming of industrialization and the Civil War. The development of the advertising agency and the rise of professionalism within its ranks is detailed, as is the impact of magazines, radio, World War II, and television.

We discuss the relationship between consumers and contemporary advertising in terms of how advertising agencies are structured, how various types of advertising are aimed at different audiences, and which trends—new technologies, audience segmentation, globalization—promise to alter those relationships.

We study the controversies that surround the industry. Critics charge that advertising is intrusive, deceptive, inherently unethical when aimed at children, prone to foster monopolies, and corrupting of the culture. We look at industry defenses too.

Finally, in the media literacy skills section we discuss advertisers' use of intentional imprecision and how to identify and interpret it.

A Short History of Advertising

Your roommates had the advantage. They know that U.S. advertisers spend $160 billion a year trying to get your attention and influence your decisions. They also know that the typical person sees 250 ads a day and more than 2 million ads by the time he or she is 25 years old. There are a lot of ads and a lot of advertisers, so pitches are showing up in some unusual places. Many public schools sell ad space on their lunch menus. Police cars in Crown Point, Indiana, carry ads on their trunks. Some golf courses sell ads at the bottom of the plastic cup that sits in the holes. Airplane snacks often come in plastic bags filled with ads and other promotions. Most professional hockey teams sell the space under their ice to sponsors. Gasoline pumps carry ads for just about every product there is, and we've come to expect, and accept, product commercials before the movie we've just paid $8 to see. Sports stadiums now carry sponsors' names—take me out to 3Com Park! Qualcomm Stadium! International Edison Stadium! Houlihans Stadium! Coke is the official drink of Ocean City, Maryland. Ford is the official truck, Speedo the official bathing suit, and Naya Canadian the official bottled water of Los Angeles County's Department of Beaches and Harbors. MasterCard is the official credit card of South Orange, New Jersey. Only public protest halted U.S. Department of the Interior plans to have corporate advertisers "sponsor" individual

This narrow street in Salzburg, Austria, still exhibits evidence of early European advertising, which often took the form of artistically designed signs announcing the nature of the business below.

national parks in 1996. We see ads on door hangers, in the mail, behind the batter at a baseball game, on basketball backboards in city parks, on suspended video monitors as we wait in line at the amusement park. We hear ads when we're on hold on the telephone. It wasn't always like this, but advertising itself has been with us for a long time.

EARLY ADVERTISING

Babylonian merchants were hiring barkers to shout out goods and prices at passersby in 3000 B.C. The Romans wrote announcements on city walls. This ad was discovered in the ruins of Pompeii:

> The Troop of Gladiators of the Aedil
> Will fight on the 31st of May
> There will be fights with wild animals
> And an Awning to keep off the sun. (Berkman & Gilson, 1987, p. 32)

By the 15th century, ads as we know them now were abundant in Europe. **Siquis**—pinup want ads for all sorts of products and services—were common. Tradespeople promoted themselves with **shopbills,** attractive, artful business cards. Taverners and other merchants were hanging

This early 18th-century tobacco label shows that the British had already mastered the use of celebrities in their advertising.

eye-catching signs above their businesses. In 1625 the first **newsbook** containing ads, *The Weekly News,* was printed in England. From the beginning, those who had products and services to offer used advertising.

Advertising came to the Colonies via England. British advertising was already leaning toward exaggeration and hyperbole, but colonial advertising was more straightforward. We saw in Chapter 4 that Ben Franklin was selling advertising space in his *Philadelphia Gazette.* This 1735 ad is typical:

> A Plantation containing 300 acres of good Land, 30 cleared, 10 or 12 Meadow and in good English Grass, a house and barn & c. [creek] lying in Nantmel Township, upon French-Creek, about 30 miles from Philadelphia. Inquire of Simon Meredith now living on the said place. (Sandage, Fryburger, & Rotzoll, 1989, p. 21)

Advertising, however, was a small business before the Civil War. The United States was primarily an agricultural country at that time, with 90% of the population living in self-sufficiency on farms. Advertising was used by local retailers primarily to encourage area residents to come to their businesses. The local newspaper was the major advertising medium.

INDUSTRIALIZATION AND THE CIVIL WAR

The Industrial Revolution and the Civil War altered the social and cultural landscape and brought about the expansion of advertising. By the 1840s the telegraph made communication over long distances possible. Railroads linked cities and states. Huge numbers of immigrants were welcomed to the United States to provide labor for the expanding factories. Manufacturers wanted access to larger markets for their goods. Advertising copywriter Volney B. Palmer recognized in 1841 that merchants needed to reach consumers beyond their local newspaper readership. He contacted several Philadelphia newspapers and agreed to broker the sale of space between them and interested advertisers. Within 4 years Palmer had expanded his business to Boston, and in 1849, he opened a branch in New York. The advertising agency had been invented.

The Civil War sped industrialization. More factories were needed to produce war material, and roads and railroads were expanded to move that material as well as troops. As farm workers went to war or to work in the new factories, more farm machinery was needed to compensate for their departure. That meant that more factories were needed to make more machinery, and the cycle repeated.

By the early 1880s the telephone and the electric light had been invented. That decade saw numerous innovations in manufacturing as well

Reaction to the deception and outright lies of patent medicine advertising—such as this 1880 piece for Pratts Healing Ointment—led to important efforts to professionalize the industry.

He Cut off his Nose to Spite his Face.

This man is a Grammar Master of the old school. He does not believe in the "New Methods." He will not send for our **Illustrated Catalogue of School Aids and Material,** although if he would mention that he reads the "Ads" in the POPULAR EDUCATOR we would mail it to him without charge. Said a prominent teacher the other day: "I never dealt with any other firm as prompt and business-like in all their methods as Milton Bradley Co., Springfield, Mass., and their material is always excellent." The majority of teachers use it, and you will surely want some of it this year. Do not attempt to begin school without our Catalogue. Send 12 cents for our new Number Builder for desk-work in figures. Remember that we shall soon publish a Manual for Primary Work in Ungraded Schools.

MILTON BRADLEY CO.

October, 1889   **Springfield, Mass.**

as an explosion in the type and availability of products. In one year alone, 1880, there were applications for more than 13,000 U.S. copyrights and patents. Over 70,000 miles of new railroad track were laid in the 1880s, linking cities and towns of all sizes. With more producers chasing the growing purchasing power of more consumers, manufacturers were forced to differentiate their products—to literally and figuratively take the pickle out of the barrel and put it in its own recognizable package. Brands were born: Quaker Oats, Ivory Soap, Royal Baking Powder, and many more. What advertisers now needed was a medium in which to tell people about these brands.

MAGAZINE ADVERTISING

We've seen in Chapter 5 how expansion of the railroads, the rise in literacy, and advantageous postal rates fueled the explosive growth of the popular magazine just before the end of the 19th century. The marriage of magazines and advertising was a natural. Cyrus H. K. Curtis, who founded the *Ladies' Home Journal* in 1883, told a group of manufacturers:

> The editor of the Ladies' Home Journal thinks we publish it for the benefit of American women. This is an illusion, but a very proper one for him to have. The real reason, the publisher's [Curtis's] reason, is to give you who manufacture things American women want, a chance to tell them about your product. (Sandage et al., 1989, p. 32)

By the turn of the century magazines were financially supported by their advertisers rather than by their readers, and aspects of advertising we find common today—creativity in look and language, mail-order ads, seasonal ads, and placement of ads in proximity to content of related interest—were already in use.

THE ADVERTISING AGENCY AND PROFESSIONALISM

In the years between the Civil War and World War I, advertising had rapidly become more complex, more creative, and more expensive, and it was conducted on a larger scale. Advertising agencies had to expand their operations to keep up with demand. Where Palmer offered merely to broker the sale of newspaper space, F. Wayland Ayer (whose firm is now the oldest ad agency in the United States) began his "full service" advertising agency in 1877. He named his firm N. W. Ayer and Sons after his father because, at only 20 years old, he felt that clients would not trust him with their business. Ayer (the son) provided clients with ad campaign planning, created and produced ads with his staff of artists and writers, and placed them in the most appropriate media. Some other big agencies still operating today started at this time, including J. Walter Thompson, William Esty, and Lord & Thomas.

During this period, three factors combined to move the advertising industry to establish professional standards and to regulate itself. First was the reaction of the public and the medical profession to the abuses of patent medicine advertisers. These charlatans used fake claims and medical data in their ads to sell tonics that at best were useless, and at worst, deadly. The second was the critical examination of most of the country's important institutions, led by the muckrakers (Chapter 5). The third factor was the establishment in 1914 of the Federal Trade Commission (FTC), which had among its duties monitoring and regulating advertising. A number of leading advertising agencies and publishers mounted a crusade against gross exaggeration, false testimonials, and other misleading forms of advertising. The Audit Bureau of Circulation was established to verify circulation claims. The Advertising Federation of America, the American Association of Advertising Agencies, the Association of National Advertisers, the Direct Mail Advertising Association, and the Outdoor Advertising Association all began operation at this time.

ADVERTISING AND RADIO

The first radio ad, as we've seen in Chapter 7, was broadcast on WEAF in 1922 (the cost was $50 for a 10-minute spot). Radio was important to advertising in many ways. First, although people both inside and outside government were opposed to commercial support for the new medium, the general public had no great opposition to radio ads. In fact, in the prosperous Roaring Twenties, many welcomed them; advertising seemed a natural way to keep radio "free." Second, advertising agencies virtually took over broadcasting, producing the shows in which their commercials appeared. The ad business became show business. The 1923 variety show *The Eveready Hour,* sponsored by a battery maker, was the first regularly broadcast sponsored series. Ad agency Blackett-Sample-Hummert even developed a new genre for its client Proctor & Gamble—the radio soap opera. Finally, money now poured into the industry. That money was used to expand research and marketing on a national scale, allowing advertisers access to sophisticated nationwide consumer and market information for the first time. The wealth that the advertising industry accrued from radio permitted it to survive during the Depression.

The Depression did have its effect on advertising, however. The stock market crashed in 1929, and by 1933 advertising had lost nearly two thirds of its revenues. Among the responses were the hard sell—making direct claims about why a consumer *needed* a product—and a tendency away from honesty. At the same time, widespread unemployment and poverty bred a powerful consumer movement. The Consumer's Union, which still publishes *Consumer Reports,* was founded in 1936 to protect people from unscrupulous manufacturers and advertisers. And in 1938 Congress passed the Wheeler-Lea Act, granting the Federal Trade Commission extended powers to regulate advertising.

WORLD WAR II

The Second World War, so important in the development of all the mass media, had its impact on advertising as well. Production of consumer products came to a near halt during the war (1941–1945), and traditional advertising was limited. The advertising industry turned its collective skills toward the war effort, and the limited product advertising typically adopted a patriotic theme.

Several national advertising and media associations joined to develop the War Advertising Council. The council used its expertise to promote numerous government programs. Its best known campaign, however, was on behalf of the sale of war bonds. The largest campaign to date for a

Using Media to Make a Difference

Saving the Grand Canyon

Advertising can often move people to do good. Robert Glatzer (1970) recounts the story of how advertising saved the Grand Canyon. In 1966 the Bureau of Reclamation of the U.S. Department of the Interior sought Congressional approval to build two dams on the Colorado River that would back water up 100 miles, creating a vast lake stretching upstream into the Grand Canyon. The lake would have ended at a spot just below the national park's stunning and justly famous South Rim. With a coalition of House and Senate members backing the plan, its passage was virtually assured.

David Brower, executive director of the Sierra Club, a small conservation group, was horrified. He went to advertising professionals Jerry Mander and Howard Gossage and asked their help in derailing the plan through advertising. Mander wrote the first ad, "Now Only You Can Save the Grand Canyon From Being Flooded—For Profit," and spent $10,000 to place it in the June 9 *New York Times* and *Washington Post.* Not only do these two papers have a sizable readership of educated people, but they are read by virtually every legislator and government official in Washington, D.C. Within one

single item, the war bond program helped sell 800 million bonds, totaling $45 billion. When the war ended, the group, now called the Advertising Council, directed its efforts toward a host of public service campaigns on behalf of countless nonprofit organizations (see the box "Saving the Grand Canyon"). Most of us have read or heard, "This message is brought to you by the American Ad Council."

week, 3,000 new memberships had flowed into the Sierra Club. At $14 each, they boosted the available campaign funds—at the time down to $8,000—to $50,000.

A second effect of the ad was that by noon of the day it appeared, the Internal Revenue Service announced that it would investigate, and possibly revoke, the tax exempt status of the Sierra Club for its "substantial" political activity. It was the first time the IRS had taken such an action against a nonprofit group. In response, thousands of new members joined to support the club in the months that followed.

In July Mander penned an eloquent, now famous ad that he placed in a number of intellectual magazines, from *The National Review* on the political right to *Ramparts* on the left. Almost immediately *Scientific American* and dozens of other magazines and newspapers asked permission to reprint the ad at no cost to the Sierra Club. The piece generated enough money for Mander and Gossage to buy a third ad in the *Times*.

Did the ads make a difference? Several Congress-people reported that the volume of mail they received on this issue exceeded that on all other topics, including the war in Vietnam. Sierra Club membership reached 50,000, and the club received more than a quarter of a million dollars in new memberships and gifts. These events combined to make it a political power. When the allocation of money for the dams finally came to a vote in the spring of 1967, it was defeated in the Senate 70 to 12.

Consumer products go to war. Advertisers and manufacturers joined the war effort. These GIs are enjoying a Coke on Leyte Island in the Pacific in a 1945 *Collier's* ad.

...Yank friendliness comes back to Leyte

Naturally Filipinos thrilled when their Yankee comrades-in-arms came back to the Philippines. Freedom came back with them. Fair play took the place of fear. But also they brought back the old sense of friendliness that America stands for. You find it quickly expressed in the simple phrase *Have a Coke.* There's no easier or warmer way to say *Relax and be yourself.* Everywhere *the pause that refreshes* with ice-cold Coca-Cola has become a symbol of good will—an everyday example of how Yankee friendliness follows the flag around the globe.

* * *

Our fighting men meet up with Coca-Cola many places overseas, where it's bottled on the spot. Coca-Cola has been a globe-trotter "since way back when".

"Coke" = Coca-Cola
You naturally hear Coca-Cola called by its friendly abbreviation "Coke". Both mean the quality product of The Coca-Cola Company.

COPYRIGHT 1945, THE COCA-COLA COMPANY

The impact of World War II on the size and structure of the advertising industry was significant. A high excess-profits tax was levied on manufacturers' wartime profits that exceeded prewar levels. The goal was to limit war profiteering and ensure that companies did not benefit too greatly from the death and destruction of war. Rather than pay the heavy tariff, manufacturers reduced their profit levels by putting income back into their businesses. Because the lack of raw materials made expansion or recapitalization difficult, many companies invested in corporate image advertising. They may not have had products to sell to the public, but they knew that the war would end someday and that stored up goodwill would be important. One result, therefore, was an expansion in the number and size of manufacturers' advertising departments and of advertising agencies. A second result was a public primed by that advertising anticipating the return of consumer goods.

ADVERTISING AND TELEVISION

There was no shortage of consumer products when the war ended. The nation's manufacturing capacity had been greatly expanded to meet the needs of war, and now that manufacturing capability was turned toward the production of consumer products for people who found themselves with more leisure and more money (Chapter 2). People were also having more children and, thanks to the GI Bill, were able to think realistically about owning their own homes. They wanted products to enhance their leisure, please their children, and fill their houses.

Advertising was well positioned to put products and people together, not only because agencies had expanded during the war but also because of television. Radio formats, stars, and network structure had moved wholesale to the new medium. Television soon became the primary national advertising medium. Advertisers bought $12 million in television time in 1949; two years later they spent $128 million.

Television commercials, by virtue of the fact that consumers could see and hear the product in action, were different from the advertising of all other media. The ability to demonstrate the product—to do the torture test for Timex watches, to smoothly shave sandpaper with Gillette Foamy—led to the **unique selling proposition (USP)**—that is, highlighting the aspect of a product that set it apart from other brands in the same product category. Once an advertiser discovered a product's USP, it could drive it home in repeated demonstration commercials. Inasmuch as most brands in a given product category are essentially the same—that is, they are **parity products**—advertisers were often forced to create a product's USP. Candy is candy, for example, but M&Ms are unique—they melt in your mouth, not in your hand.

Some observers were troubled by this development. Increasingly, products were being sold not by touting their value or quality but by emphasizing their unique selling propositions. Ads were offering little information about the product, yet people were increasing their spending. This led to growing criticism of advertising and its contribution to the consumer culture (more on this controversy later in the chapter). The immediate impact was the creation of an important vehicle of industry self-regulation. In response to mounting criticism in books like *The Hidden Persuaders* (Packard, 1957), and concern over increasing scrutiny from the Federal Trade Commission, the industry in 1971 established the National Advertising Review Board (NARB) to monitor potentially deceptive advertising. The NARB, the industry's most important self-regulatory body, investigates consumer complaints as well as complaints made by an advertiser's competitors.

Among the earliest demonstration ads, Timex took many a licking but kept on ticking.

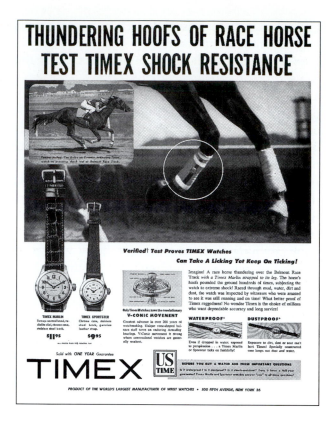

THE EVOLUTION OF TELEVISION COMMERCIALS

The history of television commercials themselves is interesting because it highlights the interdependence between medium and advertising message. We saw in Chapter 8 how advertisers and their ad agencies produced early television shows, only to lose that function after the quiz show scandal in 1959. Once advertisers no longer owned program content, it became impossibly expensive to be the sole sponsor of a network broadcast. The networks were demanding a great deal of money to offset their investment in a program. In this climate it was more efficient and more profitable for advertisers to spread commercials across a number of programs, reaching many more viewers. The networks, profiting from this new state of affairs, began selling commercial time in 60-second segments. With many different "spot" commercials for many different products in the same show, the nature of the commercials themselves changed. A spot had to stand out and be remembered—greater creativity came to television advertising.

In addition, because a number of commercials in an individual program or on a given night of television were selling the same or similar products, and because many of these products were essentially the same in quality and cost, the USP became even more important, as did the need to boost **brand awareness**—identification of a product with a particular manufacturer. Brand identification was achieved through slogans and jingles: "You'll wonder where the yellow went when you brush your teeth with Pepsodent."

In television's early days commercials were highly product-oriented. This focus changed, however, as a result of government regulation of cigarette companies, then television's biggest advertisers. Responding to mounting challenges from health groups, in 1971 the FCC banned cigarette commercials from the airwaves. With the loss of this important category of advertisers, the networks quickly discovered that too few advertisers could afford to buy a 60-second spot on a popular prime time program.

Lowering the price of advertising time was a possible solution, but rising production costs for network shows made this difficult. In 1953, for example, a one-hour episode of *Studio One* cost CBS $30,000 to produce. In 1975, *Gunsmoke* cost that same network $230,000 for one hour. The networks' solution was to split the 60-second spots into more affordable 30-second segments. Now an even greater number of advertisers could afford television. At the same time, the networks could make more money by selling two 30-second spots at more than the price of one full minute. Each minute of advertising time became more profitable. The networks had solved *their* problem, but advertisers had a new one—their commercials were now aired among twice as many competing messages. In 1965 every network television commercial was a full 60 seconds, although 23% were **piggybacked** (that is, a single sponsor presented two products in the same minute). By 1975 only 6% were a full minute long.

The number of commercial spots grew, and so too did the number of commercial minutes allowed on television. In 1967, for example, there were an estimated 100,000 commercial minutes aired on the networks. By 1974 there were 105,622 commercial minutes—5,600 *additional* minutes on the three commercial networks alone. As the number of spots grew and their length shrank, commercials became less about the products—there was too little time to give any relevant information—and more about the people who use them. Image advertising came to television.

Today the price of commercial time continues to rise, production costs for programming continue to increase, the number of commercials on the air continues to grow, the air time available for advertising continues to expand, and as a result, the length of commercial spots continues to shrink. Fifteen- and even 10-second spots are now common. More and more spots crammed into a commercial break produces **clutter.** How does an advertiser get heard and seen above the clutter? The answer for many contemporary television advertisers is to give even less information about the product and place greater emphasis on style, image, graphics, and look. Today's television ads can cost as much as $1 million a minute to produce. One television writer explained the impact of this development on the medium itself:

> The switch to 15-second commercials seems to be nothing more than a complicated story about the inner workings of the broadcast industry, another tale of the pursuit of the almighty dollar. But it's more important than you

might think. Because commercials influence the fabric of television, they, in turn, influence the fabric of everything else. When ads change, it's a sign that television is changing, as well as the culture. (Stark, 1985, p. A24)

Later in this chapter we'll see that many critics—both inside and outside the media—disagree on the benefits of this change.

Advertising and Its Audiences

The typical U.S. citizen will spend more than one year of his or her life just watching television commercials. It is a rare moment when we are not in the audience of some ad or commercial. This is one of the many reasons advertisers have begun to place their messages in many venues beyond the traditional commercial media, hoping to draw our attention. We confront so many ads every day that we overlook them, and they become invisible. As a result, many people only become aware of advertising when it somehow offends them.

CRITICISMS AND DEFENSES OF ADVERTISING

Advertising does sometimes offend, and it is often the focus of criticism. But industry defenders argue that:

- Advertising supports our economic system; without it new products could not be introduced and developments in others could not be announced. Competitive advertising of new products and businesses powers the "engine" of our economy, fostering economic growth and creating jobs in many industries.
- People use advertising to gather information before making buying decisions.
- Ad revenues make possible the "free" mass media we use not only for entertainment but for the maintenance of our democracy.
- By showing us the bounty of our capitalistic, free enterprise society, advertising increases national productivity (as people work harder to acquire more of these products) and improves the standard of living (as people actually acquire more of these products).

The first defense is a given. Ours is a capitalistic society whose economy depends on the exchange of goods and services. Complaints, then, have less to do with the existence of advertising than with its conduct and content. The second defense assumes that advertising provides information. But much—critics would say most—advertising is void of useful information about the product. The third defense assumes that the only way media can exist is through commercial support, but many nations around the world have built fine media systems without heavy advertiser

This gym may be the home of Cougar pride, but it is also home to a large Wendy's ad. Advertising in schools and on educational materials is now common—and quite controversial.

support (Chapter 15). To critics of advertising, the fourth defense—that people work hard only to acquire more things and that our standard of living is measured by what material things we have—draws an unflattering picture of human nature.

SPECIFIC COMPLAINTS

Specific complaints about advertising are that it is often intrusive, deceptive, and, in the case of children's advertising, inherently unethical. Advertising is said to foster monopolies and demean or corrupt the culture.

Advertising Is Intrusive Many critics fault advertising for its intrusiveness. Advertising is everywhere, and it interferes with and alters our experience. Giant wall advertisements change the look of cities. Ads beamed by laser light onto night skies destroy evening stargazing. School learning aids provided by candy makers that ask students to "count the Tootsie Rolls" alter education. Many Internet users complain about the commercialization of the new medium and fear advertising will alter its free, open, and freewheeling nature.

Advertising Is Deceptive Many critics say that much advertising is inherently deceptive in that it implicitly and sometimes explicitly promises to improve people's lives through the consumption or purchase of a sponsor's products. Jamieson and Campbell (1997) described this as the "If . . . then" strategy: "A beautiful woman uses a certain brand of lipstick in the ad, and men follow her everywhere. Without making the argument explicit, the ad implies that if you use this product you will be beautiful, and if you are beautiful (or use this product), you will be more attractive to men" (p. 242). They called the opposite strategy "if not. . . . then not." When Hallmark says "When you care enough to send the very best," the implication is that when you do not send Hallmark you simply do not care.

Advertising promises health, long life, sexual success, financial success, companionship, popularity, and acceptance. Industry defenders argue that people understand and accept this as allowable exaggerations, not as deception.

Yet many **infomercials**—program-length commercials designed to look like news or entertainment programs—are clearly designed to deceive. For example, many television stations and cable channels run a "program" called *Special Report: Preventing Violent Crime*. Featuring an anchorman at his desk and gripping footage of crime in progress, the show is actually a 30-minute commercial for the Nova XR 5000 stun gun. The "program" *Consumer Challenge* investigates different brands of sunglasses. BluBlocker invariably wins the approval of the experts. The show is in actuality a BluBlocker commercial.

Media Echoes

Boosting Smoking among Children

In the 1980s as U.S. levels of smoking continued to decline, RJR Nabisco introduced a new ad campaign for its Camel brand cigarettes. The campaign featured a sun-bleached, cool, and casual camel who possessed human qualities. Joe Camel, as he was called, was debonair, in control, and the center of attention, whether in a pool hall, on a dance floor, leaning against his convertible, or lounging on the beach. He wore the hippest clothes. He sported the best sunglasses. RJR Nabisco said it was trying a new campaign to boost brand awareness and corner a larger portion of a dwindling market. But antismoking groups saw in Joe Camel the echo of Edward Bernays's strategy to open smoking to an untapped market (Chapter 9). They accused the company of attempting to attract young smokers—often adding that these were the

life-long customers the tobacco company needed to replace those it was killing.

The battle heated up in 1991, and an entire issue of the *Journal of the American Medical Association* was devoted to the impact of smoking on the culture. One of the articles reported on a study of Joe Camel's appeal to youngsters. Researcher Dr. Joseph DiFranza had discovered that Joe Camel was the single most recognizable logo in the country. Children as young as 3 years old could recognize Joe, and more kids could identify him than could identify Mickey Mouse.

RJR Nabisco attempted to discredit the study and its author and claimed that it had a First Amendment right to advertise its legal product any way it wanted. Nonetheless, soon after the publication of the *JAMA*, antismoking activist Janet Mangini filed a lawsuit in

Advertising Exploits Children The average child sees more than 20,000 television commercials a year and countless more in magazines and, increasingly, even on school materials (Stead, 1997). Critics contend that children are simply not intellectually capable of interpreting the intent of these ads, nor are they able before the age of 7 or 8 to rationally judge the worth of the advertising claims (see the box "Boosting Smoking Among Children"). This makes children's advertising inherently unethical. Television advertising to kids is especially questionable because children consume it in the home—with implicit parental approval, and most often without parental supervision. The question ad critics ask is, "If parents would never allow living salespeople to enter their homes to sell their children products, why do they allow the most sophisticated salespeople of all to do it for 20 minutes every hour every Saturday morning?"

Critics see another example of advertisers' exploitation of children in **toy-based children's television programming.** Young children have a hard enough time understanding television genre conventions, but when they are presented with programs that feature characters that are also toys, that difficulty is increased. How does a 5-year-old, for example, tell where the program ends and the commercial begins in shows like *Voltron, Men in Black, 101 Dalmatians, Animaniacs,* and the *Smurfs*? These appear to be little more than 30-minute commercials disguised as kid shows.

San Francisco against the tobacco company. Several California counties and cities joined the suit, alleging that the Joe Camel campaign violated state consumer protection laws designed to protect minors from false or misleading tobacco advertising.

Just before it was to go to trial in 1997, the country's second largest tobacco company, while admitting no wrongdoing, agreed to settle out of court with a payment of $10 million. It also agreed to a court order to suspend the Joe Camel campaign, the first time in history that a tobacco company had done so. What may have encouraged the cigarette company to cooperate were internal memos in the hands of the court that would later be made public. An R. J. Reynolds Tobacco memo from 1975 said: "To ensure increased and long-term growth for Camel Filter, the brand must increase its share penetration among the 14–24 age group" ("Kids Are Getting Lost," 1998, p. 10A). Other memos identified target smokers as young as 12 years old.

Edward Bernays said that had he known about the health risks involved with smoking he would not have planned the Lucky Strike "Torches of Liberty" campaign back in 1929. What justification for the Joe Camel campaign would you give if you were part of the ad team that developed the character, or if you worked for an ad agency that placed the ads, or if you were the editor at a magazine that ran them?

Joe Camel was ubiquitous . . . and controversial.

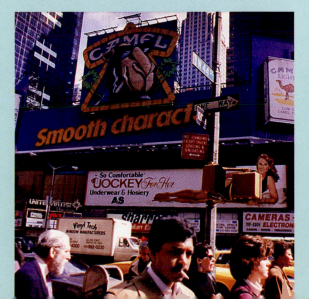

Challenging Advertising: Adbusters and Uncommercials

The Media Foundation operates out of Vancouver, British Columbia, with the goal of increasing public awareness of overconsumption and overcommercialization. Naturally, advertising is one of its primary targets. The group publishes a quarterly magazine called *Adbusters,* maintains an active Web site *(http://www.adbusters.org),* and sponsors events like the annual late-November "Buy Nothing Day" and the mid-April "TV Turnoff Week" (26 state governors officially endorsed this event in 1997). The group also makes print and video "uncommercials" (public service announcements that challenge well-known actual commercials), which are available at no cost to those who wish to use them to, as the Media Foundation likes to call it, "culturejam," or challenge the prevailing commercial culture.

Sometimes this anticommercial advocacy group has trouble getting its message out. In 1996 ABC, CBS, and NBC all refused to sell airtime to the group for its 30-second uncommercial announcing that year's "Buy Nothing Day," even though the Media Foundation was prepared to pay the full commercial rate to air the spot. Said an NBC spokesperson, "We don't want the business. We don't want to accept any advertising that's inimical to our legitimate business interests" (*www.adbusters.org*). In 1997, when the three networks refused to run an uncommercial for "TV Turnoff Week," for which the foundation was again willing to pay top commercial rates, an NBC executive said, "Our business is about turning on TV, not turning off TV. We have absolutely no intention of running these spots" (*www.adbusters.org*).

Sometimes, however, the Media Foundation is quite successful. In the fall of 1997 it was the subject of an hour-long PBS documentary called *Adfluenza.* Its Joe Chemo uncommercials and antismoking posters (parodying Joe Camel) appear in thousands of stores, schools, medical and health offices, and other public places. Many cable access stations run the uncommercials, and they occasionally appear on local commercial stations as well.

Whether or not you believe this effort is effective or even necessary, if you believe in freedom of expression, you have to ask yourself whether it is proper for the commercial television networks to refuse to carry Media Foundation uncommercials. Overcommercialization is a sometimes controversial public issue. If broadcasters feel comfortable refusing to air a side of the debate that they feel is "inimical" to their "legitimate business interests," two questions arise. First, what other expressions do they deny because it runs counter to their business interests? Second, how can debate on this important issue ever flourish?

Through its efforts, the Media Foundation has put these questions in the public forum. How do you defend your position on them?

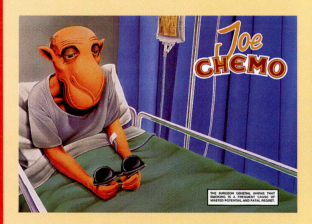
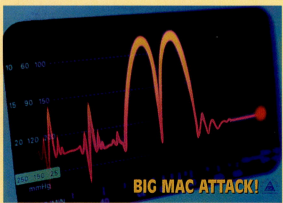

The Media Foundation's uncommercials offer alternative interpretations of some of our culture's most recognizable advertising.

Advertising Is Conducive to Monopolies   As we've seen, advertising's defenders argue that advertising is necessary to create informed, discriminating consumers to sustain our capitalistic economic system. Yet critics claim that advertising, as it is practiced, has just the opposite effect and, as a result, leads to the creation of monopolies (see the box "Challenging Advertising: Adbusters and Uncommercials"). Ad critic Richard Draper (1986) argues that, in fact, information-light advertising leads to monopoly:

> Perfect competition requires highly standardized products, many buyers and sellers, and "perfect information." Every buyer knows what every seller proposes to charge for every product and feature. Price competition, the inevitable result, forces sellers to use their resources efficiently. Consumers benefit doubly—first, because all their products are as cheap as possible, and, second, because the sum of society's wealth is greater than it would be in an imperfect market. . . .
>
> The theory of monopoly concedes that advertising deflects consumers from the rational aim of buying in the cheapest market and makes them, instead, want a certain brand, irrespective of cost. (Since the company that produces the brand is the only one that can do so, it has a "limited monopoly.") (p. 15)

In other words, Nike can demand and get $180 for a pair of basketball shoes and Evian can make a profit selling water at $2 a bottle because they have an advertising-created, USP-defined monopoly on Nike and Evian (Figure 10–1).

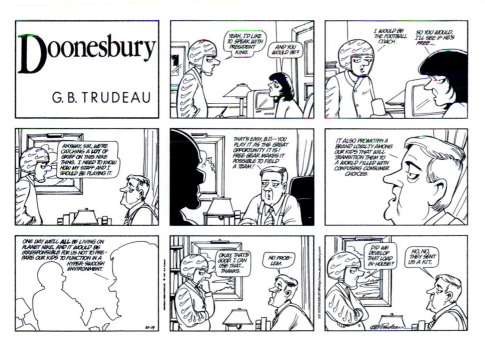

Figure 10–1 Large advertisers such as Nike have come under much criticism for their intrusion into virtually all aspects of people's lives. Here Garry Trudeau ponders life on Planet Nike. Doonesbury © 1997 G. B. Trudeau. Reprinted with permission of Universal Press Syndicate. All Rights Reserved.

Advertising Demeans and Corrupts Culture   In our culture we value beauty, kindness, prestige, family, love, and success. As human beings we need food, shelter, and the maintenance of the species, in other words, sex. Advertising succeeds by appealing to these values and needs. The basis for this persuasive strategy is the **AIDA approach**—to persuade consumers, advertising must attract *attention*, create *interest*, stimulate *desire*, and promote *action*. According to industry critics, however, problems arise when important aspects of human existence are reduced to the consumption of brand name consumer products. Freedom is choosing between a Big Gulp and a canned soda at 7-Eleven. Being a good mother is as simple as buying a bottle of Downy Fabric Softener. Prestige is driving an Oldsmobile. Success is drinking Chivas Regal. Love is giving your husband a shirt without ring-around-the-collar or your fiancée a diamond worth two months' salary.

Critics argue that ours has become a **consumer culture**—a culture in which personal worth and identity reside not in ourselves but in the products with which we surround ourselves. The consumer culture is corrupting because it imposes new definitions that serve the advertiser and not the culture on traditionally important aspects of our lives. If love, for example, can be bought rather than being something that has to be nurtured, how important can it be? If success is not something an individual values for the personal sense of accomplishment but rather is something chased for the material things associated with it, how does the culture evaluate success? Name the five most successful people you know. How many teachers did you name? How many social workers? How many wealthy or famous people did you name?

Critics contend that the consumer culture also demeans the individuals who live in it. A common advertising strategy for stimulating desire and suggesting action is to imply that we are inadequate and should not be satisfied with ourselves as we are. We are too fat or too thin, our hair is in need of improvement, our clothes are all wrong, and our spouses don't respect us. Personal improvement is only a purchase away (Figure 10–2).

Scope and Nature of the Advertising Industry

The proliferation of the different types of sales pitches described in the opening vignette is the product of an avalanche of advertising. Advertisers are exploring new ways to be seen and heard, to stand out, to be remembered, and to be effective. With so many kinds of commercial messages, the definition of advertising must be very broad. For our purposes,

> advertising is mediated messages paid for by and identified with a business or institution that seeks to increase the likelihood that those who consume those messages will act or think as the advertiser wishes.

Figure 10–2 Advertising critics fear that our growing consumer culture will produce people who define their self-worth and personal identity by the products they own rather than by who they are, as portrayed in this *Jump Start* cartoon. Jumpstart reprinted by permission of United Features Syndicate, Inc.

In 1995 advertisers spent nearly $162 billion to place their messages before the U.S. public, $355 billion to reach the world's consumers. These amounts do not include the billions of dollars spent in the planning, production, and distribution of those ads. An overwhelming proportion of all this activity is conducted through and by advertising agencies.

THE ADVERTISING AGENCY

There are approximately 6,000 ad agencies operating in the United States, employing roughly half a million people (Figure 10–3). Fewer than 500 agencies annually earn more than $1 million. Many agencies also produce the ads they develop, and virtually all buy time and space in various media for their clients. Production is billed at an agreed-upon price called a **retainer;** placement of advertising in media is compensated through **commissions,** typically 15% of the cost of the time or space. Commissions account for as much as 75% of the income of larger agencies.

Ad agencies are usually divided into departments, the number determined by the size and services of the operation. Smaller agencies might contract with outside companies for the services of these typical ad agency departments:

- *Administration* is the agency's management and accounting operations.
- *Account management* is typically handled by an account executive who serves as liaison between agency and client, keeping communication flowing between the two and heading the team of specialists assigned by the agency to the client.
- The *creative department* is where the advertising is developed from idea to ad. It involves copywriting, graphic design, and often the actual production of the piece, for example radio, television, and Web spots.
- The *media department* makes the decisions about where and when to place ads and then buys the appropriate time or space (Figure 10–4). The effectiveness of a given placement is judged by its **cost per thousand (CPM),** the cost of reaching 1,000 audience members. For

Figure 10–3 Largest U.S.-based Ad Agencies, 1996. Source: *Advertising Age,* April 21, 1997.

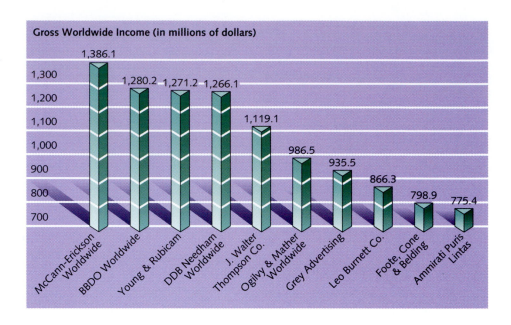

Gross Worldwide Income (in millions of dollars)

1,386.1
1,280.2 1,271.2 1,266.1
1,119.1
986.5
935.5
866.3
798.9 775.4

McCann-Erickson Worldwide · BBDO Worldwide · Young & Rubicam · DDB Needham Worldwide · J. Walter Thompson Co. · Ogilvy & Mather Worldwide · Grey Advertising · Leo Burnett Co. · Foote, Cone & Belding · Ammirati Puris Lintas

Figure 10–4 Percentage of Total U.S. Ad Revenue Spent on Different Media, 1995. Source: *Statistical Abstracts of the U.S. 1996,* p. 574.

Miscellaneous
(includes commercial messages such as those on the Internet, in farm publications, vinyl bus wraps, banners towed behind airplanes, and countless other venues)

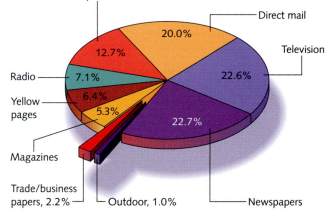

Direct mail

Television

20.0%

22.6%

Radio — 7.1%

12.7%

Yellow pages

6.4%

5.3%

22.7%

Magazines

Trade/business papers, 2.2% — Outdoor, 1.0% — Newspapers

example, an ad that costs $20,000 to place in a major newspaper and is read by 1 million people has a CPM of $20.

- *Market research* tests product viability in the market, the best venues for commercial messages, the nature and characteristics of potential buyers, and sometimes the effectiveness of the ads.

- As we saw in the last chapter, many larger agencies have *public relations departments* as well.

TYPES OF ADVERTISING

The advertising produced and placed by ad agencies can be classified according to the purpose of the advertising and the target market. Some types of advertising you may be familiar with include:

Institutional or corporate advertising. Companies do more than just sell products; companies also promote their names and reputations. If a company name inspires confidence, selling its products is easier. Some institutional or corporate advertising promotes only the organization's image, such as, "FTD Florists support the U.S. Olympic Team." But some advertising sells the image at the same time it sells the product: "You can be sure if it's Westinghouse."

Trade or professional advertising. Typically found in trade and professional publications, messages aimed at retailers do not necessarily push the product or brand but rather promote product issues of importance to the retailer—volume, marketing support, profit potential, distribution plans, and promotional opportunities.

Retail advertising. A large part of the advertising we see every day focuses on products sold by retailers like Sears and Macy's. Ads are typically local, reaching consumers where they live and shop.

Promotional retail advertising. Typically placed by retailers, promotional advertising does not focus on a product but rather on a promotion, a special event held by a retailer. "Midnight Madness Sale" and "Back to School Sale" are two promotions that often benefit from heavy advertising, particularly in newspapers.

Industrial advertising. Advertising products and services directed toward a particular industry is usually found in industry trade publications. For example, *Broadcasting & Cable,* the primary trade magazine for the television industry, runs ads from program syndicators hoping to sell their shows to stations. It also runs ads from transmitter and camera manufacturers.

National consumer advertising. National consumer advertising constitutes the majority of what we see in popular magazines and on television. It is usually product advertising, commissioned by the manufacturer—McDonald's, Honda, Cheerios, Sony, Nike—aimed at potential buyers (Figure 10–5).

Direct market advertising. Product or service advertising aimed at likely buyers rather than at all consumers is called direct market advertising. These targeted consumers are reached through direct mail, catalogues, and telemarketing. This advertising can be personalized—"Yes, BRUCE FRIEDBERG, you can drive a Lexus for less than you think"—and customized. Computer data from credit card and other purchases, ZIP codes, telephone numbers, and organizational memberships are a few of the ways consumers are identified.

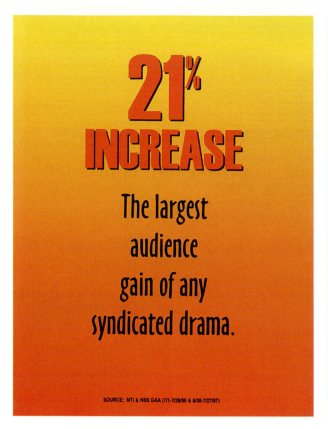

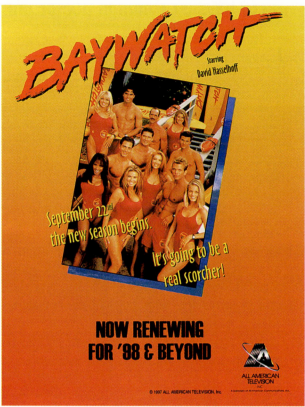

Through this industrial ad, appearing in *Broadcasting & Cable Magazine,* a program syndicator hopes to sell its series to local stations.

Figure 10–5 Top Five U.S. Consumer Advertisers, 1995. Source: *Adbusters,* Spring 1997.

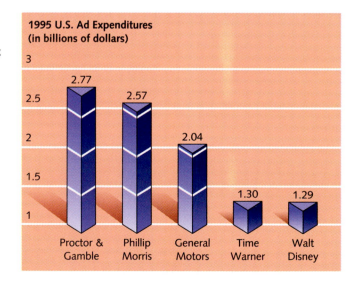

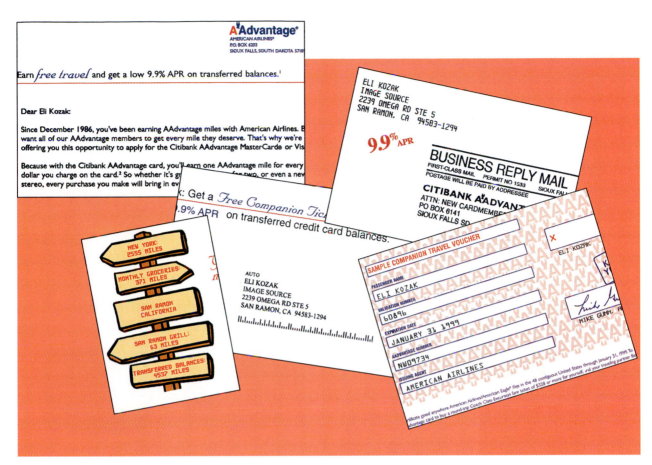

Public service advertising. Advertising that does not sell commercial products or services but promotes organizations and themes of importance to the public is public service advertising. The Heart Fund, the United Negro College Fund, and ads for MADD are typical of this form. They are usually carried free-of-charge by the medium that houses them.

THE REGULATION OF ADVERTISING

The FTC is the primary federal agency for the regulation of advertising. The FCC regulates the commercial practices of the broadcasting industry, and individual states can police deceptive advertising through their own regulatory and criminal bureaucracies. In the deregulation movement of 1980, oversight by the FTC changed from regulating unfair and deceptive advertising to regulating and enforcing complaints *against* deceptive advertising.

The FTC has several options for enforcement when it determines that an advertiser is guilty of deceptive practices. It can issue a **cease-and-desist order** demanding that the practice be stopped. It can impose fines. It can order the creation and distribution of **corrective advertising.** That

In this direct marketing package, the advertiser has not only personalized the pitch—Dear Eli Kozak—but targeted this consumer's particular interests in restaurants, travel, and other consumer goods and services. American Airlines reserves the right to change the AAdvantage program at any time without notice. American Airlines is not responsible for products or services offered by other participating companies.

Public service advertising allows advertisers to use their skills to serve society.

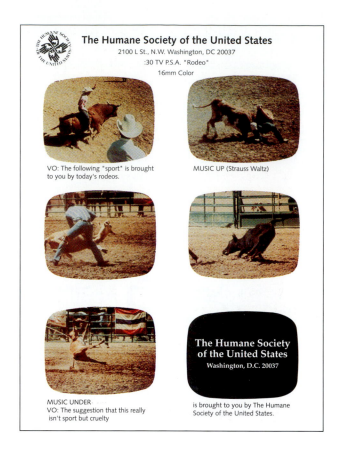

is, a new set of ads must be produced by the offender that corrects the original misleading effort. Offenders can challenge FTC decisions in court, and they are innocent until proven guilty. Meanwhile, the potentially unethical advertising remains in the marketplace.

One of the greatest difficulties for the FTC is finding the line between false or deceptive advertising and **puffery**—that little lie that makes advertising more entertaining than it might otherwise be. "Whiter than white" and "stronger than dirt" are just two examples of puffery. On the assumption that the public does not read commercials literally—the Jolly Green Giant does not exist; we know that—the courts and the FTC allow a certain amount of exaggeration.

The FTC and courts, however, do recognize that an advertisement can be false in a number of ways. An advertisement is false if it:

- Lies outright. For years Wonder Bread was the bread that "builds strong bodies 12 ways." When the FTC asked Wonder Bread to name them, it could not. Listerene mouthwash was long advertised as "preventing colds and sore throats or lessening their severity." It does neither.

- Does not tell the whole truth. "Each slice of Profile Bread contains half the calories of other breads" was the claim of this brand. True, each slice did have about half the calories. But each slice was half as thick as a normal slice of bread.

- Lies by implication, using words, design, production device, sound, or a combination of these. Television commercials for children's toys now end with the product shown in actual size against a neutral background (a shot called an **island**). This is done because production techniques such as low camera angles and close-ups can make these toys seem larger or better than they actually are.

MEASURING THE EFFECTIVENESS OF ADVERTISING

It might seem reasonable to judge the effectiveness of an ad campaign by a subsequent increase in sales. But many factors other than advertising influence how well a product fares, including changes in the economy, product quality, breadth of distribution, and competitors' pricing and promotion strategies. As a result, "for most advertisers most of the time, the answer to the essential question, 'What are you getting for your advertising expenditure?' must be 'I'm not sure' "(Sandage et al., 1989, p. 370). Agency clients, however, find this a less than comforting response. Advertisers, therefore, turn to research to provide greater certainty.

A number of techniques may be used before an ad or ad campaign is released. **Copy testing**—measuring the effectiveness of advertising messages by showing them to consumers—is used for all forms of advertising. It is sometimes conducted with focus groups, collections of people brought together to see the advertising and discuss it with agency and client personnel. Sometimes copy testing employs **consumer juries.** These people, considered to be representative of the target market, review a number of approaches or variations of a campaign or ad. **Forced exposure,** used primarily for television advertising, requires advertisers to bring consumers to a theater or other facility (typically with the promise of a gift or other payment) where they see a television program, complete with the new commercials. People are asked their brand preferences before the show, and then after. In this way, the effectiveness of the commercials can be gauged.

Once the campaign or ad is before the public, a number of different tests can be employed to evaluate the effectiveness of the ad. In **recognition tests** people who have seen a given publication are asked, in person or by phone, whether they remember seeing specific ads. In **recall testing** consumers are asked, again in person or by phone, to identify which print or broadcast ads they most easily remember. This recall can be unaided, where the researcher offers no hints ("Have you seen any interesting commercials or ads lately?"), or aided, where the researcher identifies a specific class of products ("Have you seen any interesting pizza commercials lately?"). In recall testing, the advertisers assume that an easily recalled ad is an effective ad. **Awareness tests** make this same assumption, but they are not aimed at specific ads. Their goal is to measure the cumulative effect of a campaign in terms of "consumer consciousness" of a product. A likely question in an awareness test, usually made by telephone, is: "What brands of laundry detergent can you name?"

What these research techniques lack is the ability to demonstrate the link that is of most interest to the client—did the ad move the consumer to buy the product? Their value lies in helping advertisers understand how people react to specific ads and advertising strategies, aiding advertisers in avoiding costly mistakes, and assisting advertisers in planning and organizing immediate and later campaigns.

Current Trends in Advertising

Many of the same forces reshaping the media industries are having an impact on the advertising industry as well.

NEW TECHNOLOGIES

The production of advertising has inevitably been altered by computers. Computer graphics, morphing (digitally combining and transforming images), and other special effects are now common in national retail television advertising. Computer databases and computerized printing have fueled the rapid growth of direct market advertising, and we saw in Chapter 5 that computerized printing has made possible zoned and other specialized editions of national magazines. But it is **cyberadvertising**—placing commercials on various online sites—that has recently attracted a large amount of industry interest.

For years the online information service Prodigy has put ads on its videotext pages. Today, a growing number of Internet Web sites come to home computer screens framed by **banners,** or online billboards. Many Web sites, Microsoft and NBC's *http://www.msnbc.com,* for example, include ads between pages that the viewer must pass through when moving through the site. Yet despite the trend, the research company Jupiter Communications reported Web advertising revenues of $312 million for 1996, a relatively small proportion of the ad industry's total dollar volume. This is so because online advertising still looks relatively static when compared to the more familiar television commercial, and because its effectiveness is as yet unproven.

As improvements in audio and video delivery occur, however, and as advertisers become more sure of its worth, this form of advertising will no doubt increase. For example, some advertisers are making free audio and video software available to those who wish to download it to watch **intermercials,** which are attractive, lively commercials that run while peo-

<figure>Figure 10–6 Critics of online commerce fear that the Internet will become little more than "more television" once advertisers take it over. © 1997 Washington Post Writers Group. Reprinted with permission.</figure>

ple are waiting for Web pages to download. Some advantages of online advertising are already being exploited. Online users can be connected to a sponsor's own site through a link between the ad and that site. Once there, they can make purchases with the touch of a key. Online ads can be personalized with consumers' names and localized with advertisers' locations. Computer networks make possible ads on demand, in essence cybercatalogues that can be user-selected (Figure 10–6). As a result, various analysts predict that advertisers will spend from $3.1 billion to $5 billion on the Internet by the year 2000 (Blumenthal, 1997). A fuller discussion of online advertising is presented in Chapter 14.

INCREASED AUDIENCE SEGMENTATION

As the number of media outlets for advertising grows, and as audiences for traditional media are increasingly fragmented, advertisers have refined their ability to reach and speak to ever narrower audience segments. Computer technology facilitates this practice, but segmentation exists apart from the new technologies. The ethnic composition of the United States is changing, and advertising is keeping pace. African Americans comprise just over 12% of the total U.S. population, and Hispanics 11%. A September 1997 Census Bureau report indicated that middle- and upper-income African Americans and Hispanics were indistinguishable from Whites in terms of such economic indicators as home ownership and consumer purchasing. It also concluded that the average household income for African Americans exceeded all previous levels and that of Hispanic households was growing at a rate five times faster than that of all other citizens. Asians and Pacific Islanders constitute the fastest growing ethnic segment of the population, and 65% of the Native American population lives in the general community rather than on reservations. Together these groups control billions of dollars of discretionary income and are increasingly targeted by advertisers. Figure 10–7 shows how national advertising

The growing U.S. Hispanic population is increasingly targeted by advertisers, both in English and Spanish language media. Here, these kids want their Cheerios.

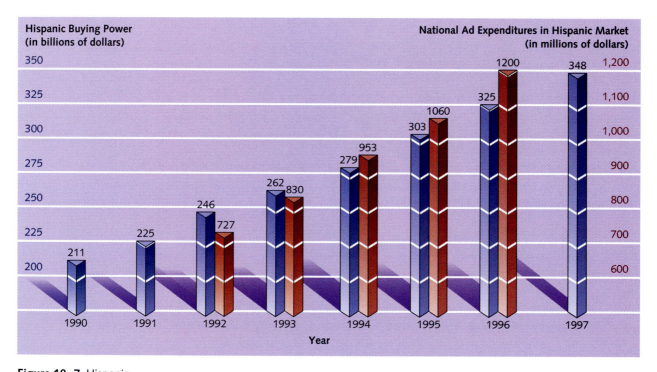

Figure 10–7 Hispanic Buying Power/Ad Expenditures. Sources: Selig Center for Economic Growth, University of Georgia, June 18, 1997; *Hispanic Business Magazine, San Jose Mercury News,* October 2, 1997.

expenditures have paralleled the growth of buying power—defined as disposable personal income after taxes that a family has available to spend on goods and services—for one ethnic group.

PSYCHOGRAPHICS

Demographic segmentation—the practice of appealing to audiences defined by varying personal and social characteristics such as race/ethnicity, gender, and economic level—has long been part of advertisers' strategy.

But advertisers are making increased use of **psychographic segmentation**—that is, appealing to consumer groups of varying lifestyles, attitudes, values, and behavior patterns.

Psychographics entered advertising in the 1970s and is receiving growing attention as advertisers work to reach increasingly disparate consumers in increasingly segmented media. **VALS,** a psychographic segmentation strategy that classifies consumers according to values and lifestyles, is indicative of this lifestyle segmentation. Developed by SRI International, a California consulting company, it divides consumers into nine VALS segments. Each segment is characterized by specific values and lifestyles, demographics, and, of greatest importance to advertisers, buying patterns. The segments, including some of their demographic identifiers, are:

Need-Driven Consumers

Survivors: Concerned with safety and security, dependent; low income, low education; price and need are important in buying decisions.

Sustainers: Struggle for survival, distrustful; live in poverty, little education; price is important, but sometimes buy impulsively.

Outer-Directed Consumers

Belongers: Conforming, conventional, nostalgic; middle to low income, hold blue collar jobs; spend for home and family, but sometimes for fads as well.

Emulators: Ambitious, macho, upwardly mobile; urban, young, moderate income; into "in" items, imitation, and conspicuous consumption.

Achievers: Materialistic, want success, fame, and comfort; suburban and urban, excellent income, good education; buy top of the line, use products to demonstrate success; buy luxury, gift, and innovative items.

Inner-Directed Consumers

I-Am-Me: Individualistic, dramatic, impulsive, experimental; young, single, student or beginning job; buy to display tastes, experiment with fads, like the far-out.

Experiential: Artistic, crave direct experience, active; under 35, good education, have young families; consider product before buying; buy for sports, home pursuits, crafts, and introspection.

Societally Conscious: Socially responsible, live simply, favor smallness of scale and inner growth; excellent education, all ages and places of living; buy simply, frugally, and environmentally.

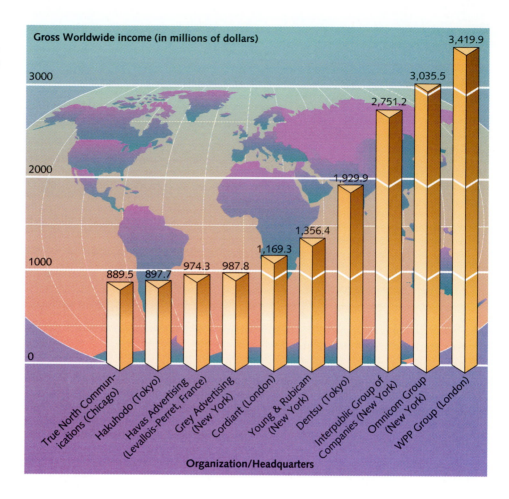

Figure 10–8 World's Ten Largest Ad Organizations, 1995. Source: *Advertising Age,* April 21, 1997.

Gross Worldwide income (in millions of dollars)

- True North Communications (Chicago): 889.5
- Hakuhodo (Tokyo): 897.7
- Havas Advertising (Levallois-Perret, France): 974.3
- Grey Advertising (New York): 987.8
- Cordiant (London): 1,169.3
- Young & Rubicam (New York): 1,356.4
- Dentsu (Tokyo): 1,929.9
- Interpublic Group of Companies (New York): 2,751.2
- Omnicom Group (New York): 3,035.5
- WPP Group (London): 3,419.9

Organization/Headquarters

Integrated: Psychologically mature, tolerant, possess world perspective; good to excellent income, excellent education, all jobs and places of living; buy esthetically, environmentally, favor one-of-a-kind items. (Berkman & Gilson, 1987)

GLOBALIZATION

As media and national economies have globalized, advertising has adapted. Figure 10–8 shows the world's 10 largest ad organizations—agencies and their international subsidiaries (regardless of local name). Notice that although five have U.S. headquarters, only two of the U.S.-owned agencies from Figure 10–3 (Young & Rubicam and Grey Advertising) appear. U.S. agencies are increasingly merging with, acquiring, or affiliating with agencies from other parts of the world. In addition to the globalization of media and economies, a second force driving this trend is the demographic fact that by the year 2000, 80% of the world's population will live in developing countries. The advertising industry is prepared to put its clients in touch with these consumers.

DEVELOPING MEDIA LITERACY SKILLS
Interpreting Intentional Imprecision

Advertisers often use intentional imprecision in words and phrases to say something other than the precise truth, and they do so in all forms of advertising—profit and nonprofit, scrupulously honest and less so. There are three categories of intentional imprecision: unfinished statements, qualifiers, and connotatively loaded words and expressions.

We are all familiar with *unfinished statements,* such as the one for the battery that "lasts twice as long." Others include "You can be sure if it's Westinghouse," "Magnavox gives you more," and "Easy Off makes oven cleaning easier." A literate advertising consumer should ask, "Twice as long as *what?*" "Of *what* can I be sure?" "Gives me more of *what?*" "Easier than *what?*" Better, more, stronger, whiter, faster—all are comparative adjectives whose true purpose is to create a comparison between two or more things. When the other half of the comparison is not identified, intentional imprecision is being used to create the illusion of comparison.

Qualifiers are words that limit a claim. A product *helps* relieve stress, for instance. It may not relieve stress as well as rest and better planning and organization. But once the qualifier "helps" appears, an advertiser is free to make just about any claim for the product because all the ad really says is that it helps, not that it does anything in and of itself. It's the consumer's fault for misreading. A product that makes a task *virtually* effort-free is not one that saves you work. In fact, the qualifier "virtually" does not mean "almost" or "the same as"; it means "not the same as"—as in "virtual reality." A product may *fight* grime, but there is no promise that it will win. In the statement, "Texaco's coal gasification process could mean you won't have to worry about how it affects the environment," "could" relieves the advertiser of all responsibility. "Could" does not mean "will." Moreover, the fact that you *could stop worrying about the environment* does not mean the product does not harm the environment—only that you could stop worrying about it.

Some qualifiers are more apparent. "Taxes not included," "limited time only," "only at participating locations," "prices may vary," "some assembly required," "additional charges may apply," and "batteries not included" are qualifiers presented after the primary claims have been made. Often these words are spoken quickly at the end of radio and television commercials, or they appear in small print on the screen or at the bottom of a newspaper or magazine ad.

Other qualifiers are part of the product's advertising slogan. Boodles gin is "the ultra-refined British gin that only the world's costliest methods could produce. Boodles. The world's costliest British gin." After intimating that the costliest methods are somehow necessary to make the best gin, this advertiser qualifies its product as the costliest "British" gin. There may be costlier, and possibly better, Irish, U.S., Russian, and Canadian gins. Many sugared children's cereals employ the tactic of displaying the cereal on a table with fruit, milk, and toast. The announcer says or the copy reads, "Coco Yummies are *a part of* this complete breakfast"—so is the tablecloth. But the cereal, in and of itself, adds little to the nutritional completeness of the meal. It is "a part of" it.

Advertising is full of words that are *connotatively loaded*. Best Western Hotels never has to explain what makes them "best." A *best selling product* may not be the best in its product class, only the one with the best advertising campaign and distribution system. A product that has more of "the pain relieving medicine doctors prescribe most" merely contains more aspirin. Products that are "cherry-flavored" have no cherries in them. A product that is high in "food energy" is in fact high in calories. Advertisers want consumers to understand the connotations of these words and phrases, not their actual meanings.

Intentional imprecision is puffery. It is not illegal; nor is it sufficiently troubling to the advertising industry to warrant self-regulatory limits. But puffery is neither true nor accurate, and its purpose is to deceive. This means that the responsibility for correctly and accurately reading advertising that is intentionally imprecise rests with the media literate consumer.

Chapter Review

Advertising has been practiced for thousands of years and came to the Colonies via England. Industrialization and the Civil War led to more leisure, more discretionary income, and greater urbanization and industrialization, all of which fueled the growth of advertising. Magazines provided a national medium for ads, and advertising agencies quickly developed to meet the needs of the industry's growing scale. As the industry matured during this time, it began to professionalize itself.

Radio moved advertising closer to show business and also allowed the industry to survive the Depression, a period in which advertising came under additional scrutiny from dollar-conscious consumers.

World War II reduced the number of consumer products that could be advertised, but advertising continued in the form of image advertising, another boon to the ad agency business. Then came television, which changed the nature of advertising content just as the commercials themselves changed the nature of the medium.

The 6,000 U.S. advertising agencies make money through retainers or commissions for placing ads. They have some or all of these departments: administration, account management, creative, media, market research, and public relations. They place some or all of these types of ads: institutional or corporate, trade or professional, retail, promotional retail, industrial, national consumer, direct market, and public service. Advertisers judge the effectiveness of their work in a number of ways, but understanding the vital link between consumers' seeing the ad and their buying behavior is at best tenuous.

Agencies and the industry as a whole are being reshaped by new communication technologies, such as computerized databases, computerized printing, and online advertising. Audiences for advertising, as for most media, are increasingly fragmented along demographic and psychographic lines, and globalization has come to advertising as well.

Despite its central role in the U.S. economy, advertising is often criticized for being intrusive and deceptive, and for unethically targeting children, fostering monopolies, and debasing the culture. These criticisms are supported by citing the industry's practice of using words and phrases that do not mean what the audience is led to believe they mean.

Questions for Review

1. Why are we seeing so many ads in so many new and different places?
2. What are siquis, shopbills, and newsbooks?
3. What impact did industrialization and the Civil War have on the advertising industry?
4. What impact did the coming of magazines, radio, and television have on the advertising industry?
5. In what ways can an ad be false?
6. What was the excess-profits tax? How did it benefit advertising agencies?
7. What are the departments in a typical advertising agency? What does each do?
8. What are the different categories of advertising and the goal of each?
9. Name some trends influencing contemporary advertising. How does each do so?
10. How can words be used to deceive in advertising?

Questions for Critical Thinking and Reflection

1. If you owned an advertising agency, would you produce advertising aimed at children? Why, or why not?
2. If you were an FTC regulator, what extent of puffery would you allow? Where would you draw the line between deception and puffery? Give examples.
3. Do you think U.S. culture is overly materialistic? If you do, what role do you think advertising has had in creating this state of affairs?
4. Can you identify yourself among the VALS segments? If you can, how accurately does that segment describe your buying habits?
5. What do you think of contemporary television advertising? Are its creativity and technological sophistication adequate substitutes for information about the product?

Important Resources

Alfino, M., Caputo, J. S., & Wynard, R. (Eds.). (1998). *McDonaldization revisited: Critical essays on consumer culture.* **New York: Praeger.** A collection of essays from scholars representing different disciplines, different theoretical approaches, and different countries. Each examines the latest thinking about commercialism and the consumer culture.

Advertising Age. The self-proclaimed "international newspaper of marketing," this weekly tabloid examines advertising from both agency and media sides from a global perspective.

Adweek. The very latest in industry news with much insider information about advertising people and agencies. The magazine contains a lot of attractive and interesting ads for magazines and other media hoping to attract the business of its readers.

Journal of Advertising. This quarterly scientific journal publishes academic and scholarly articles on many aspects of advertising—legal issues, ethics, effects, practices, and ad effectiveness. Some essays are very technical, but many make for interesting, challenging reading.

Kern-Foxworth, M. (1994). *Aunt Jemima, Uncle Ben, and Rastus: Blacks in advertising, yesterday, today, and tomorrow.* **New York: Praeger.** As the title suggests, a detailed study of racial stereotyping in advertising. It provides important historical contexts as well as an analysis of how the ad industry will handle this sensitive issue in the future.

O'Barr, W. M. (1994). *Culture and the ad: Exploring otherness in the world of advertising.* **Boulder, CO: Westview Press.** A fascinating examination of the cultural and personal influences of advertising written in layperson's terms. It is highlighted by a fascinating collection of old and new ads.

Schudson, M. (1984). *Advertising, the uneasy persuasion: Its dubious impact on American society.* **New York: Basic Books.** Only a little dated, the classic critical examination of advertising's contribution to the consumer culture.

Advertising Information Web Sites

Better Business Bureau's Children's Advertising Review Unit	*http://www.bbb.org/advertising/childrensMonitor.html*
Better Business Bureau's National Advertising Division	*http://www.bbb.org/advertising/advertiserAssist.html*
American Association of Advertising Agencies	*http://www.commercepark.com/AAAA/AAAA.html*
Advertising World	*http://advweb.cocomm.utexas.edu/world/*
Institute of Practitioners in Advertising	*http://www.ipa.co.uk/*
American Advertising Federation	*http://www.aaf.org/*
Worldwide Ad Network	*http://members.aol.com/WorldAdNet/index.htm*
Adweek	*http://www.adweek.com*
Adage	*http://adage.com*
Adbusters	*http://www.adbusters.org*

part 4

Mass Mediated Culture in the Information Age

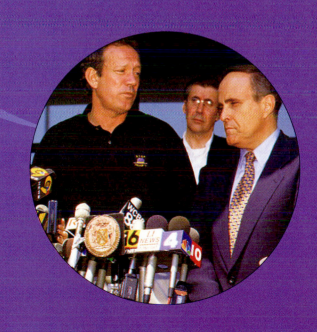

Theories of Mass Communication

"I know this isn't listed on the syllabus. But let's call it a pop quiz."

Your instructor has surprised you. "Will this count in our final grade?" you ask. You are seared by the professorial stare.

"Put everything away except a piece of paper and a pen."

You do as instructed.

"Number your paper from 1 to 6. Items 1 through 3 are true–false. One. Most people are just looking out for themselves. Two. You can't be too careful in dealing with people. Three. Most people would take advantage of you if they got the chance. Now, number four. How much television do you watch each week?"

Not too tough, you think, you can handle this.

Your prof continues, "You must answer number 5 out loud. What's the moon made of?"

You and several classmates respond, "Cheese!"

"Finally, number 6. Draw the outline of a dime as close to actual size as possible."

In this chapter we examine mass communication theory. After we define theory and discuss why it is important, we see how the various theories of mass communication that are prevalent today developed. We then study several of the most influential contemporary theories before we discuss the relationship between media literacy and mass communication theory. These theories and their application form the basis of our understanding of how media and culture affect one another, the topic of Chapter 12.

Defining Mass Communication Theory

Mass communication theories are explanations and predictions of social phenomena that attempt to relate mass communication to various aspects of our personal and cultural lives or social systems. Your responses to the six quiz questions, for example, can be explained (possibly even predicted) by several different mass communication theories.

The first four items are a reflection of cultivation analysis—the idea that people's ideas of themselves, their world, and their place in it are shaped and maintained primarily through television. People's responses to the three true–false items can be fairly accurately predicted by the amount of viewing they do (question 4). The more people watch, the more likely they are to respond "true" to these unflattering comments about others.

Your response to the question about the moon's composition can be explained by a theory called social construction of reality, which argues that people learn to behave in their social world through interaction with it. In other words, people in a given society or culture communicate, using signs and symbols, to construct a common reality that allows them to act meaningfully and efficiently in different settings. Many of us said "cheese" because we respond according to the "reality" that we constructed using our media's stories. We know intellectually that the moon is not made of cheese, but in this quiz setting we respond not as we've been educated but as we've been enculturated.

The solution to the dime-drawing task is predicted by attitude change theory. Almost everyone draws the dime too small. Because a dime is an inconsequential coin, we perceive it as smaller than it really is, and our perceptions guide our behavior. Even though every one of us has real-world experience with dimes, our attitudes toward that coin shape our behavior regarding it.

To understand mass communication theory, you should recognize these important ideas:

1. As we've just seen, *there is no one mass communication theory*. There is a theory, for example, that describes something as grand as how we give meaning to cultural symbols and how these symbols influence our behavior (symbolic interaction), and there is a theory that explains something as individual as how media influence people in times of change or crisis (dependency theory). Mass communication theorists have produced

a number of **middle-range theories** that explain or predict specific, limited aspects of the mass communication process (Merton, 1967).

2. *Mass communication theories are often borrowed from other fields of science.* The social construction of reality theory (the cheese question) comes from sociology. Attitude change theory (the dime question) is borrowed from psychology. Mass communication theorists adapt these borrowed theories to questions and issues in communication. People's behavior with regard to issues more important than the size of a dime—democracy, ethnicity, government, and gender roles, for example—is influenced by the attitudes and perceptions presented by our mass media.

3. *Mass communication theories are human constructions.* People create them, and therefore their creation is influenced by human biases—the times in which we live, the position we occupy in the mass communication process, and a host of other factors. Broadcast industry researchers, for example, have developed somewhat different theories to explain how violence is learned from television than have university researchers.

4. Because theories are human constructions and the environments in which they are created constantly change, *mass communication theories are dynamic;* they undergo frequent recasting, acceptance, and rejection. For example, theories that were developed before television and computer networks became mass media outlets have to be reexamined and sometimes discarded in the face of these new media.

A Short History of Mass Communication Theory

The dynamic nature of mass communication theory can be seen in its history. All bodies of knowledge pass through various stages of development. Hypotheses are put forth, tested, and proven or rejected. Eventually a uniform theory or **paradigm** results—that is, a theory that summarizes and is consistent with all known facts. However, over time new facts come to light and our knowledge and understanding increase. This often leads to a **paradigm shift**—a fundamental, even radical, rethinking of what we believe to be true (Kuhn, 1970). Mass communication theory is particularly open to such paradigm shifts due to three factors:

- *Advances in technology or the introduction of new media* fundamentally alter the nature of mass communication. The coming of radio and movies, for example, forced rethinking of theories based on a print-oriented mass communication system.
- *Calls for control or regulation* of these new technologies require, especially in a democracy like ours, an objective, science-based justification.

- As a country committed to protecting *democracy and cultural pluralism,* we ask how each new technology or medium can foster our pursuit of that goal.

The paradigm shifts that have resulted from these factors have produced four major eras of mass communication theory: the era of mass society theory, the era of the scientific perspective, the era of limited effects theory, and the era of cultural theory. The first three may be considered early eras; the last is the era in which we currently find ourselves.

THE ERA OF MASS SOCIETY THEORY

As we've seen, several important mass media appeared or flourished during the second half of the 19th century and the first decades of the 20th century. Mass circulation newspapers and magazines, movies, talkies, and radio all came to prominence at this time. This was also a time of profound change in the nature of U.S. society. Industrialization and urbanization spread, African Americans and poor southern Whites streamed northward, and immigrants rushed across both coasts in search of opportunity and dignity. People in traditional seats of power—the clergy, politicians, and educators—feared a disruption in the status quo. The country's peaceful rural nature was beginning to slip further into history. In its place was a cauldron of new and different people with new and different habits, all crammed into rapidly expanding cities. Crime grew, as did social and political unrest. Many cultural, political, educational, and religious leaders thought the United States was becoming too pluralistic. They charged that the mass media catered to the low tastes and limited reading and language abilities of these newcomers by featuring simple and sensationalistic content. The media needed to be controlled to protect traditional values.

The successful use of propaganda by totalitarian governments in Europe, especially Germany's National Socialist Party (the Nazis), provided further evidence of the overwhelming power of media. Media needed to be controlled to prevent similar abuses at home.

The resulting paradigm was **mass society theory**—the idea that the media are corrupting influences that undermine the social order and that "average" people are defenseless against their influence. To mass society theorists, "average" people were all those who did not hold their (the theorists') superior tastes and values. The fundamental assumption of this paradigm is sometimes expressed in the **hypodermic needle theory** or the **magic bullet theory.** The symbolism of both is apparent—media are a dangerous drug or a killing force that directly and immediately penetrate a person's system.

Mass society theory is an example of a **grand theory,** one designed to describe and explain all aspects of a given phenomenon. But clearly not all average people were mindlessly influenced by the evil mass media. People made consumption choices. They interpreted media content, often in personally important ways. Media did have effects, often good ones. No single theory could encompass the wide variety of media effects claimed by mass society theorists, and the theory eventually collapsed under its own weight.

THE ERA OF THE SCIENTIFIC PERSPECTIVE

Paradigm shifts usually happen over a period of time, and this is true of the move away from mass society theory. But media researchers often mark the beginning of the scientific perspective on mass communication as occurring on the eve of Halloween 1938. On that night actor and director Orson Welles broadcast his dramatized version of the H. G. Wells science fiction classic, *The War of the Worlds,* on the CBS radio network. Produced in what we would now call docudrama style, the realistic radio play in which Earth came under deadly Martian attack frightened thousands. People fled their homes in panic. Proof of mass society theory, argued elite media critics, pointing to a radio play with the power to send people into the hills to hide from aliens.

Research by scientists from Princeton University demonstrated that, in fact, 1 million people had been frightened enough by the broadcast to

Agnes Ayers swoons in Rudolph Valentino's arms in the 1921 movie *The Sheik.* Mass society theorists saw such common entertainment fare as debasing the culture through its direct and negative effects on helpless audience members.

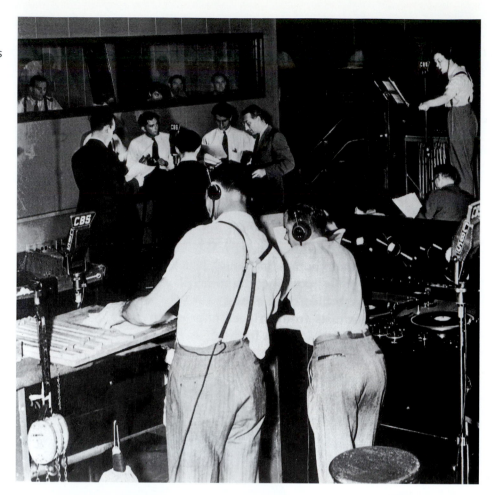

Orson Welles directs *War of the Worlds.* The 1938 Halloween broadcast of this science fiction classic helped usher in the era of the scientific study of mass communication.

take some action, but the other 5 million people who heard the show had not, mass society theory notwithstanding. More important, however, these scientists determined that different factors led some people to be influenced and others not (Lowery & DeFleur, 1995).

The researchers had the benefit of advances in survey research, polling, and other social scientific methods developed and championed by Austrian immigrant Paul Lazarsfeld. The researchers were, in fact, his students and colleagues. Lazarsfeld (1941) argued that mere speculation about the impact of media was insufficient to explain the complex interactions that comprised mass communication. Instead, well-designed, sophisticated studies of media and audiences would produce more valuable knowledge.

Limited Effects Theories   Using Lazarsfeld's work, researchers identified those individual and social characteristics that led audience members to be influenced (or not) by media. What emerged was the view that media influence was limited by *individual differences* (for example, in intelligence and education), *social categories* (such as religious and political affiliation), and *personal relationships* (such as friends and family). The theories that

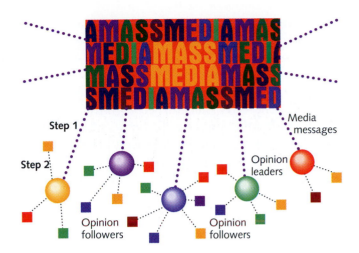

Figure 11–1 Model of Two-Step Flow of Media Influence. Media influence passes from the mass media, through opinion leaders, to opinion followers. Because leaders and followers share common personal and social characteristics, the potential influence of media is limited by their shared assumptions, beliefs, and attitudes.
Source: After E. Katz & P. F. Lazarsfeld (1955), *Personal Influence*, New York: Free Press.

emerged from this era of the first systematic and scientific study of media effects, taken together, are now called **limited effects theories.**

Two-Step Flow Theory   Lazarsfeld's own **two-step flow theory** of mass media and personal influence is a well-known product of this era and an example of a limited effects theory (Katz & Lazarsfeld, 1955). His research on the 1940 presidential election indicated that media influence on people's voting behavior was limited by **opinion leaders,** people who initially consumed media content on topics of particular interest to them, interpreted it in light of their own values and beliefs, and then passed it on to **opinion followers,** people like them who had less frequent contact with media (Figure 11–1).

Two-step flow theory has been rethought since Lazarsfeld's time. For example, television, virtually unavailable in 1940, has given everyone a more or less equal opportunity to consume media content firsthand. There is no doubt that opinion leaders still exist—we often ask friends what they've read or heard about a certain movie, book, or CD—but their centrality to the mass communication process has diminished.

THE ERA OF LIMITED EFFECTS THEORY

During and after World War II, the limited effects paradigm and several theories it supported became entrenched, controlling research and thinking about media until well into the 1960s. And as was the case with virtually all the media and support industries we've studied, the war itself was crucial to the development of mass communication theory during this era.

Memories of World War I were still very much alive, and not all Americans were enthused about entering another seemingly remote world conflict. Those who joined or were drafted into the armed forces apparently knew very little about their comrades-in-arms from different regions of the country and from different backgrounds. German propaganda seemed to prove the view of mass society theorists who claimed that mass media wielded remarkable power. The Office of War Information (OWI), therefore, set out to change public opinion about the wisdom of entering the war, to educate the military about their fellow soldiers and sailors, and to counter Nazi propaganda. Speeches and lectures failed. So, too, did informational pamphlets. The OWI then turned to filmmakers such as Frank Capra (Chapter 6) and radio personalities such as Kate Smith (Chapter 7) for their audience appeal and looked to social scientists to measure the effectiveness of these new media campaigns.

The Army established the Experimental Section inside its Information and Education Division, staffing it with psychologists who were expert in issues of attitude change. Led by Carl Hovland, these researchers tested the effectiveness of the government's mass communication campaigns. Continuing its work at Yale University after the war, this group produced some of this century's most influential communication research. Their work led to development of **attitude change theory,** which explains how people's attitudes are formed, shaped, and changed through communication and how those attitudes influence behavior (Hovland, Lumsdaine, & Sheffield, 1949).

Attitude Change Theory   Among the most important attitude change theories are the related ideas of dissonance and selective processes. **Dissonance theory** argues that when confronted by new information people experience a kind of mental discomfort, a dissonance. As a result, we consciously and subconsciously work to limit or reduce that discomfort through three interrelated **selective processes.** These processes help us "select" what information we consume, remember, and interpret in personally important and idiosyncratic ways:

- **Selective exposure** (or **selective attention**) is the process by which people only expose themselves to or attend to those messages consistent with their preexisting attitudes and beliefs. How often do you read the work of a newspaper columnist who occupies a different place on the political spectrum from you? You're more likely to read those articles that confirm what you already believe. It's quite common for someone who buys a new car, electronic component, or other expensive item to suddenly start to see more of that product's advertising. You've spent a lot of money; that creates dissonance. The ads confirm the wisdom of your decision, reducing dissonance.

- **Selective retention** assumes that people remember best and longest those messages that are consistent with their preexisting attitudes and beliefs. Television viewers, for example, remember much more detail from the convention broadcasts of the political party to which they are philosophically closer than they do the broadcasts of competing parties.

- **Selective perception** predicts that people will interpret messages in a manner consistent with their preexisting attitudes and beliefs.

Line drawing used in the 1945 Allport and Postman study of rumor. Psychologists Allport and Postman demonstrated the operation of the selective processes. When groups of White Americans were asked to whisper from one to another the subject of this drawing, the knife invariably shifted from the hand of the White aggressor to that of the African American defender. Can you explain this result in terms of dissonance theory and the selective processes?

When your favorite politicians change positions on an issue, they're flexible and heeding the public's will. When those you don't like do so, they're flip-flopping and have no convictions.

The dominant paradigm at the time of the development of dissonance theory was limited effects theory; thus, the selective processes were seen as limiting media impact because content is selectively filtered to produce as little attitude change as possible. Contemporary mass communication theorists accept the power of the selective processes to limit the influence of media content when it is primarily informational. But because so much content is symbolic rather than informational, other theorists see the selective processes as relatively unimportant when it comes to explaining media's contribution to some important cultural effects. You will recognize these differing perspectives on media's power in the distinction made in Chapter 1 between the transmissional and ritual views of mass communication.

Here is an example of the distinction between informational and symbolic content and the way they relate to the selective processes. Few television stations would broadcast lecture programs by people who openly espouse the racist opinion that people of color are genetically more prone to commit crime. If we were to see such a show, however, the selective processes would likely kick in. We would change to another channel (selective exposure). If we did watch, we would interpret the ideas as loony or sick (selective perception); later we would quickly forget the arguments (selective retention).

Susan Smith had the country fooled for 9 days after claiming that an African American carjacker had stolen her car and drowned her children. The Associated Press wire service caption for this photo read, "David and Susan Smith arrive at the Union County Sheriff's office in Union, SC, Thursday, October 27, 1994. The Smiths' children were kidnapped Tuesday night after a carjacker took Mrs. Smith's car at gunpoint and told her to get out, but would not allow her to remove her two children, Alexander, 14 months old and Michael, 3 years." It was eventually learned that Smith had murdered her own children.

Fortunately, the media rarely offer such overtly racist messages. The more likely situation in contemporary television is that the production conventions and economic and time demands of television news production lead to the common portrayal of certain people as more likely to be involved in violence and crime. It is easier and cheaper, for example, for stations to cover downtown violent crime—it's handy, it's visual, and it needs no significant research or writing—than to cover nonviolent crime, even though 90% of all felonies in the United States are nonviolent. As a result of these largely symbolic portrayals of crime, our selective processes do not have an opportunity to reshape the "information" in these news reports. There is little information, only a variety of interesting images.

Cultural theorists (we'll meet them later in this chapter) point to the 1990 shooting by Charles Stuart of his pregnant wife and the 1994 drowning by Susan Smith of her own two children as proof of the power of television to shape attitudes toward race. In both crimes most of the public and police—even thoughtful people of good will—easily accepted Stuart's and Smith's claims that African Americans had committed these crimes, although in both cases the murders were actually perpetrated by these White "victims." Before the truth was uncovered, Stuart—who killed his wife and unborn child to free himself for an affair with a coworker—was visited in the hospital by a parade of politicians lamenting urban violence.

Smith—who killed her children because her boyfriend did not want kids—was front page news as a mother who had suffered the ultimate loss, the death of her children.

Reinforcement Theory   The selective processes, however, formed the core of what is arguably the most influential book ever published on the impact of mass communication. In *The Effects of Mass Communication*, written in 1960 by the eminent scientist and head of social research for CBS Broadcasting Joseph Klapper, the core of the limited effects paradigm is articulated firmly and clearly. Klapper's theory is based on social science evidence developed prior to 1960 and is often called **reinforcement theory** (see the box "Klapper's Reinforcement Theory"). It was very persuasive at a time when the nation's social fabric had yet to feel the full impact of the social change brought about by the war. In addition, flush with enthusiasm and optimism for the technology and science that had helped the United States defeat the Axis powers, the public could see little but good coming from the media technologies, and they trusted the work of Klapper and other scientists.

In retrospect, the value of reinforcement theory may have passed with its 1960 publication date. With rapid postwar urbanization, industrialization, and the increase of women in the workplace, Klapper's "nexus of mediating factors and influences" (church, family, and school) began to lose their traditional socializing role for many people. During the 1960s, a decade both revered and reviled for the social and cultural changes it fostered, it became increasingly difficult to ignore the impact of media. Most important, however, all the research Klapper had studied in preparation for his book was conducted before 1960, the year in which it is generally accepted that television became a mass medium. Almost none of the science he examined in developing his reinforcement theory considered television.

The Uses and Gratifications Approach   Paradigms do not shift easily. Limited effects researchers were unable to ignore obvious media effects such as the impact of advertising, the media's role in sustaining sentiment against the war in Vietnam and in spreading support for civil rights and the feminist movement, and increases in real-world crime that appeared to parallel increases in televised violence. They turned their focus to media consumers to explain how influence is limited. The new body of thought that resulted, called the **uses and gratifications approach,** claimed that media do not do things *to* people; rather, people do things *with* media. In other words, the influence of media is limited to what people allow it to be.

Because the uses and gratifications approach emphasizes *audience members'* motives for making specific consumption choices and the consequences of that intentional media use, it is sometimes seen as being too apologetic for the media industries. In other words, when negative media effects are seen as the product of audience members' media choices and use, the media industries are absolved of some responsibility for the content they produce or carry. Media simply give people what they want. This approach is also criticized because it assumes not only that people know why they make the media content choices they do but also that they can clearly articulate those reasons to uses and gratifications researchers. A third criticism is that the approach ignores the fact that much media consumption is unintentional—when we read the newspaper for election news, we can't help but see ads. When we go to an action movie, we are presented with various representations of gender and ethnicity that have nothing to do with our choice of that film. A fourth criticism is that the approach ignores media's cultural role in shaping people's media choices and use (Figure 11–2).

Despite these criticisms, the uses and gratifications approach served an important function in the development of mass communication theory by stressing the reciprocal nature of the mass communication process. That is, scientists began to take seriously the idea that people are important in the process—they choose content, they make meaning, they act on that meaning.

Agenda Setting During the era of limited effects, several important ideas were developed that began to cast some doubt on the assumption that media influence on people and cultures was minimal. These ideas are still

Klapper's Reinforcement Theory

Klapper himself called his theory "phenomenistic theory." But it is more commonly called reinforcement theory because of its emphasis on media's limited power. Klapper (1960) provided this summary of his theory in his classic book, *The Effects of Mass Communication:*

1. Mass communication *ordinarily* does not serve as a necessary and sufficient cause of audience effects, but rather functions among and through a nexus of mediating factors and influences.

2. These mediating factors are such that they typically render mass communication a contributory agent, but not the sole cause, in the process of reinforcing existing conditions.

3. On such occasions as mass communication does function in the service of change, one of two conditions is likely to exist. Either

   a) The mediating factors will be found to be inoperative and the effect of the media will be found to be direct; or

   b) The mediating factors, which normally favor reinforcement, will be found to be themselves impelling toward change.

4. There are residual situations in which mass communication seems to produce direct effects, or directly and of itself to serve certain psycho-physical functions.

5. The efficacy of mass communication, either as a contributory agent or as an agent of direct effect, is affected by various aspects of the media and communication themselves or of the communication situation. (p. 8)

Can you find hints of limited effects theory in Klapper's summary? Klapper did admit that mass communication could have effects, even direct effects, beyond reinforcement. According to him, under what conditions might this occur?

DENNIS THE MENACE

"BOY! SHE SURE HAS A LOT OF SKIN, HUH, DAD?"

Figure 11–2 This Dennis the Menace cartoon demonstrates two criticisms of the uses and gratifications approach. Someone who chooses to read the newspaper may not intentionally select this cartoon but see it nonetheless. In addition, someone who chooses to read this cartoon for its humor will still be confronted with the idealized cultural image of women. Dennis the Menace ® used by permission of Hank Ketcham and © by North America Syndicate.

respected and examined even today. Among the most influential is **agenda setting,** a theory that argues that media may not tell us what to think, but media certainly tell us what to think *about*. Based on their study of the media's role in the 1968 presidential election, Maxwell McCombs and Donald Shaw wrote in 1972,

> In choosing and displaying news, editors, newsroom staff, and broadcasters play an important part in shaping political reality. Readers learn not only about a given issue, but how much importance to attach to that issue from the amount of information in a news story and its position. . . . The mass media may well determine the important issues—that is, the media may set the "agenda" of the campaign. (p. 176)

The agenda-setting power of the media resides in more than the amount of space or time devoted to a story and its placement in the broadcast or on the page. Also important is the fact that there is great consistency between media sources across all media in the choice and type of coverage they give an issue or event. This consistency and repetition signal to people the importance of the issue or event.

Researchers Shanto Iyengar and Donald Kinder (1987) tested the application of agenda setting theory to the network evening news shows in a series of experiments. Their conclusions supported McCombs and

Shaw. "Americans' views of their society and nation" they wrote, "are powerfully shaped by the stories that appear on the evening news" (p. 112). But Iyengar and Kinder took agenda setting a step or two further. They discovered that the position of a story affected the agenda setting power of television news. As you might expect, the lead story on the nightly newscast had the greatest agenda setting effect, in part because first stories tend to have viewers' full attention—they come before interruptions and other distractions can occur. The second reason, said the researchers, is that viewers accept the broadcasters' implicit categorization of the lead story as the most important. Iyengar and Kinder also tested the impact of vivid video presentations, discovering that emotionally presented, powerful images tended to undercut the agenda setting power of television news because the images focused too much attention on the specific situation or person in the story, rather than on the issue.

Dependency Theory In 1975 Melvin DeFleur and Sandra Ball-Rokeach offered a view of potentially powerful mass media, tying that power to audience members' dependence on media content. Their **dependency theory** is composed of several assertions:

- The basis of media's influence resides in the "relationship between the larger social system, the media's role in that system, and audience relationships to the media" (p. 261).

- The degree of our dependence on media and their content is the "key variable in understanding when and why media messages alter audience beliefs, feelings, or behavior" (p. 261).

- In our modern industrial society we are increasingly dependent on media (a) to understand the social world; (b) to act meaningfully and effectively in society; and, (c) to find fantasy and escape or diversion.

- Our level of dependency is related to (a) "the number and centrality (importance) of the specific information-delivery functions served by a medium"; and (b) the degree of change and conflict present in society (p. 263).

Limited effects theory has clearly been left behind here. Dependency theory argues that, especially in our complex and changing society, people become increasingly dependent on media and media content to understand what is going on around them, to learn how to behave meaningfully, and to escape. Think of a crisis, a natural disaster, for example. We immediately turn to the mass media. We are dependent on the media to understand what is going on around us, to learn what to do (how to behave), and even sometimes for escape from the reality of the situation. Now think of other, more personal crises—reaching puberty, attending high school, beginning dating, or having a child. Dependency theory can explain or predict our media use and its impact in these situations as well.

Social Learning Theory While mass communication researchers were challenging the limited effects paradigm with ideas such as agenda setting and dependency theory, psychologists were expanding **social learning theory**—the idea that people learn through observation—and applying it to mass media, especially television.

Social learning theory argues that people model (copy) the behaviors they see and that **modeling** happens in two ways. The first is **imitation,** the direct replication of an observed behavior. For example, a child might see cartoon cat Tom hit cartoon mouse Jerry with a stick and then hit his sister with a stick. The second form of modeling is **identification,** a special form of imitation in which observers do not copy exactly what they have seen but make a more generalized but related response. For example, the child might still be aggressive toward his sister but dump a pail of water on her head rather than hit her with a stick.

The idea of identification was of particular value to mass communication theorists who studied television's impact on behavior. Everyone admits that people can imitate what they see on television. But not all do, and when this imitation does occur in dramatic instances—for example, when someone hijacks a plane after seeing it done on a made-for-TV movie—it is so outrageous that it is considered an aberration. Identification, although obviously harder to see and study, is the more likely way that television influences behavior.

Social learning theorists demonstrated that imitation and identification are products of three processes:

Observational learning. Observers can acquire (learn) new behaviors simply by seeing those behaviors performed. Many of us who have never fired a handgun could do so because we've seen it done.

Inhibitory effects. Seeing a model, a movie character, for example, punished for a behavior reduces the likelihood that the observer will perform that behavior. In the media we see Good Samaritans sued for trying to help someone, and it reduces our willingness to help in similar situations. That behavior is inhibited by what we've seen.

Disinhibitory effects. Seeing a model rewarded for prohibited or threatening behavior increases the likelihood that the observer will perform that behavior. This is the basis for complaints against the glorification of crime and drugs in movies, for example. Behaviors that people might not otherwise make, those that are inhibited, now become more likely to occur. The behaviors are disinhibited.

The Era of Cultural Theory

The obvious and observable impact television has on our culture; the increased sophistication of media industries and media consumers; entrenched social problems such as racial strife; the apparent cheapening

Peter Arnett in Baghdad. Mass society theory was alive and well in the 1990s as critics claimed that CNN's Peter Arnett was feeding Iraqi propaganda to helpless U.S. television viewers.

of the political process; and the emergence of calls for controls on new technologies like cable, VCR, satellite, and computer networks are only a few of the many factors that have forced mass communication theorists to rethink media's influence. Clearly, the limited effects idea is inadequate to explain the media impact we see around us every day. But just as clearly, mass society theory tells us very little.

It's important to remember that prominent theories never totally disappear. Joseph McCarthy's efforts to purge Hollywood of communists in the 1950s, for example, was based on mass society notions of evil media and malleable audiences, as were the 1991 attacks on CNN reporter Peter Arnett's broadcasts from Baghdad during the Persian Gulf War. Unsuspecting viewers would be swayed by this obvious Iraqi propaganda, said the critics (who never explained why they themselves were resistant to it, a perfect example of the third person effect discussed in Chapter 2). In the 1996 Congressional debates and hearings leading up to the Telecommunications Act requirements of a television ratings system and the V-chip, broadcast industry spokespeople consistently raised limited effects and reinforcement theory arguments.

But the theories that have gained the most support among today's media researchers and theorists are those that accept the potential for powerful media effects, a potential that is *either* enhanced or thwarted by audience members' involvement in the mass communication process.

Important to this perspective on audience–media interaction are the **cultural theories.** Stanley Baran and Dennis Davis (1995) wrote that these theories share

> the underlying assumption that our experience of reality is an ongoing, social construction, not something that is only sent, delivered, or otherwise transmitted to a docile public. . . . Audience members don't just passively take in and store bits of information in mental filing cabinets, they actively process this information, reshape it, and store only what serves culturally defined needs. (p. 291)

This book's focus on media literacy is based on cultural theories, which say that meaning and, therefore, effects are negotiated by media and audiences as they interact in the culture. Several theories of mass communication reside under the cultural theories umbrella.

SYMBOLIC INTERACTION

Mass communication theorists borrowed another important theory from the psychologists, **symbolic interaction.** This is the idea that cultural symbols are learned through interaction and then mediate that interaction. In other words, people give things meaning, and that meaning controls their behavior. The flag is a perfect example. We have decided that an array of red, white, and blue cloth, assembled in a particular way, represents not only our nation but its values and beliefs. The flag has meaning because we have given it meaning, and that meaning now governs certain behavior toward the flag. We are not free to remain seated when a color guard carries the flag into a room. We are not free to fold it any way we choose. We are not free to place it on the right side of a stage in a public meeting. This is symbolic interaction.

Communication scholars Don Faules and Dennis Alexander (1978) define communication as "symbolic behavior which results in various degrees of shared meaning and values between participants" (p. 23). In their view, symbolic interaction is an excellent way to explain how mass communication shapes people's behaviors. Accepting that these symbolic meanings are negotiated by participants in the culture, mass communication scholars are left with the questions, What do the media contribute to these negotiations, and how powerful are they?

Symbolic interaction theory is frequently used when the influence of advertising is being studied because advertisers often succeed by encouraging the audience to perceive their products as symbols that have meaning beyond their actual function. This is called **product positioning.** For example, what does a Cadillac mean? Success. A Porsche? Virility. General Foods International Coffees? Togetherness and intimacy.

SOCIAL CONSTRUCTION OF REALITY

If we keep in mind James Carey's cultural definition of communication from Chapter 1—communication is a symbolic process whereby reality is produced, maintained, repaired, and transformed—we cannot be surprised that mass communication theorists have been drawn to the ideas of sociologists Peter Berger and Thomas Luckmann. In their 1966 book, *The Social Construction of Reality,* they never mention mass communication, but they offer a compelling theory to explain how cultures use signs and symbols to construct and maintain a uniform reality.

Social construction of reality theory argues that people who share a culture also share "an ongoing correspondence" of meaning. Things generally mean the same to me as they do to you. A stop sign, for example, has just about the same meaning for everyone. Berger and Luckmann call these things that have "objective" meaning **symbols**—we routinely interpret them in the usual way. But there are other things in the environment to which we assign "subjective" meaning. These things they call **signs.** In social construction of reality, then, a car is a symbol of mobility, but a Cadillac or Mercedes Benz is a sign of wealth or success. In either case the meaning is negotiated, but for signs the negotiation is a bit more complex.

Through interaction in and with the culture over time, people bring together what they have learned about these signs and symbols to form **typification schemes**—collections of meanings assigned to some phenomenon or situation. These typification schemes form a natural backdrop for people's interpretation of and behavior in "the major routines of everyday life, not only the typification of others . . . but typifications of all sorts of events and experiences" (Berger & Luckmann, 1966, p. 43). When you enter a classroom, you automatically recall the cultural meaning of its various elements—desks in rows, chalkboard, lectern. You recognize this as a classroom and impose your "classroom typification scheme." You know how to behave: address the person standing at the front of the room with courtesy, raise your hand when you have a question, talk to your neighbors in whispers. These "rules of behavior" were not published on the classroom door. You applied them because they were appropriate to the "reality" of the setting in your culture. In other cultures, behaviors in this setting may be quite different.

Social construction of reality is important to researchers who study the effects of advertising for the same reasons that symbolic interaction has proven valuable. But it is also widely applied when looking at how media, especially news, shape our political realities.

Crime offers one example. What do politicians mean when they say they are "tough on crime?" What is their (and your) reality of crime? It is likely that "crime" signifies (is a sign for) gangs, drugs, and violence. But the statistical (rather than the socially constructed) reality is that there is 10 times more white collar crime in the United States than there is violent crime. Now think "welfare." What reality is signified? Is it big corporations seeking money and tax breaks from the government? Or, is it unwed, unemployed mothers, unwilling to work, looking for a handout? Social construction theorists argue that the "building blocks" for the construction of these "realities" come primarily from the mass media.

CULTIVATION ANALYSIS

Symbolic interaction and social construction of reality provide a strong foundation for **cultivation analysis,** which says that television "cultivates" or constructs a reality of the world that, although possibly inaccurate, becomes accepted simply because we as a culture believe it to be true. We then base our judgments about and our actions in the world on this cultivated reality provided by television.

Although cultivation analysis was developed by media researcher George Gerbner and his colleagues out of concern over the effects of television violence, it has been applied to countless other television cultivated realities such as beauty, sex roles, religion, the judicial process, and marriage. In all cases the assumptions are the same—television cultivates realities, especially for heavy viewers.

Cultivation analysis is based on five assumptions:

1. *Television is essentially and fundamentally different from other mass media.* Unlike books, newspapers, and magazines, television requires no reading ability. Unlike the movies, television requires no mobility or cash; it is in the home, and it is free. Unlike radio, television combines pictures and sound. It can be consumed from people's very earliest to their last years of life.

2. *Television is the "central cultural arm" of U.S. society.* Gerbner and his colleagues (Gerbner, Gross, Jackson-Beeck, Jefferies-Fox, & Signorielli, 1978) wrote that television, as our culture's primary storyteller, is "the chief creator of synthetic cultural patterns (entertainment and information) for the most heterogeneous mass publics in history, including large groups that have never shared in any common public message systems" (p. 178). The product of this sharing of messages is the **mainstreaming** of reality, moving individual and different people toward a shared, television-created understanding of how things are.

3. *The realities cultivated by television are not necessarily specific attitudes and opinions but rather more basic assumptions about the "facts" of life.* Television does not teach facts and figures; it builds general frames of reference. Return to our earlier discussion of the portrayal of crime on television. Television newscasts never say, "Most crime is violent, most violent crime is committed by people of color, and you should be wary of those people." But by the choices news producers make, television news presents a broad picture of "reality" with little regard for how its "reality" matches that of its audience.

4. *The major cultural function of television is to stabilize social patterns.* That is, through television images the existing power relationships of the culture are reinforced and maintained. Gerbner and his colleagues made this argument:

> The repetitive pattern of television's mass-produced messages and images forms the mainstream of the common symbolic environment that cultivates the most widely shared conceptions of reality. We live in terms of the stories we tell—stories about what things exist, stories about how things work, and stories about what to do—and television tells them all through news, drama, and advertising to almost everybody most of the time. (1978, p. 178).

Because the media industries have a stake in the political, social, and economic structures as they exist, their stories rarely challenge the system that has enriched them.

5. *The observable, measurable, independent contributions of television to the culture are relatively small.* This is not a restatement of limited effects theory. Instead, Gerbner and his colleagues explained its meaning with an "ice-age analogy":

> Just as an average temperature shift of a few degrees can lead to an ice age . . . so too can a relatively small but pervasive influence make a crucial difference. The "size" of an effect is far less critical than the direction of its steady contribution. (Gerbner, Gross, Morgan, & Signorelli, 1980, p. 14)

In other words, even though we cannot always see media effects, they do occur and eventually will change the culture in possibly profound ways.

CRITICAL CULTURAL THEORY

A major influence on modern mass communication theory comes from European scholarship on media effects. **Critical cultural theory**—the idea that media operate primarily to justify and support the status quo at the expense of ordinary people—is openly political and is rooted in **neo-Marxist theory.** "Old-fashioned" Marxists believed that people were oppressed by those who owned the factories and the land (the means of production). They called the factories and land the *base.* Modern neo-Marxist theorists believe that people are oppressed by those who control the culture, the *superstructure*—in other words, the mass media.

Modern critical cultural theory encompasses a number of different conceptions of the relationship between media and culture. But all share these identifying characteristics:

- *They tend to be macroscopic in scope.* They examine broad, culturewide media effects.

- *They are openly and avowedly political.* Based in neo-Marxism, their orientation is from the political left.

- *Their goal is at the least to instigate change in government media policies; at the most, to effect wholesale change in media and cultural systems.* Critical cultural theories logically assume that the superstructure, which favors those in power, must be altered.

- *They investigate and explain how elites use media to maintain their positions of privilege and power.* Issues like media ownership, government–media relations, and corporate media representations of labor and disenfranchised groups are typical topics of study for critical cultural theory because they center on the exercise of power.

The Frankfurt School   The critical cultural perspective actually came to the United States in the 1930s when two prominent media scholars from the University of Frankfurt escaped Hitler's Germany. Theodor Adorno and Max Horkheimer were at the heart of what became known as the **Frankfurt School** of media theory (Arato & Gebhardt, 1978). Their approach, centered in neo-Marxism, valued serious art (literature, symphonic music, and theater) and saw consumption of art as a means to elevate all people toward a better life. Typical media fare—popular music, slapstick radio and movie comedies, the soft news dominant in newspapers—pacified ordinary people while assisting in their repression.

Adorno and Horkheimer's influence on U.S. media theory was minimal during their lifetimes. The limited effects paradigm was about to blossom, neo-Marxism was not well received, and their ideas sounded a bit too much like mass society theory claims of a corrupting and debasing popular media. More recently, though, the Frankfurt School has been "rediscovered," and its influence can be seen in the two final examples of contemporary critical theory, British cultural theory and news production research.

British Cultural Theory   There was significant class tension in England after World War II. During the 1950s and 1960s, working class people who had fought for their country were unwilling to return to England's traditional notions of nobility and privilege. Many saw the British media—with broadcasting dominated by graduates of the best upper-crust schools, and newspapers and magazines owned by the wealthy—as supporting longstanding class distinctions and divisions. This environment of class conflict produced theorists such as Stuart Hall (1980), who first developed the idea of media as a public forum (Chapter 1) where various forces fight to shape perceptions of everyday reality. Hall and others in British cultural studies trusted that the media *could* serve all people. However, because of ownership patterns, the commercial orientation of the media, and sympathetic government policies toward media, the forum was dominated by the reigning elite. In other words, the loudest voice in the give and take of the cultural forum belonged to those already well entrenched in the power structure.

British cultural studies theory today provides a home for much feminist research and research on popular culture both in Europe and in the United States.

News Production Research Another interesting strand of critical cultural theory is **news production research**—the study of how economic and other influences on the way news is produced distort and bias news coverage toward those in power. W. Lance Bennett (1988) identified four common news production conventions used by U.S. media that bolster the position of those in power:

1. *Personalized news.* Most news stories revolve around people. If a newspaper wants to do a report on homelessness, for example, it will typically focus on one person or family as the center of its story. This makes for interesting journalism (and increased ratings or circulation), but it reduces important social and political problems to soap opera levels. The two likely results are that these problems are dismissed by the public as specific to the characters in the story, and the public is not provided with the social and political contexts of the problem that might suggest avenues of public action.

2. *Dramatized news.* News, like other forms of media content, must be attractively packaged. Especially on television, this packaging takes the form of dramatization. Stories must have a hero and a villain, a conflict must be identified, and there has to be a showdown. Again, one problem is that important public issues take on the character of a soap opera or a western movie. But a larger concern is that political debate is trivialized. Fundamental alterations in tax law or defense spending or any of a number of important issues are reduced to Bill Clinton versus Newt Gingrich, the White House versus Congress. This complaint is often raised about media coverage of campaigns. The issues that should be at the center of the campaign become lost in a sea of stories about the "horse race"—who's ahead; how will a good showing in New Hampshire help Candidate X in her battle to unseat Candidate Y as the front-runner?

3. *Fragmented news.* The daily time and cost demands of U.S. journalism result in newspapers and broadcasts composed of a large number of brief, capsulated stories. There is little room in a given report for perspective and context. Another contributor to fragmented news, according to Bennett (1988), is journalists' obsession with objectivity. Putting any given day's story in context—connecting it to other events of the time or the past—would require the reporter to make decisions about which links are most important. Of course, these choices would be subjective, and so they are avoided. Reporters typically get one comment from somebody on one side of the issue and a second comment from the other side, juxta-

pose them as if they were equally valid, and then move on to tomorrow's assignment.

4. *Normalized news*. The U.S. news writing convention typically employed when reporting on natural or man-made disasters is to seek out and report the opinions and perspectives of the authorities. When an airplane crashes, for example, the report invariably concludes with the words, "The FAA was quickly on the scene. The cockpit recorder has been retrieved, and the reason for this tragedy will be determined soon." In other words, what happened here is bad, but the authorities will sort it out. Journalists give little independent attention to investigating any of a number of angles that a plane crash or flood might suggest, angles that might produce information different from that of officials.

The result of news produced according to these conventions is daily reassurance by the media that the system works if those in power are allowed to do their jobs. Any suggestions about opportunities for meaningful social action are suppressed.

DEVELOPING MEDIA LITERACY SKILLS
Applying Mass Communication Theory

There are many more theories of mass communication than we've covered here. Some apply to the operation of media as part of specific social systems. Some examine mass communication at the most micro-level; for example, How do viewers process individual television scenes? This chapter has focused on a relatively small number of theories that might prove useful to people trying to develop their media literacy skills. Remember

A news conference following the TWA flight 800 crash. According to news production research, the official, normalizing voice is an automatic part of all news coverage of natural and man-made disasters.

Gerbner's Three Bs of Television

After years of developing cultivation analysis theory, George Gerbner (1990, p. 261) was able to articulate the "three Bs of television":

1. Television BLURS the traditional distinctions of people's view of their world.

2. Television BLENDS people's realities into the cultural mainstream.

3. Television BENDS that mainstream reality to its own and its sponsors' institutional interests.

He then wrote of this power:

> The historical circumstances in which we find ourselves have taken the magic of human life—living in a universe erected by culture—out of the hands of families and small communities. What has been a richly diverse hand-crafted process has become—for better or worse, or both—a complex manufacturing and mass-distribution enterprise. This has abolished much of the provincialism and parochialism, as well as some of the elitism, of the pretelevision era. It has enriched parochial cultural horizons. It also gave increasingly massive industrial conglomerates the right to conjure up much of what we think about, know, and do in common. (p. 261)

Gerbner's tone gives away his opinion as to whether television's impact has been "for better or worse, or both." Discussion of the effects of television has been in the cultural forum since this medium was first developed. What is your opinion?

George Gerbner.

Art Silverblatt's (1995) elements of media literacy in Chapter 2. Among them were understanding the process of mass communication and accepting media content as a "text" providing insight into ourselves and our culture. Among the media literacy skills we identified was an understanding of and respect for the power of media messages. Good mass communication theory speaks to these elements and skills. Good mass communication theorists study them. Media literate people, then, are actually good mass communication theorists. They apply the available conceptions of media use and impact to their own content consumption and the way they live their lives.

George Gerbner's ideas are described a bit further in the box "Gerbner's Three Bs of Television," which also makes clear how important Gerbner believes it is to be a literate television viewer, that is, to understand the medium's power. Awareness of television's influence led this distinguished and influential mass communication theorist to become one of the founders of the Cultural Environment Movement, an activist media literacy organization introduced in Chapter 2.

Chapter Review

There is no one mass communication theory. Instead, there are many mass communication theories, explanations and predictions of social phenomena relating mass communication to various aspects of our personal and cultural lives or social systems. Many are borrowed from other disciplines. They are human constructions, and they are dynamic.

Theories are often identified by paradigms; mass communication theory paradigms shift because new technologies and media are introduced, because there needs to be an objective basis for their control, and because media's impact must be understood in a nation committed to preserving democracy and pluralism.

Mass communication theory has passed through four eras. The era of mass society includes such notions as mass society theory and hypodermic needle theory. Both see media as all powerful and audiences as more or less defenseless. The era of the scientific perspective, ushered in by the 1938 *War of the Worlds* radio broadcast, saw the development of objective, social science-based mass communication theories such as two-step flow theory. Taken together, the theories from this era are called limited effects theories.

The era of limited effects saw the entrenchment of limited effects beliefs. Attitude change theory, including dissonance theory and the selective processes, is typical of this time, as is Joseph Klapper's reinforcement theory. When limited effects theorists could no longer ignore seemingly powerful media influence, they turned to the uses and gratifications approach to explain how audience members allow media to affect them or not. Important theories claiming powerful media effects began during this era. Agenda setting (the media may not tell us what to think, but what to think about) and dependency theory (media influence is a function of people's dependence on me-

dia content) are applied even today. So, too is social learning theory—the idea that people can learn behaviors by observing them.

Contemporary mass communication theory can be called the era of cultural theory. Potentially powerful media effects are seen as either enhanced or thwarted by audience members' involvement in the mass communication process. Viewing media influence as negotiated between media and audience members, these theories see reality as socially constructed. Symbolic interaction is the idea that people give symbols meaning and that those symbols control behavior. Social construction of reality argues that reality is a social construction that depends on a correspondence of people's meanings for things in their shared world.

Cultivation analysis, developed by George Gerbner and his colleagues, claims that television "cultivates" or constructs a reality of the world that, although possibly inaccurate, becomes the accepted reality simply because we as a culture believe it to be the reality. Heavy viewers are more susceptible to cultivation than are light viewers.

Critical cultural theory, based in neo-Marxism, sees media as agents used in the cause of entrenched elites. Two interesting examples, British cultural studies and news production research, demonstrate the core philosophy of this theory, that regular people are disadvantaged by media systems as they currently exist.

There are many more mass communication theories than can be discussed in one textbook chapter, but media literate people, like mass communication theorists, develop their awareness of the impact of media, understand the process of mass communication, and accept media content as a text that provides insight into ourselves and our culture.

Questions for Review

1. What are paradigms and paradigm shifts?
2. What are the four eras of mass communication theory?
3. Who are Paul Lazarsfeld, Carl Hovland, Joseph Klapper, and George Gerbner? What is

the contribution of each to mass communication theory?
4. How did the *War of the Worlds* radio broadcast influence the development of mass communication theory?

5. What are dissonance theory and the selective processes?
6. According to uses and gratifications, what is the relationship between media and audience members?
7. What is the distinction between imitation and identification in social learning theory?

8. What assumptions about people and media are shared by symbolic interaction and social construction of reality?
9. What are the five assumptions of cultivation analysis?
10. What are the characteristics of critical cultural studies?

Questions for Critical Thinking and Discussion

1. Did you draw your dime too small? Whether you did or not, can you explain your behavior in this seemingly simple situation?
2. Many observers today hold to limited effects theories. Are you one? If you are, why? If you are not, why not?
3. Do media set the agenda for you? If not, why not? If they do, can you cite examples from your own experience?

4. Can you find examples of magazine or television advertising that use ideas from symbolic interaction or social construction of reality to sell their products? How do they do so?
5. Can you give examples of Gerbner's Three Bs of Television from your own viewing? How do you think they affect your and others' views of the world?

Important Resources

Arato, A., & Gebhardt, E. (1978). *The essential Frankfurt School reader.* **New York: Urizen Books.** The classic collection of original writing from and commentary on the Frankfurt School. People interested in issues from the effects of popular music to the use of the Internet will find useful commentary here.

Bandura, A. (1971). *Psychological modeling: Conflicting theories.* **Chicago, IL: Aldine Atherton.** The classic articulation of social learning theory written by its dominant thinker and researcher. Not only are all aspects of social learning thoroughly covered, but alternative views are aired.

Blumer, H. (1969). *Symbolic interactionism.* **Englewood Cliffs, NJ: Prentice-Hall.** The classic expression of symbolic interaction.

Blumler, J. G., Katz, E., & Gurevitch, M. (1974). Utilization of mass communication by the individual. In J. G. Blumler & E. Katz (Eds.), *The uses of mass communications:*

Current perspectives on gratifications research. **Beverly Hills, CA: Sage.** The original articulation of uses and gratifications from the researchers who developed and championed the theory.

Hall, S. (1982). The rediscovery of "ideology": Return of the repressed in media studies. In M. Gurevitch, T. Bennett, J. Curran, & J. Woollacott (Eds.), *Culture, society and the media.* **New York: Methuen.** A provocative and readable essay in which Hall lays out the theoretical as well as the political basis for British cultural studies.

Hovland, C. I., Janis, I. L., & Kelley, H. H. (1953). *Communication and persuasion.* **New Haven, CT: Yale University Press.** This collection of essays and original research is the classic work on which a generation of attitude change and dissonance theory research and theory is based.

Mass Communication Theory Web Sites

American Communication Association	*http://www.uark.edu/depts/comminfo/www/aca.html*
Association for Education in Journalism and Mass Communication	*http://www.aejmc.sc.edu/online/home2.html*
International Communication Association	*http://www.cahdq.org*
National Communication Association	*http://natcom.org*
Marxism and the Fundamental Problems of the 20th Century	*http://www.socialequality.com/*
Gary DeMar's Anti-Marxism Page	*http://www.foerunner.com/*

Mass Communication Research and Effects

"They'll never pick me," you thought, "I'm a student." But here you are . . . on jury duty. Three teenage kids torched a subway token booth after seeing the movie *Money Train* on cable television. They were caught at the scene red-handed, so they aren't claiming innocence. Instead, their defense is that the media are the real culprits; *Money Train* and television made them do it.

You listen as the prosecutor tells you and your eleven colleagues that similar appeals have been rejected in the past. A boy in Florida named Ronnie Zamora killed an elderly neighbor and said he was just imitating *Kojak*. Some boys gang raped two little girls after seeing a similar attack on an NBC made-for-television movie, *Born Innocent*. Both times juries like yours refused to place the blame on the media. Millions of people had seen the same content, those juries reasoned, and they didn't kill anyone, rape anybody, or set fire to anything.

Then you listen to the defense. These are good kids. They've never been in trouble. But they'd seen thieves in the movie squirt a flammable liquid into a token booth and set it afire, causing the clerk to open the door to escape. The defendants did what the movie had taught them to do, only this time the clerk didn't get out in time. She was burned to death. The lawyer asks, "Where would these children have gotten such an idea? Their parents didn't teach them this. Why did they think it was possible? Why did they think no one would get hurt?" The attorney then quotes former Senate Majority Leader Bob Dole's comments on the floor of the U.S. Senate after a series of similar attacks occurred when the movie was in the theaters. "Those who work in Hollywood's corporate suites must also

Kids who had seen the movie *Money Train* recreated this crime in real life. Was the film to blame?

be willing to accept their share of the blame," said the Republican who would eventually run for president. "Is this how they want to make their livelihoods? Is this their contribution to society?" ("Hollywood Feels Heat," 1995, p. A3).

The attorney turns, looking directly at you, and says, "This is the question you must decide. You must determine how much blame the filmmaker and distributor must take for this sad incident. You must decide how much they contributed to this tragedy."

That makes sense, too, you think. There's no doubt that the kids got the idea from the movie. But the DA is right too. Millions of other people saw the movie, and none of them copied what they'd seen. You realize you'd better pay attention. This isn't going to be easy.

In this chapter we investigate several media effects issues that are perplexing. Does watching television and film violence lead to increased viewer aggression? Do media promote the use of illegal drugs or increased alcohol consumption? What influence do media portrayals of gender and racial stereotypes have on people's attitudes and perceptions? How have media altered political campaigns? Do the media have positive effects?

Before we take on these complex issues, we must understand the different types of research and how these methods can be used to investigate these questions. Then we will discuss how a literate media consumer should interpret poll and survey data.

Mass Communication Research and the Effects Debate

Whether the issue is online hate groups, televised violence, or a decline in the quality of political discourse, the impact of the media is hotly debated today. In the last three years alone, the Telecommunications Act was passed, which creates new rules for children's television and regulates televised violence; a television program content rating system was introduced; the Child Pornography Act was passed, which is designed to protect kids from online images of sex; Congress is discussing how to control cigarette advertising and filtering software on school and library computers; and the Supreme Court dismissed the Communications Decency Act, which was intended to control Internet content. The assumption behind all efforts at control of media use and content is that media have effects. But the presence, strength, and operation of those effects have long been controversial.

THE EFFECTS DEBATE

The debate over media's impact has several dimensions. Here the limited or minimal effects position is stated first, followed by the counterargument.

1. *Media content has limited impact on audiences because it's only make-believe; people know it isn't real.*

The counterarguments: (a) News is not make-believe (at least it's not supposed to be), and we are supposed to take it seriously. (b) Most film and television dramas (for example, *ER* and *NYPD Blue*) are intentionally produced to seem real to viewers, with documentary-like production techniques such as handheld cameras and uneven lighting. (c) Much contemporary television is expressly *real*—reality shows such as *COPS* and *America's Most Wanted* and talk shows such as *The Jerry Springer Show* purport to present real people. (d) Advertising is supposed to tell the truth. (e) Before they develop the intellectual and critical capacity to know what is not real, children confront the world in all its splendor and vulgarity through television, what television effects researchers call the **early window.** To kids, what they see is real. (f) To enjoy what we consume, we **willingly suspend disbelief;** that is, we willingly accept as real what is put before us.

2. *Media content has limited impact on audiences because it is only play or just entertainment.*

The counterarguments: (a) News is not play or entertainment (at least it's not supposed to be). (b) Even if media content is only play, play is very important to the way we develop our knowledge of ourselves and our world. When we play organized sports, we learn teamwork, cooperation, the value of hard work, obedience to authority, and respect for the rules. Why should play be any less influential if we do it on the Internet or at the movies?

The mirror that media hold up to culture is like a fun-house mirror—some things appear bigger than they truly are, some things appear smaller, and some disappear altogether.

3. *If media have any effects at all, they are not the media's fault; media simply hold a mirror to society and reflect the status quo, showing us and our world as they already are.*

The counterargument: Media hold a very selective mirror. The whole world, in all its vastness and complexity, cannot possibly be represented, so media practitioners must make choices. For example, according to the Center for Media and Public Affairs, coverage of murder on the three evening network news shows *rose* 721% from 1993 to 1996, even though the actual U.S. homicide rate *fell* 20% in the same period. At best, media hold a fun-house mirror to society and distort what they reflect. Some things are overrepresented, others underrepresented, and still others disappear altogether.

4. *If media have any effect at all, it is only to reinforce preexisting values and beliefs. Family, church, school, and other socializing agents have much more influence.*

The counterarguments: (a) The traditional socializing agents have lost much of their power to influence in our complicated and fast-paced world. (b) Moreover, reinforcing effects are not the same as having no effects. If media can reinforce the good in our culture, media can just as easily reinforce the bad. Is racism eradicated yet? sexism? disrespect for others? If our media are doing no more than reinforcing the values and beliefs that already exist, then they are as empty as many critics contend. Former Federal Communications Commission member Nicholas Johnson has long argued of television in particular that the real crime is not what television is doing *to* us but what it could be doing *for* us, but isn't.

5. *If media have any effects at all, they are only on the unimportant things in our lives such as fads and fashions.*

The counterarguments: (a) Fads and fashions are not unimportant to us. The car we drive, the clothes we wear, and the way we look help define us; they characterize us to others. In fact, it is media that have helped make fads and fashions so central to our self-definition and happiness. Kids don't kill other kids for their $150 basketball shoes because their mothers told them that Air Jordans were cool. (b) If media influence only the unimportant things in our lives, why are billions of dollars spent on media efforts to sway opinion about social issues such as universal health care and nuclear power?

The grist for these debates over media effects comes from scientists who test the explanations and predictions of various mass communication theories using **research**—the objective search for knowledge. Research is conducted by media industry researchers and by academic researchers. A variety of research methods is available for this inquiry. Some are better suited to individual theories and questions than others, and some methods are more objective than others. This is one reason so much controversy exists about our willingness to accept the presence and extent of media effects. Not only do people research media impact from different perspectives or paradigms as we saw in Chapter 11, but they do so using different tools and with different degrees of objectivity. (Critical cultural theory, for example, is openly subjective.) Nonetheless, mass communication researchers have produced reasonable answers to many of the most important issues of media effects, and they have done so using a variety of quantitative and qualitative research methods worthy of our examination.

QUANTITATIVE RESEARCH METHODS

Quantitative research methods utilize numbers-based observations in the analysis of the mass communication process. The three methods most common to this type of research are experiments, surveys, and content analyses.

Experiments   **Experiments** are best utilized when testing **causal relationships**—the direct impact of one or more variables on one or more other variables. Expressed as a question, such relationships ask, Do alterations in X, in and of themselves, produce alterations in Y? Here X is the **independent variable,** the phenomenon that is manipulated (or altered or varied). Y is the **dependent variable,** the phenomenon whose change, as a result of variation in X, is measured. In a typical experiment about attitude change, for example, different groups of **participants**—the people in an experiment—are provided with different versions of the same content. (The common word for participants for decades has been "subjects"; however, the American Psychological Association now recommends use of the word "participants" to convey the idea that people are actively involved in the experiment.) One group may hear a lecture on seat belt safety, and the second might see a film on the same subject; the medium of presentation is varied or manipulated and therefore is the independent variable *(X)*. The participants' attitudes about seat belt safety are then measured using a series of questions; attitudes are the dependent variable *(Y)*.

Important to the logic of the experiment is the presence of a **control group,** participants who do not encounter the independent variable. In our attitude change experiment, the two groups who have heard and seen different versions of the content are the **experimental conditions;** they encounter the manipulated independent variable. A third group hears and sees no presentation at all; it is the control group. When all participants' attitudes toward seat belt safety are measured, any differences are assumed to be caused by the medium of presentation (lecture versus film).

But it is not enough to compare the attitudes of the two experimental conditions. The control group must also be considered. If the attitude scores differ for all three groups, the experimenter can logically claim that the observed differences in attitude are, in fact, produced by manipulations of the independent variable. If the control and one experimental group show no difference, the experimenter can claim that one mode of presentation is not only less effective than the other but that it has little impact on attitude change. After all, the attitudes of those exposed to the lectures, for example, were the same as those of the people who received no argument at all.

Experiments have three primary advantages:

- They can *establish causality,* important when studying the effects of mass communication.

- They *offer the researcher control;* the impact of extraneous variables can be neutralized (for example, by randomly assigning participants to each of the groups in an experiment).

- They *can be replicated.* This means that any researcher can duplicate the experiment, using different participants at a different time, to see whether the causal relationship does indeed exist. If the experiment cannot be repeated, its conclusions are assumed to be invalid.

Experiments have some important disadvantages as well. Control and the demonstration of causality make for sound experiments, but experi-

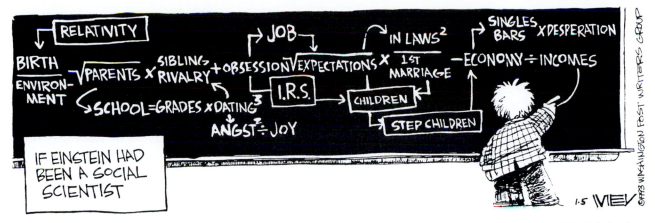

ments often occur in *artificial settings*. People don't typically confront safety messages in isolation from other content as they did in our example of an experiment. The lecture is more likely to be part of a driver education class, and the film might be a public service announcement during a television show. Related to the problem of artificiality of setting is the fact that experiments *often identify short-term effects;* that is, the demonstrated effects last only for the duration of the experiment.

In addition, answering questions about seat belt safety does not really tell us what people will do while driving. People's attitudes may be exhibited in behavior, but we don't actually know whether they will or will not use their seat belts.

Another danger is referred to as the **Hawthorne effect.** Participation in an experiment, in and of itself, can alter participants' behavior. Being observed changes the way people act.

Finally, experiments are often criticized for their lack of **generalizability.** How can the causal relationship demonstrated in the laboratory (an artificial setting) be assumed to operate in the larger real-world environment?

There are different techniques for overcoming these drawbacks. One is the use of **field** or **natural experiments**—experiments conducted in participants' actual environments, most often in the course of normal social events. For example, researchers interested in the impact of access to cable television on newspaper reading might interview a number of people from a town that has had cable for some time (experimental condition 1) and then interview people from a town that has yet to get cable (experimental condition 2). The independent variable is access to cable; the dependent variable is the amount of time participants spend reading the newspaper.

To reduce artificiality and achieve generalizability, the experimenter has sacrificed control—there is no control group. Other factors may be present that the experimenter cannot control. For example, one town may have a better newspaper than the other, or a higher level of educational achievement, or perhaps a recall of the school board has generated interest in newspaper accounts of the election.

Sometimes field experiments do employ manipulation in actual settings. For example, one televised antismoking campaign might be presented to one city's high school and a second campaign to the high school of a different city. Nevertheless, control is certainly not as easily obtained as with laboratory experiments (Figure 12–1).

Surveys **Surveys** are similar to the public opinion polls we see reported in the media. Both use sampling techniques and ask questions, but surveys are much more sophisticated than polls. They are designed to scientifically describe phenomena and their relationships in the actual environment at a given time. Surveys allow mass communication researchers to measure characteristics, opinions, or behaviors of a population by studying a small sample from that group, then generalizing back to the **population,** which is the group under scrutiny.

The logic of the survey assumes that it is impossible or impractical to observe all members of a given population. For example, how can a researcher deliver questionnaires to all television viewers or even interview all registered Republicans in Idaho who did not vote in the last presidential election? Surveys must depend instead on **samples** of **respondents** drawn from the population and considered representative of that population. Representativeness is achieved in a number of ways. Typically, respondents are drawn randomly from the population. In such a **random sample** each respondent has an equal chance of being included. In the Republican voters example, voter records would be used to identify all of Idaho's registered Republicans who did not vote in the last presidential election. Then a number is chosen at random from a table of random numbers or from the last two digits of the serial number of the third five-dollar bill in the researcher's wallet—the goal is to exclude any possible researcher influence in choosing the sample. That number is then used to identify the first respondent; if it is 27, the 27th name on the list becomes respondent number one. Then a second number is similarly chosen. If that number turns out to be 12, then every 12th name on the list is included in the random sample.

Often, however, researchers have reason to believe that a random sample will not identify adequate numbers of respondents with characteristics considered important to the question at hand. For example, the researchers might want to ensure that they have relatively equal numbers of men and women in their sample of Idaho Republicans. The population can first be divided according to gender and then randomly sampled. This is a **stratified random sample.**

Well-conducted surveys require that researchers follow a number of essential steps. They must:

1. Generate questions that not only get at the issue under examination but are not ambiguous, vague, or biased.

2. Select a sample that is large enough and representative enough for generalizations about the population to be made.

3. Organize the questionnaire to ensure that respondents do not become fatigued or frustrated and that the order of the questions does not bias people's answers.

4. Choose the most effective method of surveying the sample.

The researcher has several methods to choose from when surveying the sample. *Face-to-face interviews* allow for greater depth and detail, but they are expensive and time consuming, and the presence of the researcher can shape respondents' answers. *Telephone interviews* are inexpensive and convenient, but depth and detail are difficult to obtain. Also, the phone is a notoriously poor provider of random samples. Many people, especially females and wealthy people, have unlisted numbers; some people, especially the poor, do not have phones; answering machines and caller-ID are frequently used to screen out unwanted calls; and people are increasingly unwilling to participate in phone interviews. Refusal rates of 50% are not uncommon in contemporary phone polls and surveys, which raises serious questions about randomness and, therefore, generalizability. *Mail surveys* are inexpensive and permit collection of detailed information, but the typical return rate is about 20%, even when a stamped, preaddressed return envelope is provided. An 80% refusal rate again raises serious questions of randomness and generalizability.

Surveys offer three main advantages to mass communication researchers:

- They are particularly *useful for describing the characteristics of large populations.* A properly drawn sample of 1,200 to 5,000 households, for example, allows the Nielsen Company to generalize its ratings data to all U.S. television homes. Social scientists enjoy this same luxury.

- They are *flexible.* A well-designed questionnaire can have numerous questions about one or a number of topics.

- They are *ideal for identifying and measuring the extent of the relationships between two or more phenomena.*

These strengths lead us to the fundamental drawback of surveys. They are generally *not useful in demonstrating causality,* an important aspect of much mass communication research. A survey can ask questions about the amount of time respondents watch televised violence, and it can also ask about respondents' attitudes toward capital punishment. What the researcher cannot do is conclude that higher levels of watching televised violence *cause* higher levels of acceptance of the death penalty. At best, a survey can identify this relationship and indicate to what extent changes in one are paralleled by changes in the other. This strength of relationship is called **correlation.** Preference for televised violence may be correlated with acceptance of the death penalty. But which causes which? Surveys cannot answer this question particularly well.

Content Analysis   Scientists interested in media audiences use experiments and surveys. But some researchers are interested in media content. They use a method called **content analysis**—the objective, systematic, and quantitative description of the content of communication. It's one thing to intuitively believe that there is more gunplay on prime time television than there is in the real world; it is another to prove it. Researchers must demonstrate the presence and frequency of appearance of specific types of content in mass communication to effectively assert that that content has an impact on its consumers. George Gerbner's cultivation analysis (Chapter 11), for example, begins with the detailed, precise, and systematic categorization and counting of incidents of violence (or other forms of televised behavior). Content analysis is often used in violence and attitude change research and in studies of the impact of media on gender, ethnic, and racial stereotyping.

The strength of content analysis resides in its *efficiency and ease.* Once researchers have access to the content in question, they then develop a valid and reliable category scheme and count the number of times a piece of content fits each category. Researchers doing content analysis do not have to find participants, secure a characteristic sample of respondents, or maintain control over extraneous variables. Content analysis also allows researchers to *study trends* in mass communication over long periods of time as well as over geographic space. The portrayal of women's occupations in U.S. films can be studied from 1900 to today. It can also be studied by comparing U.S. films to films of other countries. Finally, content analysis is *unobtrusive.* The content does not respond to the researcher, as in surveys, or to the artificial experimental setting.

Content analysis has three drawbacks. The first is its *inability to measure latent rather than manifest content.* Manifest content is what we see. A woman in a 1950s film may be an airline pilot; that is the film's manifest content. But the latent or embedded content is the way she is presented in that occupation. The filmmaker, for example, might portray her as incompetent and out of her league. Content analysis would definitely consider this piece of content as a woman in a traditionally male profession; however, it might not make clear that her portrayal in that job was designed to discredit such activity rather than celebrate it. The two more important problems for many mass communication researchers are that content analysis *does not explain why a certain type of content exists* and that it *does not explain what effect a certain type of content has on the audience.* Researchers who use content analysis counter these arguments by saying that the method is simply not used to answer those kinds of questions.

QUALITATIVE RESEARCH METHODS

Much research does not rely on a quantitative assessment of the mass communication process. Rather, it is **qualitative research;** that is, it is focused on examining aspects of the process in their natural contexts. Most common are historical research, critical or text-based research, and ethnographic research.

Historical Research   Researchers often study the history of components of the mass communication process. They want to know why the regulatory structure of the broadcast industry developed as it did, or what led to the development of increased professionalism in advertising and public relations, or what public reaction was to D.W. Griffith's *The Birth of a Nation*. This is **historical research,** the objective examination of phenomena in their own time. This is as important in the study of mass communication as it is in any other discipline. Not only are those who ignore history doomed to repeat it, but practitioners and media literate audience members alike should have a historically accurate context against which to judge mass communication's contemporary operation.

Historical researchers depend on **primary sources,** material contemporary to the object under investigation, and **secondary sources,** relevant reports and material produced after the period in question, usually by other historians. Typical primary sources are the oral histories of people who were involved in the event under examination, diaries and other personal documents from the time, contemporary newspaper and other media accounts, organizational and institutional documents and records, and government records. Mass communication historians have the good fortune of studying a relatively young field and generally have a wide array of primary materials available.

Historical researchers must possess two important skills: (1) They must be able to mentally adopt the attitudes and feelings of the people of the time being studied and understand the circumstances so they can make appropriate interpretations of what they find; and (2) they must be able to find patterns among the mountains of detail they uncover describing the issue under study.

Critical/Textual Research   Researchers interested in the cultural messages embedded in mass communication content employ critical or text-based research methods. They examine content for the meaning it holds. The bedrock belief of this method of inquiry is that a culture's texts are inseparable from the realities of the lives of the people of that culture. In other words, one way to know and understand a culture and its people is to study the stories the culture tells about itself. You'll recognize this as an element of media literacy from Chapter 2.

Critical or text-based mass communication researchers make two important assumptions about media content:

What does the television show *The Beverly Hillbillies* tell researchers about U.S. values and beliefs? What myths are embodied in this program?

1. *Media content is a modern culture's literature.* Movies, television shows, popular music, and magazine ads are today's literature just as surely as the novel was in the 19th century. Throughout high school and college we are asked to read, study, and analyze literature from different times and different places. We read *The Scarlet Letter* to learn about the values and beliefs of Colonial America. Shakespeare's plays offer insight into 16th century Europe. We find a culture's view of itself—of its own reality—in its literature. Our contemporary literature exists not only in books but in all our outlets of expression.

2. *Media content makes cultural values and the relationships between those values perceptible.* Phenomena such as bravery, patriotism, racism, sexism, freedom, love, and marriage exist in the culture in many forms, and they often exist out of our immediate awareness. But through inclusion in our stories, we can see these elements highlighted; we can see what meanings the culture attributes to them. For example, we rarely reflect on our own and the larger culture's definition of patriotism until it becomes part of a media news account or a dramatic performance.

Some critical researchers make a third important assumption:

3. *Meaning does not reside in the text but is created during the act of "reading."* The author's meaning may not be the reader's meaning because audience members create meaning in interaction with the content producer.

The research of Janice Radway (1984) demonstrates these three assumptions. She studied popular contemporary romance novels (assumption 1) and discovered that their formulaic characters and story lines rest firmly on our culture's patriarchal myths of men as strong, aggressive, and heroic and women as weak, passive, and dependent (assumption 2). The male-dominated social order is presented as natural and just, and women's identities are based on their relationship with the men around them. Radway then interviewed romance novel fans and discovered that these women often engaged in **oppositional decoding,** interpreting the content in a manner counter to its apparent intent (assumption 3). These readers identified with male characters or with female characters who refused to be submissive to men.

The strength of critical research is its **phenomenology;** that it studies media content as it is. Critics find its weakness is its assumption that the relationships and values embedded in media content are also part of the larger culture. Those who see media as "only make-believe" deny that assumption. Those who accept the presence of media effects generally demand more proof of causality, or the direction of influence. That is, they question whether content affects culture or culture affects content. Using the Radway example, researchers interested in effects might ask, Do media representations of the male-dominated social order cause it to exist in the culture, or does its existence in the culture cause it to appear in the content Radway studied?

Ethnographic Research   Some researchers who admit media's power but also believe the audience produces effects find experiments too artificial, surveys too broad and impersonal, and critical analysis too subjective. They choose instead to examine media effects through **ethnographic research**—naturalistic examinations of audiences in specific and natural places. Borrowed from cultural anthropology, this research method is used to study the way people incorporate media "into their ongoing motives and goals. There is an interest in accounting for the actual unfolding of everyday interactions with media. There is, accordingly, a commitment to systematically investigating the situational contexts in which media are encountered and exploited" (Lindlof, 1987).

Ethnographic research encompasses many diverse activities. One is **participant-observer research,** in which the researcher joins a group (for example, several friends watching television in a dormitory room) or enters a setting (for example, a television news operation) and—while participating in its ongoing activities—chronicles those activities and the interactions surrounding them. Another research activity is collecting and analyzing diaries maintained by audience members whose consumption of content in a given situation, for example, during a natural disaster or during the first few days of a televised event such as the 1991 Gulf War, is of interest. A third is observation and record keeping by an **unobtrusive observer.** Here, for example, a researcher may simply sit in a corner and observe a family watching television, recording its conversations on tape and afterwards asking the family members questions.

Proponents of ethnographic inquiry point to its strengths:

1. *It is natural.* Ethnographic research examines people's interaction with media in settings where that interaction naturally occurs, thereby capturing a more realistic view of the particular aspect of the mass communication process under investigation.

2. *It gives the audience a voice.* Participants are not forced to respond to researcher created or provided content or to answer predetermined questions written by survey researchers. Instead, people are free to react in their own way to what they read, hear, or see.

3. *It allows for more depth of understanding* than quantitative methods. It focuses on individual media consumers or individual media settings.

Critics point to one primary weakness: Ethnographic methods *do not allow for sufficient generalization.* What does one family watching television, or one group of dorm dwellers, or one news operation tell us about other families, other college-age viewers, or other news organizations? A second weakness is that even the most skilled observer alters a "natural setting" by the simple fact of his or her presence. Akin to the Hawthorne effect in experimental studies, observation may well alter the processes under scrutiny.

The Effects of Mass Communication

Regardless of the method employed, mass communication research is designed to illuminate different aspects of the mass communication process. Experiments may be best for demonstrating effects. Surveys may be best for assessing the presence and extent of effects in the environment. Textual analyses may be best for identifying large cultural themes. Ethnographic research may be best for providing detailed analyses of specific audiences. Debate persists. Yet together these methods have provided scientists, industry professionals, and audience members with more or less definitive explanations of how, when, and to what extent media effects occur.

VIOLENCE

No media effects issue has captured public, legislative, and industry attention like the relationship between media portrayals of violence and subsequent aggressive behavior. Among the reasons for this focus are the facts that violence is a staple of both television and movies and that the United States experienced an upsurge in real violence in the 1960s, just about the time television entrenched itself as the country's dominant mass

Ernest Borgnine in Sam Peckinpah's *The Wild Bunch* (1969). In trying to differentiate itself from the television industry, the movie industry turned to graphic violence, fueling the debate over media violence and subsequent real-world aggression.

medium and that movies turned to increasingly graphic violence to differentiate themselves from and to compete with television.

The prevailing view during the 1960s was that *some* media violence affected *some* people in *some* ways *some* of the time. Given the dominance of the transmissional perspective of communication (Chapter 1) and the limited effects paradigm (Chapter 11), researchers believed that for "normal" people—that is, those who were not predisposed to violence—*little* media violence affected *few* people in *few* ways *little* of the time. However, increases in youth violence, the assassinations of Robert F. Kennedy and Reverend Martin Luther King Jr., and the violent eruption of cities during the civil rights, women's rights, and anti-Vietnam War movements led to creation of the Surgeon General's Scientific Advisory Committee on Television and Social Behavior in 1969. After two years and $1 million worth of research, the committee (whose members had to be approved by the television networks) produced findings that led Surgeon General Jesse L. Steinfield to report to the U.S. Senate:

> While the . . . report is carefully phrased and qualified in language acceptable to social scientists, it is clear to me that the causal relationship between televised violence and antisocial behavior is sufficient to warrant appropriate and immediate remedial action. The data on social phenomena such as television and violence and/or aggressive behavior will never be clear

enough for all social scientists to agree on the formulation of a succinct statement of causality. But there comes a time when the data are sufficient to justify action. That time has come. (Ninety-Second Congress, 1972, p. 26)

Despite the apparent certainty of this statement, disagreement persists over the existence and extent of the media's contribution to aggressive behavior. Few would argue that media violence *never* leads to aggressive behavior. The disagreement is about what circumstances are needed for such effects to occur, and to whom.

Under What Circumstances? A direct causal relationship between violent content and aggressive behavior—the **stimulation model**—has been scientifically demonstrated in laboratory experiments. So has the **aggressive cues model**—the idea that media portrayals can suggest that certain classes of people, for example, women or foreigners, are acceptable targets for real-world aggression, thereby increasing the likelihood that some people will act violently toward people in these groups.

Both the stimulation and aggressive cues models are based on social learning theory (Chapter 11). Fueled by the research of psychologists such as Albert Bandura, social learning theory has made several additional contributions to the violence debate.

Social learning theory deflated the notion of **catharsis,** the idea that watching violence in the media reduces people's innate aggressive drive. Social scientists were already skeptical: viewing people eating does not reduce hunger; viewing people making love does not reduce the drive to reproduce. But social learning theory provided a scientific explanation for the research that did show a reduction in aggression after viewing violence. This phenomenon was better explained not by some cathartic power of the media but by inhibitory effects. That is, as we saw in Chapter 11, if media aggression is portrayed as punished or prohibited, it can indeed lead to the reduced likelihood that that behavior will be modeled.

Some people, typically media industry practitioners, to this day defend catharsis theory. But nearly 30 years ago, respected media researcher and theorist Joseph Klapper, who at the time was the head of social research for CBS television, told the U.S. Senate, "I myself am unaware of any, shall we say, hard evidence that seeing violence on television or any other medium acts in a cathartic . . . manner. There have been some studies to that effect; they are grossly, greatly outweighed by studies as to the opposite effect" (Ninety-Second Congress, 1972, p. 60).

Social learning theory introduced the concept of **vicarious reinforcement**—the idea that observed reinforcement operates in the same manner as actual reinforcement. This helped direct researchers' attention to the context in which media violence is presented. Theoretically, inhibitory and disinhibitory effects operate because of, respectively, negative and positive vicarious reinforcement. That is, seeing the bad guy punished is sufficient to inhibit subsequent aggression on the part of the viewer. Unfor-

These scenes from Albert Bandura's media violence research are typical of the laboratory response to portrayals of media violence that social learning researchers were able to elicit from children.

tunately, what researchers discovered is that in contemporary film and television when the bad guys are punished they are punished by good guys who out-aggress them. The implication is that even when media portray punishment for aggressive behavior they may in fact be positively reinforcing that very same behavior.

Social learning theory introduced the concept of **environmental incentives**—the notion that real-world incentives can lead observers to ignore the negative vicarious reinforcement they have learned to associate with a given behavior.

In 1965 Bandura conducted a now classic experiment in which nursery school children saw a video aggressor, a character named Rocky, punished for his behavior. The children subsequently showed lower levels of aggressive play than did those who had seen Rocky rewarded. This is what social learning would have predicted. Yet Bandura later offered "sticker-pictures" to the children who had seen Rocky punished if they could perform the same actions they had seen him perform. They all could. Vicarious negative reinforcement may reduce the likelihood that the punished behavior will be performed, but that behavior is still observationally learned. It's just that, at the same time it is observed and learned, observers also learn not to make it. When the real world offers sufficient reward, the originally learned behavior can be demonstrated.

For Whom? The compelling evidence of social learning researchers aside, it's clear that most people do not exhibit aggression after viewing film or video violence. There is also little doubt that those predisposed to violence are more likely to be influenced by media aggression. Yet viewers need not necessarily be predisposed for this link to occur, because at anytime anyone can become predisposed. For example, experimental research indicates that frustrating people before they view media violence can increase the likelihood of subsequent aggressive behavior.

But the question remains, Who, exactly, is affected by mediated violence? If a direct causal link is necessary to establish effects, then it can indeed be argued that some media violence affects some people in some ways some of the time. But if the larger, macro-level ritual view is applied, then we all are affected because we live in a world where there is more violence than there might be without mass media. We live in a world, according to cultivation analysis (Chapter 11), where we are less trusting of our neighbors and more accepting of violence in our midst. We experience **desensitization.** This need not be the case. As researcher Ellen Wartella (1997) said, "Today, we find wide consensus among experts that, of all the factors contributing to violence in our society, violence on television may be the easiest to control" (p. 4) (see the box "National Television Violence Study").

Using Media to Make a * Difference

National Television Violence Study

A number of leading mass communication researchers recently conducted the National Television Violence Study, applying content analysis to a large sample of television programming (Wartella, 1997). The goals of the project were to identify the context in which televised violence is presented and to identify the nature and extent of that televised violence. In the 1994/95 television season the study analyzed 2,500 hours of programming, constituting 2,700 programs from 23 cable and broadcast channels. It was the largest and most representative sample of television content ever subjected to content analysis.

Defining violence as "any overt depiction of a credible threat of physical force or the actual use of such force intended to physically harm an animate being or group of beings . . . [or] . . . certain depictions of physically harmful consequences against an animate being or group that occur as a result of unseen violent means" (p. 3), the researchers released these findings in February 1996.

- *Violence is a predominant theme on television.* More than half of all shows studied contained violence; one third contained more than nine violent interactions (and one interaction, for example a bank robbery, could consist of numerous individual violent acts).

- *Perpetrators engage in repeated violence.* Nearly 60% of the violence is committed by characters who engage in repeated acts of aggression.

- *Televised violence often involves guns.* One quarter of all televised violence is committed with a gun.

DRUGS AND ALCOHOL

Concern about media effects reaches beyond the issue of violence. The claims and counterclaims surrounding media portrayals of drugs and alcohol parallel those of the violence debate.

The wealth of scientific evidence linking media portrayals of alcohol consumption, especially in ads, to increases in youthful drinking and alcohol abuse is sufficient to have moved another Surgeon General, Antonia C. Novello, to declare at a 1991 press conference:

> Of the 20.7 million 7th through 12th grade students nationwide, 10.6 million students drink . . . 8 million drink weekly and . . . 454,000 binge once a week. . . . For the longest time, sex, glamour, and action have been used as time-honored techniques to sell everything from toothpaste to laundry detergent. But let's remember, your laundry detergent doesn't affect your alertness and your toothpaste doesn't break down your barriers against risky behavior. Alcohol does. And alcohol, when mixed with the exhilaration and turmoil of youth, is a brew that can lead to disaster. . . . Current research has documented that youth are especially attracted to ads which *make lifestyle appeals* with attractive role models, imaginary peers, and attractive lifestyles to emulate; *make sexual appeals* about attracting, watching, and

- Across all channels and genres, *aggressors go unpunished.* In 75% of all the violent scenes studied, the violent characters get away with their acts.

- *The consequences of violence are not realistically presented.* Fewer than one half of the observed violent interactions presented victims experiencing signs of pain. Only one in six programs depict any long-term consequences such as limping or bandages.

- *Violence is frequently presented as humorous.* More than one third of the violent scenes involved the humorous presentation of aggression.

- *Violent programming almost never offers an antiviolence message.* Only 4% of the programs that depicted violence stressed its uselessness and destructiveness.

From a social learning perspective, what do these findings suggest about the television violence–viewer aggression link? Do you think such large-scale analyses of television violence make a difference to the public or to broadcast industry and regulatory professionals? Do they just tell people what they already know? Should they spur industry self-analysis and correction? Should they generate corrective legislation?

NBC's *Homicide: Life on the Street.*

What does this magazine ad say about drinking? About attractiveness? About people of color? About having fun? About men? About women? Are you satisfied with these representations of important aspects of your life?

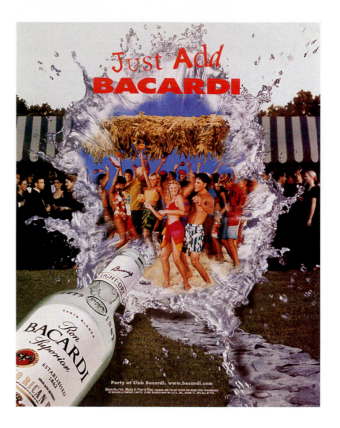

even conquering the opposite sex; *use sports figures* who usually are heroes to youth; and, *show risky activities,* leading many people, and in particular the young, to think that it is not only acceptable for people to drink while participating in that activity, but that it is also safe to do so. (emphasis in original, p. 4)

There is a good deal of scientific research—typically from alcohol industry scientists—that discounts the causal link between media portrayals and real-world drinking. Again, researchers who insist on the demonstration of this direct causal relationship will rarely agree on media's influence on behavior. The larger cultural perspective, however, suggests that media portrayals of alcohol, both in ads and in entertainment fare, tell stories of alcohol consumption that predominantly present it as safe, healthy, youthful, sexy, necessary for a good time, effective for dealing with stress, and essential to ceremonies and other rites of passage.

The same scenario exists in the debate over the relationship between media portrayals of nonalcohol drug use and behavior. Relatively little contemporary media content presents the use of illegal drugs in a glorifying manner. In fact, the destructive power of illegal drugs is often the focus of television shows like *NYPD Blue* and *ER* and a central theme in movies like *Trainspotting* and *Boyz in the Hood*. Scientific concern has centered therefore on the impact of commercials and other media portrayals of legal over-the-counter drugs. Again, impressive amounts of experimental research suggest a causal link between this content and subsequent abuse of both legal and illegal drugs; however, there also exists research that discounts the causal link between media portrayals and the subsequent abuse of drugs. It cannot be denied, however, that media often present legal drugs as a cure-all for dealing with that pesky mother-in-law, those screaming kids, that abusive boss, and other daily annoyances.

GENDER AND RACIAL/ETHNIC STEREOTYPING

Stereotyping is the application of a standardized image or concept to members of certain groups, usually based on limited information. Because media cannot show all realities of all things, the choices media practitioners make when presenting specific people and groups may well facilitate or encourage stereotyping (see the box "African Americans in Ads").

Numerous content analyses conducted over the last 40 years have demonstrated that women and people of color are consistently underrepresented in all media; that when they are portrayed they are more often than not presented in traditional, inferior roles; that women are more likely to be presented as the victims of aggression than is the case in the real world; and that people of color are more likely to be presented as the perpetrators of crime and aggression than is the case in the real world. When women and minorities are presented favorably, they are often stereotyped as "perfect"—the "perfect Asian student" or the "perfect African American social worker." These portrayals are as narrow and limiting as the "dumb blonde" or "dangerous dark outsider."

Any of a number of theories, especially cultivation analysis, symbolic interaction, and social construction of reality (Chapter 11), can predict the probable outcome of repeated and frequent exposure to these limited and limiting representations. They influence people's perceptions, and people's perceptions influence their behaviors. Examine your own conceptions not only of women and people of color but of the elderly, lawyers, college athletes, and people sophisticated in the use of computers. What images or stereotypes come immediately to mind?

Sure, you're skeptical. You're a smart, progressive, college educated individual. Test yourself on your stereotype of people from the U.S. heartland or, conversely, of people from big urban centers. Should a lone female feel more secure walking among residents of Oklahoma City or New York City? among people from Rapid City, South Dakota, or Washington, DC? The FBI reports that the incidence of forcible rape in Oklahoma City is 73.9 per 100,000 females, three times the levels of New York City and Washington, DC. The city with the highest rate of forcible rape?—Rapid City (Zoellner, 1995, p. 8). How did you develop your stereotypes of the people who live in these places? Where did you find the building blocks to construct your realities of their lives?

African Americans in Ads

Before the civil rights movement of the 1960s, it was quite common for U.S. advertisers to include African Americans in ads intended for the larger, dominant White audience. Images of young Black children eating watermelon and plump Mammies were used to sell everything from gasoline to maple syrup. In addition, African Americans in service positions—bellhops, waiters, servants, and porters—were standard elements in ads for luxury items such as fancy hotels and sleeper railroad cars.

With increased sensitivity to issues of race and the growing financial clout of the expanding African American middle class, these insulting images disappeared.

But an issue currently being debated in the cultural forum centers on the frequent use of African American athletes in advertising. By appearing in ads, athletes like Michael Jordan, Bo Jackson, Ken Griffey, Jr., and Shaquille O'Neal all earn sums of money easily in excess of what they make for playing the sports that have made them famous. Many critics, especially from the African American community, contend that these characterizations are doubly stereotypical. For non-Blacks, they reinforce the idea that the only thing African Americans succeed at is sports and entertainment. For poor African American kids, they reinforce the belief that the best, fastest, and maybe the only way to succeed is through sports and entertainment. Education, hard work, commitment to community—those are for suckers! "Where are the African American doctors, lawyers, and teachers?" ask the critics.

What is your opinion of this criticism of African American athletes in advertising? They are famous among people of all races. They sell the products. Shouldn't that be enough?

A 1938 ad for an elevator company and a contemporary spot for hot dogs.

These three images—Barbara Billingsley as Beaver Cleaver's mom, Charlie's Angels, and Queen Latifah—show how women have been portrayed over time on television. Researchers believe that repeated and frequent exposure to such representations as these influences people's perceptions of, and therefore their behaviors toward, women. The question that is typically raised when talking about media stereotypes is, "Which came first, the culture's representation or the media representation?" Clearly, television's image of women has changed over the years, but were these different cultural views of women simply mirrored by television, or did television's constant reliance on a limited array of images of women create—or at least reinforce—the stereotypes? And even if the media do create or reinforce stereotypes, why should anyone care? Do all cultures have stereotypes of their people? What do you think?

Presidential debates have become the focus of much research on the media's contribution to the electoral process. Here, John F. Kennedy and Richard M. Nixon face off in history's first series of televised presidential debates.

POLITICAL CAMPAIGNS AND VOTING

Media impact on political campaigns and voting was at the center of some of mass communication's earliest research. The two-step flow model (Chapter 11), for example, was the product of research on the 1940 presidential election conducted by Paul Lazarsfeld and his colleagues. Given that television had yet to develop into a true mass medium and that the notion of limited effects held sway, the overall conclusion drawn from this early work was that media had little *direct* impact on campaigns and voting and, when and if they did, that the impact was in the form of reinforcement.

But with the fuller diffusion of television and the interest generated in that medium by the 1960 Kennedy–Nixon debates, thinking about media and campaigns began to change. For example, research after those inaugural televised debates began to focus on how candidates used media for image building and the subsequent "cheapening" of campaigns as personalities became more important than issues. Another important development in contemporary thinking about media and campaigns was agenda setting (Chapter 11), introduced after research on the 1968 presidential elections. Agenda setting was used to explain how media can influence campaigns and voting. Media helped set the issue agenda for the campaign, and that agenda dictated the issues on which many people ultimately based their voting decisions.

The growing influence of television news throughout the 1960s and 1970s naturally turned attention to its role in the electoral process. Early thinking saw news reports as more important than political ads in shaping preferences because of the perceived impartiality of news reporting.

But recent research has demonstrated dramatic declines in the amount of time given to candidates' positions in typical news programs. Candidates now concentrate on more visually interesting, content free *pseudo-events* that have no real informational or issue meaning but exist merely to attract media attention. Candidates recognize that the public tends to trust news more than commercials. The goal of pseudo-events, therefore, is to earn candidates and their campaigns media coverage while allowing the campaigns to control the content of that coverage.

Contemporary research and theory confirms that media and campaigns do indeed have important effects. On the microlevel, media coverage of candidates and campaigns tends to reconfirm support among already committed voters and to solidify support among those leaning toward particular candidates. The macrolevel view criticizes media—especially television with its sound bites and attack ads—as debasing and trivializing the electoral process, turning off voters, and generating disinterest (at best) or disgust (at worst) with the political process.

This situation has given rise to a number of proposals for improvement. Primary among them is campaign reform. Since the media, again, especially television, have become essential to modern campaigning, raising money to buy media time and space is a full-time obsession for many politicians. This state of affairs has led to widespread suspicion among voters that the money raised to buy media access for a candidate ultimately buys access to the candidate for the source of the money. A second suggestion—one embraced by the Fox television network among others and touted by President Clinton in his 1997 State of the Union address—is that broadcasters should make free time available to candidates and campaigns, reducing the influence of money and increasing the length of time candidates have to present full, cogent explanations of their positions. A third suggestion is that the United States should follow the British election practice of not only granting free air time to candidates but also limiting all campaigning—personal and mediated—to a specified period, say three or six months, before election day. Campaigning outside this "run up" to the election would be illegal.

PROSOCIAL EFFECTS

Virtually every argument that can be made for the harmful or negative effects of media can also be applied to the ability of media to do good. A sizable body of science exists that clearly demonstrates that people, especially children, can and will model the good or prosocial behaviors they see in the media, often to a greater extent than they will the negative behaviors. Research on the impact of media portrayals of cooperation and constructive problem solving (Baran, Chase, & Courtright, 1979) and other "good" behaviors indicate that much more than negative behavior can be socially learned from the media.

Research has shown that prosocial media content can influence behavior just as easily as can antisocial behavior. Critics contend, however, that there are simply too few examples of good content like *The Waltons*, pictured here.

DEVELOPING MEDIA LITERACY SKILLS

Interpreting Sample Size and Margin of Error

Survey researchers and public opinion pollsters often report their findings in the popular media. To be media literate, people need to know something about how that reporting is best done. The surveys and polls we all see and hear reported are often criticized for the generalizations to large populations they make from seemingly small samples. However, effective sample size, surprisingly, is not related to the size of the population. Instead, it is a function of the amount of uncertainty researchers are willing to accept in their results. Scientists have determined mathematically that a predictable, built-in level of error accompanies all samples of a given size. This is sometimes called **estimated sampling error** or **error term** or, most commonly, **margin of error.**

For example, survey data may show that candidate A leads candidate B by 51% to 49%, but in reality B may lead A. This means that when survey or poll data are reported, researchers must also include the sample size and the margin of error. We often do see margin of error reported as "+/− 3%."

A sample of 100 respondents comes with a margin of error of 10 points. If the researchers in our example had used a sample of this size, candidate A's percentage might be as high as 61% or as low as 41% (51 + 10 = 61; 51 − 10 = 41). Candidate B's percentage could be anywhere between 59% and 39% (49 + 10 = 59; 49 − 10 = 39).

The convention, then, is to choose a sample size that is both economically and efficiently measurable while still giving researchers a margin of error they can tolerate. As a reader of surveys and polls, you must always assess the impact of the margin of error on the results you see reported.

Here are some sample sizes and their accompanying margins of error. Remember, except in the special circumstance when some small, particular population is under scrutiny, the size of the population is unimportant because, mathematically, samples of these sizes are always accompanied by given levels of variation or error:

Sample Size	Margin of Error
400	+/− 5%
600	+/− 4%
1,100	+/− 3%
2,400	+/− 2%
9,600	+/− 1%

Chapter Review

The debate over media effects focuses on a number of issues. Are media effects limited by the fact that audiences know content is only make believe? Is impact limited because media are used only as entertainment? Does media content simply reflect society as it is? Do media effects typically exist only in the form of reinforcement? Can media affect more than the unimportant aspects of people's lives?

Social scientists use research to test for the presence of media effects. A variety of quantitative methods, including experiments, surveys, and content analyses, and qualitative techniques, including historical research, critical research, and ethnographic research, are employed. Experiments utilize experimental and control conditions to measure the impact of independent variables on dependent variables. They sacrifice generalizability for control and the ability to demonstrate causality. Surveys—telephone, mail, and face-to-face interviews—use samples drawn from populations. They sacrifice causal explanations for generalizability

and breadth. Content analyses provide detailed and systematic examinations of media content.

Historical research is the objective examination of phenomena in their own time; it relies on primary and secondary sources. Critical or text-based research treats media content as the literature of the culture that produced it and assumes that the content makes perceptible cultural objects and the relationships between those objects. Ethnographic research is conducted in a number of ways, for example participant-observer studies, the chronicles of unobtrusive observers, and the examination of people's diaries. The goal is to study the mass communication process in the settings where it occurs.

These research methods have been applied to answering a number of effects questions. The impact of mediated violence is the best-known effects issue. The causal relationship between violent media content and subsequent aggressive behavior has been demonstrated for decades, giving rise to the stimulation and aggressive cues models of media's influence on aggressive behavior. Social learning theory has been central to demonstrating the operation of both vicarious reinforcement and environmental incentives. Catharsis, the idea that viewing mediated aggression reduces people's innate aggressive drives, has been discredited.

Effects researchers have also made important discoveries, paralleling the discoveries of the violence researchers, about the relationship between media representations of drugs and alcohol and subsequent behavior. Disagreement exists, however, regarding the interplay of content and behavior. Those who adopt the wider, macro-level ritual view of mass communication more readily accept media's influence on people's behavior than do those who hold to more transmissional views.

Two other effects issues that have attracted scientific attention are the impact of media portrayals of different groups of people (stereotyping) and the impact of media, especially television, on political campaigns. Links between attitudes and media portrayals have been demonstrated. None of this, however, is meant to imply that media content cannot have good or prosocial effects. Research demonstrates this as well.

Understanding sample size and error term when interpreting survey and poll results is an important media literacy skill.

Questions for Review

1. Define research, causal relationship, independent variable, dependent variable, control group, Hawthorne effect, and generalizability.
2. What are some typical quantitative research methods? What are some typical qualitative research methods?
3. What is the difference between participants and respondents?
4. What are the strengths and weaknesses of experiments? of surveys?
5. What are the three methods of collecting survey information? What are the advantages and disadvantages of each?
6. What is oppositional decoding?
7. What are the strengths and weaknesses of ethnographic research?
8. What are the stimulation and aggressive cues models of media violence? What is catharsis?
9. What are vicarious reinforcement and environmental incentives? How do these ideas figure in the media violence debate?
10. What is margin of error?

Questions for Critical Thinking and Discussion

1. If you were on the jury in the opening vignette, how do you think you would decide? Why?
2. Conduct your own content analysis of any of the effects issues we've discussed. How is violence portrayed on your favorite prime time drama? in your favorite action film? What beer and wine ads have you seen on television? What alcohol ads can you remember from your favorite magazine? How are alcohol and drinking presented?
3. If you were to become a mass communication researcher, do you think you'd lean toward quantitative or qualitative research methods? Why?
4. Do you pay attention to alcohol advertising? Do you think it influences your level of alcohol consumption? Does it influence the "value" you place on alcohol in social settings?
5. How did you do on the heartland–big city experiment? Why do you think you responded as you did?

Important Resources

Babbie, E. (1998). *The practice of social research.* **Belmont, CA: Wadsworth.** A well-written, student-level sociological overview of research, both its how-to and the philosophy that supports different methods.

Bowers, J. W., & Courtright, J. A. (1984). *Communication research methods.* **Glenview, IL: Scott, Foresman and Company.** An excellent overview of social science research written specifically for students interested in communication research.

Critical Studies in Mass Communication. One of the best mass communication journals, publishing much significant theoretical and effects research.

Eagleton, T. (1983). *Literary theory: An introduction.* **Minneapolis, MN: University of Minnesota Press.** Written primarily for literature or English students, this is a popular and readable analysis and how-to of text-based research.

Greenberg, B. S., Brown, J. D., & Buerkel-Rothfuss, N. L. (1993). *Media, sex, and the adolescent.* **Cresskill, NJ: Hampton Press.** Covers a number of issues, with excellent comments on stereotyping.

Journal of Broadcasting and Electronic Media. Another important mass communication journal, this one focusing on broadcasting and other electronic media.

Journal of Communication. A publication of the International Communication Association offering many scholarly and commentary articles from a wide variety of perspectives on many mass communication issues.

Journalism and Electronic Media Quarterly. A fine scholarly journal presenting research that goes well beyond issues of the impact of journalistic content.

Kerlinger, F. N. (1986). *Foundations of behavioral research.* **New York: Holt, Rinehart and Winston.** Considered by many to be the classic research text; written at a relatively sophisticated level.

Media Research and Effects Information Web Sites

Consortium of Social Science Associations	*http://www.apsanet.org/Related/cossa.html*
American Psychological Association	*http://www.apa.org/*
American Sociological Association	*http://www.asanet.org/*
Surgeon General of the United States	*http://support1.med.navy.mil/BUMED/sg.htm*
The Roper Center for Public Opinion Research	*http://www.icpsr.umich.edu/GSS/about/credits/roper.htm*
The Center on Alcohol Advertising	*http://www.usakids.org/sites/caa.html*

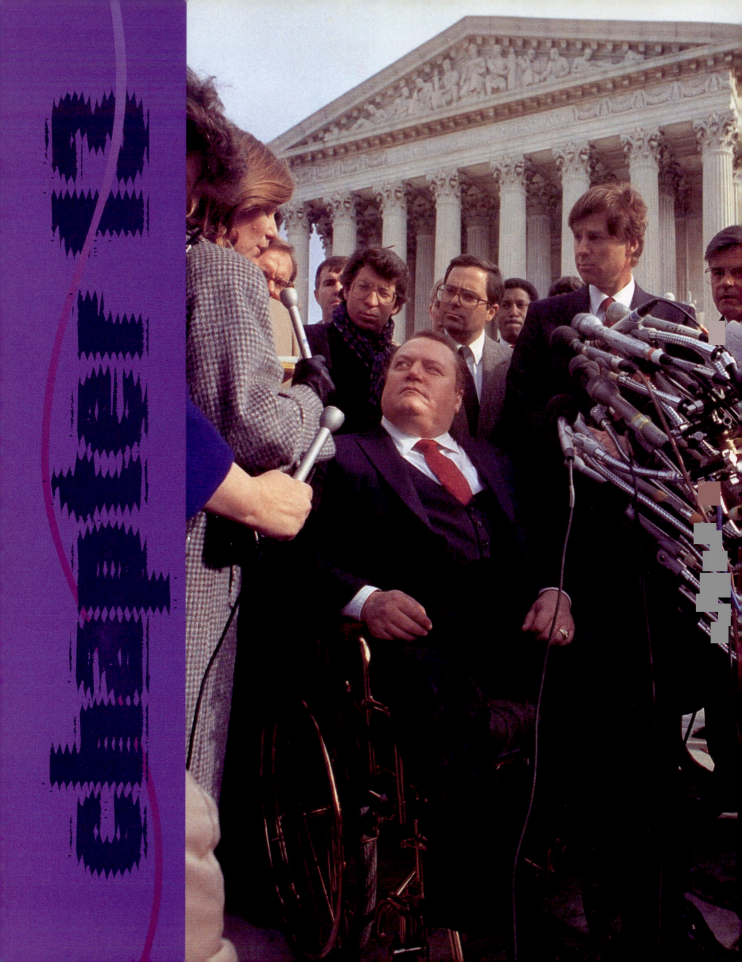

Media Freedom, Regulation, and Ethics

Y ou ran an aggressive campaign to win this job—President of Student Government. It was to have been a great resumé line, a chance to hone your leadership skills, and a way to send a few dollars of student fee money to groups that were doing some good for the campus. You never expected to be embroiled in controversy. Similar events took place at the University of Pennsylvania and at George Mason University just a few years ago. Now it's happened on your campus, and you must decide who is right and who is wrong.

The facts are before you. Your campus has a well-respected and large African American Studies program. Although some students question its place in the curriculum, many others from all over campus and of all racial and ethnic origins sign up for these classes. Through student fees your campus also funds a number of publications. Some are avowedly political, and all shades of the political spectrum are represented. One magazine, *Campus Review,* is quite conservative and often quite funny.

In its most recent issue *CR* (as it's known on campus) published course listings from the African American Studies program in parody form. Its description of "Racism in American Society" was so full of openly racist and denigrating words and images that the campus community was disgusted. *CR* meant to offend, and it succeeded. The day the issue hit the stands, groups of students—African American, Latino, and White—grabbed up copies, tossed them into a large pile, doused them with gasoline, and set them on fire.

You've listened to hours and hours of testimony, but the arguments boil down to two seemingly correct positions. From the protesters: racism has no place on a college campus. This insulting, degrading trash does nothing to further dialogue between people; it only divides. The magazine behaved unethically; it must be punished. From *CR*: we have a First Amendment right to publish what we want as long as it is neither libelous nor obscene. The existence of departments like the African American Studies program is an issue of public debate on many campuses, including our own. All we did was publish a humorous take on the controversy. Those who destroyed our magazines behaved unethically; they must be punished.

Now you, Student Government Big Shot, must decide.

This opening vignette is drawn from events on the campus of Cornell University (Hentoff, 1996, p. 7B). Cornell punished no one: not those who had written the offensive parody; not those who had stolen magazines from the racks and set them ablaze. The solution satisfied few. One student wrote to the campus newspaper, "If our voices and opinions were valued on this campus, our actions would not have been required." But First Amendment supporters on both the political right and the left were infuriated. Nat Hentoff, syndicated columnist and long-time writer on freedom of expression issues, quoted a judge involved in a similar situation at George Mason University: "The First Amendment does not recognize exceptions for bigotry, racism, and religious intolerance."

This dispute highlights two important lessons offered in this chapter. First, the First Amendment protects expression we don't like—*especially* expression we don't like. Second, decisions to publish or broadcast potentially troublesome material are far more often a matter of ethics than of law. In our vignette *CR* had a legal right to publish its racist parody. What, however, were its ethical obligations?

In this chapter we look at how the First Amendment has been defined and applied over time. We study how the logic of a free and unfettered press has come into play in the area of broadcast deregulation. We also detail the shift in the underlying philosophy of media freedom from libertarianism to social responsibility theory. This provides the background for our examination of the ethical environment in which media professionals must work as they strive to fulfill their socially responsible obligations.

A Short History of the First Amendment

The U.S. Constitution mentions only one industry by name as deserving special protection, the press. Therefore, our examination of media regulation, self-regulation, and ethics must begin with a discussion of its "First Freedom."

As we saw in Chapter 4, the first Congress of the United States made freedom of the press a priority. The First Amendment to the new Constitution expressly stated that "Congress shall make no law . . . abridging the freedom of speech, or of the press." As a result, government regulation of the media must not only be unobtrusive but also must be sufficiently justified to meet the limits of the First Amendment. Media industry self-regulation must be sufficiently effective to render official restraint unnecessary, and media practitioners' conduct should be ethical in order to warrant this special protection.

EARLY SENTIMENT FOR A FREE PRESS

Democracy—government by the people—requires a free press. The framers of the Bill of Rights understood this because of their experience with the European monarchies from which they and their forebears had fled. They based their guarantee of this privileged position to the press on **libertarianism,** the philosophy that people cannot govern themselves in a democracy unless they have access to the information they need for that governance. Libertarian philosophy is based on the **self-righting principle,** which was forcefully stated in 1644 by English author and poet John Milton in his book *Areopagitica.* Milton argued from two main points:

- The free flow or trade of ideas serves to ensure that public discourse will allow the truth to emerge.

- Truth will emerge from public discourse because people are inherently rational and good.

But as we also saw in Chapter 4, even the First Amendment and libertarian philosophy did not guarantee freedom of the press. The Alien and Sedition Acts were passed a scant eight years after the Constitution was ratified. And Milton himself was to become the chief censor of Catholic writing in Oliver Cromwell's English government.

DEFINING AND REFINING THE FIRST AMENDMENT

Clearly the idea of freedom of the press needed some clarification. One view was (and is) housed in the **absolutist position,** which is expressed succinctly by Supreme Court Justice Hugo Black: "No law means no law." Yet the absolutist position is more complex than this would suggest. Although absolutists accept that the First Amendment provides a central and fundamental wall of protection for the press, several questions about its true meaning remained to be answered over time. Let's look at some of history's answers.

What Does "No Law" Mean? The First Amendment said that the U.S. Congress could "make no law," but could state legislatures? city councils? mayors? courts? Who has the power to proscribe the press? This issue was settled in 1925 when the Supreme Court, in *Gitlow v. New York*, stated that the First Amendment is "among the fundamental personal rights and 'liberties' protected by the due process clause of the Fourteenth Amendment from impairment by the states" (Gillmor & Barron, 1974, p. 1). Given that, "Congress shall make no law" should be interpreted as "government agencies shall make no law." Today, "no law" includes statutes, laws, administrative regulations, executive and court orders, and ordinances from government, regardless of locale.

What Is "The Press?"   Just what "press" enjoys First Amendment protection? We saw in Chapter 6 that the Supreme Court in its 1952 *Burstyn v. Wilson* decision declared that movies were protected expression. In 1973 Justice William O. Douglas wrote in *CBS v. Democratic National Committee,*

> What kind of First Amendment would best serve our needs as we approach the 21st century may be an open question. But the old fashioned First Amendment that we have is the Court's only guideline; and one hard and fast principle has served us through days of calm and eras of strife, and I would abide by it until a new First Amendment is adopted. That means, as I view it, that TV and radio . . . are all included in the concept of "press" as used in the First Amendment and therefore are entitled to live under the laissez faire regime which the First Amendment sanctions. (Gillmor & Barron, 1974, pp. 7–8)

Advertising, or commercial speech, enjoys First Amendment protection. This was established by the Supreme Court in 1942. Despite the fact that the decision in *Valentine v. Chrestensen* was unanimous, some justices argued for a "two-tiered" level of protection, with commercial expression being somewhat less worthy of protection than noncommercial expression. But others argued that this was illogical because almost all media are, in fact, commercial, even when they perform a primarily journalistic function. Newspapers, for example, print the news to make a profit.

In its 1967 *Time, Inc. v. Hill* decision the Supreme Court applied similar logic to argue that the First Amendment grants the same protection to entertainment content as it does to nonentertainment content. Is an entertainingly written news report less worthy than one that is dully written? Rather than allow the government to make these kinds of narrow and ultimately subjective judgments, in the last five decades of media development the Supreme Court has consistently preferred expanding its definition of protected expression to limiting it.

What Is "Abridgment?"   Even absolutists accept the idea that limits can be placed on the time, place, and manner of expression—as long as the restrictions do not interfere with the substance of the expression. Few, for example, would find it unreasonable to limit the use of a sound truck to broadcast political messages at 4 o'clock in the morning. But the Supreme Court did find unconstitutional an ordinance that forbade all use of sound amplification except with the permission of the chief of police in its 1948 decision in *Saia v. New York.* The permissibility of other restrictions, however, is less clear cut.

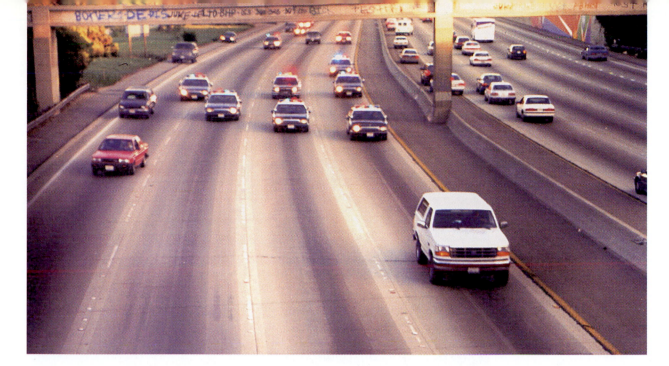

The O.J. Simpson trial raised public and legal concern over the influence of pre-trial publicity—for example, the internationally televised, low-speed, white Bronco chase—and media coverage of court proceedings.

CLEAR AND PRESENT DANGER   Can freedom of the press be limited if the likely result is damaging? The Supreme Court answered this question in 1919 in *Schenck v. United States*. In this case involving the distribution of a pamphlet urging resistance to the military draft during World War I, Justice Oliver Wendell Holmes wrote that expression could be limited when "the words used are used in such circumstances and are of such a nature as to create a clear and present danger that they will bring about the substantive evils that Congress has a right to prevent." Justice Holmes added, "Free speech would not protect a man in falsely shouting fire in a theater and causing panic." This decision is especially important because it firmly established the legal philosophy that there is no absolute freedom of expression; the level of protection is one of degree.

BALANCING OF INTERESTS   This less than absolutist approach is called the **ad hoc balancing of interests.** That is, in individual First Amendment cases several factors should be weighed in determining how much freedom the press is granted. In his dissent to the Court's 1941 decision in *Bridges v. California,* a case involving a *Los Angeles Times* editorial, Justice Felix Frankfurter wrote that free speech and press is "not so absolute or irrational a conception as to imply paralysis of the means for effective protection of all the freedoms secured by the Bill of Rights. . . . In the cases before us, the claims on behalf of freedom of speech and of the press encounter claims on behalf of liberties no less precious."

FREE PRESS VERSUS FAIR TRIAL   One example of the clash of competing liberties is the conflict between free press (First Amendment) and fair trial (Sixth Amendment). This debate typically takes two forms: (1) Can pretrial

Media intrusion in the 1935 Bruno Hauptmann kidnapping trial led to the banning of radio transmissions and photographers from the courtroom. Hauptmann is seated in the center, hands crossed.

publicity deny citizens judgment by 12 impartial peers, thereby denying them a fair trial? (2) Should cameras be allowed in the courtroom, supporting the public's right to know, or do they so alter the workings of the court that a fair trial is impossible?

Courts have consistently decided in favor of fair trial in conflicts between the First and Sixth Amendments. But it was not until 1961 that a conviction was overturned because of pretrial publicity. In *Irvin v. Dowd* the Court reversed the death sentence conviction of confessed killer Leslie Irvin because his right to a fair trial had been hampered by press coverage that labeled him "Mad Dog Irvin" and reported crimes he had committed as a juvenile, his military court-martial, his identification in a police lineup, his failure to pass a lie detector test, his confession to six killings and numerous robberies, and his willingness to trade a guilty plea for a life sentence. Of 430 potential jurors screened before the trial by attorneys, 370 said they already were convinced Irvin was guilty. Nonetheless, although "tainted" by pretrial publicity, four of the 370 were seated as jurors. The Court determined that Irvin's trial was therefore unfair.

Print reporters have long enjoyed access to trials, but broadcast journalists have been less fortunate. In 1937, after serious intrusion by newspaper photographers during the 1935 trial of Bruno Hauptmann, accused of kidnapping the baby of trans-Atlantic aviation hero Charles Lindbergh, the American Bar Association (ABA) adopted canon 35 as part of its Code of Judicial Ethics. This rule forbade cameras and radio broadcasting of trials. In 1963 the ABA amended the canon to include a prohibition on television cameras. This, however, did not settle the issue of cameras in the courtroom.

Texas was one of three states that did not subscribe to canon 35. When the conviction for theft, swindling, and embezzlement of Texas financier Billy Sol Estes was overturned by the Supreme Court because of "the insidious influence" (Justice William Douglas's words) of cameras on the conduct of the trial, the debate flared again. Justice Tom Clark wrote for the majority:

> The free press has been a mighty catalyst in awakening public interest in governmental affairs, exposing corruption among public officers and employees and generally informing the citizenry of public events and occurrences, including court proceedings. While maximum freedom must be allowed the press in carrying on this important function in a democratic society its exercise must necessarily be subject to the maintenance of absolute fairness in the judicial process. (*Estes v. State of Texas*)

Television cameras, then, were out. But Justice Clark continued, "When advances in (broadcast journalism) permit reporting . . . by television without their present hazards to a fair trial we will have another case." Cameras were back in if they posed no hazard to the principle of fair trial.

In 1972 the ABA replaced canon 35 with canon 3A(7), allowing some videotaping of trials for specific purposes but reaffirming its opposition to the broadcast of trial proceedings. But in 1981 the Supreme Court, in *Chandler v. Florida*, determined that television cameras in the courtroom were not inherently damaging to fairness, and different states have adopted different standards on the issue. So common has the televising of court proceedings become that Court TV, a cable channel programming nothing but real trials and commentary on them, was launched in 1991.

LIBEL AND SLANDER   **Libel,** the false and malicious publication of material that damages a person's reputation (typically applied to print media), and **slander,** which is oral or spoken defamation of a person's character (typically applied to broadcasting), are not protected by the First Amendment. If a report (a) defames a person, (b) identifies that person, and (c) is published or broadcast, it loses its First Amendment protection.

A report accused of being libelous or slanderous, however, is protected if it meets any one of three tests. The first test is *truth*. Even if a report damages someone's reputation, if it is true, it is protected. The second test is *privilege*. Coverage of legislative, court, or other public activities may contain information that is not true or that is damaging to someone's reputation. The press cannot be deterred from covering these important news events for fear that a speaker or witness's comments will open it to claims of libel or slander. The third test is *fair comment;* that is, the press has the right to express opinions or comment on public issues. For example, theater and film reviews, however severe, are protected, as is commentary on other matters in the public eye.

For public figures, however, a different set of rules applies. Because they are in the public eye, public figures are fair game for fair comment.

But does that leave them open to reports that are false and damaging to their reputations? The Supreme Court faced this issue in 1964 in *New York Times Co. v. Sullivan.* In 1960 the Committee to Defend Martin Luther King bought a full-page ad in the *New York Times* asking people to contribute to Dr. King's defense fund. The ad detailed abuse of Dr. King and other civil rights workers at the hands of the Montgomery, Alabama, police. L. B. Sullivan, one of three elected commissioners in that city, sued the *Times* for libel. The ad copy was not true in some of its claims, he said, and because he was in charge of the police, he had been "identified."

The Supreme Court ruled in favor of the newspaper. Even though some of the specific facts in the ad were not true, the *Times* had not acted with **actual malice.** The Court defined the standard of actual malice for reporting on public figures as *knowledge of its falsity* or *reckless disregard* for whether it is true or not.

PRIOR RESTRAINT   There is much less confusion about another important aspect of press freedom, **prior restraint.** This is the power of the government to *prevent* the publication or broadcast of expression. U.S. law and tradition make the use of prior restraint relatively rare, but there have been a number of important efforts by government to squelch content before dissemination.

In 1931 the Supreme Court ruled in *Near v. Minnesota* that freedom from prior restraint was a general principle. It also determined that it was not an absolute principle. Two of the four exceptions it listed were in times of war when national security was involved and when the public order would be endangered by the incitement to violence and overthrow by force of orderly government. These exceptions were to become the basis of two landmark prior restraint decisions. The first, involving the *New York Times,* dealt with national security in times of war; the second, focusing on protecting the public order, involved publishing instructions for building an atomic bomb.

On June 13, 1971, at the height of the Vietnam War, the *New York Times* began publication of what commonly became known as the Pentagon Papers. The papers included detailed discussion and analysis of the conduct of that unpopular war during the administrations of Presidents Kennedy and Johnson. President Nixon's National Security Council (NSC) had stamped them Top Secret. Believing that this was an improper restriction of the public's right to know, NSC staff member Daniel Ellsberg gave copies to the *Times.* After the first three installments had been published, the Justice Department, citing national security, was able to secure a court order stopping further publication. Other newspapers, notably the *Washington Post* and *Boston Globe,* began running excerpts while the *Times* was silenced until they, too, were enjoined to cease.

On June 30 the Supreme Court ordered the government to halt its restraint of the *Times*'s and other papers' right to publish the Pentagon Papers. Among the stirring attacks on prior restraint written throughout its decision was Justice Hugo Black's:

The New York Times

LATE CITY EDITION
Weather: Chance of showers today,
tonight. Partly sunny tomorrow.
Temp. range: today 74-94; Wed.
72-91. Temp. Hum. Index yesterday
82. Full U.S. report on Page 44.

VOL. CXX...No. 41,431   © 1971 The New York Times Company   NEW YORK, THURSDAY, JULY 1, 1971   15 CENTS

SUPREME COURT, 6-3, UPHOLDS NEWSPAPERS ON PUBLICATION OF THE PENTAGON REPORT; TIMES RESUMES ITS SERIES, HALTED 15 DAYS

Nixon Says Turks Agree To Ban the Opium Poppy

By JOHN HERBERS

WASHINGTON, June 30—President Nixon announced today that Turkey had agreed to eliminate with a year her production of opium poppies, which account for about two-thirds of the illegal heroin reaching the United States.

Mr. Nixon, in a brief announcement made at delivered in the White House press room, said that as a result of negotiations between the United States and Turkey's Governments, Premier Nihat Erim had agreed to ban altogether the cultivation of opium poppies by June, 1972.

He said the joint announcement, made simultaneously in Washington and Ankara, "represents by far the most significant breakthrough that has been achieved in stopping the source of supply of heroin in our worldwide offensive against dangerous drugs."

Continued on Page 22, Column 1

Soviet Starts an Inquiry Into 3 Astronauts' Deaths

By BERNARD GWERTZMAN

PRESIDENT CALLS STEEL AND LABOR TO WHITE HOUSE

He Asks Both Sides to Meet With Him Tuesday Before Contract Talks Start

By PHILIP SHABECOFF

WASHINGTON, June 30—President Nixon has called negotiators of the steel companies and steelworkers union to meet with him next Tuesday before they sit down to begin contract negotiations, a White House spokesman announced today.

It will be the first time that the President will have met with labor and management in any industry prior to nationwide contract negotiations, according to Ronald L. Ziegler, the White House press secretary.

Discussion Issues Listed

Mr. Ziegler said that the President had called the meeting to discuss general economic developments and trends in the world steel markets.

Earlier today, the chairman

Pentagon Papers: Study Reports Kennedy Made 'Gamble' Into a 'Broad Commitment'

By HEDRICK SMITH

The Pentagon's study of the Vietnam war concludes that President John F. Kennedy transformed the "limited-risk gamble" of the Eisenhower Administration into a "broad commitment" to prevent Communist domination of South Vietnam.

Although Mr. Kennedy resisted pressures for putting American ground-combat units into South Vietnam, the Pentagon analysts say, he took a series of actions that significantly expanded the American military and political involvement in Vietnam but nonetheless left President Lyndon B. Johnson with as bad a situation as Mr. Kennedy inherited.

"The dilemma of the U.S. involvement dating from the Kennedy era," the Pentagon study observes, was to use "only limited means to achieve excessive ends."

Moreover, according to the study, prepared in 1967-68 by Government analysts, the Kennedy tactics deepened the American involvement in Vietnam piecemeal, with each step minimizing public recognition that the American role was growing.

The expansion of that role, over three decades, is traced in the 3,000 pages of the Pentagon's study, which is accompanied by 4,000 pages of documents on the Vietnam era. Previous articles in The Times's presentation of this material have recounted President Johnson's movement to war in 1964 and 1965.

President Kennedy made his first fresh commitments to Vietnam secretly. The Pentagon study discloses that in the spring of 1961 the President ordered 400 Special Forces troops and 100 other American military advisers sent to South Vietnam. No publicity was given to either move.

Small as the numbers seem in retrospect, the Pentagon study comments that even the first such expansion "signaled a willingness to go beyond the 685-man limit on the size of the U.S. [military] mission in Saigon, which, if it were done openly, would be the first formal breach of the Geneva agreement." Under the interpretation of that agreement in effect since 1956, the United States was limited to 685 military advisers in Vietnam. Washington, while it did not sign the accord, pledged not to undermine it.

On May 11, 1961, the day on which President Kennedy decided to send the Special Forces, he also ordered the start of a campaign of clandestine warfare against North Vietnam, to be conducted by South Vietnamese agents directed and trained by the Central Intelligence Agency and some American Special Forces troops. [See text, action memorandum, May 11, 1961, Page 3.]

The President's instructions, as quoted in the documents, were, "In North Vietnam . . . [to] form networks of resistance, covert bases and teams for

Continued on Page 6, Column 1

The Times today resumes its series of articles on the Pentagon's secret study of the Vietnam war. The study was obtained through the investigative reporting of Neil Sheehan, and the articles were researched and written over three months by Mr. Sheehan and other staff members. The fourth and fifth articles, both by Hedrick Smith, are published today and from an account of decisions in the Kennedy Administration.

Three pages of documentary material covering the Kennedy policy begin on Page 3, and documents on the 1963 coup begin on Page 9. A summary of the three earlier articles, covering the Johnson Administration, appears on Page 15.

BURGER DISSENTS

First Amendment Rule Held to Block Most Prior Restraints

Decision, concurring opinions, dissents start on Page 17.

By FRED P. GRAHAM

WASHINGTON, June 30 — The Supreme Court freed The New York Times and The Washington Post today to resume immediate publication of articles based on the secret Pentagon papers on the origins of the Vietnam war.

By a vote of 6 to 3 the Court held that any attempt by the Government to block news articles prior to publication bears "a heavy burden" of presumption against its constitutionality."

In a historic test of that principle — the first effort by the Government to enjoin publication on the ground of national security — the Court declared that "the Government has not met that burden."

The brief judgment was read to a hushed court room by Chief

The *New York Times* heralds its victory in its First Amendment dispute with the Nixon Administration over the publication of the *Pentagon Papers.*

In the First Amendment the Founding Fathers gave the free press the protection it must have to fulfill its essential role in our democracy. The press was to serve the governed, not the governors. The Government's power to censor the press was abolished so that the press would remain forever free to censure the Government. The press was protected so that it could bare the secrets of government and inform the people. Only a free and unrestrained press can effectively expose deception in government. *(New York Times v. United States)*

Then came the case of the magazine *The Progressive.* In 1979 the magazine announced its intention to publish instructions on how to make a hydrogen bomb. President Jimmy Carter's Justice Department successfully obtained a court order halting publication, even though the article was based on information and material freely obtained from public, nonclassified sources. Before the case could come to court, several newspapers published the same or similar material. The Justice Department immediately abandoned its restraint, and 6 months later *The Progressive* published its original article.

OBSCENITY AND PORNOGRAPHY   Another form of press expression that is not protected is **obscenity.** Two landmark Supreme Court cases established the definition and illegality of obscenity. The first is the 1957 *Roth v. United States* decision. The court determined that sex and obscenity were not synonymous, a significant advance for freedom of expression. It did, however, legally affirm for the first time that obscenity was unprotected expression. The definition or test for obscenity that holds even today was expressed in the 1973 *Miller v. State of California* decision. Chief Justice Warren Burger wrote that the basic guidelines must be:

> (a) whether the average person, applying contemporary community standards, would find that the work, taken as a whole, appeals to the prurient interest, (b) whether the work depicts or describes, in a patently offensive way, sexual conduct specifically defined by the applicable state law, and (c) whether the work, taken as a whole, lacks serious literary, artistic, political, or scientific value.

The problem for the courts, the media, and the public, of course, is judging content against this standard. For example, what is patently offensive to one person may be quite acceptable to others. What is serious art to one may be serious exploitation to another. And what of an erotic short story written online by an author in New York City but accessed and read by people in Peoria, Illinois? Whose community standards would apply?

An additional definitional problem resides in **pornography,** expression calculated solely to supply sexual excitement. Pornography is protected expression. The distinction between obscenity and pornography may, however, be a legal one. Sexually explicit content is pornography (and pro-

Media Echoes

Larry Flynt and Protection for Expression We Don't Like

In the 18th century, newspaper publisher John Peter Zenger's freedom to publish was tested in a famous court case, as we saw in Chapter 4. In the late 20th century, admitted pornographer Larry Flynt has had more than one day in court, but his 1988 Supreme Court appearance might be the most important for the First Amendment.

The November 1983 issue of Flynt's raunchy magazine *Hustler* included a parody of a series of Campari Liqueur ads. The real ads featured celebrities talking about their "first time" trying the drink, clearly a play on the more usual understanding of the expression. The Hustler take-off depicted an intoxicated Jerry Falwell—minister, televangelist, and founder of the Moral Majority—confessing that his "first time" was with his mother in an outhouse. Falwell sued for $45 million,

eventually winning $200,000 for intentional infliction of emotional distress. A federal Court of Appeals upheld the judgment.

Flynt appealed to the Supreme Court. The justices' 1988 unanimous decision supported the man who, in an earlier trial, had worn only an American flag used as a diaper. The case reaffirmed the protection of parody. But *Hustler Magazine v. Falwell,* called by Flynt "the most important First Amendment case in the history of this country," made an even stronger point. As Flynt himself stated, "If the First Amendment will protect a scumbag like me, then it will protect all of you. Because I'm the worst."

Chief Justice Rehnquist made the case for the protection of expression we don't like a bit more delicately:

tected) until a court rules it illegal; then it is obscene (and unprotected). The difficulty of making such distinctions can be seen in Justice Potter Stewart's famous declaration, "I may not be able to come up with a definition of pornography, but I certainly know it when I see it" and his dissent in *Ginzburg v. United States,* "If the First Amendment means anything, it means that a man cannot be sent to prison merely for distributing publications which offend a judge's sensibilities, mine or any others" (as cited in Gillmor & Barron, 1974, p. 362).

Clearly, the issues of the definition and protection of obscenity and pornography may never be clarified to everyone's satisfaction (see the box "Larry Flynt and Protection for Expression We Don't Like").

OTHER ISSUES OF FREEDOM AND RESPONSIBILITY

The First Amendment has application to a number of specific issues of media responsibility and freedom.

Indecency   Obscenity and pornography are rarely issues for broadcasters. Their commercial base and wide audience make the airing of such potentially troublesome programming unwise. However, broadcasters frequently do confront the issue of **indecency**. According to the FCC, indecent language or material is that which depicts sexual or excretory activities in a

At the heart of the First Amendment is the recognition of the fundamental importance of the free flow of ideas. Freedom to speak one's mind is not only an aspect of individual liberty, but essential to the quest for truth and the vitality of the society as a whole. In the world of debate about public affairs, many things done with motives that are less than admirable are nonetheless protected by the First Amendment.

What do you think of this Supreme Court decision? Shouldn't there be limits on what can appear in the media? For example, was the attack on Falwell's mother necessary? Where should a media outlet draw the line? Where should the courts? Where should the culture?

Larry Flynt before the Supreme Court.

The music of such bands as Gwar is relegated to the safe harbor of late night radio to which children are not usually listening.

way that is offensive to contemporary community standards. The commission censured a Denver radio station in its 1960 Mile High Broadcasting decision because one of the station's disc jockeys persisted in uttering "smutty and suggestive" language. In 1978 the FCC censured New York's noncommercial WBAI-FM, owned by Pacifica Broadcasting, for that station's midday airing of George Carlin's recorded comedy monologue, "Seven Dirty Words You Can Never Say on Television." Although the routine was played as part of a serious program about the nature of the English language, and although there was only one complaint made, the commission thought the utterance of those seven words was indecent. The station challenged the FCC's actions in court, appealing all the way to the Supreme Court, which ruled in favor of the commission. Shock jock Howard Stern earned his parent company, Infinity Broadcasting, a $600,000 fine in 1992 for his indecent expression as well as other fines equaling that amount since then.

Situations such as these have led to the development of the concept of **safe harbor,** times of the broadcast day (typically 10 P.M. to 6 A.M.) when children are not likely to be in the listening or viewing audience. In the concept of safe harbor, the FCC recognizes that potentially offensive content, because it is in fact protected expression, should be available to those who wish to see and hear it. But in its role of trustee (Chapter 7), the commission feels it has not only the right but also the obligation to protect those listeners and viewers who do not want such content for themselves or their children.

Deregulation   The difficulty of balancing the public interest and broadcasters' freedom is at the heart of the debate over deregulation and the relaxation of ownership and other rules for radio and television. As we saw in Chapter 8, changes in ownership rules have been controversial, but relaxation of the regulation of broadcasters' public service obligations and other content controls have provided even more debate.

The courts have consistently supported the FCC's right to evaluate broadcasters' performance in serving the public interest, convenience, and necessity. Naturally, that evaluation must include some judgment of the content broadcasters air. Broadcasters long argued that such "judgment" amounted to unconstitutional infringement of their First Amendment freedom. Many listeners and viewers saw it as a reasonable and quite small price to pay for the use of their (the public's) airwaves.

The Supreme Court resolved the issue in 1943 in *National Broadcasting Co. v. United States*. NBC argued that the commission was no more than a traffic cop, limited to controlling the "flow of traffic." In this view, the regulation of broadcasters' frequency, power, times of operation, and other technical matters was all that was constitutionally allowable. Yet the Court turned what is now known as the **traffic cop analogy** against NBC. Yes, the justices agreed, the commission is a traffic cop. But even traffic cops have the right to control not only the flow of traffic but its composition. For example, drunk drivers can be removed from the road. Potentially dangerous "content," like cars with faulty brakes, can also be restricted. It was precisely this traffic cop function that required the FCC to judge content. The commission was thus free to promulgate rules such as the **Fairness Doctrine,** which requires broadcasters to cover issues of public importance and to be fair in that coverage, and **ascertainment,** which requires broadcasters to ascertain or actively and affirmatively determine the nature of their audiences' interest, convenience, and necessity (see the box "The Red Lion Decision and the Rights of the Audience").

The Fairness Doctrine, ascertainment, and numerous other regulations, such as rules on children's programming and overcommercialization, disappeared with the coming of deregulation during the Reagan Administration. License renewal, for example, was once a long and difficult process for stations, which had to generate thousands of pages of documents to demonstrate that they not only knew what their audiences wanted and needed but had met those wants and needs. The burden of proof in their efforts to keep their licenses rested with them. Had they been fair? Had they kept commercial time to acceptable levels? What was their commitment to news and public affairs? Now deregulated, renewal is conducted by postcard.

The deregulation drive began in earnest with President Reagan's FCC Chair Mark Fowler in the 1980s. Fowler rejected the trustee model of broadcast regulation. He saw many FCC rules as an unconstitutional infringement of broadcasters' rights and believed that "the market" was the audience's best protector. He said that special rules for the control of broadcasting were unnecessary, likening television, for example, to just another home appliance. He called television no more than "a toaster with pictures."

This view is not without its critics. Members of Congress charged with FCC and media oversight, such as Massachusetts's Edward Markey, Michigan's John Dingell, and Colorado's Timothy Wirth, as well as many economists, legal experts, and public interest group leaders, condemned what they saw as the government abandoning viewers and listeners to the bottom-line demands of the financial marketplace. They point, for example, to the 50% drop in the number of radio stations airing news and public affairs that occurred during Fowler's years at the commission, as well as increases in the amount of advertising on Saturday morning television (Wilke, Vamos, & Maremont, 1985). Congress has attempted to "reregulate" in some areas on content; the 1996 Telecommunications Act has provisions regarding children's programming and violent television (Chapter 8). Nonetheless, ever since Commissioner Fowler's initial aggressive stance, the trustee model of commission oversight, which he called a "series of legal fictions" (Fowler & Brenner, 1982, p. 205), has been increasingly eroded.

Using Media to Make a Difference

The Red Lion Decision and the Rights of the Audience

Throughout this book we've seen how media have been used to make a difference, for example, to fight for causes or to alert people to problems. In the specific case of broadcasting, however, it was not decided until the 1960s exactly how much power individuals had in gaining access to broadcasting so they could use it to make a difference. The question was a simple one: did broadcasters hold their licenses for the purpose of satisfying their own goals, economic and otherwise, or

could ordinary citizens expect that they, too, would have access to radio and television?

In November 1964, small AM/FM radio station WGCB in Red Lion, Pennsylvania, aired its weekly installment of "The Christian Crusade." The show's host, Reverend Billy James Hargis, offered his review of a book written by a man named Fred J. Cook. Hargis did not enjoy Cook's book, *Goldwater—Extremist of the Right,* an analysis of the career of conservative politician Barry Goldwater. In his comments on the work, Hargis accused Cook of a number of offenses—lying, being fired from his job as a reporter, being left wing. To Cook this amounted to a personal attack, and under FCC rules he was entitled to time to reply.

The station owner, Red Lion Broadcasting Company, offered to sell time to Cook or, if the writer would plead poverty, to give him free time. Cook refused, claiming the *right* to reply. FCC rules said that reply time must be free in cases of personal attack. The station (and virtually the entire broadcast industry that

Broadcast deregulation produced a rush of toy-based Saturday morning children's shows, such as *GI Joe,* something that critics claimed was inherently unfair to children who could not recognize them as program-length commercials.

bankrolled its defense) argued that this free time requirement was an infringement of broadcasters' First Amendment rights. As a result, the stakes were high. The question before the courts was nothing less than an affirmation or denial of the FCC's power to promulgate rules regarding public access to airwaves that the public, in fact, owned.

In 1966 the United States Court of Appeals for the Seventh Circuit in Chicago District ruled in favor of the station. But the FCC persisted and, in 1967, the United States Court of Appeals for the District of Columbia overturned that decision, siding with Cook and the commission. Red Lion Broadcasting and the Radio Television News Directors Association appealed to the Supreme Court.

On June 9, 1969, the justices delivered what has become known as the Red Lion Decision. Justice Byron White expressed the Court's support for Mr. Cook and the FCC this way:

There is nothing in the First Amendment which prevents the Government from requiring a licensee to share his frequency with others and to conduct himself as a proxy or fiduciary with obligations to present those views and voices which are representative of his community and which would otherwise, by necessity, be barred from the airwaves. . . . [T]he people as a whole retain their interest in free speech by radio and their collective right to have the medium function consistently with the ends and purposes of the First Amendment. . . . It is the purpose of the First Amendment to preserve an uninhibited marketplace of ideas in which truth will ultimately prevail, rather than to countenance monopolization of that market, whether it be by the Government itself or a private licensee. *(Red Lion Broadcasting v. United States)*

Justice White's most memorable and meaningful comment on the clash between broadcaster and audience rights remains: *"It is the right of the viewers and listeners, not the right of the broadcasters, which is paramount."*

Copyright   The First Amendment protects expression. **Copyright**—identifying and granting ownership of a given piece of expression—is designed to protect the creator's financial interest in that expression. Recognizing that the flow of art, science, and other expression would be enhanced by authors' financial interest in their creation, the framers of the Constitution wrote Article I, Section 8 (8), granting authors exclusive rights to their "writings and discoveries." A long and consistent history of Supreme Court decisions has ensured that this protection would be extended to the content of the mass media that have emerged since that time.

The year 1978 saw an extensive rewriting of U.S. copyright law. Copyright now remains with creators (in all media) for the span of their lives, plus 50 years. During this time, permission for the use of the material must be obtained from the copyright holder and, if financial compensation (a fee or royalty) is requested, it must be paid. Once the copyright expires, and if the creator does not renew it, the material passes into **public domain,** meaning it can be used without permission.

The exception to copyright is **fair use,** instances where material can be used without permission or payment. Fair use includes (1) limited noncommercial use, such as photocopying a passage from a novel for classroom use; (2) use of limited portions of a work, such as excerpting a few lines or a paragraph or two from a book for use in a magazine article; (3) use that does not decrease the commercial value of the original, such as videotaping a daytime football game for private, at-home evening viewing; and (4) use in the public interest, such as an author's use of line drawings of scenes from an important piece of film. This latter situation occurred in a dispute over the Zapruder home movie of the 1963 assassination of President Kennedy. A writer used sketches based on the Zapruder film in a book examining the investigation of the Kennedy killing.

Two specific applications of copyright law pertain to recorded music and cable television. Imagine the difficulty cable companies would have in obtaining permission from all the copyright holders of all the material they import and deliver to their subscribers. Yet the cable operators do make money from others' works—they collect material from original sources and sell it to subscribers. The solution to the problem of compensating the creators of the material carried by cable systems was the creation of the Copyright Royalty Tribunal, to which cable companies pay a fee based primarily on the size of their operations. These moneys are subsequently distributed to the appropriate producers, syndicators, and broadcasters.

Now imagine the difficulty songwriters would have in collecting royalties from all who use their music—not only film producers and radio and television stations, but bowling alleys, supermarkets, and restaurants. Here the solution is the **music licensing company.** The two biggest are the American Society of Composers, Authors and Performers (ASCAP) and Broadcast Music Inc. (BMI). Both collect fees based on the users' gross receipts and distribute the money to songwriters and artists.

Social Responsibility Theory

As we saw at the beginning of this chapter, the First Amendment is based on the libertarian philosophy that assumes a fully free press and a rational, good, and informed public. But we have also seen in this and previous chapters that the media are not necessarily fully free. Government control is sometimes allowed. Corporate control is assumed and accepted. During the 1930s and 1940s, serious doubts were also raised concerning the public's rationality and goodness. As World War II spread across Europe at the end of the 1930s, libertarians were hard pressed to explain how Nazi propaganda could succeed if people could in fact tell right from wrong. As the United States was drawn closer to the European conflict, calls for greater government control of press and speech at home were justified by less-than-optimistic views of the "average American's" ability to handle difficult information. As a result, libertarianism came under attack for being too idealistic.

Time magazine owner and publisher Henry Luce then provided money to establish an independent commission of scholars, politicians, legal experts, and social activists who would study the role of the press in U.S. society and make recommendations on how it should best operate in support of democracy. The Hutchins Commission on Freedom of the Press, named after its chairperson University of Chicago Chancellor Robert Maynard Hutchins, began its work in 1942 and, in 1947, produced its report, "The Social Responsibility Theory of the Press" (see Davis, 1990).

Social responsibility theory is a **normative theory**—that is, it explains how media should *ideally* operate in a given system of social values—and it is now the standard for U.S. media. Other social and political systems adhere to different normative theories, and these will be detailed in Chapter 15.

Social responsibility theory asserts that media must remain free of government control, but in exchange media must serve the public. The core assumptions of this theory are a cross between libertarian principles of freedom and practical admissions of the need for some form of control on the media (McQuail, 1987):

- Media should accept and fulfill certain obligations to society.

- Media can meet these obligations by setting high standards of professionalism, truth, accuracy, and objectivity.

- Media should be self-regulating within the framework of the law.

- Media should avoid disseminating material that might lead to crime, violence, or civil disorder or that might offend minority groups.

- The media as a whole should be pluralistic, reflect the diversity of the culture in which they operate, and give access to various points of view and rights of reply.

- The public has a right to expect high standards of performance, and official intervention can be justified to ensure the public good.
- Media professionals should be accountable to society as well as to their employers and the market.

In rejecting government control of media, social responsibility theory calls for responsible, ethical industry operation, but it does not free audiences from their responsibility. People must be sufficiently media literate to develop firm yet reasonable expectations and judgments of media performance. But ultimately it is practitioners, through the conduct of their duties, who are charged with operating in a manner that obviates the need for official intrusion.

Media Industry Ethics

A number of formal and informal controls, both external and internal to the industry, are aimed at ensuring that media professionals operate in an ethical manner consistent with social responsibility theory. Among the formal controls are laws and regulations, codified statements of what can and can't be done and what content is permissible and not permissible, and industry codes of practice. Among the informal controls are pressure groups, consumers, and advertisers. We have seen how these informal controls operate throughout this text. Our interest here is in examining media's internal controls, or ethics.

DEFINING ETHICS

Ethics are rules of behavior or moral principles that guide our actions in given situations. The word comes from the Greek *ethos*, which means the customs, traditions, or character that guide a particular group or culture. In our discussion, ethics specifically refers to the application of rational thought by media professionals when they are deciding between two or more competing moral choices.

For example, it is not against the law to publish the name of a rape victim. But is it ethical? It is not illegal to stick a microphone in a crying father's face as he cradles the broken body of his child at an accident scene. But is it ethical?

The application of media ethics almost always involves finding the *most morally defensible* answer to a problem for which there is no single correct or even best answer. Return to the grieving father. The reporter's job is to get the story; the public has a right to know. The man's sorrow is part of that story, but the man has a right to privacy. As a human being he deserves to be treated with respect and to be allowed to maintain his dignity. The reporter has to decide whether to get the interview or leave the grief-stricken man in peace. That decision is guided by the reporter's ethics.

THREE LEVELS OF ETHICS

Because ethics reflect a culture's ideas about right and wrong, they exist at all levels of that culture's operation. **Metaethics** are fundamental cultural values. What is justice? What does it mean to be good? Is fairness possible? We need to examine these questions to know ourselves. But as valuable as they are for self-knowledge, metaethics provide only the broadest foundation for the sorts of ethical decisions people make daily. They define the basic starting points for moral reasoning.

Normative ethics are more or less generalized theories, rules, and principles of ethical or moral behavior. The various media industry codes of ethics or standards of good practice are examples of normative ethics. They serve as real-world frameworks within which people can begin to weigh competing alternatives of behavior. Fairness is a metaethic, but journalists' codes of practice, for example, define what is meant by fairness in the world of reporting, how far a reporter must go to ensure fairness, and how fairness must be applied when being fair to one person means being unfair to another.

Ultimately, media practitioners must apply both the big rules and the general guidelines to very specific situations. This is the use of **applied ethics,** which is our focus for the remainder of this section.

APPLYING MEDIA ETHICS

In April 1992 media professionals were given an opportunity to apply their ethics in a very real, very public situation involving AIDS. AIDS is a disease that carries a stigma of suspicion and, for many, the idea that the disease is a "curse" invoked by sex and drug abuse.

Tennis champion Arthur Ashe, a man of undisputed dignity and humanity, had overcome racial barriers to become a great athlete. He had eventually retired from tennis because of heart problems and later tested positive for HIV, the virus that causes AIDS, which he had contracted through a blood transfusion during one of his several surgeries. As a human being, Ashe had the right to personal and medical privacy. When a reporter from *USA Today* contacted Ashe, asking questions about rumors of his infection, Ashe felt he had no choice but to go public before the newspaper did. Ashe held a news conference at which he had this to say about media ethics:

> I have it on good authority that my status was common knowledge in the medical community, especially here in New York City, and I am truly grateful to all of you, medical and otherwise, who knew, but either didn't even ask me or never made it public.
>
> What I actually came to feel about a year ago was that there was a silent and generous conspiracy to assist me in maintaining my privacy.
>
> Then sometime last week, someone phoned *USA Today* and told the paper. After several days of checking it out, *USA Today* decided to confront

Tennis legend Arthur Ashe is shown here with his wife Jeanne at the news conference during which he revealed that he had AIDS. Some people believe that he should have been remembered as a great champion (bottom photo). Others feel that his newsworthiness cost him his privacy.

me with the rumors. It put me in the unenviable position of having to lie if I wanted to protect our privacy. No one should have to make that choice. ("Ashe: Privacy at Stake," 1992, p. 2A)

The response from the media community was divided. Jack Shafer, editor of the Washington, DC, *City Paper*, wrote, "My heart goes out to Ashe for whatever anguish the news stories caused him, but news stories cause anguish all the time." *USA Today* columnist DeWayne Wickham countered, "Journalism teeters on the edge of a very slippery slope when, by confronting Ashe with rumors of his infection, and thus forcing him to go public or lie, it attempts to pass off voyeurism for news judgment" ("Arthur Ashe AIDS Story," 1992, p. 17).

Ashe died ten months later.

BALANCING CONFLICTING INTERESTS

In applying ethics, the person making the decisions is called the **moral agent.** For moral agents, sticky ethical issues invariably bring together conflicting interests, for example, the public's right to know versus Arthur Ashe's right to privacy.

Media ethicist Louis Day (1997) identified six sets of individual or group interests that often conflict:

- The interests of the moral agent's *individual conscience*; media professionals must live with their decisions.
- The interests of the *object of the act*; a particular person or group is likely to be affected by media practitioners' actions.
- The interests of *financial supporters*; someone pays the bills that allow the station to broadcast or the newspaper or magazine to publish.
- The interests of *the institution*; media professionals have company loyalty, pride in the organization for which they work.
- The interests of *the profession*; media practitioners work to meet the expectations of their colleagues; they have respect for the profession that sustains them.
- The interests of *society*; media professionals, like all of us, have a social responsibility. Because of the influence their work can have, they may even have greater responsibilities than do many other professionals.

In mass communication, these conflicting interests play themselves out in a variety of ways. Some of the most common, yet thorniest, require us to examine such basic issues as truth and honesty, privacy, confidentiality, personal conflict of interest, profit and social responsibility, and protection from offensive content.

Heads rolled at NBC News soon after the broadcast of this artificially induced explosion on *Dateline.* But what was the ethical violation? Wasn't it true that GMC trucks like this one sometimes exploded on impact?

Truth and Honesty Can the media ever be completely honest? As soon as a camera is pointed at one thing, it is ignoring another. As soon as a video editor combines two different images, that editor has imposed his or her definition of the truth. Truth and honesty are overriding concerns for media professionals. But what is truth? In 1992 *Dateline NBC* reported on the safety problems of GMC pickups. Many people believed the trucks were prone to explode in a crash because of deficiencies in design. In fact, several of the trucks had done so. For the story, however, program producers hired a company to stage what would happen in a wreck; in other words, they re-created what they believed to be the truth. To ensure the proper footage, the firm used spark igniters to guarantee the blast. GMC threatened to sue NBC. NBC apologized. The president of the news division was forced to resign, and several people were fired. The broadcast report was not false; the videotaped truck exploded, as had other similar vehicles. But was it honest?

Privacy   Do public figures forfeit their right to privacy? in what circumstances? Are the president's marital problems newsworthy if they do not get in the way of the job? Who is a public figure? When are people's sexual orientations newsworthy? Do you report the names of women who have been raped or the names of juvenile offenders? What about sex offenders? How far do you go to interview grieving parents? When is secret taping permissible?

Our culture values privacy. We have the right to maintain the privacy of our personal information. We use privacy to control the extent and nature of interaction we have with others. Privacy protects us from unwanted government intrusion.

The media, however, by their very nature, are intrusive. Privacy proves to be particularly sensitive because it is almost a metaethic, a fundamental value. Yet the applied ethics of the various media industries allow, in fact sometimes demand, that privacy be denied (see the box "Privacy for Public Figures: The Case of Princess Diana").

Confidentiality   An important tool in contemporary news gathering and reporting is **confidentiality,** the ability of media professionals to keep secret the names of people who provide them with information. Without confidentiality, employees could not report the misdeeds of their employers for fear of being fired; people would not tell what they knew of a crime for fear of retribution from the offenders or unwanted police attention. The anonymous informant nicknamed "Deep Throat" would never have been free to divulge the Nixon White House involvement in the Republican break-in of the Democratic Party's Watergate campaign offices were it not for the promise of confidentiality from *Washington Post* reporters Carl Bernstein and Bob Woodward.

But how far should reporters go in protecting a source's confidentiality? Should reporters go to jail rather than divulge a name? About half the states have established **shield laws,** legislation that expressly protects reporters' rights to maintain sources' confidentiality in courts of law. There is no shield law in federal courts, and most journalists want it that way. Their fear is that once Congress makes one "media law" it may want to make another. For example, media professionals do not want the government to legislate the definition of "reporter" or "journalist."

The ethics of confidentiality are also tested by reporters' frequent use of quotes and information from "unnamed sources," "sources who wish to remain anonymous," and "inside sources." Often the guarantee of

Privacy for Public Figures: The Case of Princess Diana

In August 1997 the chauffeur-driven automobile carrying England's Princess Diana and her companions was involved in a late night crash in a Paris tunnel. Dead were the Princess, her friend Dodi Fayed, and the driver. Diana's bodyguard was critically injured. Reports immediately surfaced that the limousine had been traveling at a very high rate of speed to escape a horde of pursuing **paparazzi**—freelance celebrity photographers. Some witnesses claimed that a cameraperson on a motorbike had cut in front of the speeding Mercedes to slow it down, resulting in the tragedy. Others contended that several paparazzi descended on the wreck snapping pictures rather than giving assistance to the victims. Several had their cameras confiscated, and five were arrested by Paris police for failure to render aid.

Later revelations that the driver had been drinking did little to soften the international outcry against the photographers. They were called privacy-invading jackals and vermin by those who had been targets of their attention and by the world's mainstream press.

The paparazzi defended themselves with a number of arguments. Princess Diana was a public figure and therefore newsworthy. She had openly and often courted media attention both for selfish reasons (to win public support during her marital difficulties) and for good causes (fighting AIDS and banning land mines). The paparazzi were reporters, journalists. The fact that they were freelance, that is, not employed by a specific news organization, should not mean they were less worthy of press freedom. Virtually every

news operation of any standing in the world employs people like them. Moreover, even the so-called mainstream press regularly paid for the product of their efforts. They did what they did because people wanted their kind of news coverage.

Many news operations were unconvinced. In England, France, Germany, and the United States, several media outlets declared that they would never again purchase paparazzi photos and videos. In Great Britain, where there is no First Amendment, the head of the national press council called for severe restrictions on the movement and functioning of these freelancers.

Eventually, in December of that same year, the British press council announced voluntary rules prohibiting paparazzi from photographing or videotaping situations where the subjects could "reasonably expect" privacy. In the United States several celebrities announced a campaign to invade the privacy and harass the families of paparazzi they thought guilty of these trespasses, and Senator Dianne Feinstein of California introduced an anti-paparazzi bill in the Senate, the Personal Privacy Protection Act.

This freedom of the press versus privacy debate remained in the cultural forum for months. What is your opinion? How much privacy do public figures relinquish in exchange for fame? How guilty in Diana's death is the public that eagerly consumes news and pictures of the private lives of the well known? Do you think the restrictions placed on the paparazzi by the British press council could be established in the United States? Should they be?

Princess Diana's fatal car wreck.

anonymity is necessary to get the information, but is this fair to those who are commented on by these nameless, faceless newsmakers? Don't these people—even if they are highly placed and powerful themselves—have a right to know their accusers?

Personal Conflict of Interest   As we've seen, ethical decision making requires a balancing of interests. But what of a media professional's own conflicts of interest? Should media personalities accept speaking fees, free travel, and other gifts from groups and corporations that they may later have to examine? Is it proper for media personalities to fail to disclose the sources and amounts of such gifts? Columnist George Will has written and spoken on television against Clinton Administration plans to impose tariffs on Japanese luxury cars. Is it a conflict of interest that his wife ran a PR firm among whose clients was the Japanese Automobile Manufacturers Association?

Other conflict of interest issues bedevil media professionals. **Checkbook journalism,** in which sources are paid for information or interviews, undermines source reliability. The interests in conflict here are truth and money—might not sources embellish their accounts to demand higher fees? Conflicts of interest also arise when media professionals' personal values, if put into action (for example, marching in a pro-choice demonstration) conflict with their obligation to show balance (for example, in reporting on a series of anti-choice protests).

Profit and Social Responsibility   The media industries are just that, industries. They exist not only to entertain and inform their audiences but also to make a profit for their owners and shareholders. What happens when serving profit conflicts with serving the public?

In 1994 ABC's *Day One* ran an investigation called "Smoke Screen," detailing tobacco industry efforts to manipulate the levels of nicotine in cigarettes. Its reward was a 16-month, multimillion dollar court fight with cigarette maker Philip Morris, which sued the network for $10 billion. The network defended the accuracy of the report and its value to the public. Outside experts agreed that the network would prevail.

In August 1995, however, ABC stunned observers by settling out of court and issuing an apology for the story. Many people believed that because ABC was about to become part of the Disney communications empire it needed to cut its financial losses so as to be more highly valued by its new corporate heads. ABC's decision came under even more scrutiny in the following months as tobacco industry documents released by the court demonstrated that the story, as the network had maintained, was true and correct.

Balancing profit and social responsibility is a concern not just for journalists. Practitioners in entertainment, advertising, and public relations often face this dilemma. Does an ad agency accept as a client the manufacturer of sugared children's cereals even though doctors and dentists

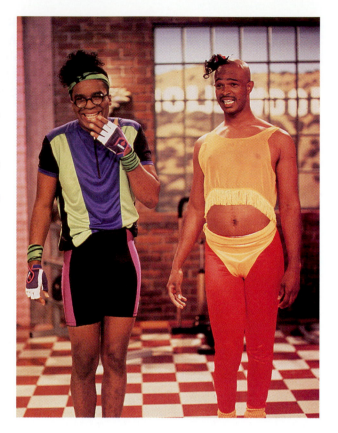

In Living Color's Men on Film. *In Living Color,* still airing in syndication, was a successful show on the Fox Network. Its appeal was primarily to young, urban viewers. It made money for its performers, producers, network, and advertisers. Does this justify what many people felt were denigrating and offensive portrayals of homosexual men and African Americans?

consider these products unhealthy? Does a public relations firm accept as a client the trade office of a country that forces prison inmates to manufacture products in violation of international rules? Does a production company distribute the 1950s television show *Amos 'n Andy* knowing that it embodies many offensive stereotypes of African Americans?

Moreover, balancing profit and the public interest does not always involve big companies and millions of dollars. Often, a media practitioner will face an ethical dilemma at a very personal level. What would you do in this situation? The editor at the magazine where you work has ordered you to write an article about the 14-year-old daughter of your city's mayor. The girl's addiction to amphetamines is a closely guarded family secret, but it has been leaked to your publication. You believe that this child is not a public figure. Your boss disagrees, and the boss *is* the boss. By the way, you've just put a down payment on a lovely condo, and you need to make only two more installments to pay off your new car. Do you write the story?

Offensive Content   Entertainment, news, and advertising professionals must often make decisions about the offensive nature of content. Other than the particular situation of broadcasters discussed earlier in this chapter, this is an ethical rather than a legal issue.

Offensive content is protected. Logically, we do not need the First Amendment to protect sweet and pretty expression. Freedom of speech and freedom of the press exist expressly to allow the dissemination of material that *will* offend. But what is offensive? Clearly, what is offensive to one person may be quite satisfactory to another. Religious leaders have attacked Mighty Mouse cartoons for their glorification of drug usage (Mighty's flower sniffing was akin to snorting cocaine, they reasoned) and the film *The Lion King* for messages hidden in the dust clouds. Television stations and networks regularly bleep cuss words that are common on cable television and in the schoolyard. Our culture sanctions the death penalty but is unwilling to view it on television. Where do we draw the line? *How* do we draw the line? Do we consider the tastes of the audience? Which members of the audience—the most easily offended? Then what of the rights of the others? These are ethical, not legal, determinations.

CODES OF ETHICS AND SELF-REGULATION

To aid practitioners in their moral reasoning, all major groups of media professionals have established formal codes or standards of ethical behavior. Several of these are reprinted in Appendix A: the Society of Professional Journalists' *Code of Ethics*, the American Society of Newspaper Editors' *Statement of Principles*, the Radio-Television News Directors Association's *Code of Broadcast News Ethics*, the American Advertising Federation's *Advertising Principles of American Business*, and the Public Relations Society of America's *Code of Professional Standards for the Practice of Public Relations*. These are prescriptive codes that tell media practitioners what they should do.

To some, these codes are a necessary part of a true profession; to others, they are little more than unenforceable collections of clichés that restrict constitutional rights and invite lawsuits from outsiders.

In addition to industry professional codes, many media organizations have formulated their own institutional policies for conduct. In the case of the broadcast networks, these are enforced by **Standards and Practices Departments.** Local broadcasters have what are called **policy books.** Newspapers and magazines standardize behavior in two ways: through **operating policies** (which spell out standards for everyday operations) and **editorial policies** (which identify company positions on specific issues). Many media organizations also utilize **ombudsmen,** practitioners internal to the company who serve as "judges" in disputes between the public and the organization. Some media organizations subscribe to the small number of existing **media councils,** panels of people from both the media and the public who investigate complaints against the media from the public and publish their findings.

These mechanisms of normative ethics are a form of self-regulation, designed in part to forestall more rigorous or intrusive government regulation. In a democracy dependent on mass communication, they serve an

To many readers, this Benetton ad was offensive. Yet its message—that race should not matter—certainly is not. Why do you think the ad was so controversial and, eventually, pulled from distribution?

important function. We are suspicious of excessive government involvement in media. Self-regulation, however, has certain limitations:

- *Media professionals are reluctant to identify and censure colleagues who transgress.* To do so might appear to be admitting that problems exist; whistle-blowers in the profession are often met with hostility from their peers.

- *The standards for conduct and codes of behavior are abstract and ambiguous.* Many media professionals see this flexibility as a necessary evil; freedom and autonomy are essential. Others believe the lack of rigorous standards renders the codes useless.

- *As opposed to those in other professions, media practitioners are not subject to standards of professional training and licensing.* Again, some practitioners view standards of training and licensing as limiting media freedom and inviting government control. Others argue that licensing has not had these effects on doctors and lawyers.

- *Media practitioners often have limited independent control over their work.* Media professionals are not autonomous, individual professionals. They are part of large, hierarchically structured organizations. Therefore, it is often difficult to punish violations of standards because of the difficulty in fixing responsibility.

Critics of self-regulation argue that these limitations are often accepted willingly by media practitioners because the "true" function of self-regulation is "to cause the least commotion" for those working in the media industries (Black & Whitney, 1983, p. 432). True or not, the decision to perform his or her duties in an ethical manner ultimately rests with the individual media professional. As media ethicists Jay Black and Ralph Barney (1985) explain, an ethical media professional

> must rationally overcome the status quo tendencies . . . to become the social catalyst who identifies the topics and expedites the negotiations societies need in order to remain dynamic. (p. 36)

DEVELOPING MEDIA LITERACY SKILLS
Accepting Reports Based on Anonymous Sources

We have seen how culture is created and maintained through communication, and that, increasingly, mass communication is central to that process. The need for literacy among media consumers, and for ethical performance among media industry practitioners, should be obvious. Yet neither is a simple enterprise. Developing sophisticated media literacy skills is hampered by a number of impediments, and even when media practitioners *do* make ethical decisions, they are not always the right or best decisions for everyone involved.

The process of mass communication is messy, chaotic, sometimes out of balance, and often troublesome. As unsettling as this can be, the alternative—external or government control—is unacceptable to most U.S. citizens. Yet calls for control are invariably based on the claim that either audiences or media industries (or both) cannot be trusted. Audience members and practitioners therefore share an additional responsibility, the need to preserve freedom in mass communication. They can best do this through the literate consumption and ethical production and distribution of content.

The 1998 sex scandal that embroiled the Clinton White House offers not only a good test of that shared responsibility but a harbinger of how the new computer network technologies (Chapter 14) make meeting that responsibility even more difficult.

Many major news operations avoid the use of unidentified or anonymous sources, although they can sometimes be quite valuable, as we have seen earlier in this chapter. The danger is that sources' requests for anonymity might be based more on their desire to disguise inaccuracy and falsehood than on their need for protection. When the use of such a source is necessary to a journalistic investigation, these organizations will not use the information the anonymous sources provide unless there is corroboration from at least one other source. In addition, major journalistic operations have a series of internal checks and balances—reporters, a hierarchy of editors, and ombudspeople—to ensure that the material they publish is factual, even when the source cannot be identified. As a result, media literate people can make their own decisions on whether to accept the account. They can evaluate the ethical standards applied by media professionals. Some readers and viewers may not accept information from anonymous sources; some may. But at least all understand that the publication or station that produced a given story did its best to assure veracity and accuracy. The Internet, however, poses a particular challenge to media literate people.

Much of the reporting on the alleged moral and ethical lapses of the Clinton White House not only was based on information provided by unnamed or anonymous sources but was also not subjected to the news industry's normal internal, ethical checks and balances. Several of the most dramatic stories originated with *The Drudge Report,* an online newspaper published by Matt Drudge and made available for free by America Online to its subscribers.

Drudge, whose only previous media experience was working in a CBS gift shop, has no editors to check his work. He has no advertisers dependent on his credibility for their own. Bound by none of the conventional institutional controls faced by most journalists—"no editors casting a skeptical eye over one's copy, no in-house counsel sweating over the possibility of lawsuits, no publisher worrying about confrontations with aggrieved sources at a dinner party" (Levy, 1998, p. 78)—Drudge operates free of traditional notions of media ethics and, therefore, assessment. *The Drudge Report* released the story that Clinton aide Sidney Blumenthal was a wife beater. Sources were "unnamed top GOP operatives." There was no corroboration, and Drudge printed his story without talking to Blumenthal. The story was false, and Drudge later retracted it. Yet before the retraction, the traditional media were forced to report, if not the charge, at least the fact that an online newspaper had made the charge. If any one news organization had done otherwise, it would have been accused, at worst, of protecting the president and his staff or, at best, of failing to report a story carried by other reputable sources. Meanwhile, Mr. Blumenthal and his wife were the focus of false and embarrassing scrutiny, and the White House suffered another hit to its reputation.

Drudge then used unnamed "investigators" for his report on sexual episodes involving President Clinton, White House intern Monica Lewinsky, former presidential assistant Dick Morris, and a prostitute. No other journalist has been able to substantiate the story.

The old standards no longer apply. As *Newsweek* media writer Steven Levy reported, with online "journalists" like Drudge, "unchecked allegations are news simply because they are alleged" (1998, p. 78). Media literate people must develop their own standards for accepting reports based on anonymous sources, and they must apply them with diligence across all media, making sure that they understand how different media bring with them varying degrees of commitment to ethical performance.

Chapter Review

The First Amendment, based on the libertarian philosophy, guarantees freedom of press and speech. Supported by the 14th Amendment, it protects the press from official intrusion by all levels of government. That protection carries to all media but can be suspended in cases of clear and present danger and when competing interests must be balanced, for example, in free press versus fair trial conflicts. Some expression, primarily libel, slander, and obscenity, are not protected. Pornography, however, is protected expression. In almost no case is prior restraint acceptable.

Indecent expression, although protected, is limited in broadcasting and is typically relegated to late night hours. Yet broadcasters' First Amendment rights were at the heart of deregulation, resulting in, among other things, the demise of the Fairness Doctrine and ascertainment.

Copyright does not protect the expression of ideas; rather, it protects the creator's financial interest in that expression, considered an important incentive in maintaining the free and ongoing flow of art, science, and other public speech. The 1978 copyright law set new rules and formalized exceptions such as use of material once it has passed into the public domain and fair use.

Because the press is not totally free, libertarianism gave way in the 1940s to social responsibility theory, the idea that to earn their freedom the media must perform responsibly. Self-regulation demands that media professionals balance conflicting interests. This balancing often produces dilemmas best resolved by applying ethics, rules of behavior or moral principles that guide actions in given situations. Ethics operate at three levels: metaethics, normative ethics, and applied ethics. Applying ethics requires balancing the conflicting interests of moral agents' consciences, people affected by their actions, their financial supporters, the institutions for which they work, their profession, and society as a whole. In mass communication these interests sometimes collide in the areas of truth and honesty, privacy, confidentiality, personal conflict of interest, profit and social responsibility, and offensive content.

Media practitioners are aided in their moral decision making by formal codes of conduct and their own institutional policies of conduct. These forms of self-regulation are controversial, however. They are seen by some as necessary and by others as limiting, abstract, and unenforceable.

Questions for Review

1. What are the basic tenets of libertarianism? How do they support the First Amendment?
2. What is the relationship between the First and 14th Amendments?
3. Name important court cases involving the definition of "no law," "the press," "abridgment," clear and present danger, balancing of interests, and prior restraint.
4. What are libel and slander? What are the tests of libel and slander? How do the rules change for public officials?
5. Define obscenity, pornography, and indecency.
6. What are ethics? What are the three levels of ethics?
7. What are some of the individual and group interests that often conflict in the application of media ethics?
8. What is confidentiality? Why is confidentiality important to media professionals and to democracy?
9. What are some examples of personal and professional conflict of interest faced by media practitioners?
10. What are some forms of media self-regulation? What are the strengths and limitations of self-regulation?

Questions for Critical Thinking and Discussion

1. Are you a libertarian? That is, do you believe that people are inherently rational and good and that they are best served by a fully free press? Defend your position.
2. What is your position on pornography? It is legally protected expression. Would you limit that protection? When?
3. How much regulation or, if you prefer, deregulation do you think broadcasters should accept?
4. Of all the groups whose interests must be balanced by media professionals, which ones do you think would have most influence over you?
5. In general, how ethical do you believe media professionals to be? Specifically, print journalists? television journalists? advertising professionals? public relations professionals? television and film writers? direct mail marketers?

Important Resources

Bittner, J. R. (1994). *Law and regulation of electronic media.* **Englewood Cliffs, NJ: Prentice-Hall.** A thorough explanation of the political, economic, and technological bases for U.S. regulation of the electronic media. This college textbook is strong on history and on contemporary analysis.

Broadcasting and the Law, Censorship News, and ***Media Law Bulletin.*** Three excellent periodicals that, among them, offer reprints, condensations, and commentary on current and ongoing media law and regulation topics.

Foerstel, H. N. (1997). *Free expression and censorship in America.* **Westport, CT: Greenwood Publishing.** A thorough encyclopedia of names, cases, and issues involving the First Amendment and censorship that presents the history of this ongoing conflict as well as its contemporary status.

Media Law Reporter. This monthly publication reprints most and digests some federal court, state court, and administrative agency (such as the FCC) decisions regarding the mass media. Reprints and digests are then collected and published in an annual volume.

Seib, P., & Fitzpatrick, K. (1997). *Journalism ethics.* **New York: Harcourt Brace College Publishers.** Written for college students, this text deals with the human side of ethics, that is, how those making the decisions do so. Two of its most useful chapters are on the compassionate journalist and developing more ethical journalism.

Media Regulation Information Web Sites

The Freedom Forum First Amendment Center (at Vanderbilt University)	*http://www.fac.org/default.htm*
The American Civil Liberties Union	*http://www.aclu.org*
The Center for Democracy and Technology	*http://www.cdt.org*
The Electronic Frontier Foundation	*http://www.eff.org*
The Electronic Privacy Information Center	*http://www.epic.org*
The Thomas Jefferson Center for the Protection of Free Expression	*http://www.tjcenter.org/whatsnew.html*
The Federal Communications Commission	*http://www.fcc.gov/*

The Federal Trade Commission	*http://www.ftc.gov/*
The U.S. Supreme Court Database	*http://court.it-services.nwu.edu/oyez/*
First Amendment Cyber-Tribune (FACT)	*http://w3.trib.com/FACT/*
Fairness and Accuracy in Reporting	*http://www.igc.org/fair/*

The Internet

Tomorrow you go to court to defend yourself. And all you did was tell the truth.

Your troubles began when you saw the computer school's television commercials and newspaper ads. Learn computer animation, they said, create Web pages, develop CD-ROM, get a high-paying job. You visited the school's offices and saw all sorts of sophisticated equipment. The problem, though, is that you never saw those computers again. You enrolled. They had your money. And you were taught only a few of the things the ads promised. You certainly did not get that high-paying job.

When you tried to get your money back, the school refused. When you tried to buy a 15-second spot on the local television station, the sales manager declined to sell you time. The newspaper said no as well, citing its First Amendment right to refuse ads it considers "inappropriate." That's what gave you the idea. The First Amendment protects your rights too. You took what few skills you had been taught and built a Web site explaining how and why you thought you had been cheated. You asked others who had similar experiences with the school to access the page and tell their stories. Thirty disgruntled students soon chimed in.

And then the school sued you for libel, claiming that you had damaged its good name and sullied its reputation. But all you did was tell your story. The school has its own Web page touting its value. Why can't you have a Web page offering an alternative view? The school has the money to buy ads anywhere it wants. You don't. The Internet is your only means of expression. If you can be silenced there, you will have no voice at all.

In this chapter we study the history of the Internet, beginning with the development of the computer and leading to the military applications that ultimately produced the Net. Then we take a detailed look at the Internet as it exists today. We examine its formats and its capabilities, especially the popular World Wide Web. The number and nature of today's Internet users are discussed, as are the growing efforts of online advertisers and sellers to reach these consumers.

The Net's freedom and openness raise a number of important First Amendment issues. We study how many users see the Internet as granting them power equal to that enjoyed by owners of more traditional media, efforts at control of Internet expression, pornography on the Web, and online copyright issues. Finally, in developing our media literacy skill, we discuss improving our online literacy, both as e-mail senders and as e-mail receivers.

A Short History of the Internet

The **information superhighway** (worldwide digital data networks) is an apt name for today's computer communication systems for many reasons. One is historical. The superhighway's primary component, the Internet, much like the interstate truck and automobile highway system that crisscrosses the United States, is an outgrowth of the Cold War.

In the 1950s, to better respond to a feared invasion from the communists, President Dwight Eisenhower ordered a system of high-speed roads built. He based his vision on the German highway system, the Autobahn, which had allowed the Nazis to move their armies so effectively during World War II. With the new superhighways in place, no matter where an enemy attacked the United States, the military could respond effectively and rapidly.

In 1962 the Air Force wanted another "highway," one that would effectively and rapidly move information instead of armies. The military wanted to maintain the ability to transfer information, even under enemy attack. The resulting system was the beginning of what we now call the **Internet,** or the Net, a global network of interconnected computers that communicate freely and share and exchange information. Before we delve into the details of this network of computers, we should first consider the origin of computers themselves.

DEVELOPMENT OF THE COMPUTER

Computers began with counting. Fingers, sticks, and stones made way for the first calculator, the **abacus**—a counting device composed of a fixed number of balls or other markers on a series of parallel rods—which was first used by the Egyptians around 460 B.C.E.

More complex mathematical calculations required development of a sophisticated number system. John Napier, the inventor of logarithms, introduced Europe to his decimal-based arithmetic system in the latter half of the 16th century. For the more complex calculations this system made possible, a calculator more sophisticated than the abacus was needed.

A Japanese abacus.

In the mid-17th century, French philosopher Blaise Pascal and German inventor Wilhelm Schickard independently produced plans for a mechanical calculator using linked series of toothed cogs. In 1694, however, German philosopher and mathematician Gottfried Leibnitz designed and produced a working mechanical calculator that permitted not only addition and subtraction but multiplication and division as well. He was an early advocate for the value of computing machines, writing, "For it is unworthy of excellent men to lose hours like slaves in the labor of calculation which could safely be relegated to anyone else if machines were used" (as cited in Goldstine, 1972, p. 8).

The title "Father of the Computer," however, goes to Englishman Charles Babbage. Lack of money and unavailability of the necessary technology stymied his plan to build an Analytical Engine, a steam-driven computer. But in 1836 Babbage did produce designs for a "computer" that could conduct algebraic computations using stored memory and punch cards for input and output. His work provided inspiration for those who would follow.

Over the next 100 years a number of mechanical and electromechanical computers were attempted, some with success. But Colossus, developed by the British to break the German's secret codes during World War II, was the first electronic **digital computer.** It reduced information to a **binary code**—that is, a code made up of the digits 1 and 0. In this form information could be stored and manipulated. The first "full-service" electronic computer, ENIAC (Electronic Numerical Integrator and Calculator), based on the work of the University of Iowa's John W. Atanasoff, was introduced

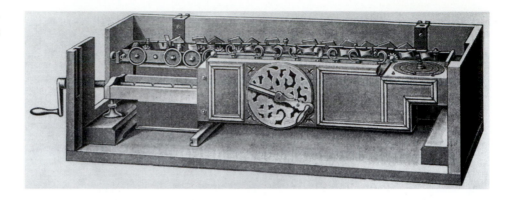

A drawing of an early version of Gottfried Leibnitz's counting machine.

by scientists John Mauchly and John Presper Eckert of the Moore School of Electrical Engineering at the University of Pennsylvania in 1946. ENIAC hardly resembled the computers we know today: 18 feet tall, 80 feet long, and weighing 60,000 pounds, it was composed of 17,500 vacuum tubes and 500 miles of electrical wire. It could fill an auditorium and ate up 150,000 watts of electricity. Mauchly and Eckert eventually left the university to form their own computer company, later selling it to the Remington Rand Corporation in 1950. At Remington they developed UNIVAC (Universal Automatic Computer), which, when bought for and used by the Census Bureau in 1951, became the first successful commercial computer.

The commercial computer explosion was ignited by IBM. Using its already well-entrenched organizational system of trained sales and service professionals, IBM helped businesses find their way in the early days of the computer revolution. One of its innovations was to sell rather than rent computers to customers. As a result of IBM's success, by 1960 the computer industry could be described as "IBM and the Seven Dwarfs"—Sperry, Control Data, Honeywell, RCA, NCR, General Electric, and Burroughs (Rosenberg, 1992, p. 60).

MILITARY APPLICATIONS

In 1957 the Soviet Union launched Sputnik, Earth's first human-constructed satellite. The once undisputed supremacy of the United States in science and technology had been usurped, and U.S. scientists and military officials were in shock. The Advanced Research Projects Agency (ARPA) was immediately established to sponsor and coordinate sophisticated defense-related research. In 1962, as part of a larger drive to promote the use of computers in national defense, ARPA commissioned Paul Baran of the Rand Corporation to produce a plan that would allow the U.S. military to maintain command over its missiles and planes if a nuclear attack knocked out conventional means of communication. The military thought a decentralized communication network was necessary. In that way, no matter where the bombing occurred, other locations would be available to launch a counterattack. Among Baran's plans was one for a "packet switched network." He wrote,

Packet switching is the breaking down of data into datagrams or packets that are labeled to indicate the origin and the destination of the information and the forwarding of these packets from one computer to another computer until the information arrives at its final destination computer. This (is) crucial to the realization of a computer network. If packets are lost at any given point, the message can be resent by the originator. (As cited in Kristula, 1997, p. 1)

The genius of the system Baran envisioned is twofold: (1) common communication rules (called protocols) and common computer languages would allow any type of computer, running with any operating system, to communicate with another; and (2) destination or delivery instructions embedded in all information sent on the system would allow for instantaneous "detours" or "rerouting" if a given computer on the network became unavailable. This, as any computer network user knows, is how the Internet actually works.

Using Honeywell computers at Stanford University, UCLA, the University of Santa Barbara, and the University of Utah, the switching network, called ARPANET, went online in 1969 and became fully operational and reliable within one year. Other developments soon followed. In 1972, an engineer named Ray Tomlinson created the first e-mail program. In 1974 Stanford University's Vinton Cerf and the military's Robert Kahn coined the term "the Internet." In 1979 a graduate student at the University of North Carolina, Steve Bellovin, created USENET and, independent of Bellovin, IBM created BITNET. These two networking software systems allowed virtually anybody with access to a Unix or IBM computer to connect to others on the growing network. By the time the Internet Society was chartered and the World Wide Web was released in 1992, there were more than 1.1 million **hosts**—computers linking individual personal computer users to the Internet. Today there are more than 15 million hosts worldwide serving a seemingly limitless number of users.

A sixties-vintage IBM mainframe computer. The personal computer in your home probably carries more computing power than this giant machine.

THE PERSONAL COMPUTER

A crucial part of the story of the Internet is the development and diffusion of personal computers. IBM was fantastically successful at exciting businesses, schools and universities, and other organizations about computers. But IBM's and other companies' **mainframe** and **mini-computers** employed **terminals,** and these stations at which users worked were connected to larger, centralized machines. As a result, the Internet at first was the province of the people who worked in those settings.

When the semiconductor (or integrated circuit, or chip) replaced the vacuum tube as the essential information processor in computers, its tiny size, absence of heat, and low cost made possible the design and production of small, affordable **personal** or **micro computers** (PCs). This, of course, opened the Net to anyone, anywhere. In a *New York Times* story entitled "Out Damned Geek! The Typical Web User Is No Longer Packing a Pocket Protector," University of Michigan marketing professor Sunil Gupta declared, "It's the end of geekdom. This technology is still available only to technologically literate households, but it has moved beyond the university and corporate domination of the past" (Lohr, 1995, p. 39).

The leaders of the personal computer revolution were Bill Gates and the duo of Steve Jobs and Stephen Wozniak. As a college freshman in 1975, Gates saw a magazine story about a small, low-powered computer, the MITS Altair 8800, that could be built from a kit and used to play a simple game. Sensing that the future of computing was in these personal computers, and that the power of computers would reside not in their size but in the software that ran them, Gates dropped out of Harvard Univer-

An early computer chip and today's Pentium II. Microprocessors continue to get smaller, more powerful, and faster.

sity and, with his friend Paul Allen, founded Microsoft Corporation. They licensed their **operating system**—the software that tells the computer how to work—to MITS. With this advance, people no longer had to know sophisticated operating languages like FORTRAN and COBOL to use computers. At nearly the same time, in 1977, Jobs and Wozniak, also college dropouts, perfected Apple II, a low-cost, easy-to-use microcomputer designed specifically for personal rather than business use. It was immediately and hugely successful, especially in its development of **multimedia** capabilities—advanced sound and image applications. IBM, stung by its failure to enter the personal computer business, contracted with Microsoft to use the Microsoft operating system in its IBM PC, first introduced in 1981. All of the pieces were now in place for the home computer revolution.

The Internet Today

John Chambers, president of Cisco Systems, an Internet networking company, spoke in 1998 of the "Internet Revolution":

> The Internet will change how people live, work, play, and learn. The Industrial Revolution brought together people with machines in factories, and the Internet revolution will bring together people with knowledge and information in virtual companies. And it will have every bit as much impact on society as the Industrial Revolution. It will promote globalization at an incredible pace. But instead of happening over 100 years, like the Industrial Revolution, it will happen over seven years. (As cited in Friedman, 1998, p. 6B)

The Internet is most appropriately thought of as a "network of networks" that is growing at an incredibly fast rate. These networks consist of **LANs** (**L**ocal **A**rea **N**etworks), connecting two or more computers, usually within the same building, and **WANs** (**W**ide **A**rea **N**etwork), connecting several LANs in different locations. When people access the Internet from a computer in a university library they are most likely on a LAN. But when several universities (or businesses or other organizations) link their computer systems, their users are part of a WAN.

As the popularity of the Internet has grown, so has the number of Internet **providers** (sometimes called **servers**), companies that offer Internet connections at monthly rates depending on the kind and amount of access needed. Some of the better known providers include America Online, Prodigy, and the wireless provider Ricochet.

USING THE INTERNET

It is only a small overstatement to say that computers are rarely used for computing anymore because the Net has given the computer so much more versatility.

E-mail (Electronic Mail)   With an Internet **e-mail** account, users can communicate with anyone else online, any place in the world, with no long distance fees (just applicable local phone connection charges). Most e-mail programs allow people to:

- List mail received and sent
- Read or delete an item from the list of documents received

- Print or save a document as a file
- Store frequently used names and addresses
- Automatically attach signatures at the end of letters
- Send replies, with portions of the original message in the reply
- Forward mail by simply readdressing it
- Attach other files to mail
- Send a document to any number of people at once

Each person online has a unique e-mail address that works just like a telephone number. There are even online "Yellow Pages" and "White Pages" to help users find other people by e-mail.

Mailing Lists   E-mail can also be used to join mailing lists, bulletin boards, or discussion groups that cover a huge variety of subjects. The lists are often incorrectly called "LISTSERVs," which is the name of the free software program used to run most of them. Users simply subscribe to a group, and then all mail posted (sent) to that group is automatically forwarded to them by the host computer. The lists are typically produced by a single person or central authority such as a university, foundation, or public interest group. A listing of discussion groups can be obtained by e-mail from *listserv@ubvm.cc.buffalo.edu.*

USENET   **USENET,** also known as network news, is an internationally distributed bulletin board system. Users enter messages, and within a day or so, the messages are delivered to nearly every other USENET host for everyone to read.

The best way to find a mailing list or discussion group is to access a document called "Publicly Accessible Mailing Lists," which is posted regularly on the USENET newsgroup site *news.answers*. It is also available by anonymous FTP (file transfer protocol): *ftp://rtfm.mit.edu/pub/usenet-by-group/news.answers/mail/mailing-lists.*

FTP (File Transfer Protocol)   Information other than e-mail can also be transferred to and from the Internet. **File transfer protocol (FTP)** is an Internet application that allows users to send complete files between other computers and their own. *Downloading* describes the activity in which users transfer files *from* an outside computer *to* their own. *Uploading* describes the task whereby users transfer files *from* their own computers *to* others. But how does a user find out what information exists and where to get it? Some information archives (secret government files and specific corporation databases, for example) are secured and can only be accessed by appropriate personnel. But most information on the Internet is available to the public for access. There are several ways to find information about different areas of interest; among them are Archie, Gopher, Veronica, and WAIS.

Archie   Because the Internet has no center, no central card catalog is possible. A reasonable facsimile, however, is created every month at a number of locations by a service and search program called **Archie.** Over a period of a month, the Archie service scans most Internet sites and generates a list of FTP files and directory names, forming a database. Most of the identified sites offer anonymous register (no permission is required for access). Simply put, the information is public, and anyone can gain it freely and anonymously. The resulting database is then duplicated (mirrored) on several other Archie servers, all of which contain the same information. To access Archie, simply Telnet (discussed later in this chapter) to any one of these several sites:

archie.sura.net   archie.unl.edu
archie.rutgers.edu   archie.internic.net
                           archie.ans.net

Gopher and Veronica: The Internet as Research Library   **Gopher** is a tool for burrowing or tunneling through file databases on the Internet. Gopher is based on menus that point to other menus, which ultimately point to specific documents, whether text, picture, animation, sound file, or search program on the same or other computers. **Veronica** (**V**ery **E**asy **R**odent-**O**riented **N**et-Wide **I**ndex to **C**omputerized **A**rchives) builds a searchable index of Gopher menus in much the same way that Archie builds an index of FTP files. Archie tells users where files are; then they must get to the files using FTP. The output of a Veronica search, however, is a custom Gopher menu. Veronica is thus both a search and a retrieval tool. The homebase for Veronica is *gopher://veronica.scs.unr.edu/11/veronica.*

WAIS   Archie searches file names in directories of anonymous FTP servers. Veronica searches key words in Gopher menus. Neither, however, examines documents themselves, only their listings in a directory or menu. But **WAIS** (**W**ide **A**rea **I**nformation **S**ervers, pronounced "waze"), are specifically document-oriented and examine the *indexes* of the text of documents on a particular database. As a result, the WAIS database can include anything that can be indexed with words. It searches for key words and ranks documents according to the number and placement of "hits," or occurrences of these key words. Like Veronica, WAIS offers a menu from which users can then retrieve documents.

Telnet (rlogin) remote login   **Telnet** lets users log into other computers on the Net as if they were connected to them directly. Whereas Archie, Veronica, and WAIS allow for information transfer, Telnet actually electronically "transports" the user *into* the site's system. For example, a user can Telnet into a university system, and, after connecting properly, the user's home machine will act as if it is a computer *on* that university's network rather than being an outside machine trying to simply download information.

THE WORLD WIDE WEB

Thus far, we have discussed how documents are linked to e-mail addresses, FTP file libraries, Gopher menus, WAIS databases, and Telneting to machines. Another way of accessing information files is via the **World Wide Web** (usually referred to as "the Web"). The Web is not a physical place, nor a set of files, nor even a network of computers. The heart of the Web lies in the protocols (common communication rules and languages) that define its use. The World Wide Web (WWW) uses hypertext transfer protocols (HTTP) to transport files from one place to another. What makes the World Wide Web unique is the striking appearance of the information when it gets to your computer. In addition to text, the Web presents color, images, sounds, and video. This, combined with its ease of use, makes the Web the most popular aspect of the Internet for the large majority of users. One 1995 estimate (*www.anamorph.com/docs/stats/stats*) said that at that time there were 27,000 Web sites, and the number was doubling every day. This growth rate would have been difficult to maintain, inasmuch as it means there would have been 35,360,668,635 Web sites on February 1, 1998—5.89 sites per living human. Nonetheless, there is no doubt that the Web is the single fastest growing neighborhood on the Net.

The ease with which users can access the Web is a function of a number of components—hosts, URLs, browsers, search engines, and home pages.

Hosts (Computers Connected to the Internet) Other than e-mail transactions, most Internet activity consists of users accessing files on remote computers. To reach these files, users must first gain access to the Internet through "wired-to-the-Net" hosts. These hosts are often called service providers or servers.

Whether they offer access to others (hosts) or not, all computers *directly* connected to the Internet are identified by numbers that represent location and routing information. To make these identification numbers more convenient and user-friendly, they are often given one or more names. For example, the number for one San Jose State University computer is 130.654.62.2, but its name is *athens.sjsu.edu*.

When using the World Wide Web, it helps to understand how names are constructed. The rightmost part of the name is its **zone.** There are two kinds of zone information. One is *geographical*, such as *mx* for Mexico, *us* for the United States, and *uk* for the United Kingdom. The other is *organizational* and signifies the nature of the activity conducted by that site's creators. These are:

Zone	Type of Organization
com	Commercial organization
edu	Educational institution
gov	Government body or department
int	International organization (mostly NATO)
mil	Military site

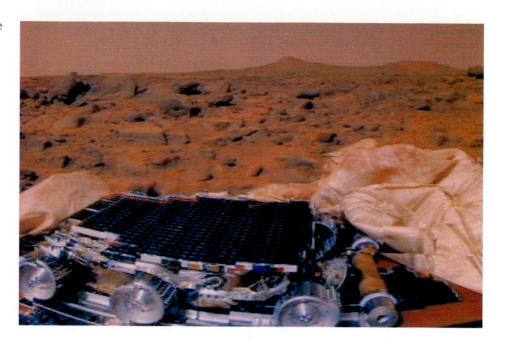

NASA's Pathfinder Web site welcomed millions of daily visitors from around the world during its July 1997 transmissions from the surface of Mars. The *New York Times* announced that, with this event, the World Wide Web had "arrived."

net	Networking organization
org	Anything that doesn't fit elsewhere, such as a professional organization, especially nonprofit organizations

Once users gain access to a host computer on the Internet, they then have to find the exact location of the file they are looking for *on* the host. Each file or directory on the Internet (that is, on the host computer connected to the Internet) is designated by a **URL** (Uniform Resource Locator). URLs indicate:

- The program for accessing a file (or the protocol that will be used)
- The path to that file within the file directory of that computer
- The name of the file or directory in question

Here are some typical URLs:

Use	URL Identifier	Example
E-mail	*mailto:*	*mailto:sbaran@email.sjsu.edu*
FTP	*ftp://*	*ftp://scholar.lib.vt.edu/*
Gopher	*gopher://*	*gopher://gopher.vt.edu*
Telnet	*telnet://*	*telnet://vtls.vt.edu*
Usenet News	*news:*	*news:comp.infosystems.www*
WWW (HTTP)	*http://*	*http://www.yahoo.com*

Browsers **Browsers** are software programs loaded onto the user's computer and used to download and view Web files. Browsers take separate files (text files, image files, and sound files) and put them all together for viewing. Netscape and Internet Explorer are two of the most popular Web browsers.

Search Engines Finding information on the Web is becoming easier thanks to the growing number of companies creating Web- or Net-search software. These programs are sometimes called **search engines, spiders,** or **Web crawlers.** They all provide on-screen menus that make their navigation as simple as pointing and clicking. The most popular search engines are:

ALTA VISTA	*http://www.altavista.digital.com/*
AOL NetFind	*http://www.aol.com/netfind/*
EXCITE	*http://www.excite.com/*
HOTBOT	*http://www.hotbot.com*
INFERENCE	*http://www.inference.com*
INFOSEEK	*http://www.infoseek.com/*
LYCOS	*http://www.lycos.com/*
MAGELLAN	*http://www.mckinley.com/*
NETSCAPE	*http://www.netscape.com/home/internet-search.html*
WEBCRAWLER	*http://www.webcrawler.com/*
YAHOO	*http://www.yahoo.com/*

Home Pages Once users reach the intended Web site, they are greeted by a **home page**—the entryway to the site itself. It contains not only the information the site's creators want visitors to know but provides **hyperlinks** to other material in that site as well as to material in other sites on other computers linked to the Net anywhere in the world (Figure 14–1).

CYBER . . .

All of this online activity occurs in the realm of **cyberspace**—a space filled with the technologies and activities associated with or dependent on computers. "Cyber" has become the shorthand expression for just about anything touched by the computer world. For example, we read of cyberdemocracy; we shop at the cybermall; heavy users are called cyberjunkies, cybergeeks, or cyberpunks.

The origin of this expression is in dispute. One camp attributes it to William Gibson's futuristic 1984 novel *Neuromancer*. Gibson, who also wrote the book and movie script *Johnny Mnemonic*, first visited the Internet in 1995. But his earlier use of the word *cyberspace* struck a chord with computer network users who adopted it as their own. In *Neuromancer*, cyberspace described the technologically created reality that existed in the minds of Gibson's characters who were physiologically hooked to computers.

A second view is that the computer and telecommunications industries simply adapted the expression from the scientific movement originating in

Figure 14–1 Web Pages to Check Out

http://www.mapblast.com/	Mapblast! allows you to create and customize your own map . . . as long as it is in the USA. It promises to add European cities soon.
http://www.cliffie.nosc.mil/~NATLAS/atlas/	Thinking on a larger scale? Visit the Atlas of the World.
http://www.fourmilab.ch/earthview/ vplanet.html	If that isn't enough, the Earth and Moon Viewer goes one step further.
http://slugfest.kaizen.net/	If you like to box, try a little fisticuffs with the likes of Madonna, Mr. Rogers, or ex-President Bush at this site.
http://www.whitehouse.gov	This takes you to speeches and other federal government agencies.
http://ericir.syr.edu/Main.html	Educational Resources Information Center (ERIC) is a huge database of ideas, stories, lesson plans, education technology, textbooks, literature, and other educational media.
http://www.nta.no/telektronikk/	This web site provides a place for you to publish your academic papers.
http://www.timein.com/vibe/	*Vibe* is the online counterpart to the paper magazine.
http://www.hotwired.com/	Much like *Wired Magazine*, its site is a designer's dream (or nightmare, depending on your tastes).
http://www.monster.com/home.html	Monster Board has much job-related data: company profiles, recruitment information for recent college graduates, and a full set of employment classifieds.
http://www.pizzahut.com/	This isn't a commercial, just an example of what the Web can do. Order a pizza from Pizza Hut and have it delivered no matter where you are!
http://www.mall2000.com/date/date.html	When pizza just isn't enough, there is a personal ads site.
http://sunsite.unc.edu/expo/expo/ busstation.html	The EXPO Ticket Office is an exhibition of some of the best sites on the Web. Click on the map of famous sites to decide where you want to visit. Grab your free ticket and take a shuttle bus to one of its web-wide exhibits.
http://www.unitedmedia.com/comics/ dilbert	The ultimate comic for the cybercrowd is Scott Adams' *Dilbert*. Naturally, he's online.

A typical and often visited home page.

William Gibson

the 1960s, **cybernetics**—the use of information to control or govern systems and environments that house them. Regardless of the roots of the expression, the cyberworld excites millions of users.

The Internet and Its Users

In earlier medium-specific chapters we discussed the relationship between those media and their audiences, for example, "Radio and Its Audiences." But Internet audiences are also content creators. At any time—or even at the same time—a person may be reading Internet content and *creating* content as well. E-mail and chat rooms are obvious examples of online users being both audience and creators, but others exist as well. For example, multiple user domains (MUDs) allow entire alternative realities to be simultaneously constructed and engaged (Chapter 15), and computer screens that have multiple open windows allow users to "read" one site while creating another, sometimes using the just-read material. We will discuss the impact of this alteration in the traditional mass communication process in more detail in the next chapter. For now, however, instead of audience, we will talk about the Internet and its *users*.

ESTIMATING THE NUMBER OF USERS

It is almost impossible to tell exactly how many users there are on the Internet. People who own computers are not necessarily linked to the Internet, and people need not own computers to use the Net. Some users access the Net through machines at school, the library, or work. Estimates range from 20 to 100 million Internet users. Computer graphics system developer and artist Simon Biggs (1996) set the number at "30,000,000 and doubling every six months" (p. 322). One commercial forecasting company, the Yankee Group, projected 200 million users by the year 2000 (O'Connor & Wasserman, 1996). Bob Metcalf, founder of the computer networking company 3Com, has argued in the pages of the magazine *InfoWorld* that there are so many users that congestion will soon crash the Internet (cited in Marshall, 1996).

Existing research, however, does give some indication of contemporary Internet usage. The November 6, 1995, issue of *Advertising Age* reported that there were 40 million U.S. homes with personal computers. Twenty-two million of those had **modems** (devices that translate digital computer information into an analog form so it can be transmitted through telephone lines), suggesting that they also have Internet access. In that same year, a Nielsen Company telephone survey of 4,200 U.S. respondents aged 16 years and older produced these results (O'Connor, 1995):

- 37 million people have Internet access
- 24 million use the Internet

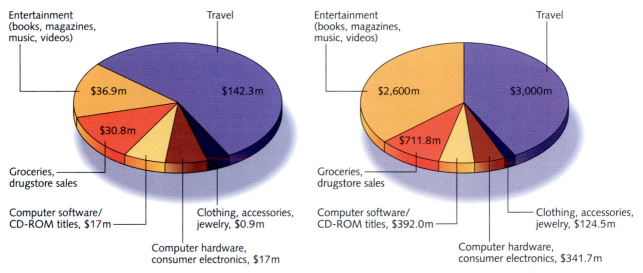

1994
$244.9 million (actual)

Entertainment (books, magazines, music, videos) — $36.9m

Travel — $142.3m

$30.8m

Groceries, drugstore sales

Computer software/CD-ROM titles, $17m

Clothing, accessories, jewelry, $0.9m

Computer hardware, consumer electronics, $17m

2000
$7,170.0 million (projected)

Entertainment (books, magazines, music, videos) — $2,600m

Travel — $3,000m

$711.8m

Groceries, drugstore sales

Computer software/CD-ROM titles, $392.0m

Clothing, accessories, jewelry, $124.5m

Computer hardware, consumer electronics, $341.7m

Figure 14–2 The Great Cybermall—What Sells Online. While not likely to replace actual shopping anytime soon, virtual shopping is expected to grow significantly over time. Here are 1994 online sales figures and industry predictions for the year 2000. Source: Jupiter Communications, 1996 Home Shopping Report.

- 18 million use the World Wide Web
- Of those who had used the Internet within one day of being surveyed, 66% had connected from work
- Two thirds of Internet users are men, and they account for 77% of the online time consumed
- The average user spends 5.5 hours a week on the Internet
- Users are primarily well educated and well off; 25% have an annual income over $80,000, and two thirds are college graduates
- 5 million of the 24 million total users link to the Net primarily for Web access; 4.5 million primarily for e-mail

A later Nielsen survey, this one conducted in conjunction with an online advertising and sales company, demonstrated not only the growth of the Internet but its potential value to advertisers. The Spring 1997 CommerceNet/Nielsen Internet Demographic Study set the number of U.S. and Canadian Internet users over 16 years of age at 23% of the population, or 50.6 million people. Of these, nearly 37 million use the Internet and the Web to search for products and services, and 5.6 million users actually purchase products and services online (Figure 14–2).

CYBERADDICTION

Some Internet users are literally addicted to the online experience. At its 1997 annual meeting in Chicago, the American Psychological Association labeled the problem "Pathological Internet Use." Naturally, the online community calls it **cyberaddiction.**

Cyberaddicts, about 10% of Internet users, average 38 hours a week online and typically get less than four hours of sleep because of their late-night connection. Most likely to get hooked are **newbies,** people new to the Net and inexperienced in its customs and conventions. Psychologists indicate that the Internet's addictive lure resides in:

- Its anonymity; users have more confidence when assuming a secret identity

- The sense of community that develops between communicating users, something many people may have difficulty finding in their real-world lives

- The ease with which online relationships can develop, often much greater than in the real world where such things as looks, social skill, and money can matter too much

- A sense of control; addicts can control this vast, sophisticated computer world much better than they can their everyday lives

- The fact that the Net's "bodiless state of communication enables users to explore altered states of being that foster emotions that (are) new and richly exciting," not unlike drugs, alcohol, and gambling, three more traditional addictions (Swartz, 1997, p. A1).

Cyberaddictive behavior can lead to isolation, depression, and, in some cases, destructive behavior, for example, committing fraud in securing access to keep the habit alive. Those with problems can visit any one of more than 60 online addiction counseling sites or the growing number of real-world addiction centers such as the one at the University of Maryland.

Commercialization of the Internet

The growing number of users and their apparent willingness to go online to find commercial information and buy products have been at the heart of the debate about the future of the Internet.

THE NATURE OF THE DEBATE

The Internet was developed, nurtured, and popularized by **hackers,** people interested in technology, information, and communication through computers. In *Road Warriors: Dreams and Nightmares Along the Information Highway* (1995), Daniel Burstein and David Kline argue that the Internet and business are poor partners. They compared the characteristics of the Internet to those of the companies that were increasingly using the Internet to conduct their business:

Internet Characteristics	Business Characteristics
Free	For profit
Egalitarian	Hierarchical
Decentralized	Systematized
Ad hoc	Planned
Open	Proprietary
Experimental	Pragmatic
Autonomous	Accountable
Anarchic	Organized

These two sets of characteristics and the values they represent, Burstein and Kline wrote, would inevitably clash. Internet hackers, geeks, and innovators have ironically become the "traditionalists" in this debate. These users fear that business will turn the information superhighway into an electronic shopping mall and that this commercialization of what was once the freest of communication technologies will lead to growing privatization and control. Commerce, they claim, cannot function amid chaos and disorder, but it is just that anarchy that has made the Internet so exciting. Nobody needs permission to get on or off the Internet. Nobody can tell a user what to say. Howard Rheingold (1994), prolific author of books and articles about new communication technologies, likens the online traditionalists to the original U.S. western "homesteaders," in danger of being driven out by the "railroad and cattle barons" of the communications industry.

Online traditionalists point to the history of television. In the medium's early stages, there were predictions and promises of a new medium of expression, education, and entertainment. Politics and political discourse, for example, would be transformed as people became aware of and involved in public affairs. The reality, the online traditionalists contend, is that television, with its commercial support, profit orientation, and lowest common denominator mentality, has cheapened politics and political discourse. Given this view, it is no surprise that a 1995 survey detailed in *Advertising Age* reported that two thirds of the U.S. adult respondents said "no" when asked whether advertising should be allowed on the Internet (Fawcett, 1996).

Defenders of online commerce argue, however, that the Internet will always be accessible and open. There is no spectrum scarcity to limit access, as there is in broadcasting, so the television analogy is inappropriate. In addition, because very small amounts of money are required for individuals to access and use the Internet, especially in contrast to the budget needed to start and run a broadcast or cable operation or a newspaper or magazine, the commercial orientation of those media will never fully overtake the Net. It is precisely this commercial potential of the Internet, they contend, that will keep the cost of access low and its value high. Regardless of the position taken, there is little doubt that the online world is increasingly characterized by commercialization (see the box "Commercializing the Net: The Green Card Incident").

Commercializing the Net: The Green Card Incident

In April 1994 husband and wife attorneys Laurence Canter and Martha Siegel decided to advertise online from their home office in Scottsdale, Arizona. They promoted their services via the Internet to aliens interested in acquiring a green card. To accomplish this, they created a computer program called Masspost. As the name would suggest, it mass e-mailed their commercial to *every* active bulletin board on the Net. Then it e-mailed it again. And again.

Users worldwide were furious over the couple's **spam**—a mass mailing of Internet messages to users whether they want them or not. (The term comes from the likely outcome of tossing a block of that canned meat into a fan.) The Internet community responded with thousands of **flames**—angry e-mail messages.

When the attorneys refused to cease their advertising, other users escalated their counterattacks. An Australian sent in 1,000 phony requests for information every day. Others threatened to visit the attorneys and inflict physical harm. Canter and Siegel's fax machine started to spit page after page of blank paper. They began to receive magazine subscriptions they had never ordered. A Norwegian user wrote a program that became known as Cancelbot, which chased the lawyers' ads around the Net, erasing them whenever it made contact. So heavy was the volume of e-mail to the Canter/Siegel computer address that within three days of their first Masspost, the host machine at their Internet provider had crashed 15 times. The provider, Internet Direct of Phoenix, canceled the lawyers' account.

Was it worth it? Canter and Siegel said yes. The ad generated more than $100,000 in new business, won them numerous television news and talk show interviews, and brought them to the attention of Harper-Collins, which published their book *How to Make a Fortune on the Information Superhighway.*

The attorneys' advertising brought the commercialization of the Internet into the cultural forum. What they did was legal. It was consistent with the no-holds-barred freedom of the Internet. It was technologically sophisticated—they'd written the Masspost program themselves. They should have been Internet heroes.

But to the Internet community they were villains, "the most hated couple in cyberspace," according to the July 25, 1994, *Time* magazine. They had abused the freedom of the Net. They had cheapened and commercialized the people's technology for their own selfish ends. After all, the people's taxes had paid for it. To the Internet community, Canter and Siegel's action may have been *legal,* but it was *unethical.*

What do you think? How would you have counseled Canter and Siegel if they had come to you with their idea? How would you have reacted had you been the recipient of their unwanted ads? What if you were someone in need of their services but, at the same time, a traditional, keep-the-Internet-free user? Would your attitude be different?

ONLINE ADVERTISING AND SELLING

Commerce has been part of the Internet almost from the start of its popular use. E-mail has long been seen as a way to deliver certain commercial services, for example, booking travel and hotel reservations, online banking, and ordering from online catalogues. But three developments have encouraged fuller commercial exploitation of the Net.

The first was the increase in the number of people who were online. Naturally, this increase made Internet advertising and sales more profitable for businesses. A second was the introduction and rapid acceptance of the World Wide Web. Exciting graphics, sound, and even motion could be used to promote and display products—a huge advance over the useful but static information available for e-mail commerce. The Web's ease of use and instant links to related products and ordering instructions and information allowed consumers to respond immediately to online advertising. The third development was the availability in the mid-1990s of trustworthy **encryption**—or coding and decoding—technologies that made the online use of credit and bank card numbers, addresses, social security numbers, and other sensitive information safer for both seller and buyer.

Online advertising and selling have not taken off as rapidly as critics feared or proponents hoped. Online advertising, as we saw in Chapter 10, is hampered by relatively unsophisticated animation and sound (compared to television). Many Internet users see advertising as cluttering the screen and delaying their access to the material they really want to see. Newspaper and magazine readers can quickly turn the page when confronted with unwanted advertising or, using a table of contents, they can go directly to the material they want to read. Unwanted online advertising surrounds much wanted material, and because its images and text are downloaded along with the wanted content, it slows access. Advances in computer technology that improve the quality of sound and images and speed their delivery will ease these situations for online advertisers and their customers.

Online selling is also hampered by a number of other factors. The first is the nature of online customers. Marketing studies indicate that "serious" Net and Web users tend to be male and highly educated. These folks tend not to be shoppers, online or otherwise. Because of their computer sophistication, they are the users who tend to be most disenchanted with the relative unsophistication of online commerce. A second problem is a lingering fear about security. In 1996 several companies, including Visa and Mastercard, agreed to a Net-wide encryption standard called Secure Electronic Transaction Protocol. Online sellers hope that this industry-assured security will allay consumers' concerns.

A third difficulty is the need for buyers to see, feel, and even smell many of the products they buy. Music, software, and airline tickets pose little problem for online buyers. But other products, such as clothes and cars, often require a real- rather than a virtual-world test. Online sellers believe that many price-sensitive shoppers will accept this disadvantage as the cost benefits of electronic shopping become better known.

Finally, there is the issue of trust. Online commerce is still in its infancy. People have little fear that their mail catalogue orders will not be shipped. They believe that the accounting will be accurate and that if the goods are not delivered, or if they are damaged or otherwise unsatisfactory, the catalogue dealer will make it right. This level of confidence is still lacking for many people in their online transactions. Trust, say advocates of online selling, will come with time.

The Internet and the First Amendment

By its very nature the Internet raises a number of important First Amendment issues. There is no central location, no on and off button for the Internet, making it difficult to control for those who want to do so. For free expression advocates, however, this freedom from control is the medium's primary strength. The anonymity of its users provides their expression—even the most radical, profane, and vulgar—great protection, giving voice to those who would otherwise be silenced. This anonymity, say advocates of strengthened Internet control, is a breeding ground for abuse. But opponents of control counter that the Net's affordability and ease of use make it our most democratic medium. Proponents of control argue that this freedom brings with it responsibilities that other media—and those who create their content—understand but that are ignored by many online. Internet freedom of expression issues, then, fall into two broad categories. The first is the Net's potential to make the First Amendment's freedom of the press guarantee a reality for greater numbers of people. The second is the problem of setting boundaries of control.

FREEDOM OF THE PRESS FOR WHOM?

Veteran *New Yorker* columnist A. J. Liebling, author of that magazine's "Wayward Press" feature and often called the "conscience of journalism," frequently argued that freedom of the press is guaranteed only to those who own one. Theoretically, anyone can own a broadcast outlet or cable television operation. But the number of outlets in any community is limited, and they are unavailable to all but the richest people and corporations. Theoretically, anyone can own a newspaper or magazine, but again

Using Media to Make a Difference

Fighting for Freedom: The Blue Ribbon Campaign

As the Telecommunications Act of 1996 worked its way toward passage, Internet users became concerned about one of its provisions, the Communications Decency Act (CDA). They saw it as an absolute threat to the fundamental freedom of expression provided by their beloved medium. It called for banning "indecent and obscene" material from the Net in the name of protecting children.

Internet and free speech advocates were outraged. Because the Net is open to everyone, adults as well as children, the true effect of the legislation, they argued, would be the total erasure of this content from the Internet. The Internet would be reduced from a medium of full and free expression to one carrying content suitable only for young children. It was, pure and simple, censorship.

To fight the bill, the Electronic Frontier Foundation (EFF), civil liberty groups, other grassroots organizations, and millions of users spontaneously joined in a massive, worldwide protest. Using the very medium under attack, they developed and publicized their offensive against the CDA. Web sites were converted so they displayed black backgrounds in symbolic protest. The programming code needed for the transformation was sent electronically and downloaded by users. A blue ribbon became the symbol for the protest, and opponents of the legislation were encouraged to place it on their pages. The ribbon graphic and necessary computer code for its display were sent online and free to anyone who wished to use them. The names, addresses, phone numbers, and e-mail addresses of U.S. legislators were dis-

the expense involved makes this an impossibility for most people. Newsletters, like a soap-box speaker on a street corner, are limited in reach, typically of interest to those who already agree with the message, and relatively unsophisticated when compared to the larger commercial media.

The Net, however, turns every user into a potential mass communicator (see the box "Fighting for Freedom: The Blue Ribbon Campaign"). Equally important, on the Internet every "publisher" is equal. The Web sites of the biggest government agency, the most powerful broadcast network, the newspaper with the highest circulation, the richest ad agencies and public relations firms, the most far-flung religion, and the lone user with an idea or cause sit figuratively side by side. Each is only as powerful as its ideas.

This chapter's opening vignette is based on the true story of 30-year-old Keith DeJarnet, a 1996 graduate of the multimedia program of Masters Institute, a California vocational school that annually trains 1,000 students in a number of professional programs. Dissatisfied with his education, unable to get a job, and lacking access to the very media where the Institute advertises, DeJarnet "broadcast" his own commercial detailing his experience and asking others who felt similarly to contact the appropriate state regulatory agencies at the addresses he gave. The Net was his only avenue of public expression. Newspapers and broadcast stations are legally permitted to deny advertising space or time to anyone they wish. It is their First Amendment right. As Liebling would say, they own the presses.

tributed to millions of users with instructions to let them know how they felt about the CDA.

Congress wasn't swayed. The House and Senate both passed the bill, although there was significant opposition from many members, both conservatives and liberals. On February 8, 1996, President Bill Clinton signed the controversial law, only to have a unanimous decision of the Supreme Court declare it unconstitutional in June 1997.

The campaign had been unsuccessful in persuading U.S. legislators, but to the extent that the Supreme Court responds to public opinion, perhaps it did work. Yet those who became and remain part of the Blue Ribbon Campaign for Online Freedom of Speech, Press, and Association prefer to believe that it was the law's obvious unconstitutionality, not their efforts, that killed it.

Nonetheless, the campaign remains a powerful online movement for free expression, putting up the fourth most visited Web page in the world, *http://www.eff.org/blueribbon.html.*

The Blue Ribbon Campaign

Within three days of the launch of his site, the school filed a libel suit against DeJarnet. But soon after, a judge threw the case out of court, writing: "The thrust of the Web page endeavors to facilitate petitions to the government. The court finds that there has been an adequate showing that the Web page did involve a public issue." DeJarnet's attorney added, "Masters is a multimillion-dollar corporation. Keith DeJarnet is a poor working stiff" (as cited in Jordan, 1997, p. 1B).

Web sites like DeJarnet's are sometimes dismissed as **gripe sites**—pages designed to counter or challenge another person or institution, typically one having more power than the site's creator. The motives for their launch range from a desire to change the world to the need to get even. For example, worldwide hamburger, marketing, and advertising giant McDonald's is challenged by McSpotlight *(http://www.envirolink.org/mcspotlight/)*. The amount and sources of outside income of political candidates are tracked by the Center for Public Integrity *(http://www.essential.org/cpi/)*. Once-secret tobacco company documents and other antismoking data are published online by the Tobacco Control Archives *(http://galen.library.ucsf.edu/tobacco/)*.

CONTROLLING INTERNET EXPRESSION

Freedom, or more specifically the abuse of freedom, is behind the argument for greater control of the Internet. The very same medium that can empower users who wish to challenge those more powerful than themselves can also be used to lie and cheat. The Internet does not distinguish between true and false, biased and objective, trivial and important. Once misinformation has been loosed on the Net, it is almost impossible to catch and correct it (Figure 14–3).

For example, in 1997 America Online (AOL) was forced to fight Net-spread rumors that its software allowed its employees to spy on its customers. The e-mail, sent to millions of addresses, was signed "A former AOL employee" and claimed that AOL employees can access users' hard drives and snoop at or steal whatever information they wished. Company and Internet security experts called it a hoax, but only after it was read by people around the world.

Individuals can also be victimized by cybermisinformation. In September 1997, a photo purportedly showing Princess Diana's crushed body in the Paris car wreck that took her life was posted on the Web. Although obviously a fraud—the supposed rescue workers and their vehicles were unlike any in France—75,000 users a day accessed the site, and several French and Italian newspapers and broadcasters published and aired the photo.

A person need not be famous to be the target of online lying. In 1996 the FBI was forced to investigate an e-mail offer of online child pornography sent to millions of users under the name of an unwitting Silicon Valley computer scientist. Someone was using the Net in an attempt to destroy the scientist's reputation. In 1997 Los Angeles attorney Russell

Doonesbury
G. B. TRUDEAU

Figure 14–3 Rumors, lies, and innuendo spread far, wide, and fast on the Internet. Doonesbury ©1997 G. B. Trudeau. Reprinted with permission of Universal Press Syndicate. All Rights Reserved.

Allyn was victimized by someone involved in a dispute with one of his clients. Thousands of insulting and abusive e-mails were sent under Allyn's name to people with whom he does business. The calls of complaint to his office closed his business for days.

Lies have always been part of human interaction; the Internet only gives them greater reach. There is little that government can do to control this abuse. Legal remedies already exist in the form of libel laws and prosecution for fraud. Users can help by teaching themselves to be more attentive to return addresses and by ignoring messages that are sent anonymously or that have suspicious origins. There is an Internet-based solution as well. Computer security specialists at the U.S. Department of Energy maintain a Web site designed to track and debunk online misinformation *(http://ciac.llnl.gov/ciac/CIACHoaxes.html)*.

PORNOGRAPHY ON THE WORLD WIDE WEB

Most efforts at controlling the Internet are aimed at indecent or pornographic Web content. We saw in Chapter 13 that indecent and pornographic expression is protected. The particular concern with the Internet, therefore, is shielding children.

Although the Communications Decency Act has been declared unconstitutional, another portion of the massive 1996 telecommunications law does survive, the Child Pornography Act. It forbids online transmission of any image that "appears to be of a minor engaging in sexually explicit conduct." Proponents argue that the impact of child porn on the children involved, as well as on society, warrants this legislation. Opponents argue that child pornography *per se* is already illegal, regardless of the medium. Therefore they see this law as an unnecessary and overly broad intrusion into freedom of expression on the Net. In August 1997 a U.S. federal court upheld the law.

The primary battleground, then, is in the realm of protecting children from otherwise legal content. The Net, by virtue of its openness and accessibility, raises particular concerns. Children's viewing of sexually explicit material on cable television can theoretically be controlled by parents. Moreover, viewers must specifically order this content and typically pay an additional fee for it. The purchase of sexually explicit videos, books, and magazines is controlled by laws regulating vendors. But computers sit in homes, schools, and libraries. Children are encouraged to explore their possibilities. A search for the novel *Little Women,* for example, can turn up *"Asian Sexy Adult Video . . . Super Hard-core: So Obscene. So Dirty"* (as cited in Early, 1997, p. 10).

Proponents of stricter control of the Net liken the availability of smut on the Internet to a bookstore or library that allows porn to sit side-by-side with books that children *should* be reading. In actual, real-world bookstores and libraries, professionals, whether book retailers or librarians, apply their professional judgment in selecting and locating material, ideally striving for appropriateness and balance. Children are the beneficiaries of their professional judgment. No such professional selection or evaluation is applied to the Internet. Opponents of control accept the bookstore/library analogy but argue that, as troubling as the online proximity of all types of content may be, it is a true example of the freedom guaranteed by the First Amendment.

One solution is technology. Filtering software, such as Net Nanny, can be set to block access to Web sites by title and by the presence of specific words and images (see the box "Rating the Web"). Few free speech advocates are troubled by filters on home computers, but they do see them as problematic when used on more public machines, for example, in schools and libraries. They argue that software that can filter sexual content can also be set to screen out birth control information, religious sites, and discussions of racism. Virtually any content can be blocked. This, they claim, denies other users—adults and mature teenagers, for example—their freedoms.

COPYRIGHT (INTELLECTUAL PROPERTY OWNERSHIP)

Another freedom of expression issue that takes on a special nature on the Internet is copyright. Copyright protection is designed to ensure that those who create content are financially compensated for their work (Chapter 13). The assumption is that more "authors" will create more content if assured of monetary compensation from those who use it. When the content is tangible (books, movies, videotapes, magazines, CDs), authorship and use are relatively easy to identify. But in the cyberworld, things become a bit more complex. John Perry Barlow (1996), a cofounder of the Electronic Frontier Foundation, explains the situation:

> The riddle is this: If our property can be infinitely reproduced and instantaneously distributed all over the planet without cost, without our knowledge, without its even leaving our possession, how can we protect it? How are we going to get paid for the work we do with our minds? And, if we can't get paid, what will assure the continued creation and distribution of such work? (p. 148)

Technically, copyright rules apply to the Internet as they do to other media. Material on the Net, even on electronic bulletin boards, belongs to the author, so its use, other than fair use, requires permission and possibly payment. The problem is that because material on the Internet is not tangible, it is easily, freely, and privately copied. This renders it difficult, if not impossible, to police those who do copy.

Another confounding issue is that new and existing material is often combined with other existing material to create even "newer" content. This makes it difficult to assign authorship. If a user borrows some text from one source, combines it with images from a second, surrounds both with a background graphic from a third, and adds music sampled from many others, where does authorship reside?

To deal with these issues, the Clinton Administration in 1995 established the Working Group on Intellectual Property Rights, a committee, according to some critics, that was designed to ensure the extension of copyright to the Internet on behalf of existing copyright holders. It offered several solutions to the dilemma:

- Development of "copyright management systems," sophisticated software that would allow copyright holders to search users' hard drives for unauthorized material.

- Outlawing decryption devices and software designed for the unauthorized translation of materials that have been encrypted, that is, coded at the source to be readable only by an end-user with appropriate decoding software.

- Holding online service providers such as AOL responsible for the copyright infringement of their customers.

Groups committed to maximizing freedom of expression on the Internet see these controls as an example of the **commodification of information**—making information a tangible, salable thing. They find fault with all three solutions. They argue that the first is an invasion of privacy that is not warranted by the scope of the problem. The second allows encryption companies to become "information monopolies," controlling who can see what for what price. The third, in effect, makes Internet providers "copyright cops" rather than companies with which users do business.

What the debate over Internet copyright represents—like concern about controlling content that children can access, commercialization of the Net, and efforts to limit troublesome or challenging expression—is a clash of fundamental values that has taken on added nuance with the coming of computer networks. We will return to this situation in greater detail in Chapter 15.

DEVELOPING MEDIA LITERACY SKILLS
Using E-Mail Effectively

Our previous literacy discussions focused on "reading" content that is received. But because the Net's unique nature allows people to be both source and audience, this chapter's discussion must deal with the development of media literacy skills for both senders and receivers.

Media Echoes

Rating the Web

We've seen how the film and television industries (Chapters 6 and 8) developed self-regulatory rating schemes to alert audiences about the nature of their content. In both instances voluntary adoption of these codes was a response designed to forestall more overt government regulation. What happened in the film industry in 1968 and in television programming in 1996 is echoed in the online world.

In June 1997, when the Supreme Court unanimously struck down the Communications Decency Act, people inside and outside the Internet industry, as well as members of the Clinton Administration, began the call for a Web rating system.

Most proponents of a Web rating system see technology, in the form of filtering software, as an appropriate solution to their worries. They see it as similar to the television content ratings system, which is tied to the blocking technology of the V-chip. Opponents of rating Web content call these filters **censorware**, but given that individual users can control the level of filtering they deem appropriate for their own households, there is less industry and user resistance to this screening method than there was to that used for television.

Rating proponents envision two forms of filtering—existing rating schemes and specific interest group ratings. As examples of the latter, the National Organization for Women can develop its own ratings scheme, the Catholic Diocese of St. Louis its own, and the Moral Majority its own. Software already exists for setting individual labeling and filtering codes.

Among preexisting filtering software, the three most utilized are the Recreational Software Advisory Council on the Internet (RSAC), SafeSurf, and Net Shepherd.

RSAC is a nonprofit organization that asks Web sites to rate themselves on a scale from 0 to 4 for tolerance of sex, nudity, strong language, and violence. The higher the number, the more of each type of content is

WHEN YOU ARE A SENDER

Like the Internet that carries it, e-mail is free and open, but communication, online or otherwise, has ramifications. Users often err in allowing the ease of use and *apparent* impersonal nature of e-mail to affect their normal ways of communicating. E-mail, although delivered digitally through an unimaginable number of technological links, is *not* impersonal. When you sign it, it's *yours*. It reflects you—who you are, and what you think of the recipients. To avoid troublesome miscommunication, use care in creating e-mail messages:

1. Before you begin writing, *consider the destination*. Issues of formality, amount of supporting explanation, evidence or documentation for arguments, and other content issues should be determined, in advance, by an understanding of who will read your message—for example, friend or foe, superior, peer, or subordinate.

2. The Net is open and free. Before you write, *anticipate unintended readership*. Bosses can read people's e-mail at work. Even in nonwork settings, without your permission or knowledge recipients can transfer your words to others with one stroke of a key. These others might be people you wish had never seen what you have to say.

present. Users set their own screening levels on the RSAC-provided software.

SafeSurf is a commercial company that monitors a self-rating system that labels sites by suitable age ranges as well as by the amount of content such as nudity and drug use. It has rated more than 50,000 sites.

Net Shepherd is a search engine-based filtering system. It periodically surveys Web site users to establish ratings in four categories of the sites they access: Maturity Level (for example, adult, general age, child), Quality (up to four stars), Type (news, sports, music), and Trusted/Untrusted (if the rating applies to all pages of the site, the rating is Trusted; if not, it is Untrusted). Net Shepherd currently rates more than 500,000 sites.

The use of ratings, labels, and filters is in its infancy, but most of the industry is behind the movement. Internet Explorer (from Microsoft) and Netscape Communicator already include a label reading capability in their browser software. Search engines Yahoo, Excite, Lycos, and Infoseek have committed to adding the feature to their tools.

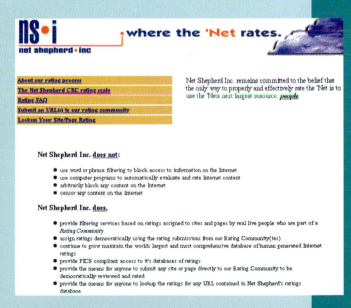

Net Shepherd is one of a number of free web content rating schemes on the net.

3. *Employ courtesy.* If you would not insult a recipient to his or her face, don't do it online. The distance between you and your recipients is nonexistent in the cyberworld because messages are delivered instantaneously. However, there is no instant, direct feedback that allows you to adjust when you sense miscommunication. Craft your messages as if they were face-to-face conversations.

Face-to-face conversations benefit from the participants' ability to see and hear nuance—a raised eyebrow, a sarcastic tone of voice, different inflections. E-mail offers no such convenience. So e-mail users have developed a system for expressing emotional nuance in their communication using **smileys**—graphic representations of emotion or other conversational nuance. Just ask your browser to search on "smileys."

4. *Use care when producing sensitive content.* If you must criticize, confront, evaluate, or otherwise commit important and potentially problematic content to the Net, take a breather. For example, type your message, but print it out and read it in hard copy before you send it. This can be a form of "counting to 10." It can also allow you to read, reread, and edit your words on paper, which many people find more natural than doing so on-screen.

5. *Focus on the task.* E-mail's simplicity of use creates the danger of easily made or thoughtless mistakes. When you are creating e-mail messages, make that your only activity. A mispunched key, for example, can send messages to the wrong places. Remember, a problematic face-to-face conversation can be instantly corrected. E-mail lives in people's in-boxes for a long time and can also be forwarded to others.

6. *The rules of grammar still apply.* Many users think of e-mail as a way to send off quick notes, saving more important messages for face-to-face communication or letters. But your e-mail represents you. Even a note composed of only a few lines, if it contains some misspelling or a comma or two dropped or out of place, can be taken as a sign of a careless person, one unconcerned about how he or she appears, one unwilling to extend the respect of a well-crafted message to the recipient.

7. *When interpersonal problems arise, get offline.* Many users hide behind their e-mail. Especially when miscommunication leads to confrontation, hashing things out online (where nuance, irony, humor, and other tools of good interpersonal communication are sometimes wasted) may not be in your best interest. At work, walk down the hall and visit the other person. With friends, or where distance intervenes, pick up the phone. Older technologies like the shoe and the telephone do have some advantages.

8. *Don't be a spammer.* It's simply too easy to send unnecessary copies of your message to everyone in your dorm, at your place of work, or on a preconstructed distribution list. Use discretion. Who *needs* to get your e-mail? They should be the primary recipients. If you insist on sending to others who *might* find the information interesting, indicate "FYI," "spam," or other notation on the subject line to alert them to its low priority.

WHEN YOU ARE A RECEIVER

Users can never be certain of the level of technological, grammatical, or interpersonal communication skill or sophistication possessed by those who communicate with them online. E-mail receiving, then, also requires development of certain skills.

1. *Avoid knee-jerk reactions.* We've already seen that despite its benefits, electronic communication lacks many of the factors that make more traditional forms of communication flexible and less open to error. Accept the fact that not all e-mail senders are as skilled as you.

2. *Don't be a slave to e-mail.* Instant, virtually no-cost communication from friends and colleagues around the corner and around the world makes e-mail fascinating, and for some, as we've seen, possibly addicting. Check your e-mail only once or twice a day. Respond in a timely fashion to the most important messages, saving the others for more thoughtful response.

3. *Use the technology.* Several e-mail managing systems exist that can sort or even delete incoming messages based on specified keywords or locations. Claris Emailer, Microsoft's Inbox, Cyberdog, and Eudora are the better known products. These allow you to establish priorities for what gets read and when, saving time and patience.

4. *Use care when subscribing* to lists or joining discussion groups and chat lines. As valuable as they are, they mark you as someone interested in a given issue or topic. You may—in fact, you most likely will—become the recipient of many more messages than you had anticipated once you identify yourself in a particular way online.

5. *Separate personal and work e-mail.* The ease of the Net often masks its intrusive power. Your employer most likely will not welcome the use of your work time to send personal messages. Your home life will be richer and less stressful if you apply the same standard of separation there.

Chapter Review

The first electronic digital computer was developed during World War II to break secret code. The first full-service electronic computer, introduced in 1946, was ENIAC. Computers quickly made their way into U.S. business and commercial life, largely through the efforts of IBM.

The Internet is the product of the military's desire to maintain U.S. defenses after a nuclear attack. Decentralization was the key to allowing communication to continue no matter where an attack occurred. The solution, then, was a network of computer networks—the Internet. Once personal or micro computers entered the picture, the Internet became accessible to millions of non-institutional users. Its capabilities include e-mail, mailing lists, USENET, FTP, Archie, Gopher and Veronica, WAIS, and Telnet. But its fastest growing application is the World Wide Web. The Web's popularity is fueled by its ease of use.

It is difficult to accurately measure the number of Internet users. Estimates range from 20 million to 200 million. Typically, the average Net user is relatively well off and highly educated. Some users, however, can become addicted to the Net.

The growing number of people online has inevitably led to efforts to advertise on and sell by Internet. This commercialization of the online world is greeted with disdain by traditional Net users, who fear that their medium will lose its freedom and energy to corporate takeover. Online advertising and selling, however, are not progressing as fast as proponents had hoped, due to a number of factors including relatively unsophisticated moving images and sound, intrusiveness of ads, consumer fears about the security of credit card and other sensitive information, and lack of buyer trust in this new way of doing business.

The Net's nature also raises a number of First Amendment issues. It transforms every user into a potential mass communicator, making freedom of the press a reality for everyone. But critics contend that this freedom is often abused because individuals are not bound by the kinds of economic and legal restraints that tend to impose responsibility on larger, commercially oriented media. The major free expression battles in cyberspace revolve around containing online pornography, protecting children from inappropriate content, and protecting copyright. None is easily solved, but improved technology may provide some solutions.

Media literacy skills for computer networks are different from those for more traditional media. Because the Internet allows people to be both sender and audience, literacy applies to users' construction as well as reception of content. This fundamental alteration in the way we have traditionally considered the mass communication process—where media organizations and audiences occupy well-defined and mutually exclusive parts of the model—is the focus of the next chapter.

Questions for Review

1. What is the importance of each of the following people to the development of the computer: Blaise Pascal, Wilhelm Schickard, Gottfried Leibnitz, Charles Babbage, John Atanasoff, John Mauchly, and John Presper Eckert?
2. What were the contributions of Paul Baran, Bill Gates, Steve Jobs, and Steven Wozniak to the development and popularization of the Internet?
3. What are digital computers, micro computers, and mainframe computers?
4. What services or capabilities are offered by the Internet?
5. What factors have led to the popularity of the World Wide Web?
6. What factors make the Internet potentially addicting?
7. What are the differing positions on the commercialization of the Internet?
8. What factors have delayed the success of online advertising and selling?
9. What are the differing positions on Internet copyright?
10. Both proponents and opponents of greater control over Internet content see advances in technology as one solution to their disagreement. What are they? How do they work?

Questions for Critical Thinking and Discussion

1. Are you online? How often do you go online? How well do you fit the basic demographic picture of the typical online user? If you are dissimilar, in what ways?
2. Do you believe that commercialization of the Internet is a worthy price to pay for its continued success and diffusion? Explain.
3. Have you ever shopped online? Describe the experience.
4. What controls should be placed on gripe sites, if any? Do you see them, by whatever name, as a way of distributing power in the culture between traditional media outlets and ordinary individuals? Why, or why not?
5. Compare your e-mail habits before you read this chapter to the hints offered in the media literacy section. How literate a sender and receiver are you?

Important Resources

Aspray, W., & Campbell-Kelly, M. (1997). *Computer: A history of the information machine.* **New York: Basic Books.** A thorough examination of the technological and entrepreneurial successes in the development of the computer. The book also offers interesting histories of other facets of the computer world, such as inside looks at companies like IBM and Microsoft and applications like the Web.

Bettig, R. V. (1997). The enclosure of cyberspace. *Critical Studies in Mass Communication, 14,* **138–157.** Although this is a serious, scholarly examination of commercialization, commodification, and concentration of ownership in cyberspace, the writing makes it accessible for most students. Bettig discusses these phenomena in terms of their relevance to mass communication theory.

InfoWorld. Calling itself "the voice of enterprise computing," this magazine's orientation is clearly toward people working in the computer industry. Despite (or as a result of) that, it is a good source for finding out what's next in both hardware, software, and networking.

internet world. This slick magazine calls itself "the Internet Authority." It offers monthly articles on Web development, Internet business, and other Internet-related news. Aimed more at companies that do business online than at everyday users, it is still a valuable resource for users.

the net. Continuing the trend of Internet magazines to ignore upper-case letters, this self-proclaimed "ultimate Internet guide" is slick, readable, and targeted at users.

Shenk, D. (1997). *Data smog: Surviving the information glut.* **New York: Harper Edge.** About the people and societies of the information age, this book focuses on the impact of too much data (information overload) on the culture.

St. Jude, Sirius, R. U., & Nagel, B. (1995). *Cyberpunk handbook: The real cyberpunk fakebook.* **New York: Random House.** Often funny, often self-critical, this handbook for making one's way in the world of cyberpunk offers a nice look into the values and mores of those who live to be online.

Strate, L., Jacobson, R., & Gibson, S. B. (1996). *Communication and cyberspace.* **Cresskill, NJ: Hampton Press.** Some of the articles in this collection of essays are quite sophisticated, but several should be appropriate (though challenging) for interested students. Topics range from who will control cyberspace to the debate over the direction of the information superhighway.

WEB Magazine. As the name makes clear, this magazine serves those who regularly surf the Web. Graphically interesting and well written, it can appeal to newbies and hard core cyberpunks.

Wired. Either "the hottest magazine in computing" or a jumbled mess of self-aggrandizing ruminations by hackers with attitude, depending on who's doing the describing. Worth a look, nonetheless. Its essays on free speech issues are particularly provocative.

Internet Information Web Sites

Internet statistics	*http://www.asiresearch.com*
	http://www.mids.org/mids
The Electronic Frontier Foundation (Internet freedom issues)	*http://www.eff.org*
AC Nielsen Internet Advertising Marketing Research	*http://www.nielsen.com.au/AdAudit*
Internet parent guide	*http://www.ed.gov/pubs/parents/internet*
Cyberaddiction	*http://www.unc.edu/courses/jomc191/addiction/interadd.html*
	http://www.albany.edu/library/internet/addiction.html

The Changing
Global Village

William Gibson and Marshall McLuhan have been two of your intellectual heroes ever since you started college. Gibson is the "Godfather of Cyberspace" and author of *Neuromancer* and *Johnny Mnemonic,* and McLuhan is the author of *Understanding Media: The Extensions of Man* and originator of some of your favorite expressions like "hot and cool media" and "the medium is the message." But now, as you see it, Gibson and McLuhan are in conflict.

For example, another of McLuhan's famous expressions is "the global village." You understood this to mean that as media "shrink" the world people will become increasingly involved in one another's lives. As people come to know more about others who were once separated from them by distance, they will form a new, beneficial relationship, a global village.

Then you saw Gibson interviewed on television. His vision of technology's impact on the globe was anything but optimistic. He said, "We're moving toward a world where all the consumers under a certain age will . . . identify more with their consumer status or with the products they consume than they would with an antiquated notion of nationality. We're increasingly interchangeable" (as cited in Trench, 1990).

Maybe you were wrong about McLuhan's ideas. He did his influential writing a long time ago. Where was it you read about the global village? in a magazine interview? You look it up at the library to confirm that you understood him correctly. There it is, just as you thought: "The human tribe can become truly one family and man's consciousness can be freed from the shackles of mechanical culture and enabled to roam the cosmos" ("A Candid Conversation," 1969, p. 158).

McLuhan's global village is an exciting place, a good place for people enjoying increased contact and increased involvement with one another aided by electronic technology. Gibson's nationless world isn't about involving ourselves in one another's lives and experiences. It's about electronic technology turning us into indistinguishable nonindividuals, rallying around products. We are united by buyable things, identifying not with others who share our common culture but with those who share some common goods. McLuhan sees the new communication technologies as expanding our experiences. Gibson sees them more negatively. You respect and enjoy the ideas of both thinkers. How can you reconcile the disagreement you've uncovered?

In this chapter we revisit many themes already discussed, but we do so in terms of their potential impact on the future of mass communication and the cultures that use it. McLuhan's idea of the global village, as well as several of his other notable conceptions, provide the basis for our discussion of the effects of developing technologies. As the mass communication process changes, so too will the manner in which people develop personal identities. Privacy takes on new meaning, as does democracy. We study the technology and information gaps, as well as the difference between information, knowledge, and understanding. These have important implications for technology-assisted self-governance.

We then visit other neighborhoods in the global village. As we do, we investigate the different normative theories that guide the media systems of other countries. Then we take a deeper look at two neighboring cultures that have developed markedly different media systems, Japan and China. The debate surrounding cultural imperialism is also reviewed.

Finally, our discussion of improving our media literacy takes the form of a primer for personal decision making and action in our increasingly media-saturated world.

Changes in the Mass Communication Process

In Chapter 2 we saw how concentration of ownership, globalization, audience fragmentation, and the erosion of distinctions among media were influencing the nature of the mass communication process. Each redefines the relationship between audiences and media industries. For example, we have discussed the impacts of concentration on newspaper readership; of globalization on the type and quality of films available to moviegoers; of audience fragmentation on the variety of channel choices for television viewers; and of the lack of distinction among media and how that influences the amount of advertising people see.

The Internet is different from these more traditional media. Rather than changing the relationship between audiences and industries, the Net changes the *definition* of the different components of the process and, as a result, changes their relationship. As we discussed in the last chapter, for example, a single individual can communicate online with as large an audience as can the giant, multinational corporation that produces a network television program. That corporation fits our earlier definition of a mass communication source—a large, hierarchically structured organization—but the Internet user does not. Feedback in mass communication is traditionally described as inferential and delayed, but online feedback can be, and very often is, immediate and direct. It is more similar to feedback in interpersonal communication than to feedback in mass communication.

This redefinition of the elements of the mass communication process is refocusing attention on issues such as privacy, responsibility, and democracy, which we have already discussed in terms of other, more traditional media. It has also rekindled interest in the writing and ideas of Marshall McLuhan.

THE DOUBLE EDGE OF TECHNOLOGY

The solution to the McLuhan versus Gibson dilemma in the opening vignette is one of perspective. McLuhan was writing and thinking in the relative youth of the electronic media. When *Understanding Media* was published in 1964, television had just become a mass medium, the personal computer wasn't even a dream, and Paul Baran was still envisioning ARPANET.

Gibson, writing much later in the age of electronic media, was commenting from a more experienced position and after observing real-world evidence. McLuhan was optimistic because he was speculating on what electronic media *could do*. Gibson is pessimistic because he is commenting on what he had seen electronic media *doing*.

Still, neither visionary is completely right nor completely wrong. Technology alone, even the powerful electronic media that fascinated both, cannot create new worlds or new ways of seeing them. *We* use technology to do these things. This, as we discussed briefly in Chapter 2, is why technology is a double-edged sword. Its power—for good and for bad—resides in us. The same aviation technology that we use to visit relatives halfway around the world can also be used to deliver bombs to our cities and theirs. The same communication technologies used to create a truly global village can be used to dehumanize and standardize the people who live in it.

McLUHAN'S RENAISSANCE

Marshall McLuhan's ideas are in vogue again. The Canadian English professor was at the center of the early intellectual debate over electronic media. His books—especially *The Gutenberg Galaxy* (1962), *Understanding Media: The Extensions of Man* (1964), and *The Medium Is the Massage* (1967)—generated heated comment and earned McLuhan much criticism.

The books that put Marshall McLuhan at the center of the debate over electronic communication.

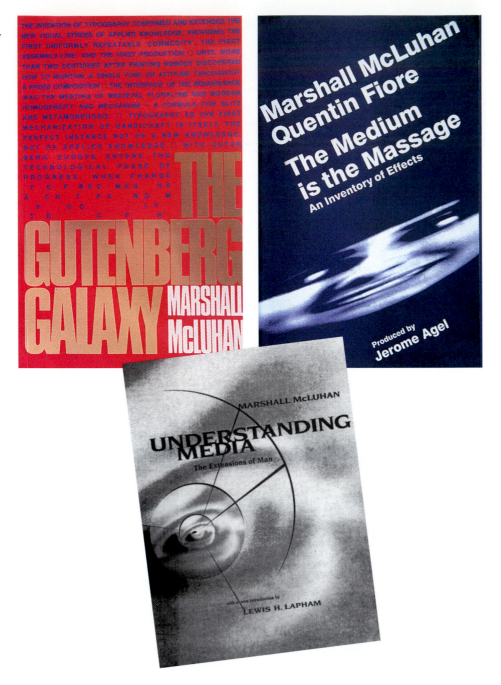

His ideas satisfied almost no one. Critics from the humanities castigated him for wasting his time on something as frivolous as television. True culture exists in "real" literature, they argued. McLuhan fared just as badly among mass communication theorists. Social scientists committed to the idea of limited media effects (Chapter 12) simply disagreed with his view of powerful media technologies, however optimistic. Others who were convinced of media's potential negative influence dismissed him as blindly

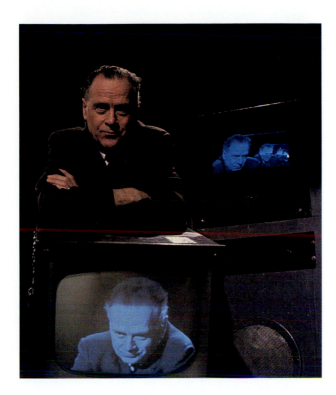

Marshall McLuhan

in love with technology and overly speculative. Social scientists demanded scientific verification of McLuhan's ideas. Labeled the "High Priest of Popcult," the "Metaphysician of Media," the "Oracle of the Electronic Age," McLuhan may simply have been ahead of his time.

What has returned McLuhan to the forefront of the cultural discussion surrounding the mass media is the Internet. McLuhan's ideas resonate with those who believe the new medium can fulfill his optimistic vision of an involved, connected global village. Those who think the potential of the Internet, like that of television before it, will never fulfill McLuhan's predictions are forced to explain their reasoning in terms of his ideas. McLuhan is back, and, as before, he is controversial. *Wired* magazine, the self-proclaimed "Bible of Cyberspace," has anointed McLuhan its patron saint. But as we saw in the opening vignette, not everyone in the cyberworld trusts the technology as much as he did.

The Global Village Many concepts survive McLuhan's 1980 death and serve as his legacy. None is more often quoted than the **global village,** the idea that the new communication technologies will permit people to become increasingly involved in one another's lives. Skeptics point out that McLuhan, with this notion, reveals his unrealistic, utopian infatuation with technology. But McLuhan himself never said all would be tranquil in the global village. Yes, he did believe that electronic media would permit "the human tribe" to become "one family." But he also realized that families fight:

> There is more diversity, less conformity under a single roof in any family than there is with the thousands of families in the same city. The more you create village conditions, the more discontinuity and division and diversity. The global village absolutely insures maximal disagreement on all points. (McLuhan & Stearn, 1967, p. 279)

Involvement does not mean harmony, but it does mean an exchange of ideas. As McLuhan said, the global village is "a world in which people encounter each other in depth all the time" (p. 280).

Media as Extensions of Our Bodies Central to McLuhan's view of how media and cultures interact is the idea that media do not *bring* the world to us but rather permit us to experience the world with a scope and depth otherwise impossible. Media, then, are extensions of our bodies. Just as clothes are an extension of our skin, permitting us to wander further from our warm caves into the cold world; just as the automobile is an extension of our feet, allowing us to travel farther than we could ever walk; television extends our vision and hearing, and computers extend our central nervous system. With television we can see and hear around the world, beyond the galaxy, into the future, and into the past. Computers process, sort, categorize, reconfigure, and clarify. McLuhan's message here is not unlike Carey's (1975) ritual view of mass communication. Communication technologies do not deliver or transmit information; they fundamentally alter the relationship between people and their world, encouraging us to construct new meanings for the things we encounter with and through them.

The Medium Is the Massage What McLuhan wants us to understand with this now-famous slogan is that, to a large degree, the content of a given medium is not as central to its impact as is its simple existence. For example, many families eat their evening meal while watching television. What they are watching is of secondary importance to the fact that the television is the center of their attention, and they are not talking with one another. In this instance, the medium—not its content—has changed the meaning of family communication and of dinner time. Similarly, it does not matter what chat rooms Internet users visit; when they are visiting their virtual friends, they are not visiting friends in the real world. The medium has changed the nature of friendship, communication, and community.

Hot and Cool Media The concept of hot and cool media has also received much attention, even serving as the thematic core for the 1969 movie *Medium Cool*. In it, a television cameraman moves with cool detachment through the turbulent 1968 antiwar protests and riots. McLuhan would agree that director Haskell Wexler got it right; television is a cool medium. For McLuhan **hot media** are high in definition—they provide a lot of information, leaving the consumer with little to do other than interpret what is presented. **Cool media,** in contrast, require the consumer to "fill in the blanks" to make meaning. Because they are cool, the consumer must make

Hot and cool media. Television is cool. Because viewers have to provide their own "heat," its pictures are more involving than the "hot" words on the printed page. Televised images of a besieged Betty Currie earned Independent Counsel Kenneth Starr far more criticism than did newspaper accounts—and presidential complaints—about his conduct during his 1998 investigation of alleged improprieties by the Clinton White House.

the heat. McLuhan says newspapers are hot and television is cool. Given his definition, this seems to make sense. Cartoons are cool as well. But McLuhan classifies movies and radio as hot. Critics find fault not so much with the idea of different media demanding different levels of engagement on the part of their audiences but with McLuhan's classifications of the different media. They see them as too personal and idiosyncratic.

The Rearview Mirror; Living in Bonanza-land When television came along, rather than finding new functions for this amazing technology—for example, redefining news and journalism or expanding the reach of expression for typically disenfranchised groups—our culture, according to McLuhan, looked in the rearview mirror. We saw what was being done by existing media and, because we are comfortable living in Bonanza-land (referring to the old western television show where things were always simple and understandable), we limited television to what we were accustomed to, radio (albeit with pictures) and movies (albeit in the home). Cable television, rather than changing the form and function of television as we knew it, has evolved (or not evolved) into more sports, more movies, more news, more sitcoms, more commercials, and more re-runs. Those who fear for the future of the Internet, the "traditionalists" of Chapter 14, worry that the Net and the Web will become "more television"; that is, they will simply offer more of what we are accustomed to on the tube—more commercials, more sex, more violence, and more lowest common denominator content.

Not everyone agrees with McLuhan's perspectives on media, yet they are being freshly discussed and debated, even though he presented them nearly 40 years ago. McLuhan's ideas provide the background for our own look at the global village. First, we discuss issues that relate to our immediate neighborhood, the United States. Then we look at other parts of the village, geographically distant countries facing many of the same challenges.

Reconceptualizing Life in the Global Village

What happens to people in the global village? Does greater involvement with others mean a loss of privacy? What becomes of personal identity when it is built and extended through media? If national identities are disappearing, what of cultural and ethnic identity? These are only a few of the questions confronting us as we attempt to find the right balance between the good and the bad that comes from the new communication technologies.

PERSONAL IDENTITY

As we discussed in Chapter 1, people develop their identities in part through interaction with their culture and with others in it. If that interaction changes, then so too must the identities it fosters. The question, then, is what kind of identities people can build when new communication technologies infinitely extend the senses—sight, speech, and hearing—once used in more traditional interaction with the culture and others in it? Let's look at one example from the Internet.

A **MUD** (multi-user domain) is an online, virtual "community" where users are encouraged to create their own identities, which then interact singly or in groups with other virtual citizens of that community. Individuals create their own look. They can appear tall, short, beautiful, or with the head of a lion and a mane of snakes. They also create their own rooms or spaces in the MUD. Users can then invite others into their virtual homes, condos, offices, or backyards. In MUDs, identity is constructed through communication with others who are always unseen (except as their MUD alter egos) and most often unknown. The purpose of the MUD is to allow people to experiment with their identities, to shed old ones and try out new ones.

MUDs are virtual environments expressly designed for the creation of virtual identities. But they also serve as a metaphor for the way computer networks allow modern people to build their actual identities, according

Figure 15–1 Despite widespread enthusiasm for today's computer network technologies, some people *are* stopping to ponder how these changes will affect our experiences and ourselves.

to MIT sociology professor Sherry Turkle (1995). Turkle writes of online "worlds without origin," places that "allow people to generate experiences, relationships, identities, and living spaces that arise only through interaction with technology" (p. 21). Rather than experiencing these things in everyday, actual environments, we experience them in a new environment, one characterized by "eroding boundaries between the real and virtual, the animate and inanimate, the unitary and multiple self" (p. 10).

Whether in a MUD, in a chat room, using e-mail, or in an interactive Web site conversation with an author, politician, or movie star, users are experiencing life—their own and others'—in ways markedly different from before. Are we as honest with our online friends as we are with our face-to-face cohorts? Are we less polite to those we cannot see? Are our cyber-identities more aggressive, more sexy, or less thoughtful than our real-world identities? The potential exists for the online expansion of individual personality, just as it exists for the online denial of who and what we really are (Figure 15–1). Individual users must make their own decisions on the Net; and this, argue committed Internet users, is the medium's greatest promise.

PRIVACY

The issue of privacy in mass communication has traditionally been concerned with individuals' rights to protect their privacy from invasive, intrusive media (Chapter 13). For example, should newspapers publish the names of rape victims and juvenile offenders? When does a person become a public figure and forfeit some degree of privacy? In the global village, however, the issue takes on a new character. Where Supreme Court Justice Louis Brandeis could once argue that privacy is "the right to be left alone," today privacy is just as likely to mean "the right to maintain control over our own data." Privacy in the global village has two facets. The first is protecting the privacy of communication we wish to keep private. The second is the use (and misuse) of private, personal information willingly given online.

Protecting Privacy in Communication The 1986 Electronic Communication Privacy Act guarantees the privacy of our e-mail. It is a criminal offense to either "intentionally [access] without authorization a facility through which an electronic communication service is provided; or intentionally [exceed] an authorization to access that facility." In addition, the law "prohibits an electronic communications service provider from knowingly divulging the contents of any stored electronic communication." The goal of this legislation is to protect private citizens from official abuse; it gives e-mail "conversations" the same protection that phone conversations enjoy. If a government agency wants to listen in, it must secure permission, just as it must get a court order for a telephone wiretap.

If a person or company feels that more direct protection of communication is necessary, encryption is one solution, but it is controversial. As we saw in Chapter 14, encryption is the electronic coding or masking of information that can be deciphered only by a recipient with the decrypting key. According to the FBI and the Clinton Administration, however, this total privacy is an invitation for terrorists, drug lords, and mobsters to use the Net to threaten national security. Their proposal is the **Clipper Chip,** an encryption system that permits secure communication, but to which the government maintains the key. Opponents argue that the Clipper Chip renders encryption meaningless (as long as the key exists, it can be used) and that it will be used not only to thwart terrorists and criminals but also to investigate private citizens. The Internal Revenue Service might want to look at people's business and financial transactions. The Immigration and Naturalization Service might want to see what resident aliens are saying to their relatives back home. The merits of the system are still being debated.

"Authorized" interception of messages is another problem for privacy. Courts have consistently upheld employers' rights to intercept and read their employees' e-mail. Employers must be able to guarantee that their computer systems are not abused by the people who work for them. Thoughtful companies solve the problem by issuing clear and fair guidelines on the use of computer networks. Therefore, when they do make unannounced checks of employees' electronic communication, the employee understands that these checks do occur, why they occur, and under what circumstances they can lead to problems.

Protecting Privacy of Personal Information Every online act leaves a "digital trail," making possible easy "**dataveillance**—the massive collection and distillation of consumer data. . . . Information gathering has become so convenient and cost-effective that personal privacy has replaced censorship as our primary civil liberties concern" (Shenk, 1997, p. 146). Ironically, we participate in this intrusion into our privacy. Because of computer storage, networking, and cross-referencing power, the information we give to one entity is easily and cheaply given to countless, unknown others (Figure 15–2).

One form of dataveillance is the distribution and sharing of personal, private information among organizations other than the one for whom it was originally intended. Information from every credit card transaction (online or at a store), credit application, phone call, supermarket or other purchase made without cash (for example, with a check, debit card, or "club" card), newspaper and magazine subscription, and cable television subscribership is digitally recorded, stored, and most likely sold to others. The increased computerization of medical files, banking information, job applications, and school records produces even more salable data. Eventually, anyone who wants to know something about a person can simply buy the necessary information—without that person's permission or even knowledge. These data can then be used to further invade people's privacy. Evening meals and family conversations at home can be interrupted by

PHILADELPHIA DAILY NEWS
Philadelphia
USA

Figure 15–2 In spite of his look of surprise, this consumer willingly gave away the personal information that is now stored and distributed by computers.

targeted phone solicitations. Employers can withhold jobs for reasons unknown to applicants. Insurance companies can selectively deny coverage to people based on data about their grocery choices (see the box "Defending Privacy: The Case of Lotus MarketPlace"). So troublesome has the problem become that the Federal Trade Commission "censured" the Internet industry in a June 1998 report to Congress "for doing little to insure adequate consumer privacy protection online" ("FTC faults Net" 1998, p. 1C). The FTC's own study of 1,400 Web sites revealed that "85% collect personal information but only 14% provide any notice about what they do with the data. Only 2% provide such notice with a comprehensive privacy policy" (p. 4C).

Recognizing the scope of data collection and the potential problems that it raises, Congress passed the 1974 Federal Privacy Act, restricting governments' ability to collect and distribute information about citizens. The act, however, expressly exempted businesses and other nongovernmental organizations from control. This stands in stark contrast to the situation across the Atlantic. In European Union countries it is illegal for an organization of any kind to sell the name and other personal information of a customer or client for any reason without that person's permission.

A second form of dataveillance is the electronic "tracking" of the choices we make when we are on the Web, called our **click stream.** Despite the anonymity online users think they enjoy, every click of a key can be, and often is, recorded and stored. This happens whether or not the user actually enters information, for example, a credit card number to

Using Media to Make a Difference

Defending Privacy: The Case of Lotus MarketPlace

In January 1993 software manufacturer Lotus Development Corporation and credit reporting agency Equifax Incorporated joined to announce the introduction of their new CD-ROM, *Lotus MarketPlace: Households.* This database package was designed for Macintosh computers and contained the names, ad-dresses, household incomes, buying habits, and other financial information about more than 120 million U.S. citizens in 80 million households.

The target audience was small businesses interested in developing their own specialized mailing lists and other marketing strategies. The price was a reasonable $695, allowing small companies access to huge amounts of data once available only to the richest big companies.

A groundswell of grassroots opposition immediately formed. Within two days of its release more than 30,000 people—some privacy and consumer advocates, many ordinary citizens—used e-mail, faxes, and telephone calls to Lotus and Equifax to demand that their information—*their* information—be deleted. *MarketPlace* was immediately pulled from distribution. Lotus President and CEO Jim Manzi said in an online company press remake a purchase or a Social Security number to verify identity. Software exists that records what sites users visit, what they look at in those sites, and how long they stay at a given place in that site as they click from Web page to Web page. In and of itself, this is not a problem, because all the Web site reads about the user is a computer address. But once a user enters personal information, that "anonymous" address has a name.

Since 1996, Congress, the Federal Trade Commission, and public interest groups have attempted to draft legislation that will offer greater protection for online privacy. They have been largely unsuccessful because of resistance on two fronts. Businesses and individuals who trade in access to information obviously will not back laws that limit their profit potential. But many Internet users as well fiercely oppose even well-intentioned government intrusion in the workings of the Net.

Two forms of industry self-regulation are in place. One, offered by the Electronic Frontier Foundation and CommerceNet, an association of Internet businesses, is eTRUST. Web sites, if they agree to certain restrictions on their collection and use of user information, will earn the eTRUST "seal of approval," presumably making them more attractive to privacy-conscious users.

A second effort at self-regulation was sanctioned by the Clinton Administration. Beginning in January 1998, 14 companies, including Lexis-Nexis and the biggest credit reporting companies in the United States, agreed to block dissemination of all personal information to anyone but "qualified customers." The 14 companies account for more than

lease, "While we believe that the actual data content and controls built into the product preserved consumer privacy, we couldn't ignore the high level of consumer concern. . . . After examining all of the issues we have decided that the cost and complexity of educating consumers about the issues is beyond the scope of Lotus as an information provider" (Manzi, 1991).

People used the media to make a difference. E-mail, fax, and even that "old" technology, the telephone, were marshaled to protect people's privacy. But exactly what difference did they really make?

In *The Social Impact of Computers,* Professor Richard Rosenberg (1992) wrote, "The removal of *MarketPlace* from the marketplace represents an important success of the privacy advocacy movement and augurs well for the future protection of privacy" (p. 215). A different view was offered by journalist and social critic David Shenk

(1997). "The triumph . . . was a mirage," he wrote.

In fact, every single scrap of data featured in Lotus *MarketPlace* was already publicly available and regularly being drawn on for marketing purposes—and still is. . . . Without realizing it, the *MarketPlace* consumer protesters were giving a lift to their chief enemies in the privacy wars: *Fortune 500* companies. After the *MarketPlace* implosion, the rest of the industry let out an audible sigh of relief that the consumer revolt had barely even scratched their surface, and other companies quickly took steps to improve public relations and operate more quietly. . . . Lotus's major mistake, then, was to let its product become too visible, to let it look too much like Big Brother. (pp. 147–148)

With whom do you agree? Was the victory real or imagined?

90% of all online personal information selling. The voluntary plan has two serious handicaps, according to privacy advocates. First is the definition of "qualified." Government agencies and private investigators would seem to be qualified. But under *all* conditions and situations? Do all government agencies operate with the best of intentions all the time? Who can determine if a private investigator's inquiries are legitimate, or possibly the basis for blackmail? The second problem is that individual users must request to "opt out"; that is, they must contact each of the participating companies and ask that their information be guarded.

For those uneasy with government regulation as well as industry self-regulation, there is a technological solution. Users can download—for free—The Anonymizer *(http://www.anonymizer.com)*, software that blocks information from the recording eyes of Web sites.

VIRTUAL DEMOCRACY

The Internet is characterized by freedom and self-governance, which are also the hallmarks of true democracy. It is no surprise, then, that computer technology is often trumpeted as the newest and best tool for increased democratic involvement and participation. Presidential candidate Ross Perot used the promise of an "electronic town hall" as a centerpiece of his 1992 campaign. Vice President Al Gore conducted history's first interactive, computer network *news* conference on January 13, 1994. It was not a *press* conference, in the traditional sense, because the people themselves, rather than their representatives in the media, could query Mr. Gore. Several states are studying the possibility of online voting. The judge in the November 1997 Boston trial of British au pair Louise Woodward issued his ruling to the public, press, and involved parties via the Internet. Among Newt Gingrich's first official acts after becoming Speaker of the U.S. House of Representatives in 1995 was to order that all Congressional documents be available online on a Web site *(http://thomas.loc.gov/)* he dubbed Thomas, after Thomas Jefferson. Virtually every politician of any standing, including the president, vice president, senate majority leader, and speaker of the house, maintains at least an e-mail address if not a full Web page.

This enthusiasm for a technological solution to what many see as increased disenchantment with politics and the political process mirrors that which followed the introduction of radio and television. A September 3, 1924, *New Republic* article, for example, argued that the high level of public interest in the broadcast of the 1924 political party conventions brought "dismay" to "the most hardened political cynic" (as cited in Davis, 1976, p. 351). The November 1950 *Good Housekeeping* claimed that television would bring greater honesty to politics because "television is a revealing medium, and it is impossible for a man or a woman appearing before those cameras to conceal his or her true self" (p. 359). In 1940 NBC founder and chairman David Sarnoff predicted that television would enrich democracy because it was "destined to provide greater knowledge to larger numbers of people, truer perception of the meaning of current events, more accurate appraisals of men in public life, and a broader understanding of the needs and aspirations of our fellow human beings" (as cited in Shenk, 1997, p. 60).

Some critics argue that the Internet will be no more of an asset to democracy than have been radio and television because the same economic and commercial forces that have shaped the content and operation of those more traditional media will constrain just as rigidly the new. Communication scientist Everette Dennis (1992) condensed the critics' concern into two overarching questions: (1) Will computer networks be readily accessible to all people—even if it means depending on institutions such as schools, churches, and community organizations—or only to some? and (2) Once the technology is in place and people have access to it, are they going to know how to use it?

The Technology Gap An important principle of democracy is "one person, one vote." But if democracy is increasingly practiced online, those lacking the necessary technology and skill will be denied their vote. This is the **technology gap**—the widening disparity between the communication technology haves and have-nots. As we saw in Chapter 14, the typical Internet user is financially well off and is well educated. These people have the money to buy the hardware and software needed to access the Net as well as to pay for that connection, have the kind of jobs that allow time for learning and using the Net, and have the necessary sophistication to do both. That leaves out many, if not most, U.S. citizens.

Ironically, the technology gap may be exacerbated by the sheer popularity of the Internet. Monthly **flat rate billing** has become the standard form of paying for Internet access. For example, in October 1996 America Online (AOL) converted its billing to a flat monthly rate of $19.95, abandoning its previous practice of charging for time connected. It was forced to do so because many of its competitors were employing this attractive and generous practice.

But many in the telecommunications industry argue that flat rate billing will eventually damage the Internet. With no financial incentive to limit the time they spend online, more people will spend more time on the Internet. The Net therefore becomes more crowded and operates more slowly, limiting its efficiency and effectiveness and angering users. AOL, for example, experienced a number of system failures due to heavy use after its change in pricing. Calling flat rate billing "bad business," many industry insiders predict that **pay-as-you-go pricing** will eventually become necessary and, as a result, will become the industry standard. Those who make the most use of the information superhighway, the logic argues, should pay the highest toll.

Among the planned solutions are fees based on the length of time connected (like billing for long-distance telephone calls), pay-as-you-go billing

Computers in the Schools

One often-cited solution to the technology and information gaps is bringing computers and computer networks to primary and secondary schools. The idea is that everyone, regardless of ability to pay, can learn to use a computer and then get online. Republican presidential candidate Bob Dole proposed auctioning the broadcast spectrum in 1996, using some of the proceeds to "wire every school in America" (Chapter 9). The Clinton Administration made "getting every school in America on the Information Superhighway" a cornerstone of its educational reform strategy. Speaker of the House Newt Gingrich and futurist writer Alvin Toffler argue that the road to cyberdemocracy passes through the schools. According to the *Statistical Abstracts of the United States,* 97.5% of U.S. elementary and secondary schools had micro computers in 1994, up from 77.7% in 1985. Twenty-eight percent were connected to the Internet.

Who could argue with a fine idea like increasing young people's access to computers in their schools? In fact, many people do. The issue is not as clear-cut as most technophiles believe. No one doubts that computers can be a useful educational tool. But many education professionals suggest caution in their application. Their concerns:

1. *There is no relationship between school spending on computers and test scores on basic skills like math and reading.* Caught up in the euphoria over the Net and the Web, many schools invested heavily in technology with little attention paid to how it complements or fits in to different curricula. What traditional, proven instructional materials aren't being bought? What skills aren't being taught?

2. *Little thought is sometimes given to technical and other support of computers and networks after purchase and installation.* Schools rushed to get on the superhighway, ignoring the cost of staying on it. In addition, upgrading teachers' skills to allow them to better employ the technology in teaching is often ignored.

3. *The focus on learning for its own sake has been dimmed.* Much of the rush toward computers in the schools is based on the desire to prepare students for specific jobs in the information society. Turning schools into vocational centers where "future workers" are trained may be a laudable goal to some, but many educators believe that schools, especially at the lower grade levels, should be imparting the joy of learning, not career preparation.

4. *The computer is a pump; school is a filter.* Computers and their networks are "pumps," designed to access, deliver, and store huge amounts of raw information at great speed. But information is not understanding. Schools, through teachers and textbooks, "filter" vast amounts of information, selecting what is most appropriate for students and organizing it in usable, understandable ways. These "polished bits of data" are the building blocks of true learning and understanding. The heavy emphasis on computer technology ignores the vital role played by "old-fashioned" pedagogical technologies like teachers, chalkboards, classroom interaction, and textbooks.

What do you think of these cautions? How aggressively, and under what circumstances, would you push for increased computer access for schoolchildren? Does your attitude depend on whether or not you have a child in elementary school?

for use during peak times, and tiered or multilevel pricing. Users wanting to maintain flat rate pricing might be limited to certain hours of the day or night. Those willing or able to pay for time connected might have greater freedom. Any of these changes, argue critics of the technology gap, will shut out or at least limit access for those who cannot afford the higher prices. The democratic ideal of one person, one vote will be reduced to one dollar, one vote. In other words, the technology gap will grow even wider.

The Information Gap Another important principle of democracy is that a self-governing people govern best with full access to information. This is the reason our culture is so suspicious of censorship. The technology gap feeds a second impediment to virtual democracy, the **information gap.** Those without the requisite technology will have diminished access to the information it makes available. In other words, they will suffer from a form of technologically imposed censorship.

Critics of the information gap point to troubling examples of other media failures to deliver important information to all citizens. Cable television subscribership is lowest among urban working-class and poor people. Many newspapers, uninterested in these same people because they do not possess the demographic profile coveted by advertisers, do not promote their papers in the neighborhoods in which they live and, in some large cities, do not even deliver there. For this same reason, there are precious few consumer magazines aimed at less well-off people. If the computer technology gap creates an even wider information gap than already exists between these audiences and other citizens, democracy will surely suffer (see the box "Computers in the Schools").

Information, Knowledge, and Understanding Some critics of the idea of online democracy are troubled by the amount of information available to contemporary citizens and the speed with which it comes. Add to this the difficulty of assessing the veracity of much online information (Chapter 14), and they argue that the cyberworld may not be the best place to practice democracy.

For example, advocates of cyberdemocracy see the Internet as a way to let citizens have more direct access to politicians. Elected officials should hear what the people have to say. But does democracy necessarily benefit when its leaders respond directly, maybe even impulsively, to public sentiment? Until there is no more technology gap, certain voices—the poor, the uneducated, the elderly—will have less access to their leaders than those who are connected. Moreover, claim critics of cyberdemocracy, ours is a representative, deliberative democracy. It was intentionally designed to allow public representatives to talk to one another, to debate ideas and issues, to forge solutions that benefit not just their own but others' constituents as well. They claim that the political alienation felt by many citizens today is the product of politicians listening *too much* to the loudest voices (that is, special interests) and being *too responsive* to the polls. People often criticize politicians for "flip flopping" or "having no personal conviction." How can the situation improve if elected officials respond daily to the voices in the electronic town hall? Journalist Robert Wright (1995) wrote in *Time:*

> The Founders explicitly took lawmaking power out of the people's hands, opting for a representative democracy and not a direct democracy. What concerned them, especially James Madison, was the specter of popular "passions" unleashed. Their ideal was cool deliberation by elected representatives, buffered from the often shifting winds of opinion—inside-the-Beltway deliberation. Madison insisted in the Federalist Papers on the need to "refine and enlarge the public views by passing them through the medium

of a chosen body of citizens, whose wisdom may best discern the true interest of their country and whose patriotism and love of justice will be least likely to sacrifice it to temporary or partial considerations." (p. 16)

Critics also argue that cyberdemocracy, by its very virtual nature, is antidemocratic. Before the coming of VCR, cable, and satellite television, a president could ask for and almost invariably receive airtime from the three major television networks to talk to the people. Today, however, these technologies have fragmented us into countless smaller audiences. Should a president address the nation today, only a small proportion of citizens is likely to tune in. This fragmentation of the audience (Chapter 1) is exacerbated by the Internet. Not only is there now an *additional* medium to further divide the audience, but by simple virtue of the way it functions—chat rooms, bulletin boards, taste-specific Web sites—the Internet solidifies people into smaller, more homogeneous, more narrowly interested groups. This cannot be good for democracy, say some critics.

The Internet and the Web encourage people to splinter into virtual communities based on a shared interest in some given information. This renders actual communities irrelevant. No longer required to coexist with other people in the day-to-day world, cybercitizens have little need to examine their own biases. They need not question their own assumptions about the world and how it works. There is little benefit to seeking out and attempting to understand the biases and assumptions of others outside the self-chosen virtual community.

For example, writes media critic and scholar Robert McChesney (1997), among the criteria that must be met if democracy is to meet the needs of its people are "a sense of community and a notion that an individual's well-being is determined to no small extent by the community's well-being" and "an effective system of political communication, broadly construed, that informs and engages the citizenry, drawing people meaningfully into the polity" (p. 5). Where McLuhan would have seen the new electronic communication technologies doing just this, many others, often likening the Net and the Web to "talk radio writ large," fear the opposite. They worry that the Internet, like the worst examples of talk radio, will splinter people into smaller, angrier, less reflective partisans.

Other Neighborhoods in the Global Village: World Media Systems

There are other neighborhoods—other countries—in the global village. They face the same issues we've been discussing, but they often do so from a different perspective. This is because not every media system resembles that of the United States. Therefore, such things as audience expectations, economic foundations, and the regulation of mass media differ. The study of different countries' mass media systems is called **comparative analysis** or **comparative studies.**

DIFFERING NORMATIVE THEORIES

Different countries' mass media systems primarily reflect their levels of development and prosperity and the nature of their political systems. Often geography also influences the type of media system a country embraces. For example, Figure 15–3 shows the level of diffusion of radios and televisions in many different countries. The United States is prosperous; its people have much mobility and leisure and tend to live in bigger homes than the people of most other lands. As a result, there are two radios for every U.S. citizen and almost one television per person. Australia, a prosperous country, is very large. Many of its people live in quite remote parts of this nation-continent. It, too, has more than one radio per person. Uganda, a developing African nation, has almost no television, and despite the remote homes of many of its people, its lack of prosperity makes even radio ownership a rarity.

That a country's political system will be reflected in the nature of its media system is only logical. Authoritarian governments need to control the mass media to maintain power. Therefore they will have a much different media system than will a democratic country with a capitalistic, free economy. The overriding philosophy of how media should ideally operate in a given system of social values is called a normative theory. In the classic 1956 book, *The Four Theories of the Press,* Fred Siebert, Theodore Peterson, and Wilbur Schramm defined the major normative theories that can be used to classify the world's media systems. With the substitution of the developing model for the now-gone Soviet/totalitarian model, its classification scheme—authoritarian, libertarian, social responsibility, and (now) developing—is still useful.

Authoritarian Model   For different reasons, some countries have **authoritarian media systems.** Dictatorships, for example, Communist North Korea, assert full control over media because their political philosophy sees media as a "tool of the people." As such, media must serve the people. Because the people are the Communist Party, the government naturally controls this tool.

Some emerging democracies, despite claims of a free and open media system, also exhibit de facto adherence to the authoritarian model. Since 1955, for example, Argentina has had an elected president, free elections, and a capitalist-based economy. But even today its leaders argue that they must control the media on grounds of national security because the people cannot yet be trusted with too much freedom. Of course, not all its citizens agree. The result is described in the box "Freedom of the Press in Argentina."

Figure 15–3 Distribution of Radios and Televisions Around the World (1993)

Country	Population (in millions)	TVs (per person)	Radios (per person)
Angola	9	1:200.0	1:20.0
Argentina	35	1:4	1:1.0
Australia	18	1:2.0	1.5:1.0
Austria	8	1:2.8	1:1.6
Bahrain	0.5	1:2.3	1:1.7
Bangladesh	119	—	1:24.0
Belgium	10	1:4.2	1:2.2
Bolivia	7	1:16.0	1:1.8
Brazil	160	1:5.0	1:2.5
Bulgaria	9	1:3.9	1:2.5
Burundi	6	—	1:10.0
Cambodia	7	1:100.0	1:10.0
Canada	30	1:1.7	1:1.2
Chile	14	1:4.0	1:3.0
China	1,200	1:8.0	1:9.0
Columbia	34	1:5.0	1:7.0
Costa Rica	3	1:4.9	1:11.0
Czech Republic	10.5	1:2.7	1:3.3
Denmark	5	1:2.7	1:2.4
Ecuador	11	1:17.0	1:3.0
El Salvador	6	1:12.0	1:2.6
Estonia	1.6	1:2.7	1:1.7
Ethiopia	51	1:100.0	1:5.0
Finland	5	1:2.7	1:1.0
France	58	1:2.6	1:1.0
Gabon	1.1	—	1:10.0
Germany	80	1:2.6	1:2.3
Greece	10	1:4.5	1:2.4
Guatemala	10	1:18.0	1:22.0
Honduras	5	1:24.0	1:2.4
India	886	1:44.0	1:16.0
Indonesia	200	1:20.0	1:8.0
Iran	61	1:23.0	1:4.7
Iraq	18	1:18.0	1:5.0
Israel	5	1:4.1	1:2.2
Italy	58	1:3.8	1:3.4
Japan	125	1:1.6	1:1.2
Jordan	3.5	1:12.0	1:4.5

Source: Hilliard and Keith, 1996.

Libertarian Model As we saw in Chapter 13, because democracies rely on government of the people, their media must be free of official control. This is the libertarian ideal. But as we also saw in that chapter, because control can and often does come in other forms, commercial pressure, for example, a truly libertarian media system may not best serve democracy. In the United States, for example, the print media operate under the lib-

Country	Population (in millions)	TVs (per person)	Radios (per person)
Kenya	26	—	1:10.0
Kuwait	1.3	1:2.6	1:1.8
Latvia	3.8	1:2.9	1:1.2
Lebanon	3.5	1:3.4	1:1.3
Lithuania	10.5	1:2.7	1:3.3
Luxembourg	0.4	1:4.0	1:1.6
Mexico	90	1:6.6	1:5.1
The Netherlands	15	1:3.2	1:1.2
New Zealand	4	1:4.0	1.5:1.0
Nicaragua	4	1:18.0	1:4.3
North Korea	22	1:50.0	1:4.0
Oman	1.6	1:1.4	1:1.6
Pakistan	60	1:60.0	1:24.0
Panama	2.5	1:10.0	1:5.0
Paraguay	5	1:10.0	1:5.0
Peru	23	1:11.0	1:5.0
Poland	39	1:3.9	1:3.6
Qatar	0.5	1:2.5	1:2.5
Romania	23	1:6.0	1:7.3
Russia	150	1:3.2	1:1.5
Rwanda	8	—	1:10.0
Saudi Arabia	17	1:3.5	1:3.3
South Africa	42	1:11.0	1:3.0
South Korea	44	1:5.0	1:1.0
Spain	40	1:2.6	1:3.4
Sweden	9	1:2.4	1:1.2
Switzerland	7	1:2.9	1:2.6
Syria	14	1:17.0	1:4.1
Taiwan	21	1:3.2	1:1.5
Thailand	58	1:15.0	1:5.0
Uganda	20	—	1:10.0
United Arab Emirates	2.5	1:12.0	1:4.7
United Kingdom	60	1:3.0	1:1.0
United States	240	1:1.3	2:1.0
Uruguay	3	1:4.0	1:1.0
Venezuela	21	1:5.0	1:2.0
Zaire	40	—	1:10.0

ertarian ideal, whereas broadcast media are more closely regulated by government. Yet of all the nations in the world, the U.S. media system comes closest to the ideal. Advocates of the Internet, however, see that medium—free of central authority and offering near-complete freedom of expression, association, and press—as best fulfilling the goals of libertarianism. This is why they zealously resist censorship and commercialization.

Media Echoes

Freedom of the Press in Argentina

John Peter Zenger went to jail for his exercise of free expression, and his name is forever linked to the fight against official intrusion into journalism. Larry Flynt spent millions of dollars on lawyers and other legal fees to protect his magazine's right to publish unpopular expression. He was immortalized in a big-budget Hollywood movie. Few people outside Argentina, however, know the names José Luis Cabezas or Adolfo Scilingo.

Cabezas was an investigative reporter and photojournalist. He was working on a story about the cozy relationship between big-time drug traffickers and government officials and abuses in the Argentinean judicial system. In January 1997 his handcuffed body was discovered near Buenos Aires. He had been shot and burned alive.

Scilingo had been a captain in the Argentine navy and had taken part in the murder of several people who opposed the military dictatorship that ruled Argentina from 1976 to 1983. During this time, the military conducted what Argentineans call the Dirty War, killing 4,000 opponents and "disappearing" 10,000 more. Scilingo went public in 1997 with details of how he and his colleagues had kidnapped political opponents and dropped them out of cargo planes over the Atlantic Ocean. Many of those same colleagues later came to hold influential positions in the government. Scilingo further accused President Carlos Menem, Argentina's second democratically elected president, of protecting these murderers. President Menem, who upon his election had granted a blanket pardon to all military and police personnel involved in the Dirty War, often referred to reporters who criticized him and his administration as "journalistic delinquents." Menem also labeled the beatings and killings experienced by opposition journalists "occupational hazards" and publicly called for the "physical assault" of anyone who criticized his government and the reporters who published those complaints. A few days after Scilingo's revelations, he was kidnapped and beaten. His assailants carved the initials of the three reporters with whom he had spoken into his face (Barili, 1997, p. 7B).

In 1993 Amnesty International published a special report, "Argentina: Journalism a Dangerous Profession," detailing officially sanctioned abuse of journalists. In 1997 the free press organization Freedom Forum issued a report detailing 800 attacks against Argentinean media professionals during President Menem's administration, which began in 1989. No violent crime against an Argentinean journalist has ever been solved—not one. The government has removed all judges who oppose its activities and controls the police and security forces, which number 45,000 in the province of Buenos Aires alone.

The media system in Argentina can be classified as a combination private/government system. Much like the United States, there are four commercial television networks and one state-owned network. The newspapers are privately owned. There was widespread political turmoil surrounding the Cabezas and Scilingo affairs, generated largely by word-of-mouth. The media, however, were either controlled or cowed by the government.

Freedoms and the traditions on which they are based that are taken for granted in the United States and in other free countries simply do not exist for many in our global village. Should you be concerned about what happens to media professionals in places like Argentina? Isn't it enough to know that such abuse cannot occur in more traditional democracies?

The coffin of José Luis Cabezas.

Social Responsibility Model As we also saw in Chapter 13, the U.S. media system adheres more to the social responsibility model than it does to true libertarianism. Britain, however, offers a good example of a media system that was expressly developed in the **social responsibility model.** The British Broadcasting System (BBC) was originally built on the premise that broadcasting was a public trust. Long before television, BBC radio offered several services—one designed to provide news and information; one designed to support high or elite culture such as symphony music and spoken-word plays; and another designed to provide popular music and entertainment. To limit government and advertiser control, the BBC was funded by license fees based on the number of receivers people had in their homes, and its governance was given over to a nonprofit commission. Many observers point to this goal-oriented, noncommercial structure as the reason the BBC developed and still maintains the most respected news operation in the world.

Eventually, Britain, like all of Western Europe, was forced by public demand to institute a more American style of broadcasting. There are now local commercial radio stations in Great Britain, and in addition to television networks BBC1 (more serious) and BBC2 (more popular), there is commercial Channel 4 and several regional commercial networks operating under the auspices of the Independent Television Authority (ITA). There is an ITA channel for Ireland, for example, one for Scotland, one for Wales, one for southern England, and so on. But even these must accept limits on the amount of advertising they air and agree to carry specified amounts of public affairs and documentary news programming in exchange for their licenses to broadcast.

Britain's commitment to the social responsibility model extends to its print media as well. Newspaper and magazine practitioners are expected to perform their duties in a professional manner. Period. If they do not, they can be held accountable. For example, there is no First Amendment protection for journalists in Great Britain. There are no libel laws protecting media professionals, who can be sued even by public figures. Journalists are forbidden to produce reports on criminal trials when they are in progress. They can be jailed or fined for violations. But as indicated by the charges that the paparazzi and the tabloids made Princess Diana's life miserable before her death, the British print media do operate with great freedom.

Developmental Model The media systems of many Third World or developing African, Asian, Central and South American, and now former Eastern-bloc European nations best fit the **developmental model.** Here government and media work in partnership to ensure that media assist in the planned, beneficial development of the country. Content is designed to meet specific cultural and societal needs, for example, teaching new farming techniques, disseminating information on methods of disease control, and improving literacy. This isn't the same as authoritarian control. There is less censorship and other official control of content. Honduras offers an

Unlike U.S. media, British media do not enjoy First Amendment protections, but as their notorious tabloids demonstrate, they nonetheless do operate with a great deal of freedom.

THURSDAY August 20, 1992   TV: Pages 26-27   ★ ★ ★   (Republic of Ireland 40p) 25p

Today

Secret date for all Rich players
FULL STORY PAGES 4 & 5

SCANDAL

How Hola! showed Johnny Bryan planting a kiss on the Duchess of York's toes. The sensational picture is certain to mark the end of Fergie and Andrew's marriage

¡HOLA!

NO HAY POSIBILIDAD DE RECONCILIACION CON EL PRINCIPE ANDRES

SORPRESA ANTE LA EVIDENTE RELACION ENTRE SARAH FERGUSON Y JOHN BRYAN

Hola! proclaimed a royal reconciliation was impossible with this front page picture

Photos that will stun the Royals

SENSATIONAL pictures of the holiday antics of Fergie and her Texan financial adviser Johnny Bryan will today spark off a massive Royal scandal after their publication here and on the Continent.

The set of photographs —

taken as the couple relaxed in the grounds of a French villa — look certain to mark the end of the Duchess of York's marriage and stun the Queen.

And as Spaniards woke up to see the shots in Hola! magazine, the question was: Should Johnny Bryan have been allowed to stop their publication?

He fought a desperate rear-

Turn to Page 2

EXCLUSIVE:

Fergie banned by the Queen

PAGE 3

excellent example. This Central American country has government-owned as well as privately owned commercial radio and television stations. A government-authorized and controlled private commission, the Honduran Contractors of Television, coordinates much of the commercial outlets' operation. In addition, the Honduran FCC, HONDUTEL, exerts tight regulatory control over all broadcasting. Together these two bodies ensure that Honduran broadcasting meets the developmental needs of the nation as determined by the government.

COMPARING TWO NEIGHBORHOODS

Because a country's media system reflects its political and economic philosophies, the degree of prosperity it enjoys, and other factors such as geography and cultural traditions, two neighborhoods in the global village can exhibit widely different characteristics. We can see this in the media of Japan and China. It is also useful, as we compare these two Asian countries, to compare them to the United States as well.

Japan   The Japanese media system combines many elements of the U.S. and British models. In broadcasting, for example, three existing radio stations in Japan joined together in 1925 to create the network Nippon Hoso Kyokai (NHK). From the start, NHK's mission, patterned after the British, was to provide high quality and educational programming for a national audience. Its financial support, also copied from the British, came from license fees paid by listeners, but unlike the British system, payment is voluntary. The large majority of listeners and viewers willingly pay—in the Japanese culture to do otherwise would be a disgrace—but as operating and production costs have risen, the NHK finds itself dependent on annual subsidies from the federal government. Finally, again as in England, NHK's supervision was entrusted to a commission, today called the Board of Governors.

After World War II, the occupying U.S. administration oversaw writing and passage of the 1950 Broadcast Law. It reconfirmed the public service role of the NHK, but it also permitted privately owned, commercial broadcasting. Commercial broadcasting is divided into "public" and "commercial" stations. Both carry commercials, but the public stations try to emulate the NHK and are more committed to educational and cultural programming. Commercial stations look like commercial stations in the United States. They air primarily entertainment—sitcoms, action/adventure shows, and variety programs. Today NHK's 5,726 radio and television stations and the country's 2,548 commercial stations are regulated by the Japanese equivalent of the FCC, the Ministry of Posts and Telecommunication. Various laws ensure the autonomy of NHK, guaranteeing that it operates at a high standard, delivers both local and national programming, and remains free of official control. Unlike the U.S. system, however, both print and broadcast journalists must have membership in a "journalist association" to be "accredited." This form of control is subtle—the government decides who can and cannot work as a journalist—but there is significant cultural pressure against its abuse.

Most of the commercial broadcasters have united into four national networks. This occurred for a number of reasons: the need to compete with the successful and high quality NHK, the need to share the high cost of production, and geography. Much of the Japanese audience lives in remote areas, many people live on small islands, and much of the country is mountainous, requiring local rather than centralized national

This set from a Japanese television news program shows the influence of U.S television conventions. Familiar to American viewers are the good-looking male and female anchors, the nice haircuts, and the space-age backdrop.

transmission. Geography also accounts for the large number of cable operations in this island state. Japan, a country of approximately 125 million people, has 10,167 cable companies. Most retransmit distant signals for the purpose of improved reception, although a number of cable systems near large population centers are adopting the U.S. practice of buying and producing original content for cablecast. Geography has also moved the NHK into the business of direct broadcast satellite. It operates two satellite systems, BS1 and BS2, which deliver NHK programming, foreign movies, foreign news reports, and some U.S. entertainment fare. A number of commercial satellite companies, including VOW WOW and Star Channel, also serve the Japanese audience.

As in the United States, 99% of Japanese homes have television sets and, on average, each home consumes more than 8 hours of television a day (compared to the U.S. average of slightly more than 7 hours).

Print media have traditionally been central forces in Japanese political and cultural life and remain so today, more so even than in the United States. There are hundreds of national, regional, and local daily newspapers in Japan. All are commercially based. The five national papers account for half the 61 million circulation, and there are 1.85 readers per copy. Where there is 0.7 newspaper subscriptions per U.S. household, there are 1.79 in Japan.

China   The Chinese media system is based on that of its old ideological partner, the now-dissolved Soviet Union. But for a variety of reasons, China has developed its own peculiar nature. China has more than a billion people living in more than a million hamlets, villages, and cities. Despite the sophisticated life of many big cities, there is near-universal illiteracy in the countryside. Because good pulp wood is not native to China and importing it from abroad is costly, newspapers are printed on paper made from bamboo, which is expensive and of low quality. Daily circulation is 116 million copies, around one paper for every 100 citizens. As a result, print is not a major national medium. In fact, face-to-face communication remains a primary means of transmitting news and information. This process is aided by the wide distribution of **wired radio,** centrally located loudspeakers, for example, in a town square, that deliver primarily political and educational broadcasts.

As in the old Soviet regime, the media exist in China to serve the government. Founder of the Chinese Communist Party, Chairman Mao Zedong, clarified the role of the media very soon after coming to power in the wake of World War II. The media exist to propagandize the policies of the party and to educate, organize, and mobilize the masses. This is still their primary function.

American reporter E. C. Osborn established an experimental radio station in China in 1923, and official Chinese broadcasting began in 1926. Television began in 1958, and from its start it was owned and controlled by the party in the form of Central China Television (CCTV), which, in turn, answers to the Ministry of Radio and Television. Radio, now regulated by China People's Broadcasting Station (CPBS), and television stations and networks develop their own content, but it must conform to the requirements of the Propaganda Bureau of the Chinese Communist Party Central Committee.

Chinese broadcasting has never used a license fee, instead opting for direct government subsidy. But in 1979 the government approved commercial advertising as a means of supporting broadcasting. Advertising has evolved into a primary means of support. Coupled with the Chinese government's desire to become a more active participant in the global village, this commercialization has led to increased diversity in broadcast content. Some foreign content is now permitted—documentaries from the BBC, for example, and cultural programming from Western countries like Germany and Brazil. Since 1994, even U.S.-made programs have been airing alongside the more typical high-level cultural programming; *Little House on the Prairie* is a particular favorite. CNN and other satellite-delivered services are also available in major metropolitan areas. Basic government control over major media remains, however, as it does even over the Internet. In December 1997 the government began enforcing criminal sanctions against those who would use the Net to "split the country," "defame government agencies," or otherwise pose a threat to "social stability" ("China Adopts," 1997, p. C1, C4).

In China and Japan we can see how two neighboring countries can develop completely different media systems and approaches to media freedom based on their politics, economics, and even geography. There are hundreds of other neighborhoods in the global village whose media systems warrant our attention, but these two examples serve to remind us

A Chinese reading wall. The newspaper is not a major national mass medium in China—there is only one copy for every 100 people. Most read the newspaper at public postings such as this one.

of a theme that has run throughout this book—it is people, not the technologies, who determine how the mass communication process operates.

Coexisting in the Global Village: Cultural Imperialism

There are few physical borders between the different neighborhoods in the global village. Governments that could once physically prohibit the introduction and distribution of unwanted newspapers, magazines, and books had to work harder at jamming unwanted radio and television broadcasts. But they could do it, until satellite came along. Governments cannot disrupt satellite signals. Only lack of the necessary receiving technology can limit its reach. Now, with the Internet, a new receiving technology is cheap, easy to use, and on the desks of more and more millions of people in every corner of the world. As a result, difficult questions of national sovereignty and cultural diversity are being raised anew.

THE McBRIDE REPORT AND THE NWIO

The debate reached its height with the 1980 release of "The McBride Report" by the United Nations Educational, Scientific, and Cultural Organization (UNESCO). The report was named after the chairman of the commission set up to study the question of how to maintain national and cultural sovereignty in the face of rapid globalization of mass media. At

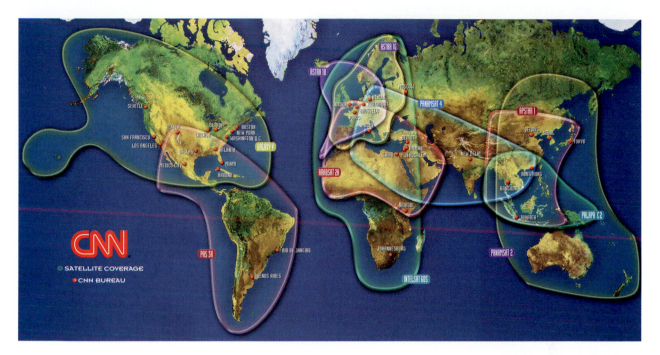

CNN uses 14 satellites to transmit to 800 million viewers in 60 countries.

the time, many Third World and communist countries were concerned that international news coverage was dominated by the West, especially the United States, and that western-produced content was dominating the media of developing countries, which lacked sufficient resources to create their own quality fare. The fear was that western cultural values, especially those of the United States, would overwhelm and displace those of other countries. These countries saw this as a form of colonialization, a **cultural imperialism**—the invasion of an indigenous people's culture by powerful foreign countries through mass media.

The McBride Report, endorsed by UNESCO, called for establishment of a New World Information Order (NWIO) characterized by several elements problematic to western democracies. In arguing that individual nations should be free to control the news and entertainment that entered their lands, it called for monitoring of all such content, monitoring and licensing of foreign journalists, and requiring that prior government permission be obtained for direct radio, television, and satellite transmissions into foreign countries. Western nations rejected these rules as a direct infringement on the freedom of the press.

Western allies of the United States may have agreed that the restrictions of the NWIO were a threat to the free flow of information, yet virtually every one had in place rules (in the form of quotas) that limited U.S. media content in their own countries. Canada, our closest cultural neighbor, required that specific proportions of all content—print and broadcast—either be produced in Canada or reflect Canadian cultural identity. The French made illegal the printing of certain U.S. words,

The McKenzie Brothers. To limit American cultural intrusion in its media, the Canadian government mandated that a specific proportion of all media content produced in its country "represent native Canadian culture." Thus, the McKenzies were born on the hit comedy series, *SCTV.* The show's joke on the regulators, of course, is that its writers thought there wasn't all that much Canadian "culture."

including "hamburger" and "cartoon" (France still maintains an official office to prosecute those who would "debase" its language). In 1989 the European Union, then called the European Community, established "Television Without Frontiers," which mandates that 50% of all content on all television channels in Europe be produced in its member countries. Even as recently as 1993, virtually all other European countries supported French resistance to those parts of the General Agreement on Tariffs and Trade (GATT) that would have eliminated or reduced tariffs on media material entering their continent from the United States.

The resistance to U.S. media would not exist among our international friends if they did not worry about the integrity of their own cultures. It is folly, then, to argue that nonnative media content will have no effect on local culture—as do many U.S. media content producers. The question today is, "How much influence will countries accept in exchange for fuller membership in the global village?" In light of instant, inexpensive, and open computer network communication, a parallel question is, "Have notions such as national sovereignty and cultural integrity lost their meaning?" For example, *The X-Files* is produced in Canada and *The Simpsons* is drawn in South Korea. The BBC broadcasts daily to a worldwide audience in 40 languages, as does Radio Beijing from China. CNN uses 14 satellites to transmit to 800 million viewers in 60 countries. Mexican soap operas dominate the television schedules of much of Latin and South America. Five of the six largest U.S. record companies have international ownership. Hollywood's Universal Studios is owned by Japanese Matsushita. MGM/UA is owned by an Italian company, Columbia Pictures by Japanese Sony, and 20th Century Fox by Rupert Murdoch's Australian corporation. Virtually every medium-specific chapter in this book, as well as those on advertising and public relations, discusses the globalization, internationalization, and concentration of those industries. As we saw in the opening vignette, respected theorists such as William Gibson and Marshall McLuhan agree that national sovereignty and cultural integrity are fast becoming anachronisms.

THE CASE FOR THE GLOBAL VILLAGE

As we also saw in the opening vignette, there are differing opinions about the benefits of this trend away from nation-specific cultures. Global village proponents see the world community coming closer together as a common culture is negotiated and, not incidentally, as we become more economically interconnected. "We are witnessing the revolution of the empowerment of the media consumer," argues Reuters Television Director Enriqué Jara (as cited in Hilliard & Keith, 1996, p. 1). There should be little fear that individual cultures and national identities will disappear, because the world's great diversity will ensure that culture-specific, special interest fare remains in demand. Modern media technology makes the delivery of this varied content not only possible but profitable. For example, native language versions of *Jeopardy* and *Wheel of Fortune* exist in virtually every Western European country.

THE CASE AGAINST THE GLOBAL VILLAGE

The global village is here, say those with a less optimistic view, and the problem is what it looks like. Professor Richard Rosenberg (1992) predicts the erosion of national sovereignty. "The advanced nations of the world, through their multi-national corporations, will greatly expand their control over the international flow of information. As a result, much of the world may become even more heavily dependent on the Western nations and Japan" (p. 331). He also predicts the demise of native cultures. "The ongoing assault on national cultures will continue, fostered by direct satellite broadcasts and worldwide information distribution networks" (p. 332).

Media critic Robert McChesney (1997) fears for worldwide democracy. "The present course," he writes, "is one where much of the world's entertainment and journalism will be provided by a handful of enormous firms, with invariably pro-profit and pro-global market political positions on the central issues of our times. The implications for political democracy, by any standard, are troubling" (p. 23).

Journalist David Shenk (1997) sees people isolated in their own little corners of the global village. He writes, "Just as a large cocktail party breaks up into a string of small conversations—and the larger the party is, the more conversations there are—so follow the people of earth when they are thrown together into one virtual village. In order to maintain intimate communication, and in order to keep up with our own sophistication, we fragment into tiny clusters within our global skyscraper" (p. 112).

THE ISSUE	THE GOOD NEWS	THE BAD NEWS	THE QUESTIONS
Technological advances have made communication easier and more democratic.	People can consume some media as wanted and needed rather than allowing media producers to schedule consumption time and content. The consumer, rather than the producer, has more control over meaning making. New technology allows participation by groups previously media-neglected (blind, handicapped, etc.). Users can participate anonymously, which leads to less prejudice (you never know who you might really be communicating with). In some cases, new technology allows communication to be accomplished at a fraction of the cost previously established by older media.	Control of much of the most influential content is in the hands of fewer and fewer people (namely, large multinational corporations). This is not democratic. Content decisions are made to fulfill economic or marketing goals, which define users of communication as simply consumers of content. Source anonymity makes it difficult to document and prosecute illegal acts. Electronic communication could lead to social fragmentation (society divided into the information rich and poor). In the information age, hardware, software, and the education to use them cost money. The difference between the "haves" and the "have-nots" will increase, placing a strain on democracy.	Can a smaller number of powerful people create havoc or revolution online (i.e., shutting down governments, bugging worldwide systems)? Should law enforcement have encryption codes on file to use under court order? Or is this an infringement of privacy and First Amendment rights? Will new technology be available to everyone? Will an information underclass form? Who will pay for information technology as it develops (private corporations, governments, users)? Who will control and regulate the information technology? Is official control necessary to ensure equal access and opportunity? Do advancements in technology result from societal need or market demands? Or is there a "technological push" -- technologies logically producing the next innovation? What is the public's role in each situation?
Technological advances have made the *creation* and *distribution* of media content easier.	Content can be duplicated and transmitted easily and without loss of quality. Individuals, *themselves,* can now be producers of media. Easier creation and distribution of content lead to more choice for media consumers. People can seek out and receive content they are interested in while ignoring other content. Information can be transmitted in "real time." A person can communicate to anywhere, from anyplace, at anytime. This affords freedom of movement and more convenience in terms of space and time. Individuals will have access to other people despite lack of physical proximity. We can finally, truly, be a global village.	Destructive (false, hateful, libelous, etc.) or even illegal communication content is also more easily created and distributed. Piracy is easier and more widespread. Questions of copyright and intellectual property are more complex, more difficult to define, and even more difficult to regulate. Too much choice leads to information overload. There is a big difference between having more information and having more understanding or comprehension. Important decisions are made based on instant information (whether it is accurate or not). There is little time for reflection and analysis. Content is sent and received without context. Reliability of sources becomes questionable. Context and continuity are lost; they are simply replaced by more "instant" content. Who wants to be available *all the time?* This "convenience" will add additional stress to life because "time off" becomes more difficult to find.	How can producers of content (corporations, artists, etc.) receive compensation for their work in a digital world of unlimited production and distribution possibilities? What will happen to security of personal information if content can be so easily copied and transmitted (privacy and security issues)? How much choice do audience members *really* want? From where is the information coming? Who will be the "authorities" creating, providing, and regulating the information (setting the agenda, etc.)? How much connection is too much? What kind of physical damage (headaches, carpal tunnel syndrome, etc.) and psychological damage (cyberaddiction, alienation, etc.) can be done by using communication too much or too often?

THE ISSUE	THE GOOD NEWS	THE BAD NEWS	THE QUESTIONS
New technology allows seamless alteration of sound and pictures.	Production and post-production are less expensive than in older media and allow unlimited possibilities for altering content. Creativity is only limited by one's imagination because technology can create the ways and means.	Images and sounds can be digitally (and invisibly) manipulated, so truth and reality are difficult to ascertain.	How will people be able to tell what is real and what is not? Will the definition of "reality" change?
New technology allows communication to be presented in a nonlinear way.	New communication technologies allow for more user control in the creation of content. Form, function, and time take on new meaning.	When immersed in a sea of data, audience members may not see a beginning, middle, or end. Communication errors are likely.	What will be the storytelling, narrative, and aesthetic conventions of the virtual real world?

Figure 15–4 The New Communication Technology Media Literacy Primer

There is no simple answer to the debate over protecting the integrity of local cultures. As we've just seen, there is even disagreement over the wisdom of doing so. Media literate people should at least be aware of the debate and its issues.

DEVELOPING MEDIA LITERACY SKILLS
Making Our Way in the Global Village

Questions raised by the new communication technologies often lack clear-cut, satisfactory answers. In fact, as the two major issues addressed in this chapter demonstrate—the impact of new communication technologies on democracy and their impact on national sovereignty and culture—different answers flow from different perspectives. For example, a world at peace with itself, its people sharing the common assumptions of a common culture, is a utopian dream. There are those who see it as attainable. But if the common culture that binds us is that of Mickey Mouse, is the harmony worth the loss of individual, idiosyncratic cultures?

Figure 15–4 offers a primer, a self-study guide, to help media literate individuals examine their own beliefs about the double edge of communication technologies. As we saw in Chapter 2, among the elements of media literacy are the development of an awareness of the impact of the media on individuals and society and an understanding of the process of mass communication. Use the primer's good news/bad news format to answer for yourself the questions that are raised, to build your awareness of media's impact, and to examine the possible influence media have on the process of mass communication.

It is important to remember that culture is neither innate nor inviolate. *We* construct culture—both dominant and bounded. Increasingly, we do so through mass communication. Before we can enter the forum where those cultures are constructed and maintained, we must understand where we stand and what we believe. We must be able to defend our positions. The hallmarks of a media literate individual are analysis and self-reflection; the primer provides a framework for exactly that.

Chapter Review

Technology is a double-edged sword. The new communication technologies generated renewed interest in the ideas of Marshall McLuhan: the global village, media as extensions of our bodies, the medium is the message, hot and cool media, and looking in the rearview mirror.

We see technology's touch in the way people use online communication to develop meaningful personal identities, MUDs being only the most obvious example. Privacy, too, takes on new meaning online. Privacy of communication—freedom from the snooping of others, including the government—can be accomplished in a number of ways, one being encryption. This secret coding, however, is problematic for many government officials. Online privacy has a second dimension—protecting the privacy of important personal information. People often willingly give up such information to unknown others. Technological data surveillance exists as well.

The new communication technologies are often touted as a boon to democracy because they permit greater citizen involvement. A more pessimistic view is that the commercialization of the Internet will make it as ineffective as more traditional media in serving participatory democracy. Critics also point to the technology and information gaps to argue that many people will be shut out of the electronic debate. Another question raised about so-called cyberdemocracy

revolves around the distinction between information and understanding. The Net's wealth of data may not necessarily produce a better-informed electorate.

Technology's ability to bring the people of the world together demands that we become better aware of the countries in which they live. Normative theories—the authoritarian, libertarian, social responsibility, and developing models—can describe the ideal operation of media systems in various countries. Japan, whose media system reflects its early reliance on Britain's social responsibility model as well as the U.S. libertarian model, has developed a system that reflects its culture. China, basing its system on the authoritarian model used by the Soviet Union of the past, reflects its culture as well.

The increased global flow of communication has rekindled the debate over cultural imperialism and whether nations can maintain their sovereignty and cultural identity in the face of a flood of foreign media. Some critics contend that the new communication technologies have made this cultural colonialization more likely; others have argued just the opposite.

The rapid changes that characterize today's communication technologies and the mass communication they foster demand that we increase our media literacy skills and that we keep ourselves aware of and open to change.

Questions for Review

1. How have new communication technologies altered the elements of the mass communication process?
2. Why is there renewed interest in Marshall McLuhan? What does he mean by the global village, media as extensions of our bodies, the medium is the message, hot and cool media, and looking in the rearview mirror?
3. What is a MUD? How does it operate?
4. What are the two primary privacy issues for online communication?
5. What are some of the arguments supporting the idea that the Internet will be a boost to participatory democracy? What are some of the counterarguments?

6. What are the technology and information gaps? What do they have to do with virtual or cyberdemocracy?
7. What are the four media system normative theories? Can you describe each?
8. What was the McBride Report? Why did most Western nations reject it?
9. What is meant by the New World Information Order?
10. What is meant by cultural imperialism?

Questions for Critical Thinking and Discussion

1. What do you think of Marshall McLuhan's ideas? How useful are they to you in deciphering the global village?
2. Have you ever participated in a MUD? If so, what was your experience? If not, what identity do you think you might adopt? Why?
3. Do you ever make personal information available online? If so, how confident are you in its security? Do you take steps to protect your privacy?
4. Do you believe that the new communication technologies will improve or damage participatory democracy? Why? Can you relate a personal experience of how the Net increased or limited your involvement in the political process?
5. Do you think that other countries, especially less developed ones, should worry about cultural imperialism? Why, or why not?

Important Resources

Barry, J. A. (1991). *Technobabble.* **Cambridge, MA: MIT Press.** Imbedded in this book-length essay on the impact of modern technology on the English language—computerese is no longer used only to describe and explain computing—is the deeper message of how cultures and technologies shape each other.

Branscomb, A. W. (1994). *From privacy to public access.* **New York: Basic Books.** A detailed discussion of the battle between private individuals and information industries to control the huge amounts of data generated by the information society.

Cate, F. H. (1997). *Privacy in the information age.* **Washington, DC: Brookings Institute.** A thorough and up-to-date examination of the scientific, legal, and sociological literature on new communication technologies and privacy. Significant attention is given to the powers and responsibilities of all important players: government, business, and individuals.

Dertouzos, M. (1997). *How the new world of information will change our lives.* **New York: Harper Edge.** The author heads MIT's Laboratory for Computer Science and employs his expertise in predicting how information technologies will remake our society, economy, culture, and individual lives. He calls it the Third Revolution.

Galtung, J., & Vincent, R. C. (1992). *Global glasnost: Toward a new world information and communication order?* **Cresskill, NJ: Hampton Press.** A historical overview of the 1970–1980 worldwide debate over the free flow of information and national sovereignty, covering all sides of the dispute while suggesting possible solutions: technological, economic, and political.

Gordon, W. T. (1997). *McLuhan for beginners.* **New York: Writers and Readers Publishing.** A funny, iconoclastic homage to one of media's great thinkers. It doesn't gloss over McLuhan's too optimistic infatuation with technology, but it does give the man his due.

Leeson, L. H. (ed.). (1996). *Clicking in: Hot links to a digital culture.* **Seattle, WA: Bay Press.** A collection of essays, some short and easy to read, others long and quite sophisticated, that examines the impact of new communication technologies on a variety of cultural issues—feminism, intellectual property, personal identity, and music and art, for example. Offering more in the way of ideas than data, it is valuable in sketching the outlines of possible technology-induced cultural change.

Mohammadi, A. (Ed.). (1997). *International communication globalization.* **Thousand Oaks, CA: Sage.** A collection of essays from scholars representing several countries and several philosophies about communication and national development and cultural sovereignty. There are interesting essays on global communication ethics and worldwide communication deregulation.

Pavlick, J. V. (1996). *New media technology: Cultural and commercial perspectives.* **Boston, MA: Allyn & Bacon.** A college-level textbook; a better discussion of all the issues—economic, political, social, cultural, and personal—that surround the emerging electronic technologies would be difficult to find.

Slouka, M. (1995). *War of the worlds: Cyberspace and the high-tech assault on reality.* **New York: Basic Books.** A small paperback replete with thoughtful and provocative counters to many of the utopian predictions of the digerati. The author is a university teacher and writes not only at a level appropriate for college students but also draws extensively on the cultural world in which students live for many of his examples.

Global Village Information Web Sites

The Center for Democracy and Technology	*http://www.cdt.org/*
Netscape's information about privacy protection	*http://home.netscape.com/newsref/std/cookiespec.html*
Links to Internet privacy issues	*http://consumer.net/linksinetpriv.htm*
UNESCO	*http://www.education.unesco.org*
NHK Broadcasting Cultural Research Institute (in English)	*http://www.nhk.or.jp/bunken/index-e.html*
BBC Broadcast House International Broadcasting History	*http://soli.inav.net/~jebraun/bbc_intl.htm*
Free Public Encryption Programs to Protect E-Mail Privacy	*http://www.pgp.com*

Appendix

Society of Professional Journalists' Code of Ethics

(originally adopted in 1926; most recently revised in 1987)

The Society of Professional Journalists believes the duty of journalists is to serve the truth.

We believe the agencies of mass communication are carriers of public discussion and information, acting on their Constitutional mandate and freedom to learn and report the facts.

We believe in public enlightenment as the forerunner of justice, and in our Constitutional role to seek the truth as part of the public's right to know the truth.

We believe those responsibilities carry obligations that require journalists to perform with intelligence, objectivity, accuracy, and fairness.

To these ends, we declare acceptance of the standards of practice here set forth:

I. RESPONSIBILITY

The public's right to know of events of public importance and interest is the overriding mission of the mass media. The purpose of distributing news and enlightened opinion is to serve the general welfare. Journalists who use their professional status as representatives of the public for selfish or other unworthy motives violate a high trust.

II. FREEDOM OF THE PRESS

Freedom of the press is to be guarded as an inalienable right of people in a free society. It carries with it the freedom and the responsibility to discuss, question, and challenge actions and utterances of our government and of our public and private institutions. Journalists uphold the right to speak unpopular opinions and the privilege to agree with the majority.

III. ETHICS

Journalists must be free of obligation to any interest other than the public's right to know the truth.

1. Gifts, favors, free travel, special treatment or privileges can compromise the integrity of journalists and their employers. Nothing of value should be accepted.

2. Secondary employment, political involvement, holding public office, and service in community organizations should be avoided if it compromises the integrity of journalists and their employers. Journalists and their employers should conduct their personal lives in a manner that protects them from conflict of interest, real or apparent. Their responsibilities to the public are paramount. That is the nature of their profession.

3. So-called news communications from private sources should not be published or broadcast without substantiation of their claims to news value.

4. Journalists will seek news that serves the public interest, despite the obstacles. They will make constant efforts to assure that the public's business is conducted in public and that public records are open to public inspection.

5. Journalists acknowledge the newsman's ethic of protecting confidential sources of information.

6. Plagiarism is dishonest and unacceptable.

IV. ACCURACY AND OBJECTIVITY

Good faith with the public is the foundation of all worthy journalism.

1. Truth is our ultimate goal.

2. Objectivity in reporting the news is another goal that serves as the mark of an experienced professional. It is a standard of performance toward which we strive. We honor those who achieve it.

3. There is no excuse for inaccuracies or lack of thoroughness.

4. Newspaper headlines should be fully warranted by the contents of the articles they accompany. Photographs and telecasts should give an accurate picture of an event and not highlight an event out of context.

5. Sound practice makes clear distinction between news reports and expressions of opinion. News reports should be free of opinion or bias and represent all sides of an issue.

6. Partisanship in editorial comment that knowingly departs from the truth violates the spirit of American journalism.

7. Journalists recognize their responsibility for offering informed analysis, comment, and editorial opinion on public events and issues. They accept the obligation to present such material by individuals whose competence, experience, and judgment qualify them for it.

8. Special articles or presentations devoted to advocacy or the writer's own conclusions and interpretations should be labeled as such.

V. FAIR PLAY

Journalists at all times will show respect for the dignity, privacy, rights, and well-being of people encountered in the course of gathering and presenting news.

1. The news media should not communicate unofficial charges affecting reputation or moral character without giving the accused a chance to reply.

2. The news media must guard against invading a person's right to privacy.

3. The media should not pander to morbid curiosity about details of vice and crime.

4. It is the duty of news media to make prompt and complete correction of their errors.

5. Journalists should be accountable to the public for their reports and the public should be encouraged to voice its grievances against the media. Open dialogue with our readers, viewers, and listeners should be fostered.

VI. PLEDGE

Adherence to this code is intended to preserve and strengthen the bond of mutual trust and respect between American journalists and the American people.

The Society shall—by programs of education and other means—encourage individual journalists to adhere to these tenets, and shall encourage journalistic publications and broadcasters to recognize their responsibility to frame codes of ethics in concert with their employees to serve as guidelines in furthering these goals.

American Society of Newspaper Editors' Statement of Principles

(adopted in 1975)

PREAMBLE

The First Amendment, protecting freedom of expression from abridgment by any law, guarantees to the people through their press a constitutional right, and thereby places on newspaper people a particular responsibility.

Thus journalism demands of its practitioners not only industry and knowledge but also the pursuit of a standard of integrity proportionate to the journalist's singular obligation.

To this end the American Society of Newspaper Editors sets forth this Statement of Principles as a standard encouraging the highest ethical and professional performance.

ARTICLE I—RESPONSIBILITY

The primary purpose of gathering and distributing news and opinion is to serve the general welfare by informing the people and enabling them to make judgments on the issues of the time. Newspapermen and women who abuse the power of their professional role for selfish motives or unworthy purposes are faithless to that public trust.

The American press was made free not just to inform or just to serve as a forum for debate but also to bring an independent scrutiny to bear on the forces of power in the society including the conduct of official power at all levels of government.

ARTICLE II—FREEDOM OF THE PRESS

Freedom of the press belongs to the people. It must be defended against encroachment or assault from any quarter, public or private.

Journalists must be constantly alert to see that the public's business is conducted in public. They must be vigilant against all who would exploit the press for selfish purposes.

ARTICLE III—INDEPENDENCE

Journalists must avoid impropriety and the appearance of impropriety as well as any conflict of interest or the appearance of conflict. They should neither accept anything nor pursue any activity that might compromise or seem to compromise their integrity.

ARTICLE IV—TRUTH AND ACCURACY

Good faith with the reader is the foundation of good journalism. Every effort must be made to assure that the news content is accurate, free from bias and in context, and that all sides are presented fairly. Editorials, analytical articles and commentary should be held to the same standards of accuracy with respect to facts as news reports.

Significant errors of fact, as well as errors of omission, should be corrected promptly and prominently.

ARTICLE V—IMPARTIALITY

To be impartial does not require the press to be unquestioning or to refrain from editorial expression. Sound practice, however, demands a clear distinction for the reader between news reports and opinion. Articles that contain opinion or personal interpretation should be clearly identified.

ARTICLE VI—FAIR PLAY

Journalists should respect the rights of people involved in the news, observe the common standards of decency and stand accountable to the public for the fairness and accuracy of their news reports.

Persons publicly accused should be given the earliest opportunity to respond.

Pledges of confidentiality to news sources must be honored at all costs, and therefore should not be given lightly. Unless there is clear and pressing need to maintain confidences, sources of information should be identified.

These principles are intended to preserve, protect and strengthen the bond of trust and respect between American journalists and the American people, a bond that is essential to sustain the grant of freedom entrusted to both by the nation's founders.

Radio-Television News Directors Association's Code of Broadcast News Ethics

The responsibility of radio and television journalists is to gather and report information of importance and interest to the public accurately, honestly and impartially.

The members of the Radio-Television News Directors Association accept these standards and will:

1. Strive to present the source or nature of broadcast news material in a way that is balanced, accurate and fair.
   a. They will evaluate information solely on its merits as news, rejecting sensationalism or misleading emphasis in any form.
   b. They will guard against using audio or video material in a way that deceives the audience.
   c. They will not mislead the public by presenting as spontaneous news any material which is staged or rehearsed.
   d. They will identify people by race, creed, nationality or prior status only when it is relevant.
   e. They will clearly label opinion and commentary.
   f. They will promptly acknowledge and correct errors.

2. Strive to conduct themselves in a manner that protects them from conflicts of interest, real or perceived. They will decline gifts or favors which would influence or appear to influence their judgments.

3. Respect the dignity, privacy and well-being of people with whom they deal.

4. Recognize the need to protect confidential sources. They will promise confidentiality only with the intention of keeping that promise.

5. Respect everyone's right to a fair trial.

6. Broadcast the private transmissions of other broadcasters only with permission.

7. Actively encourage observance of this Code by all journalists, whether members of the Radio-Television News Directors Association or not.

American Advertising Federation's Advertising Principles of American Business

1. Truth—Advertising shall reveal the truth, and shall reveal significant facts, the omission of which would mislead the public.

2. Substantiation—Advertising claims shall be substantiated by evidence in possession of the advertiser and the advertising agency prior to making such claims.

3. Comparisons—Advertising shall refrain from making false, misleading, or unsubstantiated statements or claims about a competitor or its products or services.

4. Bait Advertising—Advertising shall not offer products or services for sale unless such offer constitutes a bona fide effort to sell the advertised products or services and is not a device to switch consumers to other goods or services, usually higher priced.

5. Guarantees and Warranties—Advertising of guarantees and warranties shall be explicit, with sufficient information to apprise consumers of their principal terms and limitations or, when space or time restrictions preclude such disclosures, the advertisement shall clearly reveal where the full text of the guarantee or warranty can be examined before purchase.

6. Price Claims—Advertising shall avoid price claims which are false or misleading, or savings claims which do not offer provable savings.

7. Testimonials—Advertising containing testimonials shall be limited to those of competent witnesses who are reflecting a real and honest opinion or experience.

8. Taste and Decency—Advertising shall be free of statements, illustrations, or implications which are offensive to good taste or public decency.

Public Relations Society of America's Code of Professional Standards for the Practice of Public Relations

(most recently revised in 1988)

DECLARATION OF PRINCIPLES

Members of the Public Relations Society of America base their professional principles on the fundamental value and dignity of the individual holding that the free exercise of human rights, especially freedom of speech, freedom of assembly, and freedom of the press, is essential to the practice of public relations.

In serving the interests of clients and employers, we dedicate ourselves to the goals of better communication, understanding, and cooperation among the diverse individuals, groups, and institutions of society, and of equal opportunity of employment in the public relations profession.

We pledge:

To conduct ourselves professionally, with truth, accuracy, fairness, and responsibility to the public;

To improve our individual competence and advance the knowledge and proficiency of the profession through continuing research and education;

And to adhere to the articles of the Code of Professional Standards for the Practice of Public Relations as adopted by the governing Assembly of the Society.

CODE OF PROFESSIONAL STANDARDS FOR THE PRACTICE OF PUBLIC RELATIONS

These articles have been adopted by the Public Relations Society of America to promote and maintain high standards of public service and ethical conduct among its members.

1. A member shall conduct his or her professional life in accord with the *public interest*.

2. A member shall exemplify high standards of *honesty and integrity* while carrying out dual obligations to a client or employer and to the democratic process.

3. A member shall *deal fairly* with the public, with past or present

clients or employers, and with fellow practitioners, giving due respect to the ideal of free inquiry and to the opinions of others.

4. A member shall adhere to the highest standards of *accuracy and truth*, avoiding extravagant claims or unfair comparisons and giving credit for ideas and words borrowed from others.

5. A member shall not knowingly disseminate *false or misleading information* and shall act promptly to correct erroneous communications for which he or she is responsible.

6. A member shall not engage in any practice which has the purpose of *corrupting* the integrity of channels of communications or the processes of government.

7. A member shall be prepared to *identify publicly* the name of the client or employer on whose behalf any public communication is made.

8. A member shall not use any individual or organization professing to serve or represent an announced cause, or professing to be independent or unbiased, but actually serving another or *undisclosed interest*.

9. A member shall not *guarantee the achievement* of specified results beyond the member's direct control.

10. A member shall *not represent conflicting* or competing interests without the express consent of those concerned, given after a full disclosure of the facts.

11. A member shall not place himself or herself in a position where the member's *personal interest is or may be in conflict* with an obligation to an employer or client, or others, without full disclosure of such interests to all involved.

12. A member shall *not accept fees, commissions, gifts or any other consideration* from anyone except clients or employers for whom services are performed without their express consent, given after full disclosure of the facts.

13. A member shall scrupulously safeguard the *confidences and privacy rights* of present, former, and prospective clients or employers.

14. A member shall not intentionally *damage the professional reputation* or practice of another practitioner.

15. If a member has evidence that another member has been guilty of unethical, illegal, or unfair practices, including those in violation of this Code, the member is obligated to present the information promptly to the proper authorities of the Society for action in accordance with the procedure set forth in Article XII of the Bylaws.

16. A member called as a witness in a proceeding for enforcement of this Code is obligated to appear, unless excused for sufficient reason by the judicial panel.

17. A member shall, as soon as possible, sever relations with any organization or individual if such relationship requires conduct contrary to the articles of this Code.

Glossary

abacus   a counting device composed of a fixed number of balls or other markers on a series of parallel rods

absolutist position   regarding the First Amendment, the idea that no law means no law

acquisitions editor   the person in charge of determining which books a publisher will publish

Acta Diurna   written on a tablet, account of the deliberations of the Roman senate; an early "newspaper"

actual malice   the standard for libel in coverage of public figures consisting of "knowledge of its falsity" or "reckless disregard" for whether it is true or not

ad hoc balancing of interests   in individual First Amendment cases, several factors should be weighed in determining how much freedom the press is granted

administrative research   studies of the immediate, practical influence of mass communication

advertorial   ads in magazines and newspapers that take on the appearance of genuine editorial content

affiliate   a broadcasting station that aligns itself with a network

agenda setting   theory that argues that media may not tell us what to think but that media tell us what to think about

aggressive cues model   of media violence; media portrayals can indicate that certain classes of people are acceptable targets for real-world aggression

AIDA approach   the idea that to persuade consumers advertising must attract Attention, create Interest, stimulate Desire, and promote Action

Alien and Sedition Acts   series of four laws passed by 1798 U.S. Congress making illegal the writing, publishing, or printing of "any false scandalous and malicious writing" about the president, the congress, or the U.S. government

aliteracy   possessing the ability to read but being unwilling to do so

all-channel legislation   1962 law requiring all television sets imported into or manufactured in the United States to be equipped with both VHF and UHF receivers

AM/FM combo   two stations, one AM and one FM, simultaneously broadcasting identical content

applied ethics   the application of metaethics and normative ethics to very specific situations

Archie   an Internet service and search program

ascertainment   requires broadcasters to ascertain or actively and affirmatively determine the nature of their audiences' interest, convenience, and necessity; no longer enforced

attitude change theory   theory that explains how people's attitudes are formed, shaped, and changed and how those attitudes influence behavior

audimeter   device for recording when the television set is turned on, the channel to which it is tuned, and the time of day; used in compiling ratings

audion tube   vacuum tube developed by DeForest that became the basic invention for all radio and television

authoritarian media system   a national media system characterized by authoritarian control

average quarter-hour   how many people are listening to a broadcast station in each 15-minute day part

awareness test   ad research technique that measures the cumulative effect of a campaign in terms of a product's "consumer consciousness"

B-movie   the second, typically less expensive, movie in a double feature

banners   online advertising messages akin to billboards

Bill of Rights   the first 10 amendments to the U.S. Constitution

billings   total sale of broadcast airtime

Biltmore Agreement   settled the press war between newspapers, which had refused their services to their electronic competitors, and radio

binary code   information transformed into a series of digits 1 and 0 for storage and manipulation in computers

block booking   the practice of requiring exhibitors to rent groups of movies (often inferior) to secure a better one

blockbuster mentality filmmaking characterized by reduced risk taking and more formulaic movies; business concerns are said to dominate artistic considerations

bounded cultures groups with specific but not dominant cultures

brand awareness an advertising goal when a number of essentially similar brands populate a given product category

broadcast spectrum in the atmosphere, layers of frequencies and channels on which the FCC grants permission to transmit

broadsides (sometimes **broadsheets**) early colonial newspapers imported from England, single-sheet announcements or accounts of events

browsers software programs loaded on personal computers and used to download and view Web files

calotype early system of photography using translucent paper from which multiple prints could be made

catharsis theory that watching mediated violence reduces people's inclination to behave aggressively

causal relationships the direct impact of one or more variables on one or more other variables

cease-and-desist order demand made by a regulatory agency that a given illegal practice be stopped

censorware unflattering name given to Web content filtering software by its opponents

chained Bibles Bibles attached to church furniture or walls by early European church leaders

channel surfing travelling through the television channels focusing neither on specific programs nor on the commercials they house

checkbook journalism paying sources for information or interviewees for their interviews

cinematographe Lumière brothers' device that both photographed and projected action

circulation the number of issues of a magazine or newspaper that are sold

civic journalism modern practice of newspapers actively engaging the community in their reporting of important civic issues

clear time when local affiliates carry a network's program

click stream the series of choices made by a user on the Web

Clipper Chip U.S. government-sanctioned encryption system permitting secure communication; the government holds the translation key should it want, for good reason, to intercept that communication

clutter in television, when many individual commercials share one commercial break

CNN effect the power of television pictures to emotionally move people so powerfully that important military and political decisions are driven by those pictures rather than by well-thought-out policy considerations

collateral materials printing, research, and photographs that PR firms handle for clients, charging as much as 17.65% for this service

commissions in advertising, placement of advertising in media is compensated, at typically 15% of the cost of the time or space, through commissions

commodification of information making information a tangible, salable thing

communication the process of creating shared meaning

comparative analysis the study of different countries' mass media systems

comparative studies see **comparative analysis**

compensation network payments to affiliates for clearing content

complementary copy newspaper and magazine content that reinforces the advertiser's message, or at least does not negate it

concentration of ownership ownership of different and numerous media companies concentrated in fewer and fewer hands

concept films movies that can be described in one line

conduction system wireless communication system using signals sent through water and ground

confidentiality the ability of media professionals to keep secret the names of people who provide them with information

consumer culture where personal worth and identity reside not in the people themselves but in the products with which they surround themselves

consumer juries ad research technique where people considered representative of a target market review a number of approaches or variations of a campaign or ad

content analysis the objective, systematic, and quantitative description of the content of communication

control group subjects in an experiment who do not encounter the independent variable

controlled circulation when a magazine is provided at no cost to readers who meet some specific set of advertiser-attractive criteria

conventions   in media content, certain distinctive, standardized style elements of individual genres

cool medium   a McLuhan concept that requires consumers to "fill in the blanks" to make meaning; because media are cool, the consumer must make the heat

copy testing   measuring the effectiveness of advertising messages by showing them to consumers; used for all forms of advertising

copyright   identifying and granting ownership of a given piece of expression to protect the creators' financial interest in it

corantos   one-page news sheets on specific events, printed in English but published in Holland and imported into England by British booksellers; an early "newspaper"

corrective advertising   a new set of ads required by a regulatory body and produced by the offender that correct the original misleading effort

correlation   the strength of relationship between two or more variables

cost per thousand (CPM)   in advertising, the cost of reaching 1,000 audience members, computed by the cost of an ad's placement divided by the number of thousands of consumers it reaches

cottage industry   an industry characterized by small operations closely identified with their personnel

cover   rerecording of one artist's music by another

critical cultural theory   idea that media operate primarily to justify and support the status quo at the expense of ordinary people

critical research   studies of media's contribution to the larger issues of what kind of nation we are building, what kind of people we are becoming

cruising   see **channel surfing**

cultivation analysis   idea that television "cultivates" or constructs a reality of the world that, although possibly inaccurate, becomes the accepted reality simply because we as a culture believe it to be the reality

cultural definition of communication   communication is a symbolic process whereby reality is produced, maintained, repaired, and transformed; from James Carey

cultural imperialism   the invasion of an indigenous people's culture, through mass media, by outside, powerful countries

cultural theory   the idea that meaning and therefore effects are negotiated by media and audiences as they interact in the culture

culture   the world made meaningful; socially constructed and maintained through communication, it limits as well as liberates us, differentiates as well as unites us, defines our realities and thereby shapes the ways we think, feel, and act

cume   the cumulative audience, the number of people who listen to a radio station for at least 5 minutes in any one day

cyberaddiction   Internet users' addiction to the online experience

cyberadvertising   placement of commercials on various online sites

cybernetics   use of information to control or govern systems and environments that house them

cyberspace   technologies and activities associated with or dependent on computers

daguerreotype   process of recording images on polished metal plates, usually copper, covered with a thin layer of silver iodide emulsion

dataveillance   the massive electronic collection and distillation of consumer data

decoding   interpreting sign/symbol systems

democracy   government by the people

demographic segmentation   advertisers' appeal to audiences composed of varying personal and social characteristics such as race, gender, and economic level

dependency theory   idea that media's power is a function of audience members' dependency on the media and their content

dependent variable   phenomenon whose change as a result of manipulation of the independent variable is measured

deregulation   relaxation of ownership and other rules for radio and television

desensitization   the idea that viewers become more accepting of real-world violence because of its constant presence in television fare

desktop publishing   small-scale print content design, layout, and production made possible by inexpensive computer hardware and software

developmental model   of media systems; government and media work in partnership to ensure that media assist in the planned, beneficial development of the country

digital audio radio service (DARS)   direct home or automobile delivery of audio by satellite

digital audio tape (DAT)   introduced in the early 1970s, offers digital quality sound purity in a cassette tape format

digital computer a computer that processes data reduced to a binary code

digital recording recording based on conversion of sound into 1s and 0s logged in millisecond intervals in a computerized translation process

dime novels inexpensive late 19th- and early 20th-century books that concentrated on frontier and adventure stories; sometimes called *pulp novels*

disinhibitory effects in social learning theory, seeing a model rewarded for prohibited or threatening behavior increases the likelihood that the observer will perform that behavior

dissonance theory argues that people, when confronted by new information, experience a kind of mental discomfort, a dissonance; as a result, they consciously and subconsciously work to limit or reduce that discomfort through the selective processes

distant importation of signals delivery of distant television signals by cable television for the purpose of improving reception

diurnals daily accounts of local news printed in 1620s England; forerunners of our daily newspaper

DMX (Digital Music Express) home delivery of audio by cable

dominant culture the culture that seems to hold sway with the large majority of people; that which is normative

double feature two films on the same bill

duopoly single ownership and management of multiple radio stations in one market

e-mail (electronic mail) function of Internet allowing communication via computer with anyone else online, anyplace in the world, with no long-distance fees

early window the idea that media give children a window on the world before they have the critical and intellectual ability to judge what they see

editorial policy newspapers' and magazines' positions on certain specific issues

encoding transforming ideas into an understandable sign/symbol system

encryption coding online content at the source so that it can only be read by an end user with appropriate decoding software; used for security purposes

environmental incentives in social learning theory, the notion that real-world incentives can lead observers to ignore negative vicarious reinforcement

error term see *margin of error*

estimated sampling error see *margin of error*

ethics rules of behavior or moral principles that guide actions in given situations

ethnographic research naturalistic examinations of audiences in specific and natural places

experimental conditions the groups in an experiment who are confronted with variations in the independent variable

experiments a research method where the manipulation of variables is employed to demonstrate the presence of causal relationships

factory studios the first film production companies

fair use in copyright law, instances where material may be used without permission or payment

Fairness Doctrine requires broadcasters to cover issues of public importance and to be fair in that coverage; abolished in 1987

feature syndicates clearinghouses for the work of columnists, cartoonists, and other creative individuals, providing their work to newspapers and other media outlets

feedback the response to a given communication

fiber optics signals carried by light beams over glass fibers

field experiment experiment conducted in subjects' actual environments in the course of normal social events

File Transfer Protocol (FTP) an Internet facility allowing copying of files between computers

Financial Interest and Syndication Rules FCC rules delineating the amount of ownership the television networks are allowed in the programming they air

Fin-Syn see *Financial Interest and Syndication Rules*

First Amendment Congress shall make no law respecting an establishment of religion, or prohibiting the free exercise thereof; or abridging the freedom of speech, or of the press; or the right of the people peacefully to assemble, and to petition the Government for a redress of grievances

first-run syndication original programming produced specifically for the syndicated television market

fixed fee arrangements when PR firms perform a specific set of services for a client for a specific and prearranged fee

flack a derogatory name sometimes applied to public relations professionals

flame an angry e-mail message

flat rate billing   a flat monthly charge levied by a provider for Internet access

focus groups   small groups of people who are interviewed, typically to provide advertising or public relations professionals with detailed information

forced exposure   ad research technique used primarily for television commercials, requiring advertisers to bring consumers to a theater or other facility where they see a television program, complete with the new ads

format   a radio station's particular sound or programming content

Frankfurt School   media theory, centered in neo-Marxism, that valued serious art, viewing its consumption as a means to elevate all people toward a better life; typical media fare was seen as pacifying ordinary people while repressing them

functional displacement   when a newer medium replaces an older medium's functions, forcing that medium to find new roles in order to survive

generalizability   the question of applying demonstrated causal relationships to the larger, real-world environment

genre   a form of media content with a standardized, distinctive style and conventions

global village   a McLuhan concept; new communication technologies permit people to become increasingly involved in one another's lives

Gopher   a menu-based tool for burrowing or tunneling through files on the Internet; Gopher menus point to other menus, which ultimately point to specific documents

grand theory   a theory designed to describe and explain all aspects of a given phenomenon

grazing   watching several television programs simultaneously

greenwashing   public relations practice of countering the public relations efforts aimed at clients by environmentalists

griots   the "talking chiefs" in orally based African tribes

gripe site   Web page designed to counter or challenge another person or institution, typically one having more power than the site's creator

hackers   people interested in technology, information, and communication through computers

hard news   news characterized by factual accounting, data, and information

Hawthorne effect   when participation *per se* in an experiment alters subjects' behavior

HDTV   digital compression of television signals allowing transmission of six or seven channels of programming in a single band

historical research   objective examination of phenomena in their own time

home page   entry way into a Web site, containing information and hyperlinks to other material

hosts   computers linking individual personal computer users to the Internet

hot medium   a McLuhan concept; hot media are high in definition, providing a lot of information and leaving consumers with little to do other than interpret what is presented

hyperlink   connection, imbedded in Internet or Web site, allowing instant access to other material in that site as well as to material in other sites

hypodermic needle theory   idea that media are a dangerous drug that can directly enter a person's system

iconoscope tube   first practical television camera tube, developed in 1923

identification   in social learning theory, a special form of imitation where observers do not exactly copy what they have seen but make a more generalized but related response

ideogrammatic alphabet   a symbol- or picture-based alphabet

imitation   in social learning theory, the direct replication of an observed behavior

indecency   in broadcasting, language or material that depicts sexual or excretory activities in a way offensive to contemporary community standards

independent variable   the phenomenon that is altered or varied in an experiment

inferential feedback   in the mass communication process, feedback is typically indirect rather than direct; that is, it is inferential

infomercials   program-length commercials designed to look like news or entertainment programs

information gap   the widening disparity in amounts and types of information available to information haves and have-nots

information processing theory   theory that explains how viewers individually watch and process the news

information society   a society where the creation and exchange of information is the predominant social and economic activity

information superhighway   popular name for today's worldwide computer digital data networks

inhibitory effects in social learning theory, seeing a model punished for a behavior reduces the likelihood that the observer will perform that behavior

instant books books published very soon after some well-publicized public event

intermercials attractive, lively commercials that run while people are waiting for Web pages to download

Internet a global network of interconnected computers that communicate freely and share and exchange information

interpersonal communication communication between one or a few people

islands in children's television commercials, the product is shown simply, in actual size against a neutral background

Joint Operating Agreement (JOA) permitted when a failing paper is allowed to merge most aspects of its business with a successful local competitor, as long as editorial and reporting operations remain separate

kinescope improved picture tube developed by Zworykin for RCA

kinetograph William Dickson's early motion picture camera

kinetoscope peep show devices for the exhibition of kinetographs

LANs (Local Area Networks) networks connecting two or more computers, usually within the same building

libel the false and malicious publication of material that damages a person's reputation (typically applied to print media)

libertarianism philosophy of the press that asserts that good and rational people can tell right from wrong if presented with full and free access to information; therefore censorship is unnecessary

limited effects theory media's influence is limited by people's individual differences, social categories, and personal relationships

linotype technology that allowed the mechanical rather than manual setting of print type

liquid barretter first audio device permitting the reception of wireless voices; developed by Fessenden

literacy the ability to effectively and efficiently comprehend and utilize a given form of communication

literate culture a culture that employs a written language

lobbying in public relations, directly interacting with elected officials or government regulators and agents

macro-level effects media's wide-scale social and cultural impact

magic bullet theory the mass society theory idea that media are a powerful "killing force" that directly penetrates a person's system

mainframe computer a large central computer to which users are connected by terminals

mainstreaming in cultivation analysis, television's ability to move people toward a common understanding of how things are

margin of error the predictable and built-in level of error that accompanies all samples of a given size

mass communication the process of creating shared meaning between the mass media and their audiences

mass communication theories explanations and predictions of social phenomena relating mass communication to various aspects of our personal and cultural lives or social systems

mass medium (pl. **mass media**) when a medium carries messages to a large number of people

mass society theory the idea that media are corrupting influences; they undermine the social order, and "average" people are defenseless against their influence

media councils panels of people from both the media and the public who investigate complaints against the media and publish their findings

media literacy the ability to effectively and efficiently comprehend and utilize mass communication

medium (pl. **media**) vehicle by which messages are conveyed

metaethics examination of a culture's understanding of its fundamental values

micro computer a very small computer that uses a microprocessor to handle information (also called a **personal computer** or **PC**)

micro-level effects effects of media on individuals

middle-range theories ideas that explain or predict only limited aspects of the mass communication process

mini-computers a relatively large central computer to which users are connected by terminals; not as large as a mainframe computer

MNA reports multinetwork area television ratings based on the 70 largest markets

modeling in social learning theory, learning through imitation and identification

modem   a device that translates digital computer information into an analog form so it can be transmitted through telephone lines

montage   tying together two separate but related shots in such a way that they take on a new, unified meaning

moral agent   in an ethical dilemma, the person making the decision

muckraking   a form of crusading journalism that primarily used magazines to agitate for change

MUD   multi-user domain; an online, virtual "community" where users are encouraged to create their own identities, which then interact with other virtual citizens of that community

multimedia   advanced sound and image capabilities for micro computers

multiple points of access   ability of a literate media consumer to access or approach media content from a variety of personally satisfying directions

music licensing company   organizations that collect fees based on recorded music users' gross receipts and distribute the money to songwriters and artists

narrowcasting   aiming broadcast programming at smaller, more demographically homogeneous audiences

natural experiment   see *field experiment*

neo-Marxist theory   the theory that people are oppressed by those who control the culture, the superstructure, as opposed to the base

network   centralized production, distribution, decision-making organization that links affiliates for the purpose of delivering their viewers to advertisers

newbies   people new to the Internet and inexperienced in its customs and conventions

news production research   the study of how economic and other influences on the way news is produced distort and bias news coverage toward those in power

news staging   re-creation on television news of some event that is believed to have happened or which could have happened

newsbook   early weekly British publications that carried ads

newspaper chains   businesses that own two or more newspapers

niche marketing   aiming media content or consumer products at smaller, more demographically homogeneous audiences

nickelodeons   the first movie houses; admission was one nickel

Nipkow disc   first workable device for generating electrical signals suitable for the transmission of a scene

noise   anything that interferes with successful communication

nonduplication rule   mid-1960s FCC ruling that AM and FM license holders in the same market must broadcast different content at least 50% of the time

normative ethics   generalized theories, rules, and principles of ethical or moral behavior

normative theory   an idea that explains how media should ideally operate in a given system of social values

O&O   a broadcasting station that is owned and operated by a network

obscenity   unprotected expression determined by (a) whether the average person, applying contemporary community standards, would find that the work, taken as a whole, appeals to the prurient interest, (b) whether the work depicts or describes, in a patently offensive way, sexual conduct specifically defined by the applicable state law, and (c) whether the work, taken as a whole, lacks serious literary, artistic, political, or scientific value

observational learning   in social learning theory, observers can acquire (learn) new behaviors simply by seeing those behaviors performed

off-network   broadcast industry term for syndicated content that originally aired on a network

offset lithography   late 19th-century advance making possible printing from photographic plates rather than from metal casts

oligopoly   a media system whose operation is dominated by a few large companies

ombudsman   internal arbiter of performance for media organizations

operating policy   spells out standards for everyday operations for newspapers and magazines

operating system   the software that tells the computer how to work

opinion followers   people who receive opinion leaders' interpretations of media content; from **two-step flow theory**

opinion leaders   people who initially consume media content, interpret it in light of their own values and beliefs, and then pass it on to opinion followers; from **two-step flow theory**

oppositional decoding   interpreting media content in a manner counter to its apparent intent

oral (or **preliterate**) **culture**   a culture without a written language

overnights   television ratings data gathered from homes connected by phone lines to Nielsen computers

paparazzi   freelance photographers

papyrus   early form of paper composed of pressed strips of sliced reed

paradigm   a theory that summarizes and is consistent with all known facts

paradigm shift   fundamental, even radical rethinking of what people believe to be true for a given body of knowledge

parchment   writing material made from prepared animal skins

parity products   products generally perceived as alike by consumers no matter who makes them

participant-observer research   studies where the researcher "joins" a group or enters a setting and, while participating in its ongoing activities, chronicles those activities and the interactions surrounding them

participants   the subjects in an experiment

pass-along readership   measurement of publication readers who neither subscribe nor buy single copies but who borrow a copy or read one in a doctor's office or library

pass-by rate   percentage of homes that have access to a cable system that actually take the service

pay-as-you-go pricing   billing Internet users based on the amount of time spent online

penny press   newspapers in the 1930s selling for one penny

peoplemeter   remote control keypad device for recording television viewing for taking ratings

persistence of vision   images our eyes gather are retained by our brains for about ¹⁄₂₄ of a second, producing the appearance of constant motion

personal computer (PC)   see **micro computer**

phenomenology   study of media content as it is, as it exists

piggybacking   in television advertising, when a single sponsor presents two products in the same commercial

pixels   the smallest picture element in an electronic imaging system such as a television or computer screen

playlist   predetermined sequence of selected records to be played by a disc jockey

pocketpieces   television ratings based on a national sample, computed and reported every two weeks

policy book   delineates standards of operation for local broadcasters

population   in survey research, the group under scrutiny to which the results obtained from a sample are generalized

pornography   expression calculated solely to supply sexual excitement

positioning   advertisers' practice of encouraging the culture to perceive their products as symbols that have meaning beyond the products' actual function

preliterate culture   see **oral culture**

primary sources   in historical research, material contemporary to the object under investigation

prior restraint   power of the government to *prevent* publication or broadcast of expression

product positioning   the practice in advertising of assigning meaning to a product based on who buys the product rather than on the product itself

production values   media content's internal language and grammar; its style and quality

propaganda   generation of more or less automatic responses to given symbols

providers (Internet)   companies that offer Internet connections at monthly rates depending on the kind and amount of access needed; also called **servers**

pseudo-events   events that have no real informational or issue meaning; they exist merely to attract media attention

psychographic segmentation   advertisers' appeal to consumer groups of varying lifestyles, attitudes, values, and behavior patterns

public domain   in copyright law, the use of material without permission once the copyright expires

puffery   the little lie or exaggeration that makes advertising more entertaining than it might otherwise be

pulp novels   see **dime novels**

qualitative research   research that examines aspects of the mass communication process in their natural contexts

quantitative research   scientific methods such as experiments, surveys, and content analyses that utilize numerically based observations in the analysis of mass communication

radiation system   wireless communication system allowing reliable sending and receiving of signals through the air

random sample   a sample in which each member of a group has an equal chance of inclusion

rating percentage of a market's total population that is reached by a piece of broadcast programming

recall testing ad research technique where consumers are asked to identify which ads are most easily remembered

recognition tests ad research technique where people who have seen a given publication are asked whether they remember seeing a given ad

reinforcement theory Joseph Klapper's idea that if media have any impact at all it is in the direction of reinforcement

remainders unsold copies of books returned to the publisher by bookstores to be sold at great discount

research the objective search for knowledge

respondents participants in a survey

retainer in advertising, an agreed-upon amount of money a client pays an ad agency for a specific series of services

ritual perspective the view of media as central to the representation of shared beliefs and culture

safe harbor times of the broadcast day (typically 10 P.M. to 6 A.M.) when children are not likely to be in the listening or viewing audience

sample in survey research, respondents drawn from the population who are considered representative of that population

satellite-delivered media tour spokespeople can be simultaneously interviewed by a worldwide audience hooked to the interviewee by telephone

search engines (sometimes called **spiders**, or **Web crawlers**) Web or Net-search software providing on-screen menus

secondary service a radio station's second, or non-primary, format

secondary sources in historical research, reports and material produced after the period in question that bear on it

selective attention see **selective exposure**

selective exposure the idea that people expose themselves or attend to those messages that are consistent with their preexisting attitudes and beliefs

selective perception idea that people interpret messages in a manner consistent with their preexisting attitudes and beliefs

selective processes people expose themselves to, remember best and longest, and reinterpret messages that are consistent with their preexisting attitudes and beliefs

selective retention assumes that people remember best and longest those messages that are consistent with their existing attitudes and beliefs

self-righting principle John Milton's articulation of libertarianism

servers, Internet see **providers**

share the percentage of people listening to radio or of homes using television tuned in to a given piece of programming

shield laws legislation that expressly protects reporters' rights to maintain sources' confidentiality in courts of law

shopbills attractive, artful business cards used by early British tradespeople to promote themselves

short ordering network practice of ordering only one or two episodes of a new television series

signs in social construction of reality, things that have subjective meaning

siquis pinup want ads common in Europe before and in early days of newspapers

Sixth Report and Order fundamental blueprint for the technical operation of television, issued in 1952

slander oral or spoken defamation of a person's character (typically applied to broadcasting)

smiley in an e-mail, a graphic representation of emotion or other conversational nuance

social construction of reality theory for explaining how cultures construct and maintain their realities using signs and symbols; argues that people learn to behave in their social world through interaction with it

social learning theory idea that people learn through observation

social responsibility theory (or **model**) normative theory or model asserting that media must remain free of government control but, in exchange, must serve the public

soft news news characterized by opinion, background, and "color"

spam a mass mailing of Internet messages to users whether they want them or not

spectrum scarcity broadcast spectrum space is limited, so not everyone who wants to broadcast can; those who are granted licenses must accept regulation

spiders see **search engines**

split runs special versions of a given issue of a magazine in which editorial content and ads vary according to some specific demographic or regional grouping

spot commercial sales in broadcasting, selling individual advertising spots on a given program to a wide variety of advertisers

Standards and Practices Department the internal content review operation of a television network

stereotyping application of a standardized image or conception applied to members of certain groups, usually based on limited information

stimulation model of media violence; viewing mediated violence can increase the likelihood of subsequent aggressive behavior

stratified random sample in survey research, dividing a population according to some important characteristic before each division is randomly sampled

stripped broadcasting a syndicated television show at the same time five nights a week

subsidiary rights the sale of a book, its contents, even its characters to outside interests, such as filmmakers

survey a research method used to describe phenomena and their relationships in the actual environment at a given time

sweeps periods special television ratings times in February, May, July, and November in which diaries are distributed to thousands of sample households in selected markets

syllable alphabet a phonetically based alphabet employing sequences of vowels and consonants, that is, words

symbolic interaction the idea that people give meaning to symbols and then those symbols control people's behavior in their presence

symbols in social construction of reality, things that have objective meaning

syndicates feature services that operate as clearinghouses for the work of columnists, essayists, cartoonists, and other creative individuals

syndication sale of radio or television content to stations on a market-by-market basis

synergy the use by media conglomerates of as many channels of delivery as possible for similar content

targeting aiming media content or consumer products at smaller, more specific audiences

taste publics groups of people or audiences bound by little more than their interest in a given form of media content

technology gap the widening disparity between communication technology haves and have-nots

teletext see **videotext**

television freeze 1948 freeze in authorization of new television stations while the FCC resolved a number of technical problems

telnet an Internet tool that allows users to log onto other computers on the Net as if they were connected to them directly

terminals user workstations that are connected to larger centralized computers

theatrical films movies produced primarily for initial exhibition on theater screens

third person effect the common attitude that others are influenced by media messages, but we are not

time-shifting taping a show on a VCR for later viewing

toy-based children's television programming television programs aimed at children that feature characters that are also toys

trade books hard- or softcover books including fiction and most nonfiction and cookbooks, biographies, art books, coffeetable books, and how-to books

traffic cop analogy in broadcast regulation, the idea that the FCC, as a traffic cop, has the right to control not only the flow of broadcast traffic but its composition

transmissional perspective the view of media as senders of information for the purpose of control

trustee model in broadcast regulation, the idea that broadcasters serve as the public's trustees or fiduciaries

two-step flow theory the idea that media's influence on people's behavior is limited by opinion leaders, people who initially consume media content, interpret it in light of their own values and beliefs, and then pass it on to opinion followers who have less frequent contact with media

typification schemes in social construction of reality, collections of meanings people have assigned to some phenomenon or situation

unique selling proposition (USP) the aspect of an advertised product that sets it apart from other brands in the same product category

unobtrusive observer in ethnomethodological research, a researcher who is present at and observing a situation but who does not intrude on it

URL (**U**niform **R**esource **L**ocator) the designation of each file or directory on the host computer connected to the Internet

USENET also known as network news, an internationally distributed Internet bulletin board system

uses and gratifications approach the idea that media don't do things *to* people; people do things *with* media

V-chip popular name for television set technology allowing parents to program out specific categories of content

VALS advertisers' psychographic segmentation strategy that classifies consumers according to values and lifestyles

vast wasteland expression coined by FCC Chair Newton Minow in 1961 to describe television content

Veronica (**V**ery **E**asy **R**odent-**O**riented **N**et-Wide **I**ndex to **C**omputerized **A**rchives) an Internet tool that builds a searchable index of Gopher menus

vertical integration studios that produced their own films, distributed them through their own outlets, and exhibited them in their own theaters

vicarious reinforcement in social learning theory, the observation of reinforcement operates in the same manner as actual reinforcement

video news release preproduced report about a client or its product that is distributed on videocassette free of charge to television stations

videotext (or **teletext**) paperless newspapers or news on demand delivered by video screen

virtue ethics emphasize the moral agent's character

WAIS (**W**ide **A**rea **I**nformation **S**ervers) an Internet tool that examines the full text of all the documents on a particular database

WANs (**W**ide **A**rea **N**etworks) networks that connect several LANs in different locations

Web crawlers see **search engines**

WEB-TV online delivery of high definition television to special home receivers

Webzines online magazines

willing suspension of disbelief audience practice of willingly accepting the content before them as real

wire services news-gathering organizations that provide content to members

wired radio employed in remote areas of many developing countries; centrally located loudspeakers that deliver radio broadcasts

wireless telegraph early efforts at long-distance communication that led to development of radio

World Wide Web a tool that serves as a means of accessing files on computers connected via the Internet

yellow journalism early 20th-century journalism emphasizing sensational sex, crime, and disaster news

zapping using the remote control to switch to other content when a commercial appears

zipping fast-forwarding through taped commercials on a VCR

zone Internet address information, typically either geographic or descriptive of the type of organization

zoned editions suburban or regional versions of metropolitan newspapers

zoopraxiscope early machine for projecting slides onto a distant surface

References

A candid conversation with the high priest of popcult and metaphysician of media. (1969, March). *Playboy*, 53–74, 158.

Adams, M. (1996). The race for radiotelephone: 1900–1920. *AWA Review*, x, 78–119.

Apar, B. (1997, summer). DaViD meets Goliath. *Video Business DVD Supplement*, 10.

Arato, A., & Gebhardt, E. (1978). *The essential Frankfurt School reader*. New York: Urizen Books.

Arthur Ashe AIDS story scrutinized by columnists, editors. (1992, June). *Quill*, 17.

Ashe: Privacy at stake. (1992, April 9). *USA Today*, p. 2A.

Bagdikian, B. H. (1992). *The media monopoly* (4th ed.). Boston, MA: Beacon Press.

Baker, R. (1997, September/October). The squeeze. *Columbia Journalism Review*, 30–36.

Ball, S., & Bogatz, G. A. (1970). *The first year of Sesame Street: An evaluation*. Princeton, NJ: Educational Testing Service.

Bandura, A. (1965). Influence of model's reinforcement contingencies on the acquisition of imitative responses. *Journal of Personality and Social Psychology, 1*, 589–595.

Baran, S. J., Chase, L. J., & Courtright, J. A. (1979). *The Waltons:* Television as a facilitator of prosocial behavior. *Journal of Broadcasting, 23* (3), 277–284.

Baran, S. J., & Davis, D. K. (1995). *Mass communication theory: Foundations, ferment and future*. Belmont, CA: Wadsworth.

Barili, A. (1997, December 1). Argentina wages war against journalists. *San Jose Mercury News*, p. 7B.

Barlow, J. P. (1996). Selling wine without bottles: The economy of mind on the global Net. In L. H. Leeson (Ed.), *Clicking in: Hot links to a digital culture*. Seattle, WA: Bay Press.

Barnouw, E. (1966). *A tower of Babel: A history of broadcasting in the United States to 1933*. New York: Oxford University Press.

Bennett, W. L. (1988). *News: The politics of illusion*. New York: Longman.

Berelson, B. (1949). What "missing the newspaper" means. In P. F. Lazarsfeld & F. N. Stanton (Eds.), *Communication research, 1948-1949*. New York: Harper.

Berger, P. L., & Luckmann, T. (1966). *The social construction of reality: A treatise in the sociology of knowledge*. Garden City, NY: Doubleday.

Berkman, H. W., & Gilson, C. (1987). *Advertising: Concepts and strategies*. New York: Random House.

Bernays, E. L. (1986). *The later years: Public relations insights, 1956–1988*. Rhinebeck, NY: H&M.

Biggs, S. (1996). Multimedia, CD-ROM, and the Net. In L. H. Leeson (Ed.), *Clicking in: Hot links to a digital culture*. Seattle, WA: Bay Press.

Bittner, J. R. (1994). *Law and regulation of electronic media*. Englewood Cliffs, NJ: Prentice-Hall.

Black, J., & Barney, R. D. (1985/86). The case against mass media codes of ethics. *Journal of Mass Media Ethics*, vol. 1, 27–36.

Black, J., & Whitney, F. C. (1983). *Introduction to mass communications*. Dubuque, IA: William C. Brown.

Blumenthal, R. G. (1997, September/October). Woolly times on the Web. *Columbia Journalism Review*, 34–35.

Bogle, D. (1989). *Toms, coons, mulattos, mammies, & bucks: An interpretive history of Blacks in American films*. New York: Continuum.

Bradbury, R. (1981). *Fahrenheit 451*. New York: Ballantine. (Originally published in 1956.)

Bridges v. California 314 U.S. 252 (1941).

Broadcasting & Cable Yearbook 1997. (1997). New Providence, NJ: R. R. Bowker.

Burstein, D., & Kline, D. (1995). *Road warriors: Dreams and nightmares along the information highway*. New York: Dutton.

Carey, J. W. (1975). A cultural approach to communication. *Communication, 2*, 1–22.

CBS v. Democratic National Committee 412 U.S. 94 (1973).

Chandler v. Florida 449 U.S. 560 (1981).

China adopts new Net curbs. (1997, December 31). *San Jose Mercury News,* pp. C1, C4.

CJR Grapevine. (1997, September/October). Industry to *Might:* Drop dead. *Columbia Journalism Review, 36,* 23.

Cook, T. D., Appleton, H., Conner, R. F., Shaffer, A., Tamkin, G., & Weber, S. J. (1975). Sesame Street *revisited.* New York: Russell Sage Foundation.

Cranberg, G. (1997, March/April). Trimming the fringe: How newspapers shun low-income readers. *Columbia Journalism Review, 35,* 52–54.

Curtis, Q. (1997, March 21). The dark side of the force. *Daily Telegraph,* p. 26.

Dalton, T. A. (1997, September/October). Reporting on race: A tale of two cities. *Columbia Journalism Review, 36,* 54–57.

Davis, D. K. (1990). News and politics. In D. L. Swanson & D. Nimmo (Eds.), *New directions in political communication.* Newbury Park, CA: Sage.

Davis, R. E. (1976). *Response to innovation: A study of popular argument about new mass media.* New York: Arno Press.

Day, L. A. (1997). *Ethics in media communications: Cases and controversies.* Belmont, CA: Wadsworth.

DeFleur, M. L., & Ball-Rokeach, S. (1975). *Theories of mass communication* (3rd ed.). New York: David McKay.

Dennis, E. E. (1992). *Of media and people.* Newbury Park, CA: Sage.

deVries, H. (1997, October 11). Out & about. *TV Guide,* 20–27.

Dilenschneider, R. L., & Forrestal, D. J. (1987). *The Dartnell public relations handbook.* Chicago, IL: The Dartnell Corporation.

Draper, R. (1986, June 26). The faithless shepherd. *The New York Review of Books,* pp. 14–18.

Dunn, S. W. (1986). *Public relations: A contemporary approach.* Homewood, IL: Irwin.

Early, D. E. (1997, October 12). The information age. *West,* 10–13.

Editor & Publisher International Yearbook. (1995, 1996, 1997). New York: Editor & Publisher Company.

Effron, S. (1997, January/February). The North Carolina experiment. *Columbia Journalism Review, 35,* 12–14.

Estes v. State of Texas 381 U.S. 532 (1965).

Faules, D. F., & Alexander, D. C. (1978). *Communication and social behavior: A symbolic interaction perspective.* Reading, MA: Addison-Wesley.

Fawcett, A. W. (1996, October 16). Interactive awareness growing. *Advertising Age,* p. 20.

Filler, L. (1968). *The muckrakers: Crusaders for American liberalism.* Chicago: Henry Regnery.

Fleming, H. (1996, December 16). Valenti delivers the V-chip code. *Broadcasting & Cable,* pp. 6–7.

Foerstel, H. N. (1994). *Banned in the U.S.A.: A reference guide to book censorship in schools and public libraries.* Westport, CT: Greenwood Press.

Fowler, M. S., & Brenner, D. L. (1982). A marketplace approach to broadcast regulation. *Texas Law Review, 60,* 205–254.

Freidman, T. L. (1998, April 14). The network is the power. *San Jose Mercury News,* p. 6B.

FTC faults Net on privacy. (1998, June 4). *San Jose Mercury News,* pp. 1C, 4C.

Gerbner, G. (1990). Epilogue: Advancing on the path of righteousness (maybe). In N. Signorielli & M. Morgan (Eds.), *Cultivation analysis: New directions in media effects research.* Newbury Park, CA: Sage.

Gerbner, G., Gross, L., Jackson-Beeck, M., Jeffries-Fox, S., & Signorielli, N. (1978). Cultural indicators: Violence profile no. 9. *Journal of Communication, 28,* 176–206.

Gerbner, G., Gross, L., Morgan, M., & Signorielli, N. (1980). The "mainstreaming" of America: Violence profile no. 11. *Journal of Communication, 30,* 10–29.

Gillmor, D. M., & Barron, J. A. (1974). *Mass communication law: Cases and comments.* St. Paul, MN: West.

Ginzburg v. United States 383 U.S. 463 (1966).

Gitlin, T. (1997, March 17). The dumb-down. *The Nation,* 28.

Gitlow v. New York 268 U.S. 652 (1925).

Glatzer, R. (1970). *The new advertising.* New York: Citadel Press.

Goldstine, H. H. (1972). *The computer from Pascal to von Neumann.* Princeton, NJ: Princeton University Press.

Gremillion, J. (1995, July/August). Showdown at generation gap. *Columbia Journalism Review, 34*–38.

Hall, E. T. (1976). *Beyond culture.* New York: Doubleday.

Hall, S. (1980). Cultural studies: Two paradigms. *Media, Culture and Society, 2,* 57–72.

Harlow, R. F. (1976). Building a public relations definition. *Public Relations Review, 2,* 36.

Harris, M. (1983). *Cultural anthropology.* New York: Harper & Row.

Hentoff, N. (1996, August 18). Colleges' patronizing behavior. *San Jose Mercury News,* p. 7B.

Herhold, S. (1997, December 29). Online clash of costs vs. content: Net magazine *Salon* epitomizes fate of mind over matter. *San Jose Mercury News,* pp. 1E, 4E.

Hickey, N. (1996, July/August) What's at stake in the spectrum war? *Columbia Journalism Review,* 39–43.

Hilliard, R. L., & Keith, M. C. (1996). *Global broadcasting systems.* Boston, MA: Focal Press.

Hollywood feels heat after arson attack. (1995, November 28). *San Jose Mercury News,* p. A3.

Hoover v. Intercity Radio Co., Inc. 286 F. 1003 (1923).

Hovland, C. I., Lumsdaine, A. A., & Scheffield, F. D. (1949). *Experiments on mass communication.* Princeton, NJ: Princeton University Press.

Hustler Magazine v. Big Jerry Falwell 485 U.S. 46 (1988).

Institute for Alternative Journalism. (1996, December). Media and democracy: A blueprint for reinvigorating public life in the information age (working paper).

Irvin v. Dowd 366 U.S. 717 (1961).

Iyengar, S., & Kinder, D. R. (1987). *News that matters: Television and American opinion.* Chicago: University of Chicago Press.

Jamieson, K. H., & Campbell, K. K. (1997). *The interplay of influence: News, advertising, politics, and the mass media.* Belmont, CA: Wadsworth.

Jordan, H. (1997, October 13). Student can't be sued for libel. *San Jose Mercury News,* pp. 1B.

Joseph Burstyn, Inc. v. Wilson. 343 U.S. 495 (1952).

Katz, E., & Lazarsfeld, P. F. (1955). *Personal influence: The part played by people in the flow of communications.* New York: Free Press.

Kava, B. (1996, July 12). Longing for the days when DJs made the calls. *San Jose Mercury News,* p. 22.

Kids are getting lost in the tobacco deal shuffle. (1998, January 16). *USA Today,* p. 10A.

Kinsella, B. (1997, January 20). The Oprah effect: How TV's premier talk show host puts books over the top. *Publishers Weekly,* 276–278.

Klapper, J. T. (1960). *The effects of mass communication.* New York: Free Press.

Kristula, D. (1997, March). *The history of the Internet.* (Online). http://www.davesite.com/webstation/net-history.shtml

Kuhn, T. (1970). *The structure of scientific revolutions* (2nd ed.). Chicago: University of Chicago Press.

Kunkel, D. (1997, January 31). Why content, not the age of viewers, should control what children watch on TV. *Chronicle of Higher Education,* pp. B4–B5.

Kuralt, C. (1977). *When television was young* (videotape). New York: CBS News.

Lasswell, H. D. (1948). The structure and function of communication in society. In L. Bryson (Ed.), *The communication of ideas.* New York: Harper.

Lazarsfeld, P. F. (1941). Remarks on administrative and critical communications research. *Studies in Philosophy and Social Science, 9,* 2–16.

Leland, J. (1995, June). The irony and the ecstasy. *Newsweek,* 71.

Levy, S. (1998, February 16). New media's dark star. *Newsweek,* 78.

Lieberfarb, W. (1997, Summer). Point of view: Why the industry needs DVD. *Video Business DVD Supplement,* 14.

Lindlof, T. R. (1987). *Natural audiences: Qualitative research of media uses and effects.* Norwood, NJ: Ablex.

Lohr, S. (1995, July 3). Out damned geek! The typical Web user is no longer packing a pocket protector. *New York Times,* p. 39.

Lovell, G. (1997, December 21). Branded. *San Jose Mercury News,* pp. 7G, 14G.

Lowery, S. A., & DeFleur, M. L. (1995). *Milestones in mass communication research.* White Plains, NY: Longman.

Manzi, J. (1991, January 23). Lotus, Equifax cancel shipment of Lotus MarketPlace: Households. (Online press release).

Marshall, J. (1996, November 4). Economics, not engineering, will unclog Internet. *San Francisco Chronicle,* pp. E1, E5.

Mast, G., & Kawin, B. F. (1996). *A short history of the movies.* Boston: Allyn & Bacon.

McChesney, R. W. (1997). *Corporate media and the threat to democracy.* New York: Seven Stories Press.

McCombs, M. E., & Shaw, D. L. (1972). The agenda-setting function of mass media. *Public Opinion Quarterly, 36,* 176–187.

McLuhan, M. (1962). *The Gutenberg galaxy: The making of typographic man.* London: Routledge & Kegan Paul.

McLuhan, M. (1964). *Understanding media: The extensions of man.* New York: McGraw-Hill.

McLuhan, M., & Firoe, Q. (1967). *The medium is the massage.* New York: Random House.

McLuhan, M., & Stearn, G. E. (1967). A dialogue: Q&A. In M. McLuhan & G. E. Stearn (Eds.), *McLuhan: Hot and cool: A primer for the understanding of McLuhan and a critical symposium with a rebuttal by McLuhan.* New York: Dial Press.

McQuail, D. (1987). *Mass communication theory: An introduction.* Beverly Hills, CA: Sage.

McQuail, D., & Windahl, S. (1986). *Communication models for the study of mass communications.* New York: Longman.

Merton, R. K. (1967). *On theoretical sociology.* New York: Free Press.

Miller, M. C. (1997, March 17). The crushing power of big publishing. *The Nation,* 11–18.

Miller v. State of California 413 U.S. 463 (1966).

Mutual Film Corp. v. Ohio Industrial Commission. 236 U.S. 230 (1915).

National Broadcasting Company v. United States 319 U.S. 190 (1943).

National Communication Association (1996). *Speaking, listening, and media literacy: Standards for K through 12 education.* Annandale, VA: NCA.

The National Telemedia Council. (1992). *Telemedium, 38,* 12.

Near v. Minnesota 283 U.S. 697 (1931).

New York Times v. Sullivan 376 U.S. 254 (1964).

New York Times v. United States 403 U.S. 713 (1971).

Ninety-Second Congress. (1972). *Hearings before the Subcommittee on Communications on the Surgeon General's Report by the Scientific Advisory Committee on Television and Social Behavior.* Washington, DC: U.S. Government Printing Office.

Novello, A. C. (1991, November 4). *Youth and alcohol—advertising that appeals to youth.* Surgeon General's Press Conference.

O'Connor, R. J. (1995, October 31). Net used mainly by the well-off, survey shows. *San Jose Mercury News,* pp. 1A, 11A.

O'Connor, R. J., & Wasserman, E. (1996, November 25). E-commerce isn't yet an e-ssential way of life. *San Jose Mercury News,* pp. 1A, 13A.

Packard, V. O. (1957). *The hidden persuaders.* New York: David McKay.

Paper Tiger Television. (1981). *Paper tiger television manifesto.* New York: Paper Tiger TV.

Pavlik, J. V. (1997, July/August). The future of online journalism: Bonanza or black hole. *Columbia Journalism Review, 36,* 30–36.

The People's Communication Charter. (1996, Fall). *Cultural Environment Monitor, 1,* p. 4.

Radway, J. (1984). *Reading the romance: Women, patriarchy, and popular literature.* Chapel Hill, NC: University of North Carolina Press.

Red Lion Broadcasting v. United States 395 U.S. 367 (1969).

Rheingold, H. (1994). *The virtual community: Homesteading on the electronic frontier.* New York: Harper Perennial.

Rich, F. (1997, November 29). Seven is enough. *New York Times,* p. A25.

Rock Out Censorship. (1998, January). (Online). http://www.charink.com/roc

Romney, J. (1997, February 21). Dumber and dumber. *The Guardian,* pp. 2–3, 8–9.

Rosaldo, R. (1989). *Culture and truth: The remaking of social analysis.* Boston: Beacon.

Rosenberg, R. S. (1992). *The social impact of computers.* Boston, MA: Harcourt Brace Jovanovich.

Roth v. United States 354 U.S. 476 (1957).

Saia v. New York 334 U.S. 558 (1948).

Sampson, H. T. (1977). *Blacks in black and white: A source book on Black films.* Metuchen, NJ: The Scarecrow Press.

Sandage, C. H., Fryburger, V., & Rotzoll, K. (1989). *Advertising theory and practice.* New York: Longman.

Sarnoff, D. (1953, September 21). Address to NBC Radio Affiliates Committee in Chicago. *Broadcasting/Telecasting,* 108–112.

Schenk v. United States 249 U.S. 47 (1919).

Schiffrin, A. (1996, June 3). The corporatization of publishing. *The Nation,* 29–32.

Schwarzbaum, L. (1997, November/December). Independents' day. *Entertainment Weekly,* 8–9.

Shenk, D. (1997). *Data smog: Surviving the information glut.* New York: Harper Edge.

Siebert, F. S., Peterson, T., & Schramm, W. (1956). *Four theories of the press.* Urbana, IL: University of Illinois Press.

Silverblatt, A. (1995). *Media literacy.* Westport, CT: Praeger.

Sloan, W., Stovall, J., & Startt, J. (1993). *Media in America: A history.* Scottsdale, AZ: Publishing Horizons.

Stark, S. (1985, October 27). TV quickens the quicksell. *Boston Globe,* pp. A1, A24.

Stauber, J. C., & Rampton, S. (1995). *Toxic sludge is good for you: Lies, damn lies and the public relations industry.* Monroe, ME: Common Courage Press.

Stead, D. (1997, January 5). Corporations, classrooms and commercialism. *New York Times Magazine,* 30–47.

Steinberg, S. H. (1959). *Five hundred years of printing.* London: Faber & Faber.

Sterling, C. H., & Kitross, J. M. (1990). *Stay tuned: A concise history of American broadcasting.* Belmont, CA: Wadsworth.

Swartz, J. (1997, August 15). Cyber-addiction more than a virtual malady. *San Francisco Chronicle,* pp. A1, A12.

Taylor, D. (1991). Transculturating TRANSCULTURATION. *Performing Arts Journal, 13,* 90–104.

Tebbel, J. (1987). *Between covers: The rise and transformation of American book publishing.* New York: Oxford University Press.

Tebbel, J., & Zuckerman, M. E. (1991). *The magazine in America 1741–1990.* New York: Oxford University Press.

Time, Inc. v. Hill 385 U.S. 374 (1967).

Trench, M. (1990). *Cyberpunk.* Mystic Fire Videos. New York: Intercon Production.

Turkle, S. (1995). *Life on the screen: Identity in the age of the Internet.* New York: Simon & Schuster.

U.S. Census Bureau (1997). *Statistical Abstract of the United States.* Washington, DC: U.S. Government Printing Office.

U.S. v. Zenith Radio Corp. et al. 12 F. 2d 616 (1926).

Valentine v. Christensen 316 U.S. 52 (1942).

Walker, J., & Ferguson, D. (1998). *The broadcast television industry.* Boston, MA: Allyn & Bacon.

Walser, R. (1993). *Running with the devil: Power, gender, and madness in heavy metal.* Hanover, NH: University Press of New England.

Wartella, E. A. (1997). *The context of television violence.* Boston, MA: Allyn & Bacon.

Wilke, J., Vamos, M. N., & Maremont, M. (1985, August 5). Has the FCC gone too far? *Business Week,* 48–54.

Wright, R. (1995, January 23). Hyperdemocracy. *Time,* 14–21.

Zoellner, D. B. (1995, September/October). The truth about the Heartland. *Columbia Journalism Review,* 8.

Acknowledgments

Photo credits

Part 1 p. 1T, © Michael Newman/PhotoEdit; p. 1B, Photofest **Chapter 1** p. 2, © Reuters/Corbis-Bettmann; p. 11TL, Everett Collection; p. 11MR, © 1992 Paramount/MP & TV Photo Archive; p. 11BL, Photo by Mark Seliger. From *Rolling Stone*, April 16, 1998 by Straight Arrow Publishers Company, L.P. 1998; p. 11TR, © David Young-Wolff/PhotoEdit; p. 11BR, © Michael Newman/PhotoEdit; p. 13TL, Photo by Jon Ragel/Photofest; p. 13TR, © Stephen Sigoloff/The Kobal Collection; p. 13B, © The Kobal Collection; p. 14L, Photo © 1997 Warner Brothers; p. 14M, Photofest; p. 14R, Everett Collection; p. 15, © Reuters/Corbis-Bettmann; p. 17, © Jack Rowand/ The Kobal Collection; p. 19, © David Young-Wolff/PhotoEdit **Chapter 2** p. 34, © Mark Richards/ PhotoEdit; p. 38, © The Granger Collection, New York; p. 39, © The Granger Collection, New York; p. 40, © Corbis-Bettmann; p. 41, © The Granger Collection, New York; p. 43, © Erich Lessing/Art Resource, NY; p. 45, © UPI/Corbis-Bettmann; p. 46, © Mark Richards/PhotoEdit; p. 47, © The Granger Collection, New York; p. 53T, Photo by Larry Watson/HBO/Kobal Collection; p. 53B, Everett Collection; p. 54, © Agence France Presse/Corbis-Bettmann; p. 56T, Everett Collection; p. 56B, Capital Cities/ABC, Inc./Everett Collection **Part 2** p. 61T, © The Kobal Collection; p. 61B, © Reuters/Jerry Lampen/Archive Photos **Chapter 3** p. 62, © AP/Wide World Photos; p. 64, © The Kobal Collection; p. 66, © The Granger Collection, New York; p. 67, © Culver Pictures, Inc.; p. 70, © Ancient Art and Architecture Collection; p. 71, © The Granger Collection, New York; p. 72L, Reprinted by permission of Random House, Inc. Photo by Alán Gallegos/AG Photograph; p. 72R, Cover of *The Accidental Tourist* by Anne Tyler reproduced by arrangement with The Berkley Publishing Group, a member of Penguin Putnam Inc. All rights reserved. Photo by Alán Gallegos/AG Photograph; p. 83T, © The Kobal Collection; p. 83MR, © The Kobal Collection; p. 83ML, © Warner Books. Photo by Alán Gallegos/AG Photograph; p. 83B, © Reuters/Jerry Lampen/Archive Photos; p. 84, Courtesy Ten Speed Press, Berkeley, CA; p. 85, © Michael Newman/PhotoEdit; p. 87, Amazon.com. is a registered trademark of Amazon.com, Inc. © 1996-1997 Amazon.com, Inc. All rights reserved. p. 89, © 1997 Harpo Productions, Inc. All Rights Reserved. Photo by George Burns **Chapter 4** p. 92, © AP/Wide World Photos; p. 95, Courtesy John Frost Newspapers; p. 96, © The Granger Collection, New York; p. 98, © The Granger Collection, New York; p. 99, © The Granger Collection, New York; p. 101, © The Granger Collection, New York; p. 103, Reprinted by permission of *USA Today;* p. 106, © Robert Brenner/PhotoEdit; p. 107L, Reprinted by permission of the *Palo Alto Daily News;* p. 107R, Reprinted by permission of the *San Jose Mercury News;* p. 115, Reproduced by permission of the *San Jose Mercury News;* p. 117, *The San Francisco Chronicle* reproduced with permission.; p. 118, *The San Francisco Chronicle* and *The San Francisco Examiner* reproduced with permission. **Chapter 5** p. 122, © Alán Gallegos/AG Photograph; p. 124, Courtesy *Might* Magazine, Inc.; p. 126, © The Granger Collection, New York; p. 127, © 1923 Time Inc.; p. 129T, © Alán Gallegos/AG Photograph; p. 129B, Theodore Roosevelt Collection, Harvard College Library; p. 130TL, Printed by permission of the Norman Rockwell Family Trust. © 1958 The Norman Rockwell Family Trust; p. 130TR, © The Condé Nast Publications, Ltd.; p. 130B, © People/Time, Inc.; p. 134, This article first appeared in *SALON*, an online magazine, at http://www.salonmagazine.com. Reprinted with permission.; p. 137, Cover reprinted courtesy of *American Way*. Photo © Carol Friedman/ Outline; p. 139, Reprinted by permission of *Psychologie Heute;* p. 140, This advertisement is reprinted by arrangement with Sears, Roebuck and Co. and are protected under copyright. No duplication is permitted; p. 143, © 1997, Newsweek, Inc. All rights reserved. Reprinted by permission **Chapter 6** p. 146, Everett Collection; p. 148, © The Kobal Collection; p. 149, © The Granger Collection, New York; p. 151, © Culver Pictures, Inc.; p. 152, Photofest; p. 153, © Edison Co. 1903/MP & TV Photo Archive; p. 154, Everett Collection; p. 157, Everett Collection; p. 158, © 1927 Warner Brothers/MP & TV Photo Archive; p. 161, Photofest; p. 163, Photofest; p. 166, Everett Collection; p. 167, Everett Collection; p. 169, Photo by Michael Tackett/ © 1995 Gramercy Pictures/The Kobal Collection; p. 173, Photofest; p. 174, JVC Company of America **Chapter 7** p. 178, © Steve Freedman/Spooner/Liaison

Agency Inc.; p. 182, © AP/Wide World Photos; p. 183, © The Granger Collection, New York; p. 184, © The Granger Collection, New York; p. 185, © Culver Pictures, Inc.; p. 186, © The Granger Collection, New York; p. 189, Photofest; p. 191L, © UPI/Corbis-Bettmann; p. 191R, © Corbis-Bettmann; p. 197, From *Broadcasting/Telecasting*, Aug. 17, 1953; p. 198, © AP/Wide World Photos; p. 201, © Reuters/Sue Ogrocki/Archive Photos; p. 203, © Joseph Sia/Archive Photos; p. 204, © Steve Freedman/Spooner/Liaison Agency Inc.; p. 206, CDNOW, http://www.cdnow.com **Chapter 8** p. 210, © AP/Wide World Photos; p. 212, Photofest; p. 213, © Smithsonian Institution. Neg. #85-12139; p. 214L, © Culver Pictures, Inc.; p. 214R, © The Granger Collection, New York; p. 218, © 1986 National Broadcasting Co./The Kobal Collection; p. 219, Photofest; p. 221, © AP/Wide World Photos; p. 227, Everett Collection; p. 229T, Everett Collection; p. 229ML, Photofest; p. 229MR, Everett Collection; p. 229B, Everett Collection; p. 231, © Eric Liebowitz/HBO/Kobal Collection; p. 232, © Ken Staniforth/Fox/Kobal Collection; p. 234, © 1996 Universal/WB/MP & TV Photo Archive; p. 236, © DirecTV. Current as of April 10, 1997; p. 240, Everett Collection **Part 3** p. 243T, © Culver Pictures; p. 243B, © Bill Aron/PhotoEdit **Chapter 9** p. 244, © The Granger Collection, New York; p. 246, © Naum Kazhdan/NYT Pictures; p. 248, Courtesy Odwalla, Half Moon Bay, CA; p. 250, © The Granger Collection, New York; p. 251, © Tony Freeman/PhotoEdit; p. 253, © 1978 GM Corp. All Rights Reserved.; p. 254, © Culver Pictures, Inc.; p. 256, Everett Collection; p. 257, Everett Collection; p. 260, © Mark Richards/PhotoEdit; p. 263L, Reproduced by permission of the Starbucks Coffee Company; p. 263R, Courtesy Unocal and Baker Design Associates of Santa Monica, CA; p. 265, Courtesy Ronald McDonald House, Palo Alto, CA; p. 266, Courtesy Cambridge Consulting Corporation/USDA; p. 269, © The Granger Collection, New York; p. 270, © UPI/Corbis-Bettmann **Chapter 10** p. 276, © Bill Aron/PhotoEdit; p. 279, © Adam Woolfitt/Woodfin Camp and Associates; p. 280, © The Granger Collection, New York; p. 281, © The Granger Collection, New York; p. 282, Milton Bradley; p. 285, © Brown Brothers; p. 286, © Culver Pictures, Inc.; p. 288, © Timex/Timexpo Museum; p. 291, © Tom Kimmell; p. 293, © AP/Wide World Photos; p. 294, © The Media Foundation/Adbusters Magazine; p. 300, All American Communications; p. 302, Courtesy of The Humane Society of the United States; p. 306, © Bill Aron/PhotoEdit **Part 4** p. 313, © Courtney Kealy/Liaison Agency Inc. **Chapter 11** p. 314, © The Kobal Collection; p. 319, © The Kobal Collection; p. 320, Photofest; p. 323, Reprinted from "The Basic Psychology of Rumor," Transactions of the New York Academy of Sciences, 1945, VIII, 61–81; p. 324, © AP/Wide World Photos; p. 330, Everett Collection; p. 337, © Courtney Kealy/Liaison Agency Inc.; p. 338, Courtesy George Gerbner **Chapter 12** p. 342, Courtesy Professor Albert Bandura, Stanford University; p. 344, © AP/Wide World Photos; p. 346, Courtesy Stanley Baran; p. 354, © Glenn Embree/MP & TV Photo Archive; p. 357, Photofest; p. 359, Courtesy Professor Albert Bandura, Stanford University; p. 361, Everett Collection; p. 362, Bacardi-Martini USA Inc.; p. 364L, Ad originally appeared in *Fortune*, March 1938; p. 364R, © Jacques M. Chenet/Liaison Agency Inc.; p. 365TL, Photofest; p. 365TR, Everett Collection; p. 365B, Photofest; p. 366, Photofest; p. 368, Everett Collection **Chapter 13** p. 372, © AP/Wide World Photos; p. 377, © AP/Wide World Photos; p. 378, © Culver Pictures, Inc.; p. 381, Courtesy John Frost Newspapers; p. 383, © AP/Wide World Photos; p. 384, © Dan Dion/Liaison Agency Inc.; p. 387, Everett Collection; p. 392T, © UPI/Corbis-Bettmann; p. 392B, © Bob Straus/Woodfin Camp and Associates; p. 394, © AP/Wide World Photos; p. 396, © AP/Wide World Photos; p. 398, Everett Collection; p. 400, Concept: O. Toscani. Courtesy United Colors of Benetton **Chapter 14** p. 406 © AP/Wide World Photos; p. 409, © Baldwin H. Ward/Corbis-Bettmann; p. 410, © Culver Pictures, Inc.; p. 411, © AP/Wide World Photos; p. 412, © Archive Photos; p. 413T, © AP/Wide World Photos; p. 413B, Courtesy Intel; p. 418, © Reuters/NASA/Archive Photos; p. 421, http://www.whitehouse.gov; p. 421B, © Robbie McClaren/SABA; p. 429, Courtesy Blue Ribbon, http://www.eff.org/blueribbon.html; p. 435, Courtesy NetShepherd. http://ratings.netshepherd.com **Chapter 15** p. 440, © Paul Chesley/National Geographic Image Collection; p. 444TL, © 1962 University of Toronto Press. Reproduced by permission of the publisher. Photo by Alán Gallegos/AG Photograph; p. 444TR, *The Medium is the Massage*, by Marshall McLuhan and Quentin Fiore, produced by Jerome Agel. © 1967 by Jerome Agel. Renewed © 1996 by Jerome Agel. All rights reserved. The book is available in a Hardwired paperback edition. Photo by Alán Gallegos/AG Photograph.; p. 444B, *Understanding Media* by Marshall McLuhan is published by MIT Press; p. 445, © Bernard Gutfryd/Woodfin Camp and Associates; p. 447, © Agence France Presse/Corbis-Bettmann; p. 462, © Atlantida/Liaison Agency Inc.; p. 464, Courtesy John Frost Newspapers; p. 466, *News Plus One* with Miss Yuko Kimura & Mr. Yuichi Mayama. © NTV; p. 468, © Dennis Cox/China Stock; p. 469, © CNN; p. 470, Everett Collection

Text and Illustration Credits
Chapter 1 Figs. 1-1, 1-2 From *The Process and Effects of Mass Communication*, Wilbur Schramm, editor. Copyright © 1954 by the Board of Trustees of the University of Illinois. Used with permission of the University of Illinois Press. **Chapter 2** p. 50 Reprinted with permission from Cultural Environment Movement. **Chapter 3** Fig. 3-3 Reprinted with permission from the March 17, 1977 issue of *The Nation* magazine. **Chapter 5** p. 143 Frank Rich, *The New York Times*, November 29, 1997. Copyright © 1997 by The New York Times Co. Reprinted by permission. **Appendix** p. 202 Reprinted with permission from Society of Newspaper Editors. p. 207 Copyright © Radio-Television News Directors Association. Reprinted with permission. p. 209 Reprinted with permission from American Advertising Federation. p. 210 Reprinted with permission from The Public Relations Society of America (PRSA).

Index